THE OXFORD HANDBOOK OF

ENERGY AND SOCIETY

THE OXFORD HANDBOOK OF

ENERGY AND SOCIETY

Edited by

DEBRA J. DAVIDSON

and

MATTHIAS GROSS

OXFORD

UNIVERSITY PRESS

OXFORD
UNIVERSITY PRESS

Oxford University Press is a department of the University of Oxford. It furthers
the University's objective of excellence in research, scholarship, and education
by publishing worldwide. Oxford is a registered trade mark of Oxford University
Press in the UK and certain other countries.

Published in the United States of America by Oxford University Press
198 Madison Avenue, New York, NY 10016, United States of America.

© Oxford University Press 2018

CIP data is on file at the Library of Congress
ISBN 978–0–19–063385–1

1 3 5 7 9 8 6 4 2

Printed by Sheridan Books, Inc., United States of America

Contents

PART III   CONSUMPTION DYNAMICS

PART IV   PERSPECTIVES ON ENERGY EQUITY AND ENERGY POVERTY

PART V ENERGY AND PUBLICS

PART VI ENERGY (RE)TAKES CENTER STAGE IN POLITICS

PART VII EMERGING TRENDS
IN THE ENERGY-SOCIETY RELATIONSHIP

ABOUT THE EDITORS

Debra J. Davidson is Professor of Environmental Sociology in the Department of Resource Economics and Environmental Sociology at the University of Alberta. Her primary areas of teaching and research include the social dimensions of energy and food systems, with special interest in the impacts on, and the observed and potential institutional transformation in, energy and food systems due to climate change. She is co-author of *Challenging Legitimacy at the Precipice of Energy Calamity*, with Mike Gismondi (Springer, 2011), and co-editor of *Consuming Sustainability: Critical Social Analyses of Ecological Change* with Kierstin Hatt (Fernwood, 2005). Recent articles have been published in *Science, Society and Natural Resources, British Journal of Sociology, Global Environmental Change*, and *Agriculture, Food and Human Values*, among other journals. She also served as Lead Author on the 5th Assessment Report of the Intergovernmental Panel for Climate Change, Working Group II, with contributions to Chapter 26: *North America*; the *Technical Summary*; and the *Summary for Policymakers*. Dr. Davidson's current research projects are focused on urban agriculture and food security, the social impacts of hydraulic fracturing, and discourse analysis of the political framing of fossil fuel development. Dr. Davidson received her PhD from the Department of Rural Sociology, University of Wisconsin-Madison, in 1998.

Matthias Gross is Professor of Environmental Sociology at Helmholtz Centre for Environmental Research in Leipzig, and by joint appointment, the University of Jena, Germany. His recent research focuses on the changing role of civil society, alternative energy systems, the sociology of engineering, real world experiments, ecological restoration and design, as well as risk, knowledge, and ignorance. He is a founding editor of the journal *Nature + Culture*. Dr. Gross's book publications in English include *Ignorance and Surprise: Science, Society, and Ecological Design* (MIT Press, 2010), *Renewable Energies* (Routledge, 2015, with Rüdiger Mautz), the *Routledge International Handbook of Ignorance Studies* (edited with Linsey McGoey, 2015), and *Green European: Environmental Behaviour and Attitudes in Europe in a Historical and Cross-Cultural Comparative Perspective* (Routledge, 2017, co-editor with Audrone Telesiene). He is currently chair of the *European Sociological Association*'s Research Network "Environment and Society" (RN12) and the German Sociological Association's Section on "Environmental Sociology." Dr. Gross received his PhD from the Department of Sociology, Bielefeld University, Germany, in 2001.

Contributors

Mauro Berni University of Campinas, Brazil

Marilyn A. Brown Georgia Institute of Technology

Karl-Michael Brunner Vienna University of Economics and Business

Paul S. Ciccantell Western Michigan University

Neilton Fidelis da Silva Federal University of Rio de Janeiro

Martin David Helmholtz Centre for Environmental Research—UFZ

Debra J. Davidson University of Alberta

Ana Delicado University of Lisbon

Jennifer Dodge State University of New York, Albany

Cyria Emelianoff Université du Maine, Le Mans, France

Marcos A. V. Freitas Federal University of Rio de Janeiro

Paul K. Gellert University of Tennessee-Knoxville

Paula Graham Memorial University of Newfoundland

Matthias Gross Helmholtz Centre for Environmental Research—UFZ

José Alexandre Hage Federal University of São Paulo, Brazil

Ana Horta University of Lisbon

Sampsa Hyysalo Aalto University, Helsinki, Finland

Jouni K. Juntunen Aalto University, Helsinki, Finland

Janet A. Lorenzen Willamette University

Sylvia Mandl Vienna University of Economics and Business

Paulo Manduca University of Campinas and Universidade Paulista—UNIP, Brazil

David Mares Rice University and University of California, San Diego

Nils Markusson Lancaster University

Iure Paiva Federal University of Paraiba, Brazil

Marcio Giannini Pereira Federal University of Rio de Janeiro

Thomas Pfister Zeppelin University

Sybille Roehrkasten Institute for Advanced Sustainability Studies (IASS), Potsdam

Harald Rohracher Linköping University, Sweden

Perry Sadorsky York University

Jalel Sager University of California, Berkeley

Martin Schweighofer Zeppelin University

Jack D. Sharples European University at St. Petersburg

Christine Shearer CoalSwarm, San Francisco

Jillian Rene Smith Memorial University of Newfoundland

Benjamin K. Sovacool University of Sussex

Jennie C. Stephens Northeastern University

Mark C. J. Stoddart Memorial University of Newfoundland

Harriet Thomson Manchester University

Ion Bogdan Vasi University of Iowa

John Vogler Keele University

Aleksandra Wagner Jagiellonian University, Kraków

Richard York University of Oregon

CHAPTER 1

....

A TIME OF CHANGE, A TIME FOR CHANGE

Energy-Society Relations in the Twenty-first Century

....

DEBRA J. DAVIDSON AND MATTHIAS GROSS

ENERGY, simultaneously ubiquitous and invisible, is the current upon which cultures, economies, polities, technology, and relations of social power have ridden throughout human history. Invisible, but eminently directional, that current describes a historic trajectory ever uphill. Just as increased energy inputs enrich our ecosystems in increasingly complex webs, so too has there been a clear relationship between energy consumption and social complexity, despite significant leaps in efficiency (Smil, 2010; Tainter, 1988). As noted by Urry (2014, p. 9), "contemporary cultures presuppose huge concentrations of energy so as to power the modern world and its machines." Securing access to energy over time is a key task for ensuring the survival of any society, but at least since the close of World War II, those fortunate enough to live in Western, developed countries have had the luxury of complacency—so long as the lights turn on and the gas station is open, most people in the West could leave it to a handful of engineers, politicians, and corporate executives to figure out the details outside the limelight. The 1973 oil crisis did capture attention, but at least in the USA it was mainly understood as political crisis—a response to US support for Israel during the Yom Kippur War—rather than an oil supply crisis per se. That attention was all too brief; the solar panels installed on the White House by Jimmy Carter later in the 1970s were ceremoniously removed by Ronald Reagan. Taking society's cue, sociologists too largely ignored energy, although there have always been those on the outskirts who have attempted to draw the discipline's attention for a century.

That current, always turbulent, is beginning to shift in ways that have begun to jar scholars, politicians, and business executives alike. The political, social, and economic importance of energy has come to the fore at the beginning of the twenty-first century, and there are no signs of it receding again into the background. First, as has been made strikingly clear in international climate negotiations, this current is made up of a few main channels and many small streams, with the populations of a small number of developed countries consuming vastly more energy resources than the remainder, with over a billion people today lacking secure access to electricity (see, e.g., Chapter 17 of this volume). As has been noted repeatedly in these negotiations, developing countries have a right to enjoy the benefits of fossil-fuelled economic development, too. And yet, as has also been noted, energizing the rest of the world up to the standards enjoyed in the highest-income countries is not climatologically, ecologically, or even geologically possible with fossil fuels (Smil, 2010). Even for those developed economies, there is a rapidly receding confidence in our ability to continue to rely on conventional fossil fuels to foster economic growth. Remaining global reserves of fossil fuels are indeed quite large, but they consist primarily of unconventional sources, including shale, heavy oil, bitumen, and kerogen. The economic costs of their exploitation, not to mention the environmental and social costs—through methods like oil-sands mining, hydraulic fracturing, deep-sea drilling, gas-to-liquids and coal-to-liquids processes— are currently higher than those same costs associated with conventional deposits, and they may well continue to escalate in the future in the absence of substantial technological advances or alternatives. Regardless of their quantity or quality, burning them currently accounts for upward of 70% of the greenhouse gas emissions that have been attributed to rapid climate change.

However, there are few indications that fundamental shifts in the current consumption patterns and energy-intensive lifestyles that characterize modern societies will emerge with ease. To the contrary, the world's hunger for energy appears to be following an upward trajectory, and fossil fuels remain the most readily accessed, due in no small part to preexisting political and physical infrastructures that have evolved to support those fuel types. The present challenge is considerable: to effect a socio-technical transition to energy-society relations that are greenhouse-gas-emission free, while also minimizing other environmental impacts, and at the same time ensuring equitable access to energy resources. Whereas the Industrial Revolution was effectively an energy revolution, as coal and oil were used to industrialize and mobilize the Western world, contemporary transitions will necessarily be equally revolutionary. As with earlier energy transitions, doing so promises to both require and facilitate concomitant transformation of forms of social organization that may very well leave no social subsystem unaffected. One important driver of this transition is political-economic in nature, and given the political power of fossil-fuel interests today, any efforts toward transition away from reliance on such fuels have been and will continue to be fiercely resisted. Investment decisions that shape the direction of research and development are also pertinent. A third key driver pertains to the organization of energy access: our current, highly centralized systems of energy production and delivery increasingly are being called into question, and in some cases are being replaced by decentralized modes of energy production, including small-scale, community-based, and cooperative models. Other drivers are subtler, described by discourses and cultures of energy that follow unpredictable pathways, yet strongly shape everything from legislation to consumption practices.

NEW POLITICAL REALITIES

The reluctant acceptance by members of the international political elite of the inevitability and severity of the impacts of climate change has marked forever a fundamental shift in the politics of energy. The title of Jörg Friedrich's recent book, *The Future Is Not What It Used to Be* (2013), describes a notable decline in confidence in our prospects for continuation of the economic progress enjoyed by the West since the close of World War II. Historical trajectories of economic growth stop here, and twenty-first-century societies seem to be left with a rather poor set of choices: put the brakes on the economy, or set the climate to boil.

The crux of the issue is a dilemma dubbed the *carbon bubble*: representing the carbon content of remaining fossil-fuel reserves that must be kept in the ground to prevent dangerous levels of global warming. According to an analysis published in *Nature* (McGlade & Ekins, 2015), a third of global oil reserves, half of natural gas reserves, and over 80% of coal reserves should remain unused from 2010 to 2050 in order to meet the target of limiting global warming below 2°C. The implications for the world's economies in general are alarming. Fossil fuels are used to heat and electrify homes, offices, and factories, and, perhaps most crucially, to move things. The mobility of people, material goods, and currencies defines contemporary societies to such an extent that there are almost no activities that are significant in the modern world that do not entail movement of some kind, virtually all of which depends upon oil (Urry, 2012). But the implications of the carbon bubble also have a far more specific character: much of those fossil fuels are already "owned" by energy companies, whose portfolios depend on their expected future exploitation; ergo, a bursting of this bubble would render some of the largest and most powerful corporations in the world, and many petro-states, penniless. As quipped by Biel (2014, p. 186), "in a bizarre way, wealth flows to those who cause the most entropy," and collective efforts to restrain that entropy constitutes a direct threat to those interests.

This context sheds light on the increasingly acerbic politicization of climate science. As research by McCright and Dunlap (2010) indicates, efforts by members of the US federal government to manipulate climate science at the behest of conservatives goes back decades. None of this should come as a surprise since, as noted by Friedrichs (2013: p. ix), "when our entire way of life is at stake, the struggle over knowledge is bound to be political." Global social movement attention to climate change has nonetheless continued to grow alongside these efforts. And, sharing less of the limelight, but no less consequential, growing resistance in civil society to fossil-fuel development has also emerged, taking the form of divestment campaigns, local resistance to pipelines and hydraulic fracturing, and a growing number of legal efforts to hold government and industry accountable. Personal- and community-level experiments in low carbon transition are also growing in number, and with the increasing availability of small-scale renewable electricity-generation technologies, many consumers have become "prosumers," demanding more control over the goods and services that they consume (Wood, 2016). Attention by civil society to energy and climate change is significant, and already has generated results: a number of nations, states and provinces, and municipalities have instituted bans on hydraulic fracturing; fossil-fuel divestment campaigns continue to grow in number and effectiveness; and protests such as No Dakota Access Pipeline (#NODAPL), which 10 years ago would likely not have attracted even national attention, has generated an international response.

Underlying this momentum, however, lurks an elephant: optimism regarding prospects for a smooth and rapid renewable energy transition are increasingly recognized as overly naïve. Research by York (2010), among others, illustrates that expanding the use of non-fossil-fuel energy sources does not necessarily suppress the use of fossil-fuel energy sources. In response, Geels (2014) urges his transition-focused colleagues to focus not just on up-scaling green alternatives. As he argues, ironically, the prevalence of academic attention among transition theorists on new innovations in renewable energy "may serve to protect existing regimes by detracting attention from the fossil fuel burning problem" (Geels, 2014, p. 37). In short, environmental social scientists need an equally ambitious research program focused on preventing existing fossil-fuel reserves from being burned. There is no better example of this than the inflated subsidies committed to fossil fuels. According to a recent International Monetary Fund (IMF) Report, pre-tax basis subsidies for petroleum industries reached $480 billion in 2011. When the negative externalities from energy development and consumption are factored in, that subsidy rises to $1.9 trillion. Favoritism toward fossil fuels is not the only constraint; even renewable energy alternatives generate opposition or introduce challenges of their own, and are, furthermore, also associated with environmental impacts (Shaw, 2011), and thus, as Venderheiden (2011) reminds us, the politics of energy involves selecting from among a set of imperfect options, and some scholars believe that many of the alternative energy resources are simply not up to the job of powering our current global economies (e.g., Baghat, 2008).

Even further backstage are enduring political issues that are not in the limelight (but then again, they never have been) as the geopolitics of fossil fuels has more often than not been a behind-the-scenes affair. The consistent backstage position of oil geopolitics is, in and of itself, remarkable: struggles to control world energy resources played a role in both world wars and the Iraq War (Amineh & Houweling, 2007). The need to secure transport routes has always been the centerpiece of maritime military movements, constituting heavy state revenue commitments. Marriott and Minio-Paluello (2014) note that the "oil roads" that run from extracting states to consuming states have remained remarkably constant over the decades. These researchers describe the pipeline routes from the Caspian region to EU markets as a tangled web, laid atop a checkerboard of unstable and conflicting states, with Iran, Russia, Kazakhstan, Azerbaijan, and Turkmenistan squabbling over control of production, and this mass relocation of fossil fuels requires constant coordination of logistical and financial resources. Meanwhile, the emergence of both new producing states, including several underdeveloped African nations like Algeria and Angola, and new consuming states like China has disrupted a decades-old geopolitical regime previously dominated by a small set of Organization of Petroleum Exporting Countries (OPEC) and the United States. China may have plenty of coal, but must import oil to support its rapid industrialization. Production in the extreme periphery, like Nigeria, has had disastrous social, economic, and ecological effects (Watts, 2008).

NEW MATERIAL REALITIES

While energy and society relations are in many ways socially constructed, with numerous social factors shaping demand, supply, and delivery of energy resources—many of which will be explored in detail in the chapters to follow—those resources still have a physical (and ecological) reality that comes into play in markets, politics, and cultures. Underlying this materiality is a simple fact: one cannot produce or create energy, but can only transform it from one source into another. A power plant does not produce energy, or "power," but rather transforms it, as when nuclear energy is transformed into electrical energy. Energy is not something that simply disappears or "evaporates"; it is merely transformed, either by itself or by human activity, and is thus always a part of social life. Through the process of transformation, from a raw material into a product that can be used, another transformation takes place, from more concentrated and organized, to more dissipated and disorganized forms. Interest in this entropic law has been largely limited to energy scholars, although a number of social scientists, from Marx to Georgescu-Roegen, have given it attention. Today, the arguments of these scholars that entropy is far more than esoteric are beginning to resonate.

That resonance is associated with a new material context that is unprecedented for our century-long relationship with fossil fuels. The concept of "peak" fossil fuels (e.g., Kerr, 2011; Murphy & Hall, 2010) has been largely misrepresented in public and political discourse to imply that we are running out of oil, gas, and coal reserves. As energy analysts are quick to point out, the earth's crust is still replete with the stuff. But the quality of those reserves has been in decline since the first moment of extraction, and continued reliance on fossil fuels portends an increasing intensity of investment and ecological impact as the quality and accessibility of remaining reserves declines (Davidson, 2018; Davidson & Andrews, 2013). This historic trend is alarming for environmental reasons—the explosion on British Petroleum's Macondo drilling rig has been attributed to corporate negligence, but the fact that the well was drilled to an unprecedented depth of nearly 25,000 ft (7.6 km) rendered such an accident more likely, and more disastrous. Why would British Petroleum choose to drill at such a depth? Simply because more accessible reserves are becoming harder to find (Smith-Nonini, 2016), to the extent to which we may no longer be able to rely on increases in fossil-fuel-based energy consumption to support growth. As noted by Moore (2011, pp. 22), our turn toward lower quality fuels "has brought with it a monstrous turn towards toxification on a gigantic scale—from unprecedented oil spills to the 'hydraulic fracturing' of natural gas exploitation to coal's mountaintop removals, energy production in late capitalism increasingly manifests as a qualitative leap forward in the erosion of the conditions of human, never mind extra-human, well-being."

This historic trend is just as alarming for economic reasons. Again referring to Moore (2011), the prospect of discovering new global reserves capable of underwriting the next century's progress at anything close to the pace enabled by the capture of fossil fuels during the previous century is slim. The recent boom in fracking has been hailed loudly by proponents as the rebirth of energy independence in places like the United States, but for those with any understanding of the limited quality of shale reserves, and the costs of their exploitation, this moment in the history of fossil fuels is more accurately conceived as the retirement party (Berman, 2015; Love & Isenhour, 2016). Over the past few years, energy companies have adjusted to current economic realities by taking on increased debt, while petro-states lower royalties and offer other forms of subsidy, but these management strategies clearly have their own limits. Why does this matter to our economies? "If the dollar is pegged to anything today, it is pegged to a barrel of oil" (Sager, 2016, pp. 38–39).

NEW EPISTEMOLOGICAL REALITIES

Energy is in many ways a special field of study. Energy is an inherent, intrinsic aspect of social change that can be seen not only as the glue that holds together different elements of the social order, but also as a force that helps to transform them, by facilitating the creation of new social arrangements. Energy also sets the boundaries by which such transformations must abide. The structuration of energy access is a complex problem that touches on many areas of science and culture. Access to energy and the development of innovative new technologies are interlinked with geology and engineering, as well as economic and political processes, and cultural patterns of energy use. The social sciences have in many ways remained on the sidelines of inquiry, but that appears to be starting to change.

The genre of energy and society research in the social sciences has evolved quite dramatically over the past century, a course that began with the prevalence of structural, political economy treatments. To these were added social-psychological attitude studies, particularly during the 1980s oil embargo, which motivated efforts to stimulate conservation in the West. Toward the end of the twentieth century, the field began to open up considerably, with the inclusion of cultural studies, social practice and actor-network theories, multilevel systems transition theories, and, most recently, a return to those original materialist accounts, but with the integration of recent advances in complexity theory, among other insights. This historical trajectory has brought forth a conceptually and methodologically exciting field that is well represented in the chapters in this volume. The developments in social analysis of the energy-society relationship that have emerged have the potential to fertilize the discipline of sociology and related fields with pertinent new ideas and findings germane to contemporary politics and economics, while simultaneously advancing social theory.

Sociology has not always been fertile ground for the consideration of energy and society relations. Major parts of the discipline were founded on principles of what Catton and Dunlap (1978) called human exemptionalism—the belief that social processes can only be explained by other social processes—and thus adherents to the discipline for the most part neglected the role of energy in society, as well as any other causal mechanisms other than those originating in the social sphere (McKinnon, 2010). The handful of scientists speaking to energy-society relations came from neighboring fields in the social sciences—like anthropology and economics—or even further afield, in the natural sciences. Wilhelm Ostwald, having coined the term *sociological energetics*, was a chemist by training; Howard T. Odum developed the concept of *emergy*—an effort to capture the embodied energy in all material components of social life—from his disciplinary home in ecology. Herbert Spencer, despite his development of a concept of *energetic sociology*, was more of an evolutionary biologist and philosopher than a sociologist in today's understanding. Spencer developed an ambitious theory of social evolution based on the principles of energy—an effort largely lost on contemporary scholars due to strong criticism of other aspects of his work. Leslie White was also an anthropologist, and drew heavily from the natural sciences to develop his understanding of the material (energetic) bases of social, and in particular economic, change (Love & Isenhour, 2016).

William Cottrell's work, published in book form in 1955, is among the few works focused on energy to emerge from sociology prior to the 1980s, and continues to be held in high regard among energy and society scholars today. Cottrell provided a history of social development from low-energy societies to modern industrial societies, placing particular emphasis on the explanatory power of the forms of energy available, and the role of technology in determining that availability. Many current sociologists and others have continued to find merit in the work of economist Georgescu-Roegen (e.g., O'Hara, 2009; Sager, 2016). Georgescu-Roegen was quite preoccupied by energy's entropic character, and its implications for economies and societies, in which we continually yet fruitlessly attempt to oppose this force (Georgescu-Roegen, 1971). As noted by both Georgescu-Roegen and Cottrell, economic growth necessitates an increase in overall material and energetic flows; equally important, power is intimately associated with control over energy, and shifts in energy availability and form thus have enormous disruptive potential.

More recently, the changing material circumstances discussed in the preceding have reinvigorated materialist approaches, integrated with more recent scholarship in complexity theory (e.g., Biel, 2014; Demaria & Schindler, 2016; Sager, 2016; Urry, 2004, 2014). These scholars frame energy-society relations in metabolic terms of *funds* and *flows*, path dependency and transition. John Urry (2014, p. 8) stated, "the human and physical/material worlds are utterly intertwined and the dichotomy between the two is a construct that mystifies understanding of the problem of energy." And yet he devoted much of his last decade of life to seeking that understanding (Urry, 2004, 2008, 2014). His treatment of the private automobile offers an exemplar of the integration of materialism and complexity theory. The car is strangely absent from sociology, he notes, and yet Western society has been wholly shaped physically and culturally to accommodate it. Importantly to his analysis, it is also the single most important form of personal environmental impact, and wholly dependent upon a resource access to which is in decline: oil. And yet the "car-driver"—a hybrid assemblage of activities, technologies, infrastructures, and cultures—is frustratingly resilient. Urry (2004, p. 26) notes, "what is key is not the 'car' as such but the system of these fluid interconnections."

Working our way down to the bottom of the pecking order are individual consumers. Consumer attitude studies emerged in the 1980s (e.g., Rosa et al., 1988), and attention to energy consumers has continued to grow in the ensuing decades, although today this field has expanded considerably to include, at one end of the spectrum, more sophisticated computer-based statistical behavioral modeling. Much of this work identifies a consistent "value-action-gap" between the expressed sentiments of consumers and their actual behavior, reinforcing what Jevons (1865, p. 140) quipped so long ago: "It is wholly a confusion of ideas to suppose that the economical use of fuel is equivalent to a diminished consumption. The very contrary is the truth." At the other end of the spectrum are actor-network-theory-influenced analyses that place far more emphasis on the cultural context within which consumption practices emerge. Currently the repertoire of energy and society analysis within sociology also includes a panoply of studies at all scales, but particularly, an explosion of work focused on communities, albeit with a postmodern twist. As described by Campbell and colleagues (2016, p. 136) the very concept of community has been recast within sociotechnical energy systems, highlighting the roles of spatially-delimited communities of interest and practice, described in terms of "flows of agency, capacity, and value . . . [and] the sociocultural role of power within any energy production regime." Similarly, sociologists have begun to play with the concept of energy culture, defined by Sheller (2014, p. 134) as "specific assemblages of human mobility, transport of goods (logistics), and energy circulation . . . embedded in ongoing processes of mobilizing, energizing, making and doing" (see also Stephenson et al., 2010). These conceptual innovations have been stimulated in large part by the socio-technical innovations unfolding around us, particularly the opening up of energy politics due to the increased access to decentralized and less capital-intensive forms of electricity generation, disrupting entrenched power relations (Wood, 2016). Those power relations themselves have received renewed attention, with a greater degree of focus on the role of energy itself in shaping those relations (e.g. Boyer, 2014).

While attention to energy issues is growing in sociology, as well as other areas of the social sciences and humanities, many of these efforts remain at the fringes of academic inquiries into energy. We hope that this *Handbook* will help to close that gap, while presenting an overview of a field that has achieved a considerable level of maturity and relevance.

OUTLINE OF THE BOOK

Our contributors represent the discipline of sociology primarily, but we also have included contributors in complementary fields, where we believe such complementarity is valuable to the study of energy and society. The frequency with which we have felt the need to do so reflects the necessarily interdisciplinary nature of the research inquiries involved, and the cross-fertilization across disciplines that has enriched this body of scholarship as a whole. We also have sought to bring together contributors who can provide a broad international perspective, and we have included both senior scholars as well as emerging scholars whose work we feel has strong potential to make significant new contributions to the field.

The organization of this *Handbook* was done with a number of specific objectives in mind. First, we have attempted to capture a variety of scales and methods, and a range of both conceptual and empirical analyses that define the field. We include contributions that focus on the continued importance of, and rapid changes in, the roles of individuals, communities, industries, scientists, states, and civil societies. Recent developments in energy production, consumption, politics, and governance are all highlighted, notably as they pertain to the rapidly growing sectors of renewables and non-conventional fossil fuels. The book is divided into seven parts capturing what we believe are the primary sociological fields of inquiry into energy and society today. Each part contains a handful of diverse perspectives within each of these fields, and is prefaced with a short essay synthesizing the key themes.

In Part I, "Key Contemporary Dynamics and Theoretical Contributions," we highlight sociology's response to calls on global society to radically transform its relationship with energy away from dependence on fossil fuels, or to confront the collapse of civilization's ecological foundations. Necessarily broad in scope, this field draws on complexity theory and systems thinking to grapple with society's precarious relationship with energy today. Part II, "The Persistent Material and Geopolitical Relevance of Fossil Fuels," offers a set of contemporary analyses, highlighting the renewed interest among many scholars in structural and political-economic perspectives, and the persistent material and geopolitical relevance of fossil fuels.

Part III, titled "Consumption Dynamics," highlights the elemental role played by individual consumers in energy consumption and the prospects of energy system transition. Attention is given, first, to global consumption patterns, exploring in particular geographic shifts in sites of consumption, with consumption rates growing rapidly in emerging economies. Attention then turns to research on recent empirical studies that have attempted to quantify the "behavioral wedge," the potential efficiency gains that could be realized with relatively minor shifts in household behavior, and its flip side, the so-called value-action gap, before turning to more recent work that evaluates energy consumption for a social practice lens.

Part IV, "Perspectives on Energy Equity and Energy Poverty," offers perspectives on equity, and poverty in energy access, highlighting the extent to which sources of the earth's energy resources are by no means equitably distributed. The negative social and environmental impacts of development, moreover, are borne by communities at the sites of production, while the resources themselves and the wealth they generate are most often exported for consumption elsewhere. Analyses that integrate both the sociopolitical and biophysical structures of energy-society relations raise uncomfortable questions about energy, poverty, and justice.

Part V is focused on "Energy and Publics." The role of public perceptions, their expression in politics and the market, and their emergent effects have in many circumstances had a notable influence on energy policymaking, and in ways that do not necessarily favor improvements in sustainability, energy conservation, and efficiency. This section will especially focus on agenda-setting processes for critical energy issues by using different social theoretical frameworks. We then turn in Part VI, "Energy (Re) takes Center-Stage in Politics," to the role of states and social movements to explore dynamic shifts in energy politics and governance taking place today, including the growth in number, and successes, of mobilized opposition to energy developments such as pipelines, mountaintop removal (coal), coal/open-cast mining in general, and hydraulic fracturing, as well as renewable energy developments. These encounters raise the possibility that we are experiencing the emergence of a new energy-focused global social movement, one that is independent of and yet has several implications for the politics of climate change. At the same time, significant shifts in governance have had their effect on energy politics, with de-decentralization in some cases, while in others more centralized governance structures have emerged.

We close in Part VII, "Emerging Trends in the Energy-Society Relationship," with a relatively retrospective section, contemplating emerging trends in the energy-society relationship. We are experiencing rapid shifts in several aspects of contemporary society with direct or indirect implications for the energy and society relationship. Drivers of these changes include technology, politics, and the growing political salience of climate change, among others. One compelling trend of note involves the "prosumer" movement: describing the rapid expansion of household-level micro-generation of renewable energy and citizen-led developments of new technologies, representing a dismantling of the centralized control structure that has defined energy delivery for decades. Other observations have opened up new lines of sociological inquiry, including case studies of local energy transition.

REFERENCES

Amineh, M. P., & Houweling, H. (2007). Global energy security and its geopolitical impediments: The case of the Caspian Region. *Perspectives on Global Development and Technology, 6,* 365–388.

Baghat, G. (2008). Energy security: What does it mean? And how can we achieve it? *Journal of Social, Political, and Economic Studies, 33*(1), 85–98.

Berman, A. (2015). The artificial shale boom: Interview on BNN TV (Canada). April 11. Retrieved from http://www.artberman.com/the-artificial-shale-boom-interview-on -bnn-tv-canada/

Biel, R. (2014). Visioning a sustainable energy future: The case of urban food-growing. *Theory, Culture & Society, 31*(5), 183–202.

Boyer, D. (2014). Energopower: An introduction. *Anthropological Quarterly 87*(2), 309–333.

Campbell, B., Cloke, J., & Brown, E. (2016). Communities of energy. *Economic Anthropology, 3,* 133–144.

Catton, W. R., Jr., & Dunlap, R. E. (1978). Environmental sociology: A new paradigm. *The American Sociologist, 13*(1), 41–49.

Cottrell, W. (1955). *Energy and society: The relation between energy, social changes, and economic development.* New York: McGraw-Hill.

Davidson, D. J. (2018). The effort factor: An adjustment to our understanding of social -ecological metabolism in the era of peak oil. *Social Problems.*

Davidson, D. J., & Andrews, J. (2013). Not all about consumption. *Science, 339*(15), 1286–1287.

Demaria, F., & Schindler, S. (2016). Contesting urban metabolism: Struggles over waste-to-energy in Delhi, India. *Antipode, 48*(2), 293–313.

Friedrichs, J. (2013). *The future is not what it used to be: Climate change and energy security.* Cambridge, MA: MIT Press

Geels, F. W. (2014). Regime resistance against low-carbon transitions: Introducing politics and power into the multi-level perspective. *Theory, Culture & Society, 31*(5), 21–40.

Georgescu-Roegen, N. (1971). *The law of entropy and the economic process.* Cambridge, MA: Harvard University Press.

Jevons, W. S. (1865). *The coal question: An inquiry concerning the progress of the nation, and the probable exhaustion of our coal mines.* London: Macmillan.

Kerr, R. A. (2011). Peak oil production may already be here. *Science, 331*(6024), 1510–1511.

Love, T., & Isenhour, C. (2016). Energy and economy: Recognizing high-energy modernity as a historical period. *Economic Anthropology, 3*(1), 6–16.

Marriott, J., & Minio-Paluello, M. (2014). The political and material landscape of European energy distribution: Tracking the oil road. *Theory, Culture & Society, 31*(5), 83–101.

McCright, A. M., & Dunlap, R. E. (2010). Anti-reflexivity: The American conservative movement's success in undermining climate science and policy. *Theory, Culture and Society, 27*(2–3), 100–133.

McGlade, C., & Ekins, P. (2015). The geographical distribution of fossil fuels unused when limiting global warming to 2°C. *Nature, 517,* 187–190.

McKinnon, A. M. (2010). Energy and society: Herbert Spencer's "energetic sociology" of social evolution and beyond. *Journal of Classical Sociology, 10*(4), 439–455.

Moore, J. W. (2011). Transcending the metabolic rift: A theory of crises in the capitalist world-ecology. *The Journal of Peasant Studies, 38*(1), 1–46.

Murphy, D. J., & Hall, C. S. (2010). Year in review: EROI or energy return on (energy) invested. *Annals of the New York Academy of Sciences, 1185,* 102–118.

O'Hara, P. A. (2009). Political economy of climate change, ecological destruction and uneven development. *Ecological Economics, 69*(2), 223–234.

Rosa, E. A., Machlis, G. E., & Keating, K. M. (1988). Energy and society. *Annual Review of Sociology, 14,* 149–172.

Sager, J. (2016). The crown joules: Resource peaks and monetary hegemony. *Economic Anthropology*, 3, 31–42.

Shaw, K. (2011). Climate deadlocks: The environmental politics of energy systems. *Environmental Politics*, 20(5), 743–763.

Sheller, M. (2014). Global energy cultures of speed and lightness: Materials, mobilities and transnational power. *Theory, Culture & Society*, 31(5), 127–154.

Smil, V. (2010). Science, energy, ethics, and civilization. In R. Y. Chiao, M. L. Cohen, A. J. Leggett, W. D. Phillips, & C. L. Harper, Jr. (Eds.), *Visions of discovery: New light on physics, cosmology, and consciousness* (pp. 709–729). Cambridge: Cambridge University Press.

Smith-Nonini, S. (2016). The role of corporate oil and energy debt in creating the neoliberal era. *Economic Anthropology*, 3(1), 57–67.

Stephenson, J., Barton, B., Carrington, G., Gnoth, D., Lawson, R., & Thorsnes, P. (2010). Energy cultures: A framework for understanding energy behaviours. *Energy Policy*, 38(10), 6120–6129.

Tainter, J. A. (1988). *The collapse of complex societies*. Cambridge: Cambridge University Press.

Urry, J. (2004). The "system" of automobility. *Theory, Culture & Society*, 21(4–5), 25–39.

Urry, J. (2012). Changing transport and changing climates. *Journal of Transport Geography*, 24, 533–535.

Urry, J. (2014). The problem of energy. Introduction to Special Issue: Energy & Society. *Theory, Culture and Society*, 31(5), 3–20.

Venderheiden, S. (2011). The politics of energy: An introduction. *Environmental Politics*, 20(5), 607–616.

Watts, M. (2008). Blood oil: The anatomy of a petro-insurgency in the Niger delta. *Focaal: European Journal of Anthropology*, 52, 18–38.

Wood, C. L. (2016). Inside the halo zone: Geology, finance, and the corporate performance of profit in a deep tight oil formation. *Economic Anthropology*, 3, 43–56.

York, R. (2010). Three lessons from trends in CO_2 emissions and energy use in the United States. *Society and Natural Resources*, 23(12), 1244–1252.

PART I

KEY CONTEMPORARY DYNAMICS AND THEORETICAL CONTRIBUTIONS

THE attempt to grapple with society's relationship with energy has inspired fruitful and often interdisciplinary pursuits among sociologists, as well as some of the most exciting systems-based conceptual developments one can identify anywhere in the discipline. The chapters in Part I of this volume emphasize some contemporary intellectual spaces that have served to shift our collective gaze in our inquiries into energy-society relations, and that we believe are worth watching in the coming years.

The first is unquestionably the sociopolitical upheavals wrought by growing acknowledgment of climate change's human origins and impacts, and by extension, scholars' attempts to grapple with these sociopolitical shifts. As discussed by John Vogler in Chapter 2, climate change has shifted the ground upon which political economies have rested, and has challenged our continued reliance on governments in decision-making, despite trends that may suggest the fruitfulness of other governance arrangements. Ironically, developments in international governing regimes to address climate change have far surpassed analogous efforts on the energy front: energy continues to be a comparatively domestic and private affair.

Chapters 3 and 4 describe tandem upheavals in the academy that have had a particular impact on the sociological study of energy: social practices and sustainability transitions. Both of these conceptual frameworks offer unique and valuable sociological contributions to understanding (and attempts to manage) energy-society relations. Both have also been subject to critique. Ana Horta's Chapter 3 details how substantively social practices theory departs from an entrenched (rational) actor paradigm versus social structure, to boldly resituate energy as an integral feature of all of our social activities undertaken in everyday living, while drawing empirical attention to the interactions between social and material elements and infrastructures. Sometimes intentional, sometimes not, our practices are nonetheless always embedded in sociocultural systems that dictate the norms governing those practices. In Chapter 4, Harald Rohracher describes emerging attention toward sustainability transitions based on a strong conviction that the political, economic, and cultural institutions defining our current energy-society relations must be transformed fundamentally in order to avoid fundamental lowering of standards of living and health, as well as the more catastrophic implications of climate change. This conviction has motivated renewed interest in complex systems, and the elements that aid in their transformation, namely niches in which innovations can flourish, and their potential upscaling through the multilevel systems that characterize modern societies. While in many ways the conceptual frameworks in Chapters 3 and 4 could not be more different, the common link here is growing acknowledgment of system complexity and attempts to accommodate that complexity epistemologically, while simultaneously acknowledging the dynamic role of actors. The extent to which actors are indeed *agents* in this system, however, is a point of contention among scholars involved in recent research in this vein, which has facilitated a fruitful discussion.

CHAPTER 2

ENERGY, CLIMATE CHANGE, AND GLOBAL GOVERNANCE

The 2015 Paris Agreement in Perspective

JOHN VOGLER

STUDYING the International Relations (IR) of the environment is a relatively recent academic endeavor for a discipline that has been generally more concerned with questions of war and peace, order and security. Climate change, of course, is critically associated with anthropogenic CO_2 emissions, two-thirds of which arise from energy production and use (IEA, 2015, p. 20), and IR scholars are no strangers to international conflicts over scarce hydrocarbon resources. It also has become clear in both academic and policy circles that the impacts of climate change are likely, at the very least, to provide a "threat multiplier" complicating existing conflicts and are likely to spawn entirely new international and intra-state confrontation (Detraz & Betsill, 2010; European Council, 2008). Such matters were not at the heart of IR approaches to issues of atmospheric pollution and natural resource depletion. Rather, their overriding concern, within a liberal institutionalist tradition, was to study the ways in which international cooperation and policy coordination to manage common environmental problems could be achieved within a "fragmented and often highly conflictual political system" of sovereign states in which there was no central authority (Hurrell & Kingsbury, 1992, p. 1). This is now commonly seen as an exercise in "global environmental governance"—with the management of climate change being regarded as its primary task.

However, the actual meaning of "global climate governance" is variously interpreted. For a long period in official circles, the term was merely used as a synonym for intergovernmental cooperation. Strictly speaking, the term "governance" is appropriate because there can be no government in a system composed of sovereign state entities, but the term has come to embrace the myriad private, transnational, regional, and local activities that serve to shape and control climate-related activities (Bulkeley & Schroeder, 2012; Pattberg, 2007). The apparent failure of governments to cooperate effectively in fulfilling the aspirations of the 1992 United Nations Framework Convention on Climate

Change (UNFCCC) has led to a focus on such non-state activity and frequent denial of the continuing relevance of international action (Andonova et al., 2009). This chapter attempts to redress this balance in the light of the Paris climate agreement that was achieved in late 2015. It considers the ways in which the international system has framed climate and energy issues and how international climate action—or more often, inaction—has been shaped by the seismic structural changes in the global political economy over the last three decades and by the day-to-day pursuit of national interest and prestige, which is also indissolubly connected to normative demands for climate justice in a very unequal system.

While it is true that the key decisions and actions that shape humanity's response are located at many social and economic levels and particularly involve private economic entities, there is still an important role for state governments acting in a coordinated manner. In order to avoid over- or underestimating the role of international cooperation in general and the UNFCCC climate regime in particular, it is important to establish what this might be. It has several components. First, international cooperation is required to monitor and restrict transboundary movements of pollutants and to regulate trade. Second, it is generally the case that only governments are in a position to fund the major research and aid and technology transfers upon which effective environmental action depends. It is no accident that the impressive international scientific enterprise for the production of authoritative knowledge and advice on a changing climate is named the Inter*governmental* Panel on Climate Change (IPCC). Although there are frequent optimistic references to private-sector development and adaptation funding, the bulk of this derives from coordinated government donations through international agencies such as the Global Environmental Facility of the World Bank and the more recently established Green Climate Fund. The extensive international climate architecture that will be discussed below is not integrated, with or matched, by attempts at international energy regulation. This has been rudimentary. The International Energy Agency (IEA) was a collective response to the energy security issues of the 1970s; more recently, there has been an attempt to stimulate renewables technology in the International Renewable Energy Association (IRENA) (Van de Graaf, 2013). Potentially, there is an enormous role for governments in funding and organizing the kind of energy transition that most experts argue will be required if the most damaging effects of climate change are to be avoided (Victor, 2011). Third, there is the key matter of providing governance arrangements for a global commons to cope with "market failure" at the international level, where unrestricted economic activity will lead to collective "tragedy." International standards and rules are thus required, but governments will not be prepared to restrict polluting activities within their own jurisdiction if they cannot be assured that others will do likewise. For economists, dealing with this "free-rider" problem is a key function of an international regime that directs attention to its monitoring, compliance, and enforcement arrangements (see, for example, Stern, 2007). Finally, there is the more intangible dimension of norm generation that provides the context and justification for particular actions: shared understandings on principles such as the "polluter pays" or the "precautionary principle," definitions of sustainability, what constitutes dangerous climate change, and the responsibility of the international community for loss and damage. A great deal of international activity from the 1992 Earth Summit, with its Agenda 21, to the UN's millennium goals and Article 2 of the Paris Agreement, displays such normative intent.

THE UN FRAMEWORK CONVENTION
ON CLIMATE CHANGE (1992)

In a world still divided by the second phase of the Cold War, climate change began to be recognized as a policy problem during the 1980s. This was a decade characterized by a dawning awareness of environmental problems at a global scale. Notable was the discovery of the depletion of the stratospheric ozone layer caused by emissions of chlorofluorocarbons (CFCs) and other "man-made" gases. In 1985 the Vienna Convention outlined the problem and called for international action to ban or restrict ozone-depleting chemicals. This was to occur quite rapidly with the signature of the 1987 Montreal Protocol, which soon came to be regarded as a paradigm for successful international environmental action that incorporated emergent scientific findings into an ongoing program of regulation that would successively ban production and trade in a range of ozone-depleting substances (ODS). The interconnections between the stratospheric ozone and climate regimes were established early on, not the least of which was that the ODS were in themselves powerful greenhouse gases (GHGs) (their regulation is specifically excepted from the scope of the 1992 Climate Convention). Significantly, the negotiation of a new climate treaty commenced shortly after the signature of the Montreal Protocol and adopted its legal and institutional approach—a "framework convention" to define the problem and encourage and respond to scientific findings (the IPCC was set up in 1988) and a "control protocol" to initiate concrete action. This primary framing of the climate issue seemed appropriate at the time but failed to adopt a similar targeted regulatory approach. Of course the ozone problem was very specific, involving a set of gases for which substitutes were usually available, while the problem of excess GHGs was infinitely more complex and wide-ranging, touching the very essence of a hydrocarbon-based civilization. It still might have been possible, but exceedingly difficult, to follow the Montreal model by identifying and restricting particular emission sources, such as the mining of and trade in coal. In the event, the International Negotiating Committee (INC) adopted a much looser universal approach by attempting to reduce overall national emissions of GHGs and to conserve carbon sinks (Articles 2 and 4 of the UNFCCC). Because the lion's share of anthropogenic CO_2 emissions (the principal GHG) is related to power generation and transport, this implied, but did not propose, energy policy measures. In the international transport sector, rising aviation- and shipping-related emissions were excluded from the developing climate regime on the grounds that this would cut across the remit of other international organizations (the International Civil Aviation and International Maritime organizations, ICAO and IMO). The European Union (EU) was subsequently to fail in its 2012 attempt to include international aviation emissions in its Emissions Trading Scheme, and aviation fuel and maritime bunkering remain largely uncontrolled, pending ongoing and protracted attempts by the ICAO and IMO to erect their own schemes for international carbon reduction. One further problem with the drafting of the UNFCCC was that emissions were to be calculated on a national territorial basis, which provides scope for extreme distortions in terms of assigning responsibility. Thus the physical shifts in production and pollution under economic globalization mean that while the emissions of developed economies in Europe have been reduced, they may simply have been transferred to less developed economies with a "spatial disconnect between the point of consumption and emissions in production" (Peters et al., 2011, p. 5).

Academic and popular commentary has often located the source of the climate problem in population growth and related patterns of consumption in an expanding global economy (Newell, 2012; Royal Society, 2012). These "drivers" of climate change lie well beyond the formal remit of the climate regime. For a number of religious and cultural reasons, population is not an issue that can be comfortably addressed at the international level. Consumption, rather than population growth per se, is evidently the key driver of rising GHG emissions and is inextricably linked with the economic and cultural processes of globalization. In spite of this, the UNFCCC framing of economic issues reflects the circumstances under which it was created and contains text on the beneficial effects of open markets in a globalizing economy. Unlike the ozone protocol and other international instruments, such as the Cartagena Protocol to the Convention on Biodiversity CBD, there are no evident clashes with World Trade Organization (WTO) trade rules. The latter's approach to the environmental consequences of trade is the assertion that if the "externalities" of production are priced into the costs of products, then open markets will provide the most efficient means of environmental protection and indeed the restriction of GHGs. There may be problems if national attempts at internal energy taxation designed to achieve emissions reduction targets lead to "border tax adjustments" to maintain the competitiveness of national industries in ways that are incompatible with WTO rules.

The final, and probably most significant, framing of the Climate Convention is noted in its preamble and reflected in the allocation of responsibilities to developed (as defined in Annex I) and less developed countries (LDCs). It is contained in the principle that the Parties should act to reduce GHG emissions according to their "common but differentiated responsibilities and respective capabilities" (art.3.1). In the early 1990s, the idea that it was the responsibility of developed nations to make the first moves in reducing emissions was not as controversial as it subsequently became. The climate convention itself was sponsored by the UN General Assembly, where developing countries, grouped in the G77, constituted a large majority. It was signed during the epochal United Nations Conference on Environment and Development (UNCED), more popularly known as the Rio Earth Summit, which proclaimed the norm of sustainable development. Accordingly, there could be no

North-South agreement on international environmental questions unless the development requirements and demands for "climate justice" of the South were fully taken into account. In the negotiations that drafted the climate convention, the principal antagonism was between the Europeans, who were prepared to move immediately to emission-reduction commitments, and a reluctant United States. The question of "differentiation" between the Parties was to become the major issue that dogged the development of the regime as "the respective" economic capabilities of the Parties were increasingly subject to dramatic alteration.

The Kyoto Protocol

Despite the efforts of the EU to include a GHG-reduction commitment in the 1992 UNFCCC (a reduction to 1990 levels by 2000), the only binding obligations in the Convention were related to the important preliminary step of national reporting and the drawing up of inventories. The Convention entered into force in 1994 and its first Conference of the Parties (COP I) in Berlin took the ambitious step of mandating that a new substantive and binding agreement be negotiated by 1997. This was to become the famous Kyoto Protocol. Remarkable in many ways, it included a set of varied but binding "top-down" international commitments by developed countries to reduce their emissions by an aggregate 5.2% against a 1990 baseline by the end of the first commitment period, 2008–2012. As the price of agreement, the Clinton administration successfully managed to add a set of "flexibility mechanisms" within the Protocol to assist Parties to meet their "quantified emissions limitation and reduction objectives" (QELROs). The mechanisms included complex and innovative arrangements on emissions trading and related offset mechanisms for Joint Implementation (between developed countries) and the Clean Development Mechanism (CDM). The latter enabled developed countries to gain credits against their own emissions targets by funding GHG-reducing projects in developing countries—sometimes known as internationally transferred mitigation outcomes, or ITMOs. The system continues to operate, with Chinese enterprises as a major beneficiary. Inherent possibilities of fraud and sharp practice, in mis-representing the levels of reductions, achieved required the creation of an extensive and unprecedented international compliance, enforcement, and facilitation apparatus. The Kyoto approach to emissions reduction owed much to the prevailing intellectual climate in which essentially liberal, market-based solutions had long been in vogue. The Kyoto Protocol was to stimulate the United Kingdom and then the EU as a whole, contrary to its previous policies, to adopt an Emissions Trading Scheme to cover the power-generation sector. This has subsequently been through a number of difficult iterations but remains the foundation of the Union's climate and energy policy. Elsewhere, similar carbon-trading arrangements have been established in China and North America, created and then abandoned in Australia, and are planned in no less than 39 other states (IEA, 2015, p. 23).

The Kyoto Protocol followed the Convention's principle of "common but differentiated responsibilities" in that it requires only developed countries to make emissions reductions. This was already controversial as economic globalization, in the wake of the ending of the Cold War, meant that the "respective capabilities" of the Parties and their relative share of global CO_2 emissions were beginning to shift in a process that was to accelerate into the new century. By the time of the ratification of the Protocol in 2005, it was evident that non–Annex I emissions would soon surpass those of the Annex I Parties. Adherence to an international agreement that appeared to penalize US industries in the face of their new competitors in China and elsewhere had already been condemned by an overwhelming majority of the US Senate in the 1997 Byrd-Hagel Resolution. The incoming administration of George W. Bush proceeded to denounce US signature of the Protocol and to actively oppose its provisions. This left the EU to lead the complex negotiation that turned the Protocol into a ratifiable and operational international instrument. By February 2005, this task was accomplished in the face of US opposition. The net effect of the Protocol in terms of actual emissions reductions was quite marginal, in terms of the scientific estimates of what was required to avoid dangerous climate change. In fact, the reductions achieved as a byproduct of the Montreal Protocol's removal of ODS GHGs was of the order of five times greater than that achieved within Kyoto's first commitment period (UNEP, 2011, p. 21). But as CFCs were phased out, they were often replaced by stratospheric ozone–friendly hydrofluorocarbon chemicals (HFCs). Unfortunately, these were also extremely potent GHGs. In parallel with developments in the climate convention, the Parties to the Montreal Protocol arrived at a solution to the problem in the 2016 Kigali Amendment. The claim has been made that scheduled reductions of HFCs under the Amendment will yield a reduction of 0.5°C in the temperature rise that would otherwise have occurred in the period to 2100 (UNEP, 2016).

Attempts were made to achieve a second phase of Kyoto after 2012, but in the context of the global economic downturn that began in 2008, Japan, Canada, and Russia declined to take part. The developed world commitments in Kyoto remained an important *quid pro quo* for any future participation in emissions reductions by developing countries, and the EU and its allies obliged with a 2011 agreement to adhere to a second phase of the Protocol. Advocates of Kyoto tended to admit its limitations in terms of the actual control of emissions, but stressed the longer-term importance of its institutional legacy.

COPENHAGEN (2009) AND THE SEARCH FOR A NEW AGREEMENT

Successive assessment reports of the IPCC strengthened what had become, despite some well organized climate change skepticism in the Anglo-Saxon world, an overwhelming case for international action to stabilize the global climate system. Essentially, the problem was political and economic, rather than one of disputed or inadequate scientific evidence: how to re-engage the United States and to involve all those developing countries, and notably China, that would soon be responsible for the bulk of anthropogenic GHG emissions but which also had very good reason, in terms of climate justice, to insist that the developed world should continue to pay for their historic responsibility for climate change. This normative minefield was made more lethal by the way in which justice claims and counterclaims tended to reflect short-term national energy interests. The domestic political barriers to international action were also significant. The first Obama administration was hamstrung by pressure from fossil-fuel interests and a hostile Congress. There was an awareness that any US administration would have enormous difficulties in passing federal legislation to comply with any future agreement. Likewise, the Chinese and Indians tended to conceptualize climate action as an economic burden that would impede their development and poverty-reduction priorities.

Some progress had been achieved in the 2007 Bali Plan of Action. This enabled the inclusion of the United States in the search for a new climate agreement by splitting negotiations into two tracks, one on the future of Kyoto and the other on the Convention, in which the United States could be persuaded to participate. As far as the developing countries were concerned, there was a significant recognition of the importance of "adaptation" alongside the matter that had previously dominated proceedings: the "mitigation" of emissions. Adaptation to the adverse effects of climate change, which were already beginning to be apparent, was a key national interest of those developing countries likely to be hardest hit and least able to cope. The other side of the Bali deal represented the first crack in the rigid wall of differentiated responsibilities and annexes between developed and developing Parties. Carefully limited "nationally appropriate mitigation actions" (NAMAs) for non–Annex I countries were now to be recognized. The intent was to conclude a new climate agreement at the 2009 COP to be held at Copenhagen, but the global economic downturn of 2008 was to diminish the prospect that governments would be prepared to make bold emissions pledges or to provide the funding necessary for adaptation and mitigation in the developing world.

The Copenhagen COP was an enormous and highly public disappointment—some said a disaster. The Parties had failed to negotiate a clean text to which the many national leaders who had been encouraged to come to Copenhagen (including the new US president, Barack Obama, and his Chinese and Indian counterparts) could sign their names. Instead, a hastily cobbled together "Accord" was produced in a conclave between the United States and the four BASIC countries. The BASIC group—Brazil, South Africa, India, and China—had been formed earlier in the year to represent the climate interests of the four large "emerging economies." The Accord gave some pointers to the future in that it legitimized the target of keeping global mean temperatures below a 2°C (above pre-industrial levels) threshold of "dangerous" climate change. It was also determinedly "bottom-up" in its approach, inviting Parties to state publicly the kind of emissions reductions that they were willing to undertake. In the case of China and India, these were not cuts at all, but predictions of future improvements in energy efficiency. The development and adaptation needs of many Parties were also recognized by the creation of a Green Climate Fund (GCF). A distinguishing feature of the climate convention was its relatively open and democratic character in terms of the involvement of even small countries, especially small island states, and an army of critical nongovernmental organizations (NGOs). Understandably, the cabalistic manner in which the Copenhagen Accord was drawn up was widely resented, with calls for a more open and "Party-driven" process.

In the years following the Copenhagen COP, climate diplomacy within the highly institutionalized structures of the UNFCCC moved to construct a new climate agreement that would be operative from 2020. In the interim there was to be limited participation in a second phase of the Kyoto Protocol, but it soon became clear that a new comprehensive agreement would be very different from its predecessor, involving a "bottom-up" approach to mitigation and some form of "pledge and review" process that would encourage, rather than require, Parties to make reductions in their national emissions. Such a voluntaristic strategy, mapped out originally in the Copenhagen Accord and formalized at the Cancun COP of 2010, provided a politically feasible route to engaging the relatively small group of major emitters, including the United States and the BASIC countries. By 2013, the United States and China alone accounted for around half of total global CO_2 emissions, and the EU, which pressed for a more robust agreement, accounted for a diminished share of about 11%. The bases of a new agreement were set out in the "Durban Platform" of 2011, which replaced wording on national commitments with the much looser term "intended national contributions" and set in motion a negotiating process to conclude an agreement at the Paris COP, to be held in 2015. The legal form of a new agreement was left open in order to accommodate the US government's problem with a potentially hostile Congress. It is also worth noting that in contrast to the period leading up to Copenhagen, the increasing attraction of renewable energy sources, alongside horrendous levels of urban air pollution, appears to have led to a recalculation in China and elsewhere as to the costs of making "contributions." Between 2008 and 2013, the cost of solar-power generation fell by 80% and wind power by 18% (IRENA, 2014, pp. 14–15). Widespread awareness of the increasing competitiveness of such renewable energy sources certainly assisted the negotiations for a new agreement (IEA, 2015, pp. 21–22).

In his second term, President Obama was determined to make a climate agreement part of his legacy, using executive action to cut US emissions under preexisting legislation. Climate policy also provided a cooperative element in the largely conflictual relationship with China. This yielded a November 2014 consensus between the two, expressed in the concept that contributions in the new agreement would be made ". . . in the light of different national circumstances." This phrase was to be appended to the well-worn "common but differentiated responsibilities and respective capabilities" (Paris Agreement, Art. 2.2) in a formula that allowed universal participation in mitigation efforts. By the time of the Paris COP 21, 180 countries had presented nationally defined mitigation plans.

After the events of Copenhagen and amidst fears that major players would simply abandon the UNFCCC, a new agreement, if it were to be legitimate, would also have to receive support from the majority of the international community. In the developed North, the extent to which the Convention and its procedures are valued in the South is often insufficiently understood. European Union policy has always recognized this, and the Union, after the setback to its leadership aspirations at Copenhagen, embarked on an active program of diplomacy to build support for a new agreement across the international system. This required the development of areas of the climate regime that are sometimes neglected when mitigation targets provide the headlines. Climate funding for both adaptation and mitigation was a critical element, and in the years after Copenhagen the structure and procedures of the GCF were elaborated. There were also funding pledges by developed countries, with the aim of reaching a reaching a $100 billion per annum target by 2020. Significant developments, to include sustainable management and enhancement, also occurred in the arrangements for forest preservation under the "Reducing Emissions from Deforestation and Forest Degradation in Developing Countries" program REDD+. Additionally, new procedures were set out in the 2013 Warsaw Mechanism for "loss and damage" assistance for vulnerable countries subject to the impact of actual climate change. Also important in securing developing world support for a new agreement was the undertaking by the EU, virtually alone, to commit to a second phase of the Kyoto Protocol.

After the Durban COP, ongoing dialogue between the EU and around 12 small states provided the core of what was to become the "High Ambition Coalition." As the United States and then Brazil, among others, joined in, the Coalition lent significant momentum to the final negotiation in Paris (Brun, 2016, pp. 120–121). The specifics of the Paris COP and preceding meetings demonstrated that many of the lessons arising from the previous failure at Copenhagen had been learned. In a long but transparent and inclusive process (the snappily titled Ad Hoc Group on the Durban Platform for Enhanced Action, or ADP), a usable, albeit heavily bracketed, negotiating text for the final COP at Paris was produced. This was only one part of a major diplomatic effort by France and the previous presidency, Peru, to ensure that the Paris COP would succeed. As in 2009, the COP was portrayed as an event of high political salience with preliminary interventions by the UN Secretary General and the Pope, but a repetition of the endgame at Copenhagen was avoided as heads of state and government were invited to the beginning rather than the end of the Paris meeting.

THE PARIS AGREEMENT (2015)

For two decades, the objective of the climate convention lacked precise definition, ". . . the stabilization of greenhouse gas concentrations in the atmosphere at a level that would prevent dangerous anthropogenic interference with the climate system" (Art. 2). The Copenhagen Accord, formalized at the Cancun COP of 2010, provided a 2°C threshold definition of "dangerous anthropogenic interference," but this was never suf-ficient to ensure the survival of small island states threatened with inundation. Their Alliance of Small Island States, AOSIS, demanded recognition of a 1.5°C threshold. To the surprise of many, this was partially achieved at Paris, where Parties agreed to hold ". . . the increase in the global average temperature to well below 2°C above pre-industrial levels and to pursue efforts to limit the temperature to 1.5°C" (Art. 2.1). In the same article, two other critical elements of the consensus in Paris are highlighted: the importance of adaptation, and the provision of "making finance flows consistent with a pathway towards low greenhouse gas emissions and climate-resilient development."

Since its inception, the climate regime has been dogged by the issue of differentia-tion, reflecting, of course, the underlying structural inequalities of the international system and core arguments about climate justice and historic responsibilities. The Paris Agreement represents a compromise on these issues, which has facilitated a loose but comprehensive approach. There is no mention of Annex I, and all Parties are involved in mitigation; however, the detailed wording of the agreement indicates some subtle dif-ferentiation between developed countries and the rest. For example, while developed countries "should [not shall!] continue taking the lead by undertaking economy-wide absolute emission reduction targets," LDCs and SIDs (Small Island Developing States) "may prepare and communicate strategies . . ." for low GHG development (Arts. 4.5, 4.6), while developed countries "shall" provide support for developing countries in imple-mentation (Art. 4.5). It is also significant that in comparison to the original Convention, the agreement greatly upgrades the status of "adaptation," giving it some equivalence to mitigation, backed up by promises on the scale of the GCF and by the provisions on "loss and damage" as a separate item from adaptation (Art. 8).

In US Secretary of State Kerry's view, the nationally determined contributions were in themselves "a monument to differentiation," as each country determines its "fair con-tribution," according to its respective capabilities and in the light of "its different na-tional circumstances" (ENB, 2015, p. 43). There is no defined overall emissions target similar to that set out for the developed countries in the Kyoto Protocol. Instead, the Paris Agreement is ambitious yet vague. It can be read as seeking to achieve its temper-ature control objectives by moving to an essentially de-carbonized global economy at some point after 2050. It states that the Parties should aim to reach "global peaking of greenhouse gas emissions as soon as possible" and thereafter to make "rapid reductions" so as to achieve a balance between anthropogenic emissions by sources and removals by sinks of greenhouse gases in the second half of this century" (Art. 4.1). Each successive nationally determined contribution (NDC) "will represent a progression" beyond its current NDC and ". . . and represent its highest possible ambition" (Art. 4.3). The Paris Agreement contains no direct mention of emissions trading or a global carbon price. There is some reference back to the international flexibility mechanisms that were at the heart of the Kyoto Protocol. Joint action and "internationally transferred mitiga-tion outcomes" with robust accounting rules are recognized as means to achieve NDCs. However, engagement with them by Parties is strictly voluntary, and there is even a new framework to facilitate "non-market approaches to sustainable development" (Art. 6.9).

This leads to questions of how the objectives of the Agreement can be met without any enforceable commitments. In reading the text, "shall" indicates a binding obligation, and some precise yet important disagreements at Paris centered on the alternative use of "should" or "may." The binding parts of the Paris Agreement are procedural, rather than substantive, and this provides a key to understanding how it is envisaged that the new system will operate. Parties will be required to produce and communicate NDCs in a five-year cycle. These will account for "anthropogenic emissions and removals," and there is also reference to the use of existing methods and guidance and the setting up of common time frames (Art. 4). National communications will be recorded in a public registry and subject to an "enhanced transparency framework" (Art. 13). This brings together various existing procedures within the Convention to subject national communications to expert scrutiny and review. National sensitivities to such monitoring and review activities are indicated by the stipulation that the transparency framework will be implemented in a "facilitative, non-intrusive, non-punitive manner, respectful of national sovereignty and avoid placing undue burden on parties" (Art. 13.3). There was a key disagreement between the EU, the United States, and the BASICs on the independence and extent of monitoring and verification provisions. Nonetheless, the intention to gain a clear understanding of Parties' mitigation and adaptation actions, "including clarity and tracking of progress towards achieving Parties' individual" NDCs, is clear. If there is to be enforcement, it will thus have a horizontal character, encouraging or shaming Parties to keep to and expand their contributions through publicity and the hope that they will be concerned to safeguard their reputation both at home and abroad.

The other crucial element in fulfilling the objectives of the Agreement is the assessment of Parties' actions against scientific evidence. This has always been central to the operation of the climate regime, which has operated in tandem with the IPCC and has its own Subsidiary Body for Scientific and Technological Advice SBSTA. What has been in question has been the "adequacy of commitments" in relation to Article 2 of the original Convention. The Kyoto Protocol failed to come anywhere near the level of reductions that were required, and the estimates of the impact of Parties' published intended NDCs in advance of Paris yielded a mean temperature increase of 2.7°C (UNFCCC Secretariat, 2015). Now the "contributions" of Parties will need to match against the newly demanding aspirations of the Paris Agreement—a 1.5°–2° threshold for dangerous climate change. To ensure this, the Agreement mandates a "Global Stocktake" to assess progress toward achieving its purposes. This progressive element may be regarded as an important counterbalance to the voluntary nature of self-determined contributions (Brun, 2016, p. 118). The first such "stocktake" will occur in 2023 (one will be conducted every subsequent five years), and will include funding and adaptation actions, alongside mitigation. Beyond this, there is no further detail on what will be involved, except that Parties will be expected to revise their NDCs in accordance with the outcome (Art. 14). While the "stocktake" is scheduled for 2023, the Paris Agreement entered into force in November 2016, having achieved the necessary 55 ratifications, representing 55% of global GHG emissions. Much work remained to be done in "operationalizing" the terms of the Agreement and in ensuring that pre-2020 action on reducing GHG emissions was enhanced (ENB, 2016, pp. 36–38). Despite negotiating success in Paris, the UNFCCC with its new Agreement remains a weak and limited form of commons governance. This is especially evident if comparisons are drawn to the regime for the restoration of the stratospheric ozone layer. Unlike the latter, the Paris agreement contains no mechanisms for dealing with "free-riders." Inadequately framed from the outset, the regime that emerged from Paris rejected the central targets and timetables of the Kyoto Protocol for a "pledge and review" system of the type that had been discussed and discarded during the negotiation of the original Convention. This appears to have been the inevitable price of a comprehensive agreement and has all the hallmarks of a system of sovereign states that rejects central direction and in which enforcement, if not impossible, is very difficult. On the other hand, it is also true that some vestiges of the Kyoto system remain in the form of common rules for transparency and in the facilitating (but not enforceable) compliance mechanism (ENB, 2015, p. 43). The novelty of the new system is that it creates a potential dynamic between domestic energy policies and international standards and aspirations: a "new logic of international climate politics" that "acknowledges the primacy of domestic politics in climate change" (Falkner, 2016, p. 1107). For better or worse, it will provide the framework for international climate cooperation for decades to come, and the outcome at Paris was a great deal more productive than many had predicted, both before and after Copenhagen. Then there were many rivals to the UNFCCC and attempts to "forum shop" by promoting other institutions, such as the APEC initiative or Major Economies Forum, which threatened to fatally undermine a universal approach within the UN system.

Arguably the most significant aspect of the Paris Agreement is in the way that it achieves one of the other functions of international environmental cooperation. It sets up generally agreed-upon norms and expectations of behavior for a future decarbonized global economy. In the discourse surrounding previous attempts to erect a successor to Kyoto, there were constant complaints from business that governments had failed to agree on a clear framework to facilitate climate-friendly investment decisions over the next 25–50 years. The IEA claimed that the measure of success would be the "extent to which it conveys to energy sector stakeholders a conviction that the sector is destined to change" (IEA, 2015, p. 32). Paris may provide the basis for a future investment framework, but it remains to be seen how actual decisions within both public and private energy sectors will be made and the extent to which they will reflect the ambitions of Article 4. There is some encouraging evidence that despite its acknowledged weaknesses, the Kyoto Protocol was associated with a significant upturn in investment in renewable energy (IPCC, 2014).

Under circumstances where the social and economic damage wrought by the enhanced greenhouse effect is becoming manifest, the adaptation provisions of the Agreement and its promised funding arrangements are another noteworthy contribution, alongside a long-standing concern with technology transfer and its financing (Art. 10). Here the developmental trajectory of economies that previously were uninvolved, other than as recipients and critics of the failures of the Annex I countries to live up to their historical responsibilities, will play a huge part in the long-term achievement (or otherwise)of the Agreement's objectives.

How the Paris Agreement Was Achieved and May Be Sustained

In seeking an explanation of how the international community managed to formulate a new climate agreement, the first resort would be to an analysis of coincident national interests. There is no doubt that the persistent scientific findings of the IPCCC and the evidence, for example, of very serious atmospheric pollution in Chinese cities led to some recalculation of national priorities, which often have been seen in terms of a balance between the economic costs and the environmental benefits of taking action. In the United States, the arrival of the Obama administration was marked by a clear reversal of the obstructionist approach of its predecessor. Having once been seen as an economic cost, climate policy came to be viewed in a more favorable light as the costs of alternatives to hydrocarbons fell and as economic gains from investment in solar and other technologies came to be more fully appreciated. The EU had long stressed the benefits of taking a progressive approach to climate policy, but from 2009 Chinese policymakers appear to have become more receptive to this view. India and some other developing countries continued to prioritize an absolute right to development and poverty reduction and to insist that the old industrialized countries no longer had a right to a diminishing "carbon space." The fact that all could be accommodated within the new agreement arose rather obviously from its permissive nature. Governments could now simply determine what they were prepared or could afford to contribute in terms of mitigation, and there was little question of non-compliant states free-riding on the efforts of others. Contributions would be set nationally, subject to transparency and expert analysis.

While unlike many other international issues, relative military strength and hard power do not figure in climate negotiations, there is still an important respect in which shifts in structural power have affected the development of the regime. The rise of the BASIC countries (particularly China) in relation to Europe and the United States changed the nature of climate politics in a way that was graphically demonstrated by the events of the 2009 Copenhagen COP. The old "Annex I versus the rest" division was no longer tenable under circumstances in which China had become the largest emitter and many saw the future of climate politics in a G2 agreement between the United States and China or in some form of ruling "concert" of large and economically powerful emitters. Although Sino-American agreement was doubtless important, the time and diplomatic energy that was expended in meeting the concerns of a large number of small and often insignificant (in terms of the scale of their economies and emissions) states is a remarkable feature of the UNFCCC. The regime did not collapse into a deal between a few powerful emitters, and the Paris Agreement resists analysis in simple terms of relative power.

Normative arguments about climate justice in general and the rights and survival of small island developing states played a central role in building support and momentum for the Paris Agreement. This started with the Cartagena Dialogue, which brought together a range of developed and developing countries in pursuit of a new basis for negotiation after Copenhagen, and then continued, before and during the Paris Conference, with the High Ambition Coalition. This represents a continuation of a long-term trend in which AOSIS has played a disproportionately large part in climate deliberations. Arguments for climate justice are doubtless an important motivator in themselves, but they have been unusually potent within the climate regime. In part, this derives from its relatively "democratic" character and links to the UN General Assembly, along with the effective advocacy of some of the leaders of small island states, the Maldives at Copenhagen and the Marshall Islands at Paris. For them, climate change is a matter of national survival, as their territories face inundation with the inexorable rise of global mean temperatures and resulting sea levels.

A substantial proportion of the activity within the UNFCCC is not directly related to climate issues, but rather to the pursuit of many other symbolic causes that have reputational significance. Consider, for example, this extract from the Paris preamble: "Noting the importance of ensuring the integrity of all ecosystems, including oceans . . . recognised by some cultures as Mother Earth." Or the following portmanteau clause on adaptation which should ". . . follow a country-driven, gender responsive, participatory and fully transparent approach, taking into consideration vulnerable groups, communities and ecosystems . . . guided by the best available science and, as appropriate, traditional knowledge, knowledge of indigenous peoples and local knowledge systems . . ." (Art. 7.5).

At the end of the Copenhagen COP, the Bolivarian Alliance (ALBA) Latin American states, including Cuba and Venezuela, used the occasion to make an explicitly "political" anti-imperialist point by refusing to agree the terms of the deal that had been crafted by the United States and BASIC countries. It therefore had only informal status as an "Accord." There are numerous other examples of symbolic politics within a regime that provides ample scope because of its lengthy plenary sessions, in which all Parties make formal statements, and the large public audience, made up of NGOs and others that attend the annual COPs. While this can be irritating, if not destructive, of the real work of the UNFCCC, the politics of recognition and prestige also has a positive side. It partly accounts for the tenacity with which the EU has pursued a climate leadership role in order to burnish its credentials as a significant international actor (Bretherton & Vogler, 2006). Hosting a successful COP is also regarded as a significant indicator of national status: witness the major diplomatic effort put in by France in advance of and during the Paris COP, where climate change became one of a small number of national policy priorities.

What might be regarded as the politics of esteem between governments has provided a motor for regime development (Vogler, 2016, pp. 108–130). In the early period the

EU attempted to shame others into action and emulation by announcing targets and timetables, pre- and post-Copenhagen, and there were other occasions, at the 2007 Bali COP, for instance, when a reluctant United States was persuaded/shamed into joining a virtuous consensus. Comparison and emulation lie behind the post-Copenhagen stress on the publication of contributions. In the absence of internationally agreed-upon targets and related enforcement, the regime has been designed to operate on the basis of peer pressure and emulation with its progressive five-year cycles, binding review processes and the "Global Stock-Take." National reputation was always important, but it now became the intended driver of a central mechanism of the regime by which governments will, hopefully, be held accountable not only by their international peers but by their own domestic publics.

Overall, the Paris Agreement has been hailed as a revival of multilateralism after fears of collapse and a splintering of the regime in the aftermath of Copenhagen. It entered into force on November 4, 2016, but within four days the election of President Donald Trump cast a shadow over its future. On June 1st 2017 the President announced that the United States would be withdrawing from the Agreement but the other Parties responded by re-affirming their commitment, leaving the United States isolated. It remained unclear whether the Paris Agreement would henceforth be regarded as a the high water mark of a diminishing liberal international order or whether some of its more heroic assumptions about the "ratcheting up" of efforts to de-carbonize national economies and energy systems would be fulfilled over the coming decades. Equally uncertain was the continuance of the political alignments and understandings between major emitters that had, after 20 years of stalemate, made a new climate agreement possible.

REFERENCES

Andonova, L. L. B., Betsill, M. M., & H. Bulkeley, H. (2009). Transnational climate governance. *Global Environmental Politics*, 9(2), 52–73.

Bretherton, C., & Vogler, J. (2006). *The European Union as a global actor*. London: Routledge.

Brun, A. (2016). Conference diplomacy: The making of the Paris Agreement. *Politics and Governance*, 4(3), 115–123.

Bulkeley, H., & Schroeder, H. (2012). Beyond state and non-state divides: Global cities and the governing of climate change. *European Journal of International Relations*, 18(4), 743–766.

Detraz, M., & Betsill, M. M. (2010). Climate change and environmental security: For whom the discourse shifts. *International Studies Perspectives*, 10(3), 303–320.

Earth Negotiations Bulletin (ENB). (2015). Summary of the Paris Climate Change Conference: 29 November–13 December 2015. *ENB*, 12(663), 1–47.

Earth Negotiations Bulletin (ENB). (2016). Summary of the Marrakech Climate Change Conference: 7–19 November 2016, *ENB*, 12(689), 1–39.

European Council. (2008). *Climate change and international security*. Paper from the High Representative and the Commission to the European Council, S113/08. www.consilium .europa.eu.

Falkner, R. (2016). The Paris Agreement and the new logic of international climate politics. *International Affairs*, 92(5), 1107–1125.

Hurrell, A., & Kingsbury, B. (Eds.). (1992). *The international politics of the environment.* Oxford: Clarendon Press.

Intergovernmental Panel on Climate Change (IPCC). (2014). *Climate change 2014: Mitigation of climate change. Contribution of Working Group III to the fifth assessment report of the Intergovernmental Panel on Climate Change.* Cambridge: Cambridge University Press.

International Energy Agency (IEA). (2015). *Energy and climate change: World energy outlook special report.* Paris: OECD/IEA. Retrieved from www.iea.org

International Renewable Energy Association (IRENA). (2014). *RE-thinking energy.* Abu Dhabi: IRENA. Retrieved from www.irena.org/publication.

Newell, P. (2012). *Globalization and the environment: Capitalism, ecology and power.* Cambridge: Polity Press.

Pattberg, P. (2007). *Private institutions and global governance: The new politics of environmental sustainability.* (Cheltenham, UK: Edward Elgar).

Peters, G. P., Minx, J. C., & Weber, C. L. (2011). Growth in emissions transfers via international trade from 1990 to 2008. *Proceedings of the National Academy of Sciences, 108*(21), 8903–8908.

Royal Society. (2012). *People and the planet: The Royal Society science policy report.* April 2012, DES2470. London: Royal Society.

Stern, N. (2007). *The economics of climate change: The Stern review.* Cambridge: Cambridge University Press.

UNEP. (2011). *HFCs: A critical link in protecting climate and ozone layer.* Retrieved from http.www.unep.org

UNEP. (2012). Countries agree to curb powerful greenhouse gases in largest climate breakthrough since Paris. October 15, Press Release. Retrieved from http.unep.org

UNFCCC. (2015). Paris Agreement. FCCC/CP/2015/L.9. unfccc.int/paris_agreement

UNFCCC Secretariat. (2015). Synthesis report on the aggregate effect of the intended nationally determined contributions. FCCC/CP/2015/7. unfccc.int/resource/docs/2015/cop21

Van de Graaf, T. (2013). *The politics and institutions of global energy governance.* Houndmills, UK: Palgrave Macmillan.

Victor, D. G. (2011). *Global warming gridlock: Creating more effective strategies for protecting the planet.* Cambridge: Cambridge University Press.

Vogler, J. (2016). *Climate change in world politics.* Houndmills, UK: Palgrave Macmillan.

....

CHAPTER 3

ENERGY CONSUMPTION AS PART OF SOCIAL PRACTICES

The Alternative Approach of Practice Theory

....

ANA HORTA

RESEARCH on energy consumption has been based largely on an understanding of society and energy as two separate realms. On one side, engineers measure energy use and develop the technological innovation needed to overcome energy crises and sustainability issues; on the other side, social scientists identify the barriers that impede the adoption by individuals of energy-conservation actions. As argued by Elizabeth Shove (1998), this conventional view of energy and society obscures the social character of technological change; an alternative approach that can generate new knowledge on the social structuring of energy consumption is needed. The recent development of social practices theory has provided key advances in the understanding of energy consumption. However, this new approach requires a transformation of the conventional view of energy and society as different domains to a view of energy as part of the social practices that constitute society.

This chapter provides a brief account of social practices as an alternative and promising approach to conventional social science research on energy consumption. It begins by briefly tracing the evolution of social science research on energy consumption, highlighting how it progressively flowed toward recent developments in theories of practice while trying to overcome the limitations of the dominant theoretical frameworks. The chapter then summarizes the "practice turn" in sociology and its extension to research on energy consumption. The next section is an attempt to synthesize the most prominent features of practice theory used in the field of research on energy consumption. The following section presents an example of empirical research on energy consumption, using a practice theory approach. To conclude, the main advances in the understanding of energy consumption are synthesized.

CONFLUENCE OF RESEARCH ON ENERGY CONSUMPTION AND PRACTICE THEORY

Early research on energy end uses in households tried to explain variations among the behaviors of users mainly according to economic rationality and attitudinal models. These models have been based on attitudes, values, and responses to information and energy prices. Despite the complexity of consumers' behavior, as well as controversy about the effectiveness of attitudes in predicting behavior, these factors have been considered by mainstream research as predominant influences on energy consumption. Research on energy consumption has been motivated by the need to increase energy conservation; by prioritizing the identification of key variables that might promote (or hamper) behavior change toward energy saving and/or efficiency, the most influential theories of pro-environmental behavior—that is, individualized rational actor approaches—became dominant in social science research on energy consumption. Many studies have illustrated that consumers are generally unaware of the fact that their everyday life activities imply energy use, and energy bills do not establish connections between concrete actions or technologies and consumption. This recognition that energy consumption is largely invisible to users has led to repeated calls for education: raising individuals' awareness through more information and feedback on their own energy use. However, these approaches have not been able to explain fully energy consumption, and many times the results of interventions aiming at changing consumer behavior have been inconsistent.[1] Research has shown a gap between individuals' values and what they actually do. Indeed, social groups sharing pro-environmental discourses do not necessarily practice energy-saving behaviors.

In the 1980s and 1990s, sociological research on energy consumption was scarce and also tended to rely on individualized approaches to consumers' conscious choices. Consumption was predominantly analyzed as a means of communicating to others one's lifestyle, social status, and individual identity. As summarized by Alan Warde (2014, p. 283), "the model of an active and reflexive agent predominated, implying that conscious and intentional decisions steer consumption behaviour and explain its sense and direction." However, research premised on this theoretical model, which prevailed in the sociology of consumption, failed to capture ordinary and inconspicuous activities of everyday life (Warde, 2015) and their implications for energy consumption. The recognition that sociology of consumption was not able to account for environmental issues related to inconspicuous forms of resource consumption, such as energy, and that it was necessary to shed new light on mundane routines of everyday life (Shove & Warde, 2002), was a key development, creating openings for fundamentally new conceptual and empirical directions in research.

As research revealed the cultural significance of services provided by energy use and their integration in routines (Wilhite et al., 1996), researchers were becoming more aware of the need to attend to the relationship between energy use and the organization of everyday life (Guy & Shove, 2000). As proposed by Lutzenheiser (1993), research should go beyond individualized approaches focused on prices and attitudes and, with households and communities as units of analysis, should consider energy use as a social process. At the base of this alternative approach, key notions were emerging: the need to examine actual processes and contexts of energy use in everyday life; how energy intensive habits become normalized (i.e., embedded in everyday life as taken-for-granted expectations); and how a complex mix of institutional factors (instead of individual choices of consumers) influence energy demand. A new approach was needed, one that could go beyond the individual and could analyze the systemic transformation of habits and conventions (Shove, 2003). However, despite growing interest in routine and mundane aspects of everyday life, practice theory had not yet emerged in the research then conducted (Halkier, Katz-Gerro, & Martens, 2011).

A crucial step toward this new approach was convergence with recent developments in the sociology of science and technology. These promising insights were focused on the "seamless web" of technology and society, instead of separately analyzing the social, technical, economic, or political aspects of technological development (Bijker, Hughes, & Pinch, 1987). These new studies pointed to the inextricability of technical change and social contexts, some of which were based on the idea that both nonhuman actors (such as infrastructures and technological innovations) and social actors co-evolve and play creative parts in the construction of socio-technical systems (Guy & Shove, 2000). Traditionally, social thought has not taken materiality into account, in accordance with the distinction between culture and nature; however, in the last decades several theories have challenged the boundary between society and materiality (Schatzki, 2010). Actor-network theory, for example, analyzes relations between different kinds of actors (including objects) and how their networks form the social (Latour, 2005). Based on these theoretical developments, to understand energy use in everyday life it would be necessary to analyze the interactions between social and material elements and infrastructures. Thus, instead of limiting the analysis to the understanding of the social obstacles (attitudes, ignorance or lack of economic rationality, for example) to technological innovation that hinder energy conservation, with these new insights social science research could go further—investigating the material and social contexts and circumstances in which energy demand is structured. This strand of analysis did not just reinforce the need to explore the relationship between energy use and everyday life (Guy & Shove, 2000), but also generated awareness that socio-technical systems can support escalating levels of consumption by structuring certain patterns of daily life and related consumption practices (Shove & Warde, 2002).

The Practice Turn in the Sociology of Energy Consumption

At the beginning of the twenty-first century, a small but increasing number of studies in several fields of social science had begun to investigate practices. In spite of the diversity of activities considered "practices," as well as their heterogeneous theoretical orientations, these studies shared the "practice idiom" (Rouse, 2007), considering social practices as their basic object of study. This trend, proclaimed "the practice turn in contemporary theory" (Schatzki, Knorr Cetina, & Savigny, 2001), was inspired by diverse authors, such as Pierre Bourdieu (1977), Anthony Giddens (1979, 1984), and Charles Taylor (1985), among others. The practice-oriented approach emerged as an alternative to the duality between human action (or agency) and system (or structure). As synthesized by Sherry Ortner (1984, p. 159), by accepting "that society is a system, that the system is powerfully constraining, and yet that the system can be made and unmade through human action and interaction," practice theory was a unique and promising approach, allowing the integration of Marxist and Weberian theoretical frameworks. However, a coherent and systematized overview of practice theory was lacking. Theodore Schatzki (1996) and Andreas Reckwitz (2002) contributed significantly to developing this approach, later followed and complemented by Elizabeth Shove, Mika Pantzar, and Matt Watson (2012). Other authors have also contributed to systematizing the diversity of theories of practice, as well as advocating the potential of this approach for research in several fields related to consumption and environmental sustainability (e.g., Ropke, 2009; Sahakian & Wilhite, 2014; Spaargaren, 2011; Warde, 2005, 2014; Watson, 2012), some of which specifically focus on energy consumption (Gram-Hanssen, 2011, 2014; Shove & Walker, 2014; Strengers, 2012; Walker, 2014; Wilhite, 2013, 2014).

Shove's article, "Beyond the ABC: Climate Change Policy and Theories of Social Change" (2010), represents a key contribution, exemplifying theory of practice's usefulness over the dominant paradigms of economics and psychology. In an incisive critique of the "ABC model," which she argues has been embedded in most contemporary climate change policy, Shove (2010, p. 1273) contends that the conventional focus on individual responsibility for responding to climate change is based on a "strikingly limited understanding of the social world and how it changes." The ABC model describes a well-known social psychology model proposed by Paul Stern (2000), in which individual behavior (B) is driven by attitudes and values (A), as well as contextual factors (C)—which in Shove's view stands for choice, due to this concept's central role in this framework. The model presumes that through the identification of these determinants of pro-environmental behavior, it would be possible to plan strategies of intervention targeted at providing the right motivators and overcoming the barriers to behavior change (Shove, 2010). However, as she argues, this framework is not only unable to overcome the gap between values and action, it is also unable to account for the evolution of how needs and aspirations become normalized. In contrast, by focusing on how practices evolve, a practice-based approach allows the analysis of the emergence and reproduction of patterns of consumption, as well as the social conventions sustained and changed through the evolution of practices (Shove, 2010). Crucially, practices (not individuals) are taken as the central unit of analysis. This constitutes a considerable change in social analysis. Furthermore, by focusing on how practices evolve over time, this alternative approach is suitable for understanding the dynamics of social change. Thus, as clearly put by Tom Hargreaves (2011, p. 84),

> [s]ocial practice theory, in this view, raises a series of radically different questions about how to create more sustainable patterns of consumption. The focus is no longer on individuals' attitudes, behaviours and choices, but instead on how practices form, how they are reproduced, maintained, stabilized, challenged and ultimately killed-off; on how practices recruit practitioners to maintain and strengthen them through continued performance, and on how such practitioners may be encouraged to defect to more sustainable practices.

The recognition of the potential interest of practice theory for the development of the understanding of energy consumption has led to growing adoption of this framework. Some examples of research include practices of heating and cooling (Shove, Walker, & Brown, 2013; Strengers & Maller, 2011), residential heat comfort (Gram-Hanssen, 2010; Winther & Wilhite, 2015), use of information and communication technologies (Ropke & Christensen, 2012), use of mobile phones (Horta et al., 2016), energy retrofitting of dwellings (Bartiaux et al., 2014), car driving (Ryghaug & Toftaker, 2014; Shove, Watson, & Spurling, 2015), commuting (Cass & Faulconbridge, 2016), several household practices (Bartiaux & Salmón, 2014; Friis & Christensen, 2016), or a comparison of practices at home and work (Palm & Darby, 2014). The practice turn in social science research on energy consumption has become so resonant that a considerable number of articles and conference presentations use the terminology of practice theory while not explicitly adopting this approach.

In spite of an increasing number of studies engaging with practice theory, there is still some heterogeneity in the analytical assumptions guiding their approaches. Thus, a synthesis of features common to practice theories is "somewhat hazardous" (Warde, 2014, p. 285). Still, there are some understandings that are becoming prominent in the field of study of energy consumption. The following is a tentative synthesis of these.

SOCIAL PRACTICES

According to the idealized model of practice theory proposed by Reckwitz (2002, p. 249) to systematize the diversity of theoretical approaches to social practices,

> [a] "practice" (*Praktik*) is a routinized type of behavior which consists of several elements, interconnected to one another: forms of bodily activities, forms of mental activities, "things" and their use, a background knowledge in the form of understanding, know-how, states of emotion and motivational knowledge.

Such blocks of interconnected elements, rather than the individual, are the units of analysis of practice theory. As proposed by Reckwitz (2002, p. 250), the individual is analyzed as a carrier of practices: in fact, "not only a carrier of patterns of bodily behavior, but also certain routinized ways of understanding, knowing how and desiring." Since each individual carries out multiple practices, he is "the unique crossing point of practices" and his understandings (of the world and himself) depend on his practices (Reckwitz, 2002, p. 256). Thus, to analyze a practice such as cooking or walking a dog, it is necessary to identify the connections between elements such as bodily performances or movements, mental patterns, objects handled, and specific forms of collective knowledge—in other words, routinized ways of understanding, knowing, wanting, and feeling.

This acknowledgment of the role of materiality in social life is an important feature of practice theory. Like other contemporary theories that have contested the distinction between society and nature, and the consequent neglect of materiality, practice theories acknowledge the interaction of humans and their material surroundings (Schatzki, 2010). Although there is still some controversy regarding the role of objects in social practices (Warde, 2014), the most recent developments in practice theory point to more than just analyzing the interaction between materiality and practices. Recently, Schatzki (2010, p. 128) claimed that "material phenomena are part of society," since "practices are carried on amid and determinative of, while also dependent on and altered by, material arrangements" (Schatzki, 2010, p. 130). Shove, Pantzar, and Watson (2012, p. 14) do not simply acknowledge materiality as part of practices, they emphasize it; indeed, in their simplified definition of the three elements that compose practices, materials are deemed to be one:

"By elements we mean:

- *materials*—including things, technologies, tangible physical entities, and the stuff of which objects are made;
- *competences*—which encompass skill, know-how, and techniques; and
- *meanings*—in which we include symbolic meanings, ideas, and aspirations."

Other authors have proposed that practices are constituted by somewhat different elements. Specifically regarding the study of energy consumption, Gram-Hanssen (2011) argues that the most appropriate elements of practices are (1) know-how and embodied habits, (2) institutionalized knowledge and explicit rules, (3) engagements, and (4) technologies. Strengers and Maller (2011), on the other hand, prefer to define these elements as (1) practical knowledge, (2) material infrastructures, and (3) common understandings. In both of these conceptions, materiality is included as an essential element.

Besides emphasizing the role of objects and materiality, practice theories also accentuate the role of bodies in social practices, through embodied skills, tacit knowledge, sensory knowing, habits, dispositions, or emotions, for example. Along these lines, research has included performances that "can be shown but not said, or competently enacted only when freed from verbal mediation" (Rouse, 2007, p. 515). This allows the analysis of doings that are not easily translated into words (Martens, 2012). However, as argued by Warde (2014), while this has also contributed to minimizing the relevance of

discursive consciousness and decision-making (which is characteristic of the individualistic models of action criticized by practice theories), the role of bodily processes still
need clarification.

It is important to emphasize the dynamic character of practices. According to
Schatzki (2010, p. 129), "a practice is not a set of regular actions, but an evolving domain
of varied activities linked by common and orchestrated items," such as understandings,
rules, normative teleologies, and material arrangements. The linkage between elements
has a central role in Shove, Pantzar, and Watson's view of how practices evolve: the
elements are actively combined or integrated when practices are enacted and, as the
connections between these elements are established, sustained, or broken, practices
"emerge, persist, shift and disappear" (Shove, Pantzar, & Watson, 2012, p. 14). Thus,
practices are invented when links between materials, competences, and meanings are
established. In order for practices to endure and remain effective, these connections
"have to be renewed time and again" (Shove, Pantzar, & Watson, 2012, p. 24). Practices
disappear when these links are broken or no longer maintained. When new elements
are introduced, as the result of technological innovation or as a consequence of changes
in meanings, for example, previously established links may erode and practices change
(Shove, Pantzar, & Watson, 2012). Thus, as asserted by Warde (2005, p. 140), the sources
of change are within practices themselves: "The concept of practice inherently combines
a capacity to account for both reproduction and innovation." From this point of view, an
analysis of the evolution of social practices needs to take into account the establishment
and history of connections between all the elements of practices, instead of focusing on
just one of these aspects, as in conventional histories of technology (Shove, Pantzar, &
Watson, 2012).

The establishment of connections between the elements that compose practices does
not just trace the trajectories or histories of practices (recognized as specific activities
or entities, such as driving a car or bathing), it also conditions different performances
of practices (how they are effectively reproduced in everyday life across different times
and spaces). Importantly, practices are not carried out in identical ways and can take
differentiated forms (Warde, 2005). The fact that practices are enacted in specific spaces
and times and depend on historically situated contexts contributes to the variability
of performances. As stated by Shove, Pantzar, and Watson (2012, p. 122), "each performance is situated and in some respect unique."

These notions of practices as entities and as performances have been the object of
some controversy. By centering the analysis on practices instead of individuals, practices
become conceived as "entities." Indeed, sometimes researchers have referred to practices
as "recruiting" their practitioners. However, as pointed out by Galvin and Sunikka-
Blank (2016), this conception of practices is a "heuristic device" or model constructed by
researchers to help explain complex phenomena; therefore, such assertions of practices
as entities (nearly beings) leading the action lack clarity. The underlying issue, which
has divided theories of practice, is the ontological and methodological status of practice
(Warde, 2014).[2] More radical versions of practice theory consider practices as recognizable entities, while others embrace a more limited analytical conception of practices

as performances. However, both notions can be compatible. As asserted by Southerton et al. (2012, p. 240): "practices configure performances, and practices are reproduced, and stabilized, adapted and innovated, through performances."

It should be highlighted that individuals do not passively carry out pre-formatted practices; they can improvise, experiment, and adapt to local situations (Shove, Pantzar, & Watson, 2012; Warde, 2005). In addition, since individuals carry out multiple practices, these can influence each other, and there may be dependencies and tensions between different practices. Changes in one practice may also trigger changes in related practices (Sahakian & Wilhite, 2014). These interactions between practices, as argued by Shove, Pantzar, and Watson (2012), may have consequences such as mutual adaptation, destruction, synergy, or radical transformation.

Empirical Example: Energy as an Ingredient of Mobile Phone Management

The process of formation of the practice of managing the mobile phone can be presented as an example of how energy consumption can be analyzed with a practice theory lens. The following is a reinterpretation of data from a study of the energy consumption related to the use of electronic media by teenagers in Lisbon, Portugal.[3] The data collected reveal not just how different elements are combined in the process of emergence and normalization of the practice of mobile phone management, but also how energy consumption takes part in this process.

Teenagers were chosen as a preferential group of practitioners since a previous study indicated that their energy-intensive routines of electronic media are not likely to change toward energy saving due to a strong engagement and integration of these technologies in their everyday life (Schmidt et al., 2014). The research included a survey carried out with 748 teenagers enrolled in the ninth through twelfth grades in three schools with very different socioeconomic backgrounds. Their average age was 16 years. After the survey, respondents were invited to volunteer to be interviewed. Twenty-two interviews were conducted. The survey and individual interviews took place between November 2014 and March 2015.

Adopting the conceptualization of practice theory proposed by Shove, Pantzar, and Watson (2012), this example illustrates how the establishment of connections between materials, competences, and meanings give rise to the practice of mobile phone management, with direct implications for energy use. In an initial stage, these three elements already existed in the everyday lives of these teenagers, but had not yet been integrated in a way that enabled the emergence of this practice. Indeed, at this stage users had been given their first mobile phones, but the functionality of these devices was very limited—these phones were used mostly to call their parents and let them know where they were and at what time they should be picked up from school or after-school activities. Thus, the meanings associated with these devices were mostly related to connectivity between family members, and perhaps also security or control. Even though having a mobile phone was already socially valued and thus was considered desirable by the children, their competences to use this technology were in most cases minimal.

However, changes in the material arrangements related to mobile phone use, together with changes in the meanings attributed to these technologies, have accelerated the rhythm of use. Among this sample of teenagers, this co-evolution of elements happens when they start using a smartphone and in addition have access to Wi-Fi networks. Smartphones have touch screens, advanced operating systems, and enhanced hardware, and these features allow engaging in multiple activities, such as taking photos, recording videos, browsing the Internet, playing games online, posting messages on social networks, and so on. Thus, there is the possibility of developing an increased number of practices, many of them connoting desirable meanings, particularly among young people, such as having easy access to entertainment (e.g., music, games, countless applications) and information (through web browsing), communicating with friends, or being popular. Additionally, due to an institutional framework favorable to the development of wireless infrastructures, since 2006 all public schools in Portugal have free wireless broadband access to the Internet. There is also a large number of free Wi-Fi spots, including in the main commercial and public transport spaces. Thus, these material arrangements grant access to entertainment and other meanings valued by teenagers nearly everywhere throughout their daily life. As some teenagers admit, their mobile phones have become "an addiction" (Horta et al., 2016) for themselves and almost all other teenagers they know. However, this co-evolution of material arrangements (smartphones and access to free wireless infrastructures in different spaces and times of the day, not just at home) and the meanings related to these activities demands some orchestration. Indeed, in spite of the remarkable development of mobile phones in recent years, their enhanced technological features have significantly increased their energy consumption, which is limited by batteries. Hence, the daily reproduction of practices related to mobile phones, such as social networking, listening to music, or coordinating activities with family and friends, requires the development of competences that can assure that smartphones have enough power to function. There is a need to orchestrate the practices related to mobile phone use with the battery power available. As users develop the competences, embodied skills, and dispositions for charging and managing the power of their mobile phones in order to keep their routines flowing, a new practice develops and becomes normal. The reproduction of this practice allows the successful integration of the mobile phone in practitioners' everyday life, since the normalization of this practice guarantees that the smartphone has utility for the performance of other practices. Interestingly, if the practice of managing the mobile phone does not become normalized, tension and disruption emerge, since the inoperability of the device affects and can even thwart co-dependent practices.

The practice of managing mobile phones includes actions such as regularly checking the remaining power of the device, calculating how much power will be needed to perform other practices (important phone calls or messages, for example) until the battery can be charged again, curtailing unnecessary practices (e.g., listening to music while walking), turning off functions and features when these are not necessary (such as Wi-Fi), turning on applications or features that allow power saving (through lowering the brightness of the screen and turning off wireless connections), or charging the battery earlier than necessary. Although some of these actions may increase the energy efficiency of the device, the meaning of energy saving does not seem to be part of it. Indeed, as pointed out by some of the teenagers interviewed, their concern is solely to avoid draining the battery, and for that reason they sometimes use other devices (such as computers or MP3 players) that can execute the same tasks (checking social networks or listening to music, for example) instead of their mobile phones. For the same reason, some interviewees indicated that they use their mobile phones while the devices are charging: from their point of view, this way they are not running down the battery.

This empirical example thus shows how the establishment of links between the elements of practices allows the formation of new practices, and also how different practices sharing common elements (in this case the mobile phone) are co-dependent. More important, this case illustrates how energy is as an ingredient of social practices. Thus, from this point of view, energy participates in the reproduction of social practices—not as a resource that is consumed, but rather as part of the flow of elements that compose everyday life and need to be orchestrated.

This example can also illustrate a critical methodological issue that needs to be addressed when conducting empirical research based on practice theory. As pointed out by Warde (2014), a key question results from the fact that practices are considered the unit of analysis. The need to clearly conceptualize what should be analyzed as a practice is further complicated by the need to trace clear boundaries of specific practices, especially because practices form "bundles and complexes" (Shove, Pantzar, & Watson, 2012) with other practices. An example of the ambiguity in the delimitation of the practice of mobile phone management could be whether to view not making a phone call to a friend as part of saving power or, instead, as part of friendship management, so to speak.

CONCLUSION: ADVANCES IN THE UNDERSTANDING OF ENERGY CONSUMPTION

The emergence of practice theory in social science research on energy consumption is a particularly insightful and promising conceptual turn. By focusing on the interaction between social structures and everyday life, and including materiality, practice theory provides a fruitful framework for the analysis of energy that corresponds to the research directions identified by social science.

Furthermore, as contended by Harold Wilhite (2014), after decades of ineffective policies intended to reduce energy consumption that have been based on dominant rational and economic behavioral models, practice-based approaches offer the potential for creative new energy-saving policies grounded in improved conceptual understandings of how energy is consumed in everyday practices. This alternative approach, however, introduces a particular challenge to energy policy, since it presupposes changes in social practices, and not in individuals' decisions. And, therefore, a "coordinated policy response" (Strengers & Maller, 2011, p. 166) is necessary. Indeed, a key advance in the understanding of energy consumption made possible with the contribution of practice theory is the acknowledgment that energy is an ingredient of social practices, as claimed by Shove and Walker (2014), in accordance with Schatzki's (2010) view of material phenomena as part of society. Thus, energy consumption should not be considered as something invisible that needs to be brought to light in order for consumers to reduce their energy use. Energy consumption is part of everyday life and society, and therefore the elements that constitute the practices of everyday life are what need to be changed. In fact, as clearly said by Wilhite (2013, p. 67), energy consumption should not be considered as "something performed by individuals," but rather as a "result of the interaction between things, people, knowledge, and social contexts." Practice theory thus offers an alternative to models of individual choice, and it "uncover[s] phenomena normally concealed in the cultural analysis of consumption" (Warde, 2015, p. 126). For these reasons, this alternative framework seems particularly suitable for research on sustainability and environmental issues involving the inconspicuous consumption of natural resources in everyday life.

Summing up, practice theory emerges as a useful way of understanding the relations between energy and society since it accounts for the collective structures of practices, including technological structures (Gram-Hanssen, 2014) and other material arrangements. This supposes the recognition of the fact that "energy consumption is not a practice in itself" (Gram-Hanssen, 2014, p. 94), but an intrinsic part of many daily practices that is taken for granted and is considered normal by most people. Indeed, as pointed out by Shove and Walker (2014, p. 42), energy "is best understood as part of the ongoing reproduction and transformation of society itself," instead of as an external factor; therefore, "understanding energy is first and foremost a matter of understanding the sets of practice that are enacted, reproduced and transformed in any one society" (Shove & Walker, 2014, p. 48).

NOTES

1. For more extended accounts of early research on energy consumption see Rosa, Machlis & Keating (1988); Wilhite et al., (2000); Horta et al. (2014); Frederiks, Stenner & Hobman (2015).

2. The issues related to the articulation between practices and individual performances were thoroughly criticized by Turner (1994) and were later discussed by Rouse (2007).

3. More information can be found in Horta et al. (2016). This research had the support of the Institute of Social Sciences, University of Lisbon, and was funded by the Portuguese Foundation for Science and Technology under the award EXPL/IVC-SOC/2340/2013

REFERENCES

Bartiaux, F., Gram-Hanssen, K., Fonseca, P., Ozolina, L. & Christensen, T. H. (2014). A practice-theory approach to homeowners' energy retrofits in four European areas. *Building Research & Information*, 42(4), 525–538. doi: 10.1080/09613218.2014.900253

Bartiaux, F., & Salmón, L. R. (2014). Family dynamics and social practice theories: An investigation of daily practices related to food, mobility, energy consumption and tourism. *Nature and Culture*, 9(2), 204–224.

Bijker, W. E., Hughes, T. P., & Pinch, T. J. (1987). *The social construction of technological systems.* Cambridge, MA: MIT Press.

Bourdieu, P. (1977). *Outline of a theory of practice.* Cambridge: Cambridge University Press.

Cass, N., and Faulconbridge, J. (2016). Commuting practices: New insights into modal shift from theories of social practice. *Transport Policy*, 45, 1–14.

Frederiks, E. R., Stenner, K., & Hobman, E. V. (2015). The socio-demographic and psychological predictors of residential energy consumption: A comprehensive review. *Energies*, 8, 573–609.

Friis, F., and Christensen, T. H. (2016). The challenge of time shifting energy demand practices: Insights from Denmark. *Energy Research & Social Science*, 19, 124–133.

Galvin, R., & Sunikka-Blank, M. (2016). Schatzkian practice theory and energy consumption research: Time for some philosophical spring cleaning? *Energy Research & Social Science*, 22, 63–68.

Giddens, A. (1979). *Central problems in social theory: Action, structure and contradiction in social analysis.* London: Macmillan.

Giddens, A. (1984). *The constitution of society.* Cambridge: Polity Press.

Gram-Hanssen, K. (2010). Residential heat comfort practices: Understanding users. *Building Research & Information*, 38(2), 175–186.

Gram-Hanssen, K. (2011). Understanding change and continuity in residential energy consumption. *Journal of Consumer Culture*, 11(1), 61–78.

Gram-Hanssen, K. (2014). New needs for better understanding of household's energy consumption—bahaviour, lifestyle or practices? *Architectural Engineering and Design Management*, 10(1–2), 91–107.

Guy, S., & Shove, E. (2000). *A sociology of energy, buildings and the environment: Constructing knowledge, designing practice.* Oxon: Routledge.

Halkier, B., Katz-Gerro, T., & Martens, Lydia. (2011). Applying practice theory to the study of consumption: Theoretical and methodological considerations. *Journal of Consumer Culture*, 11(1), 3–13.

Hargreaves, T. (2011). Practiceing behaviour change: Applying social practice theory to pro-environmental behaviour change. *Journal of Consumer Culture*, 11(1), 79–99.

Horta, A., Fonseca, S., Truninger, M., Nobre, N., & Correia, A. (2016). Mobile phones, batteries and power consumption: An analysis of social practices in Portugal. *Energy Research & Social Science*, 13, 15–23.

Horta, A., Willhite, H., Schmidt, L., & Bartiaux, F. (2014). Socio-technical and cultural approaches to energy consumption: An introduction. *Nature and Culture, 9*(2), 115–121.

Latour, B. (2005). *Reassembling the social: An introduction to Actor-Network Theory.* Oxford: Oxford University Press.

Lutzenheiser, L. (1993). Social and behavioral aspects of energy use. *Annual Review of Energy and the Environment, 18,* 247–289.

Martens, L. (2012). Practice "in talk" and talk "as practice": Dish washing and the reach of language. *Sociological Research Online, 17*(3), 1–11.

Ortner, S. B. (1984). Theory in anthropology since the sixties. *Comparative Studies in Society and History, 26*(1), 126–166.

Palm, J., & Darby, S. J. (2014). The meanings of practices for energy consumption: A comparison of homes and workplaces. *Science & Technology Studies, 2,* 72–92.

Reckwitz, A. (2002). Toward a theory of social practices: A development in culturalist theorizing. *European Journal of Social Theory, 5*(2), 243–263.

Ryghaug, M., & Toftaker, M. (2014). A transformative practice? Meaning, competence, and material aspects of driving electric cars in Norway. *Nature and Culture, 9*(2), 146–163.

Ropke, I. (2009). Theories of practice: New inspiration for ecological economic studies on consumption. *Ecological Economics, 68,* 2490–2497.

Ropke, I., & Christensen, T. H. (2012). Energy impacts of ICT: Insights from an everyday life perspective. *Telematics and Informatics, 29,* 348–361.

Rosa, E. A., Machlis, G. E., & Keating, K. M. (1988). Energy and society. *Annual Review of Sociology, 14,* 149–172.

Rouse, J. (2007). Practice theory. In D. M. Gabby, P. Thagard, & J. Woods (Eds.), *Handbook of the philosophy of science* (pp. 499–540). Vol. 15 (S. Turner & M. Risjord, Vol. Eds.): *Philosophy of anthropology and sociology.* Dordrecht: Elsevier.

Sahakian, M., & Wilhite, H. (2014). Making practice theory practicable: towards more sustainable forms of consumption. *Journal of Consumer Culture, 14*(1), 25–44.

Schatzki, T. R. (1996). *Social practices: A Wittgensteinian approach to human activity and the social.* Cambridge: Cambridge University Press.

Schatzki, T. R. (2010). Materiality and social life. *Nature and Culture, 5*(2), 123–149.

Schatzki, T. R., Cetina, K. K., & von Savigny, E. (Eds.). (2001). *The practice turn in contemporary theory.* London: Routledge.

Schmidt, L., Horta, A., Correia, A., & Fonseca, S. (2014). Generational gaps and paradoxes regarding energy consumption and saving. *Nature and Culture, 9*(2), 183–203.

Shove, E. (1998). Gaps, barriers and conceptual chasms: theories of technology transfer and energy in buildings. *Energy Policy, 26*(15), 1105–1112.

Shove, E. (2003). Converging conventions of comfort, cleanliness and convenience. *Journal of Consumer Policy, 26,* 395–418.

Shove, E. (2010). Beyond the ABC: climate change policy and theories of social change. *Environment and Planning A, 42,* 1273–1285.

Shove, E., Pantzar, M., & Watson, M. (2012). *The dynamics of social practice: Everyday life and how it changes.* London: Sage.

Shove, E., & Walker, G. (2014). What is energy for? Social practice and energy demand. *Theory, Culture & Society, 31*(5), 41–58.

Shove, E., Walker, G., & Brown, S. (2013). Transnational transitions: The diffusion and integration of mechanical cooling. *Urban Studies, 51*(7), 1–14.

Shove, E., & Warde, A. (2002). Inconspicuous consumption: The sociology of consumption, lifestyles, and the environment. In R. E. Dunlap, F. H. Buttel, P. Dickens, & A. Gijswijt (Eds.), *Sociological theory and the environment* (pp. 230–251). Lanham, MD: Rowman & Littlefield.

Shove, E., Watson, M., & Spurling, N. (2015). Conceptualizing connections: Energy demand, infrastructures and social practices. *European Journal of Social Theory, 18*(3), 274–287.

Southerton, D., Olsen, W., Warde, A., & Cheng, S.-L. (2012). Practices and trajectories: A comparative analysis of reading in France, Norway, the Netherlands, the UK and the USA. *Journal of Consumer Culture, 12*(3), 237–262.

Spaargaren, G. (2011). Theories of practice: Agency, technology, and culture. Exploring the relevance of practice theories for the governance of sustainable consumption practices in the new world-order. *Global Environmental Change, 21*, 813–822.

Stern, P. (2000). Toward a coherent theory of environmentally significant behavior. *Journal of Social Issues, 56*, 407–424.

Strengers, Y. (2012). Peak electricity demand and social practice theories: Reframing the role of change agents in the energy sector. *Energy Policy, 44*, 226–234.

Strengers, Y., & Maller, C. (2011). Integrating health, housing and energy policies: Social practices of cooling. *Building Research & Information, 39*(2), 154–168.

Taylor, C. (1985). *Philosophy and the human sciences: Collected papers*, Vol. 2. Cambridge: Cambridge University Press.

Turner, S. (1994). *The social theory of practices: Tradition, tacit knowledge, and presuppositions.* Chicago: University of Chicago Press.

Walker, G. (2014). The dynamics of energy demand: Change, rhythm and synchronicity. *Energy Research & Social Science, 1*, 49–55.

Warde, A. (2005). Consumption and theories of practice. *Journal of Consumer Culture, 5*(2), 131–153.

Warde, A. (2014). After taste: culture, consumption and theories of practice. *Journal of Consumer Culture, 14*(3), 279–303.

Warde, A. (2015). The sociology of consumption: Its recent development. *Annual Review of Sociology, 41*, 117–134.

Watson, M. (2012). How theories of practice can inform transition to a decarbonised transport system. *Journal of Transport Geography, 24*, 488–496.

Wilhite, H. (2013). Energy consumption as cultural practice: Implications for theory and policy of sustainable energy use. In S. Strauss, S. Rupp, & T. Love (Eds.), *Cultures of energy: Power, practices, technologies* (pp. 60–72). Walnut Creek, CA: Left Coast Press.

Wilhite, H. (2014). Insights from social practice theory and social learning theory for sustainable energy consumption. *Flux, 96*(2), 24–30.

Wilhite, H., Nakagami, H., Masuda, T., Yamaga, Y., & Haneda, H. (1996). A Cross-Cultural Analysis of Household Energy-Use Behavior in Japan and Norway. *Energy Policy, 24*(9), 795–803.

Wilhite, H., Shove, E., Lutzenhiser, L., & Kempton, W. (2000). The legacy of twenty years of demand side management: We know more about individual behavior but next to nothing about demand." In E. Jochem, J. Sathaye, & D. Bouille (Eds.), *Society, behaviour and climate change mitigation* (pp. 109–126). Dordrecht: Kluwer Academic.

Winther, T., & Wilhite, H. (2015). An analysis of the household energy rebound effect from a practice perspective: Spatial and temporal dimensions. *Energy Efficiency, 8*, 585–607.

CHAPTER 4

ANALYZING THE SOCIO-TECHNICAL TRANSFORMATION OF ENERGY SYSTEMS

The Concept of "Sustainability Transitions"

HARALD ROHRACHER

INTRODUCTION

THE way we produce and use energy plays a decisive role in some of the grand challenges our societies currently face: global warming and the need to reduce greenhouse gas emissions, the depletion of finite resources and the need to move away from a fossil-fuel-based economy, and not least, questions of global equity and justice in the way we are handling the impact of climate change and opportunities for sustainable development. Our current, unsustainable generation and use of energy are deeply entrenched in the sociocultural, economic, political, and material structures of our world-society: the infrastructures of production, transport, and housing that we have built over many decades; the geopolitical relations that have been shaped to allow for access to cheap fossil fuels; the organization of our economic systems and the global organization of production; and not least, the cultures of energy use that have become dominant in our consumer-oriented societies.

It is obvious that the immense reduction of greenhouse gas emissions required to keep global temperature rise under a level of 2°C or even 1.5°C cannot be achieved by optimizing our systems of energy, transport, or housing, or speeding up technological change. The required reduction of greenhouse gas emissions by 80% or more within the next decades can only be achieved by a radical change of our fossil-fuel dependent economies, infrastructures, and ways of living—in other words, by a transition toward much more sustainable systems of production and consumption.

Social science research may help to increase our capacity for governing such change processes toward more sustainable energy generation and use. Of particular relevance are approaches that build on the deep entanglement of technologies and innovation with sociocultural, political, and economic elements and which thus frame the problem of energy transition as a socio-technical challenge. Such interrelations have long since been at the core of social studies of science and technology, and of more economically oriented innovation studies. The study of "sustainability transitions" as part of this inter-disciplinary research field focuses on systemic, fundamental change processes toward greater sustainability. Along with the increasing social and political awareness of the need for a radical socio-technical change, this field has increasingly attracted academic attention over the past years (see Markard, Raven, & Truffer, 2012). At the core of transition studies is the ambition of a goal-oriented, transformative change. Contributing to such a goal requires a sound understanding of not only the socio-technical relations that create the stable structures characteristic of our current energy system, but also the dynamics of systemic change and of governance strategies aiming for a more sustainable energy system.

The aim of this chapter is to provide a short overview of concepts of socio-technical change and "sustainability transitions" in particular, and their relevance for the trans-formation of our energy system. Some of the main approaches in this field are the mul-tilevel perspective of innovations, strategic niche management, transition management, and "technological innovation systems" approaches. Some of these approaches will be discussed in the next section of this chapter, along with critical perspectives pointing to their limitations and "blind spots," as well as more nuanced views and conceptual improvements. The following section will then discuss a concrete example of socio-technical change in the field of renewable energy—wind power—and will reflect on some of the lessons we can draw for our understanding of transitions toward a more sustainable energy system.

STUDYING TRANSITION PROCESSES: CONCEPTUAL APPROACHES

The concept of "socio-technical transitions" to denote fundamental, systemic change processes has been developed from the late 1980s onward as a "fusion" of different approaches to analyze innovation and socio-technical change, particularly from Neo-Schumpeterian economics of innovation or evolutionary economics (e.g., Dosi et al., 1988; Freeman, 1994; Nelson & Winter, 1977), history of technology, and social studies (or social shaping) of technology approaches (e.g., Bijker, Hughes, & Pinch, 1987; Hughes, 1983). The predominantly Dutch group of scholars brought with them a strong policy orientation focusing on the development of strategies to shape socio-technical change, which was understood as a socially distributed and systemic process. Taking the idea of variation and selection from evolutionary economics and combining it with the science and technology studies understanding of a simultaneous, co-evolutionary shaping of the content and context of technologies, Schot (1992) proposed a "quasi-evolutionary model of technological change," which resulted in a three-pronged strategy to influence technological change: the development of alternative variations of technologies (experiments); the modification of the selection environment (regulation, government policies); and the creation and utilization of a technological nexus (i.e., the creation of institutional linkages between innovation processes, external policies, and long-term orientation). Also, the related concept of (socio-)technological regimes as a stable set of design configurations that have already profited from past learning processes, capital outlays, and so on (Kemp, 1994) is modeled on evolutionary economics thinking about technological paradigms and technological regimes (e.g., Dosi, 1982; Nelson & Winter, 1982). Creating protected spaces for experiments with new socio-technical constellations and for learning between producers, users, and a range of other stakeholders—the strategic management of niches (SNM)—was seen as the prevailing means by which to build up momentum and eventually overthrow existing regimes (Hoogma et al., 2002; Schot, Hoogma, & Elzen, 1994; Weber et al., 1999). Even during the formative phase of transition studies, "sustainability transitions" with a particular focus on energy, transport, and buildings took center stage in the discussions.

TRANSITIONS IN A MULTILEVEL PERSPECTIVE

These strands of research were eventually consolidated in a multilevel perspective (MLP) of socio-technical transitions, which distinguishes socio-technical transformation dynamics at different levels of structuration: niches (technological projects, emerging technologies) as a source of variety, test-bed, and an "engine for change"; regimes (such as the energy system) providing stable structures and a selection environment for innovations; and socio-technical landscapes (deeply entrenched cultural norms, values) as slowly changing socio-technical structures at the level of societies (Geels, 2005; Rip & Kemp, 1998). MLP thus points to the multidimensionality of processes of socio-technical change, to the multiplicity of actors involved in the process, and to the embeddedness of local practices and niches in various social contexts with their own specific histories and dynamics.

The central element in this concept is the meso-level of the "socio-technical regime" at which socio-technical configurations are temporarily stabilized and supported by a rule set, or "grammar," that structures the socio-technical co-evolution process. A regime is defined by the fulfillment of a societal function, such as energy, transport, or communication, and thus puts more emphasis on aspects of use and functionality than economics of innovation approaches (Geels, 2004). The regime level incorporates the mutually reinforcing technological and institutional structures of these specific societal domains and is characterized by a resistance to change (which, for example, may cause promising new technologies to fail). The way such a regime evolves "is structured by the accumulated knowledge, engineering practices, value of past investments, interests of firms, established product requirements and meanings, intra- and interorganisational relationships and government policies" (Kemp, Rip, & Schot, 2001, p. 273). Geels (2004) distinguishes between systems (resources, material aspects), actors involved in maintaining and changing the system, and the rules and institutions (not only at a regulative/legislative level, but also cognitive and normative rule sets) that guide actors' perceptions and activities.

Under specific circumstances, regimes may eventually transform into fundamentally new configurations, especially if radical innovations (technological and/or institutional) coincide with strong outside pressures on the regime (Geels & Schot, 2007). Such regime transitions are closely linked to "system innovations" (Elzen, Geels, & Green, 2004; Grin, 2008), resulting in new interrelations of technologies, institutions, actor networks, and social practices.

Socio-technical niches play a key role for the emergence of radical innovations as they provide "incubation rooms for radical novelties" and locations for learning processes, for example about technical specifications, user preferences, public policies, or symbolic meanings (Geels, 2004). Different patterns of how niches may impact on regimes, such as niche accumulation or the hybridization of niches with established technologies, have been identified (Geels, 2002; Raven, 2007), though these linking mechanisms between niches and regime still lack analytical depth (Smith, 2007). Further work has rather focused on niche-internal processes, such as the formation of social networks, the shaping of expectations and learning processes (Schot & Geels, 2008; Verbong et al., 2010), or on the growth and aggregation of niches as an interaction between local projects and increasingly global niches with an emerging community sharing cognitive, formal, and normative rules (Geels & Raven, 2006; Raven & Geels, 2010). Smith and Raven (2012; see also Raven et al., 2016) interrogate the concept of niches as "protective space" and the different ways in which niches may contribute to path-breaking innovations by shielding against mainstream selection pressures, by nurturing alternative socio-technical configurations, or by different forms of empowerment (e.g., adapting to dominant regimes through fit-and-conform, or pushing for change through stretch-and-transform strategies).

The creation of novel technologies and radical change thus is brought about not only by bottom-up processes in niches, but also by the interactions of multiple levels: niche innovations building up momentum; destabilized regimes creating windows of opportunity for niche innovations; and changes at the macro-level of socio-technical landscapes creating pressure on the regime (Schot & Geels, 2008).

Studies of transition processes have predominantly been carried out in a long-term historic perspective (as an example, see Geels, 2006), which typically results in a rather phenomenological understanding of historic patterns and dynamics of change. However, attempts have been made to differentiate specific dynamics or patterns of transitions depending on internally or externally available resources, the type of regime coordination, type of steering, timing and type of interaction between niches, landscape, and regime (Geels & Schot, 2007; Smith, Stirling, & Berkhout, 2005). The dominant understanding of transitions as punctuated equilibrium has been replaced by different transformation patterns, including more gradual transformations and adaptive regime responses—the reorientation of trajectories, endogenous renewal, emergent transformation, and purposive transition (Smith, Stirling, & Berkhout, 2005), or transformation, reconfiguration, technological substitution, and de-alignment and re-alignment (Geels & Schot, 2007). A further deepening of the understanding of niche dynamics has been achieved by taking into account couplings and interactions between different regimes or between niches and different regimes they relate to (Raven & Verbong, 2007, 2009), such as biogas generation linking energy regimes and regimes of food production and agriculture.

EXTENDING THE MULTILEVEL CONCEPT: AGENCY, POWER, PLACE

Transition studies—and particularly the multilevel perspective—have been criticized for their weak conceptualization of several key social dimensions of change. To name but a few of these debates,

- Genus and Coles (2008) as well as Smith and others (2005) have pointed to the problems of adequately dealing with questions of social agency and power. Along similar lines, Meadowcroft (2009) addresses the problem of collectively specifying the character of desired transitions that can be expected to be messy and infested with power struggles, rather than consensual as conceptualized in many treatments of transition. Moreover, as Meadowcroft (2009) rightly points out, policy instruments of transition management (visioning, experiments, etc.) are often set apart from more traditional regulatory, planning, financial, and tax-based approaches, which makes it difficult to integrate these policy instruments and their supporters into transition efforts. In general, transition management should be much more concerned with political interactions and policy processes, through which societal goals are determined, decisions enforced, and resources allocated.
- Walker and Shove (2007) question the way transition management and reflexive governance deal with the inherent contingency and ambivalence of sustainability goals and ask to bring such contradictions into "the open" to avoid obscuring the dynamics of power involved in transition practice.

- Along similar lines, Berkhout (2006) questions the possibility of normative, consensual, collective visions as a guidance of system innovations, in contrast to visions as an emergent feature of social processes (see also Garud & Gehman, 2012).
- Researchers of urban and regional change have also noted that dimensions of space and scale have so far been insufficiently integrated in the studies of transitions (Bulkeley, Castán Broto, & Maassen, 2011; Hodson & Marvin, 2009, 2011).

Beyond a broader debate on the validity of these criticisms (see Geels, 2011), the engagement with these weaknesses has also infused new dynamics into studying sustainability transition processes from new angles. The role of space and scale in transition processes, for example, has become a prominent issue in transition studies (Coenen, Benneworth, & Truffer, 2012; Raven, Schot, & Berkhout, 2012) and has led to a more differentiated view of the role of regions in sustainability transitions (e.g., Späth & Rohracher, 2010; Truffer & Coenen, 2012) and the study of urban sustainability initiatives and strategies as a key element of wider processes of change (e.g., Bulkeley et al., 2011; Bulkeley, Castán Broto, & Maassen, 2014; Rohracher & Späth, 2014; Wolfram & Frantzeskaki, 2016). Similarly, questions of power have been taken up more explicitly (Avelino & Rotmans, 2009; Avelino & Wittmayer, 2016; Geels, 2014), by, for example, shifting attention to the resistance of incumbent actors against regime change. Recent actor-network-theory-inspired approaches, such as "navigational governance" (Jørgensen, 2012), "transition mediators" (Jensen et al., 2015), and "urban green assemblages" (Blok, 2013), adopt a more conflict-oriented and actor-based view and conceive of transition strategies not so much as the (participatory) development of transition pathways, but rather take a bottom-up perspective organized around different social arenas where problems of change are interpreted and framed differently and where conflicting perspectives come to the fore.

Studying the Dynamics of Socio-Technical Change: The Development of Wind Energy in International Comparison

In this second half of the chapter, we will take a closer look at the development of wind energy as a case study in ongoing energy transition in different countries. The case of wind energy is just one concrete case within broader changes of the energy system; similar insights can be gained from studying other renewable energy technologies, electricity grid infrastructures, or the built environment. Our discussion of wind energy not only conveys an idea of how energy-society relations can be analyzed through a socio-technical lens, but also intends to emphasize the relevance of dimensions such as agency, power, and space for our understanding of the dynamics of these transitions. The analysis of wind energy should thus also indicate how the current discussion of energy transitions is moving forward in relation to the original conceptualization in the multilevel perspective.

Wind energy already has the largest share of all newly installed power generation in Europe. As the European Wind Energy Association points out, more than €26 billion have been invested in Europe in new wind power installations in 2015 alone (EWEA, 2016). This translates into an added production capacity of 12.8 gigawatts (GW), or 44.2% of total 2015 power capacity installations, an increase of 6.3% compared to 2014. Roughly a quarter of the new installations come from offshore wind energy; most of these installations use onshore wind. Wind energy now accounts for 15.6% of all power generation in Europe, with fossil-fuel power capacity meanwhile being decommissioned at a higher rate than new capacity is added. However, the differences between countries are significant, which not least points to the importance of different political, regulatory, economic, and geographic contexts. While Germany still has the highest total capacity installed by far (45 GW compared to Spain with 23 GW and the UK with 13.6 GW), the United Kingdom attracted almost half of all new investments in 2015 (€12.6 bn, compared to Germany €5.3 bn). Another shift in dynamics takes place between onshore and offshore wind installations: While investments in onshore wind generation increased by 6.3% in 2015, those in the offshore wind sector doubled compared to the year before. However, total energy generation by onshore wind is currently still about eight times as much as that from offshore wind. But offshore wind-generation costs are rapidly decreasing: Vattenfall's winning bid for the largest offshore wind farm in Denmark, Krigers Flak, set a new lowest watermark with a price of only €49.9/megawatt hour (MWh) (compared to the international average costs for offshore wind of $126/MWh or roughly €120/MWh) (Hill, 2016).

Though it now looks like an economically highly competitive technology, wind energy has by no means been a straightforward and uncontested development of innovation and market deployment. The innovation journey of wind energy over the past five or so decades is nevertheless an instructive case of how such processes of socio-technical change are shaped by institutional contexts, policy interventions, social controversies, the engagement of diverse actor groups, and various historical contingencies. Moreover, it lays bare the limitations of a conscious governance of such developments—and nevertheless at the same time highlights the great importance of concerted efforts to nurture and support such technologies against the resistance of powerful actors. Instead of trying to tell the "whole story" of wind-energy development during the past decades, we will draw attention to some selected elements that were important for the growth of this technology.

Civil Society Engagement in the Development of Wind Power

The early market introduction and upscaling of "modern" wind-energy generation in the 1970s and 1980s provides plenty of insights into the dynamics of socio-technical change, in this case particularly the potential role of user participation processes, social movements, and grassroots innovations in the growth and deployment of a new technology. Such grassroots movements were particularly important for the development of the Danish wind-power industry, which became a dominant player on the world market for many years and has put Denmark ahead of most other countries in the share of wind energy in electricity production. The development of modern, electricity-producing wind turbines began in Denmark in the early 1970s as an outcome of a societal conflict about the use of nuclear power (see Danielsen & Halkier, 1995; Jørgensen & Karnøe, 1995; Ornetzeder & Rohracher, 2013). In reaction to the first energy crises in 1974 and opposition to the planned generation of nuclear energy, a grassroots energy movement, driven by opposition to nuclear energy and organized in local groups all over the country, promoted the development of alternative energy technologies. Some of these groups, consisting of "self-builders, craftsmen, architects, engineers, teachers from folk high schools and researchers" (Danielsen & Halkier, 1995, p. 64), organized the first meetings on wind-power technologies. Later these groups also received government support and were joined by people from test stations and an emerging local industry. Moreover, these groups could build on a long tradition of practical engagement with windmill technology in Denmark going back to the eighteenth century. Experimentation and tinkering with technical designs resulted in a large variety of solutions, usually in a rather small-scale power range of 20–50 kilowatts (kW). Nevertheless, there were also projects, such as the Tvind Mill project, which aimed for larger scale technology and developed a prototype with a capacity of 2 megawatts (MW), which made use of a number of technical features that were later adopted by early producers of wind technology (e.g., fiberglass blades).

By the end of the 1970s, the first phase of innovation, dominated by grassroots entrepreneurs and do-it-yourself builders, moved on to a phase characterized by early industrialization and home-market development (Jørgensen & Karnøe, 1995). Moreover, an organizational and technical infrastructure for wind-power production and implementation was built up. In 1978 two professional interest groups were founded: the Association of Danish Wind Turbine Owners and the Association of Danish Wind Turbine Manufacturers. Along with this development, a national research program for wind energy was launched, which also included a test station for small wind turbines at Risø. The association of windmill owners was also the main driving force regarding the development of rules and standards for grid connection of wind turbines and published performance data (like breakdowns or output) of installed wind turbines on a monthly basis. This turned out to be an effective strategy to increase market transparency, which indirectly helped to improve the quality of industrial products (Garud & Karnoe, 2003). Companies such as Vestas, later the world's largest manufacturer of wind turbines, started with the serial production of wind turbines in the early 1980s. Although these companies and research institutes dominated the further development of wind energy, 75% of installed wind power capacity was still controlled by wind-power cooperatives in 1992 (Danielsen & Halkier, 1995: p. 21). The engagement of grassroots activists, driven by values supporting a renewable energy future, their experimentation with and eventual upscaling of windmills, and the gradual building of an infrastructure of supporting institutions and test laboratories were crucial for the successful take-off of wind energy in Denmark. In different forms we can see such influences of grassroots innovations, particularly in the early stages of development and dissemination, also with other technologies and energy carriers (Ornetzeder & Rohracher, 2006; Seyfang & Smith, 2007).

Garud and Karnœ (2003) compared the developmental paths of wind turbines in Denmark with those in the United States. In the United States, at that time a leading country in wind-energy development with a long history of wind-energy deployment as well, one could similarly observe the distributed action required to develop an entire techno-organizational infrastructure for wind-energy generation. One of the main differences, which in this case appears to have been decisive for success in Denmark, was the bottom-up co-development approach between testing procedures and a variety of design solutions in Denmark, and the focus on a selection of the best available technologies through test centers based on engineering science design knowledge in the United States—a difference that Garud and Karnœ (2003) have characterized as "bricolage" versus "breakthrough."

However, grassroots movements and cooperatives not only have been influential for the start-up phase of wind-energy generation in Denmark, but also have been of much wider importance for the dissemination of wind energy. A comparison of the current situation of community energy and wind-power cooperatives in Germany, Belgium, Denmark, and the United Kingdom (Bauwens, Gotchev, & Holstenkamp, 2016) shows that such bottom-up movements to collectively own and manage renewable energy projects are of relevance in all these countries, but strongly depend on specific institutional and cultural contexts. The institutional environment has tended to become more hostile toward such models in all of the investigated countries, not only through increased price volatility, with new types of feed-in tariffs and higher economic risks that are easier to bear for large corporations, but also to some extent because of the growing size of modern wind turbines, which need a stronger economic resource base than most cooperatives have. As a consequence, cooperatives peaked in Denmark around 2002 with ownership of around 40% of all existing turbines and with approximately 150,000 households owning shares in wind cooperatives. The number of household shareholders has since gone down to about 100,000 in 2004 and 50,000 in 2009, or 15% of all wind turbines, respectively. Nevertheless, the more hostile environment also led to strategic reactions of cooperatives, which started to pool resources and benefit from economies of scale, or by jointly organizing sales to the wholesale electricity markets and reducing transaction costs for individual cooperatives (Bauwens, Gotchev, & Holstenkamp, 2016, p. 146). Similar observations have been made in Austria (Schreuer, 2016), where citizen power plants have been increasingly able to mobilize resources, but at the cost of adapting to mainstream economic models and a high dependency on financial and regulatory support schemes. The "transformative capacity" of such collective models thus has diminished over time. Also a further comparison of Sweden, France, and Germany (Mignon & Rüdinger, 2016) showed how renewable energy

cooperative projects are affected by a lack of financial infrastructure, knowledge infrastructure, and an adverse institutional environment. However, cooperative ownership
of wind turbines is only one type of civil society influence on wind-energy development.
A study of the emergent US wind-energy sector from 1978 to 1992 provides evidence for
how social movement organizations create conditions for entrepreneurial engagement
in the emerging sector by constructing and propagating cognitive frameworks, norms,
values, and regulatory structures, for example by challenging existing practices and
advocating alternatives, and by embedding their values in regulatory structures (Sine &
Lee, 2009). Environmental social movements in the United States acted as institutional
entrepreneurs, facilitated access to information and resources, and provided a cognitive
frame for the future development of the energy system, which had significant direct and
indirect effects on entrepreneurial activity.

Obviously, civil society organizations are only one of many factors shaping the development and deployment of renewable energies, even if they played a crucial role in the
emerging wind-energy sector. Some other key factors that help to explain the uneven
development of wind power across different countries are, for example, different planning systems that support wind power in different ways; the design of systems for financial support, such as feed-in tariffs; the level of opposition against wind power, such
as by landscape protection organizations; and—related to our earlier discussion—local
ownership patterns, which seem to garner more public support for wind power development than remote, corporate ownership (Toke, Breukers, & Wolsink, 2008). What
becomes clear in all of these examples is how deeply entangled technical and social
elements are in the transition toward renewable energies in general, and wind power in
particular, and that these interdependencies need to be reflected in our conceptualization of such change processes.

The Contrasting Story of Offshore Wind Energy

Let us briefly shift our emphasis to a different pathway of wind-energy development
to get a better impression of how diverse such change dynamics can be, even within
the same technological field. As the short statistical overview at the beginning of the
wind-power section has shown, we have experienced recently a shift from onshore to
offshore wind energy, with high growth rates combined with rapidly falling electricity-
generation costs. In relation to onshore wind, this development has been driven much
more by electricity-sector incumbents—often multinational energy companies—and by
concerted political efforts to provide supportive regulatory and financial frameworks,
adapted electricity grid infrastructures, and research and development (R&D) support.
Again, internationally comparative studies can provide us with insights about the
factors shaping different pathways of change.

While the United Kingdom, for example, has recently experienced an almost boom-
like development (almost half of the investments in Europe in 2015), the development in
the Netherlands—also a country with high potential for offshore wind and a governance

system that has stressed the importance of offshore wind for many years—has been nearly stagnant (Kern et al., 2015). Differences in offshore wind deployment rates between these countries can be fruitfully analyzed through the lens of socio-technical niche development and different strategies of niche empowerment in these countries (see also, for further case description, Kern et al., 2014; Kern et al., 2015; Verhees et al., 2015). As mentioned earlier, Smith and Raven (2012) distinguish strategies of shielding, nurturing, and empowering of socio-technical niches. Empowerment can occur through fit-and-conform strategies (i.e., adaptation to the dominant structures of the electricity regime), or through stretch-and-transform strategies (i.e., changes in regime structures to accommodate the growing wind-energy niche).

In many respects, the offshore wind development paths in the United Kingdom and the Netherlands are similar. Plans for the construction of offshore wind plants emerged already in the 1970s, much in parallel with onshore wind development. The high potential for wind turbines at sea was obvious, and the oil crises inspired visions of a renewable energy future. Nevertheless, attempts to kick-start offshore wind development clearly followed a fit-and-conform strategy, as offshore wind turned out to be much more costly and difficult to realize than originally conceived: the focus in both countries was thus to bring generation costs down to competitive levels, and the expectation was that centralized and large-scale offshore wind parks would fit well into the prevailing structure of the electricity system. Emphasis was thus put on R&D funding and innovation policies, and not on the deployment of what was seen as prohibitively priced offshore wind power. Still, the narrative was that offshore wind parks would play a vital role in future energy systems.

Moreover, costs were not coming down nearly as quickly as expected, and various other problems emerged, in particular with the grid connection of the wind parks, and regulatory questions, such as whether transmission grid operators or the owners of the wind park would own and operate the interconnection cables. While successive Dutch governments largely remained with fit-and-conform strategies, the United Kingdom more forcefully included elements of stretch-and-transform into its policies—not only through a strong commitment to renewable energy and climate mitigation targets (with offshore wind an essential part of this), but also with more consistent policies and regulations, which facilitated the certification of new wind parks. Over time, this led to the emergence of a coalition of powerful and resourceful actors consisting of big electricity companies as well as manufacturers, which further drove the expansion of offshore wind energy. Not least, the Crown Estate, a private organization that manages public land and "rents out" pieces of seabed to wind-park operators, took on an active role as a system builder in the United Kingdom and became essential in facilitating the development of offshore wind parks. Development in the Netherlands at the same time was held back by a much more inconsistent policy regarding the concession system for wind parks and further system-building activities (Kern et al., 2015).

A variety of factors thus played a role for the creation of a protective space for offshore wind, not least the strategic linking of offshore wind to different policy goals such as climate change, employment, and industrial development, as well as a certain pressure from successful developments in other countries, particularly in Denmark (first commercial wind park deployed in 2002) and Germany. Also in these cases it had taken a rather long time of niche learning and overcoming of various technical, economic, and regulatory problems until powerful industrial actors entered the offshore wind market in strong force—in Germany only around 2008–2009 (Reichardt et al., 2016). The mix, consistency, and long-term orientation of policies and instruments to support offshore wind development has been a further key factor for successful development in all the country cases investigated (Reichardt & Rogge, 2016).

The example of wind-energy development makes one point very clear: technical development has been just one element in what has shaped the emergence and growth of wind power. At least as important have been the vision and endurance of various types of wind-power advocates, among them social movements and cooperatives; the creation of new network organizations and associations, along with an increasing alignment of expectations for the further development of wind energy; the reaction and strategies of powerful incumbents in the energy system in relation to these new technologies; public controversies and discourses around the deployment of wind energy; the creation and exchange of bodies of knowledge and competencies around wind energy; and the gradual creation and alignment of new institutional contexts of wind energy, its alignment with different types of policies and interests, and the building of an entire infrastructure of test centers, wind maps, and systems for the transport and construction of wind turbines. We thus should rather think of wind power as a socio-technical system with particular characteristics and dynamics of growth and change—characteristics that strongly depend on the dimensions listed earlier and which are shaped by spatial contexts and historical developments alike. We need to take these elements into account to gain a better understanding of the different development paths of wind energy in different countries, or the different dynamics that characterize the development of onshore and offshore wind power.

However, the growth of socio-technical niches such as wind energy is just one element in the ongoing transformation of the energy system. Analyzing these broader transition dynamics requires that we broaden our perspective even further than we have done in this chapter; we need to examine the interrelations with competing or complementary technology and application fields (see, e.g., Gross & Mautz, 2015, for a broader analysis of renewable energy transitions) and the interaction of these niches with obdurate socio-technical structures of the energy system, including strategies of incumbent utilities, institutions such as regulatory structures, and dominant cognitive frames, as well as the broader socio-political structures in which the current energy system is embedded, such as the social dynamics of consumption, international interdependencies, and the emergence of new national and international policy regimes regarding climate change, among other issues. Not least, a deeper understanding of the relations of energy and society is needed in order to critically reflect on the limitations and potential of political strategies to govern such transition processes.

REFERENCES

Avelino, F., & Rotmans, J. (2009). Power in transition: An interdisciplinary framework to study power in relation to structural change. *European Journal of Social Theory*, 12, 543–569.

Avelino, F., & Wittmayer, J. M. (2016). Shifting power relations in sustainability transitions: A multi-actor perspective. *Journal of Environmental Policy & Planning*, 18, 628–649.

Bauwens, T., Gotchev, B., & Holstenkamp, L. (2016). What drives the development of community energy in Europe? The case of wind power cooperatives. *Energy Research & Social Science*, 13, 136–147.

Berkhout, F. (2006). Normative expectations in systems innovation. *Technology Analysis & Strategic Management*, 18, 299–311.

Bijker, W. E., Hughes, T. P., & Pinch, T. (1987). *The social construction of technological systems.* Cambridge, MA: MIT Press.

Blok, A. (2013). Urban green assemblages: An ANT view on sustainable city building projects. *Science & Technology Studies*, 26, 5–24.

Bulkeley, H., Castán Broto, V., Hodson, M., & Marvin, S. (2011). *Cities and low carbon transitions.* London: Routledge.

Bulkeley, H., Castán Broto, V., & Maassen, A. (2011). Governing urban low carbon transitions. In: H. Bulkeley, V. Castán Broto, M. Hodson, & S. Marvin (Eds.,) *Cities and low carbon transitions* (pp. 29–41). London: Routledge.

Bulkeley, H., Castán Broto, V., & Maassen, A. (2014). Low-carbon transitions and the reconfiguration of urban infrastructure. *Urban Studies*, 51, 1471–1486.

Coenen, L., Benneworth, P., & Truffer, B. (2012). Toward a spatial perspective on sustainability transitions. *Research Policy*, 41, 968–979.

Danielsen, O., & Halkier, B. (1995). *Renewable energy in the Danish energy system: From small experiments to full scale energy plants, Danish contribution to the project "Express path."* Contact No. EV5V-CT92-0086, Roskilde University.

Dosi, G. (1982). Technological paradigms and technological trajectories: A suggested interpretation of the determinants and directions of technical change. *Research Policy*, 11, 147–162.

Dosi, G., Freeman, C., Nelson, R., Silverberg, G., and & Soete, L. (1988). *Technical change and economic theory.* London; New York: Pinter.

Elzen, B., Geels, F. W., & Green, K. (2004). *System innovation and the transition to sustainability.* Cheltenham, UK: Edward Elgar.

EWEA. (2016). *Wind in power: 2015 European statistics.* The European Wind Energy Association.

Freeman, C. (1994). The economics of technical change. *Cambridge Journal of Economics*, 18, 463–514.

Garud, R., & Gehman, J. (2012). Metatheoretical perspectives on sustainability journeys: Evolutionary, relational and durational. *Research Policy*, 41, 980–995.

Garud, R., & Karnoe, P. (2003). Bricolage versus breakthrough: Distributed and embedded agency in technology entrepreneurship. *Research Policy*, 32, 277–300.

Geels, F. W. (2002). Technological transitions as evolutionary reconfiguration processes: A multi-level perspective and a case-study. *Research Policy*, 31, 1257–1274.

Geels, F. W. (2004). From sectoral systems of innovation to socio-technical systems. Insights about dynamics and change from sociology and institutional theory. *Research Policy*, 33, 897–920.

Geels, F. W. (2005). *Technological transitions and system innovations: A co-evolutionary and socio-technical analysis*. Cheltenham, UK: Edward Elgar.

Geels, F. W. (2006). The hygienic transition from cesspools to sewer systems (1840–1930): The dynamics of regime transformatino. *Research Policy, 35*, 1069–1082.

Geels, F. W. (2011). The multi-level perspective on sustainability transitions: Responses to seven criticisms. *Environmental Innovation and Societal Transitions, 1*, 24–40.

Geels, F. W. (2014). Regime resistance against low-carbon transitions: Introducing politics and power into the multi-level perspective. *Theory, Culture & Society, 31*, 21–40.

Geels, F. W., & Raven, R. P. J. M. (2006). Non-linearity and expectations in niche-development trajectories: Ups and downs in dutch biogas development (1973–2003). *Technology Analysis & Strategic Management, 18*, 375–392.

Geels, F. W., & Schot, J. (2007). Typology of sociotechnical transition pathways. *Research Policy, 36*, 399–417.

Genus, A., & Coles, A.-M. (2008). Rethinking the multi-level perspective of technological transitions. *Research Policy, 37*, 1436–1445.

Grin, J. (2008). The multilevel perspective and design of system innovations. In J. C. J. M. van den Bergh & F. R. Bruinsma (Eds.), *Managing the transition to renewable energy: Theory and practice from local, regional and macro perspectives* (pp. 47–79). Cheltenham, UK: Edward Elgar.

Gross, M., & Mautz, R. (2015). *Renewable energies,* Abingdon, UK: Routledge.

Hill, J. S. (2016). Vattenfall wins rights to build largest nordic wind farm, cheapest offshore wind farm yet. *Clean Technica*. Retrieved from https://cleantechnica.com/2016/11/10/vattenfall-wins-rights-build-largest-nordic-wind-farm-cheapest-offshore-wind-farm-yet/

Hodson, M., & Marvin, S. (2009). Cities mediating technological transitions: understanding visions, intermediation and consequences. *Technology Analysis & Strategic Management, 21*, 515–534.

Hodson, M., & Marvin, S. (2011). Can cities shape socio-technical transitions and how would we know if they were? In: H. Bulkeley, V. Castán Broto, M. Hodson, & S. Marvin (Eds.), *Cities and low carbon transitions* (pp. 54–70). London: Routledge.

Hoogma, R., Kemp, R., Schot, J., & Truffer, B. (2002). *Experimenting for sustainable transport: The approach of strategic niche management*. London: Spon Press.

Hughes, T. P. (1983). *Networks of power: Electrification in Western societies 1880–1930*. Baltimore, MD: Johns Hopkins University Press.

Jensen, J. S., Fratini, C. F., Lauridsen, E. H., & Hoffmann, B. (2015). Harbour bathing and the urban transition of water in Copenhagen: Mediators, junctions and embedded urban navigation. *Environment and Planning A: Economy and Space, 47*, 554–570.

Jørgensen, U. (2012). Mapping and navigating transitions: The multi-level perspective compared with arenas of development. *Research Policy, 41*, 996–1010.

Jørgensen, U., & Karnøe, P. (1995). The Danish wind-turbine story: Technical solutions to political visions? In A. Rip, T. J. Misa, & J. Schot (Eds.), *Managing technology in society: The approach of constructive technology assessment* (pp. 57–82). London: Pinter.

Kemp, R. (1994). Technology and the transition to environmental sustainability: The problem of technological regime shifts. *Futures, 26*, 1023–1046.

Kemp, R., Rip, A., & Schot, J. (2001). Constructing transition paths through the management of niches. In R. Garud & P. Karnøe (Eds.), *Path dependence and creation* (pp. 269–299). Mahwah, NJ; London: Lawrence Erlbaum Associates.

Kern, F., Smith, A., Shaw, C., Raven, R., & Verhees, B. (2014). From laggard to leader: Explaining offshore wind developments in the UK. *Energy Policy, 69*, 635–646.

Kern, F., Verhees, B., Raven, R., & Smith, A. (2015). Empowering sustainable niches: Comparing UK and Dutch offshore wind developments. *Technological Forecasting and Social Change, 100*, 344–355.

Markard, J., Raven, R., & Truffer, B. (2012). Sustainability transitions: An emerging field of research and its prospects. *Research Policy, 41*, 955–967.

Meadowcroft, J. (2009). What about the politics? Sustainable development, transition management, and long term energy transitions. *Policy Sciences, 42*, 323–340.

Mignon, I., & Rüdinger, A. (2016). The impact of systemic factors on the deployment of cooperative projects within renewable electricity production: An international comparison. *Renewable and Sustainable Energy Reviews, 65*, 478–488.

Nelson, R. R., & Winter, S. G. (1977). In search of useful theory of innovation. *Research Policy, 6*, 36–76.

Nelson, R. R., & Winter, S. G. (1982). *An evolutionary theory of economic change*. Cambridge, MA: Harvard University Press.

Ornetzeder, M., & Rohracher, H. (2006). User-led innovations and participation processes: Lessons from sustainable energy technologies. *Energy Policy, 34*, 138–150.

Ornetzeder, M., & Rohracher, H. (2013). Of solar collectors, wind power, and car sharing: Comparing and understanding successful cases of grassroots innovations. *Global Environmental Change, 23*, 856–867.

Raven, R., Kern, F., Verhees, B., & Smith, A. (2016). Niche construction and empowerment through socio-political work: A meta-analysis of six low-carbon technology cases. *Environmental Innovation and Societal Transitions, 18*, 164–180.

Raven, R. P. J. M. (2007). Niche accumulation and hybridisation strategies in transition processes towards a sustainable energy system: An assessment of differences and pitfalls. *Energy Policy, 35*, 2390–2400.

Raven, R. P. J. M., & Geels, F. W. (2010). Socio-cognitive evolution in niche development: Comparative analysis of biogas development in Denmark and the Netherlands (1973–2004). *Technovation, 30.* 87–99.

Raven, R. P. J. M., & Verbong, G. P. J. (2007). Multi-regime interactions in the dutch energy sector: The case of combined heat and power technologies in the Netherlands 1970–2000. *Technology Analysis & Strategic Management, 19*, 491–507.

Raven, R. P. J. M., & Verbong, G. P. J. (2009). Boundary crossing innovations: Case studies from the energy domain. *Technology in Society, 31*, 85–93.

Raven, R., Schot, J., & Berkhout, F. (2012). Space and scale in socio-technical transitions. *Environmental Innovation and Societal Transitions, 4*, 63–78.

Reichardt, K., Negro, S. O., Rogge, K. S., & Hekkert, M. P. (2016). Analyzing interdependencies between policy mixes and technological innovation systems: The case of offshore wind in Germany. *Technological Forecasting and Social Change, 106*, 11–21.

Reichardt, K., & Rogge, K. (2016). How the policy mix impacts innovation: Findings from company case studies on offshore wind in Germany. *Environmental Innovation and Societal Transitions, 18*, 62–81.

Rip, A., & Kemp, R. (1998). Technological change. In S. Rayner & E. L. Malone (Eds.), *Human choice and climate change: Resources and technology* (pp. 327–399). Columbus, OH: Batelle Press.

Rohracher, H., & Späth, P. (2014). The interplay of urban energy policy and socio-technical transitions: The eco-cities of Graz and Freiburg in retrospect. *Urban Studies, 51*, 1413–1429.

Schot, J. (1992). The policy relevance of the quasi-evolutionary model: The case of simulating clean technologies. In R. Coombs, P. Saviotti, & V. Walsh (Eds.), *Technological change and company strategies: Economic and sociological perspectives* (pp. 185–200). London; New York: Harcourt Brace Jovanovich.

Schot, J., & Geels, F. W. (2008). Strategic niche management and sustainable innovation journeys: Theory, findings, research agenda, and policy. *Technology Analysis & Strategic Management, 20*, 537–554.

Schot, J., Hoogma, R., & Elzen, B. (1994). Strategies for shifting technological systems: The case of automobile system. *Futures, 26*, 1060–1076.

Schreuer, A. (2016). The establishment of citizen power plants in Austria: A process of empowerment? *Energy Research & Social Science, 13*, 126–135.

Seyfang, G., & Smith, A. (2007). Grassroots innovations for sustainable development: Towards a new research and policy agenda. *Environmental Politics, 16*, 584–603.

Sine, W. D., & Lee, B. H. (2009). Tilting at windmills? The environmental movement and the emergence of the U.S. wind energy sector. *Administrative Science Quarterly, 54*, 123–155.

Smith, A. (2007). Emerging in between: The multi-level governance of renewable energy in the English regions. *Energy Policy, 35*, 6266–6280.

Smith, A., & Raven, R. (2012). What is protective space? Reconsidering niches in transitions to sustainability. *Research Policy, 41*, 1025–1036.

Smith, A., Stirling, A., & Berkhout, F. (2005). The governance of sustainable socio-technical transitions. *Research Policy, 34*, 1491–1510.

Späth, P., & Rohracher, H. (2010). "Energy regions": The transformative power of regional discourses on socio-technical futures. *Research Policy, 39*, 449–458.

Toke, D., Breukers, S., & Wolsink, M. (2008). Wind power deployment outcomes: How can we account for the differences? *Renewable and Sustainable Energy Reviews, 12*, 1129–1147.

Truffer, B., & Coenen, L. (2012). Environmental innovation and sustainability transitions in regional studies. *Regional Studies, 46*, 1–21.

Verbong, G. P. J., Christiaens, W., Raven, R. P. J. M., & Balkema, A. (2010). Strategic niche management in an unstable regime: Biomass gasification in India. *Environmental Science & Policy, 13*, 272–281.

Verhees, B., Raven, R., Kern, F., & Smith, A. (2015). The role of policy in shielding, nurturing and enabling offshore wind in The Netherlands (1973–2013). *Renewable and Sustainable Energy Reviews, 47*, 816–829.

Walker, G., & Shove, E. (2007). Ambivalence, sustainability and the governance of socio-technical transitions. *Journal of Environmental Policy & Planning, 9*, 213–225.

Weber, K. M., Hoogma, R., Lane, B., & Schot, J. (1999). *Experimenting with sustainable transport innovations: A workbook for strategic niche management.* Seville; Enschede: IPTS.

Wolfram, M., & Frantzeskaki, N. (2016). Cities and systemic change for sustainability: Prevailing epistemologies and an emerging research agenda. *Sustainability, 8*, 144.

PART II

....

THE PERSISTENT MATERIAL AND GEOPOLITICAL RELEVANCE OF FOSSIL FUELS

....

Fossil fuels have been at the heart of geopolitics since at least World War I. During the ensuing 100 years, our growing dependence on such resources has left indelible marks on the physical, cultural, and political structures of modern societies. And the unequal geographic distribution of fossil fuel storehouses has been a linchpin of the dynamics of those political relations. But the presence of reserves does not necessarily translate into political power; rather, the relation between fossil fuels and power is far more complex, often materializing in an inverse relationship between oil dependence and democracy. In Chapter 5, Jalel Sager makes quite clear the intimate relationship between energy and economies, highlighting that as the investments required to ensure continued access to the fossil fuels used to run our economies grows, they can eat up the very surpluses generated by those economies, describing the proverbial snake eating its own tail.

David Mares extends this theme in Chapter 6, offering a compelling analysis that suggests that long-term, top-down energy planning is difficult, if not impossible. He describes how the geographic dispersion of energy resources, and of the skills and technologies required to develop them, creates interdependencies with geopolitical implications, which in turn can help or hinder, but always shape, regional economic development. Renewable energy sources are no different: their potential is likewise geographically dispersed in a non-uniform manner; they are associated with a host of their own material problems; and they too shape, and are shaped by, geopolitics. Subsidization of particular types of energy resources do not necessarily provide improvements in energy security and well-being—to the contrary, in fact: for those countries that are highly economically dependent on a small basket of petrochemical products and that have relatively weak institutions, continued reliance on these markets can be highly deleterious, leading to the "resource curse."

In Chapter 7, Paul S. Ciccantell and Paul K. Gellert offer a cautious if discouraging account indicating that while coal may have become the "bad boy" in energy discourse, it remains a substantial material resource in the world system, which continues to be manipulated by those with control over energy resources. Just as coal fueled the ascent of the United States and the United Kingdom in previous eras, so too does coal fuel the ascent of China today. These energy flows are not going to change overnight, nor are they static. As non-renewable reserves are depleted, and related technologies undergo continuous transformation, the landscape changes, but the tension between economics of scale and dis-economies of space will persist, and will continue to shape the geopolitics of energy in ways that are difficult to control.

Jack D. Sharples closes Part II by drawing much needed but rarely offered explicit attention to those dis-economies of space, and the materiality of resources. In Chapter 8, Sharples reminds us that material energy resources are just that: they are located in certain places, and their eventual consumption requires transport over routes that are not of either the seller's or the buyer's choosing. The energy security of the economies and many citizens within the European Union (EU), for example, is provided via pipelines that originate in Russia and travel through Ukraine, among other jurisdictions, linking indelibly a set of nation-states and peoples in a quagmire of interdependency in which politics, not markets and not technology, prevails.

The chapters in Part II, if anything, remind us that although much has changed, much still remains the same in the political economies of energy. These arguments pose a formidable challenge to decoupling enthusiasts. Notably, the geopolitics of energy today are as dynamic as ever, shifting dramatically as each new source of fossil fuels is brought into the marketplace, particularly sources in Africa, Latin America, and Asia. The potentially vast reserves lying beneath the Arctic mark an emerging geopolitical arena on the horizon that will be important to watch, with no less than eight countries vying for access amidst highly contested jurisdictional claims. In later parts of this volume, we will also draw attention to insights offered by post-structural approaches, by highlighting, for example, the importance of cultural history to our evolving energy-society relations.

CHAPTER 5

....

NATIONAL ENERGY SIGNATURES

Energetics, Money, and the Structure of the Global System

....

JALEL SAGER

> Above all, there is the indisputable fact that all struggles between the Great Powers have not turned idly around ideologies or national prestige but around the control of natural resources. They still do.
>
> —Georgescu-Roegen (1975, p. 350)

FOSSIL fuels and their high yield of available energy regulate the global economy and structure its hierarchy of nations. When a "pulse" of energy—over months, years, decades, or centuries—enters the global industrial system, we often see overshoot dynamics. The system enters a new mode of production, with new technical combinations. Once it does, it is extremely difficult to return to the old infrastructure, even though the energy resource that provided the pulse likely will yield less over the years (the US and its highway system provide one example of an infrastructural system conceived in a higher-yielding environment, the US oil boom of the early twentieth century). As the energy surplus, or marginal resource return, begins to diminish, output declines, slowing the rise of powerful nations,[1] and transferring growth elsewhere.

The effects of declining returns often show up in the monetary system. Tainter (1990, p. 139) gives a historical example—the debasement of Roman currency over hundreds of years after the reign of Augustus. As the surpluses available to the rulers of Rome diminished, with more spent on maintenance of lands won through conquest, reducing the precious metal content of official currency was a method of squaring the imperial accounts. While this resulted in high levels of price inflation, the soldiers were paid.

A nation's total primary energy supply and its cumulative growth only indirectly relate to that nation's net energy yield or surplus across various sources. To get at the latter, we can think about energy in terms of the overall economic surplus required to produce it. The more a nation plows its economic surplus back into energy production, the less remains for other sectors. We can take the United States as our example, and observe the "petroleum and coal products" sector in the postwar period consuming a large part of the surplus, contracting through the 1960s, and then exploding in the late 1970s and early 1980s, garnering nearly a third of our proxy measure, after-tax corporate profits. After more than a decade of enormous oil investment, its portion of the surplus disappears as prices collapse for nearly 20 years. During this period, banking begins to consume 15%–25% of the surplus.

These effects carry across international boundaries as well. Energy is not only a primary limiting factor for any advanced economy—the constraint that usually bites first—it is also the most important component of global trade and currency movements. Oil is by far the most important commodity in global trade, at roughly 15% of total export value in 2013 (total crude liquids). Coffee, the second most traded commodity by value, accounts for *only about 3% of global trade over the past decade* and is now challenged by natural gas, which went from less than 1% in 1998 to more than 2% by 2013 (UN Comtrade, 2015).

Considering its size and price volatility when compared to other commodity types, oil would logically influence exchange rates. The importance of exports to growth reinforces energy's status as the crucial factor in global economic competition. While driving local and national economies, energy costs pace global economic competition, the latter at root a race to partition ever-increasing amounts of global value (represented by, for example, monetary gold or reserves).

Figures 5.1–5.4 suggest a modern twist on Malthus (1798) and his observation that agriculture grows arithmetically and population geometrically. Money, as noted by Frederick Soddy (1933) and a number of others, grows geometrically. Energy, however,

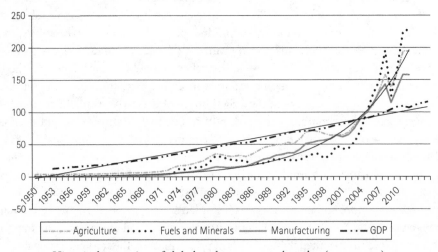

FIGURE 5.1 Historical expansion of global trade, 1950–2013, by value (2005 = 100).

Source: WTO Trade Statistics.

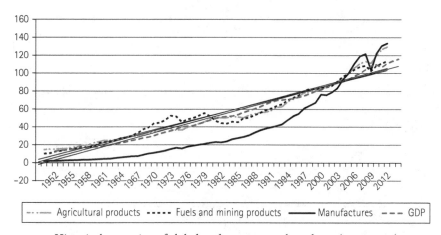

FIGURE 5.2 Historical expansion of global trade, 1950–2013, by volume (2005 = 100).

Source: WTO Trade Statistics.

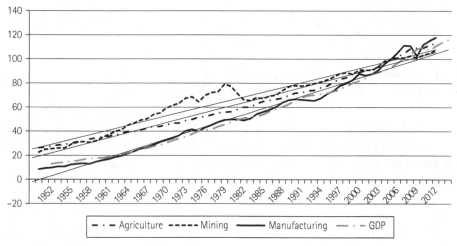

FIGURE 5.3 Historical expansion of global production by volume (2005 = 100).

Note: Oil and gas account for the vast bulk of the mining sector; the overshoot in production through the 1960s and 1970s, or "the bump," is clearly visible.

Source: WTO Trade Statistics.

subject to physical laws, generally falls short of this, whether in the cultivation of crop energy or slowing rates of oil production growth.[2] As is visible in Figures 5.2 and 5.3, the periods of 1967–1979 saw oil production rising far beyond its long-term trend rate, a pace that could not be sustained. The same overshoot dynamics that apply to populations outstripping their agricultural resources may also apply to money and debt outstripping energy. Only through a difficult period of adjustment—involving expansion then contraction of the money supply and a completely new pricing regime for energy—has this

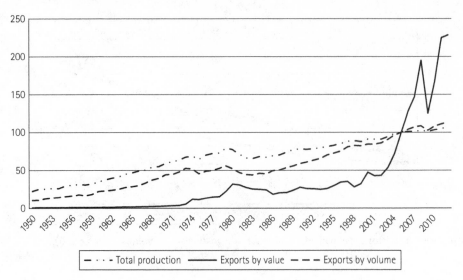

FIGURE 5.4 Comparison of global expansion in fuels and minerals by value, volume, and production (2005 = 100).

Source: WTO Trade Statistics.

imbalance been resolved, flattening out near-term energy and money growth rates while bringing on a new slate of resources from intensified exploration and development.

Through most of modern economic history, global trade has been structured by the energy sector—terms of trade adjust to energy productivity, along the lines laid out by Jevons (1866)—while energy itself became the central global flow in the late nineteenth and early twentieth centuries. Meanwhile, hegemonic states such as Great Britain and then the United States have taken responsibility for overseeing global monetary relations that guarantee and manage this system of flows (see Table 5.1). Yet a decline in energy production rates, global energy control, or a Hubbert-type peak within that hegemonic power can cause large disruptions in the global monetary and economic systems. The importance of the energy factor in production and the need for the hegemon to hold a "buffer" against production fluctuations help explain this.

As shown by the fundamental contributions of Georgescu-Roegen (1971), Odum (1971), and Cleveland et al. (1984), as well as a generation of ecological economists who followed them, *exergy* (or useful work) cannot be separated from economic activity. Despite the enduring concept of "decoupling" the two, in practice this means doing either of the following:

1. exporting energy-intensive industries to less-developed nations, producing greater articulation of the global system (this increasing complexity, or division of labor, is engendered by high-yielding energy sources (see Smith, 1904 [1776]; Tainter, 1990); or
2. substituting fuels with a higher energy "quality" or usefulness, such as primary electricity from hydropower, for those with less, such as coal (Cleveland et al., 1984).

Table 5.1 Leading Global Producers, Changing Internal
Energy Conditions

Nation	Key Source	Peak Production
Great Britain	Coal	1913
United States	Crude Oil, Natural Gas	1970?
China	Coal	Expected 2015

Note: Shale oil and gas drilling in the US has recently brought natural gas production past its previous peak in the early 1970s. Further, when natural gas plant liquids and other liquids are added to produce the metric "Total Oil Supply," the US becomes the top global producer as of 2014, with production levels apparently above those of the 1970s. The conventional crude peak, however, for now remains back in 1970 for the US.

After accounting for these two mechanisms, ecological economists such as Cleveland et al. (1984) find a deep correlation between energy and growth, as measured by changes in gross domestic product (GDP) or similar. The economic system seems structured around the growth of energy resources in a nearly organic manner.[3] This relationship continues today. Whether one uses as a metric energy surplus or yield, or growth in total primary energy supply (TPES, equivalent to energy production plus imports minus exports), the world's declining return on its fossil base provides one explanation for the declining rates of growth in the United States and the world. In Figure 5.5 we see a clear linear correlation between growth in world GDP and in TPES over the last 40 years. A similar relationship holds for the United States over the past 50 years.

Economic growth has, for much longer than the last 40 years, been inextricably linked to growth in fossil sources. Despite oscillation about the trend, despite running ever faster to stay in place, the latter proceeds inexorably in one direction. What was true for Great Britain in 1913 and the United States in 1970 has become a reality for contemporary China and the world at large: exhaustible energy supplies limit growth. The world now finds itself with sputtering expansion in its major centers—with one particularly notable exception.

The United States has added dramatically to its domestic oil and gas production since the global financial crisis. New energy sources help push economies out of recession. By coaxing an extra million barrels of oil per day from shale oil deposits in North Dakota and two million from those in Texas (see Figures 5.6 and 5.7), the United States has pushed ahead of the EU in recovery, with higher post-crisis growth rates. If China at its 2001 World Trade Organization (WTO) accession was a case of ready domestic energy waiting for capital, the US shale oil boom was one of ready capital waiting for domestic energy.

This boom in US energy production has driven the dollar/euro exchange rate toward parity and has brought a surplus of oil to global markets, halving the global market

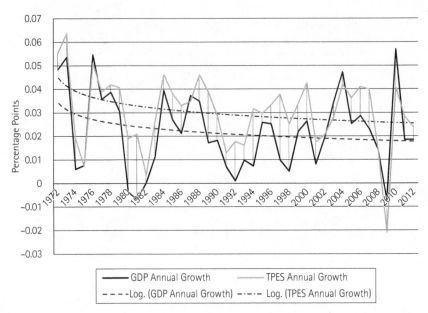

FIGURE 5.5 World GDP and total primary energy supply (TPES) annual growth, 1972–2012.

Source: Data from International Energy Agency (IEA) global energy balances and IMF International Financial Statistics.

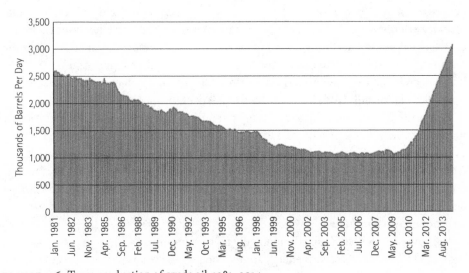

FIGURE 5.6 Texas production of crude oil, 1981–2014.

Source: US EIA.

price over the last quarter of 2014. Yet given the shorter lifespan of these types of fields (Hughes, 2013), one may fairly doubt the durability of the shale boom. Further, unconventional sources of oil and gas carry larger environmental and climatic burdens. These two factors create uncertainty around such fuels as long-term economic solutions in a climate-constrained world (see Figures 5.8 and 5.9).

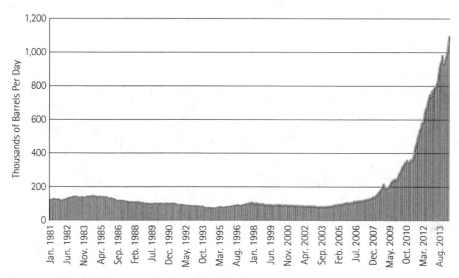

FIGURE 5.7 North Dakota production of crude oil, 1981–2014.

Source: US EIA.

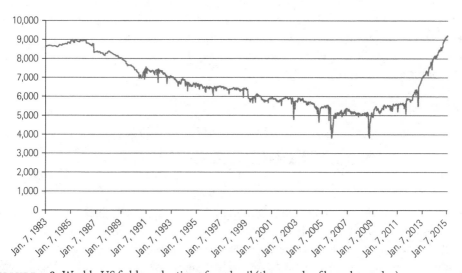

FIGURE 5.8 Weekly US field production of crude oil (thousands of barrels per day).

Note: The downward spikes ("icicles") at 2004, 2005, 2008, etc., appear to be large-scale production cuts in response to ongoing or expected price changes (likely influenced in turn by interest-rate movements).

Source: US EIA.

As a global society we cannot buy our way out of energy constraints, though energy can in many senses transcend financial constraints. One aspect of the economy is imaginary, the other real.[4] One might argue that spending on energy research allows us to transcend energy constraints. True, advances can help produce more energy yield for less energy expense, increasing our energy return on investment (EROI).[5]

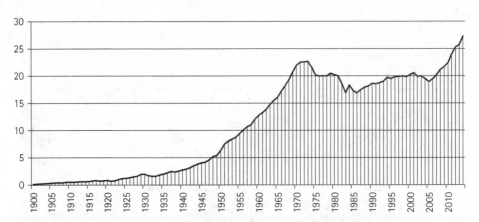

FIGURE 5.9 US natural gas production, 1900–2014 (trillion cubic feet).

Note: In 2013 about 47% of US production came from shale or tight wells.

Source: US EIA.

Renewable technologies such as solar and wind do seem to be getting more efficient in this manner, as their costs suggest. Yet the trend for exhaustible sources often works the other way, as Jevons pointed out in *The Coal Question* (1866): as mines and wells run deeper, we continually spend more energy to receive less surplus in return— technology enables us to work harder to get less—or run ever faster to stay in place, as the saying goes.[6]

SYSTEMIC CAUSATION
AND AN ECOLOGICAL APPROACH

Of course, growth is a complex phenomenon. In ecology, from which I draw inspiration for the current study, limiting factors on the growth of species within an ecosystem include energy, water, and various available nutrients. Likewise for species of firms and nations within the global ecosystem, we might imagine that limiting factors include energy, capital, and labor. The claim is not that energy magically produces an economy, but that it underlies other factors, constraining them now to a larger degree than vice versa, leaving it the primary limiting element.

The trajectory of major economies over the past 50 years correlates directly to their energy supply. Linear regressions of GDP growth on total energy supply typically produce very high coefficients. Yet what causes what? Does that question even make sense, given systemic causality (Lakoff, 2010)? In Table 5.2, I perform a series of Granger causality tests on differenced monthly US time series data (1959–2010). This provides a first approximation step to determine whether energy production gives us more future

Table 5.2 Granger Relationships on Key Variables

Lead	Lag	Cor.	Sign	Lag for Peak Strength	Granger Direction @ 12 Months
GDP	M2	0.65	Positive	–12 months	Both ways, strongly
Industrial production	GDP	0.50	Positive at peak around 0	Around 0, slightly leading	Both, strongly for Ind Pro lead
Industrial production	Oil imports	0.30	Positive peak around 0, later positive	Around 0, slightly leading	Oil import stronger predictor
Industrial production	Monetary base	0.30	Negative Peak around –1 or 2 months, later positive	–2 to 4 months	Both ways, strongly

Source: OECD, Federal Reserve Bank of St. Louis (ALFRED).

information about future economic growth or vice versa. Methods such as artificial neural network (ANN) modeling may be more appropriate to the complex, entwined, and reciprocal macro-, micro-, and physical processes at hand.

What does this mean? Relationships are reciprocal, embedded in a complex system, or nested complex systems. Energy both spurs and constrains economic growth, which in turn stimulates more energy development (toward physical limits). I share Odum's view (1973) that the economic system acts as a positive feedback loop for energy production.[7] While industrial production seems central to the analysis, demand in foreign and domestic markets, as we've been reminded by Adam Smith, Keynes, and others, drives much of the cycle.

In Figure 5.10 we see annual changes in the world's TPES (on a national level, domestic energy production plus net imports).[8] When plotted against changes in GDP, a linear fit performs as well as nonlinear fits ($r^2 = 0.66$), such as exponential or logistic curves. Here, when comparing GDP and energy in change terms, I prefer to use nominal GDP, unadjusted for inflation; given that the money supply and price inflation are crucial to the understanding of the system, for this application it seems more appropriate not to adjust GDP with the problematic consumer price index (CPI). Adjustment by such indexes can distort raw data, obscuring the very effects we search for and thus hindering scientific inquiry.

These simple statistical exercises reveal an intricate dance of energy-economy leads and lags. New energy resources spur new industrial activity, which induces monetary growth and further energy development, and so on. Untangling these cycles is difficult, as they feature systemic, rather than linear, causation. Cross-correlation tests at various time scales tend to show dynamic relationships between variables such as oil prices, industrial production, and money supply—correlations negative at one lag, positive

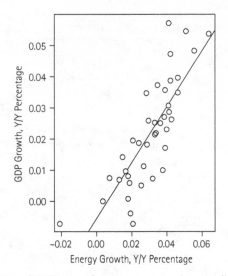

FIGURE 5.10 World GDP and TPES growth rates, 1972–2013 (nominal).

Source: Data from IEA global energy balances and IFC International Financial Statistics.

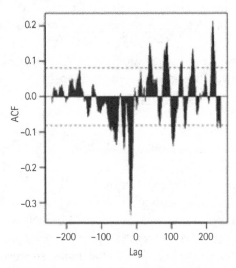

FIGURE 5.11 Cross-correlation of 12-month differenced monthly time series: Oil prices and US oil imports, 1964–2013.

Note: Maximum lag is 240 months. Oil price (UK), selected as the lead variable, does lead imports by a few months in the negative correlation, though at longer periods, oil imports hold significant information about a positive long-term correlation.

Source: EIA and International Financial Statistics.

at another, which I interpret as the interplay of negative feedback mechanisms and oscillating cycles (Figure 5.11). Further consideration of these factors will be left to other pieces, where I investigate complex relationships between energy and external balances at greater depth.

Patterns in National Energy Signatures over Time

As shown in Figure 5.5, the year 2009 saw dramatic contraction in global energy production, the largest decline in at least 40 years. This was also overshoot—a reaction to massive disturbance in the financial system, collapse of certainty and fall in expectations, following a recession in the real economy. Yet these events, like the tumultuous monetary events of the 1970s (beginning with the 1971 unilateral dollar float, known abroad as the "Nixon shock"), had energy roots in turn. These lay in the differential growth rates of nations with divergent energy trajectories, the United States and China, yoked together in a fragile financial mechanism. The 2009 event thus appears a correction, or feedback effect, of a sustained energy imbalance. Meanwhile, extremely high energy growth rates may represent positive feedback from the monetary system— low rates of interest or easy money can stimulate rapid short-term demand growth, and often does, until correction (see Frankel, 2006).

The United States and its energy profile in the 1960s provide an excellent example. Energy supplies in the 1960s and early 1970s, during a long expansion, shot far above trend for both the United States, and, as we saw in Figures 5.1–11, world mining in general, with oil the major component. The 1970s, beginning with the Nixon shock and ending with the Volcker shock, can be read as a readjustment of the US monetary system to deal with the changing global energy situation.

In short, the steep global energy trajectory from 1960 to 1972 was forcibly flattened by massive price adjustments, emerging from the energy contraction of the late 1970s to a completely different growth path from 1982 to 2005. The United States added about 35 exajoules (EJ) to its total primary energy supply between 1960 and 1978. China added about 35 EJ from 2001 to 2007. The global energy growth path flattened again in 2006, after four years of spiking oil demand from China.

In both cases, the countries went from around 45 to around 80 EJ, though China streaked past 100 EJ by 2010. It is important to note that in the case of China's rise, its growing share of global energy took place against a backdrop of global energy production increases that were on trend, while US and global energy production increases were far above trend in the 1960s and 1970s (see Figures 5.12 and 5.13). This indicates that China's unprecedented energy gain, for all the awe it induces, *merely filled in for decline in other countries during the first years of the 2000s*. After both overshoots, crises ensued, though the US 1970s path required two corrections to adjust, with attendant recessions in the 1970s–1980s. Both cases saw a massive energy price adjustment.

These price adjustments, however, depended not only on supply and demand, but in large part on the changes in—on the correction of—a monetary system *put out of balance by energy differentials and kept there*. This is the root of the "disequilibrium system" of Mundell (1961). Simply put, the artificially expensive dollar's devaluation made an energy price shock inevitable in both cases (see Figure 5.14).

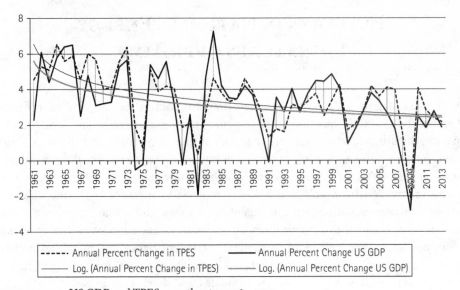

FIGURE 5.12 US GDP and TPES growth rates, 1961–2012.

Source: IMF International Financial Statistics, IEA.

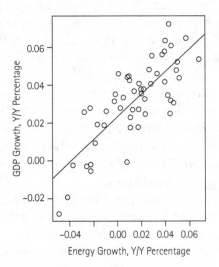

FIGURE 5.13 Linear fit: US GDP and TPES growth rates, 1961–2012.

Source: IMF International Financial Statistics, IEA.

As the global energy system grows, fairly predictably and linearly, resources are shuffled around with it. The flattening US energy signature in Figure 5.14 is typical of advanced industrial nations, with Germany and Japan (Figures 5.15 and 5.16) other exemplars of a "rise-and-decline" TPES. These nations in general saw extremely high energy growth in the 1960s and into the 1970s, with Germany and Japan peaking and declining significantly earlier than the United States.[9]

Not all countries had such gentle plateaus. Cuba's "Special Period" experience in the 1990s and 2000s, after it lost its flow of subsidized oil from the Soviet Union, shows

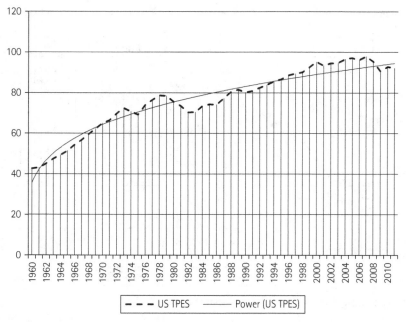

FIGURE 5.14 US total primary energy supply, 1960–2012 (exajoules [EJ]).

Source: IEA Energy Balances.

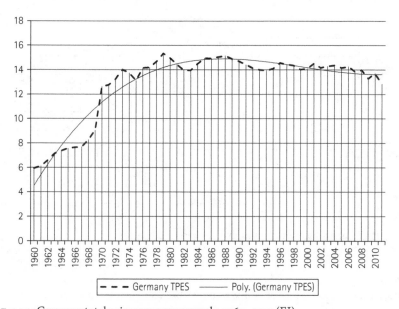

FIGURE 5.15 Germany total primary energy supply, 1960–2012 (EJ).

Source: IEA Energy Balances.

what happens to a nation whose energy supplies disappear overnight (see Figure 5.17). Most Cubans during this time lived on the edge of the minimum sufficient daily caloric intake, while the nation's transport and housing infrastructure deteriorated severely. Meanwhile, sectors with relatively light energy footprints, such as biotech and

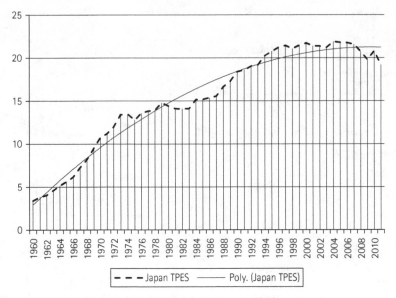

FIGURE 5.16 Japan total primary energy supply, 1960–2012 (EJ).

Source: IEA Energy Balances.

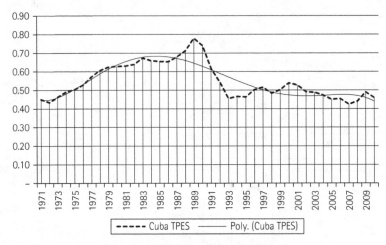

FIGURE 5.17 Total primary energy supply, Cuba, 1971–2010 (EJ).

Source: IEA Energy Balances.

education, maintained relatively high, even world-class levels (Eckstein, 2004). Here an energy shock produced total economic change. The source of that shock, however, the collapse of the Soviet Union—though perhaps originating in oil markets, according to its former prime minister (Gaidar, 2007)—was a complex political economic event.

Very few nations have experienced this type of energy signature over the past 45 years. Sustained drops in total energy are rare, and so far in this investigation have turned up only in nations whose supply was connected with the former Soviet Union. One might assume that much of the oil component of that "lost" energy was redirected to the Western world, helping to account, perhaps, for the low oil prices and related economic boom that prevailed across the United States and the West through the 1990s.

Not surprisingly, the collapse of the Soviet Union in 1991 also shows this unique, Cuba-like energy signature, with the TPES of its constituent units dropping dramatically (see Figure 5.18). We might say metaphorically that the nation's "binding energy" was released. Yet we do need to pay attention, in this case, to the colinear variables involved, and the reciprocal relationship between the Soviet economy's financial and energetic collapse.

Meanwhile, as factories closed and former Soviet Union (FSU) nations endured a bitter 1990s, China stood on the verge of the largest energy expansion in world history. Its exponential energy supply path during the second half of the twentieth century is reasonably similar to those of other developing nations, but the scope and speed of its burst during the first decade of the 2000s was unparalleled. From 2001 to 2010, China added roughly the energy supply of 1967-era United States, about 60 terajoules (TJ), to its annual use (Figure 5.19). It accounted for 30%–50% of total net global energy supply growth during these years, on average (Table 5.3). This process has recently begun slowing, however, with the Chinese Communist Party announcing that it would cap coal production around 2015, at 3.9 billion tons (Bloomberg News, 2012). Chinese coal production levels in 2014 indeed fell for the first time in the twenty-first century against 2013, with 2015 expected to be lower still (Guardian, 2015).

China's energy supply was flat during the period just before its coal-fired take-off, remaining around 50 TJ per year from 1995 to 2001 (Figure 5.19). The incredible coal drive

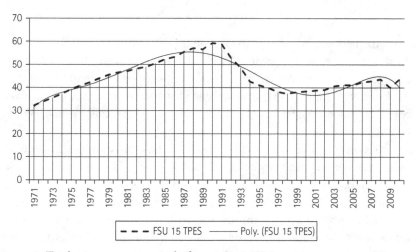

FIGURE 5.18 Total primary energy supply, former Soviet Union states, 1971–2010 (EJ

Source: IEA Energy Balances.

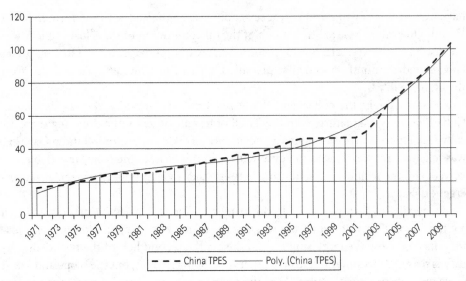

FIGURE 5.19 Total primary energy supply, China, 1971–2010 (EJ).

Source: IEA World Energy Balances.

Table 5.3 China's Share of Global Net Energy Production Increase, 2001–2009

2001	2002	2003	2004	2005	2006	2007	2008	2009	2010
22%	90%	35%	32%	36%	34%	55%	46%	N/A*	30%

Note: Global net energy production contracted in 2009.
Source: Author's calculations from IEA World Energy Balances.

of the next 10 years began virtually the moment China joined the WTO, in December 2001. In the year after its accession, China accounted for a startling 90% of new net global energy production. A vast array of new export markets changed the structure of the Chinese economy toward "labor-intensive manufactured goods," while the percentage of population engaged in agriculture dropped dramatically, from 50% in 2001 to 11.2% in 2010 (Boden, 2012, p. 13).

The global economy had swallowed a whale. China's vast middle class would eventually require a redistribution of global purchasing power. The event that heralded the end of this period, the 2008 financial crisis, stemmed in large part from its accumulated financial imbalances: "an enormous quantity of money flowed into low-income housing in the United States, both from abroad and from government-sponsored mortgage agencies such as Fannie Mae and Freddie Mac. . . . Foreign investors looked for safety. Their money flowed into securities issued by government-sponsored mortgage agencies like Fannie Mae and Freddie Mac, thus furthering the U.S. government's low-income

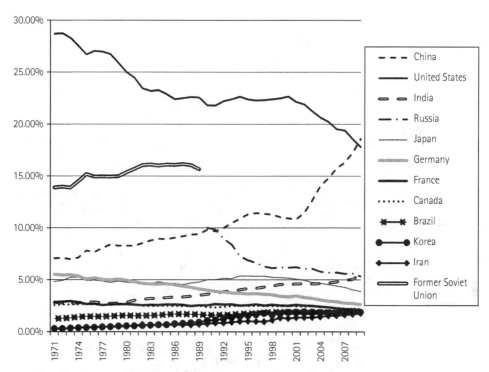

FIGURE 5.20 Share of global TPES, 1971–2009, 12 nations.

Source: IEA World Energy Balances.

housing goals" (Rajan, 2010, p. 16). In 2001 China held 10% of global central bank reserves—by 2010, it had accumulated 28%, as shown in Figure 5.21 (International Monetary Fund, 2015).

These financial imbalances arose from enormous differentials in energy productivity across the global system—mainly from China's access to enormous amounts of high-yielding coal, complemented by the low-cost energy of hundreds of millions of Chinese laborers. Yet, as we will see shortly, the importance of China's labor supply versus its coal supply has perhaps been overstated. By modeling growth with production function improvements made in ecological economics (Ayres & Warr, 2010), it may become clear that lower-cost energy (or higher-yielding energy, similar but separate concepts linked since *The Coal Question*) provided not only a massive boost, but perhaps also the brakes, for China's historic production push (see Table 5.4).

China's energy growth in 2012 was 3.85%—its lowest rate of the boom period. It is not clear what energy source, and thus what region, can substitute for the 2001–2006 pulse of energy from China, and the impetus it provided the global economic system. Shale oil in the United States, though a contested and potentially short-lived resource, is one near-term answer, with attendant political economic adjustments producing interesting times in the financial and energy worlds as of 2015.

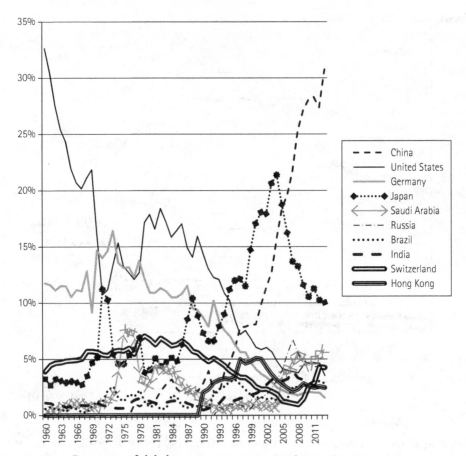

FIGURE 5.21 Percentage of global monetary reserves, 10 nations, 1960–2013.

Note: Includes monetary gold, special drawing rights, IMF holdings of member nations, and foreign exchange held by the monetary authority.

Source: IMF International Financial Statistics.

Table 5.4 Average Annual Energy Production Growth in China

2001–2003	2004–2006	2007–2009	2010–2012
7.43%	9.07%	4.89%	6.48%

Source: Author's calculations from IEA World Energy Balances.

HOW WE ARE STUCK: ENERGY YIELDS AND GLOBAL STAGNATION

The correlation of total primary energy supply with growth rates is important. This study attributes the current stagnation of the global economic system, dating from the 2008 collapse—and perhaps the 2006–2007 slowdown—in large part to falling global energy yields. The collapse itself appears to be in large part an adjustment to differential global energy productivity, given that the Chinese and US central banks prevented the monetary system from adjusting gradually in previous years, mainly through the pegged USD-Yuan and recycling. Slowing rates of energy production after the Chinese energy burst of 2001–2006 likely exacerbated the effect on a financial system geared toward rapid growth.

Despite what appear to be a large monetary expansion via US central bank policies, global growth seems stuck at levels well below that of the pre-2008 world.[10] The argument here is that global stagnation will remain unless a high-yielding new source of energy growth is identified. The global economic system requires an engine, and excepting the problematic US shale boom, we have not yet identified it.

We can look at secular stagnation in another way—too much savings, too little investment. This is the view of Keynes (1997 [1936]) on the Great Depression, and of Lawrence Summers on the Great Recession (Economist, 2015). Investors cannot find enough profitable projects, according to Summers's point of view. For Keynes this makes capital artificially scarce, given liquidity preference under current uncertainty. A true Keynesian response to this problem would involve the socialization of investment by the state, which would bridge the gap between expected returns on current projects and the "marginal efficiency of capital"—or, roughly, the going rate of profit—by raising taxes at top income brackets and engaging in a large-scale fiscal investment program. The economy-wide rate of profit would fall toward the going rate of interest (though this is nowhere near the 0% currently being awarded to savers at banks). Previously marginal projects would be matched with readily available capital, increasing investment, then employment and effective demand, and then output.

For marginal projects, energy costs can make the difference between viable and not—given interest rate responses, price shocks often attach what is effectively a private tax across the economy on the order of 5%–15%, with direct energy costs often much higher. Notably, in a time when demand for large-scale, low-carbon, or ecologically effective programs seems urgent, what Keynes saw as an unnecessary scarcity of capital keeps many of them on the drawing board. A "Green New Deal" or such would seem to require another "euthanasia of the rentiers" in order to access the capital in the rents they receive as a consequence of artificial scarcity (Keynes, 1997 [1936], p. 376). Yet rentiers today seem, if anything, less disposed to go to sleep than they were in the 1930s, evoking deeper questions of state power vis-à-vis the financial and energy industries in particular, and the corporate sector in general.

In any case, given the trajectories of the global and US energy-economic systems, the current global stagnation is no surprise. The same crisis occurs whenever energy production rates begin to peak and decline. The difference now is that the phenomenon has beset the entire world, rather than a single core or hegemonic country. Large debt-based increases to the money supply may cover declining real growth rates and keep incomes at a steady nominal level in a country such as the United States, yet this seems impracticable for the whole world. China provided, as mentioned, an enormous boost to the global economy after its December 2001 accession to the WTO. It accounted not only for a large portion of net global energy growth through its coal resources, but also acted as a stabilizer for the US currency, while providing low-cost goods that keep the US cost of living down.

When thinking about energy differentials between nations, it is important to separate total energy production, growth in energy production, and net energy yield (also "energy surplus" or EROI). The first term refers to how much energy is being produced, the second to its growth rate, and the third to what's left over after energy costs of energy production are subtracted. A nation could conceivably produce a large amount of energy—100 exajoules, for instance, about a fifth of global supply—but use 100 exajoules to do so. In that case, net energy would be zero. It is impossible for the global system as a whole to work at zero net energy, given maintenance costs, entropic degradation, and so on. Virgin resources, such as coal and oil fields, typical had energy surplus ratios of 100 or greater—this means 100 joules would cost their owners one joule or less to produce.

Since the large decreases in net energy yields up to the 1970s, the United States has for years been a net consumer, producing less energy than it uses. This requires other nations be net producers; their energy surplus is net of their own energy cost of production. From that surplus they subtract energy used domestically outside the energy industry, while the remainder may be sold abroad to consumers such as the United States. Clearly, there must be a balance between consumers and producers; a world of net consumers is not possible. Long the world's largest energy consumer, the United States has been a net consumer for several decades. Meanwhile, China became in 2007–2008 a net coal consumer, at least, for the first time. While its new energy production averaged around one-third of the global total through the first decade of the 2000s (Table 5.4), China's new consumption was about half of new global supplies in key years, as it continually increased its share of both global production and consumption.

I argue that the changing role of China, with its extraordinary energy growth in the first decade of the 2000s, lies near the root of the 2008 global financial crisis (see Rajan, 2010). From that point, with China no longer putting out a massive energy surplus onto world markets, the global energy balance looks quite different. As oil prices spiked and China became a net importer of coal for the first time in 2008, it became clear that its growth rate, which propelled global growth and US financial speculation via its capital tsunami, was unsustainable. The system built over it simply fell apart, as the great stream of money produced through the massive conversion of coal slowed. The "too little, too late" 2004–2006 US interest rate rise, with the attendant reduction of demand, was one of many contributors to the system's near collapse.

As shown above, GDP growth in the United States has declined with its rate of domestic energy use over time. The trend appeared in the 1970s, though it was not the first time a global power has seen energy limit its growth and power. England in the early twentieth century, as predicted by one of its greatest economists (Jevons, 1866), was the first major global fossil power to peak and decline. As it did so, the role of global monetary hegemon or guarantor began a long migration to the United States, which would not see its prime energy source peak until 1970.

Similar to the global situation of the 2010s, in the 1970s the United States struggled to reproduce the growth rates of the previous decade. Insofar as unpegging its currency from the Bretton Woods–era gold regime allowed it, for a time, to import far more energy on the global market than it otherwise would have been able to afford, it succeeded. Energy became extremely cheap versus its long-term trends at key points leading up to the "energy crises" of the 1970s and early 2000s. The key to this apparent contradiction is that the United States has devalued the dollar repeatedly over the past 50 years, but, especially in the "posted-price" (non-market) oil regimes of the 1970s, it takes time for energy prices to catch up with the falling value of the dollar, building up tensions in trade that produced enormous overcorrections or "price shocks." In work published elsewhere, I examine these energy price shocks in the United States, with the goal of contributing to current debates on the mechanisms through which they affect the economy.

References

Ayres, R. U., & Warr, B. (2010). *The economic growth engine: How energy and work drive material prosperity*. Cheltenham, UK: Edward Elgar.

Bloomberg News. (2012). China to restrict coal demand, output, to 3.9 billion tons. March 21. Retrieved from https://www.bloomberg.com/news/articles/2012-03-22/china-to-restrict-coal-demand-output-to-3-9-billion-tons

Boden, G. (2012). China's accession to the WTO: Economic benefits. *The Park Place Economist*: Vol. 20. Retrieved from http://digitalcommons.iwu.edu/parkplace/vol20/iss1/8

Cleveland, C. J., Costanza, R. C., Hall, A., & Kaufmann, R. (1984). Energy and the US economy: A biophysical perspective. *Science, 225*(4665), 890–897.

Eckstein, S. E. (2004). *Back from the future: Cuba under Castro*. New York: Routledge.

Frankel, J. A. (2006). *The effect of monetary policy on real commodity prices*. No. w12713. National Bureau of Economic Research.

Gaidar, Yegor. (2007). The Soviet collapse: grain and oil. *American Enterprise Institute for Public Policy Research*, April, 1-8. Retrieved from https://www.ciaonet.org/catalog/5662

Georgescu-Roegen, N. (1975). Energy and economic myths. *Southern Economic Journal, 41*, 347–381.

Georgescu-Roegen, N. (1971). *The entropy law and the economic process*. Cambridge, MA: Harvard University Press.

Hansen, J., Sato, M., & Ruedy R. (2012). Perception of climate change. *Proceedings of the National Academy of Sciences, 109*(37), E2415–E2423.

Harrison, S. G., & Weder, M. (2006). Did sunspot forces cause the Great Depression? *Journal of monetary Economics, 53*(7), 1327–1339.

Hayek, F. A. (2009 [1944]). *The road to serfdom: Text and documents—The definitive edition*. Chicago: University of Chicago Press.

Heilbroner, R. L. (2011). *The worldly philosophers: The lives, times and ideas of the great economic thinkers*. New York: Simon and Schuster.

Hogan, L., & Naughten, B. (1990). Some general equilibrium effects of declining crude oil production in Australia. *Energy Economics, 12*(4), 242–250.

Höök, M., Hirsch, R., & Aleklett, K. (2009). Giant oil field decline rates and their influence on world oil production. *Energy Policy*, 37(6), 2262–2272.

Hooker, M. A. (1996). What happened to the oil price-macroeconomy relationship? *Journal of Monetary Economics*, 38(2), 195–213.

Hornborg, A. (2009). Zero-sum world challenges in conceptualizing environmental load displacement and ecologically unequal exchange in the world-system. *International Journal of Comparative Sociology*, 50(3–4), 237–262.

Hughes, J. D. (2013). Energy: A reality check on the shale revolution. *Nature*, 494(7437), 307–308.

International Monetary Fund. (2015). *International Financial Statistics*.Washington, DC: IMF.

Jakobsson, K., et al. (2014). Bottom-up modeling of oil production: A review of approaches. *Energy Policy 64*, 113–123.

Jevons, W. S. (1878). Commercial crises and sun-spots. *Nature 19*(472), 33–37.

Jevons, W. S. (1866). *The coal question: An inquiry concerning the progress of the Nation, and the probable exhaustion of our coal-mines*. Library of Economics and Liberty, 4. Retrieved from http://www.econlib.org/library/YPDBooks/Jevons/jvnCQ0.html

Kallis, G., & Sager, J. (2015). Beyond simple explanations: Oil's role in global economic crisis. Unpublished manuscript.

Kaufmann, R. K. (1992). A biophysical analysis of the energy/real GDP ratio: implications for substitution and technical change. *Ecological Economics*, 6(1), 35–56.

Kaufmann, R. K., & Cleveland, C. J. (1991). Policies to increase US oil production: Likely to fail, damage the economy, and damage the environment. *Annual Review of Energy and the Environment*, 16(1), 379–400.

Keynes, J. M. (1997 [1936]). *General theory of employment, interest and money*. Amherst, NY: Prometheus Books.

Lakoff, G. (2010). Why it matters how we frame the environment. *Environmental Communication*, 4(1), 70–81.

Malthus, T. R. (2015 [1798]). *An essay on the principle of population*. Library of Economics and Liberty. Retrieved from http://www.econlib.org/library/Malthus/malPop.html

Mandel, E. (1972). *Decline of the dollar: A Marxist view of the monetary crisis*. New York: Monad Press.

Mankiw, G. N. (2003). *Principles of macroeconomics*. Boston: Cengage Learning.

Martínez-Alier, J., & Schlüpmann, K. (1987). *Ecological economics: Energy, environment, and society*. Oxford: Basil Blackwell.

Mill, J. S. (1848). *Principles of political economy with some of their applications to social philosophy*. London: J. W. Parker.

Mirowski, P. (1984). Macroeconomic instability and the "natural" processes in early neoclassical economics. *The Journal of Economic History*, 44(2), 345–354.

Mirowski, P. (1991). *More heat than light: Economics as social physics, physics as nature's economics*. Cambridge: Cambridge University Press.

Mitchell, T. (2009). Carbon democracy. *Economy and Society*, 38(3), 399–432.

Mundell, R. A. (1961). The international disequilibrium system. *Kyklos*, 14(2), 153–172.

Odum, H. T. (1971). *Environment, power, and society*. Vol. 130. New York: Wiley-Interscience.

Odum, H. T. (1973). Energy, ecology, and economics. *Ambio*, 2, 220–227.

Rajan, R. G. (2010). *Fault lines: How hidden fractures still threaten the world economy*. Princeton, NJ: Princeton University Press.

Samuelson, P. A., & Nordhaus, W. D. (2005). *Macroeconomics*. New York: McGrawHill.

Schrödinger, E. (1992). *What is life?: With mind and matter and autobiographical sketches.* Cambridge, UK: Cambridge University Press.

Schumpeter, J. A. (1934). *The theory of economic development: An inquiry into profits, capital, credit, interest, and the business cycle.* New Brunswick: Transaction.

Schumpeter, J. A. (2013). *Capitalism, socialism and democracy.* New York: Routledge.

Sexton, S. E., Wu, ., and Zilberman, D. (2012). *How High Gas Prices Triggered the Housing Crisis: Theory and Empirical Evidence.* Berkeley, CA: University of California, Center for Energy and Environmental Economics Working Paper Series.

Smith, A. (1904). *An inquiry into the nature and causes of the wealth of nations.* Edwin Cannan, ed. Library of Economics and Liberty. Retrieved from http://www.econlib.org/library /Smith/smWN.html

Soddy, F. (1933). *Wealth, virtual wealth and debt: The solution of the economic paradox.* New York: E. P. Dutton.

Solow, R. M. (1956). A contribution to the theory of economic growth. *The Quarterly Journal of Economics, 70,* 65–94.

Solow, R. M. (1974). The economics of resources or the resources of economics. *The American Economic Review, 64,* 1–14.

Spiro, D. E. (1999). *The hidden hand of American hegemony: Petrodollar recycling and international markets.* Ithaca, NY: Cornell University Press.

Strange, S. (1971). *Sterling and British policy: A political study of an international currency in decline.* Oxford: Oxford University Press.

Stresing, R., Lindenberger, D., & Kümmel, R. (2008). Cointegration of output, capital, labor, and energy. *The European Physical Journal B-Condensed Matter and Complex Systems, 66(2),* 279–287.

Tainter, J. (1960). *The collapse of complex societies.* Cambridge: Cambridge University Press.

The Economist. (2014). Why is stagnation bubbly? January 6. Retrieved from https://www .economist.com/blogs/freeexchange/2014/01/secular-stagnation

The Guardian. (2015). China coal production falls for first time this century. Retrieved from https://www.theguardian.com/environment/2015/jan/27/china-coal-production -falls-for-first-time-this-century

UN Comtrade. (2015). *Commodity trade statistics database.* United Nations Statistics Division. Retrieved from https://comtrade.un.org

Whale, P. B. (1937). The working of the pre-war gold standard. *Economica, 4,* 18–32.

White, L. A. (1943). Energy and the evolution of culture. *American Anthropologist, 45,* 335–356.

NOTES

1. The "shadow price" of a given factor is another way of looking at the issue. As it rises, its constraint on growth increases. At a certain level the global price matrix must readjust.

2. I ignore here the very long-term necessity of entropic degradation, as in, for example, Georgescu-Roegen (1971).

3. Howard Odum (1973, p. 223) gets at this organic relationship with his beautiful comparison of high-surplus fossil fuels to the leaves of a tree that get the most sun, produce the most energy, and come out first, enabling secondary and tertiary leaves to grow in places less opportunely placed to collect solar energy. Odum compares the latter to lower-yielding (compared to virgin fossil deposits) resources such as solar and wind energy.

4. Again, we saw the collision of financial and physical realities in Figures 5.10–5.13 on global trade; the global monetary value of traded fuel and minerals rises exponentially, their production only linearly.

5. Though Georgescu-Roegen (1971) reminds us that eventually the second law means the economic progression cannot be ever upward. This constraint might bite sooner than later. Until now the global upward trajectory in energy yield and production has mitigated the effects of local peaks, such as those in US oil (1970) and British coal (1913). However, when faced with the problem of "feeding" an economic system that requires enormous amounts of energy to maintain itself, let alone grow, it stands to reason that absent a tremendous new step forward in energy production, society will at some point see a peak in its energy production.

6. On shale fields this process of keeping production up despite rapid field decline is known as the "Red Queen," named for a character from Lewis Carroll's *Through the Looking-Glass*.

7. These positive feedback loops, modeled in neuroscience and biology as reciprocal Granger causality between two variables, help explain the outsized influence of energy on the economy.

8. The trend line for the world GDP and TPES data comes much closer to the origin than that of the United States, which has an "offset" of about 2% GDP growth (at zero energy growth) versus the rest of the world, which is closer to 0.5% offset. The meaning and importance of this is open to debate. For much of the world, energy growth is a hard limit—for individual countries such as the United States, it is easier to transcend domestic energy supplies for various reasons. Indeed, this is an important mechanism in the global system, the cause of large-scale disruption in the 1970s and 2000s.

9. Germany and Japan also overshot during the 1960s–1970s, when the great fields of Saudi Arabia and OPEC opened up. Like the United States, both nations doubled or tripled their available energy during the golden 1960s.

10. Due to excess reserves held at the Fed, this monetary expansion may be somewhat illusory. M2 has seen relatively mild growth despite the astounding rise in the US monetary base from the Troubled Asset Recovery Program (TARP) and quantitative easing.

CHAPTER 6

....

ENERGY MARKETS
AND TRADING

....

DAVID MARES

INTRODUCTION

ENERGY is fundamental for economic and social development, but efficiency in use and the characteristics of the energy matrix matter for how that development unfolds. The transformation of energy markets and their expansion via trade can help or hinder development, depending on the processes behind them and how stakeholders interact. The availability of renewable, climate-friendly sources of energy, both domestically and internationally, means that there is no inherent trade-off between economic growth and the use of fossil fuels.

This chapter discusses the role of energy in economic development, the transformation of energy markets, trade in energy resources themselves, and the geopolitical dynamics that result. Ceteris paribus, the larger markets for energy that can be developed via international trade can benefit growth and the development of more climate friendly and renewable sources of energy. But the existence of economic, political, social, and geopolitical adjustment costs means that the expansion of international energy markets to incorporate these alternatives to oil and coal will likely proceed more slowly than we wish. Further complicating the adjustment dynamic, energy production is a complex balance of environmental trade-offs, with no solutions completely free of negative impact risk. The chapter concludes by examining how the growing portfolio of renewable energy resources influences the pattern and geopolitical dynamics and consequences of the energy trade. The lesson of this chapter, in short, is that the supply of and demand for energy cannot be understood without considering the institutional context within which they occur, as well as the social and political dynamics of their setting.

THE ROLE OF ENERGY
IN ECONOMIC DEVELOPMENT

The availability and use of energy plays a fundamental role in economic development, and thus in social and political development as well since quality of life (a function of wealth, health, and values) influences societal interactions and how people relate to their government. Electricity doesn't just power equipment that increases economic productivity, it enhances personal and social life by powering light for extending the time available for reading, studying, and interacting with others, and increases the ability of local clinics to keep medicines requiring refrigeration on hand, among other things. Compared with traditional biomass or kerosene, natural gas can lessen the time for preparing meals and can increase health by reducing exposure to noxious fumes (Millan, 2003).

For the purposes of examining the role of energy in economic development, we can divide the economy into four sectors: industrial, transport, residential, and commercial. The industrial sector is the largest consumer of energy worldwide; traditional sources were wood and hydro, which were supplanted by crude oil products and natural gas (Energy Information Agency, 2016a; International Flame Research Foundation, n.d.). Transport-sector energy use is growing faster than in the other two sectors, and especially so in developing countries. In the United States, 88% of transport-sector energy derives from petroleum (gasoline, diesel, and jet fuel), with biofuels contributing 5%, natural gas 3%, and the rest from a variety of sources, including electricity (2015 data) (Energy Information Agency, 2016b). Energy sources for residential use can be categorized into traditional (biomass), transitional (kerosene, carbon, and charcoal), and modern (natural gas, hydro, and non-conventional alternatives of wind and solar) (Jimenez & Yepez-Garcia, 2016). In the commercial sector, electricity and natural gas are the dominant energy sources. An optimal mix of energy sources for a national society will vary based on natural endowments, economics, politics, culture, and values. Although global society will be better off economically and environmentally if we move to modern sources that are climate friendly, the pace of transforming national energy markets will be affected by what is optimal and/or politically viable regionally and in the short term.

The relationship between energy availability/consumption and economic development is, nevertheless, neither linear nor positive in all cases. For example, more use of energy does not necessarily contribute to economic development if it is used inefficiently. Subsidies to consumers in general, rather than to a specific category of consumer (e.g., those living in poverty), provide incentives to use more energy (e.g., drive a car two blocks rather than walk, or open a window rather than turn down the heating system) without a commensurate improvement in productivity. Subsidies can also keep society tied to dirtier and less efficient fuels, as in the Egyptian case—the country is a major exporter of liquefied natural gas (LNG) but liquefied petroleum gas (LPG) subsidies keep the use of natural gas at home at a commercial disadvantage (Gerner & Sinclair, 2006). And of course, subsidizing the use of more polluting energy resources can keep firms from adopting the most modern technologies, thereby making their production less competitive and contributing to climate change.

Greater efficiencies can produce higher growth rates with less energy use. New studies are revealing that with economic growth the efficiency of industrial and residential energy use generally rises. For example, even with an extended economic recovery from 2010 to 2035, the growth of energy use in the United States is expected to continue to slow. On a per capita basis, energy consumption is even expected to decline by an annual average of 0.5% and the energy intensity of the economy to fall by 42% in that period (Sieminski, 2015). Across time and place, part of that efficiency increase not only represents the move away from traditional fuels to transitional and modern fuels, but also is impacted by cultural practices and societal values regarding the health and environmental impacts of different fuels, as well as the distribution of income across society (Jimenez & Yepes-Garcia, 2016).

Yet, wealthier countries might also choose to pay higher prices and even reduce the rate of economic growth for environmental and climate-related reasons. Regulatory rules that require reduced energy use (such as those currently being discussed in the European Union (EU) that would cut energy use by up to 30% by 2030; Lewis 2016) can be expected to increase the efficiency of use and stimulate renewable energy use, but perhaps not sufficiently to maintain economic growth (Lewis, 2016). These regulations thus encompass social values regarding the cost of economic growth—reflected in reduced employment and high energy prices to consumers and businesses. They may also have political implications that create a dynamic in which higher unemployment and energy costs combine with other issues (e.g., migration and austerity budgets in the EU) to generate a backlash against the regulators and the adoption of new energy regulations, perhaps stimulating inefficient energy use and higher rates of growth.

The production of energy can also influence economic development negatively via what has been labeled the "resource curse" (Dunning, 2008; Haber & Menaldo, 2011; Ross, 2012). This problematic process begins when the abundance of valuable natural resources creates incentives for rent-seeking and corruption on the part of governments, the private sector, and even consumers. In this context, government officials, investors, and civil society groups focus on maximizing immediate gains, thereby disrupting the ability of a government to function efficiently and effectively, as well as the ability of firms to invest in productive and internationally competitive activities. Economic development, despite short-term growth spurts in response to a boom in the price of the natural resources (in our case, oil and natural gas), suffers therefore from forgone productive investment. The social and political disruptions generated by boom-and-bust economic cycles, corruption, and patronage also undermine the investment climate necessary for economic development. In addition, authoritarian political structures supported by natural resource revenues prevent the transition to democracy, and thus deprive the country of the long-term economic benefits of democracy.

Nonetheless, there is no "curse" inherent in natural resource wealth. As the experiences of Norway, the Netherlands, Great Britain, Canada, Australia, the United

States, and Chile demonstrate, the resource curse is not inevitable. The determinants of whether a country mishandles its natural resource wealth are institutional: transparent and accountable government institutions and civil societies with participatory cultures minimize both rent-seeking behavior and corruption. Consequently, countries that produce valuable internationally traded energy resources will more likely experience positive impacts on economic development and avoid their social, political, and economic externalities if they have strong institutions that promote good governance.

Separate, though often conflated, is the impact of being a major producer and exporter of energy on a country's exchange rate. The general phenomenon is known as the "Dutch disease"—observed in the 1970s when Dutch natural gas exports generated enough wealth to produce an appreciation in the national currency (Ismail, 2010). The result was the loss of international competitiveness of non-gas exports and inflation at home. Without some countervailing efforts (e.g., "sterilizing" the inflows of money), development of the national economy is likely to become skewed toward the product generating the inflow and less efficient because of inflation.

THE EVOLUTION OF ENERGY MARKETS

Energy markets exist in one form or another as soon as sources of energy in whatever form are bartered or sold among those utilizing them. The evolution of an energy market is influenced by geology, technology, economics, social and political dynamics, and institutional context. With so many factors influencing energy markets, it should not surprise us that energy markets have been subject to wild and unpredictable swings once the ability of the major consuming countries and their international oil companies (IOCs) to control production and exports ended in the early 1970s (Figure 6.1).

With competitive markets and newly empowered actors (communities, NGOs, national oil companies, and governments in the developing world), even a developed and mature energy market like the United States can evolve in unforeseen and dramatically different ways. In the 1990s the United States was preparing itself to become a major importer of LNG and was fearful of its dependence on oil imports. With the "shale revolution," however, within two decades the United States had developed a major capacity to produce light crude oil and natural gas, helping to send international oil markets into a tailspin and promising to turn the country into an important LNG exporter.

The shale revolution is a revealing case regarding the interaction of many variables that generate a particular developmental pathway. Beginning in the 1980s, drilling technology and procedures experienced significant advances, with coil-tubing, steerable drill bits, downhole telemetry equipment, and—in this third generation of horizontal drilling—the ability to place multiple horizontal well bores over longer distances, deeper, and with greater accuracy. Hydraulic fracturing ("fracking") techniques were developed, whereby a mixture of water, chemicals, and sand is pumped into the well to crack open the rock and release the oil and natural gas into the well (Energy Information Agency, 2012a; Helms, n.d.).

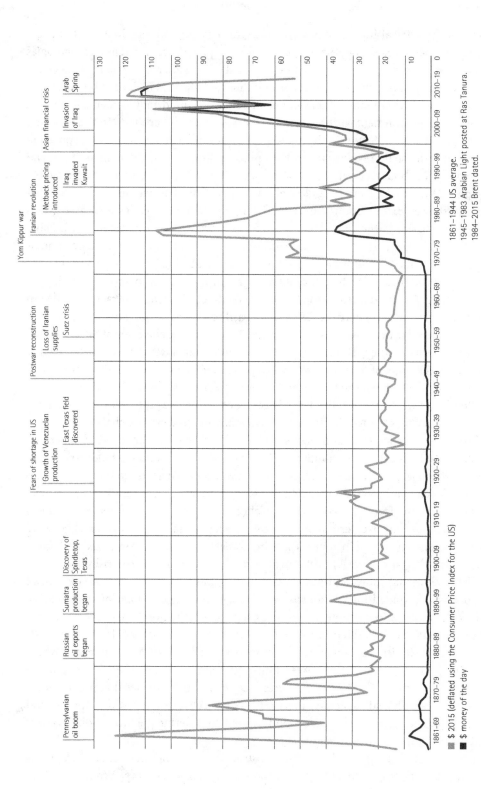

FIGURE 6.1 Crude oil prices, 1861–2015.

The technological innovations were costly to develop and use. Major oil and gas companies perceived the opportunity costs of developing the required new technologies to be too great, given their access to conventional oil and gas reserves across the globe. Small, domestic companies in the US market thus took the lead in developing and using the technology. These innovators were helped by three important elements in the domestic legal environment within which shale exploration and production (E&P) would develop, and by three factors in the domestic energy and financial markets. The question of whether the shale revolution can be reproduced outside of the United States and Canada is not about technology and skill; rather, it is whether these additional factors are present in other countries and, if not, whether equivalent factors might be developed (Arbogast & Rao, 2016; Mares, 2012). Among the three legal factors, first, access to resource basins in the United States was initially relatively cheap, given that US laws grant subsoil property rights to surface property owners rather than to the state (a situation unique to the US and some Canadian provinces). The high costs of technology and equipment were thus offset to a substantial degree by the initially low cost of purchasing the resource. A second factor is the sanctity of contracts. Leasing contracts signed with individual property owners or states were not easily overturned when the lessees discovered that the value of the gas was significantly higher than they believed at the time shale E&P was in its infancy. Though the costs of purchasing shale deposits subsequently increased, the costs of technology and equipment declined, and thus there was still a stimulus to investment. The third legal factor in promoting the shale revolution in the United States was a decentralized regulatory context that was difficult to revise, a circumstance that has limited the impact of environmental concerns on shale E&P.

Two of the three key facilitating factors in the domestic energy market were low barriers to entry and high prices for natural gas. Deregulation of the natural gas industry, which began in the 1980s and picked up speed in the 1990s, opened access to the extensive US pipeline system and created a competitive market for natural gas. Returns were initially high—despite the fact that shale wells' depletion rates are higher than for conventional wells—because market-determined gas prices were high (peaking at more than US$13 per Mcf [thousand cubic feet] in 2008). The third domestic factor, a decentralized and broad financial market, also made it possible to finance what was initially a very risky bet.

The institutional context within which the various sources of energy are developed nationally and traded internationally is a fundamental determinant of their relative prices. That institutional context prioritizes some concerns over others—for example, environmental over production interests on public, but not private, lands. The institutional context also legitimates some actors over others, such as in countries where marginalized populations have no standing to oppose central government policies taken in the name of the "national interest," compared to countries that provide local communities with veto rights over those types of projects. In other words, supply of and demand for energy cannot be understood without considering the institutional context and the social and political dynamics.

With the spread of minimally democratic structures, the empowerment of Indigenous communities, the environmental movement, and nongovernmental organizations (NGOs) seeking to defend the powerless, community buy-in is becoming increasingly important in the development of energy markets. We certainly tend to think of this when we read about protests against oil and gas exploration and transportation to market—for example, the Keystone and Dakota Access pipelines that would have transferred Canadian heavy oils and US shale oil, respectively, to US refineries (Sammonaug, 2016). The International Energy Agency has tried to overcome some of these obstacles to the development of unconventional gas, particularly shale gas, by elaborating a set of "golden rules" that call for appropriate government attention to the social and environmental issues involved, the development of transparent and credible regulations, and recognition by corporations of the need to utilize "best practices" in all of their operations (International Energy Agency, 2012).

But all of these issues are also present in the development of "green energy" projects designed to make national and international markets reach agreed-upon standards to reduce greenhouse gas emissions. For example, the development of wind and solar energy requires siting of the turbines, panels, and transmission lines, but local residents, including defenders of wildlife and unobstructed scenic panoramas, as well as those fearful of the health effects of high-voltage transmission lines, can raise the political and economic costs of a project to a level that makes it commercially non-viable. Geothermal energy can also generate concerns. In northern Mexico, water pollution—already a regional concern—is exacerbated by two geothermal plants in the region. Other negative effects of geothermal exploitation include the use of large amounts of scarce water as well as increased danger of induced seismicity, land collapse, and land pollution. In addition, waste-water management issues and the constant fluxes of sulfuric gas to the atmosphere can reduce the promised sustainability of so-called green technology (Union of Concerned Scientists, n.d.). The essential truth is that energy production is a complex balance of environmental trade-offs—with no solutions completely free of negative impact risk.

The Importance of Public Policy

Public policy creates incentives and barriers for the development of energy markets. Incentives can be regulatory, tariff, financial, even interstate agreements. Of course, the importance of public policy draws attention to the issue of the credibility of commitments made by government officials. In the literature on foreign direct investment in the natural resource sector, credibility issues are usually couched in terms of the credibility of government promises. Government promises are inherently suspect because governments generally leave office before the terms of the contracts they sign expire, raising the question of whether a new government will respect those terms. In addition, since governments have the attribute of sovereignty, they can change laws and legislation in ways that have a negative impact on contracts already signed. Although investors will be concerned with government credibility, the empowerment of local communities and other stakeholders like NGOs means that government commitments to them must also be credible for a project to be implemented at the expected costs.

Public policy also interacts with corporate policy, and here credibility issues also arise. Questions of corporate social responsibility (CSR) and the notion of a social license to operate affect both conventional and renewable energy projects (Taylor, 2016).

The institutional context of markets also matters. The transformation of energy markets is driven in large part by the competition among distinct energy sources. One of the factors that affects the use of natural gas, even though it is associated with fewer pollutants than its chief competitors for power generation (diesel and coal) or for home heating (wood), is its ability to compete on price with those alternative sources of energy. In a country like Brazil, the availability of hydroelectric power is a major determinant of the demand for natural gas because its price to the consumer is so cheap. If nuclear power plant construction in Brazil, Argentina, and Chile proceeds and the energy produced does not reflect the real cost of construction and disposal, demand for natural gas and petroleum in the Southern Cone will also be affected.

Though natural gas is cleaner than LPG (also known as propane) and can, in a competitive market, be cheaper than LPG, the development of a residential natural gas market often faces economic, social, and political challenges. Because LPG is provided in gas cylinders, its use does not require the installation of gas lines and the costs of gas connections; this makes it a valuable means of transitioning away from traditional fuels without the need for expensive distribution infrastructure, and will often be subsidized initially by governments seeking to benefit lower-income segments of society. The World Bank recognizes it as a "fuel of the poor" and advocates government policies to cushion the impact of transitioning from LPG to natural gas (Gerner & Sinclair, 2006). But of course, the amount of government subsidies raises economic, social, and political issues about who pays, how much, and for how long.

The development of natural gas markets in the United States and Western Europe was slow into the 1990s because the markets were heavily regulated, rendering them unattractive to investors (NaturalGas.org, 2013). In addition, the price of gas was tied to oil, and with falling oil prices in the 1980s–1990s, North Sea gas was not attractive to produce, thus depriving Western Europe of a regional source. Gas markets were thus developed most extensively in Asia, particularly in Japan, where LNG, even with its high price, became an important factor in diversifying domestic energy away from imported oil (Markus, 2015, pp. 94–96).

It is no surprise, therefore, that the developed natural gas–consuming countries are predominantly longtime producers of natural gas (Saudi Arabia mainly produces gas in association with oil), or in the case of Japan, rich and with no domestic sources of oil or sufficient coal (British Petroleum, 2016, Natural Gas Data slides). Producing natural gas certainly does not lead to the development of a domestic natural gas market. Most poor countries "flare," or burn off their natural gas associated with oil production, because they lack domestic markets for its consumption. The greatest gas flaring occurs in Iran and Russia, which have developed domestic gas markets but lack the infrastructure to transport significant amounts of associated gas from remote oil fields to markets. Algeria, Egypt, Peru, and Bolivia developed natural gas production specifically for export, with domestic consumption following (see Map 6.1).

MAP 6.1 Gas consumption per capita, 2015, tonnes oil equivalent.

THE DEVELOPMENT OF TRADE
IN ENERGY RESOURCES

Energy endowments are distributed unevenly across the globe, and even societies with similar resource endowments differ in their willingness to exploit these resources. In addition, demand for electricity is variable across the day and place (due to climate, demographics, income levels, distribution of economic activities, etc.), so some areas will have excess capacity at the same time that other areas will have shortages. Some areas are moving faster than others toward renewable and climate-friendly sources, the production of which is variable (e.g., wind and solar), and thus need a backup source to generate electricity on short notice; natural gas-fed combined cycle gas turbine (CCGT) plants are the ideal complement. Trade in energy resources thus can fill gaps and permit areas to be more efficient in their choice of energy resources that make up their energy matrices. The state of California is an excellent example of a state that has chosen not to exploit most of its hydrocarbon energy resources and takes advantage of its climate and neighboring supplies (from other US states, Canada, and Mexico) of renewable energy and natural gas to develop an energy matrix that is politically acceptable and serves to stimulate its dynamic economy (Clemente, 2015; Energy Information Administration, 2016b).

The importance of oil in modern economies and defense establishments led to a quick development of international trade for that commodity. Trade in natural gas took longer to develop because it was more difficult and expensive to transport, but today, with advances in LNG technology and the desire to move to a cleaner fossil fuel, the natural gas market is expanding and can be expected to mirror the reach of the global oil market (see Maps 6.2 and 6.3). The reach of these markets and their specific flows will be influenced by technology, the willingness of financial markets to fund infrastructure, the politics of government regulation and foreign policy, and societal responses to resource availability and trade. The energy trade, in short, is affected by all of the major influences on supply and demand.

The shale gas revolution will have a major impact on the future development of a global LNG market as the United States becomes an important supplier, especially to Europe. In addition, Australia's offshore Gorgon gas fields began commercial production in 2016 and are estimated to contain 35 trillion cubic feet (tcf) of gas. The emergence of these two new gas suppliers weakened prices sufficiently to slow investment in new projects, but that could result in supply shortages in the future and subsequent increases in prices. If gas prices increase sufficiently, Canada and East Africa could also increase production. Israel now has the potential to be a significant gas exporter, though investors have concerns that domestic and international politics will limit Israel's export potential, especially if weak gas prices persist (Kennedy, 2016; Sachs & Boersma, 2015). On the demand side, trade patterns might also change as Japan and Korea are expected to decrease their gas consumption (Costanza, 2016). The geological potential on a global

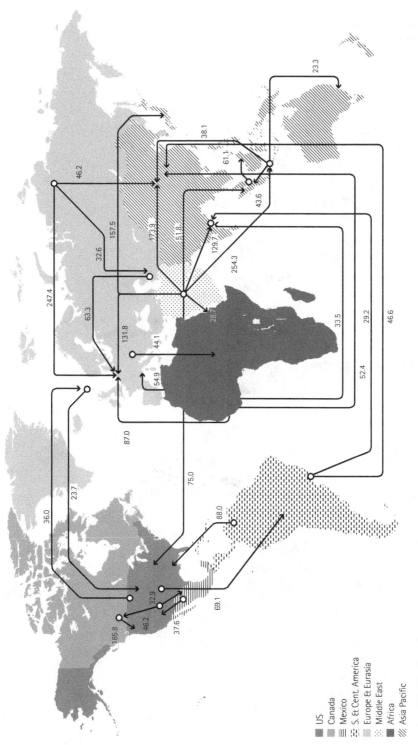

MAP 6.2 Major oil trade movements, 2015.

US
Canada
Mexico
S. & Cent. America
Europe & Eurasia
Middle East
Africa
Asia Pacific

23.3
38.1
61.1
46.2
43.6
157.5
173.9
51.8
129.7
254.3
32.6
63.3
131.8
44.1
28.7
33.5
29.2
46.6
52.4
247.4
54.9
87.0
75.0
36.0
23.7
88.0
32.9
46.2
185.8
37.6
69.1

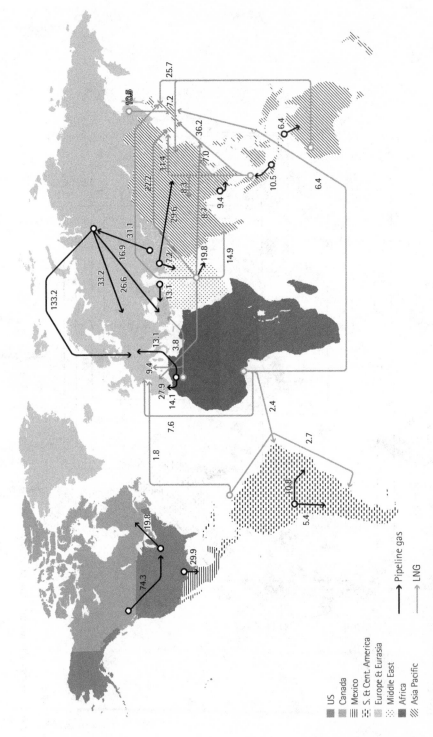

MAP 6.3 Major gas trade movements, 2015.

US
Canada
Mexico
S. & Cent. America
Europe & Eurasia
Middle East
Africa
Asia Pacific

Pipeline gas
LNG

scale for shale oil and gas to supply international markets long into the future is great, but the economic, political, and social contexts to support that production have not yet been developed outside of the United States (Energy Information Administration, 2013).

The larger the market, the more potential it has for increased efficiency, as distinct partners bring specific comparative advantages. Weather and geography can also play a role, if precipitation and heat vary across borders that can be profitably traversed by supply lines. The US-Canada energy relationship illustrates the advantages and controversies associated with a trade relationship based on economic rationales. It is the most valuable integrated energy market in the world, with energy trade valued at more than US$100 billion in 2011. As seen in Figure 6.2, the trade spans all sources of energy (hydrocarbons, hydropower, and non-hydro renewables) and includes raw materials (oil, gas, and coal) as well as electricity (Energy Information Administration, 2012). Canada's electricity is overwhelmingly generated by hydropower, and it exports 10% of its total electricity generation to the US market, covering 1.6% of US electricity retail sales (Energy Information Administration, 2015).

Though we think of trade in national terms regarding suppliers and consumers, transit countries or zones can play a significant role in the development of the trade. The conflict between Ukraine and Russia not only has generated intense mistrust in the EU regarding Russian supplies, it will likely result in Turkey becoming a new transit zone into Europe.

If the larger market created by integration is strongly shaped by regional or international political factors, the result could be less efficiency and fewer benefits for public goods. In a worst-case scenario, regional political relationships might make transparency and credibility more problematic and contribute to the "resource curse" for the energy-exporting country. For example, an energy-importing member of the integrated

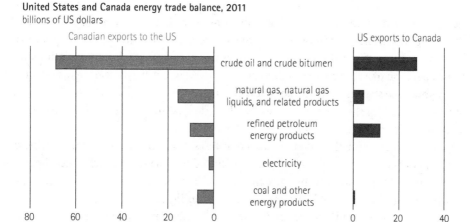

United States and Canada energy trade balance, 2011
billions of US dollars

FIGURE 6.2 United States and Canada energy trade balance, 2011.

Source: Energy Information Administration, "Canada Week: The United States and Canada share the world's most significant energy trade"; www.eia.gov/todayinenergy/detail.cfm?id=8910 November 26, 2012.

market might not want to criticize the politics in the energy-exporting member because they also share ideological or security relationships. The evolution of the Middle East and North Africa's chaotic political economy over the past half-century certainly are intimately linked to their role in the international oil and gas trade. Thus, once again we see that economic relationships in energy trade cannot be taken as necessarily beneficial locally or regionally.

CHALLENGES FOR MARKET INTEGRATION AND TRADE RELATIONSHIPS

Integrating electricity markets can be more challenging than integrating raw materials markets for economic and political reasons. The export of power can be a very important issue for developing countries in particular. If a natural resource producer can export electricity rather than coal, natural gas, or water, they are adding value to their primary resource, and thus generating more wealth from their natural endowments.

The difference between exporting higher and lower value-added energy resources may not be very important to the United States vis-à-vis Canada because they have a deep and varied economic interaction that benefits both countries. But for developing countries, that difference can be an important strategic consideration for economic development, as well as building domestic political coalitions around the issue of whether a government in office has been selling the national patrimony too cheaply. For example, Bolivians have been talking about "industrializing" their gas (turning it into electricity and petrochemicals that can be exported) for decades, and Evo Morales swept into the presidency in 2006 partly on a criticism of prior governments' gas trade policies. The problem for Bolivia, however, is that while Brazil and Argentina have been willing to pay for pipeline infrastructure to get gas to their power plants, they do not want to pay the value-added price to Bolivia that importing electricity would imply. Chile is another neighbor in need of imported energy and might be willing to pay a higher price for importing electricity. However, Chile does not even have diplomatic relations with Bolivia because of a dispute over territory conquered in a war 150 years ago, and would worry about the security of a power supply that came from Bolivia. The issue is moot anyway, since the Morales government sees withholding natural gas as a means to pressure Chile to resolve the issue of an outlet to the sea for Bolivia.

There are international markets for fuel that can serve as backups for domestic power plants that have seen their contracted supply limited; those sources will likely be more expensive and/or polluting (otherwise they would have been the primary source), but at least power can be generated. If a country is depending on power imports, however, it will be unlikely to have idle power plants that can be easily fired up when power imports suddenly drop. Consequently, power integration involves a much more delicate, intimate, deeper level of integration, and the credibility of supply contracts will be more important.

The supply-and-demand scenarios that drive integration can fluctuate dramatically over time, resulting in the disruption of specific trade flows or even their reversal. The shale revolution not only reduces the need for imported oil into the US market, it has turned the US LNG market on its head. The LNG re-gasification terminals built to receive LNG shipments are now being converted into liquefaction facilities to export LNG. The gas relationship between Bolivia and Argentina is especially dynamic: in the 1970s a pipeline was built to supply Argentina; within a decade, Argentine supplies developed to the point that the flow was reversed; a decade after that, Bolivian supplies were again feeding Argentina; and in another 20 years, the development of Argentine shale might again reverse the flows. Of course, concerns regarding the environmental effects of shale gas production or the election of another populist government could curtail shale development altogether.

Technological innovations also play a dynamic role in facilitating the creation or destruction of trade relationships. For example, in South America the initial turn to natural gas as a power source led to a pipeline system traversing the southern part of the continent. First Bolivia was going to be the gas hub, then in the 1990s it appeared that Argentina would be. The move to gas for power also supported the move to large hydropower projects and a growing electricity trade, as gas-fired thermal power plants could provide backup in drought periods. But the shale revolution and new conventional gas discoveries in Brazil, Uruguay, and Paraguay have made it possible for each country to be virtually self-sufficient in gas, though perhaps not enough to become important international exporters (Bailey, 2013, pp. 14–19).

Nevertheless, new technologies can be trumped by societal opposition. The hydropower push in Latin America and elsewhere has been slowed significantly, if not stopped, by opposition from environmentalists and local communities. They may also be successful in ending a national shale revolution before it even begins, especially if community opposition coincides with significant innovations that will make green energy more competitive with hydro and natural gas.

Government regulation is a major determinant of trade via its impact on project siting and investment climate. The decision by the Obama-led US government to not build the Keystone pipeline from Canada to the Gulf of Mexico refineries forced Canada to consider diversifying some oil trade away from the United States, motivating approval of pipelines from Alberta to the British Columbia coastline. The subsequent reversal of the Keystone decision by Trump now raises concerns about pipeline *over*capacity in Canada. The difficulty in siting an LNG re-gasification facility in southern California led to its development south of the border in Mexico, as well as the construction of a gas pipeline connecting it to the California market, and a link between Mexico and Peru for the LNG. In the 1990s, the discovery of important natural gas reserves in Bolivia led to predictions that Bolivia would become the "energy hub" for South America, but societal opposition to exports, then new regulations on foreign investment by the Evo Morales administration, as well as a focus on developing the domestic market, derailed the supply scenario for that would-be hub. Developing countries with underdeveloped markets are not the only ones that confront the issue of whether regulation should be used to develop or protect the domestic market. The United States only lifted its ban on crude oil and LNG exports once the shale revolution convinced Congress that there would be no domestic shortages (Clayton, 2013; Neuhauser, 2016).

Energy trade is also affected by the economic and ideological value that a producing country places on its natural resources. National energy resources carry with them the issue of the "just" distribution of rents. Rents are returns on investment that are higher than those that would occur in a competitive market; natural resources are subject to a variety of influences (inherent differences in costs of production, uncertainty about supply, etc.) that at times lead to the generation of significant rents. Analysts, governments, and citizens often ask whether those rents should go to the host government that owns the subsoil resource, or an international company that develops the resource. Again, this is not just a question concerning developing countries—British Chancellor of the Exchequer George Osborne noted in 2011 when discussing tax increases on North Sea oil, "It is worth bearing in mind that this oil and gas is not theirs. It is ours, as a nation" (Osborne 2011). In the current context of increased energy trade, internationally active national oil companies (NOCs), and privately owned companies from developing countries, the distribution question affects not only major international oil companies (IOCs), but also governments whose NOCs are buying and selling to each other. Demands for price revisions by one party can lead to tensions if the credibility of contracts is not high.

The issue of rent distribution also affects the vulnerability of supply. Oil and gas companies and the financial markets that raise capital for them face multiple opportunities for investment. If a country is demanding a rent distribution that is too high relative to other opportunities, the investment necessary for exploration, production, and transportation of that energy in that country will not materialize. And if a country doesn't attract that investment, it will not be able to supply its contracts (e.g., Argentina and Bolivia). The insertion of state-owned enterprises (SOEs) into markets as a means of capturing more rents directly can create supply problems, too. SOEs need to be able to recover investments and finance new expansion/facilities/maintenance, but often governments simply treat them as a means to appropriate income or subsidize partisans and will starve the SOEs of resources necessary for reinvestment.

Whether regional or international energy integration is fundamentally driven by political agreements, or by market relationships, each of those drivers generates its own problems. The question that concerns both investors and importing countries is the credibility of those commitments in the context of economic or political volatility. How much credibility will political agreements signed with volatile countries provide a partner country that needs to develop its own energy policies based on the promise of future energy security provided by a politically unstable country?

Market relationships generate their own challenges. If energy integration is based on a regional market, it means that governments cannot give priority to the domestic market. But the marketplace doesn't meet demand (i.e., the desire for something); it meets *effective* demand (i.e., the desire for something by people who have something to exchange for it), and many poor people don't have effective demand for energy. Yet in a

democracy, those without effective market demand nevertheless can have effective political demand, which market relationships must ultimately address. Market reforms in
the late 1970s and again in the 1990s stimulated the development of markets for natural
gas in Argentina, Chile, and Brazil. Vast new supplies were discovered and came online
as private and public investors responded. But that development ran into problems beginning in the late 1990s, largely for domestic reasons, as regulatory agencies failed to
keep pace with the privatization of suppliers, and citizens felt "robbed" and overcharged.

Efforts to address the issue of who pays the cost of delivering access to the benefits
of energy to disadvantaged social sectors can also greatly affect energy trade. Do the
consumers in the importing countries of Latin America foot the bill via ever higher
prices, with the likely possibility that substitution of energy sources and diversification of the energy matrix will occur, thereby diminishing the long-term wealth to be
generated from the country's energy supplies? Or do those resources come from a reassessment of the budget priorities of the government of the exporting country, which in
turn means that some domestic programs and economic sectors will see their relative
share of the budget decline? The answer is neither easy nor self-evident.

GEOPOLITICAL DYNAMICS THAT DEVELOP
FROM ENERGY TRADE PATTERNS

Trade can create dependencies and vulnerabilities, and trade in strategic resources can
generate both political power and vulnerability for governments and societies. Mutual
dependencies (aka interdependence) can be uneven and influence the relative bar-
gaining position of partners who are otherwise happy with the relationship. Trade can
also be a means of compensating a partner for providing a benefit on another matter.
Whatever the specific situation, trade influences geopolitical dynamics among partners
and between them and rivals. Energy trade is not inherently different in this respect,
and thus we can think of how energy trade brings partners closer together and is used to
dissuade or sanction rivals.

Although for most countries the geopolitical dynamics of the energy trade are linked
to specific dependencies created by those energy flows, for the United States the key
focus is on global markets. Lofty assumptions that with the current shale revolution and
the development of green energy sources the United States can disengage from the oil-
rich Middle East are mistaken. The price the United States pays for oil is globally determined, its allies will continue to import oil from this region, and US rivals will feel more
insecure if the global oil market appears to be unstable. Consequently, as long as the
global market in oil is heavily influenced by supply from this region, the United States
will maintain its interest in oil continuing to flow. China and India will become increasingly supplied from Middle Eastern oil, and their military presence in the region will
likely increase as both develop their blue water navies; the US defense establishment

will be leery of such power projections. So long as oil continues to be a major part of global energy markets, the Middle East will continue to play an important role in US, and global, geopolitics.

American sanctions on a variety of Iranian assets, services, and products predate concerns about Iran's nuclear development, and stem from the Iranian Revolution's attacks on the US embassy and support for certain terrorist actions by non-state actors. The United Nations placed its own sanctions on Iran in 2006 after the country was found by the International Atomic Energy Association (IAEA) to be in violation of its agreements under the Nuclear Non-Proliferation Treaty (NPT) regime. Iranian oil exports became a target of the sanctions in 2012 when the EU complemented the UN sanctions by adding oil imports to the list (the US imports no Iranian oil). The combination of sanctions over time created domestic economic pressure in Iran, and the government signed an agreement in 2015 that lifted many sanctions, including the oil embargo (Laub, 2015). Iran's current plans are to increase production well above pre-sanction levels, and it is certainly far too early to know the ultimate impact of the sanctions on Iranian behavior.

Governments have been cautious in imposing oil sanctions today. The administrations of Republican George W. Bush and Democrat Barak Obama refused to embargo imports of Venezuelan oil into the United States despite their opposition to the Bolivarian socialist governments in Caracas and demands by many right-wing groups in the United States. For their part, the governments of Hugo Chavez and his successor Nicolas Maduro rhetorically attacked the US government for its imperialist behavior and support of the failed coup against Chavez in 2002, but never followed through on the threat to halt oil exports to the United States. It would be difficult to know how each country would be affected by ending the relationship. The dependence of US Gulf of Mexico oil refineries on Venezuelan heavy crude, as well as the domestic and regional political backlash likely to be produced as a result of any embargo on Venezuela, means that such an embargo would have hurt the United States in addition to Venezuela. For Venezuela, even during the heyday of high oil prices, and more so today, the dollars produced by exports to the US market are fundamental for financing first the expansion and now the survival itself of the leftist Bolivarian Revolution initiated by Chavez. In short, mutual dependence makes "the oil weapon" a difficult tool to use effectively by either country.

The EU's energy matrix is not natural gas intensive, and its consumption of gas has been falling since 2010 due to slower economic growth, rising production of renewables, and cheap coal. Nevertheless, the Union imports almost 70% of the natural gas it consumes, and that raises questions about reliability of supply. In 2014, 29% of gas imports came from Russia, 23% from Norway, 4% from Algeria, and 10% in the form of LNG, although data from the major gas firms indicate that in 2015 Russian imports were second to gas from Norway (*Moscow Times*, 2015).[1]

Analysts disagree about how much vulnerability to Russian gas is produced by this situation, with some arguing that as long as options exist that can be implemented in the short term, the amount of Russian gas being imported doesn't matter. Political pundits in Washington, Brussels, and Central-Eastern Europe, however, have opposed this view. Compared with the situation in the 1990s, EU gas sources are more diversified today (Auon & Cornot-Gandolphie, 2015). Vulnerability varies by country in the EU, as East and Central European member states import more Russian gas than Western states. But in light of Russia's international behavior under Vladimir Putin, there is growing concern in Europe (probably more in Washington, DC) that any import of gas gives Putin leverage over Europe. And at some point, NATO sanctions might include Russian gas, or Russia's pivot to the Asian markets might make less Russian gas available to the EU anyway.

Because economics is on Russia's side (huge reserves and a gas pipeline infrastructure already in place) and West Europeans are actually ambivalent about natural gas in this era of climate change, the process of diversification that would further reduce Russian gas imports is likely to be erratic. Norway is concerned that EU climate change policies undermine the future of the natural gas market there, making future investments in Norwegian gas and infrastructure for transporting it less attractive. The country still has capacity, and its 2015 gas exports increased by 7%, second only to the Russian's increase of 7.7% (British Petroleum, 2016, p. 4). The Baltic Connector, an Estonia-Finland gas pipeline, is being partially financed by the EU, which hopes to create a Baltic market and integrate it with the EU as part of an Energy Union (NewEurope, 2016). The Finnish gas company, Gasum, already walked away from the project, and the Finnish government is now running it (Gasum, 2015). Shale exploration has been either too controversial to move forward (though the British government recently—October 2016—decided to authorize shale exploration) or disappointing (e.g., in Poland) to hold much promise in the foreseeable future. The EU price for carbon is also low enough for coal to compete. For its part, Russia has announced a new gas pipeline to the EU via Turkey. This would divert gas from traversing Ukraine, and thus would punish Ukraine with the loss of right of way fees, as well as increase pressure on Europeans to see Russian gas as separate from the Ukrainian dispute and to continue to depend on gas from Russia (TASS News, n.d.).

NON-HYDRO RENEWABLE ENERGY RESOURCES AND THE ENERGY TRADE

Understanding the potential impact of renewable energy on energy supplies and trade requires discarding some common myths. Renewable energy is not new, nor is it necessarily "clean" or "environmentally friendly." Harnessing the power of water generated by large dams, directly or indirectly by diverting the water into rivers to run mills, has been around for centuries. Today, the impact of large-scale hydropower projects on climate is controversial (Wockner, 2014), and the increasingly erratic rainfall that appears to be developing with climate change raises questions about its reliability. But the impact of building large dams on the ecology of a region and the way of life of the rural communities that are forcibly relocated generates sufficient, indisputable harm that the category of "non-hydro renewable energy" is increasingly being used in discussions of "green" energy.

But non-hydro renewables have their own issues and histories. Traditional energy sources of manure and wood are renewable, rivers have a long history driving mills and are renewed as long as the rains come, and windmills constitute very old technology. Burning some forms of biomass and cooking with wood can be harmful to one's health, contribute to local air pollution, and in the case of deforestation, make reducing carbon levels in the atmosphere even more difficult. Solar panels in environmentally sensitive hot places create shade and cool the ground beneath them, thus impacting the plant and animal life struggling to survive in the shadows. Wind turbines interfere with birds' flight patterns, create noise that can divert game from traditional hunting areas, and ruin vistas. The high-voltage lines needed to transport solar and wind power are also considered an eyesore, and generate health concerns among some people living near them. Mining the lithium for batteries[2] to store renewable power, finally, is far from an environmentally friendly process.

Why do these facts matter? Because they indicate that development of non-hydro renewables also has its problems, which can become economic and political costs that will affect these developing markets and trade. This is not to argue that current energy matrices and trade patterns will not be affected by non-hydro renewables—gas already has trouble competing against these alternative energy sources in the EU. But the economics of competing fuels, the regulation of the industry, the need to build political coalitions behind the new fuels, buy-in from community groups, and the role of societal norms and values will all influence whether non-hydro renewables get developed, where, and at what costs.

An illustrative case of the promise and the challenges associated with non-hydro renewables can be found in the wind corridor of Mexico's Isthmus region, especially on the Pacific side in Oaxaca. Private companies completed an environmental impact assessment that was approved by the government and that secured the approval of some Indigenous communities in the valleys to build necessary towers and transmission lines. Power generated here could feed the Mexican, US, and Central American markets if fully developed. The Tehuantepec Isthmus Wind Corridor project, however, has met resistance from other Indigenous communities and NGOs and may not reach its full development of 28 wind farms. Among the complaints are that the land used was communal, not private land, and that the noise will affect not only people, but animals, causing both to leave ancestral homelands, with negative implications for Indigenous cultures. In addition, many opponents have complained that they are paying the price for the carbon credits and the Kyoto Protocol–promoted Clean Development Mechanism, both of which subsidize polluting companies and regions and make investment in wind energy here profitable. From the perspective of some locals in Oaxaca, these efforts to offset carbon production in one area by generating clean energy in another simply transfers the costs of carbon generation to the locals elsewhere; in their view, carbon production should be eliminated in situ. In general, these protestors have no confidence in the Mexican government's credibility for assessing the environmental and social impacts of the project, nor for devising the means by which Indigenous groups can effectively exercise their rights to be consulted under international treaties signed by Mexico (Navarro & Bessi, 2016).[3]

The consumption of "other renewables" has increased significantly across the world in the twenty-first century. The largest increase of consumption has come in Europe and Eurasia, followed by the Asia Pacific. But when we consider the place of these renewables in a region's energy matrix, it is the Western Hemisphere that stands out—first North America, then South and Central America (British Petroleum, 2016, Renewable Energy slides).

Wind energy is the dominant non-hydro renewable source of electricity, followed by solar. Biofuel production increased at its slowest rate in a decade, with a fall in biodiesel production not being offset by the continuing increase in bio-ethanol production. The renewables market is developing quickly, but it is so far behind fossil fuel sources that in 2015 it accounted for only 2.8% of global energy production, though it did a bit better in terms of global power generation (6.7%) (British Petroleum, 2016, pp. 5, 39). It will certainly be some time before non-hydro renewables play a role that is significant enough to alter the geopolitical dynamics of regional or global energy trade.

Yet, non-hydro renewables do affect trading partners. California is a global leader in carbon reduction and promotes the development and use of non-hydro renewable energy sources. In 2009–2012, contrary to the expectations of many, the state economy did not suffer; in fact, it grew 4% in real terms at the same time that carbon intensity fell slightly more than 4% (Oglesby, 2015, p. 7). Governor Brown has set a 2030 goal for California of generating 50% of California's electricity from renewable sources and reducing petroleum use by 50%. One of the innovative components in California's climate change efforts is adoption of the recommendations of the Western Climate Initiative (WCI) for establishment of a cap-and-trade program with Quebec to regulate their carbon market. The first joint auction took place on November 2014 with very good results. This market is important for Mexico, as well. California already imports wind, solar, and geothermal energy from northwest Mexico and will need to help clean up its neighbor's energy matrix to reach its own carbon-reduction goals. Some Mexican border states have observer status in the WCI, and Tijuana and Mexicali participate de facto in this market because their power grid is connected to those of some California cities.

CONCLUSIONS

Energy and the markets that distribute it have always had, and will continue to have, complex and dynamic implications for geopolitics, making long-term, high-scale energy planning difficult, if not impossible. The supply of and demand for energy cannot be understood without considering the institutional context as well as social and political dynamics. Markets are very dynamic, not easily regulated to produce outcomes desired by governments and their constituencies. Demand considerations are many and varied: the reliability of supply; prices for specific energy sources that may function as competitors; and the existence of multiple markets for the energy (electric power, transportation, industrial, fertilizers/feedstocks, residential) with differing potentials domestically and regionally.

Even with regard to climate change, the topic is controversial. Should natural gas be treated as a beneficial, low-carbon transition fuel, or as a dangerous distraction, giving a false sense of security while making zero-carbon energy development more difficult? Who should pay for the negative externalities generated by wind, solar, and geothermal power, and how? The economics of competing fuels, the regulation of the industry, the need to build political coalitions behind the new fuels, buy-in from community groups, and the role of societal norms and values will all influence whether non-hydro renewables get developed, where, and at what costs.

There are many positive externalities that a country or community could tap. The development of an emerging regional market for gas where fears regarding security of supply are important (Europe vis-à-vis Russia, South American rivalries and economic instabilities) can be facilitated by the integration of regional markets into global ones where sources of supply and demand can be diversified. The transformation of a regional into an international gas market thus makes it more likely that governments and societies will be willing to alter their energy matrix and import cleaner fuels.

But the social, political, legal, institutional, and financial obstacles can loom large. In many parts of the developing world, increased investments in energy integration projects are diminished by the risks of domestic price caps, nationalization, and even access to negotiated and contracted supplies from neighboring countries. And many local communities continue to find their self-defined cultural and social norms undervalued by those who would take or make use of their local resources. These complex considerations all serve to underscore the essential fact that the development of all energy sources represents a trade-off, with benefits and costs for all.

ACKNOWLEDGMENTS

I would like to thank Debra Davidson for comments and Amanda Singh for research assistance; all responsibility is mine alone.

NOTES

1. Article reports EU officials' estimates that in 2014 Russia supplied 42% of EU gas imports.
2. Lithium is recyclable and thus scenarios of a global lithium market that parallels the unstable oil market is unlikely to develop since high prices would drive more reuse. Nevertheless, as the world needs to store more energy and lithium batteries are a major player in the storage market, more lithium will need to be mined.

3. The international treaty protecting indigenous rights to consultation is Convention 169 on Indigenous and Tribal Peoples of the International Labor Organization.

REFERENCES

Arbogast, S. V., & Rao, V. (2016, July). *Global fracking: Conference report*. Presentation at Kenan-Flagler Business School, University of North Carolina at Chapel Hill.

Aoun, M.-C., & Cornot-Gandolphie, S. (2015). *The European gas market: Looking for its golden age?* Paris: Institut français des relations internationales (IFRI).

Bailey, J. (2013, May 5). Shale and beyond: The next phase of Latin American energy integration. *World Politics Review*, 14–19.

British Petroleum. (2016). *BP Statistical Review of World Energy*, June 2016, Natural Gas Data Slides, Renewable Energy Data Slides. Retrieved from http://www.bp.com/content/dam/bp/powerpoint/energy-economics/statistical-review-2016/bp-statistical-review-of-world-energy-2016-full-slidepack.ppt

Clayton, B. (2013). The case for allowing U.S. crude oil exports. Policy Innovation Memorandum No. 34, Council on Foreign Relations.

Clemente, J. (2015). Why California is a natural gas state. *Forbes*. July 12. Retrieved from http://www.forbes.com/sites/judeclemente/2015/07/12/why-california-is-a-natural-gas-state/#47cf93e327cf

Costanza, J. (2016, June). Gas: Medium term market report 2016. Presentation at International Energy Agency, Paris.

Dunning, T. (2008). *Crude democracy: Natural resource wealth and political regimes*. Cambridge: Cambridge University Press.

Energy Information Administration, US Department of Energy. (2012a, July). What is shale gas and why is it important? *Energy in Brief*. Retrieved from http://www.eia.gov/energy_in_brief/about_shale_gas.cfm

Energy Information Administration, US Department of Energy. (2012b, November 26). Canada week: The United States and Canada share the world's most significant energy trade. Retrieved from www.eia.gov/todayinenergy/detail.cfm?id=8910

Energy Information Administration, US Department of Energy. (2013). Technically recoverable shale oil and shale gas resources: An assessment of 137 shale formations in 41 countries outside the United States. Retrieved from https://www.eia.gov/analysis/studies/worldshalegas/pdf/overview.pdf

Energy Information Administration, US Department of Energy. (2015, July 9). U.S.-Canada electricity trade increases. Retrieved from http://www.eia.gov/todayinenergy/detail.php?id=21992

Energy Information Administration, US Department of Energy. (2016a). *International energy outlook 2016*, Table F1. Retrieved from www.handbook.ifrf.net/handbook/dl.html/index.pdf?id=62&type=pdf

Energy Information Administration, US Department of Energy. (2016b, October 20). California: State profile and energy estimates. Retrieved from https://www.eia.gov/state/analysis.cfm?sid=CA

Energy Information Administration, US Department of Energy. (2016c, October 4). Use of energy in the United States explained: Energy use for transportation. Retrieved from http://www.eia.gov/energyexplained/?page=us_energy_transportation

Gasum. (2015, October 2). Finngulf terminal and Balticconnector pipeline not commercially viable. Retrieved from http://www.gasum.com/Corporate_info/News/2015/finngulf-terminal-and-balticconnector-pipeline-not-commercially-viable/

Gerner, F., & Sinclair, S. (2006). Connecting residential households to natural Gas: An economic & financial analysis. *OBA Working Paper Series Paper* No. 7 (p. 1).

Haber, S., & Menaldo, V. (2011). Do natural resources fuel authoritarianism? A reappraisal of the resource curse. *American Political Science Review, 105*(1), 1–26.

Helms, L. (n.d.). Horizontal drilling. *DMR Newsletter, 35*(1), 1–3. Retrieved from https://www.dmr.nd.gov/ndgs/newsletter/NL0308/pdfs/Horizontal.pdf

International Energy Agency. (2012). *Golden rules for a golden age of gas.* World Energy Outlook Special Report on Unconventional Gas. Paris: IEA.

International Flame Research Foundation. (n.d.). What are industrial fuels? A combustion file downloaded from the IFRF Online Combustion Handbook ISSN 1607-9116. Retrieved from www.handbook.ifrf.net/handbook/dl.html/index.pdf?id=62&type=pdf

Ismail, K. (2010, April). The structural manifestation of the "Dutch disease": The case of oil exporting countries. IMF Working Papers, Strategy, Policy and Review Department. Retrieved from http://www.resourcegovernance.org/sites/default/files/Dutch%20Disease%20(IMF)%20Newest%20Version.pdf

Jimenez, R., & Yepez-Garcia, A. (2016). Composition and sensitivity of residential energy consumption. IDB Working Paper Series No. IDB-WP-690.

Kennedy, C. (2016, March 28). Israel's game changing gas discovery dealt another blow. *Oil Price.com.* Retrieved from http://oilprice.com/Energy/Energy-General/Israels-Game-Changing-Gas-Discovery-Dealt-Another-Blow.html

Laub, Z. (2015, July 15). International sanctions on Iran. *Council on Foreign Relations.* Retrieved from http://www.cfr.org/iran/international-sanctions-iran/p20258

Lewis, B. (2016, September 9). EU regulators poised to seek deeper cut in energy use: Draft. *Reuters.* Retrieved from http://www.reuters.com/article /us-eu-energy-efficiency-idUSKCN11F20R

Mares, D. R. (2012, February). Shale gas in Latin America: Opportunities and challenges. *Energy Policy Group, Working Papers, Inter-American Dialogue.* Washington, DC.

Markus, U. (2015). *Oil and gas: The business and politics of energy* (pp. 94–96). London: Palgrave MacMillan.

Millan, J. (2003). Meeting of regional development banks and the United Nations Framework Convention on Climate Change: Basic trends in energy investment and development in LAC. Washington: Interamerican Development Bank. Retrieved from http://www.iadb.org/sds/doc/iadb%5fenergy%5fbackground.pdf

Moscow Times. (2015, May 22). Norway overtakes Russia as Europe's no. 1 gas supplier. Retrieved from https://themoscowtimes.com/articles/norway-overtakes-russia-as-europes-no-1-gas-supplier-46791

NaturalGas.org. (2013, September 20). The history of Regulation. Retrieved from http://naturalgas.org/regulation/history/

Navarro, F. S., & Bessi, R. (2016, January 20). The dark side of clean energy in Mexico. *Americas Program.* Retrieved from http://www.cipamericas.org/archives/18300

Neuhauser, A. (2016, May 16). The new U.S. energy era will be a gas: A coming shift will see America's exports of natural gas eclipse its imports for the first time in 60 years. *US News & World Report.* Retrieved from http://www.usnews.com/news/articles/2016-05-15/us-gas-exports-poised-to-surpass-imports-for-first-time-since-1957

NewEurope. (2016, August 10). Energy union: EU invests 187.5 million euro in first gas pipeline between Estonia and Finland." Retrieved from https://www.neweurope.eu/press-release /daily-news-10-08-2016/

Oglesby, R. P. (2015, January 13). California Mexico clean energy collaboration. Institute of the Americas, Cross Border Energy Forum. La Jolla, CA (p. 7).

Osborne, The Rt Hon George MP, Chancellor of the Exchequer, United Kingdom, before the Parliamentary Treasury Committee (Oral Evidence taken before the Treasury Committee on Tuesday 29 March 2011 Examination of Witnesses, questions 417–529). (2011). Transcript, as cited in Juan Carlos Boue (2014), Enforcing Pacta Sunt Servanda? Conoco-Phillips and Exxon-Mobil versus the Bolivarian Republic of Venezuela. *Journal of International Dispute Settlement*, 5, 438–474. doi: 10.1093/jnlids/idu007

Ross, M. L. (2012). *The oil curse: How petroleum wealth shapes the development of nations.* Princeton, NJ: Princeton University Press.

Sachs, N., & Boersma, T. (2015, February). The energy island: Israel deals with its natural gas discoveries. Policy Paper No. 35. *Foreign Policy at Brookings, The Brookings Institution.*

Sammonaug, A. (2016, August 26). The next Keystone? Protesters try to stop another huge oil pipeline." *Mother Jones.* Retrieved from http://www.motherjones.com/environment/2016 /08/dakota-access-bakken-pipeline-protesters-sioux

Sieminski, A. (2015, May). Annual energy outlook 2015. Presentation at Columbia University, New York, New York. Slides 2 and 5. Retrieved from https://www.eia.gov/pressroom /presentations/sieminski_05042015.pdf

TASS News Agency. (n.d.). Russia's gas giant Gazprom intends to completely abandon gas supplies to Europe through Ukraine after 2018 with the help of a new pipeline to Turkey. Retrieved from http://tass.ru/en/infographics/7275

Taylor, A. (2016, April 7). Building a social license to operate in the renewable energy sector. *Business for Social Responsibility.* Retrieved from https://www.bsr.org/en/our-insights /blog-view/building-a-social-license-to-operate-in-the-renewable-energy-sector

Union of Concerned Scientists. (n.d.). Environmental impacts of geothermal energy. Retrieved from http://www.ucsusa.org/clean_energy/our-energy-choices/renewable-energy /environmental-impacts-geothermal-energy.html#.WGSKghsrI2w

Wockner, G. (2014, August 14). Dams cause climate change, they are not clean energy. *EcoWatch.* Retrieved from http://www.ecowatch.com/dams-cause-climate-change-they -are-not-clean-energy-1881943019.html

CHAPTER 7

RAW MATERIALISM AND SOCIOECONOMIC CHANGE IN THE COAL INDUSTRY

PAUL S. CICCANTELL AND PAUL K. GELLERT

INTRODUCTION: THE RISE AND DEMISE OF COAL?

> A profound shift is happening right now in America's energy landscape. With the bankruptcy of Peabody Energy, it's clear that the coal industry is in decline, and that a massive shift in the global market favoring clean energy sources like wind and solar is underway.
>
> —Sierra Club (2016)

COAL has fueled economic development in the most dramatic and transformative cases of economic ascent over the past two and a half centuries, in Great Britain, Germany, the United States, and Japan (Bunker & Ciccantell, 2005, 2007). But today, coal seems like a relic of the old economy. The warning bells have been ringing in the past couple of years: coal is dying. The *New York Times* reported, "the coal industry is in a free fall and the banks are pulling away" (Corkery, 2016). Declining coal demand is viewed as a desirable and urgently needed turn of events by activists, citizens, and policymakers concerned about the significant contribution of coal use to global warming (Dunlap & Brulle, 2015; McGlade & Ekins, 2015).

Reliance on renewable energy sources such as wind and solar is growing in many countries, and coal extraction and consumption have fallen in recent years. Some researchers declare that we have reached "peak coal" (Romm, 2016). From the financial sector, Goldman Sachs agrees that "[p]eak coal is coming sooner than expected" (Lowrey, 2015). Furthermore, environmental organizations have been agitating for the United States to support the demise by moving "beyond coal" (Sierra Club, 2016). The scientific foundations of their politics are strong, as recent estimates project that "over 80% of current coal reserves should remain unused from 2010 to 2050 in order to meet the target of 2°C [maximum increase in global temperature]" (McGlade & Ekins, 2015). Since 2010, 230 coal-fired power plants have shut down in the United States (Sierra Club, 2016). As of 2016, coal is the raw material for only 34% of US electricity production, "the smallest share for coal in the electricity mix since 1949" (Goldenberg, 2016).

But is coal truly dying, and if so, how quickly? Coal's exhaustion has been predicted multiple times, including by Jevons in nineteenth-century England (Foster et al., 2010; Podobnik, 2005). Donald Trump pledged to revive the Appalachian coal industry during the 2016 presidential election campaign, a sharp policy break with the Obama administration. Coal continues to be a vital raw material for electricity and is highly correlated with economic growth. Moreover, due to the continuing lack of substitutes, demand for metallurgical coal for steel production has grown steadily since the late 1800s.

Taking a world-historical perspective, the evidence of decline is more contradictory over the *longue durée*. Coal is booming in some locations, and in late 2016 prices were rising as dramatically as they fell the previous years. Most fundamentally, coal's role in industrialization, economic ascent, and long-term change in the capitalist world economy is still significant. Coal has fueled generative sectors in iron and steel, railroads, steamboats, steamships, steam-powered factories, and electrification over the centuries. In doing so, coal affected prospects for ascent and state relations in successful and unsuccessful attempts at hegemonic ascent (Bunker & Ciccantell, 2005, 2007).

This chapter offers a historical-material perspective on energy and society relations by analyzing commodity chains and their effects on extractive regions, using the theoretical model of raw materialism and lengthened global commodity chains (GCCs) (Ciccantell & Smith, 2009). The chapter provides an illustration by focusing on the historical evolution and likely future trajectories of coal commodity chains in major coal-producing and consuming countries. As coal extraction and consumption have declined in the United States and Europe, both have exploded in China. China's economic ascent has radically transformed global coal and steel industries and the capitalist world economy over the past four decades. Coal still fuels the majority of China's electricity generation and remains irreplaceable for primary steel production, calling into question the potential for reducing this threat of global climate change.

In the following sections, we present our theoretical model of raw materialism and lengthened GCCs. Then we use this theoretical model to analyze the key material characteristics of the coal industry that have shaped the past, present, and future of the industry. The following sections use this theoretical model to examine the evolution of the coal industry from its origins and growth in Europe, especially Great Britain, and the United States, to its globalization after World War II, and then to the China-driven boom since the 1990s. In the final section, we analyze the key factors in the current quite complicated state of the coal industry and the possible multiple future trajectories of the industry.

RAW MATERIALISM AND LENGTHENED GLOBAL COMMODITY CHAINS

A reformulation of world-systems theory, new historical materialism, or, more bluntly, "raw materialism" as developed by Bunker and Ciccantell (2005, 2007), is vital to understanding the *longue durée* of coal.[1] Building on the works of Wallerstein (1974), Chase-Dunn (1989), and Arrighi (1994, 2007), raw materialism analyzes the contradictory roles of raw material extraction, processing, and consumption in shaping the long-term evolution of the capitalist world-economy and its constituent national economies, as well as attendant socioeconomic and socio-ecological impacts. This perspective reformulates world-systems analysis to stress the importance of control over and organization of raw materials sectors as a systemic characteristic of the operation of the world-system. Equally important, this approach provides a lens to examine spatially based "disarticulations" (Bair & Werner, 2011) that occur alongside articulations or incorporation into global commodity chains. Therefore, the struggles by less powerful states, firms, and social groups and classes to capture benefits from raw materials extraction are also important to historical dynamics.

Raw materialism works "outward" from the bio- and geophysical mechanics of matter and space that are crucial to efforts to build "generative sectors" in order to ascend the world-economic hierarchy. While opposing models of "environmental determinism," the key contribution of this theoretical model and research methodology lies precisely in its "raw materialism": the goal is to understand the material bases of power and inequality in the capitalist world-economy by beginning from first principles of chemistry, physics, geology, and hydrology.

As with much environmental sociology, the goal is to understand how relationships between society and nature have been shaped by these biogeophysical processes and how humans have learned about, adapted to, and, to varying extents, reshaped putatively separate "natural" processes. As such, raw materialism captures the "intertwined histories of struggles over raw materials and the development of capitalism" (Abramsky, 2007, p. 163). This nature-society nexus, which Foster (2010) and his colleagues examine via rifts in the universal metabolism of nature and Moore (2015) calls the web of life, is the central focus of both the theoretical model and the analytic method.

Raw materialism also works from a world-systems perspective in emphasizing how innovation and change in the capitalist world-economy at any point in time is found in those societies with rapidly growing economies that (from a post hoc perspective) have the potential to rise to challenge other economies for core or even hegemonic status. These rapidly growing economies face a host of challenges at this nature-society nexus. Ironically, both economies of scale and what Bunker and Ciccantell (2005) dubbed "dis-economies of space" are at work in the dynamics of the raw materials sectors. The raw materials used in the largest volumes present the greatest challenges to and best opportunities for achieving economies of scale and related reductions in unit costs and energy inputs. These economies of scale, however, drive a contradictory increase in transport costs. The closest, cheapest, and most secure reserves of raw materials are rapidly depleted as the scale of production increases, forcing states and firms to seek more distant supplies. Over time, the tension between the economies of scale and dis-economies of space expands as innovations in transport reduce material, energy, and labor inputs per unit of output and innovations in production that control for heat, pressure, and chemical mixtures make each unit stronger and lighter. These technological "fixes," however, generate expansions of scale that expand the system of accumulation even further while also relying on and disrupting socio-ecological relations (Bunker & Ciccantell, 2005).

There is an inherent contradiction between *economies* of scale, with emphasis on the economic, and *dis-economies*, with emphasis equally on the economic and the socio-ecological. Resolving this contradiction requires more than simple technological innovations. In a small number of cases, the organizational and institutional innovations have fostered "generative sectors" (Bunker & Ciccantell, 2005) that not only create backward and forward linkages (as in the concept of a leading sector). They also stimulate a broad range of technical skills and learning; formal institutions designed and funded to promote them; diversified instrumental knowledge held by interdependent specialists about global supplies of raw materials; financial institutions adapted to the requirements of large sunk costs in a variety of social and political contexts; specific formal and informal relations between firms, sectors, and states; and legal distinctions between public and private and between different levels of public jurisdiction (Bunker & Ciccantell, 2005). Importantly, generative sectors rest on the creation of national and global commodity chains (Ciccantell & Smith, 2009). These GCCs tightly link the rising economy to extractive peripheries and, via processes of unequal exchange, generate growing levels of economic and political inequality (Bunker, 1984; Jorgenson & Rice, 2012). Yet, surprisingly, generative sectors are not necessarily the most profitable sectors (Bunker & Ciccantell, 2003). Instead, generative sectors provide the material building blocks, cost reductions across many sectors to increase competitiveness, and patterns of state-sector-firm relations and other institutions that combine to drive economic ascent.

Using this approach, Bunker and Ciccantell (2005, 2007) explained causal similarities across the five most spectacular cases of systemically transformative economic ascent over the past five centuries: Holland, Great Britain, the United States, Japan, and China. Leaving aside the Dutch period, coal has been an essential ingredient of industrialization, economic ascent, and long-term change in the capitalist world economy. Coal has fueled generative sectors in iron and steel, railroads, steamboats, steamships, steam-powered factories, and electrification over the centuries. These generative sectors in Great Britain and the United States—as well as Germany in its aspiration to hegemony—drove economic ascent and created patterns of state-sector-firm relations. Coal resources were used to fuel urbanization and industrialization, then steam power to dewater coal mines as the most accessible deposits near the surface were depleted, and then transformed coal-fired steam power for use in factories, railroads, and steamships that in turn sustained Great Britain's hegemonic position throughout the nineteenth and early twentieth centuries. It is important to note that the generative sectors did not, however, resolve the socio-ecological contradictions of coal extraction.

Subsequent ascendant economic powers also relied on coal for electrification and growth. Appalachian coal supported US efforts to follow the British model of industrialization on a larger continental scale. Thus, even in the "age of oil" when an "energy shift" had been made from coal to petroleum by some accounts, we find a critical role played by coal (Mitchell, 2013; Podobnik, 2005). China's industrialization drive during the mid-twentieth century, especially its rapid ascent since the 1980s, has also been fueled by domestic coal reserves. Given the stupendous scale of its expansion, China came to rely on imports, including from the Japanese-created coal GCC, to supply what is now the world's largest steel industry.

Coal has not only been important to rising hegemons. It has affected core economies that did not rise to hegemonic status, for example leading Great Britain, the United States, failed challenger for hegemony Germany, and other countries to build systems of coaling stations around the world during the late 1800s. Also, domestic coal supplies affected industrialization and militarization in Germany and Japan. We identify four strategies of rapidly growing economies to acquire essential raw materials, in light of depletion dynamics and dis-economies of space. The first is state and military domination, like the Japanese empire's conquest of Manchuria, but also in acquisition of domestic territories. Second, states may "steal" raw materials peripheries (Ciccantell, 2009) from earlier ascendant economies that have already undertaken the arduous tasks of building infrastructure and creating political, organizational, and legal forms that facilitate the incorporation of peripheries into the world economy. Third, one can create new "greenfield" investments in raw materials. Fourth, one can increase the scale of extraction via technologies, although that strategy faces feedbacks of dis-economies of space. Coal also has been important to peripheral states in the world-system. Particularly during periods of material expansion, firms and elites in the periphery have taken advantage of openings provided by rising powers. For example, higher prices for rapidly increasing volumes of exports motivate investments in production for export, while actors in raw materials peripheries come to see the new ascendant as a potential ally in their attempts to promote resource nationalism and economic development (Ciccantell, 2009; Kaup & Gellert, 2017). Rightly or wrongly, coal is viewed as a potential generative sector for India, Indonesia, and other rising economies today, despite environmental and social problems created by this industry.

In addition, raw materialism provides a lens to examine spatially based disarticulations (Bair & Werner, 2011). Disarticulation is defined by the marginalization or outright elimination of particular nodes from a GCC. Rather than see disarticulation as simply the obverse of articulation, we need to pay attention to "the relationship between inclusion and exclusion as ongoing processes that are constitutive of commodity chains," as Bair and Werner (2011, p. 992) recommend. Articulations, disarticulations, and rearticulations can be driven by capitalist accumulation strategies, depletion dynamics, and contestation. Local residents and their allies may oppose the construction of a particular commodity chain in a particular place, or groups may contest or resist the reproduction of a location as a node of a GCC. In such cases, labor movements, social movement organizations, or other groups seek to achieve their goals despite opposition from firms and states.

Coal commodity chains have long contained sites of resistance. Coal was particularly important in shaping patterns of labor relations during the struggle over unionization, wages, and worker safety; the resolution of the long periods of contestation became the template for labor relations in other industries and became the basis of the political power of unions and coal-extracting regions (Bunker & Ciccantell, 2005, 2007). Miners' unions in Europe, the United States, and elsewhere are the historically most important actors of resistance to the expansion of coal commodity chains, but at times, they have supported expansion (Gaventa, 1980). Contemporary examples of resistance include opposition to mountaintop-removal mining in Appalachia and protests over the loss of land to coal mining in India, port worker conflicts, and the battle over the Keystone XL pipeline and oil sands, whose expansion competes with coal (Ciccantell & Smith, 2009; Sowers, Ciccantell, & Smith, 2014). Environmental opposition to the climate impacts of coal use is another prominent form of resistance to coal commodity chains, including efforts to get universities and other organizations to divest their investments in coal and other fossil-fuel firms (Greenpeace, 2015).

MATERIAL CHARACTERISTICS OF COAL

While coal may seem like an antiquated "old economy" material of little importance in the twenty-first century, our raw materialist world-systems analysis demonstrates two key facts. First, earlier materials and generative sectors do not disappear over the *longue durée*. Coal did not disappear after Great Britain's economic ascent or after the first decades of US ascent, and coal has played a critical role in Japan's post–World War II ascent and in China's ascent since the 1980s (Bunker & Ciccantell, 2005, 2007). Second, despite its declining importance in the United States and much of Europe today, coal remains a critical component of economic growth in many countries, including China and India.

In building a raw materialist perspective, it is vital to recognize four key material characteristics of coal that shape its past, present, and future uses in the capitalist world economy: (1) "naturally" produced qualities of coal that shape human uses; (2) "naturally" produced locations and volumes of coal availability; (3) evolving patterns of human use of coal; and (4) prices and costs of coal.

First, the most salient qualities of coal from the point of view of human use are the ability to burn coal to produce heat and thereby power in various forms, and the potential to use this heat and the release of carbon from burning to smelt metal ores into forms more useful to humans. The energy content of coal is directly proportional to its carbon content; in general, the higher the carbon content, the better it is for industrial use and the more carbon is released when it is burned. Coals are ranked from lowest to highest quality based on carbon content: peat, lignite, sub-bituminous, bituminous, and anthracite. Other qualities are also important, such as volatile matter content, especially sulfur, which pollutes and can make steel brittle, and moisture content, which reduces the energy content and adds to transport costs (McGraw-Hill, 1992, p. 50). Different coals are differentially efficient in generating heat and electricity, but all types of coal can be burned to generate electricity. The easy substitutability of thermal coals has fostered competition between firms and between coal-extracting countries. In contrast, only a very limited range of bituminous coals with very particular qualities can be used to smelt iron ore to produce steel (McGraw-Hill, 1992). Therefore, the substitutability of metallurgical coal from different deposits is significantly more difficult.

Second, geologic and environmental processes over millions of years produced huge volumes of various types of coals in many locations around the globe. This widespread availability contrasts sharply with the locational concentration of most geologic resources. In fact, most countries today have at least some coal in the ground, although proved recoverable reserves—defined as coal deposits that have been studied by firms and/or states to determine their size and the likely economic costs of extracting the coal—are concentrated in five countries: China, the United States, India, Australia, and Russia. Together, these five have 72.4% of the world's current proved recoverable reserves (BP, 2016, p. 30).

Proved reserves are a volatile and politically shaped variable, however. Expanding demand stimulates exploration and may lead to a dramatic increase of known reserves. In 1962, the World Power Conference estimated that total proven world coal reserves were 572.7 billion metric tons (Brubaker, 1967, p. 191); by 1989, British Petroleum estimated that world total proven coal reserves were 1,174 billion short tons[2] (EIA, 1990, p. 279). This doubling occurred despite world coal production of 98 billion metric tons in this period. Proven reserves have since declined by 16% to 982,743 million short tons as of 2013, while total coal production from 1990 to 2013 was more than 120 billion tons (see Table 7.1).

Global proven coal reserves are sufficient for 120 years of production at current levels of human use (IEA, 2015, p. II.27). The duration of availability of proven coal reserves now far exceeds the time frame during which scientists tell us climate change must be addressed (Dunlap & Brulle, 2015). One of the most fundamental misreadings of the materiality of raw materials is the use of data on reserves to claim that "the world is running out of resource X." Proven coal reserves are not simply a "natural" characteristic, but a statement about social activity to "discover" them, shaped by the current state of technology and the economics of extracting those deposits, geopolitical conditions of trade between raw materials–consuming nations and potential suppliers, as well as the willingness of states to allow and promote exploration and extraction within their borders, and a variety of other social conditions and processes. A closer approximation of the total of naturally produced coal in the earth (although still conditioned by the current social state of geologic knowledge, exploration technology, and geopolitics) is the current estimate of the world's total coal *resources* of 22.1 trillion tons, or more than 18 times greater than proven coal *reserves* (IEA, 2015, p. II.27). In geologic terms, there are many centuries' worth of coal in the ground. Peak coal is a materially unfounded claim.

Table 7.1 Proven Coal Reserves in Millions
of Short Tons of Anthracite, Bituminous,
Sub-bituminous, and Lignite

	1962	1989	2013
United States	72,000	268,000	261,572
Japan	5,723	939	382
Australia	1,800	99,800	84,216
Canada	42,000	7,520	7,255
Indonesia	n/a	3,296	30,883
China	n/a	184,117	126,214
India	0	68,507	66,799
World	572,700	1,174,000	982,743

Sources: BP Statistical Review of World Energy (2016, p. 30) for 2013 converted to short tons.

1962: World Power Conference (1962), World Power Conference Survey of Energy Resources, 1962, Table II, pp. 20–22. London: WPC, pp. 20–22, cited in Brubaker (1967, p. 191).

1989: EIA (1990, p. 279).

Note: n/a refers to data that are unavailable or unknown.

Third, as a global commodity, coal is affected by price. The expansion of extraction, consumption, and trade of coal in the context of the evolution of the capitalist world economy have driven a series of booms and busts. Historically, there was neither an oligopoly's producer price nor an established market such as the London Metals Exchange for coal, although some organized markets have been established in recent years. Long-term contracts and spot purchases continue to be the two key price-setting mechanisms (Hobbs, 2015). Prices for both metallurgical and steam coal have historically been linked to broader economic cycles, as well as the price of oil. Since the mid-twentieth century, coal prices doubled during the Korean War boom in 1951–1952 but then remained relatively stable (fluctuating in a band of $10/ton) during the 1950s and 1960s. Coal prices tripled between 1973 and 1975 during the first oil price shock, but fell by roughly 50% during the oil price collapse in the mid-1980s. Prices continued to decline by another 50%+ during the 1990s and early 2000s, but China's economic ascent reversed this decline. Coal prices reached historic highs in 2011 at the height of China's boom, but fell by 40%–50% between 2014 and early 2016 (BP, 2016; EIA, 2012; IEA, 1982, 1983, 1992, 2001, 2015, 2016). Coal prices are once again rising in late 2016, a topic to which we will return. The prolonged period of low prices from the mid-1980s through 2003 was a difficult time for the industry in many countries, while the China boom over the following decade was an unprecedented period of prosperity; falling prices between

2014 and early 2016 provoked a serious crisis in the industry, particularly in Appalachia but also in Indonesia, Australia, and other coal-extracting regions, prompting much of the discussion about the demise of coal.

COAL, INDUSTRIALIZATION, AND GLOBALIZATION

Coal has an incredibly long history. In China, mining dates back to 475 BCE and metallurgy to the eleventh century (Wu, 2015), but it was not until the Industrial Revolution and European expansionism in the 1800s that coal became one of the energy commodities consumed in greatest total volume, progressively substituting for animals, wood, and wind as a source of heat and power during the nineteenth century. Its contribution to labor productivity, reduced turnover time, and accelerated accumulation of capital has only been possible to the extent that coal was available in great volume at low prices. This combination of high volume and low value meant that coal deposits were the primary determinant of early industrial location, with iron- and later steel-processing plants and factories located near coal deposits (Harris, 1988; Isard, 1948). Early coal commodity chains were quite short, with coal consumption for heating or smelting metals taking place near the site of extraction, but coal has become globalized since the 1950s and now a quarter of all coal is shipped long distance (Shulman, 2015). The subsequent state–raw material sector–firm relations that emerged were shaped by its material and geophysical properties, and geographic locations, in concert with the geopolitics of capitalist world-system structures and dynamics (Arrighi, 1994; Bunker & Ciccantell, 2007).

Coal's long-standing importance to states and firms is demonstrated by their historic investments in data collection (Table 7.2). British data began in 1655 (Mitchell, 1988a, p. 240–250); data on Europe and the United States began in the early 1800s (Mitchell, 1998b, 1998c).

Coal production has paralleled the economic ascent of each of these countries. German production surpassed British production during Germany's efforts to overcome British hegemony in the first half of the twentieth century; US production surpassed both the United Kingdom and Germany as the United States ascended toward a hegemonic position. Coal production began to decline in the United Kingdom during the Thatcher neoliberal era of the 1980s and has since almost disappeared. German coal production has fallen by more than 50% since 1990 as the result of environmental concerns, and the United States is the most recent case of the onset of decline during the early twenty-first century.

Trade flows of coal have traced the hegemonic transitions from nineteenth-century dominance by the United Kingdom, to the twentieth-century rise of the United States (IEA, 1983: p. 3). Since the 1950s, coal has become one of the most globalized industries

Table 7.2 Long–Term Coal Output Data in Millions of
Metric Tons

Year	United Kingdom	Germany	United States
1830	30.5	1.8	0.8
1840	42.6	3.9	2.2
1850	62.5	6.8	7.6
1860	87.9	18.4	18.2
1870	115	34	36.7
1880	149	59.1	72
1890	185	89.2	143.2
1900	229	149.5	245
1910	269	222.5	455
1920	233	220	596
1930	248	289	487
1940	228	409	465
1950	220	328.2	508
1960	197	467.7	394
1970	147	481	556
1980	130	475.1	753
1990	94	464.4	937
2000	31	206	972
2010	18	183	996
2015	8.5	185	812

Source: Mitchell (1998a, pp. 426–433) for Europe; Mitchell
(1998b,311–313) for US; 1950–1980 includes East and West
Germany; EIA (2016) for 2000–2015.

in the world, with 1,383 million tons traded internationally in 2014 (IEA, 2015). The globalization of the coal industry resulted directly from US-led Cold War efforts to "reverse
course" and assist Japan's reindustrialization as a geopolitical bulwark in Asia, building
state-sector-firm relations that led to Japan's economic ascent over several decades
(Bunker & Ciccantell, 2005, 2007). Japanese firms and its state, supported by US and
World Bank financial assistance, created a new model of domestic development based in
the steel, shipbuilding, and shipping industries.

From the 1950s through the 1980s, Japanese steel firms and the Japanese state created
a truly global coal industry. Coal extraction was fomented in socially remote areas of
Australia, Canada, South Africa, and several other nations (Bunker & Ciccantell,
2007). As a result, world coal trade doubled from 1960 to 1980, as Table 7.3 shows. Coal
trade then doubled again in the following 20 years, with substitution of coal for oil in

Table 7.3 World Hard Coal Trade
(Millions of Metric Tons)

Year	Amount
1960	132
1970	167
1980	263
1990	400
2000	594
2010	1,076
2015	1,311

Source: IEA (1982, 1992, 2001, 2016).

electricity generation following the two oil price shocks, which helped to drive this increase. Even more remarkably, world trade almost doubled again in the following decade and by another 30% by 2015. China's economic ascent since the 1980s drove the rapid growth of the global coal industry and coal trade since the 1990s.

The same system of state-sector-firm coordination and transport-cost reduction that was so beneficial to Japan progressively drove down prices and rents for coal and transferred billions of dollars in investment and subsidization costs onto its raw materials peripheries. Japanese strategies fomented a huge excess capacity in the metallurgical coal industry as new firms and mines entered production based on expectations of continually rising Japanese demand and steadily increasing prices. For a variety of reasons, emphatically not depletion of raw materials, Japan went into economic stagnation in the 1990s (Bunker & Ciccantell, 2007). Intense global competition and excess capacity lowered raw materials prices and reduced or eliminated rents (as demonstrated by the halving of real costs of importing coal into Japan between 1959 and 1998 from US$86.65 in 1992 dollars to US$43.63 (Ciccantell & Bunker, 2005, pp. 188–189), putting intense pressure on exporting firms to reduce costs or face bankruptcy. The resulting restructuring from the late 1980s through the early 2000s bankrupted firms, closed mines, and devastated communities (Bunker & Ciccantell, 2007). Coal mining did not recover until the 2000s, when the mining supercycle spurred by Chinese growth turned things around.

China Boom and Coal

After a century of foreign incursions, the British state-sponsored opium trade, and civil wars, China's economy and people were among the poorest in the world in the mid-twentieth century. Coal, steel, transport, and other linked industries grew during the early twentieth century under the aegis of invading imperial powers, most importantly the Japanese. The Communist Party emphasized the continued development of these industries from the 1950s through the 1980s. As the Communist Party sought to rebuild and secure the country after 1949, coal became the primary fuel for economic development. Steel mills were relatively small scale and often were located far inland for security purposes. Rural areas supplied coal and iron ore, and the coal industry became one of the most important employers in rural China. The mines and steel mills were linked by a limited and antiquated railroad transport system that severely limited interregional trade and raised costs of production; this transport system also made imports and exports of resources extremely difficult (Ciccantell, 2009; Hogan, 1999a;Serchuk, 2001).

Since the opening of the economy in 1978, China's economic ascent has been driven both by low-cost manufacturing labor and by generative sectors in coal and steel (Table 7.4 and 7.6). China's rapid economic ascent drove a dramatic expansion of coal extraction in China and globally and radically transformed the capitalist world-economy.

A few key points are readily apparent. First, despite growing international concern over the unsustainability of fossil-fuel use, global hard-coal production has almost doubled since 2000. Second, much of this increase is due to the tripling of coal extraction in China. Efforts to address global climate change, such as the COP 21 Paris Agreement, thus confront a harsh reality: China and the world economy have become heavily dependent on coal in the last 15 years. Reversing this growing coal dependence is a tremendous material, technological, economic, and political challenge that will not be easy to overcome. Third, China became the world's largest coal producer in the 1980s and now produces more than half of the world's hard coal. Coal mining has played a central role in employment, capital accumulation, and fueling linked industries to sustain

Table 7.4 Hard Coal Production in Millions of Metric Tons of Anthracite, Bituminous, and Sub-bituminous

	World	China	China's Share of the World
1946	1,217	11	0.9%
1950	1,434	42	2.9%
1960	1,990	397	19.9%
1970	2,207	354	16.1%
1980	2,809	620	22.1%
1990	3,566	1,050	29.4%
2000	3,638	1,171	32.2%
2010	6,329	3,140	49.6%
2015	6,899	3,527	51.1%

Source: IEA (2001, 2016).

China's rapid industrialization (Lei, Cui, & Pan, 2013), helping drive China's economic ascent.

The tenfold increase in coal consumption in both China and India drove the huge increase in global consumption, translating into an increase in world coal consumption of 156% over the past four decades, as Table 7.5 shows, despite falling consumption in Organisation for Economic Co-operation and Development (OECD) Europe and the United States.

The growth of Chinese steel, coal, and electricity production and consumption transformed the low price and stagnant demand situation of coal-producing firms and regions in the 1990s. Rapidly growing metallurgical coal consumption by China's steel industry transformed China from a metallurgical coal exporter to an importer in the first decade of the 2000s. Chinese coal imports soaked up existing excess coal capacity and stimulated a huge investment rush in Canada, Australia, and other coal-mining regions (Morrison, 2004). From a low of US$39.69 in 2000 CIF (delivered to) Japan (BP, 2016), metallurgical coal contract prices rose to exceed US$100 per ton, and spot prices exceeded US$150 per ton by 2004 (Wailes, 2004) and rose to US$229.12 CIF Japan in 2011.[3] During the first decade and a half of the 2000s, coal firms reopened mines previously closed because of uncompetitively high costs and invested in mining projects that earlier had been economically unattractive (Bunker & Ciccantell, 2007; Ciccantell, 2009; Hayes, 2004; Morrison, 2004; Wailes, 2004). Metallurgical coal prices fell from their 2011 peak to US$93.85 CIF Japan in 2015 (BP, 2016) and continued to fall in early 2016. Steam coal prices followed a similar trajectory, rising from US$34.58 in 2000 CIF Japan to a peak of US$133.61 CIF Japan in 2011 and then falling to US$79.47 in 2015, and

Table 7.5 Coal Consumption in Millions of Tons of Anthracite, Bituminous, Sub-bituminous, and Lignite)

	World	United States	OECD Europe	China	India
1973	3,093	505	1,056	414	77
1980	3,756	650	1,157	626	107
1990	4,638	815	1,155	1,049	220
2000	4,748	966	817	1,337	357
2010	7,135	949	749	3,221	683
2014	7,923	835	726	3,909	906

Notes: Revisions to Chinese government data on coal consumption in 2015 indicate that this table may understate Chinese coal consumption at least since 2000 by 0%–14% a year (Buckley, 2015; Tan & Mathews, 2015).

Table 7.5 includes lignite coal consumption; lignite production is not included in Table 7.4.

Source: IEA (2015).

continuing to fall in early 2016 (BP, 2016). However, in the second half of 2016, thermal and especially metallurgical coal prices rose dramatically. Spot prices for metallurgical coal reached US$270 per ton in October 2016, compared to US$70 a ton in November 2015. Spot prices for thermal coal in October 2016 exceeded US$100 per ton, twice the price of thermal coal in early 2016 (Els, 2016; Mining Journal, 2016). Closed coal mines in Australia are being reopened, as are mines in Canada and a number of other coal-producing countries (Jamasmie, 2016d; Richardson, 2016c, 2016d).

Chinese government policies for coal, steel, and linked industries called for them to be key components of expanding China's role as part of the broader process of economic reform (Dorian, 1999; Schneider et al., 2000). Chinese steel production increased from a minor role in global terms to become the world's largest producer, producing almost half of the world's steel (Table 7.6). Just as was the case for Great Britain, Germany, the United States, and Japan, steel became a generative sector for China's economic ascent.

Chinese government policy since the late 1990s has sought to close small, globally uncompetitive steel mills and build new coastal steel mills using the latest technology and least costly globally available coal and iron ore, rather than relying on lower quality, higher cost domestic resources, as was formerly done under state policies of domestic economic self-sufficiency (Hogan, 1999a). To supply these steel mills, imports of far higher quality Australian, Brazilian, and other imported iron ore increased rapidly, and several ports serving coastal steel mills were expanded to accommodate very large bulk carriers (Hogan, 1999a, 1999b; International Bulk Journal, 2002, pp. 27–28).

During 2016, facilities representing 21 million tons of small-scale, technologically outdated, and uncompetitive steel capacity were shut down by midyear, and the Chinese government's target was 45 million tons of capacity closures by the end of 2016

Table 7.6 Steel Production in Millions of Tons

	China	World	China's Share of the World
1950	0.55	189	0.3%
1960	20.3	381	5.3%
1970	20.0	655	3.1%
1980	27.2	715	3.8%
1990	51.5	770	6.7%
1995	89.8	758	11.8%
2000	128.5	898	14.3%
2005	353	1,140	31.0%
2010	637	1,430	44.6%
2014	823	1,670	49.3%
2015	804	1,600	50.3%

Source: usgs.gov; worldsteel.com for 2014, 2015.

(Bloomberg, September 29, 2016). A total of 500,000 steel mill workers are expected to be reassigned to other work because of these efforts (Associated Press, 2017). China became the world's largest importer of iron ore and, more recently, moved from being an exporter of coal to an importer to supply its steel mills and electricity-generating facilities, utilizing a global system of raw materials supply created by Japan during its economic ascent (Bunker & Ciccantell, 2007). Coal imports have grown rapidly, as Table 7.7 shows.

China has also been working to "steal" Japan's raw materials peripheries (Ciccantell, 2009; Moyo, 2012; Nayar, 2004). For Australia, Indonesia, Canada, and other coal-exporting countries, China's ascent and India's growth and the integration of these coal peripheries into coal commodity chains linked to China and India are increasingly making these extractive peripheries look like successful cases of stealing peripheries from earlier ascendants (Ciccantell, 2009). The growth of thermal coal and electricity as part of China's economic ascent has been similarly dramatic.

As Table 7.8 shows, despite massive investments in hydroelectric dams, wind farms, and other renewable energy sources, coal-fired electricity production dominates. The Chinese government invested US$103 billion in renewable energy sources in 2015 and has 26 nuclear reactors under construction in 2016, with a further 40 being planned and another 100+ proposed (Jamasmie, 2016a). These massive investments are only starting to make inroads into reducing the overwhelming role of coal, although China has committed in the 2015 Paris COP Agreement to peaking CO_2 emissions and increasing the share of non-fossil fuels to 20% by 2030 (C2ES, 2015; Green & Stern, 2016).

China has followed the Japanese model of coastal greenfield heavy industrialization to supply other industries at low cost (Hogan, 1999a; Todd, 1996), as state policies have focused on deepening industrialization in steel, shipbuilding, and other heavy industries. China's coal-mining sector, however, has faced and continues to face several serious challenges. China's efforts to follow Japan's model of ascent confront efforts by

Table 7.7 Coal Imports in Millions of Tons

	China	India
1960	0.06	0.01
1970	0.0	0.004
1980	1.99	0.55
1990	2.0	5.1
2000	2.1	24.5
2010	184	121
2014	292	239
2015	204	222

Source: IEA (2001, 2015, 2016).

Table 7.8 Electricity Generation in Billions of Kilowatt-Hours in China

	Total	Fossil Fuel Derived	Share of Fossil-Fuel-Derived Electricity
1980	285	228	80%
1985	391	299	76.5%
1990	590	465	78.8%
1995	956	756	79.1%
2000	1,281	1,041	81.3%
2005	2,373	1,925	81.1%
2010	3,975	3,132	78.8%
2015	5,618	4,210	74.9%

Source: eia.gov

the existing hegemon, the United States, and other competitors, including the European Union (EU), Japan, Russia, and even India. In material terms, much of China's large coal reserves are of relatively low quality and often face challenging mining conditions, making domestic coal more expensive and less useful than imported coal. These often small-scale, low-technology mines are extremely dangerous for workers; China has been the world's deadliest location for coal miners for years, officially but questionably dropping below 1,000 deaths in 2015 (RFA, 2015).

Further, this low-quality coal is heavily polluting, contributing to the very serious environmental and human health problems due to poor air quality in Chinese cities. These material characteristics and the sociopolitical responses to these problems in China have helped motivate Chinese government policies to close small, inefficient, dangerous, and low-quality coal mines (Peng, 2015; Shi, 2013), including 150 million tons of capacity in 2016 (Bloomberg, September 29, 2016). Current government plans call for closing 1,000 coal mines by the end of 2016 and a total of 4,300 by 2019, cutting production capacity by 700 million tons and eliminating one million jobs. In the last five years, 7,250 small coal mines have been closed, eliminating 500 million tons of capacity. Despite these cuts, at the end of 2015, China had 11,000 coal mines with a capacity of 5.7 billion tons per year (Jamasmie, 2016b). This process has been uncertain and contentious, but reduction continues to be a major government policy goal, with the preferred alternative being the creation of large coal-power bases operated by much larger, more efficient firms that integrate coal mining and electricity generation (Peng, 2015; Rui, Morse, & He, 2015). Chinese Premier Li in April 2016 stated that "the transformation and upgrading of traditional growth drivers and the elimination of obsolete capacity in steel and coal must be hastened, as arrangements are made to resettle and ensure basic living and work for those affected in the process" (Tan, 2016), with an estimated 1.3 million coal miners to be reassigned to other work by the government (Associated Press, 2017). The economic and social consequences of closing and/or ending state support for inland coal, steel, and other industries, especially in the Northeast, are also a potential internal limitation of China's ascent (Ciccantell & Bunker, 2004). However, the success of these efforts to cut back capacity contributed to a rise in thermal and metallurgical coal prices in the second half of 2016. In response, state-owned coal companies agreed in late September to reverse course and increase coal output in order to reduce costs for steel mills (Topf, 2016a). An earlier government restriction on coal mines to 276 days of output for the year was relaxed to allow additional production in the hope of reducing domestic coal prices (Cooper, 2016).

This incredible growth in coal mining, imports, and consumption in China has been increasingly recognized in recent years as the cause of a variety of very serious problems. Air pollution from coal-consuming power plants and steel mills poison air in many cities (AJOT, 2016; Jamasmie, 2016c; Topf, 2016b). Many coal mines operate under a murky legal status and often with little effort to protect worker safety or control negative environmental impacts. Many steel mills and coal mines are profitable only due to the high demand and prices of much of the past decade in China, as well as the lack of investment in modern equipment and workplace safety. Coal is still often used for household heating and cooking as well. In recent years, particularly as Chinese economic growth has slowed, government policy has shifted to encouraging the closure of high-cost and highly polluting steel mills and coal mines, consolidating steel and coal firms into a much smaller number of stronger firms, encouraging the import of higher quality coal from Australia, Canada, Indonesia, and other countries, and fostering the rapid growth of alternative sources of power, including hydroelectric dams, natural gas, wind, and solar power. However, reversing the recent doubling of China's dependence on coal makes it very difficult for these goals to be achieved.

CONCLUSION: THE FUTURE(S) OF COAL

The raw materialist lengthened GCC model begins from a focus on the material process of economic ascent in the capitalist world economy. The key problem for rapidly growing economies over the past five centuries has been obtaining raw materials to support economic development. Successfully resolving this challenge rests on access to raw materials peripheries and the creation of generative sectors. Processes of economic ascent and economic and geopolitical competition with existing hegemons have driven long-term change in the capitalist world-economy over the past five centuries. The most successful cases of ascent have restructured and globalized the world economy, incorporating and reshaping economies, ecosystems (including human populations), and space. The historical sequence of rapidly ascending economies from Holland to Great Britain, to the United States, to Japan, and finally to China has led to dramatic increases in the scale of production and trade, building generative sectors in coal, iron and steel, petroleum, railroads, ocean shipping, and other raw materials and transport industries, and—with the exception of allied local elites—has impoverished their raw materials peripheries (Bunker & Ciccantell, 2005, 2007).

This materially and spatially grounded approach allows analysis of the economic, social, and environmental dimensions of commodity chains at each node, as well as providing a lens to examine spatially based disarticulations (Bair & Werner, 2011) and contestations over extraction, processing, transport, consumption, and waste disposal across these chains (Ciccantell & Smith, 2009; Sowers, Ciccantell, & Smith, 2014). This model thus emphasizes long-term historical change in the world-system as a whole and in particular places and times, and it allows world-systemic comparative analyses that provide nested and historical comparisons across commodity chains. The grounding in material process also focuses attention on local, regional, and global environmental impacts of these lengthened GCCs. Coal's repeated role in previous centuries as a generative sector in Great Britain, Germany, the United States, Japan, and China is revealed in our raw materialist lengthened GCC analysis.

The medium-term future of coal is likely to include multiple trajectories of extraction and use in different locations. Whether China will make a transition to a less coal-intensive future is one of the most important questions about these multiple trajectories. Despite the perceived "death of coal," the reality of coal consumption is far more complicated. Per capita coal consumption has bifurcated dramatically since the 1980s. In the OECD countries (mostly core countries, but including some semi-peripheral countries in recent decades), per capita coal consumption has fallen almost 20% since 1990, while in China and India it has tripled. As a result, world per capita coal consumption has continued to increase, with consumption 23% higher in 2015 than in 1990, despite competition from other fuels for electricity generation, most notably natural gas and renewable sources, and efforts to reduce coal consumption due to concern over climate change (Table 7.9).

The decline of coal extraction and consumption in the United States and much of Europe is often attributed to efforts to address climate change. However, much of the driving force behind this transition comes not from enlightened attitudes toward the impacts of climate change or political pressures by environmental organizations, but

Table 7.9 World Per Capita Coal Consumption in Tons of Coal Equivalent per Person

	OECD	World	China	India
1973	1.31	0.54	0.33	0.08
1980	1.41	0.57	0.46	0.09
1990	1.43	0.60	0.65	0.15
2000	1.35	0.56	0.79	0.2
2010	1.24	0.73	1.77	0.33
2015	1.05	0.74	2.03	0.44[a]

Source: IEA, 2016Note: a = 2014 data

instead from growing competition from cheap natural gas, often produced by hydraulic fracturing (fracking) (Culver & Hong, 2016).

Despite the perceived death of coal in some locations, including serious concerns about the future of coal in Australia—the world's largest coal exporter (Cleary, 2015)—coal prices underwent a significant increase during the second half of 2016. A number of coal firms have emerged from bankruptcy in more stable financial condition, investors have bought mines put up for sale by mining companies exiting the coal industry, and interest in reopening closed mines and investing in new mines is growing. Perhaps the single most controversial coal mine project in the world is the Carmichael mine in Australia proposed by the Adani Group of India. The mine in Queensland could eventually produce 60 million tons of thermal coal for export to Adani's coal-fired power plants in India (Richardson, 2016a). The project has faced strong opposition in Australia over its environmental impacts, including potentially damaging the Great Barrier Reef for a related port expansion. Some Australian banks have stated that they will not participate in financing the project, but the state government in Queensland is working to remove obstacles to the mine's construction (Cooper, 2015; Richardson, 2016b).

As this case implies, after China and Australia, the next most critical location for shaping the future of coal is India. Domestic coal production and consumption are increasing, as are imports of coal. India is partially following the Chinese model of using both less expensive and higher quality imported raw materials and lower quality domestic supplies, with a mixture of state firms and private Indian capital with state support, in key heavy-industry sectors like coal and steel. However, other economic sectors in India are more open to foreign capital than was the case earlier in China's developmental trajectory. Similar conflicts are taking place in India, as was the case in China, as the state supports raw materials extraction, processing, transport, and energy infrastructures that force mass relocations and loss of land rights on often rural local populations and that impose severe economic and human health impacts on particular locations and populations (Lahiri-Dutt, 2014).

However, following the models of earlier ascendant economies, even in terms of fomenting what have historically been key generative sectors in the most successful cases of ascent, does not guarantee success. Coal and steel have been generative sectors driving China's economic ascent. Older models may prove to be surpassed by new technological and organizational innovations by other competitors; also, successful sustained ascent is a relational process of competition with the existing hegemon and other ascendant economies. The strategies, successes, and failures of other ascendant economies and the existing hegemon shape the technological, organizational, socioeconomic, and political parameters that determine global competitiveness, and more successful rivals can effectively circumscribe the best policy choices and largest investments of other competitors. The outcomes of these developmental efforts are highly contingent on the strategies of other competing economies, and the long-term sustainability of China's efforts to continue its economic ascent by following the Japanese model is far from assured. The challenges confronting China's coal industry and its broader development model, however, raise serious concerns about the future trajectory of China's economic ascent. The Chinese government's COP 21 commitments and air pollution and human health concerns are pushing it to move forward with this process of closing coal mines and seeking to reduce coal consumption. These competing commitments to economic growth and decreasing coal dependence add further complexity to any prediction about the future trajectory of China's development.

The materiality of coal's future also presents a mixed and complex picture of the likely futures of coal. Several factors make it likely that coal will remain tremendously important in a variety of locations for years to come. Coal remains abundant, widespread, easy to extract, easy to use, and relatively cheap. Large-scale technologies of extraction and consumption are widely available, and their use will provide significant employment opportunities. Electric power and steel remain essential ingredients in economic development. The infrastructure for coal production, export, transport, and consumption is readily available in many countries, even if efforts to expand coal ports are confronting significant resistance in the western United States and Australia.

Other sociomaterial factors militate against a rosy future for coal, particularly its CO_2 emissions intensity, regional air pollution, and the poverty and environmental costs in coal-mining communities. Thus, while material characteristics lead many to use coal as a basis for economic development, socio-environmental impacts suggest against that development strategy. Once a formidable source of protection, unions today are struggling and have even joined with firms to support cost-cutting efforts to "save" jobs. Finally, the political importance of traditional coal-producing regions and contested visions of ecological justice and ameliorating global warming in many core political contexts makes the industry an ongoing battleground.

NOTES

1. The initial formulation of this theoretical model in the late 1990s used the term "raw materialism," which was eventually replaced with the less emphatic term "new historical materialism." This term reflects the intellectual foundation in world-systems theory and the classical political economy of Marx. In this chapter we revert back to "raw materialism" to re-emphasize the importance of matter and space to political economy.
2. One metric ton is equal to 1.1 short tons.
3. CIF is an abbreviation of cost, insurance, and freight and refers to transactions in which the importer pays these costs of transporting goods.

REFERENCES

Abramsky, K. (2007). The underground challenge: Raw materials, energy, the world-economy, and anticapitalist struggle: Reflections on "Globalization and the race for resources" by Stephen Bunker and Paul Ciccantell. *Review (Fernand Braudel Center)*, 30(2), 161–169.

American Journal of Transportation (AJOT). (2016, October 16). China's poisonous coal capital is spending millions to go green. Retrieved from Ajot.com. https://www.ajot.com/news/chinas-poisonous-coal-capital-is-spending-millions-to-go-green

Arrighi, G. (1994). *The Long twentieth century: Money, power, and the origins of our times.* London: Verso.

Arrighi, G. (2007). *Adam Smith in Beijing: Lineages of the 21st century.* New York: Verso.

Bair, J., & Werner, M. (2011). The place of disarticulations: Global commodity production in La Laguna, Mexico. *Environment and Planning A, 43*(5), 998–1015.

Bloomberg. (2016, September 29). China punishes coal, steel companies in overcapacity cut drive. *Bloomberg News.* Retrieved from https://www.bloomberg.com/news/articles /2016-09-29/china-punishes-coal-steel-companies-in-overcapacity-cut-drive

BP. (2016). *BP statistical review of world energy 2016.* Retrieved from http://www.bp.com /content/dam/bp/pdf/energy-economics/statistical-review-2016/bp-statistical-review-of -world-energy-2016-full-report.pdf

Brubaker, S. (1967). *Trends in the world aluminum industry.* Baltimore, MD: Johns Hopkins University Press.

Buckley, C. (2015, November 3). China burns much more coal than reported, complicating climate talks. *New York Times.* Retrieved from https://www.nytimes.com/2015/11/04/world /asia/china-burns-much-more-coal-than-reported-complicating-climate-talks.html

Bunker, S. G. (1984). Modes of extraction, unequal exchange, and the progressive underdevelopment of an extreme periphery: The Brazilian Amazon, 1600–1980. *American Journal of Sociology, 89*(5), 1017–1064.

Bunker, S. G., & Ciccantell, P. S. (2003). Generative sectors and the new historical materialism: Economic ascent and the cumulatively sequential restructuring of the world economy. *Studies in Comparative International Development, 37*(4), 3–30.

Bunker, S. G., & Ciccantell, P. S. (2005). *Globalization and the race for resources.* Baltimore, MD: Johns Hopkins University Press.

Bunker, S. G., & Ciccantell, P. S. (2007). *East Asia and the global economy: Japan's ascent, with implications for China's future.* Baltimore, MD: Johns Hopkins University Press.

C2ES. (2015). China's contribution to the Paris Climate Agreement. Center for Climate and Energy Solutions. Retrieved from http://www.c2es.org/docUploads/chinas-contributions -paris-climate-agreement.pdf

Chase-Dunn, C. (1989). *Global formation: Structures of the world-economy.* Cambridge, MA: Blackwell.

Ciccantell, P. S. (2009). China's economic ascent via stealing Japan's raw materials peripheries." In H.-F. Hung (Ed.), *China and the transformation of global capitalism* (Chapter 6, pp. 109–129). Baltimore, MD: Johns Hopkins University Press.

Ciccantell, P. S., & Bunker, S. G. (2004). The economic ascent of China and the potential for restructuring the capitalist world-economy. *Journal of World-Systems Research, 10*(3), 565–589.

Ciccantell, P. S., & Bunker, S. G. (2005). Japan's economic ascent and its extraction of wealth from its raw materials peripheries. In P. Ciccantell, D. Smith, & G. Seidman (Eds.), *Nature, raw materials and political economy* (pp. 187–208). New York: Elsevier.

Ciccantell, P. S., & Smith, D. A. (2009). Rethinking global commodity chains: Integrating extraction, transport and manufacturing. *International Journal of Comparative Sociology, 50*(June/August), 361–384.

Cleary, P. (2015, October). Coal crash: How long can Australia ride in the coal wagon? *The Monthly Essays.* Retrieved from https://www.themonthly.com.au/issue/2015/october /1443621600/paul-cleary/coal-crash

Cooper, M. (2015, September 3). Australian bank NAB rules out funding Adani's Australian coal export project. *Platts.* Retrieved from https://www.platts.com/latest-news/coal/perth /australian-bank-nab-rules-out-funding-adanis-26199435

Cooper, M. (2016, September 8). China to relax 276-day limit on coal mine operations, say market sources. *Platts*. Retrieved from https://www.platts.com/latest-news/coal/perth /china-to-relax-276-day-limit-on-coal-mine-operations-27666179

Corkery, M. (2016, March 20). As coal's future grows murkier, banks pull financing. *New York Times*. Retrieved from http://www.nytimes.com/2016/03/21/business/dealbook/as-coals -future-grows-murkier-banks-pull-financing.html?_r=1

Culver, W., & Hong, M. (2016). Coal's decline: Driven by policy or technology? *The Electricity Journal, 29*, 50–61.

Dorian, J. (1999). Mining in China: An update. *Mining Engineering, 51*(2), 35–44.

Dunlap, R., & Brulle, R. (Eds.). (2015). *Climate change and society: Sociological perspectives.* New York: Oxford University Press.

Els, F. (2016). Iron ore jumps to 6-month high, coking coal binge continues. Retrieved from www.mining.com/author/frik/

EIA. 1990. *Annual energy review 1990.* Washington, DC: US Energy Information Agency.

EIA. 2012. *Annual energy review 2012.* Washington, DC: US Energy Information Agency.

EIA. 2016. *Quarterly coal production.* US Energy and Information Agency. Retrieved from http://www.eia.gov/coal/production/

Foster, J. B., Clark, B., & York, R. (2010). *The ecological rift: Capitalism's war on the earth.* New York: Monthly Review Press.

Gaventa, J. (1980). *Power and powerlessness: Quiescence and rebellion in an Appalachian Valley.* Chicago: University of Illinois Press.

Goldenberg, S. (2016, February 4). US electricity industry's use of coal fell to historic low in 2015 as plants closed. *The Guardian*. Retrieved from http://www.theguardian.com /environment/2016/feb/04/us-electricity-industrys-use-of-coal-fell-to-historic-low-in -2015-as-plants-closed

Green, F., & Stern, N. (2016). China's changing economy: Implications for its carbon di- oxide emissions. *Climate Policy*. Retrieved from http://dx.doi.org/10.1080/14693062 .2016.1156515

Greenpeace. (2015). Coal's terminal decline. Retrieved from http://www.greenpeace.org /international/Global/international/publications/climate/2015/Coals-Terminal-Decline.pdf

Harris, J. R. (1988). *The British iron industry 1700–1850.* Houndmills, UK: Macmillan Education.

Hayes, J. (2004). Canadian metallurgical coal market expanding. *CIM Bulletin, 97*(1082), 15–16.

Hobbs, H. (2015, October 27). How to secure your coal supply. *World Coal*. Retrieved from https://www.worldcoal.com/coal/27102015/how-to-secure-your-coal

Hogan, W. (1999a). *The steel industry of China: Its present status and future potential.* Lanham, MD: Lexington Books.

Hogan, W. (1999b). The changing shape of the Chinese industry. *New Steel, 15*(11), 28–29.

International Energy Agency (IEA). (1982, 1983, 1992, 2001, 2015, 2016). *Coal information.* Paris: OECD.

International Bulk Journal. (2002). China has its irons in the fire. (May), 25–28.

Isard, W. (1948). Some locational factors in the iron and steel industry since the early nine- teenth century." *Journal of Political Economy, 63*(3), 203–217.

Jamasmie, C. (2016a). China to reach target in cutting coal overcapacity by year-end. Retrieved from www.mining.com/author/cecilia

Jamasmie, C. (2016b). Chinese coal miners to work less hours this year in bid to reduce supply glut. Retrieved from www.mining.com/author/cecilia

Jamasmie, C. (2016c). Extreme pollution forces China to shut down hundreds of coal, steel op- erations. Retrieved from www.mining.com/author/cecilia

Jamasmie, Cecilian. 2016d. "All these Australian mines are reopening thanks to the rally in coal prices." Retrieved from www.mining.com/author/cecilia

Jorgenson, A., & Rice, J. 2012. The sociology of ecologically unequal exchange in comparative perspective. In S. Babones & C. Chase-Dunn (Eds.), *Routledge handbook of world-systems analysis* (pp. 431–439). New York: Routledge.

Kaup, B., & Gellert, P. K. (2017). Cycles of resource nationalism: Hegemonic struggle and the incorporation of Bolivia and Indonesia. *International Journal of Comparative Sociology, 58*(4), 275–303.

Lahiri-Dutt, K. (2014). Introducing coal in India: Energising the nation. In K. Lahiri-Dutt (Ed.), *The coal nation: Histories, politics and ecologies of coal in India* (pp. 1–37). Aldershot, UK: Ashgate.

Lei, Y., Cui, N., & Pan, D. (2013). Economic and social effects analysis of mineral development in China and policy implications. *Resources Policy, 38*, 448–457.

Lowrey, D. (2015). Goldman makes case for "peak coal," expects pricing pressure and demand, output fall. *SNL.* Retrieved from https://www.snl.com

McGlade, C., & Ekins, P. 2015. The geographical distribution of fossil fuels unused when limiting global warming to 2 °C. *Nature, 517*, 187–190. doi: 10.1038/nature14016

McGraw-Hill. (1992). *McGraw-Hill encyclopedia of science and technology* (7th ed.). New York: McGraw-Hill.

Mining Journal. (2016, October 19). Thermal coal breaks through US$100/tonne. *Mining Journal.* Retrieved from http://www.mining-journal.com/bulks/news/1174610/thermal-coal-breaks-ususd100-tonne

Mitchell, B. R. (1988). *British historical statistics.* Cambridge: Cambridge University Press.

Mitchell, B. R. (1998a). *International historical statistics: Europe 1750–1993.* New York: Macmillan Reference.

Mitchell, B. R. (1998b). *International historical statistics: The Americas 1750–1993.* New York: Macmillan Reference.

Mitchell, T. (2013). *Carbon democracy: Political power in the age of oil.* London: Verso.

Moore, J. W. (2015). *Capitalism in the web of life: Ecology and the Accumulation of Capital.* London: Verso.

Morrison, K. (2004, April 23). Voracious demand fuels miners' challenge. *Financial Times,* 24.

Moyo, D. (2012). *Winner take all: China's race for resources and what it means for the world.* New York: Basic Books.

Nayar, B. R. (2004). The geopolitics of China's economic miracle. *China Report, 40*(1), 19–47.

Peng, W. (2015). The evolution of China's coal institutions. In M. Thurber & R. Morse (Eds.), *The global coal market: Supplying the major fuel for emerging economies* (pp. 37–72). Cambridge: Cambridge University Press.

Podobnik, B. (2005). *Global energy shifts: Fostering sustainability in a turbulent age.* Philadelphia: Temple University Press.

RFA. (2015, March 16). China cuts coal mine deaths, but count in doubt. *Radio Free Asia.* Retrieved from http://www.rfa.org/english/commentaries/energy_watch/china-coal-deaths-03162015103452.html/

Richardson, N. (2016a, September 23). Adani to start work on Australian Carmichael coal mine in 2017. *Platts.* Retrieved from https://www.platts.com/latest-news/coal/sydney/adani-to-start-work-on-australian-carmichael-26552843

Richardson, N. (2016b, October 10). Australian state government trims red tape for Adani's Carmichael coal project. *Platts.* Retrieved from https://www.platts.com/latest-news/coal/sydney/australian-state-government-trims-red-tape-for-26565760

Richardson, N. (2016c, October 11). Glencore to resume production at Australian Collinsville coal mine by early 2017. *Platts*. Retrieved from https://www.platts.com/latest-news/coal /sydney/glencore-to-resume-production-at-australian-collinsville-27685026

Richardson, N. (2016d, October 14). Australia's Bloomfield ramps up output at reopened Rix's Creek North coal mine. *Platts*. Retrieved from https://www.platts.com/latest-news/coal /sydney/australias-bloomfield-ramps-up-output-at-reopened-27688520

Romm, J. (2016, January 14). We might have finally seen peak coal. *Climate Progress*. Retrieved from http://thinkprogress.org/climate/2016/01/14/3739164/global-coal-pe/

Rui, H., Morse, R., He, G. (2015). Developing large coal-power bases in China. In M. Thurber & R. Morse (Eds.), *The global coal market: Supplying the major fuel for emerging economies* (pp. 73–122). Cambridge: Cambridge University Press.

Schneider, K., Zhonghu, W., Lin, D., & Tulpule, V. (2000). *Supplying coal to South East China: Impacts of China's market liberalisation*. Canberra: ABARE.

Serchuk, A. (2001). Chinese steel: Rousing the phoenix. *Modern Metals*, 57(1), 32–43.

Shi, X. (2013). China's small coal mine policy in the 2000s: A case study of trusteeship and consolidation. *Resources Policy*, 38, 598–604.

Shulman, P. (2015). *Coal and empire: The birth of energy security in industrial America*. Baltimore, MD: Johns Hopkins University Press.

Sierra Club. (2016). Open letter to coal industry and coal analysts. Retrieved from https: //www.sierraclub.org/sites/www.sierraclub.org/files/blog/Openlettertocoalindustry%20 %281%29.pdf

Sowers, E., Ciccantell, P. S., & Smith, D. A. (2014). Comparing critical capitalist commodity chains in the early twenty-first century: Opportunities for and constraints on labor and political movements. *Journal of World-Systems Research*, 20(1), 112–139.

Tan, H., & Mathews, J. (2015). The revision of China's energy and coal consumption data: A preliminary analysis. *Asia-Pacific Journal*, 13 46(2), 1–9.

Tan, K. (2016 April 12). Chinese premier stresses need for structural reforms in steel, coal sectors. *Platts*. Retrieved from https://www.platts.com/latest-news/metals/singapore /chinese-premier-stresses-need-for-structural-26416256

Associated Press. (2017). China to Cut 500K Coal, Steel Jobs. Retrieved from https://www.ien .com/supply-chain/news/20853562/china-to-cut-500k-coal-steel-jobs

Todd, D. (1996). Coal shipment from northern China and its implications for the ports. *The Dock and Harbour Authority*, 76(868), 49–58.

Topf, A. (2016a, September 25). Chinese coal companies to boost thermal coal output to placate steel mills. Retrieved from www.mining.com/author/andrewtopf/

Topf, A. (2016b). Higher coal use could cause droughts in Asia. Retrieved from www.mining .com/author/andrewtopf/

Wailes, G. (2004). Export metallurgical coal mine costs. *AusIMM Bulletin*, 2, 44–45.

Wallerstein, I. (1974). *The modern world-system I*. New York: Academic Press.

Wu, S. (2015). *Empires of coal: Fueling China's entry into the modern world order, 1860–1920*. Stanford, CA: Stanford University Press.

CHAPTER 8

THE INTERNATIONAL POLITICAL ECONOMY OF EASTERN EUROPEAN ENERGY SECURITY

Russia, Ukraine, and the European Union

JACK D. SHARPLES

INTRODUCTION

As noted in the introduction to this part of the volume, fossil fuels have retained persistent material and geopolitical importance. Consumption of fossil fuels underpins transportation, electricity generation, and industrial activity around the world. The uneven distribution of those fossil-fuel resources necessitates international trade in coal, oil, and natural gas—trade that has both significant economic and political value. While the economic value of that trade is based upon the exchange of large volumes of commercially valuable resources, the political value of that trade derives from the dependence of states on either imports that make up for a lack of domestic resources, or economic dependence on revenues from the export of those resources.

For the European Union (EU), natural gas remains a key component of many member states' primary energy mixes, while Russia remains the most significant external supplier of natural gas to the EU market. A significant proportion of natural gas exported from Russia to the EU is delivered via the territory of Ukraine. This brings Russia, the EU and its member states, and Ukraine into a trilateral relationship in the sphere of natural gas. In both 2006 and 2009, disputes between Russia and Ukraine over their bilateral gas relations resulted in interruptions in Russian gas deliveries to the EU via Ukraine. Then, during the winter of 2013–2014, a new Russia-Ukraine gas dispute emerged, which led to a dramatic reduction in Ukrainian imports of Russian gas and increased EU concerns over the security of Russian gas supplies delivered via Ukraine. This dispute highlights the complex interdependency of political and economic processes that affect the production, transportation, and consumption of energy materials. This chapter aims to address the question of whether the concerns over regional energy security in Eastern Europe that have arisen since 2013 are caused by market failure, or by commercial trade falling victim to regional political tensions, with specific reference to the trilateral gas relationship between Russia, Ukraine, and the EU. In doing so, this chapter begins with an examination of the development of the EU gas market over the past decade, before identifying ongoing trends in the role of Russian gas supplies and Ukrainian gas transit in the EU gas market. The third section of this chapter analyzes the repeated crises in Russia-Ukraine gas relations, and addresses the key question of whether they are caused by market failure, or by markets falling victim to political developments. The final section then examines the prospects for overcoming the energy security challenges posed by the crises in Russia-Ukraine gas relations by analyzing the prospects for Ukraine's integration into the EU gas market and the development of market mechanisms for the continued regional trade in natural gas.

THE DEVELOPMENT OF THE EU GAS MARKET AND THE LEGAL FRAMEWORK FOR NATURAL GAS TRADE AND TRANSIT

An analysis of the international political economy of regional energy security in Eastern Europe with a focus on natural gas must begin by defining the market, in order to assess whether that market is failing or falling victim to regional political developments. This chapter is concerned with the EU gas market and the prospects for integrating Ukraine into the EU gas market through Ukraine's membership in the European Energy Community.

As illustrated in the Figures 8.1, 8.2 and 8.3, natural gas plays a substantial role in EU energy consumption. While natural gas accounted for approximately 22% of total EU energy consumption (also referred to as "total primary energy supply") in 2014, the shares of natural gas in EU heat generation (37%), industrial energy consumption (32%), and residential energy consumption (41%) were significantly higher, and the share of natural gas in electricity generation (14%) was lower.

Furthermore, natural gas indirectly accounted for an additional 7% of EU industrial energy consumption and 5% of EU residential energy consumption. This is because electricity accounted for roughly 35% and 20% of industrial and residential energy consumption, respectively, while heat accounted for around 6% of both industrial and residential energy consumption. Therefore, heat and electricity generated from natural gas should be included in addition to direct consumption of natural gas. In

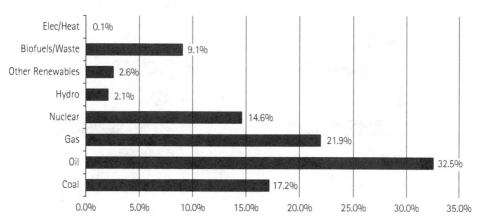

FIGURE 8.1 EU-28 total primary energy supply by fuel (2014).

Data source: IEA, 2016a, 2016b.

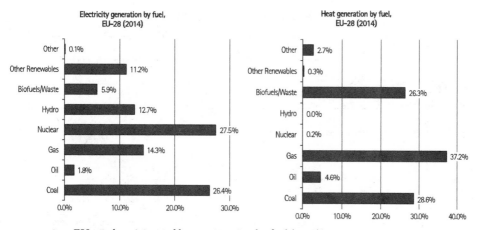

FIGURE 8.2 EU-28 electricity and heat generation by fuel (2014).

Data source: IEA, 2016a, 2016b.

this context, the importance of natural gas in EU energy consumption can hardly be underestimated.

In terms of ongoing trends, EU total primary energy consumption grew until the middle of the first decade of the 2000s, and then entered into a period of decline. The consumption of natural gas and the share of natural gas in EU electricity generation followed a similar pattern. The decline in European gas consumption that took place between 2009 and 2014 can be attributed to a combination of the broader European economic recession, increases in energy efficiency in industrial and household energy consumption, and the growing share of renewable energy sources in electricity generation (European Environment Agency, 2016; Honoré, 2014; IEA, 2016c, 2016d).

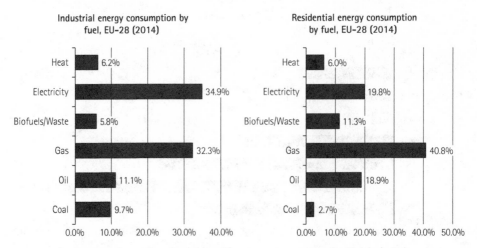

FIGURE 8.3 EU-28 industrial and residential energy consumption by fuel (2014).

Data source: IEA, 2016a, 2016b.

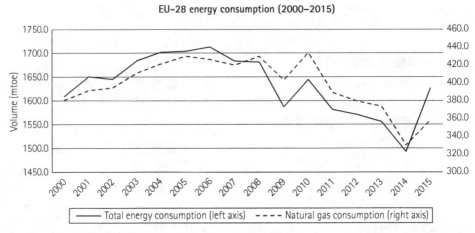

FIGURE 8.4 EU-28 total energy consumption and natural gas consumption, 2009–2015 (in million tonnes of oil equivalent, mtoe).

Data source: Eurostat, 2017b

However, data from Eurostat show that the decline in EU gas consumption has been reversed over the past two years. In the calendar year 2015, total gas consumption and consumption of gas for power generation were higher than in 2014, and data for January–August 2016 shows that this trend is continuing (Figure 8.4) (Eurostat, 2017a, 2017b).

Looking to the future, it is notable that coal is being gradually phased out of EU energy consumption for environmental reasons, and in the wake of the Fukushima nuclear disaster, several EU member states have adopted policies to abandon electricity generation from nuclear power over the coming decade. Therefore, it is likely that natural gas will retain a substantial role in EU energy consumption. Indeed, it is possible that the upturn in gas demand in 2015–2016 may signal the beginning of this trend.

The EU gas market today is the result of decades of development. In 1973, five countries (Germany, Italy, the Netherlands, Romania, and the United Kingdom) accounted for 88% of EU-28 gas production. In the same year, EU gas production was sufficient to meet 95% of EU gas demand (IEA, 2016e, pp. II.4–5, II.8–9). There was no "market" as such. Gas consumption was concentrated in the producing states, with additional volumes being exported to neighboring countries under long-term, bilateral contracts with the price of natural gas being index-linked to the price of oil (Konoplyanik, 2012, pp. 45–47). By 2015, natural gas production in the EU was sufficient to meet just 32% of EU gas demand, with only the Netherlands acting as a substantial exporter of gas to neighboring countries (IEA, 2016e, pp. II 4–5, II.8–9).

The past four decades have seen the emergence of a single EU gas market, although the process of developing that market is not yet complete (Stern & Rogers, 2014). The end of socialism in Central and Eastern Europe in 1989–1991 and the expansion of the EU itself intensified economic relations between states that are now members of the Union, including in the sphere of natural gas. A series of directives drafted by the European Commission and approved by the European Parliament and Council in 1998, 2003, and 2009 created a common regulatory framework for the trade of natural gas within the EU single market (European Parliament and Council, 1998, 2003, 2009). The aim of these directives, and other supporting regulations, has been to create a market in which companies may trade freely with each other and transport natural gas across international borders within a single market, with the same freedom that they would have if they were operating in a single country.

This legal framework has been expanded beyond the EU, through the European Energy Community (EC). The EC was established by an international treaty in 2005, with the treaty entering into force in 2006. All EU members are also members of the EC, in addition to eight "contracting parties": Albania, Bosnia and Herzegovina, Kosovo, Former Yugoslav Republic of Macedonia (FYRM), Moldova, Montenegro, Serbia, and Ukraine (Energy Community, 2016a). According to the EC secretariat, "The key aim of the organization is to extend the EU internal energy market to South East Europe and beyond on the basis of a legally binding framework" (Energy Community, 2016a).

A final part of the legal framework governing energy trade in Eastern Europe is the Energy Charter Treaty (ECT). The ECT has several aims. The most relevant for this chapter are "non-discriminatory conditions for trade in energy materials, products and energy-related equipment based on WTO rules, and provisions to ensure reliable cross-border energy transit flows through pipelines, grids and other means of transportation" and "the resolution of disputes between participating states" (Energy Charter Secretariat, 2016a). The ECT was signed in December 1994 and entered into force in April 1998. The ECT has been signed and ratified by all 28 EU member states, as well as Albania, Bosnia and Herzegovina, FYRM, Moldova, Montenegro, and Ukraine. Belarus has signed but not ratified the ECT, and is applying it provisionally (Energy Charter

Secretariat, 2016a). Russia has also signed but not ratified the ECT, but ended its provisional application in October 2009 (Energy Charter Secretariat, 2016b).

In commercial terms, the EU gas market has developed into a more flexible trading arena. The long-standing method of gas trade is the "Groningen model," based on long-term (15–35 years) bilateral contracts between exporters and importers, with prices index-linked to the price of oil (to make up for the lack of market signals), and "take-or-pay" clauses to protect both suppliers and consumers. The "take-or-pay" clause stipulates that the importer must purchase a set percentage of the nominal contractual volume, or face a financial penalty. In the past, this was often approximately 80%–90% of the contractual volume, although today clauses of around 60%–70% are more common. Equally, in the event of an increase in demand by the importing party, suppliers must supply up to 120% of the nominal contractual volume, at the agreed contractual price. So-called destination clauses (also known as "territorial restrictions") prevented importing companies from re-exporting imported gas supplies. This allowed exporting companies to place barriers between national markets and to offer different prices to different national markets, depending on their levels of competitiveness, while depriving the importing companies of price arbitrage opportunities (Energy Charter Secretariat, 2007, pp. 143–174; Konoplyanik, 2012, pp. 45–47).

Across much of Europe, this model has been replaced by "hub trading," whereby suppliers offer volumes at trading hubs, and consumers are able to purchase set volumes without signing long-term contracts. The price of gas at these hubs (the "spot price") is determined by the balance between supply and demand (so-called gas-on-gas competition), thus removing the link to oil prices (Franza, 2014, pp. 11–20; Stern & Rogers, 2014). According to the International Gas Union, 64% of wholesale gas trade volumes in Europe in 2015 were priced on the basis of gas-on-gas competition, while oil-indexed pricing accounted for 30% of wholesale gas trade volumes (International Gas Union, 2016, pp. 39–40).

Crucially, hub trading can break the direct link between gas-exporting companies and companies that purchase gas for their own consumption by allowing the emergence of "third parties"—companies that either import gas on long-term contracts and re-sell their excess volumes, or companies that purchase gas solely in order to re-sell that gas for a profit. Such hub trading is not evenly developed across the European gas market. It is most developed in Northwestern Europe (UK, Netherlands, and Germany), and least developed in Southeastern Europe (Heather, 2015, pp. 17–23; Platts, 2016).

Even where bilateral contracts remain in place, the past five to ten years has seen significant renegotiation of these contracts. By the latter part of the first decade of the 2000s, destination clauses had been removed from long-term contracts between Western European energy companies and their major supply partners (Norway, Algeria, Nigeria, and Russia) (Chyong, 2015, pp. 12–13; Fernandez & Palazuelos, 2014, pp. 502–505; Wäktare, 2007). The removal of destination clauses is also one of three outstanding issues in the European Commission anti-monopoly investigation into the Russian state-owned gas-exporting company, Gazprom, and its relations with gas-importing companies in 10 EU member states in the Baltic, Central, and Southeastern regions of the Union (European Commission, 2015). In response to this investigation, Gazprom submitted a series of commitments to the European Commission in December 2016. In March 2017, the European Commission announced that it was satisfied with the proposals, and sought the views of "customers and stakeholders" before making those commitments legally binding. One of those commitments is the removal of destination clauses from all of Gazprom's gas supply contracts with its European customers (European Commission, 2017).

Recent years have also seen the introduction of spot-pricing mechanisms into long-term contracts that were previously oil-indexed. For example, in 2013, the Norwegian gas exporter, Statoil, negotiated with its customers in Northern Europe to switch from oil-indexation to gas hub-price indexation in its long-term gas supply contracts (Financial Times, 2013). The following year, Gazprom revised its contract with the Italian Eni, switching from oil-indexation to spot price indexation in its long-term contract (Financial Times, 2014b).

Finally, even the premise of the "take-or-pay" clause has been challenged. In 2012, a commercial court in Vienna ruled that RWE Transgaz was not bound by the "take-or-pay" clause in its long-term gas supply contract with Gazprom, due to the fundamental change in market conditions that led to a wide discrepancy between oil-indexed and European hub gas prices (Reuters, 2012).

This change in market conditions influenced Gazprom's own strategy of renegotiating contracts with its customers. As Henderson and Mitrova (2015, p. 49) note, "During the period 2009–2014 nearly 60 gas supply contracts were reviewed with 40 clients, providing price discounts, easing of take-or-pay obligations, and the introduction of a spot component." In June 2014, Cedigaz offered a similar assessment, noting that all companies supplying gas to the European market were facing up to changing conditions:

> Negotiations of Gazprom contracts (or arbitration decisions) representing a volume of at least 60 billion cubic meters (bcm) per year (one-third of the volume of Gazprom contracts listed in the Cedigaz database) have been reported. The result has been a decrease in prices, with price discounts in the range of 10%–20%, often accompanied by a reduction of TOP (take-or-pay) obligations. But Gazprom was not the sole provider to face tough renegotiations of its long-term contracts; all major European suppliers were either brought to the negotiating table or subjected to arbitration. (Cedigaz, 2014)

Clearly, the past decade has seen a decisive shift in the European gas market, away from the original long-term bilateral contracts governed by the "Groningen model," to more flexible trading arrangements. As shall be discussed later, this has created a contrast between the flexible, multilateral, market-based gas trade in Western Europe and the traditional, bilateral gas relations conducted in Eastern Europe.

The Role of Russian Gas Supplies and Ukrainian Gas Transit on the EU Gas Market

As natural gas demand in the EU outpaced the growth of EU gas production, the Union as a whole became more gas import-dependent. The pattern of imports broadly follows the same trend identified earlier in terms of gas consumption in the EU, with a period of growth followed by decline from 2010 to 2014, before growing again in 2015. In terms of major suppliers of natural gas to the EU, Russia, Norway, and Algeria remain dominant, accounting for 80%–90% of EU gas imports over the past decade. Imports from Libya and Egypt peaked between 2006 and 2010, while imports from Qatar grew strongly from 2008, peaking in 2011. Liquefied natural gas (LNG) imports from other suppliers reached a high point between 2006 and 2012, before falling off to a level similar to that of Libya and Egypt combined. These trends are illustrated in Figures 8.5 and 8.6.

Russian gas is delivered to the EU via three routes: Ukraine, Belarus, and via the Nord Stream pipeline, which runs under the Baltic Sea directly from Russia to Germany. Until 2011, transit via Ukraine typically accounted for approximately 75% of Russia's gas deliveries to the EU (not including direct deliveries from Russia to Finland, Estonia, Latvia, and Lithuania), with transit via Belarus accounting for the remaining 25%. Since then, the volume of gas transit via Ukraine has fallen due to two key developments.

First, Gazprom increased its deliveries of gas via Belarus from 31 bcm in 2011 to 37 bcm in 2014. Part of the reason behind this may be Gazprom's two-step purchase of the owner-operator of the Belarusian gas transmission system, Beltransgaz, in 2007 and 2010 (Gazprom, 2013). Second, the Nord Stream pipeline was launched in two stages

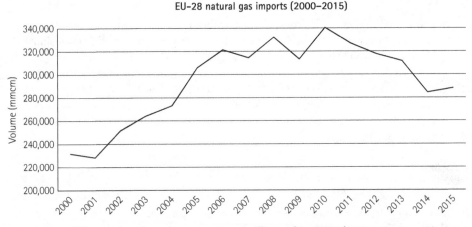

FIGURE 8.5 EU natural gas imports, 2000–2015 (million cubic meters).

Data source: Eurostat, 2016, 2017a.

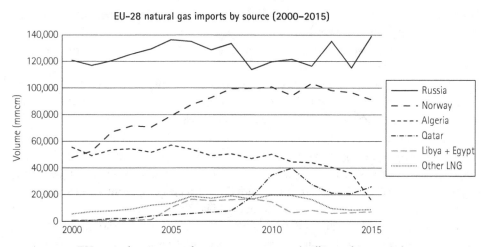

FIGURE 8.6 EU natural gas imports by source, 2000–2015 (million cubic metres).

Data source: Eurostat, 2016, 2017a.

in 2011 and 2012, and was used to deliver 34 bcm in 2014—volumes that were previously delivered via Ukraine. Together, these two developments shifted 40 bcm per year of transit away from the Ukrainian route. As a result, the transit of Russian gas to the EU via Ukraine declined from 87 bcm in 2011 to 46 bcm in 2014. In percentage terms, the share of Ukraine in Russian gas deliveries to the EU fell from 74% to 40% between 2011 and 2014, while the share of Nord Stream rose from zero to 30%, and the share of Belarus rose from 26% to 32% (IEA, 2016f; Sharples, 2015).

As illustrated by Figure 8.6, Russia has retained its role as the largest external supplier of natural gas to the EU. While transit via Ukraine no longer accounts for the absolute majority of Russian gas deliveries to the Union, it is still the largest route by transit volume. Therefore, when considering the international political economy of energy security in Eastern Europe, with specific reference to trade in natural gas, the trilateral relationship between Russia, Ukraine, and the EU plays a key role in ensuring regional energy security.

Sowing the Seeds of the 2013–2014 Gas Dispute: Russia-Ukraine Gas Relations, 2006–2013

In 2006, Ukraine imported natural gas only from Russia, and was both a major export market for Russian gas and the most important delivery route for Russian gas supplies to the EU. Gas relations between Russia and Ukraine were conducted primarily by two state-owned companies: Gazprom from Russia and Naftogaz from Ukraine. These commercial relations were underpinned by intergovernmental agreements. Contracts for gas supplies from Russia to Ukraine were renewed annually, on the basis of commercial negotiations between Gazprom and Naftogaz, and political negotiations between the Russian and Ukrainian governments.

Yet January 2006 also saw the first major crisis in gas relations between Russia and Ukraine. The two sides failed to agree upon a renewal of the Gazprom-Naftogaz contract by the expiry of the previous contract at midnight on December 31, 2005. The result was a suspension of Gazprom deliveries to Naftogaz for several days, which resulted in a brief interruption in Gazprom's deliveries to the EU via Ukraine (Stern, 2006). Three years later, the situation was repeated with more serious consequences. This time, Gazprom's exports to Ukraine were suspended for three weeks, resulting in a longer interruption in Gazprom's gas deliveries to the EU via Ukraine. That dispute was resolved with the signature of a new, 10-year gas supply contract between Gazprom and Naftogaz and a parallel 10-year gas transit contract for the regulation of Russian gas deliveries to the EU via Ukraine. Both of these contracts were leaked and published by *Ukrainska Pravda* (Pirani, Stern, & Yafimava, 2009; *Ukrainska Pravda* 2009a, 2009b).

The contracts that resolved the 2009 dispute laid the foundations for the 2013 dispute, for four reasons. First, the price at which Gazprom would sell gas to Naftogaz was index-linked to the prices of heavy fuel oil and gasoil (two types of oil products, which are used as liquid fuels for non-road machinery, such as agricultural and construction vehicles, as a shipping fuel, and in industrial plants). The price of these fuels are heavily influenced by international oil prices (IEA, 2009, pp. 19, 23; Pirani, Stern, & Yafimava, 2009, p. 46). In January 2009, those oil prices were at a relatively low point, following their decline in the second half of 2008. As oil prices recovered in 2009–2010, and then remained above $100 a barrel from February 2011 to the middle of 2015, the contractual price of Gazprom's supplies to Naftogaz rose and stabilized at a level estimated to be 10% higher than the price of Russian gas supplies to Germany (Aleksashenko, 2014; EIA, 2016).

Second, the contract specified delivery volumes of 40 bcm in 2009 and 52 bcm per year thereafter, although the "take-or-pay" clause gave Naftogaz the flexibility to reduce its purchases by a set amount. From 2010, Naftogaz was obliged to purchase at least 80% of the contractual volume (42 bcm) or face financial penalties. Naftogaz was also allowed to purchase up to 120% of the contractual volume at the contractually agreed-upon price (Pirani, Stern, & Yafimava, 2009, p. 46; Ukrainska Pravda, 2009a). The contractual volume, which was designed to cover 100% of Ukraine's gas import needs, was based on estimates of Ukraine's future gas consumption, derived from data on Ukraine's gas consumption in the preceding years. However, the impact of the global economic recession on Ukraine in 2009–2010 resulted in a further sharp decline in Ukrainian gas consumption (Figure 8.7), and therefore imports, thus leaving Naftogaz contractually obliged to purchase gas that it did not need.

Third, the gas transit contract stipulated that Gazprom would deliver at least 110 bcm of natural gas via Ukraine each year. From 2010, the transit fee is approximately $2.04 per thousand cubic meters per 100 kilometers, plus an element based on 2009 gas prices that added a further $0.60 (Pirani, Stern, & Yafimava, 2009, p. 27; *Ukrainska Pravda*,

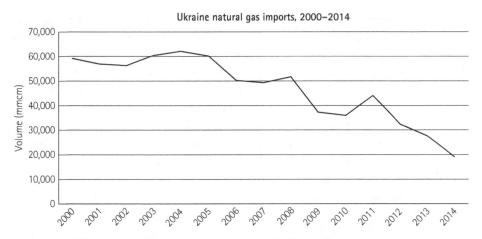

FIGURE 8.7 Ukraine natural gas imports, 2000–2014 (million cubic meters).

Data source: Eurostat, 2016.

2009b).[1] Given that the (very rough) average distance of gas transit across Ukraine is 1,000 kilometers, the transit of 110 bcm at a price of $2.64 would generate revenues of $2.9 billion per year for the Naftogaz subsidiary, UkrTransGaz, which manages Ukraine's gas pipeline network. However, as discussed earlier, Gazprom has diverted substantial export volumes away from the Ukrainian route since 2011, resulting in the transit of approximately 46 bcm to Europe in 2014. If transit via Ukraine to Turkey is included, the figure rises to 59 bcm, or 54% of the volume stipulated by the transit contract (IEA, 2016f). If the transit fee were the same in 2014 as in 2010, actual transit revenues would be $1.57 billion. This reduction of transit revenues for Naftogaz and its subsidiary, UkrTransGaz, is clearly financially substantial.

Fourth, the two sides retained a willingness to engage in the political negotiation of gas prices. When the January 2009 gas supply contract was signed, it was agreed that Naftogaz would benefit from a price discount for the first year (Pirani, Stern, & Yafimava, 2009, p. 26; *Ukrainska Pravda*, 2009a). By the time the discount expired in January 2010, higher oil prices meant that the shift from discounted to non-discounted prices was substantial.

In order to retain the discount, the Ukrainian president at the time, Viktor Yanukovich, signed the Kharkiv Accords, in which the Ukrainian government agreed to extend the lease of the Sevastopol naval base in Crimea (home of Russia's Black Sea Fleet since the collapse of the Soviet Union) from 2017 to 2042, in exchange for a 30% discount (up to $100 per thousand cubic meters) in the price at which Russian gas was supplied to Ukraine. That discount was facilitated by the suspension of the levying of export duties on Russian gas sold to Ukraine, and brought the price of Gazprom's gas sales to Naftogaz down from an estimated $255 per thousand cubic meters (mcm) to approximately $179 per mcm. In their analysis of the agreement, Pirani, Stern, and Yafimava characterize it as "essentially political. . . . Both sides have gone back to mixing commercial gas issues with political, non-gas issues" (Pirani, Stern, & Yafimava, 2010, pp. 2, 7, 17–18).

Overall, gas relations between Gazprom and Naftogaz continued to be conducted in accordance with the Groningen model—a model of bilateral gas contracts that was designed to overcome the lack of market development and the lack of competition among suppliers, and between suppliers and customers. While this model served Russia, Norway, and Algeria well for several decades from the 1960s onward, its ability to do so was based on the acceptance of this model by all parties and the separation of gas trade from political relations. Furthermore, from the mid-1980s to the beginning of the first decade of the 2000s, relatively low international oil prices (EIA, 2016) meant that oil indexation was not perceived by importers as commercially disadvantageous.

By the early 2010s, much of the European gas market had moved on to a more competitive, market-oriented footing, with multilateral relations between a range of suppliers and customers. By contrast, gas relations between Russia and Ukraine continued to be conducted on a bilateral basis, with oil indexation being used as a contractual mechanism to overcome the lack of market signals. Crucially, during the crisis of 2013–2014, Russia-Ukraine gas relations were conducted at a time of high oil prices and relatively low spot gas prices in Europe (EIA, 2016). This left Naftogaz dissatisfied with the fact that it was paying higher prices for Russian gas than European companies further west, which were benefiting from a more competitive gas market. In other words, Naftogaz no longer accepted the Groningen Model as the basis for its gas imports from Russia.

Furthermore, Russia-Ukraine gas relations were politically negotiable, with discounts being traded for political concessions. This is particularly problematic in the context of Gazprom's reliance on Ukrainian transit for its lucrative exports to the EU, and Naftogaz's dependence on transit revenues to fund its Russian gas imports. Indeed, the crises of 2006 and 2009 emerged (at least in part) from Gazprom's attempts to take advantage of its position as monopoly supplier to extract maximum economic rent from its exports to Ukraine, and Naftogaz's attempts to leverage its role as a transit provider to negotiate discounted gas import prices. The inherent instability of this model left the Russia-Ukraine gas trade particularly vulnerable to the influence of developments in the political relationship between Russia and Ukraine.

The Crisis in Political Relations Between Russia and Ukraine since 2013

The political crisis in Russia-Ukraine relations erupted in November 2013. The last-minute refusal of Ukrainian president Viktor Yanukovich to sign an Association Agreement with the EU resulted in protests on the streets of Kyiv. The anti-government protests developed into the EuroMaidan movement and led to Yanukovich's effective resignation, after which he fled to Russia, in February 2014. An interim government was established, and Petro Poroshenko was elected president of Ukraine in May 2014.

During the period between the emergence of protests in Kyiv and Poroshenko's election, the crisis spread to other areas of Ukraine (BBC, 2014b).

At the end of February 2014, armed gunmen seized key buildings in Crimea, and in March a referendum in favor of independence from Ukraine and unification with Russia was passed with a reported 97% in favor of the motion. That same month, Russian president Vladimir Putin signed a decree formally incorporating Crimea into the Russian Federation. In April, protestors occupied government buildings in the eastern Ukrainian cities of Luhansk and Donetsk, before declaring independence in May, as fighting broke out across the Luhansk and Donetsk regions. In July, Malaysian Airlines flight MH17 was shot down over rebel-held territory (BBC, 2014b). The EU regarded the situation in Crimea as an illegal annexation by Russia, and reacted with asset freezes and travel bans against "persons responsible for actions which undermine or threaten the territorial integrity, sovereignty and independence of Ukraine" (Council of the EU, 2014a). In the same month, the EU imposed economic sanctions on Russia, "[i]n view of Russia's actions destabilising the situation in eastern Ukraine" (Council of the EU, 2014b). This reflects the view of the EU that Russia has provided both troops and material support to the rebels, although the Russian government claims that the only Russian soldiers in Eastern Ukraine were "volunteers," the only professionals were "military intelligence experts," and the only material aid delivered was humanitarian (*Guardian*, 2015).

At the beginning of September 2014, a ceasefire (the Minsk Agreement) was agreed between the Russian-backed separatists and the Ukrainian government (BBC, 2014a). After the first ceasefire collapsed, a new agreement (Minsk II) was agreed in February 2015. Low-level fighting continued, and a new ceasefire agreement was reached on September 1, 2016 (BBC, 2016). The latest ceasefire has effectively "frozen" the conflict, with the separatists still in control of substantial parts of the Donetsk and Luhansk regions of eastern Ukraine. This, combined with the continued Ukrainian government opposition to the Russian annexation of Crimea, means that political relations between Ukraine and Russia remain tense, as do relations between the EU and Russia.

THE RUSSIA-UKRAINE GAS DISPUTE OF 2013–2014: COMMERCIAL FAILURE OR COMMERCE AS A VICTIM OF POLITICS?

By 2013, gas relations between Russia and Ukraine faced several challenges, as discussed earlier. Disagreements over gas prices, contractual volumes, and transit volumes meant that the gas supply and gas transit contracts signed in January 2009 no longer reflected commercial reality. Because Naftogaz was purchasing less than the minimum volumes stated by the "take-or-pay" clause in its contract with Gazprom, Naftogaz was effectively ignoring the terms of that contract. By building Nord Stream and reducing its transit via Ukraine, Gazprom was ignoring the terms of its gas transit contract with UkrTransGaz.

The political crisis exacerbated these issues. In December 2013, the Russian government offered support to President Yanukovich in the form of a gas price discount and a substantial loan to the Ukrainian government, by buying $15 billion of Ukrainian government bonds, in several tranches. The change of government in Ukraine in February 2014 led to the discount and loan being canceled (Rushton, 2014). The annexation of Crimea also led to the cancellation of the Kharkiv Accords in April 2014 (*Financial Times*, 2014a). The removal of these discounts significantly increased the price at which Gazprom sold gas to Naftogaz, from $268 per mcm to $485 per mcm (*Financial Times*, 2014c).

From November 2013, Naftogaz also started accumulating debts to Gazprom (Pirani et al., 2014, pp. 2–6). Part of the reason is that while Naftogaz and Gazprom agreed on the volumes of gas that were provided, disagreement on prices (particularly since the removal of the discounts) meant disagreement on the total amount that Naftogaz should pay to Gazprom. Therefore, the crisis had the dual impact of intensifying the preexisting price dispute and signaling the end of politically negotiated gas price discounts for Ukraine.

Regarding the contractual volumes (i.e., the amount of gas that Naftogaz was obliged to purchase from Gazprom), two key points must be made. First, the decline in Ukrainian gas demand after 2009 was influenced significantly by the broader contraction of the Ukrainian economy. The reliance of the Ukrainian economy on heavy industry, which was itself traditionally underpinned by imports of Russian gas, meant that the dramatic contraction of industrial activity (especially steel production) from 2008 onward caused a substantial drop in Ukrainian gas demand. According to Naftogaz, total gas consumption in Ukraine fell dramatically from around 70 bcm in 2007 to just 34 bcm in 2015, within which industrial gas consumption fell from 33 bcm to 12 bcm (Naftogaz, 2016a; Naftogaz Europe, 2016, 2017; Sutela, 2012).

A second key point to make is that a combination of the high price of Ukraine's gas imports from 2010 onward, and the development of a diplomatic crisis in Ukraine-Russia relations from 2013 onward, gave the Ukrainian government and Naftogaz additional political motivation to further reduce Ukraine's gas consumption, specifically in order to reduce its gas imports from Russia. This situation was exacerbated by the dysfunctional manner in which Naftogaz was importing gas at wholesale prices, and then reselling it in Ukraine at "retail" prices, either directly to consumers through its own subsidiaries, or to other energy companies.

In Western Europe, it is usually the case that the "wholesale" price is lower than the "retail" price, meaning that the company that imports and then resells the gas to consumers can make a profit. This has not been the case in Ukraine. Rather, Naftogaz has been purchasing gas at high wholesale prices, and then reselling that gas at lower, state-regulated, retail prices inside Ukraine. Because it made a financial loss doing so, Naftogaz was effectively subsidized by the Ukrainian government from the national budget.

In order to encourage consumers to use less gas and to allow Naftogaz to both reduce its imports and improve its profitability, the new Ukrainian government enforced substantial increases in state-regulated retail gas prices for households, industrial enterprises (including electricity generators), and district heating companies between 2014 and 2016. Indeed, Rozwałka and Tordengren (2016, pp. 13–18) estimate that, in 2012, household consumers and district heating companies (DHC) were paying Naftogaz retail prices of $50 and $100 per mcm, respectively, while Naftogaz was paying $495 per mcm to import gas wholesale. This meant that Naftogaz was taking a loss of $395–445 on every mcm of gas that it imported and then resold inside Ukraine.

By mid-2016, the wholesale price that Naftogaz was paying for its gas imports, and the retail prices paid by households, industrial enterprises, and district heating companies, had converged at approximately $200 per mcm. In October 2016, Naftogaz announced that it would raise industrial gas prices to 7,380 hryvnia ($281) per mcm. This meant that domestic gas consumption no longer required subsidies from the Ukrainian government to cover the cost of wholesale imports, and thus had become sustainable (*Kyiv Post*, 2016; Rozwałka & Tordengren, 2016, p. 3). Furthermore, the decline in Ukrainian gas demand noted earlier showed that these higher prices had encouraged Ukrainian gas consumers to become more energy efficient and to reduce their gas consumption.

In parallel with the overall decline in Ukrainian gas demand and, by extension, Ukrainian gas imports, Naftogaz began to diversify its gas imports away from Gazprom. In 2013, Naftogaz imported 2 bcm of natural gas from the European market via Poland and Hungary. In August 2014, Naftogaz began importing gas from Slovakia, leading to a total of 5 bcm of imports from the European market (as opposed to imports from Russia) in 2014. Using the same three routes, Naftogaz's European imports doubled to 10 bcm in 2015 and reached 6 bcm in the first nine months of 2016 (IEA, 2016f). By contrast, Gazprom reports that its exports to Ukraine fell from 45 bcm in 2011 to 8 bcm in 2015 (Gazprom, 2016, p. 82). Gazprom's exports to Ukraine then ceased entirely, and on November 25, 2016, Naftogaz celebrated one year without the purchase of gas from Gazprom (Naftogaz, 2016b).

Finally, the decline in the transit of Russian gas via Ukraine would have occurred even without the crisis in relations between Russia and Ukraine. Not only did Gazprom launch the Nord Stream pipeline, it also increased its usage of the Yamal-Europe pipeline via Belarus and its usage of the Soviet-era Belarusian gas pipeline network for the delivery of gas to Poland (and onward to Germany) (IEA, 2016f). While Gazprom's purchase of Beltransgaz and construction of Nord Stream predated the Russia-Ukraine crisis of 2013–2014, the political crisis did allow Gazprom to justify its diversification of delivery routes.

In order to resolve their disputes, Gazprom and Naftogaz each launched arbitration cases in June 2014 at the Arbitration Institute of the Stockholm Commercial Court. The decision to hold the arbitration proceedings in Stockholm reflects the fact that neither the Energy Charter Treaty (ECT) nor Energy Community (EC) dispute resolution mechanisms can be used, as Russia is no longer provisionally applying the ECT and is not a member of the EC. The hearings were completed in December 2016 (Naftogaz,

2016c), and an interim ruling was made in May 2017. In November 2017, the Stockholm arbitration tribunal announced that final rulings on the gas supply contract and transit contract would be made in December 2017 and February 2018 respectively. However, also in November 2017, Gazprom challenged the interim ruling—a move which could further delay the final rulings (Interfax Energy, 2017; Vedomosti, 2017).

In brief, Naftogaz is seeking to revise the existing contract by canceling the "take-or-pay" clause, canceling the "destination clause," and revising the pricing formula by both reducing the "base price" and replacing oil indexation with spot-price indexation. Naftogaz also claims that it overpaid for its gas imports from Russia since 2010, and is seeking a rebate. For its part, Gazprom is seeking to collect unpaid gas bills from 2013 to 2015, unpaid bills for gas delivered to Eastern Ukraine since 2014, and to enforce the contractual financial penalties stipulated by the "take-or-pay" clause in the gas supply contract (Radchenko, 2016; Wilson & Lowery, 2014).

Therefore, we can conclude that despite the seriousness of the recent crisis in political relations between Russia and Ukraine, difficulties in the Russia-Ukraine gas relationship had already existed, and were merely exacerbated by the political crisis. Indeed, the problem is not market failure, but the very absence of a market and an associated legal framework that covers Russia (the supplier), Ukraine (importer and transit state), and the EU (as the destination market for Russia's gas exports). This raises the question of whether the establishment of market mechanisms and an associated regulatory framework could ease concerns over regional energy security, with specific reference to the Russia-Ukraine-EU trilateral gas relationship.

Overcoming the Challenges: Prospects for Ukraine's Integration into the EU Gas Market

At the formal level, Ukraine has been a member of the Energy Community since February 1, 2011 (Energy Community, 2016b). According to an Energy Community brief on Ukraine, "Ukraine managed to achieve an impressive record in transposing the Third Energy Package, thus becoming the first Contracting Party of the Energy Community with a significantly developed regulatory framework of the natural gas market" (Energy Community Secretariat, 2016). In April 2015, the Ukrainian government passed the Law of Ukraine on the Natural Gas Market, which laid the foundations for transposing EU gas and electricity market legislation—specifically the EU Third Energy Package—into Ukrainian law (Energy Community Secretariat, 2016; Rozwałka & Tordengren, 2016, p. 8).

At the domestic level, price increases for industrial, district heating, and residential consumers between 2014 and 2016 meant that revenues from domestic sales were able to cover the cost of wholesale imports, thus rendering such imports sustainable without subsidies from the Ukrainian government budget. At the international, whole-sale import level, Naftogaz has successfully diversified its gas imports away from Russia. However, this has been achieved through a substantial reduction in domestic gas consumption.

As noted earlier, in 2015, total Ukrainian gas consumption of 34 bcm was met through domestic production of 19 bcm, imports from Europe of 10 bcm, and imports from Russia of 8 bcm. The physical capacity of pipelines importing gas from the European market via Poland, Hungary, and Slovakia is 15 bcm per year (IEA, 2016f). If Naftogaz intends to continue its policy of not importing gas from Gazprom, this can only be achieved by holding Ukrainian gas consumption at its 2015 level and importing gas from Europe at full capacity. Yet the resumption of gas purchases by Naftogaz from Gazprom need not be problematic. The crucial point is that, by introducing alternative sources and (by extension) competition to the Ukrainian gas import market, Naftogaz and the Ukrainian government would be able to place the Ukrainian gas market on a commer-cial footing.

Looking to the future, the transit of Russian gas will likely continue after the ex-piry of the Gazprom-UkrTransGaz gas transit contract in 2019. While the current, ongoing Russia-Ukraine gas dispute has not affected the transit of Russian gas via Ukraine, it is worth remembering that the previous interruptions in gas transit via Ukraine were caused by disputes relating to the Gazprom-Naftogaz gas supply contract. Therefore, under conditions of continuing gas transit via Ukraine, transit would be best secured by establishing sound commercial relations between Gazprom and Naftogaz (Chyong, 2014).

The reform of the domestic Ukrainian gas market and increased commercial viability of Naftogaz are essential to this process. The ongoing Gazprom-Naftogaz arbitration case could deliver a final resolution of the dispute, and could lay the groundwork for a new commercial relationship to replace the arrangements governed by the existing gas supply and gas transit contracts. The negotiation of that future commercial relation-ship may yet prove contentious, and as such it represents a fork in the road: It could re-sult in the renewal of the dispute, with the two sides failing to agree on new contractual arrangements, or it could result in the two parties reaching a more sustainable agree-ment that better represents the commercial reality of the contemporary gas trade in Eastern Europe.

CONCLUSION

Tensions regarding the security of natural gas supplies in the trilateral relationship between Russia, Ukraine, and the EU between 2013 and 2016 were the result of both commercial challenges and the influence of regional political developments. When the dispute emerged during the winter of 2013–2014, it was already clear that the ex-isting Gazprom-Naftogaz gas supply and gas transit contracts no longer reflected the commercial reality of their relations. Indeed, the lack of market influence meant that Naftogaz was left paying a much higher price for its Russian gas imports than both companies that were purchasing their gas on trading hubs in the EU and Western European companies that were able to negotiate short-term discounts on their supplies from Gazprom, in light of the disparity between hub-based and oil-indexed prices on the EU gas market.

Furthermore, both sides had already begun to diversify away from each other: Gazprom had constructed the Nord Stream pipeline, while Naftogaz began "testing the waters" of increasing its gas imports from the EU market. The crisis in political relations between Russia and Ukraine that developed during the winter of 2013–2014 merely intensified existing trends. For Ukraine, diversification away from Russia gas supplies and integration into the EU gas market became a strategic political priority. From the Russian perspective, Gazprom may feel more justified in having constructed the Nord Stream pipeline, and indeed in investing in potential future pipelines that may further reduce its dependence on gas transit via Ukraine.

Looking to the future, the ability of Naftogaz (and other Ukrainian gas importers) to purchase significant volumes of natural gas from the EU market will depend on the effective functioning of the EU gas market, and on Ukraine's integration into that market. Such integration began with Ukraine's accession to the Energy Community in 2011 and Ukraine's first substantial gas imports from a western direction in 2013, and is likely to continue. The security of Russian gas transit via Ukraine will be improved by the resolution of commercial disputes between Gazprom and Naftogaz, and even the tensions in this relationship will be reduced in line with the reduction of their mutual dependence

To conclude, given Ukraine's integration into the EU gas market, the continuation of Russia's role as a major supplier of natural gas to the EU, and the continuation of the transit of Russian gas via Ukraine, Eastern European energy security in the sphere of natural gas will be strongly influenced by the degree of regional market-building, even in the context of challenging regional political dynamics.

NOTE

1. All uses of the symbol $ refer to US dollars unless otherwise noted.

REFERENCES

Aleksashenko, S. (2014, July 22). Is there a solution? *Carnegie Moscow Centre Commentary*. Retrieved from http://carnegie.ru/commentary/?fa=56209

BBC. (2014a, September 5). Ukraine and pro-Russia rebels sign ceasefire deal. *BBC News*. Retrieved from http://www.bbc.com/news/world-europe-29082574

BBC. (2014b, November 14). Ukraine crisis: timeline. *BBC News*. Retrieved from http://www.bbc.com/news/world-middle-east-26248275

BBC. (2016). Ukraine crisis: New ceasefire "holding with eastern rebels." *BBC News.* Retrieved from http://www.bbc.com/news/world-europe-37243434

Cedigaz. (2014, June 25). *CEDIGAZ, the International Centre for Natural Gas Information, has released today the updated edition of its Long-Term Gas Supply Contracts by Pipelines in Europe* [Press release]. Retrieved from http://www.cedigaz.org/documents/2014/PR%20-%20LT%20Gas%20supply%20contracts%20by%20pipelines%20in%20Europe.pdf

Council of the EU. (2014a, March 17). *EU adopts restrictive measures against actions threatening Ukraine's territorial integrity* [Press release]. Retrieved from http://www.consilium.europa.eu/uedocs/cms_data/docs/pressdata/EN/foraff/141603.pdf

Council of the EU. (2014b, July 31). *Adoption of agreed restrictive measures in view of Russia's role in Eastern Ukraine* [Press release]. Retrieved from http://www.consilium.europa.eu/workarea/downloadAsset.aspx?id=27446

Chyong, C. K. (2014). Why Europe should support reform of the Ukrainian gas market—Or risk a cut-off. *European Council on Foreign Relations Policy Brief,* September. Retrieved from http://www.ecfr.eu/page/-/ECFR113_UKRAINE_BRIEF_131014_SinglePages.pdf

Chyong, C. K. (2015). Markets and long-term contracts: The case of Russian gas supplies to Europe. *Energy Policy Research Group Working Paper,* Cambridge University. Retrieved from http://www.eprg.group.cam.ac.uk/wp-content/uploads/2015/12/1524-Text.pdf

EIA. (2016). *Europe spot Brent price FOB.* Retrieved from http://www.eia.gov/dnav/pet/hist/LeafHandler.ashx?n=PET&s=RBRTE&f=D

Energy Charter Secretariat. (2007). *Putting a price on energy: International pricing mechanisms for oil and gas.* Brussels: Energy Charter Secretariat. Retrieved from http://www.energycharter.org/fileadmin/DocumentsMedia/Thematic/Oil_and_Gas_Pricing_2007_en.pdf

Energy Charter Secretariat. (2016a). *The Energy Charter Treaty.* Retrieved from http://www.energycharter.org/process/energy-charter-treaty-1994/energy-charter-treaty/

Energy Charter Secretariat. (2016b). *Members and observers: The Russian Federation.* Retrieved from http://www.energycharter.org/who-we-are/members-observers/countries/russian-federation/

Energy Community. (2016a). *The Energy Community: Who we are.* Retrieved from https://www.energy-community.org/portal/page/portal/ENC_HOME/ENERGY_COMMUNITY/Who_are_we

Energy Community. (2016b). *Energy Community members: Ukraine.* Retrieved from https://www.energy-community.org/portal/page/portal/ENC_HOME/MEMBERS/PARTIES/UKRAINE

Energy Community Secretariat. (2016, March 9). Spotlight on Ukraine. *Energy Community Country Brief,* Issue 3. Retrieved from https://www.energy-community.org/portal/page/portal/ENC_HOME/DOCS/4058387/2DA01F3623B07BC3E053C92FA8C0CFDA.pdf

European Commission. (2015, April 22). *Antitrust: Commission sends Statement of Objections to Gazprom for alleged abuse of dominance on Central and Eastern European gas supply markets* [Press release]. Retrieved from http://europa.eu/rapid/press-release_IP-15-4828_en.htm

European Commission. (2017, March 13). *Antitrust: Commission invites comments on Gazprom commitments concerning Central and Eastern European gas markets* [Press release]. Retrieved from http://europa.eu/rapid/press-release_IP-17-555_en.htm

European Environment Agency. (2016). *Primary energy consumption by fuel.* Retrieved from http://www.eea.europa.eu/data-and-maps/indicators/primary-energy-consumption-by-fuel-6/assessment-1

European Parliament and Council Directive (1998) 98/30/EC of 22 June 1998 concerning common rules for the internal market in natural gas. Retrieved from http://eur-lex.europa.eu/legal-content/EN/TXT/?uri=uriserv:OJ.L_.1998.204.01.0001.01.ENG

European Parliament and Council Directive (2003) 2003/55/EC of the Council of 26 June 2003 concerning common rules for the internal market in natural gas and repealing Directive 98/30/EC. Retrieved from http://eur-lex.europa.eu/legal-content/EN/TXT/?uri=celex:32003L0055

European Parliament and Council Directive (2009) 2009/73/EC of 13 July 2009 concerning common rules for the internal market in natural gas and repealing Directive 2003/55/EC. Retrieved from http://eur-lex.europa.eu/legal-content/EN/ALL/?uri=CELEX%3A32009L0073

Eurostat. (2016). *Imports of gas: Annual data (nrg_124a)*. Retrieved from http://appsso.eurostat.ec.europa.eu/nui/show.do?dataset=nrg_124a&lang=en

Eurostat. (2017a). *Supply of gas: Monthly data (nrg_103m)*. Retrieved from http://appsso.eurostat.ec.europa.eu/nui/show.do?dataset=nrg_103m&lang=en

Eurostat. (2017b). *Gross inland energy consumption by fuel type (thousand tonnes of oil equivalent)*. Retrieved from http://ec.europa.eu/eurostat/tgm/refreshTableAction.do?tab=table&plugin=1&pcode=tsdcc320&language=en

Fernandez, R., & Palazuelos, E. (2014). A political economy approach to the European Union Gas Model: Continuities and changes. *Journal of Common Market Studies, 52*(3), 495–511.

Financial Times. (2013, November 19). Statoil breaks oil-linked gas pricing. *Financial Times*. Retrieved from https://www.ft.com/content/aad942d6-4e25-11e3-b15d-00144feabdc0

Financial Times. (2014a, April 2). Putin tears up lease for Sevastopol naval base. *Financial Times*. Retrieved from https://www.ft.com/content/5a610a56-ba85-11e3-8b15-00144feabdc0

Financial Times. (2014b, May 23). Eni in spot market gas deal with Gazprom. *Financial Times*. Retrieved from https://www.ft.com/content/3b79b0e4-e284-11e3-a829-00144feabdc0

Financial Times. (2014c, June 2). Gazprom delays threat to disrupt Ukraine gas supplies. *Financial Times*. Retrieved from https://www.ft.com/content/c2b545ae-ea28-11e3-8dde-00144feabdc0

Franza, L. (2014). *Long-term gas import contracts in Europe: The evolution in pricing mechanisms*. The Hague: Clingendael International Energy programme. Retrieved from http://www.clingendaelenergy.com/inc/upload/files/Ciep_paper_2014-08_web_1.pdf

Gazprom. (2013, April 5). *Beltransgaz to be renamed Gazprom Transgaz Belarus* [Press release]. Retrieved from http://www.gazprom.com/press/news/2013/april/article159735/

Gazprom. (2016). Gazprom in figures 2011–2015. Moscow: Gazprom. Retrieved from http://www.gazprom.com/f/posts/12/001311/gazprom-in-figures-2011-2015-en.pdf

Guardian. (2015, December 17). Putin admits Russian military presence in Ukraine for first time. *The Guardian*. Retrieved from https://www.theguardian.com/world/2015/dec/17/vladimir-putin-admits-russian-military-presence-ukraine

Heather, P. (2015). *The evolution of European traded gas hubs*. Oxford: Institute for Energy Studies. Retrieved from https://www.oxfordenergy.org/wpcms/wp-content/uploads/2016/02/NG-104.pdf

Henderson, J., & Mitrova, T. (2015). *The political and commercial dynamics of Russia's gas export strategy*. Oxford: Institute for Energy Studies. Retrieved from https://www.oxfordenergy.org/wpcms/wp-content/uploads/2015/09/NG-102.pdf

Honoré, A. (2014). *The outlook for natural gas demand in Europe.* Oxford: Institute for Energy Studies. Retrieved from https://www.oxfordenergy.org/wpcms/wp-content/uploads/2014 /06/NG-87.pdf

IEA (2009). *Oil definitions.* Paris: IEA. Retrieved from www.iea.org/interenerstat_v2/meeting /2009/Oil.pdf

IEA (2016a). *European Union 28: Energy balances for 2014.* Retrieved from https://www.iea.org /statistics/statisticssearch/report/?year=2014&country=EU28&product=Balances

IEA. (2016b). *European Union 28: Electricity and heat for 2014.* Retrieved from https://www.iea .org/statistics/statisticssearch/report/?year=2014&country=EU28&product=Electricityand Heat

IEA. (2016c). *Electricity generation by fuel 1990–2014: European Union 28.* Retrieved from http://www.iea.org/stats/WebGraphs/EU282.pdf

IEA. (2016d). *Key natural gas trends.* Paris: IEA. Retrieved from https://www.iea.org /publications/freepublications/publication/KeyNaturalGasTrends-1.pdf

IEA. (2016e). *Natural gas information (2016 edition).* Paris: IEA. Retrieved from http://wds.iea .org/wds/pdf/Gas_documentation.pdf

IEA. (2016f). *Gas trade flows in Europe.* Retrieved from https://www.iea.org/gtf/#

Interfax Energy. (2017, November 15). Stockholm court extends timeline for Gazprom-Naftogaz ruling. *Interfax Energy.* Retrieved from http://interfaxenergy.com/gasdaily/article/28410 /stockholm-court-extends-timeline-for-gazprom-naftogaz-ruling

International Gas Union. (2016). *2016 IGU wholesale gas price survey.* Fornebu, Norway: IGU. Retrieved from http://www.igu.org/sites/default/files/node-news_item-field_file/IGU _WholeSaleGasPrice_Survey0509_2016.pdf

Konoplyanik, A. (2012). Russian gas at European energy market: Why adaptation is inevitable. *Energy Strategy Reviews, 1*(1), 42–56.

Kyiv Post. (2016, October 21). Naftogaz raises gas price for industrial consumers by 15–16 percent for November. *Kyiv Post.* Retrieved from https://www.kyivpost.com/ukraine-politics /naftogaz-raises-gas-price-industrial-consumers-15-16-percent-november.html

Naftogaz. (2016a). *Gas consumption.* Kyiv: Naftogaz. Retrieved from http://www.naftogaz .com/www/3/nakweben.nsf/0/89BCADFD7E7A8320C2257FCD00373B9E?OpenDocumen t&Expand=1.5&

Naftogaz. (2016b, November 25). *Naftogaz open letter: A year without gas imports from Russia* [Press release]. Retrieved from http://www.naftogaz.com/www/3/nakweben.nsf/0/371FE97 DD813E51FC225807600517667?OpenDocument&year=2016&month=11&nt=News&

Naftogaz. (2016c, December 6). *Stockholm arbitration completes hearing of dispute between Naftogaz and Gazprom* [Press release]. Retrieved from http://www.naftogaz-europe.com /article/en/StockholmarbitrationcompleteshearingofdisputebetweenNaftogazandGazprom

Naftogaz Europe. (2016, February 23). *Gas consumption dynamics in Ukraine in 2004– 2015* [Press release]. Retrieved from http://www.naftogaz-europe.com/article/en /gasconsdyn2015eng

Naftogaz Europe. (2017, January 10). *Natural gas supplies to Ukraine* [Press release]. Retrieved from http://www.naftogaz-europe.com/article/en/NaturalGasSuppliestoUkraine

Pirani, S., Stern, J., & Yafimava, K. (2009). *The Russo-Ukrainian gas dispute of January 2009: A comprehensive assessment.* Oxford: Institute for Energy Studies. Retrieved from https://www.oxfordenergy.org/wpcms/wp-content/uploads/2010/11/NG27-TheRusso UkrainianGasDisputeofJanuary2009AComprehensiveAssessment-JonathanSternSimon PiraniKatjaYafimava-2009.pdf

Pirani, S., Stern, J., & Yafimava, K. (2010). *The April 2010 Russo-Ukrainian gas agreement and its implications for Europe.* Oxford: Institute for Energy Studies. Retrieved from https://www.oxfordenergy.org/wpcms/wp-content/uploads/2011/05/NG_42.pdf

Pirani, S., Henderson, J., Honoré, A., Rogers, H., & Yafimava, K. (2014). *What the Ukraine crisis means for gas markets.* Oxford: Institute for Energy Studies. Retrieved from https://www.oxfordenergy.org/wpcms/wp-content/uploads/2014/03/What-the-Ukraine-crisis-means-for-gas-markets-GPC-3.pdf

Platts. (2016, May 9). Gas spot, hub linked prices rose to 64% in Europe in 2015: IGU. *Platts.* Retrieved from http://www.platts.com/latest-news/natural-gas/london/gas-spot-hub-linked-prices-rose-to-64-in-europe-26437515

Radchenko, V. (2016). *Legal battles between Russia and Ukraine (Presentation at Vienna Forum on European Energy Law, 14–15 April 2016).* Brussels: Energy Community. Retrieved from https://www.energy-community.org/portal/page/portal/ENC_HOME/DOCS/4132479/31F06AA1FCF.23773E053C92FA8C00010.pdf

Reuters. (2012, October 24). RWE in landmark win over Gazprom crucial contract clause. *Reuters.* Retrieved from http://uk.reuters.com/article/gazprom-rwe-dispute-idUKL5E8LOAWW20121024

Rozwałka, P., & Tordengren, H. (2016). *The Ukrainian residential gas sector: A market untapped.* Oxford: Institute for Energy Studies. Retrieved from https://www.oxfordenergy.org/wpcms/wp-content/uploads/2016/07/The-Ukrainian-residential-gas-sector-a-market-untapped-NG-109.pdf

Rushton, K. (2014, March 4). Russia cancels Ukraine's gas discount and demands $1.5bn. *The Telegraph.* Retrieved from http://www.telegraph.co.uk/finance/newsbysector/energy/oilandgas/10676228/Russia-cancels-Ukraines-gas-discount-and-demands-1.5bn.html

Sharples, J. (2015). *Gazprom monitor annual review: Presentation at the Brussels Energy Club (16 December)* [MS PowerPoint]. Retrieved from https://www.academia.edu/33803668/Presentation_of_the_Gazprom_Monitor_at_the_Brussels_Energy_Club_-_Presentation_Slides_January_2017

Stern, J. (2006). *The Russian-Ukrainian gas crisis of January 2006.* Oxford: Institute for Energy Studies. Retrieved from https://www.oxfordenergy.org/wpcms/wp-content/uploads/2011/01/Jan2006-RussiaUkraineGasCrisis-JonathanStern.pdf

Stern, J., & Rogers, H. (2014). *The dynamics of a liberalised European gas market: Key determinants of hub prices, and roles and risks of major players.* Oxford: Institute for Energy Studies. Retrieved from https://www.oxfordenergy.org/wpcms/wp-content/uploads/2014/12/NG-94.pdf

Sutela, P. (2012). *The underachiever: Ukraine's economy since 1991.* Carnegie Endowment for International Peace. Retrieved from http://carnegieendowment.org/2012/03/09/underachiever-ukraine-s-economy-since-1991-pub-47451

Ukrainska Pravda. (2009a, January 22). Gazovoe soglashenie Timoshenko-Putina. Pol'nyi tekst. *Ukrainska Pravda.* Retrieved from http://www.pravda.com.ua/rus/articles/2009/01/22/4462671/

Ukrainska Pravda. (2009b, January 22). Kontrakte o tranzite gaza Rossijskogo gaza + dopsoglashenie ob avanse "Gazproma." *Ukrainska Pravda.* Retrieved from http://www.pravda.com.ua/rus/articles/2009/01/22/4462733/

Vedomosti. (2017, November 14). Gazprom appealed against Stockholm arbitration award in dispute with Naftogaz. *Vedomosti.* Retrieved from https://www.vedomosti.ru/business/news/2017/11/14/741663-gazprom

Wäktare, E. (2007). Territorial restrictions and profit sharing mechanisms in the gas sector: The Algerian case. *European Commission Competition Policy Newsletter*, 3, 19–21. Retrieved from http://ec.europa.eu/competition/publications/cpn/2007_3_19.pdf

Wilson, J., & Lowery, W. (2014, June 20). A quick look at the Gazprom/Naftogaz gas contract dispute. *National Law Review*. Retrieved from http://www.natlawreview.com/article/quick-look-gazpromnaftogaz-gas-contract-dispute

PART III

....

CONSUMPTION
DYNAMICS

....

In Part III we move from production to its flip side—consumption—and in that process bring to the fore the role of actors in energy-society relations. While the autonomy of individual consumers can at times be overemphasized (it is minuscule compared to that of industry and business), consumers nonetheless do play an elemental role in energy consumption and the prospects of energy system transition, as highlighted in a number of recent empirical studies that have attempted to quantify the "behavioral wedge," the potential efficiency gains that could be realized with relatively minor shifts in household behavior. The availability of cheap energy in high-income countries has fostered energy-consumptive goods, markets, and lifestyles, and high expectations among citizens of these countries for the protection of such lifestyles has had a notable impact on politics in places like the United States. While per capita consumption has largely stabilized in high-income countries, moreover, the expansion of middle classes in rapidly industrializing countries like China has and will continue to have foreboding effects on energy supply and demand, as well as our efforts to mitigate climate change.

Studies of consumer behavior have advanced considerably in recent years. Researchers continue to grapple with what appears to be a consistent inelasticity in energy-consumption behaviors—the so-called value-action gap—despite growing environmental awareness, but, as noted by Ana Delicado, sociological inquiries have moved beyond social-psychological studies of individuals to situate those actors within a larger sociocultural context in which practices are (re)produced. At the same time, it is important to remain aware of the limits of individual responsibility, the focus of the final chapter of Part III.

Richard York begins this section in Chapter 9, exemplifying first and foremost the vast inequities in energy consumption globally. To a great extent, these inequities in energy access are just as noteworthy as those in wealth. Importantly, York makes clear with current data that the historical trajectory of efficiency improvements bears no inevitable relation to overall consumption—both are perfectly capable of increasing simultaneously. Notably, as later chapters will further substantiate, observed increases in renewable energy utilization have not replaced fossil-fuel consumption.

In Chapter 10, Perry Sadorsky draws our attention to cities, now home to the majority of us, which are currently the sites of 75% of global energy consumption. Not only is this a reflection of population; urbanization is also associated with increases in per capita consumption. This is not entirely new; concentrations of people have led to vast increases in energy consumption since the Roman Empire. But it may well be newly disconcerting as we consider options for transition in energy-society relations. The relationship between cities and energy consumption are complex, however, expanding way beyond direct consumption in economic activities. This means not only that there is no simple answer to reducing the amount of energy consumed in cities, but also that there are several avenues for doing so.

Marilyn A. Brown and Benjamin K. Sovacool dig down to focus on the consumer in Chapter 11. Middle- and upper-income households are responsible for a sizable share of the energy pie, and are often the target of transition proponents, but the authors highlight the formidable constraints on the ability of consumers to reduce their consumption, despite expressed concern about the environmental and climatological effects of our consumption practices. This value-action gap is so perplexing to social scientists that the authors identify no less than 50 distinct conceptual frameworks introduced to explain this phenomenon, all of which note the many structural conditions within which consumption takes place but which are beyond the control of individual consumers.

Following this, Thomas Pfister and Martin Schweighofer employ a social practices perspective to make the case that "energy systems are much more than technological hardware." In fact, if one wants to understand the relationship of any given society to energy, and the likely future of that relationship, we must start with culture. There is more to this perspective than the rather superficial conclusion that energy transition must involve cultural change, however. Rather, the authors bring to the center of analysis the expression of energy-society relationships through specific assemblages of material, knowledge, and practices, enabled and sanctioned through cultural institutions. Change thus necessarily implicates all three of these domains.

In Chapter 13, Janet A. Lorenzen picks up where Brown and Sovacool left off, focusing squarely on just what those structural constraints are. Presenting the results of an analysis of qualitative interviews with three distinct groups, all of which are motivated to change their practices for various reasons, Lorenzen shows just how problematic is the narrative that "we are all responsible / if we all do a little together we can accomplish a lot." Not only are households *not* the primary consumers (the residential sector accounts for just 24% of total energy end use in the United States)—and this narrative draws attention away from those who are—but also, let's face it, in most Western industrial societies, we are locked in, with systems of provision, regulation, and institutional support placing hard limits on the effectiveness of voluntary measures. Even if we assume optimistically that the vast majority of consumers are motivated, and that motivation can be sustained, consumers face economic, cultural, organizational, and societal barriers to doing so; our prioritization of household-based voluntary measures to support a shift in energy-society relations ultimately only serves to draw attention and resources away from those actors and locations where the potential for meaningful change lies.

....

CHAPTER 9

ENERGY CONSUMPTION
TRENDS ACROSS THE GLOBE

....

RICHARD YORK

ALL societies, like all living things, require energy. Therefore, finding energy sources has been an unavoidable concern of all societies, be they Paleolithic tribes that sought out wood to cook with, or twenty-first-century post-industrial nations that build wind farms to power their Internet servers. In many respects, societies can be characterized by how much energy they consume and the sources of energy they utilize. In our era of anthropogenic climate change, caused in major part by the burning of fossil fuels, the degradation of most major river systems around the world from hydroelectric dams, and radioactive contamination from nuclear waste and accidents at nuclear power plants, understanding the energy use of societies could not be more important.

In this chapter, I examine global and national-level trends in how much energy societies use and what sources of energy are exploited. In my presentation, I offer some explanations for the political and economic forces driving trends in energy use. I begin with a brief summary of long-term changes in energy use, and then I focus on examining three major features of energy use in recent decades and their implications. First, I examine the growth of energy use and electricity consumption around the world, and note the striking diversity across nations. Second, I review trends in aggregate energy efficiency of national economies, and I show how improvements in efficiency have not been particularly effective at suppressing energy use. Third, I look at the development of renewable energy sources and consider the degree to which this development has affected fossil-fuel use.

HISTORICAL ENERGY TRENDS

....

One remarkable thing about humans is the extraordinary variability of energy consumption across societies. This variability generally increased over the course of human history, and became especially dramatic following the Industrial Revolution, when some societies came to consume vast quantities of energy, while other societies subsisted on very modest levels of energy consumption (Smil, 1994). Although coal and peat have been exploited sporadically since at least antiquity, fossil fuels did not start to become major global energy sources until the end of the eighteenth century, after which coal consumption grew exponentially (Smil, 1994). By the time petroleum became a major energy source toward the end the nineteenth century, fossil fuels were the dominant energy sources in industrializing nations. Biomass, such as wood and animal- and vegetable-based oils, became less important as sources of energy as fossil-fuel use grew explosively, although in an absolute sense biomass consumption levels remained high and grew over the industrial era, though their proportion of the energy supply declined rapidly. Animal power, for industry (where, for example, oxen turned wheels for energy) and for transportation (e.g., horses), declined rapidly in economic importance with the expansion of the coal-powered steam engine, the train, and the automobile.

Over the course of the twentieth century, electricity became an especially important form of energy for industrializing societies, powering cities and factories. Power plants fueled by fossil sources, particularly coal, provided much of this electricity. However, large dams and, starting in the latter part of the twentieth century, nuclear plants produced a large amount of electricity in many nations. More recently, wind and solar sources have begun to contribute noticeably, although typically still very modestly, to electricity production in some nations. Of course, despite the importance of electricity, energy for mechanical power (such as for engines in automobiles, planes, ships, and trains) and for heating still comes in large part from the immediate combustion of fossil fuels.

GLOBAL SHIFTS IN ENERGY CONSUMPTION

Energy use and electricity consumption have grown steadily around the world and in most nations in recent decades. However, the patterns of growth have varied substantially across nations. Some nations have seen their levels of consumption plateau, and even dip slightly, while others, mostly those that are rapidly industrializing, have seen their energy consumption grow dramatically. These different patterns of change across nations have resulted in a shift in the share of energy consumption in different parts of the world in the past few decades.

Table 9.1 shows the population, gross domestic production (GDP) per capita, energy use total and per capita, and electricity consumption total and per capita for the world as a whole and for the 20 most populous nations/economies in the world in 2013, where the European Union is counted as a single economy.[1] The 20 most populous nations/economies contain 76.4% of the world population, 77.1% of global energy use, and 77.5% of global electricity consumption, and represent nations from all levels of "development,"

Table 9.1 Population, Energy Use, and Electricity Consumption in the World and the 20 Most Populous Nations/Economies,[a] 2013

Nations and World	Population (millions)	GDP per capita (US$)	Energy Use[b]	Energy Use, per Capita[c]	Electricity Consumption (TWh)	Electricity Consumption p.c. (KWh)
World	7,176	9,900	13,593	1,894	22,277	3,104
China	1,357	5,652	3,022	2,226	5,107	3,762
India	1,279	1,604	775	606	979	765
European Union	508	33,844	1,626	3,200	3,067	6,036
United States	316	49,849	2,188	6,916	4,110	12,988
Indonesia	251	3,571	214	850	198	788
Brazil	204	11,797	294	1,438	517	2,529
Pakistan	181	1,087	86	475	82	450
Nigeria	173	2,462	134	773	25	142
Bangladesh	157	882	34	216	46	293
Russia	144	11,616	731	5,093	938	6,539
Japan	127	44,328	455	3,570	998	7,836
Mexico	124	9,317	191	1,546	255	2,057
Philippines	98	2,422	45	458	68	692
Ethiopia	95	423	48	507	6	65
Vietnam	90	1,522	60	668	117	1,306
Egypt	88	2,654	78	885	149	1,697
Iran	77	5,763	228	2,960	224	2,899
Turkey	76	11,103	116	1,528	209	2,745
Congo, Dem. Rep.	73	351	21	292	8	110
Thailand	67	5,613	134	1,988	167	2,471

[a] The European Union is counted as a single "nation," and its individual members are not listed separately. These 20 nations include over 76% of the world population and account for over 77% of both world energy use and world electricity consumption.

[b] Megatonnes of oil equivalent.

[c] Kilograms of oil equivalent.

from very poor nations such as the Democratic Republic of Congo to the most affluent nations, such as the United States and Japan. Therefore, the trends in these 20 economies dominate global trends and represent the diversity of patterns across all nations. As can be seen in Table 9.1, China has the highest energy use and electricity consumption in the world, with over 3,000 megatonnes of oil equivalent (Mtoe) and over 5,000 terawatt hours (TWh), respectively, in 2013. The United States and the European Union are the other two economies with highest levels of energy use and electricity consumption.

Other nations, even though populous, use a tiny fraction of world energy resources, with energy use and electricity consumption being, for example, only 21 Mtoe and 8 TWh, respectively, in the Democratic Republic of Congo and 34 Mtoe and 46 TWh, respectively, in Bangladesh.

Since 1990, these nations/economies have shown a variety of trends, as can be seen in Table 9.2, which presents average annual growth rates in energy use (total and per capita) and electricity consumption (total and per capita) for three periods: 1990–2001 (the end of the twentieth century); 2001–2008 (the start of the twenty-first century before the global recession); and 2008–2013 (following the onset of the global recession). It is noteworthy that rates of growth in electricity consumption are typically substantially higher than rates for energy use. This is largely due to the well-established fact that electricity consumption is more closely connected with industrialization and economic growth than energy use in general, and investments in expanding electricity production have been a central part of development plans in most nations since World War II (Mazur, 2013). Table 9.3 presents growth rates for population and GDP per capita (inflation adjusted). The trends in these factors help to explain the trends in energy use and electricity consumption, as I will discuss in the following.

Looking at the world as a whole, the effect of the global recession (generally considered to have started in December 2007) is clear, where energy use and electricity consumption, in total and per capita terms, are noticeably lower in the period 2008–2013 than in 2001–2008. However, it also is evident that there was a slower growth regime in the 1990s, when growth rates in energy use and electricity consumption were lower than they were after the global recession. Thus, growth in energy and electricity consumption accelerated in the twenty-first century.

We can gain insight into the global trends by examining how patterns differ across nations. The collapse of the Soviet Union and the Eastern Bloc around 1990 led to dramatic economic decline in those regions throughout the subsequent decade, with concomitant drops in industrial production and energy use. This is clearly apparent for Russia, where over the course of the 1990s it averaged a 3.0% annual decline in energy use (matching the decline in GDP per capita) and a 2.3% decline in electricity consumption (see Table 9.2). These declines in the former Eastern Bloc suppressed growth in global energy consumption and GDP. In the 1990s there were also intense civil wars in parts of Africa, notably Rwanda and the Democratic Republic of Congo. However, due to global inequalities, levels of energy consumption in these nations are so low as to not appreciably affect global trends. Nonetheless, it is noteworthy that the DRC saw energy use and electricity consumption drop noticeably in per capita terms over the course of the 1990s, although total national levels of these grew due to rapid population growth.

In addition to the pattern of decline and growth in the former Eastern Bloc, global trends were largely driven by two contrasting patterns across a few dominant nations/economies. On the one hand, the European Union and the United States saw their rates of growth in GDP, electricity consumption, and energy use drop in the twenty-first century, and this drop became more pronounced following 2008. This may be due in part to structural changes that occur in "advanced" economies, where internal industrial

Table 9.2 Average Annual Growth Rates (%) in Energy Use and Electricity Consumption, in Total and per Capita Terms, in the World and the 20 Most Populous Nations/Economies,[a] 1990–2013

Nations and World	Energy Use			Energy Use per Capita			Electricity Consumption			Electricity Consumption per Capita		
	2008–2013	2001–2008	1990–2001	2008–2013	2001–2008	1990–2001	2008–2013	2001–2008	1990–2001	2008–2013	2001–2008	1990–2001
World	2.2	2.7	1.3	0.9	1.4	-0.1	3.0	3.9	2.5	1.8	2.6	1.0
China	7.7	8.4	2.8	7.2	7.8	1.8	9.4	13.2	8.1	8.9	12.5	7.0
India	5.2	4.2	3.5	3.9	2.6	1.6	7.8	6.9	5.4	6.3	5.2	3.4
European Union	-1.5	0.2	0.5	-1.8	-0.2	0.3	-0.8	1.3	1.5	-1.0	1.0	1.3
United States	-0.8	0.3	1.4	-1.6	-0.6	0.2	-0.2	1.6	2.2	-1.0	0.7	1.0
Indonesia	2.8	2.3	4.4	1.4	1.0	2.9	8.1	6.2	10.5	6.7	4.8	8.8
Brazil	3.4	3.8	2.9	2.4	2.6	1.3	3.8	4.7	3.3	2.8	3.4	1.7
Pakistan	0.9	3.4	3.8	-1.2	1.3	1.3	2.4	4.4	5.5	0.3	2.3	2.9
Nigeria	3.4	3.3	2.8	0.6	0.6	0.3	5.1	10.5	1.2	2.3	7.7	-1.3
Bangladesh	4.9	4.2	4.2	3.7	2.7	2.0	9.0	10.4	10.2	7.7	8.8	7.9
Russia	1.2	1.4	-3.0	1.1	1.7	-2.9	0.5	2.5	-2.3	0.4	2.8	-2.1
Japan	-1.7	-0.4	1.4	-1.6	-0.5	1.1	-0.6	0.5	2.0	-0.5	0.4	1.7
Mexico	1.1	2.9	1.8	-0.3	1.4	0.0	3.1	2.7	5.6	1.5	1.3	3.8
Philippines	2.1	0.7	2.7	0.6	-1.1	0.3	4.9	3.7	5.8	3.3	1.8	3.4
Ethiopia	5.0	3.3	3.3	2.3	0.4	0.0	12.4	9.4	4.8	9.6	6.4	1.5
Vietnam	4.3	6.8	5.0	3.2	5.6	3.4	11.1	14.8	13.6	9.9	13.5	11.8
Egypt	1.4	6.8	3.2	-0.7	4.9	1.2	4.9	7.2	6.0	2.7	5.2	4.0
Iran	2.2	6.3	6.1	1.0	5.1	4.5	5.1	6.9	6.8	3.8	5.7	5.1
Turkey	3.4	5.0	2.6	1.7	3.6	1.0	4.1	7.4	6.8	2.5	6.0	5.2
Congo, Dem. Rep.	2.7	3.7	1.8	-0.6	0.5	-1.3	5.5	4.1	0.2	2.1	0.8	-2.9
Thailand	4.4	5.5	5.3	4.1	4.8	4.3	3.5	5.6	8.2	3.2	4.9	7.1

[a] The European Union is counted as a single "nation," and its individual members are not listed separately. These nations include over 76% of the world population and account for over 77% of both world energy use and world electricity consumption.

Table 9.3   Average Annual Growth Rates of Population and GDP per Capita (Inflation Adjusted), 1990–2013, for the World and the 20 Most Populous (In 2013) Nations/Economies

Nations and World	Population			GDP per Capita		
	2008–2013	2001–2008	1990–2001	2008–2013	2001–2008	1990–2001
World	1.2	1.2	1.5	0.9	2.1	1.2
China	0.5	0.6	1.0	8.4	10.4	9.1
India	1.3	1.6	1.9	6.1	5.5	3.5
European Union	0.2	0.4	0.2	–0.4	1.7	2.0
United States	0.8	0.9	1.2	0.2	1.3	2.0
Indonesia	1.3	1.4	1.5	4.3	4.0	2.6
Brazil	0.9	1.3	1.6	2.2	2.7	0.9
Pakistan	2.1	2.1	2.5	0.9	3.0	1.2
Nigeria	2.7	2.6	2.5	3.1	7.2	–0.4
Bangladesh	1.2	1.5	2.1	4.7	4.2	2.5
Russia	0.2	–0.3	–0.1	0.9	7.1	–3.0
Japan	–0.2	0.1	0.3	0.4	1.1	0.8
Mexico	1.5	1.4	1.8	0.4	1.2	1.4
Philippines	1.6	1.8	2.3	3.6	3.3	0.5
Ethiopia	2.6	2.8	3.3	7.5	5.1	0.0
Vietnam	1.1	1.1	1.6	4.6	5.7	5.8
Egypt	2.1	1.8	1.9	1.1	3.1	2.2
Iran	1.2	1.2	1.6	–0.5	4.6	1.5
Turkey	1.6	1.3	1.6	2.1	4.5	1.1
Congo, Dem. Rep.	3.3	3.2	3.2	3.1	2.3	–8.2
Thailand	0.3	0.7	1.0	3.1	4.4	3.2

production has declined, as cheaper manufactured goods are imported from less developed nations. Japan appears to have gone through this transition somewhat earlier than the United States and the European Union, having had low rates of growth in GDP, energy use, and electricity consumption since 1990. On the other hand, China and, to a lesser extent, India shifted to explosive rates of growth in GDP, electricity consumption, and energy use in the first decade of the 2000s, having had only modest rates in the 1990s. Additionally, the global recession had a more modest effect in India and China than it did in affluent nations.

These patterns are reflected in the ongoing shift in which economies are responsible for the largest shares of energy use and electricity consumption in the world. As Table 9.4 shows, China and India combined moved from being responsible for only 13.4% of global energy use and 7.3% of global electricity consumption in 1990 to accounting for 27.9% of

Table 9.4 World Share of Energy Use and Electricity Consumption in the European
Union, United States, and Japan versus in China and India, 1990–2013

	Energy Use (% world total)		Electricity Consumption (% World Total)	
Year	China and India	EU, US, and Japan	China and India	EU, US, and Japan
2013	27.9%	31.4%	27.3%	36.7%
2001	16.2%	39.2%	12.2%	51.8%
1990	13.4%	45.6%	7.3%	55.3%

Table 9.5 Correlations with Growth in Energy Use and Electricity Consumption
for the 20 Most Populous Nations/Economies (as of 2013) in the World

	Correlations with Population Growth Rate		Correlations with GDP per Capita Growth Rate	
Period	Energy Use, Total	Electricity Consumption, Total	Energy Use per Capita	Electricity Consumption per Capita
2008–2013	.220	.404	.796*	.861*
2001–2008	.166	.271	.592*	.766*
1990–2001	.447*	.169	.625*	.757*

* *p*-value <.05 (two-tailed test)

Note: *N* = 20 for each period.

global energy use and 27.3% of electricity consumption in 2013. Conversely, the European Union, the United States, and Japan moved from being the sites of 45.6% of global energy use and 55.3% of global electricity consumption in 1990 to 31.4% and 36.7%, respectively. The largest part of this shift—from the three major affluent economies in the world to the two largest rapidly industrializing nations—occurred in the twenty-first century, and the rate of change is striking. Since the European Union, the United States, Japan, China, and India combined now account for nearly 60% of global energy use and close to two-thirds of global electricity consumption, these five economies stand out as being the dominant players behind global trends.

Some of the key factors that explain national and global trends in energy use and electricity consumption have been alluded to earlier, most notably demographic and economic factors. Table 9.5 shows the correlations between the growth rates in population and GDP per capita and growth rates in energy use and electricity consumption for each of the three periods examined here for the 20 nations/economies listed in Tables 9.1–9.3. Population growth has a positive correlation with growth in both total energy use and total electricity consumption in each period, although these correlations are modest, and only the one for 1990–2001 for energy use is statistically significant with a two-tailed test at the .05 alpha level. There is a much closer connection between growth in GDP per capita and per capita levels of both energy use and electricity consumption. These correlations are all positive and statistically significant. Both correlations with GDP per capita are stronger in the most recent period (.796 for energy use per capita and .861 for electricity consumption per capita), and the correlations are generally somewhat stronger with electricity consumption than with energy use. These correlations are consistent with the findings from more rigorous analyses that have clearly established that population and GDP are two of the main drivers of a variety of environmental impacts, including energy use and carbon dioxide emissions (Jorgenson & Clark, 2012; Rosa et al., 2015; York, 2007). Of course, the connections between economic and demographic trends are often complex. It is also noteworthy that declines in fertility, which change the age structure of the population, can lead to growth in GDP per capita, so that growth in energy use is not infrequently higher in nations with lower population growth rates than in those with higher population growth rates. For example, in both China and India, growth in GDP per capita, energy use, and electricity consumption have been higher in the twenty-first century than at the end of the twentieth century, even though their population growth rates have been lower (see Tables 9.2 and 9.3).

Although energy use and electricity consumption growth rates have been modest in affluent nations in this century, while they have been high in many less developed nations, China most notably, it is important to not lose sight of the stark inequalities that continue to exist. Cross-national inequalities are best understood by examining per capita levels. The United States has the highest level of energy use (nearly 7,000 kg oil equivalent [kgoe]) and electricity consumption (nearly 13,000 KWh) in per capita terms among the 20 nations/economies I examine here, and these levels are many times the levels in many other nations (see Table 9.1). Even though China and India have experienced high rates of growth, their levels of energy use and electricity consumption are still much lower than those in the United States in per capita terms. In 2013, US per capita energy use and electricity consumption were, respectively, 3.1 and 3.5 times those in China and 11.4 and 17.0 times those in India (calculated from the data presented in Table 9.1). There are contrasts that are even more extreme. For example, the United States used 32 times more energy per capita than Bangladesh and consumed 200 times more electricity per capita than Ethiopia in 2013 (see Table 9.1). So, even though patterns of growth have been changing around the world, the affluent nations of the world are still responsible for large shares, particularly in per capita terms, of global resource consumption.

It is also important to recognize that where energy is used is not the same as where the goods and services that come from that use are consumed. For decades, manufacturing has shifted from core, affluent nations to less developed nations, and the manufactured goods are to a large extent imported back into the affluent nations. In effect this is a process, sometimes called "off-shoring," whereby the pollution from industry is moved to poorer nations, allowing affluent nations to continue to maintain high levels of consumption without experiencing the concomitant environmental degradation within their borders. Ehrlich and Holdren (1971) famously referred to the erroneous assumption that the environmental impacts a nation causes are contained within its own national boundaries as the "Netherlands fallacy." This is in reference to the fact that wealthy nations like the Netherlands consume vastly more natural resources than can be produced within their borders by importing resources from elsewhere. For this reason, some analyses focus on "ecological footprints" of nations, which are estimates based on where goods and services are consumed, rather than where resources are extracted and/or transformed into final products (e.g., York, Rosa, & Dietz, 2003). Thus, we should not assume that rising energy use in poorer nations necessarily means that people in those nations are themselves consuming more for their own uses. This point suggests the importance of examining the global economy as a whole, rather than focusing on individual nations in isolation.

Efficiency and Renewables to the Rescue?

In light of the fact that global energy consumption has been growing at an accelerated pace in the twenty-first century, despite growing awareness of the large environmental impacts that stem from energy consumption (climate change, pollution, nuclear waste, etc.), a key question is whether there are processes in motion that might help to curtail energy consumption and/or reduce the impact of energy use. In particular, is there potential for improvements in energy efficiency and the expansion of clean, renewable energy sources to stem the tide of environmental degradation?

Although improvements in efficiency have been touted for a long time as holding the potential to reduce energy consumption while allowing the economy to continue to grow (Hawken, Lovins, & Lovins, 1999), the standard, and apparently paradoxical, historical trend since the dawn of the industrial era is of steady, simultaneous growth in energy consumption and energy efficiency (York & McGee, 2016). This counterintuitive relationship, where improvements in energy efficiency are associated with growth in energy consumption, has become known as the Jevons paradox, in reference to the nineteenth-century economist William Stanley Jevons, who first observed that improvements in the efficiency of steam engines were associated with increasing coal consumption, since efficiency gains made the reliance on coal-powered technologies more cost-effective (York & McGee, 2016). This paradoxical association between total consumption and efficiency has been observed on a variety of scales, from the energy use of specific technologies (e.g., steam engines) to the resource efficiency of national economies (York & McGee, 2016). For example, Grant et al. (2014) show that power plants in the United States with high thermal efficiency typically have higher carbon dioxide emissions.

The pattern characteristic of the Jevons paradox is common, although not universal, with respect to trends in energy consumption and energy efficiency in national economies. The energy efficiency of national economies is typically measured as economic output (GDP) per unit of energy consumption. Instead of efficiency, it is common to focus on the energy intensity of economies, where intensity is simply the inverse of efficiency (i.e., intensity is units of energy consumed per unit of economic output). Thus, declining intensity corresponds with rising efficiency. The Jevons paradox can be seen in energy trends in the world as a whole in recent years. Between 1990 and 2013, the energy intensity of the global economy declined (i.e., energy efficiency improved) by 18%, while total and per capita energy use grew by 55% and 14%, respectively, and the correlation between energy intensity and per capita energy use is –.746 ($N = 24$, p <.05, two-tailed test). The trends in China have had a substantial effect on the global pattern. From 1990 to 2013 in China, total and per capita energy use increased by nearly 250% and 190%, respectively, while energy intensity declined by over 60% (see Figure 9.1). Stated another way, over a period of less than a quarter century, per capita energy use in China increased by nearly a factor of 3, while energy intensity declined by close to a factor of 3—that is, China had a dramatic improvement in energy efficiency and yet at the same time its energy consumption grew explosively. The correlation in China between efficiency and per capita consumption, at –.734 ($N = 24$, p <.05, two-tailed test), is very similar to that for the world as a whole.

These close correlations, of course, do not necessarily mean the connection is directly causal, but they do suggest that efficiency/intensity is not a good indicator of energy conservation or environmental performance. There are likely multiple processes that explain the Jevons paradox, and these processes likely vary over time and across different

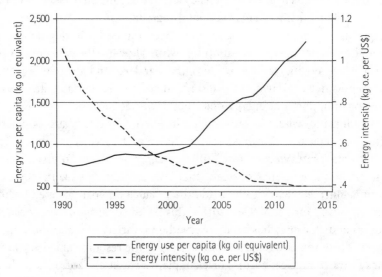

FIGURE 9.1 Trends in energy use per capita (kg of oil equivalent) and energy intensity (energy use in kg of oil equivalent per US$ inflation adjusted to year 2010) in China, 1990–2013.

circumstances. In a basic mathematical sense, this pattern emerges due to different growth rates in GDP and energy use. If energy use is growing, but GDP is growing faster, intensity is declining in parallel with expanding energy use. This highlights the fact that declining intensity (i.e., rising efficiency) does not necessarily imply a trend toward absolute reductions in energy use. It is important to note, of course, that the pattern in China, although common around the world, is not seen everywhere. Japan provides a clear example, where from 1990 to 2013 energy intensity and per capita energy use tracked each other fairly closely (see Figure 9.2) and were positively correlated at .652 (N = 24, p <.05, two-tailed test). A key point to take from these patterns is that intensity/efficiency tells us little about total or per capita energy use, and we should not assume that improvements in efficiency are necessarily indicative of a "greening" of the economy.

The quantity of energy consumed is, of course, not the only aspect of energy use that is of interest. The composition of energy production is obviously very important as well. Given their contribution to global climate change, fossil fuels are an especially problematic energy source, and there is understandably widespread interest in shifting energy production to non-carbon and renewable energy sources. Here I focus on the electrical sector, since that is where non-fossil fuel sources have the greatest potential to be used, and I examine trends in four sources of electricity production: fossil fuels, nuclear, hydro, and non-hydro renewables (henceforward, I'll refer to the latter simply as "renewables"). Renewables have expanded dramatically in recent years, accelerating in the twenty-first century. From 1990 to 2001, worldwide electricity production from renewables grew more than 40%, from about 160 TWh to 230 TWH, but by 2013 it had reached roughly 1,300 TWh, more than five times what it was in 2001. However, despite this rapid growth, (non-hydro) renewables provided little more than 5% of

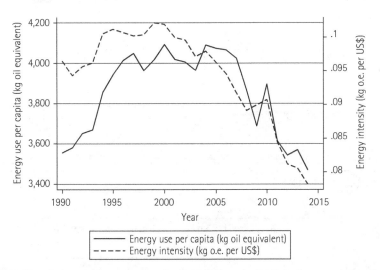

FIGURE 9.2 Trends in energy use per capita (kg of oil equivalent) and energy intensity (energy use in kg of oil equivalent per US$ inflation adjusted to year 2010) in Japan, 1990–2013.

world electricity production in 2013 (although this is up from about 1.5% in 2001) (see Figure 9.3).

The rise in renewables has failed to suppress fossil fuel use. In fact, the share of world electricity that comes from fossil fuel sources *increased* in the twenty-first century, from 64% in 2001 to over 66% in 2013 (see Figure 9.3), and this represents a large increase in absolute terms (over 50% growth) since, as I noted earlier, total electricity consumption grew substantially over this period. The persistence of fossil fuel use is consistent with York's (2012) finding that non-fossil energy sources do not effectively displace fossil fuel sources, but rather to a substantial degree are added to them, rather than replacing them. If anything, it appears that renewables were more prone to take the place of nuclear energy, which fell from about 17% of world electricity production in 2001 (which is approximately the same share it had throughout the 1990s), to less than 11% in 2013 (see Figure 9.3). This drop in the percentage of electricity production does not indicate that nuclear electricity generation declined markedly, but rather it remained approximately constant over this period, while production from other energy sources grew. Hydroelectric power grew at roughly the same pace as total electricity production, retaining approximately the same share (around 16%) of world electricity production throughout the beginning of the twenty-first century (see Figure 9.3).

Despite the rapid growth in renewables, it does not appear that the world is on a trend away from dirty energy. In fact, not only do fossil fuels remain the dominant

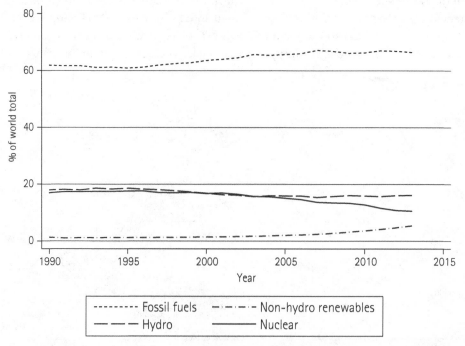

FIGURE 9.3 Sources of world electricity production, 1990–2013.

energy source in the world, the impacts associated with their extraction appear to be escalating. Davidson and Andrews (2013) observe that the "ecological footprint" of energy extraction has increased since the mid-twentieth century. Because the most easily accessible and highest-grade resources are typically extracted first, as time goes on the exploitation of more "extreme" forms of energy becomes necessary to maintain growing energy consumption. For example, increasing amounts of oil come from tar sands, which are particularly energy intensive to extract, there has been a rise in mountaintop-removal coal mining, which devastates ecosystems, and there is more offshore, ocean-floor oil drilling (Bell, 2014). Technological advances in the fossil-fuel industry, such as high-volume hydraulic fracturing ("fracking"), have allowed for more unconventional gas and oil development, but there are high environmental costs associated with these new technologies, especially fracking, including pollution of groundwater, leaks of methane (a more potent greenhouse gas than carbon dioxide), and increases in earthquakes (Ladd, 2017). Thus, there does not seem to be a general overall trend to cleaner energy.

It is also worth noting that even renewable energy sources have substantial environmental impacts (Sovacool & Dworkin, 2014; Zehner, 2012). For example, hydroelectric dams destroy river ecosystems and can increase methane emissions, wind turbines require a substantial amount of material to manufacture and they (and the access roads and other infrastructure that goes with them) take up land, and the manufacture of solar panels requires a lot of energy and produces a substantial amount of toxic waste. There is no unproblematic energy source, which highlights the importance of total amounts of energy consumption.

Conclusion

In general terms, the trends and patterns discussed here can be summarized in four main points. First, energy use and electricity consumption continue to rise around the world, and the rates of growth are higher in the twenty-first century than they were at the end of the twentieth century, even following the onset of the global recession in 2008. Second, in recent years rates of growth in energy use and electricity consumption declined in the most affluent nations and accelerated in some developing nations, most notably China and India. This has led to a major geographic shift in the locations where energy resources are consumed. Third, the energy efficiency of the global economy and that of many nations has generally improved steadily in recent decades, sometimes quite dramatically, but this typically has not led to noticeable suppression of energy consumption in most nations. Fourth, energy production from renewable energy sources has grown rapidly worldwide in the twenty-first century, but it has not substantially displaced fossil fuels, the production of which is in fact on the rise, in part due to new extraction technologies.

Note

1. All of the data presented here come from (or were calculated using) the World Development Indicators online DataBank (World Bank 2016). The energy and electricity data originate from the International Energy Agency, and the population and GDP per capita (measured in US$ inflation adjusted to the year 2010) data are World Bank estimates. Electricity consumption measures the production of power plants (including heat), less transmission, distribution, and transformation losses, from primary sources. Energy use measures all forms of primary energy before transformation to other end-use fuels (such as electricity and refined petroleum products). A notional thermal efficiency of 33% is assumed for converting nuclear electricity into oil equivalents and 100% efficiency for converting hydroelectric power.

References

Bell, S. E. (2014). Energy, society, and the environment. In K. A. Gould & T. L. Lewis (Eds.), *Twenty lessons in environmental sociology* (2nd ed., pp. 137–158). Oxford University Press.

Davidson, D., & Andrews, J. (2013). Not all about consumption. *Science, 339*, 1286–1287.

Ehrlich, P., & Holdren, J. (1971). Impact of population growth. *Science, 171*, 1212–1217.

Grant, D., Bergstrand, K. J., Running, K., & York, R. (2014). A sustainable 'building block'? The paradoxical effects of thermal efficiency on U.S. power plants' CO_2 emissions. *Energy Policy, 75*, 398–402.

Hawken, P., Lovins, A., & Lovins, L. H. (1999). *Natural capitalism: Creating the next industrial revolution.* New York: Little, Brown.

Jorgenson, A. K. & Clark, B. (2012). Are the economy and the environment decoupling? A comparative international study, 1960–2005. *American Journal of Sociology, 18*(1), 1–44.

Ladd, A. E. (Ed.). (2017). *Fractured communities: Risk, impacts, and protest against hydraulic fracking in U.S. shale regions.* New Brunswick, NJ: Rutgers University Press.

Mazur, A. (2013). *Energy and electricity in industrial nations: The sociology and technology of energy.* London: Earthscan.

Rosa, E. A., Rudel, T. K., York, R., Jorgenson, A. K., & Dietz, T. (2015). The human (anthropogenic) driving forces of global climate change. In R. E. Dunlap and R. J. Brulle (Eds.), *Climate change and society: Sociological perspectives* (pp. 47–91). New York: Oxford University Press.

Smil, V. (1994). *Energy in world history.* Boulder, CO: Westview.

Sovacool, B. K., & Dworkin, M. H. (2014). *Global energy justice: Problems, principles, and practices.* Cambridge: Cambridge University Press.

World Bank. (2016). *World development indicators.* Retrieved from http://databank.worldbank .org/data/reports.aspx?source=world-development-indicators

York, R., & McGee, J. A. (2016). Understanding the Jevons paradox. *Environmental Sociology, 2*(1), 77–87.

York, R. (2012). Do alternative energy sources displace fossil fuels? *Nature Climate Change, 2*(6), 441–443.

York, R. (2007). Demographic trends and energy consumption in European Union Nations, 1960–2025. *Social Science Research, 36*(3), 855–872.

York, R., Rosa, E. A., & Dietz, T. (2003). Footprints on the Earth: The environmental consequences of modernity. *American Sociological Review, 68*(2), 279–300.

Zehner, O. (2012). *Green illusions: The dirty secrets of clean energy and the future of environmentalism.* Lincoln: University of Nebraska Press.

CHAPTER 10

··

SHIFTS IN ENERGY CONSUMPTION DRIVEN BY URBANIZATION

··

PERRY SADORSKY

INTRODUCTION

··

> Regardless of the source, energy is a major factor for development. It is
> needed for transport, industrial and commercial activities, buildings and
> infrastructure, water distribution, and food production. Most of these ac-
> tivities take place in or around cities, which are on average responsible for
> more than 75% of a country's Gross Domestic Product (GDP) and there-
> fore the main engines of global economic growth. To run their activities,
> cities require an uninterrupted supply of energy. They consume about 75%
> of global primary energy and emit between 50 and 60% of the world's total
> greenhouse gases. (http://unhabitat.org/urban-themes/energy/)

THE year 2007 marked an important milestone as, for the first time in history, the
world's urban population passed 50% (United Nations, Department of Economic and
Social Affairs, 2014). This was a dramatic increase from the 1950s, when only one-third
of the world's population lived in urban areas. Furthermore, it is expected that by 2050,
two-thirds of the world's population will live in urban centers. This increase in urbanization brings new opportunities and new challenges with respect to business, society, and
the economy, as increases in urbanization are associated with higher economic growth
and greater economic development (Beall & Fox, 2009; Henderson, 2010). One particular area of interest is how urbanization (broadly defined as the percentage of the population living in urban areas) affects energy consumption. This is of particular concern
for emerging economies because the greatest increase in urbanization is coming from
emerging economies. If urbanization leads to greater energy consumption or less energy

efficiency, then questions arise concerning how future energy needs are going to be met. It is also the case that the impact of urbanization on energy consumption is likely have a negative impact on the natural environment as long as fossil fuel is the primary energy source. Since the principal emission from the burning of fossil fuels is carbon dioxide (CO_2), the impact of urbanization on energy consumption will have impacts on policies designed to curb greenhouse gas emissions. If urbanization leads to reductions in energy consumption or at least increases in energy efficiency, then there will be a lesser overall impact on future energy needs and the natural environment. The purpose of this chapter is to review the existing literature on the relationship between urbanization and energy consumption at the macro level and provide some directions for future research.

This chapter is organized as follows. The next sections set out the conceptual framework and some empirical observations on the relationship between energy consumption and urbanization. These are followed by sections that provide a more detailed review of the empirical evidence linking energy consumption with urbanization. The chapter concludes with observations concerning some limitations from existing empirical studies, suggestions for future research, and policy implications.

CONCEPTUAL FRAMEWORK FOR HOW URBANIZATION AFFECTS ENERGY CONSUMPTION

Conceptually there are several channels by which urbanization can impact energy use (Jones, 1989, 1991; Madlener & Sunak, 2011; Parikh & Shukla, 1995; Sadorsky 2014a, 2013). The production channel refers to the impact that urbanization has on production through the concentration of economic activity. With increases in urbanization, the production of economic output shifts from less energy-intensive agriculture to more energy-intensive manufacturing, resulting in an increase in energy use. Urban centers also offer economies of scale in production, which can help to reduce energy use and energy intensity. A further shift from a manufacturing-based economy to a service-based economy will lower energy intensity. In the United States, for example, energy consumption per real dollar of GDP is currently 58% lower than it was in 1950 (US Energy Information Agency, 2013). This decline in energy intensity occurred at a time of rising urbanization and falling industrialization. Urbanization in the United States in 1950 was 64%, while today it is 81%. Moreover, the percentage of US workers employed in industrial jobs peaked at 35% in 1950, while today it is 20%. Second, urbanization creates a transportation channel as raw materials and food are transported into the urban manufacturing center and the resulting manufactured goods are transported to other destinations. This increase in transportation activity increases the demand for energy. Properly designed urban centers with a well-functioning mass transit can offset some of the increased demand for transportation fuel if commuters take mass transit rather than driving their own car. Third, there is an infrastructure channel as growing cities build up their infrastructure. The construction of new infrastructure is energy intensive, but once built, modern infrastructure can be more energy efficient and environmentally sustainable than older infrastructure if newer technology is used to operate the infrastructure and buildings are LEEDS certified. (Leadership in Energy and Environmental Design [LEED] is a green building-rating system used in 150 countries around the world.) Fourth, there is a consumer demand channel. Urban centers are wealthier than rural areas, and consumption patterns change as urban consumers become wealthier and use more energy-intensive products like air conditioning, cars, and refrigerators. In summary, urbanization leads to more economic activity and energy use. Economies of scale and energy-efficient transportation and infrastructure can reduce energy use, which makes it difficult to predict what the overall impact of urbanization is on energy intensity.

The relationship between energy use and urbanization also plays a vital role in the historical literature on the rise and fall of great civilizations because great civilizations are enormous consumers of energy. The rise and fall of the Roman Empire provides a good example of how the energy needs of great empires can lead to their collapse (Rifkin, 2002). Roman conquests in Macedonia (167 BC), Syria (63 BC), and Gaul (52 BC) were very successful and brought the Romans vast riches in the form of minerals, treasure, cropland, forests, and slave labor. These riches created a flow of available energy into the Empire. The establishment of the Roman province of Egypt (30 BC) represented the end of the expansionary period of the Roman Empire. Egypt had a highly developed urban economy and was a major producer of grain. After defeats by the Germans, the Roman Empire transformed from a conquest-based empire to a colonizing empire; at this point, the Roman Empire started to experience the effects of the second law of thermodynamics (energy can only be changed from usable to non-usable). With no new sources of energy, Rome had to find new ways to fund basic services. The fall of the Roman Empire is often attributed to many factors, including the decadence of the ruling class, corruption, exploitation of the people, and military defeat by the Germanic tribes. All of these factors were important, as was the decline in energy. At the beginning of the Roman Empire, Italy and the surrounding Mediterranean regions were heavily forested. The trees were cut down and the lumber sold, and the deforested land was used to grow crops and graze livestock. At first the new cropland was fertile and produced high yields. Later, over-grazing and over-farming reduced crop yields. The importance of agriculture to the Roman Empire cannot be underestimated. During the later period of the Roman Empire, agriculture provided 90% of government revenue. With increasing urbanization, fewer people were left to work the land, and in some of the more distant provinces large amounts of farmland were abandoned as people moved to cities. Land still being farmed experienced diminishing returns as overworked soil produced declining yields. Roman rulers responded by imposing crippling taxes on agriculture in order to keep up the tax base. In the early fourth century, serfdom was created to bind peasants to the land and prevent further movement of people. Eventually Rome became a city without enough food to feed the people. Marauding invaders, lack of food, decaying infrastructure, and bad decision-making marked the last days of the Roman Empire. Rome, a city that was once home to over one million people, had fewer than 30,000 in the sixth century.[1]

A First Look at the Empirical Relationship Between Energy Consumption and Urbanization

As a useful starting point, scatter plots and regression analysis are used to examine the relationship between energy use and urbanization for a large group of countries. First, it is important to provide some definitions regarding terminology. There are differences between *energy consumption* and *energy demand*. This distinction is the most clear in the case of electricity. For example, electricity consumption is measured in kilowatt hours (kWh). Electricity consumption is the total amount of electricity used (a stock). Electricity demand, measured in kilowatts (kW), is the immediate rate of consumption (a flow). For example, one 100-Watt light bulb burning for 10 hours consumes one kWh. By comparison, 10 100-Watt light bulbs burning for one hour consume one kWh. In both cases, the energy consumption is one kWh. In the second case, however, the demand is 10 times greater. Many socioeconomic macro empirical studies employ energy use data from the World Bank. According to the World Bank, energy use is primary energy before transformation to other end-use fuels. This is equal to indigenous production plus imports and stock changes, minus exports and fuels supplied to ships and aircraft engaged in international transport. The World Bank measures energy use in kilogram of oil equivalent per capita.

Country-level data on energy use (kg of oil equivalent per capita) and urbanization (% of the population living in urban areas) are collected from the World Bank World Development Indicators (World Bank, 2016). Scatter plots and regression lines for the years 1990 and 2010 are shown in Figures 10.1 and 10.2, respectively. Energy consumption per capita is expressed in natural logs. For both years, there is a positive correlation between energy use per capita and urbanization. Linear regression analysis is used to determine the strength of this relationship. In 1990, a one-unit increase in urbanization is associated with a 3.7% increase in energy use per capita (Table 10.1). By comparison, in 2010, a one-unit increase in urbanization is associated with a 3.4% increase in energy use per capita. The estimated coefficient on urbanization is positive, statistically significant, and very similar in magnitude across the two years. The R^2 values show a slightly higher fit for the 1990 results. The scatter plots and regression results provide convincing evidence for a positive relationship between energy use and urbanization.

It is also useful to conduct this type of analysis for different groupings of countries. For example, how does the relationship between energy consumption and urbanization

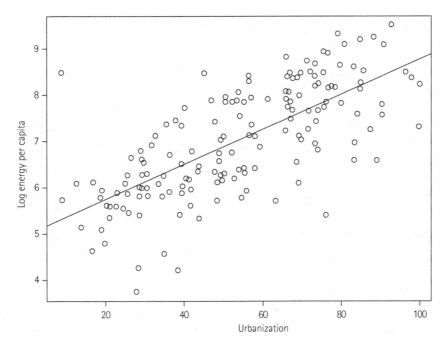

FIGURE 10.1 The relationship between energy use and urbanization, 1990 (all countries).

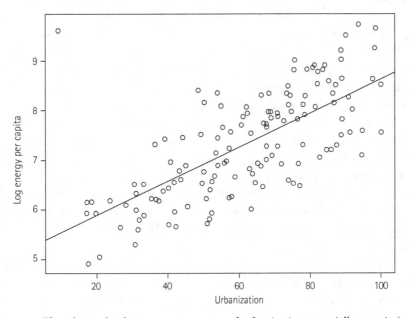

FIGURE 10.2 The relationship between energy use and urbanization, 2010 (all countries).

Table 10.1 Regression Results of Log Energy Use on Urbanization

	All		High Income		Not High Income	
	1990	2010	1990	2010	1990	2010
Const	4.993	5.220	7.591	8.040	5.079	5.401
	(25.428)	(17.762)	(13.239)	(6.410)	(27.343)	(32.751)
Urban	0.037	0.034	0.009	0.005	0.031	0.025
	(11.190)	(7.854)	(1.172)	(0.357)	(7.578)	(8.908)
R^2	0.498	0.484	0.073	0.025	0.345	0.410
Obs	160	138	48	46	112	92

Heteroskedasticity robust *t* statistics are in parentheses. The number of observations denotes the number of countries. Const refers to the intercept term, Urban refers to the urbanization variable, and Obs refers to the number of observations.

vary between high-income countries and non-high-income countries? High-income countries are classified according to the World Bank's income classification of high-income Organisation of Economic Co-operation and Development (OECD) countries or high-income non-OECD countries. The impact of urbanization on energy consumption is small, with estimated coefficients between 0.005 and 0.009 (Table 10.1). Also notice that these estimated coefficients are positive but statistically insignificant. By comparison, the estimated coefficient on the urbanization variable is positive and statistically significant for non-high-income countries. A one-unit increase in urbanization increases per capita energy consumption in non-high-income countries by 3.1% in 1990 and 2.5% in 2010. The impact of urbanization on energy consumption is much larger for non-high income countries. Plots of these relationships are shown in Figures 10.3–10.6.

For completeness, regression results of log energy on log urbanization are also presented (Table 10.2). This is desirable because the estimated coefficient on the log urbanization variable can be interpreted as an elasticity, which is how most existing empirical studies present results. For the data set using all of the countries, a 1% increase in urbanization leads to a 1.57% increase in per capita energy consumption in 1990 and a 1.49% increase in per capital energy consumption in 2010 (Table 10.2). For the high-income countries, notice that the estimated coefficient on the log urbanization variable is statistically insignificant in both 1990 and 2010. For the non-high-income countries, the estimated coefficient on the log urbanization variable is positive and statistically significant in both 1990 and 2010.

The results from Tables 10.1 and 10.2 indicate that the strongest evidence for urbanization affecting energy consumption comes from the non-high-income countries. This seems reasonable because urbanization in high-income countries does not change

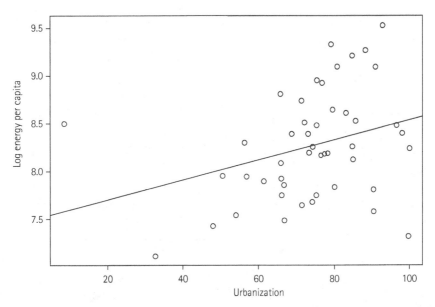

FIGURE 10.3 The relationship between energy use and urbanization, 1990 (high-income countries).

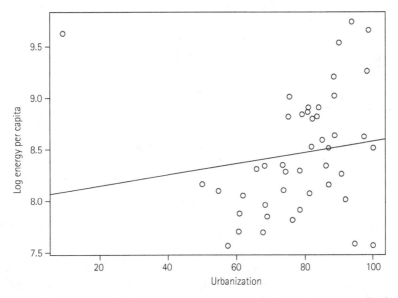

FIGURE 10.4 The relationship between energy use and urbanization, 2010 (high-income countries).

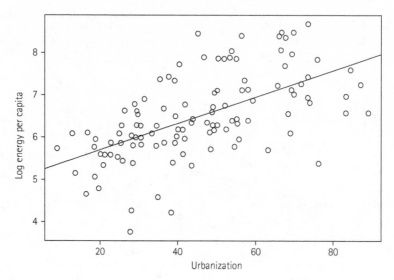

FIGURE 10.5 The relationship between energy use and urbanization, 1990 (not high-income countries).

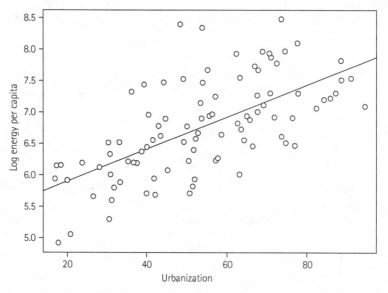

FIGURE 10.6 The relationship between energy use and urbanization, 2010 (not high-income countries).

very much. It is also important to point out that these results are for simple bivariate regressions, which provide measures of correlation between per capita energy consumption and urbanization but do not control for other important factors like income and industrialization. The effect of controlling for these other factors would be to reduce the magnitude of the estimated urbanization coefficient.

Table 10.2 Regression Results of Log Energy Use on Log Urbanization

	All		High Income		Not High Income	
	1990	2010	1990	2010	1990	2010
Const	0.920	1.309	7.107	8.838	1.823	2.063
	(0.987)	(0.761)	(1.930)	(1.235)	(2.929)	(3.882)
Log urban	1.572	1.490	0.269	-0.085	1.256	1.205
	(6.727)	(3.585)	(0.315)	(-0.052)	(7.476)	(8.911)
R^2	0.439	0.380	0.032	0.003	0.345	0.424
Obs	160	138	48	46	112	92

Heteroskedasticity robust t statistics are in parentheses. The number of observations denotes the number of countries. Const refers to the intercept term, Log urban refers to the natural log of the urbanization variable, and Obs refers to the number of observations.

EMPIRICAL EVIDENCE ON THE IMPACT OF URBANIZATION ON ENERGY CONSUMPTION

Most of the economic and sociological empirical research on the impact of urbanization on energy consumption uses regression-based statistical techniques. Common approaches are to analyze a cross section of data for many countries, a time series analysis for one country, or a panel data analysis for a group of countries. When conducting empirical analysis, differences between research findings can arise because of differences in data, empirical approach, or choice of country or region under study. In the case of research investigating the impact of urbanization on energy consumption, most of the evidence points to a positive relationship between energy consumption and urbanization, and the results tend to be strongest for developing economies.

Jones (1989, 1991) provides some of the earliest evidence on the impact of urbanization on energy use. Jones (1989) studies the impact of urbanization on energy use for a cross section of 59 developing countries. Several measures of energy use are considered, including energy use per capita and energy per dollar of GDP. Energy use is further classified as *modern* or *total*, with *modern* referring to commercially traded fossil fuels, and *total* including traditional fuels like wood and biomass along with modern fuels. Explanatory variables include income, industrialization, and urbanization. Using data for 1980, he finds urbanization elasticities ranging between 0.30 and 0.48. Jones (1991) uses a similar data set to investigate the impact of urbanization on energy intensity and finds an urbanization elasticity of 0.35. Like the papers by Jones (1989, 1991), the 1995 work by Parikh and Shukla is also a seminal paper on the relationship between energy use and urbanization. Parikh and Shukla (1995) study the impact of urbanization on energy consumption for a pooled data set of developed and developing countries over the period 1965–1987. They find that urbanization elasticities range between 0.28 and 0.47.

Burney (1995) uses data from 1990 on 93 countries to investigate the impact of socio-economic variables on electricity consumption. Using ordinary least squares (OLS) and random coefficients (RC) techniques, he finds that urbanization has a positive impact on electricity consumption. Larivière and Lafrance (1999) investigate the relationship between per capita electricity consumption and urban density for cities in the province of Quebec, Canada. Using data for the year 1991, they find that electricity consumption per capita is lower in high-density cities. Liddle (2004) investigates the impact of urbanization and population density on per capita road transportation energy use. He finds that both urbanization and population density have a negative impact on per capita road transportation energy use. Holtedahl and Joutz (2004) use vector error correction models (VECMs) to estimate residential electricity demand in Taiwan between 1955 and 1995 as a function of income, price, urbanization, weather, and oil prices. They argue that urbanization is a useful variable to include in the analysis because it can capture non-income effects. The estimated coefficient on urbanization is positive and statistically significant in both the short and long run.

York (2007a) uses a STIRPAT (STochastic Impacts by Regression on Population, Affluence, and Technology) model to analyze the impacts of population and urbanization on energy consumption in 14 European Union countries. The data set covers the period 1960–2000, and estimation is by panel-corrected standard errors (PCSE). Urbanization and population both have positive and statistically significant impacts on energy consumption. The urbanization elasticity is around 0.5, while the population elasticity is around 2.0. Energy consumption projections to 2025 show that an expected decline in population growth will reduce future EU energy consumption. York (2007b) uses panel regression to estimate the impact of socioeconomic factors on energy production for 14 Southeast Asian countries. Socioeconomic factors like economic development, urbanization, and export intensity each contribute to higher energy production.

Mishra et al. (2009) use panel regression techniques to study the relationship between energy consumption and other important variables like GDP and urbanization for nine Pacific Island countries over the period 1980–2005. They find that urbanization has a negative impact on energy use in New Caledonia. For Fiji, French Polynesia, Samoa, and Tonga, urbanization has a positive impact on energy use. Jorgenson et al. (2010) use first difference OLS techniques to model the relationship between energy consumption and urbanization for a panel of 57 developed countries over the period 1990–2005. They find that the growth in urbanization has a positive and significant impact on energy-demand growth. They also find a negative association between energy demand and the percentage of the population living in slums.

Poumanyvong and Kaneko (2010) study the impact of urbanization on energy use for a panel of 99 countries for the years 1975–2005. Using panel regression techniques, they find the impact of urbanization on energy use varies by income group. They find that for low-income groups, urbanization decreases energy use. For middle- and high-income groups, urbanization increases energy use.

Adom et al. (2012) model the impact of income, industrialization, and urbanization on electricity demand in Ghana. They estimate the model using autoregressive distributed lag (ARDL) techniques on data for 1975–2005. They find that urbanization has a positive and significant impact on electricity demand in the short and long run. Fang et al. (2012) use a STIRPAT model to test the effect of energy service company activities on energy use. First difference and generalized method of moment (GMM) techniques are applied to a data set of 94 countries over the period 1981–2007; they find that urbanization has a slight negative impact on total primary energy use for high-income countries and a statistically insignificant impact on energy use for low-income countries. Using integrated assessment models, Krey et al. (2012) find that for the case of China and India, the direct relationship between residential energy demand and urbanization is not very strong. The impact of urbanization on energy use is indirectly affected by the relationship between labor productivity and economic growth. Using general equilibrium models, O'Neill et al. (2012) also find that the direct impact of urbanization on energy use is not very strong. The impact of urbanization on energy use is indirectly affected by the relationship between labor supply and economic growth. Poumanyvong et al. (2012) use a STIRPAT model to determine the impact of income, population, industrialization, and urbanization on national transport and road energy use for a panel of 92 countries covering the period 1975–2005. Models are estimated using fixed effects. They find that urbanization has a positive and significant impact on road energy use. Urbanization elasticities are slightly larger than one for high-income countries, and less than one for low- and middle-income countries.

Sadorsky (2013) investigates the impact of urbanization and industrialization on energy intensity using an unbalanced panel of 76 developing economies over the period 1980–2010. Static and dynamic models are estimated using several different econometric approaches that allow for cross-sectional dependence. Homogeneous parameter estimates are obtained from pooled ordinary least squares (POLS) and fixed effects (FE) panel regression techniques. Heterogeneous parameter estimates are obtained from mean group (MG) estimators (Pesaran & Smith, 1995) common correlated effects mean group (CCEMG) estimators (Pesaran, 2006) and augmented mean group (AMG) estimators (Eberhardt & Bond, 2009). Long-run income elasticities are in the range of −0.45% to −0.35%, while long-run industrialization elasticities are in the range of 0.07 to 0.12. Long-run urbanization elasticities are in the range of −0.02 to 2.11, indicating considerable variability across different estimation techniques. The main conclusion is that while the income and industrialization elasticities are fairly precisely estimated, the impact of urbanization on energy intensity is mostly positive but somewhat mixed. Reductions in energy intensity can occur as long as the negative impact of income on energy intensity is large enough to overcome the positive impacts on energy intensity from industrialization and urbanization.

Sadorsky (2014a) uses pooled mean group estimators to study the impact of urbanization and industrialization on per capita energy consumption for a panel of 18 emerging economies. These countries are chosen from the Morgan Stanley Capital International (MSCI) list of emerging countries. The data set is an unbalanced panel covering the years 1971–2008. In the long-run income and industry structure, both have positive and statistically significant impacts on energy consumption, while urbanization has a negative and significant impact. This paper is one of the few to find that urbanization has a negative and statistically significant impact on per capita energy consumption.

Salim and Shafiei (2014) analyze the impact of urbanization on renewable and nonrenewable energy consumption for a panel of OECD countries covering the period 1980–2011. They use panel co-integration and panel causality methods to analyze the relationship between urbanization and energy consumption. Population and urbanization each have positive and statistically significant long-run impacts on non-renewable energy consumption. Urbanization has a positive but insignificant impact on renewable energy consumption, while population has a positive and statistically significant impact. Wang (2014) uses decomposition analysis on annual data from 1980 to 2011 to determine the impact of urbanization on residential energy consumption and production energy consumption for China. Residential energy consumption grows slower in urban areas compared with rural areas.

Creutzig et al. (2015) use a unique data set of 274 cities to look at how socioeconomic factors affect city energy use. Economic activity and heating degree days have positive impacts on energy use and greenhouse gas (GHG) emissions, while population density and fuel prices each have negative impacts. They find that economic activity, transport costs, geographic factors, and urban form account for 35% of urban direct energy use, 88% of urban transport energy use, and 70% of GHG emissions. If current urban trends continue, urban energy use will triple between 2005 (240 EJ) and 2050 (730 EJ). Reducing greenhouse gas emissions will require carefully planned policies on urban planning and transportation. For mature affluent cities, compact urban form and higher gasoline prices can help to reduce residential and transport energy use. For cities in developing countries, compact urban form and transport planning can help to increase urban density and provide alternatives to high-carbon travel patterns.

Kennedy et al. (2015) study the energy and material flows of 27 megacities. Megacities are cities with greater area populations in excess of 10 million people. These 27 megacities accounted for 460 million people in 2010, which corresponds to 6.7% of global population. The combined GDP of these megacities was 14.6% of global GDP, while these megacities accounted for 12.6% of global waste production. The total energy consumption of the 27 megacities accounted for 6.7% of global energy consumption, which is the same as the percentage of the world's population living in the 27 megacities. One of the important findings of this study is that electricity use is strongly correlated with building floor area, and this helps to explain the correlation between per capita electricity use and urbanization.

Ma (2015) investigates the impact of urbanization on energy intensity for a panel of 30 Chinese provinces over the period 1986–2011. Models are estimated using panel regression techniques that accommodate cross-sectional dependence. Several measures of energy intensity are considered, including total energy intensity, coal energy intensity, and electricity energy intensity. In general, urbanization has a positive impact on energy intensity, although the effect is not always statistically significant.

Zhao and Wang (2015) use vector error-correction models (VECMs) on data spanning 1980 to 2012 to study the relationship between urbanization and energy consumption in China. They find evidence of a long-run equilibrium relationship between energy consumption, urbanization, and GDP. In the long run, a 1% increase in urbanization will increase energy consumption by 0.50%. There is evidence of unidirectional Granger causality from urbanization to energy consumption.

Belloumi and Alshehry (2016) investigate the impact of urbanization on energy intensity in Saudi Arabia using data for the period 1971–2012. They find that energy intensity, income, industrialization, and urbanization are co-integrated (these variables form a long-run equilibrium). Urbanization has a positive impact on energy intensity in both the short and long run.

Rafiq et al. (2016), building on the work of Sadorsky (2013, 2014b), investigate the impact of urbanization and trade openness on energy intensity and CO_2 emissions in a panel of 22 rapidly urbanizing economies (Angola, Bangladesh, Costa Rica, China, Ghana, Ethiopia, Indonesia, India, Lebanon, Jordan, Mongolia, Malaysia, Namibia, Mozambique, Panama, Nigeria, Sudan, Singapore, Thailand, Tanzania, Zambia, and Vietnam). The annual data set covers the period 1980–2010. Models are estimated using several panel regression approaches that take into account cross-sectional dependence like MG, CCEMG, and AMG. Urbanization is found to have a positive and significant impact on energy intensity but an insignificant impact on CO_2 emissions. These results are consistent with those of Sadorsky (2013) for energy intensity and Sadorsky (2014b) for CO_2 emissions.

Shahbaz et al. (2016) study the impact of globalization on energy consumption in India. Recent co-integration techniques are applied to analyze the annual data over the period 1971–2012. Urbanization is also included in their analysis. They find a long-run equilibrium relationship between per capita energy consumption, per capita GDP, financial development, urbanization, and different measures of globalization. Urbanization is found to have a positive and statistically significant impact on Indian per capita energy consumption. Long-run urbanization elasticities range between 0.5 and 0.8.

Wang et al. (2016) use annual data for 1990 to 2012 to study the impact of urbanization on energy consumption in China. The analysis is conducted for the country as a whole as well as three main sub-areas. Urbanization is an important driver in increasing energy consumption, but the impact of urbanization on energy demand is not as strong as the effect of car ownership and economic development.

In summary, the empirical literature on the impact of urbanization on energy consumption is fairly consistent in showing that urbanization has a positive impact on energy consumption. Long-run urbanization elasticities are generally in the 0.5 to 1.0 range, indicating that a 1% increase in urbanization increases energy use by 0.5% to 1%. These results are reasonably robust to the choice of data set (time series, panel data, or cross section) and estimation technique (single equation methods or panel data methods).

TESTING FOR CAUSALITY BETWEEN ENERGY CONSUMPTION AND URBANIZATION

While much of the published research looks at the impact of urbanization on energy consumption, there is a related literature looking at the causal relationship between these two variables. More specifically, tests are conducted for Granger causality (Granger 1969). These are statistical tests to determine whether movements in one variable precede movements in another variable. If the interest is in testing Granger causality between two variables, say X and Y, then there are four possible outcomes: (1) X Granger causes Y; (2) Y Granger causes X; (3) bidirectional feedback between the two variables; or (4) neutrality (no finding of a Granger causal relationship). Many studies that test for Granger causality are solely focused on the outcome of the tests and not the size or magnitude of an individual effect.

With regard to the dynamic relationship between energy consumption and urbanization, the reasoning for how and why urbanization can affect energy consumption was set out in the conceptual section earlier in this chapter. What about the possibility of energy consumption affecting urbanization? Energy consumption can affect urbanization through rural-urban migration patterns. For example, energy demand associated with manufacturing can increase urbanization if higher paying jobs in urban areas attract rural residents (Liddle & Lung, 2014). Access to electricity in urban areas brings about a higher quality of life, which provides an incentive for people to move to urban areas.

Halicioglu (2007) uses autoregressive distributed lag (ADRL) and error correction model (ECM) methods to study the relationship between residential electricity consumption and urbanization in Turkey over the period 1968–2005. He finds no evidence of causality between electricity consumption and urbanization. Liu (2009) explores the relationship between urbanization and energy consumption in China using data for the years 1978–2008. Autoregressive distributed lag and factor decomposition methods are used to analyze the data. Evidence of Granger causality is found running from urbanization to energy consumption in both the short run and long run.

Hossain (2011) analyzes the dynamic relationship between CO_2 emissions, energy consumption, economic growth, trade, and urbanization for a panel of nine newly industrialized countries (Brazil, China, India, Malaysia, Mexico, Philippines, South Africa, Thailand, and Turkey). The data set covers the period 1971–2007, and models are estimated using panel regression techniques. While there is no evidence of long-run causality between any of the variables, there is evidence of some short-run causal relationships. In particular, there is evidence of a short-run causal relationship from economic growth and trade openness to CO_2 emissions, from economic growth to energy consumption, from trade openness to economic growth, from urbanization to economic growth, and from trade openness to urbanization.

Gam and Ben Rejeb (2012) investigate the dynamic relationship between electricity consumption and urbanization in Tunisia. Using Granger causality and ECM methods applied to data from 1976 to 2006, they find evidence of bivariate feedback between electricity consumption and urbanization. Michieka and Fletcher (2012) use the Toda and Yamamoto (1995) version of Granger causality to study the dynamic relationship between electricity production from coal sources and urbanization in China for the period 1971–2009. They find evidence of Granger causality from urbanization to electricity consumption.

Shahbaz and Lean (2012) use ADRL and Granger causality methods to test for causality between energy consumption and urbanization in Tunisia over the period 1971–2008. They find that energy consumption Granger causes urbanization. Al-mulali et al. (2013) test for Granger causality between per capita energy consumption and urbanization for 20 Middle East and North Africa (MENA) countries using data for the period 1980–2009. They find evidence of bidirectional feedback between energy consumption and urbanization. Solarin and Shahbaz (2013) use ADRL and Granger causality methods to investigate the dynamic relationship between per capita electricity consumption and urbanization in Angola for the years 1971–2009. They find evidence of bidirectional causality between electricity consumption and urbanization.

Liddle and Lung (2014) use recently developed panel regression techniques to test for Granger causality between electricity consumption and urbanization in panels classified as high-, middle-, and low-income countries. The data set covers the years 1971–2009. Results are further provided for total electricity consumption, as well as industrial and residential electricity consumption. The strongest results show causality running from electricity consumption to urbanization. They conclude that the employment and quality-of-life opportunities associated with access to electricity cause urbanization.

The literature on testing for causality between energy consumption and urbanization is somewhat mixed, with most papers finding a causal relationship from urbanization to energy consumption and some papers finding evidence of feedback. Some recent research has found evidence of a causal relationship running from electricity consumption to urbanization.

LIMITATIONS OF EXISTING EMPIRICAL STUDIES

There are a number of limitations of existing empirical studies. Research that focuses on the Granger causal relationship between energy consumption and urbanization is somewhat limited if no effort is made to provide relative magnitudes of the effect under study. Granger causality is a statistical concept that helps to determine whether movements in one variable occur before or after movements in a different variable. This type of analysis is useful for building predictive models, but in the energy and urbanization literature this is rarely done. Predictive modeling of the energy consumption and urbanization relationship is one area that could benefit from further research.

Many studies use STIRPAT models to investigate the impact of urbanization on energy consumption. This approach, which has been applied to time series data for individual countries or cross-section and time series data for groups of countries, is useful in determining the sign, magnitude, and statistical significance of the impact of urbanization on energy use. While new econometric techniques or data sets open up the possibility of future research, one area that is sadly lacking is the connection between empirical results and policy recommendations. Many empirical studies, after finding a positive and statistically significant estimated coefficient on the urbanization variable, conclude by stating that if left unchecked, urbanization is going to increase energy consumption. This is logically true but not very informative beyond stating the obvious. Given the global trend to increased urbanization, it is reasonable to rule out reducing urbanization as a viable means of reducing energy consumption. More research needs to be done for finding ways to reduce energy consumption or to encourage fuel switching in the face of increasing urbanization. Case studies, simulations, and benchmarking tools are ways to do this. Here a distinction needs to be made between developed countries and developing countries because developing countries face less carbon lock-in effects. Zhou et al. (2015), for example, have designed an Excel-based benchmarking tool to evaluate Chinese cities on their environmental performance. Siemens's Green City Index is another example of ranking cities according to their environmental sustainability (Siemens AG, 2012; Birch, 2015). The Green City Index collects data from 30 different indicators, which are assembled into main categories like CO_2 emissions, energy use, buildings, land use, transportation, water and sanitation, waste management, air quality, and environmental governance. To date, 120 cities around the world have been evaluated. The major regions of the world include Europe (Copenhagen, Stockholm, Oslo), Latin America (Curitiba), Asia (Singapore), North America (San Francisco, Vancouver, New York City), and Africa. For Europe and North America, the top three cities based on a numeric score are listed in parentheses. For the other regions, the cities listed as "well above average" are included in parentheses. Africa has no city that is classified as above average in the Green City Index.

While there is a literature looking at the impact of urbanization on energy use and energy intensity, there is much less known about how urbanization affects energy efficiency. Unlike energy use (kg of oil equivalent) or energy intensity (units of energy per units of GDP), energy efficiency is not directly measurable and must first be estimated. One way to conduct this type of analysis is to use analytical tools especially designed for efficiency estimation. For example, data envelope analysis (DEA) can be used to construct an energy efficiency score for each country, and then the impact of urbanization on these energy efficiency scores can be investigated. DEA is a non-parametric empirical approach that uses inputs and outputs of decision-making units (DMU) to construct efficiency scores showing how efficient the DMUs are at using inputs to produce outputs (Cooper, Seiford, & Tone, 2007).

Conclusions and Policy Implications

Urbanization and industrialization are two important concepts from modernization theory that affect the consumption of energy. Conceptually, urbanization can affect energy use through the production channel, the transportation channel, the infrastructure channel, and the consumer demand channel. The existing literature is fairly consistent in showing a strong positive relation from urbanization to energy consumption. Long-run urbanization elasticities are typically in the range of 0.5 to 1.0. There is also a smaller branch of research that shows support for the feedback hypothesis between energy consumption and urbanization. Under the feedback hypothesis, increases in urbanization increase energy consumption, and increases in energy consumption increase urbanization. There are a number of implications stemming from these results.

Urbanization in most developed countries has plateaued, which is important because the impact on energy consumption from any further urbanization is likely to be small. Even though urbanization in developed countries is unlikely to change much in the coming decades, there is still room for improvement over how urban centers in developed countries use energy.

It is important to point out that within developed countries there are variations in urbanization. Canada, France, and the United States, for example, each have urbanization around 80%. By comparison, German and Italy have urbanization around 75% and 70%, respectively. These values show that there is no tendency to long-run convergence in urbanization. For each country, urbanization will eventually reach a value that does not change, but these values will be different across countries. Developing countries, however, are going through rapid increases in urbanization. In the case of China, for example, urbanization was 20% in 1980 and 55% in 2015. In Nigeria, urbanization was 22% in 1980 and increased to 48% in 2015. For developing countries, greater urbanization is going to have a substantial impact on energy consumption. This brings about questions of securing a stable and dependable source of energy to meet future energy demand, and how to deal with current and future environmental concerns. Since most energy is supplied from fossil fuels, increased energy demand from urbanization is going to raise questions about how to deal with the CO_2 emissions released from the burning of fossil fuels.

Kovacevic (2016), for example, describes how changes in demographics and urbanization are going to affect spending patterns and energy use for years to come. The Unites States has 87 million millennials (aged 16–35 years), while China has five times as many (415 million). China's millennial population is larger than the combined working populations in Canada, the United States, and Western Europe. Chinese millennials have earned 107 million college degrees, which is much more than any previous generation. These well-educated millennials are looking forward to an increased quality of life from living comfortably in urban areas. This will increase the demand for energy-intensive products like homes, air conditioners, refrigerators, and automobiles. China is already the world's largest auto market, with 25 million automobiles sold in 2015. This is remarkably because in China only 22% of the population has a driver's license. This increase in quality of life is going to create a huge demand for energy. Air pollution, climate change, and technology are three forces shifting future energy needs toward green energy. Between 2014 and 2030, China is expected to build 1000 GW of green energy capacity. This will be equivalent to 90% of the current US electricity grid.

There are several ways by which cities can reduce their dependence on energy. The first step is for a city to introduce a comprehensive energy plan (CEP), supported in a nonpartisan and legal way, on how to make a city an environmentally sustainable city. The plan should involve all of the major stakeholders (individuals, business, government) and encourage public and private sponsorship. This is important so that targets and goals are not treated as short term but rather as long-run sustainable initiatives. The energy plan can be stand alone or part of a larger sustainable governance plan like what is used in constructing the Siemens Green City Index. The focus of a CEP should be on reducing energy consumption, reducing energy intensity, increasing renewable energy consumption, reducing CO_2 emissions, increasing mass transportation, and making buildings more energy efficient. Where ever possible, energy reduction, fuel switching (from fossil fuel to renewable), and energy efficiency should be encouraged. Consumers and producers should be given incentives to make these adjustments, in combination with government policy targeted at fuel switching from fossil fuels to renewables. Carbon taxes, although unpopular politically, could be very useful in encouraging fuel switching. Transportation and buildings are two areas that should be given priority in the CEP. A well-thought-out mass transit program can help to reduce energy consumption by getting commuters into buses and trains and encouraging ride sharing and carpooling. The goal is to get as many single-occupancy cars off the road as possible. Incentives to use more widespread adoption of electric cars should be done in accordance with a fuel-switching program for the generation of electricity. Incentives for commuters to use mass transit can come from higher fuel prices and road tolls applied to vehicles entering a city. Dedicated bike lanes into, out of, and around cities can also help commuters who want to use bicycles in a safe environment.

Rapid development in the adoption of electric cars will also have implications for the relationship between urbanization and energy consumption. Tesla, which is currently seen as the maker of sleek sporty electric cars, has ambitions to become an ecosystem provider of electric vehicles (cars, trucks, and buses), charging stations, solar rooftop power units, and batteries to store solar power. Essentially, Tesla wants to be a one-stop shopping center for the ecosystem lifestyle. Solar power rooftop units, an example of distributed energy, will allow consumers to generate some of their own electricity, which will reduce demand from the power grid. Solar-generated electricity not immediately consumed can be stored in batteries for later use. While solar rooftop units do not currently generate enough electricity to allow houses to be completely independent of the electricity grid, technology is changing quickly. In the future it may be possible for solar rooftop units to generate enough electricity to meet household needs. Cities can facilitate the adoption of these developments by encouraging the installation of solar rooftop units and ensuring access to power-charging stations for electric vehicles. Power-charging stations could be coupled with existing gasoline stations. In addition, some cities are already experimenting with self-driving electric taxis as a way to reduce CO_2 emissions and reduce traffic gridlock. In the future, car ownership in urban areas may actually decrease as individuals rely more on self-driving electric taxis connected to ride-sharing programs like Uber.

NOTE

1. More generally, Chew (2001) provides evidence on how urbanization and deforestation have led to the collapse or transformation of many great civilizations.

REFERENCES

Adom, P. K., Bekoe, W., & Akoena, S. K. K. (2012). Modelling aggregate domestic electricity demand in Ghana: An autoregressive distributed lag bounds cointegration approach. *Energy Policy, 42*, 530–537. doi:10.1016/j.enpol.2011.12.019

Al-mulali, U., Fereidouni, H. G., Lee, J. Y. M., & Sab, C. N. B. C. (2013). Exploring the relationship between urbanization, energy consumption, and CO2 emission in MENA countries. *Renewable and Sustainable Energy Reviews, 23*, 107–112. doi:10.1016/j.rser.2013.02.041

Beall, J., & Fox, S. (2009). *Cities and development*. New York: Routledge.

Belloumi, M., & Alshehry, A. (2016). The impact of urbanization on energy intensity in Saudi Arabia. *Sustainability, 8*(4), 375. doi:10.3390/su8040375

Birch, H. (2015). Where is the world's greenest city? | Cities | The Guardian. *The Guardian*. Retrieved from https://www.theguardian.com/cities/2015/apr/02/where-is-the-worlds -greenest-city-ecofriendly

Burney, N. A. (1995). Socioeconomic development and electricity consumption a cross-country analysis using the random coefficient method. *Energy Economics, 17*(3), 185–195. doi:10.1016/0140-9883(95)00012-J

Chew, S. C. (2001). *World ecological degradation: Accumulation, urbanization, and deforestation, 3000BC–AD2000*. Walnut Creek, CA: AltaMira Press.

Cooper, W., Seiford, L., & Tone, K. (2007). *Data envelopment analysis: A comprehensive text with models, applications, references and DEA-solver software*. Dordrecht: Springer.

Creutzig, F., Baiocchi, G., Bierkandt, R., Pichler, P.-P., & Seto, K. C. (2015). Global typology of urban energy use and potentials for an urbanization mitigation wedge. *Proceedings of the National Academy of Sciences of the United States of America, 112*(20), 6283–6288. doi:10.1073 /pnas.1315545112

Eberhardt, M., & Bond, S. 2009. Cross-sectional dependence in nonstationary panel models: A novel estimator. *MPRA Working Paper 17870*. Retrieved from https://mpra.ub.uni -muenchen.de/17692/

Fang, W. S., Miller, S. M., & Yeh, C.-C. (2012). The effect of ESCOs on energy use. *Energy Policy, 51*, 558–568. doi:10.1016/j.enpol.2012.08.068

Gam, I., & Rejeb, J. B. (2012). Electricity demand in Tunisia. *Energy Policy*, *45*, 714–720. doi:10.1016/j.enpol.2012.03.025

Granger, C. W. J. (1969). Investigating causal relations by econometric models and cross-spectral methods." *Econometrica*, *37*(3), 424. doi:10.2307/1912791

Halicioglu, F. (2007). Residential electricity demand dynamics in Turkey. *Energy Economics*, *29*(2), 199–210. doi:10.1016/j.eneco.2006.11.007

Henderson, J. V. (2010). Cities and development. *Journal of Regional Science*, *50*(1), 515–540. doi:10.1111/j.1467-9787.2009.00636.x

Holtedahl, P., & Joutz, F. L. (2004). Residential electricity demand in Taiwan. *Energy Economics*, *26*(2), 201–224. doi:10.1016/j.eneco.2003.11.001

Hossain, M. S. (2011). Panel estimation for CO_2 emissions, energy consumption, economic growth, trade openness and urbanization of newly industrialized countries. *Energy Policy*, *39*(11), 6991–6999. doi:10.1016/j.enpol.2011.07.042

Jones, D. W. (1989). Urbanization and energy use in economic development. *Energy Journal*, *10*(4), 29–44. Retrieved from http://www.jstor.org/stable/41322370?seq=1#page_scan_tab _contents

Jones, D. W. (1991). How urbanization affects energy-use in developing countries. *Energy Policy*, *19*(7), 621–630. doi:10.1016/0301-4215(91)90094-5

Jorgenson, A. K., Rice, J., & Clark, B. (2010). Cities, slums, and energy consumption in less developed countries, 1990 to 2005. *Organization & Environment*, *23*(2), 189–204. doi:10.1177/1086026610368376

Kennedy, C. A., Stewart, I., Facchini, A., Cersosimo, I., Mele, R., Chen, B., Uda, M., et al. (2015). Energy and material flows of megacities. *Proceedings of the National Academy of Sciences*, *112*(19), 5985–5990. doi:10.1073/pnas.1504315112

Kovacevic, G. (2016). *My electrician drives a Porsche? Investing in the rise of the new spending class*. Austin, TX: Greenleaf Book Group Press.

Krey, V., O'Neill, B. C., van Ruijven, B., Chaturvedi, V., Daioglou, V., Eom, J., et al. (2012). Urban and rural energy use and carbon dioxide emissions in Asia. *Energy Economics*, *34*(December), S272–S283. doi:10.1016/j.eneco.2012.04.013

Larivière, I., & Lafrance, G. (1999). Modelling the electricity consumption of cities: Effect of urban density. *Energy Economics*, *21*(1), 53–66. doi:10.1016/S0140-9883(98)00007-3

Liddle, B. (2004). Demographic dynamics and per capita environmental impact: using panel regressions and household decompositions to examine population and transport. *Population and Environment*, *26*(1), 23–39. doi:10.1023/B:POEN.0000039951.37276.f3

Liddle, B., & Lung, S. (2014). Might electricity consumption cause urbanization instead? evidence from heterogeneous panel long-run causality tests. *Global Environmental Change*, *24*, 42–51. doi:10.1016/j.gloenvcha.2013.11.013

Liu, Y. (2009). Exploring the relationship between urbanization and energy consumption in China using ARDL (autoregressive distributed lag) and FDM (factor decomposition model). *Energy*, *34*(11), 1846–1854. doi:10.1016/j.energy.2009.07.029

Ma, B. (2015). Does urbanization affect energy intensities across provinces in China? Long-run elasticities estimation using dynamic panels with heterogeneous slopes. *Energy Economics*, *49*, 390–401. doi:10.1016/j.eneco.2015.03.012

Madlener, R., & Sunak, Y. (2011). Impacts of urbanization on urban structures and energy demand: What can we learn for urban energy planning and urbanization management?" *Sustainable Cities and Society*, *1*(1), 45–53. doi:10.1016/j.scs.2010.08.006

Michieka, N. M., & Fletcher, J. J. (2012). An investigation of the role of China's urban population on coal consumption. *Energy Policy, 48,* 668–676. doi:10.1016/j.enpol.2012.05.080

Mishra, V., Smyth, R., & Sharma, S. (2009). The energy-GDP nexus: Evidence from a panel of Pacific Island countries. *Resource and Energy Economics, 31*(3), 210–220. doi:10.1016/j.reseneeco.2009.04.002

O'Neill, B. C., Ren, X., Jiang, L., & Dalton, M. (2012). The effect of urbanization on energy use in India and China in the iPETS model. *Energy Economics, 34*(December), S339–S345. doi:10.1016/j.eneco.2012.04.004

Parikh, J., & Shukla, V. (1995). Urbanization, energy use and greenhouse effects in economic development. *Global Environmental Change, 5*(2), 87–103. doi:10.1016/0959-3780(95)00015-G

Pesaran, M. H. (2006). Estimation and inference in large heterogeneous panels with a multifactor error structure. *Econometrica, 74*(4), 967–1012.

Pesaran, M. H., & Smith, R. (1995). Estimating long-run relationships from dynamic heterogeneous panels. *Journal of Econometrics, 68*(1), 79–113. doi:10.1016/0304-4076(94)01644-F

Poumanyvong, P., & Kaneko, S. (2010). Does urbanization lead to less energy use and lower CO_2 emissions? A cross-country analysis. *Ecological Economics, 70*(2), 434–444. doi:10.1016/j.ecolecon.2010.09.029

Poumanyvong, P., Kaneko, S., & Dhakal, S. (2012). Impacts of urbanization on national transport and road energy use: Evidence from low, middle and high income countries. *Energy Policy, 46,* 268–277. doi:10.1016/j.enpol.2012.03.059

Rafiq, S., Salim, R., & Nielsen, I. (2016). Urbanization, openness, emissions and energy intensity: A study of increasingly urbanized emerging economies. *Energy Economics, 56,* 20–28. doi:10.1016/j.eneco.2016.02.007

Rifkin, J. (2002). *The hydrogen economy.* New York: Tarcher/ Putnam.

Sadorsky, P. (2013). Do urbanization and industrialization affect energy intensity in developing countries? *Energy Economics, 37,* 52–59. doi:10.1016/j.eneco.2013.01.009

Sadorsky, P. (2014a). The effect of urbanization and industrialization on energy use in emerging economies: Implications for sustainable development. *American Journal of Economics and Sociology, 73*(2), 392–409. doi:10.1111/ajes.12072

Sadorsky, P. (2014b). The effect of urbanization on CO_2 emissions in emerging economies. *Energy Economics, 41,* 147–153. doi:10.1016/j.eneco.2013.11.007

Salim, R. A., & Shafiei, S. (2014). Urbanization and renewable and non-renewable energy consumption in OECD countries: An empirical analysis. *Economic Modelling, 38,* 581–591. doi:10.1016/j.econmod.2014.02.008

Shahbaz, M., & Lean, H. H. (2012). Does financial development increase energy consumption? The role of industrialization and urbanization in Tunisia. *Energy Policy, 40,* 473–479. doi:10.1016/j.enpol.2011.10.050

Shahbaz, M., Mallick, H., Mahalik, M. K., & Sadorsky, P. (2016). The role of globalization on the recent evolution of energy demand in India: Implications for sustainable development. *Energy Economics, 55*(March), 52–68. doi:10.1016/j.eneco.2016.01.013

Siemens AG. (2012). The Green City Index. Munchen. Retrieved from https://www.siemens.com/entry/cc/features/greencityindex_international/all/en/pdf/gci_report_summary.pdf

Solarin, S. A., & Shahbaz, M. (2013). Trivariate causality between economic growth, urbanisation and electricity consumption in Angola: Cointegration and causality analysis. *Energy Policy, 60,* 876–884. doi:10.1016/j.enpol.2013.05.058

Toda, H. Y., & Yamamoto, T. (1995). Statistical inference in vector autoregressions with possibly integrated processes. *Journal of Econometrics*, *66*(1), 225–250. doi:10.1016/0304-4076(94)01616-8

US Energy Information Agency. (2013). U.S. energy intensity projected to continue its steady decline through 2040—Today in energy—U.S. Energy Information Administration (EIA). Retrieved from http://www.eia.gov/todayinenergy/detail.php?id=10191

United Nations, Department of Economic and Social Affairs, Population Division. (2014). World urbanization prospects: The 2014 revision, highlights (ST/ESA/SER.A/352). Retrieved from https://esa.un.org/unpd/wup/publications/files/wup2014-highlights.pdf

Wang, Q. (2014). Effects of urbanisation on energy consumption in China. *Energy Policy*, *65*, 332–339. doi:10.1016/j.enpol.2013.10.005

Wang, Q., Wu, S., Zeng, Y., & Wu, B. (2016). Exploring the relationship between urbanization, energy consumption, and CO2 emissions in different provinces of China. *Renewable and Sustainable Energy Reviews*, *54*, 1563–1579. doi:10.1016/j.rser.2015.10.090

World Bank. (2016). World development indicators. Retrieved from http://databank.worldbank.org/data/home.aspx

York, R. (2007a). Demographic trends and energy consumption in European Union Nations, 1960–2025. *Social Science Research*, *36*(3), 855–872. doi:10.1016/j.ssresearch.2006.06.007

York, R. (2007b). Structural influences on energy production in South and East Asia, 1971–2002. *Sociological Forum*, *22*(4), 532–554. doi:10.1111/j.1573-7861.2007.00034.x

Zhao, Y., & Wang, S. (2015). The Relationship between urbanization, economic growth and energy consumption in China: An econometric perspective analysis. *Sustainability*, *7*(5), 5609–5627. doi:10.3390/su7055609

Zhou, N., He, G., Williams, C., & Fridley, D. (2015). "ELITE cities: A low-carbon eco-city evaluation tool for China. *Ecological Indicators*, *48*, 448–456. doi:10.1016/j.ecolind.2014.09.018

CHAPTER 11

THEORIZING THE BEHAVIORAL DIMENSION OF ENERGY CONSUMPTION

Energy Efficiency and the Value-Action Gap

MARILYN A. BROWN AND BENJAMIN K. SOVACOOL

MUCH of the public has become increasingly aware and concerned about global climate change, yet patterns of consumption have failed to drive down greenhouse gas (GHG) emissions. Understanding and closing this value-action gap is essential to realizing the ambitious GHG reduction commitments of the 2016 Paris Agreement. This chapter focuses intently on human behavior and energy efficiency, notably the "gap" that often occurs between values and actions concerning energy consumption.

Abundant evidence shows that consumers are gaining greater understanding of the value and need for sustainable energy practices, as repeatedly demonstrated in numerous surveys over the past decade (Brechin & Bhandari, 2011; Capstick et al., 2014; Frederiks, Stenner, and Hobman, 2015; McCright et al., 2016). This trend is fortuitous because of the urgent need to understand and enable household and societal engagement in GHG mitigation. National pledges will be more achievable if interventions take into account beliefs, attitudes, and values that influence energy choices, along with contextual factors and social norms (Stern et al., 2016). Recognizing this, policy initiatives are increasingly focused on the facilitation of sustainable individual behaviors, motivated by the fact that households make purchases and decisions that are responsible for a large portion of the national energy and carbon emission budgets. In the United States and Europe, about one-third of total energy use and carbon emissions results from direct household energy use (Bertoldi, Hirl, & Labanca, 2012; Dietz et al., 2009; Vandenbergh et al., 2010).

Many homes in the industrialized world boast an inventory of equipment to meet household "needs," including microwaves, ovens, dishwashers, water heaters, refrigerators, washers, dryers, tropical fish tanks, massage chairs, ice makers, stereos, electric can openers, electric blankets, electric clocks, and the hallowed "beer fridge." Worldwide, households own approximately one billion personal automobiles, requiring material inputs such as steel, plastic, and glass that must be manufactured and assembled in energy-intensive processes (Sovacool, Brown, & Valentine, 2016). The energy requirements for the production, transportation, and disposal of appliances, food, goods, and services for households amount to about half of total household energy use in Europe (Kok, Benders, & Moll, 2006). Choices made in the purchase of such goods and services can be more or less energy-polluting, depending on the selections made and how they are used (UNEP, 2008).

Despite consistently high levels of reported concern, there exists a well-documented misalignment between energy-related behaviors and the personal values of consumers, challenging analysts and policymakers. Even with adequate knowledge of how to save energy and a professed desire to do so, many consumers still fail to invest in cost-effective energy-efficient purchases and behaviors. While expressing strong beliefs about the negative consequences of global warming and dependence on fossil fuels, and while strongly approving alternative and renewable energy sources, people do not seem to have translated these opinions into practical actions to limit the fossil energy used in their domestic consumption, lifestyles, and travel behaviors. Despite widespread pro-green attitudes, consumers frequently purchase non-green alternatives. The significant gap between the public's level of concern about climate change and the actions taken by individuals to address climate change appears to be a major impediment to achieving more sustainable consumption patterns (Stoknes, 2014).

This chapter examines the literature on the value-action gap to determine its implications for improving household energy efficiency. We begin by defining the value-action gap and characterizing what is known about its size.

DEFINITION AND EVIDENCE OF ENERGY EFFICIENCY'S VALUE-ACTION GAP

The *value-action gap* refers to the discrepancy between the values and attitudes of an individual and his or her actions. More colloquially, it is the difference between what people say they value and what they do.

Our focus in this chapter is on energy efficiency's value-action gap: the difference between the values and attitudes of individuals and their energy-efficient actions—that is, behaviors that affect the quantity of energy consumed to deliver a given level of energy services (Brown & Wang, 2015). Energy efficiency can be increased by purchasing appliances, equipment, and cars that are more efficient, or by modifying practices and behavior. Energy-efficient purchases might involve replacing an incandescent or fluorescent bulb with a light emitting diode (LED) lamp or buying a hybrid-electric car. Energy efficiency can also be increased with practices and behaviors such as using smart thermostats with motion sensors to reduce space heating and cooling when homes are empty, and carpooling or substituting walking for driving. We are not focusing on energy conservation, which involves reducing energy consumption at the expense of comfort or convenience—the warm beer and cold shower phenomenon—because these actions typically produce a loss of utility. In contrast, energy efficiency encompasses investments and actions that achieve a stream of energy-bill savings and pollution-emissions reductions in the future, with no sacrifice of comfort or convenience.

Evidence of an energy-efficiency value-action gap can be deduced from the broader environmental literature that has relied primarily on self-reported environmental values and self-reported environmental actions (Chung & Leung, 2007). For decades, economists, engineers, and policy analysts have described a phenomenon in energy markets that came to be known as the "energy paradox" or the "efficiency gap" (Golove & Eto, 1996; Hirst & Brown, 1990; Jaffe & Stavins, 1994). Engineering/economic analyses showed that technologies exist that could potentially reduce the energy use of consumer durables (light bulbs, air conditioners, water heaters, furnaces, building shells, and automobiles) and producer goods (motors, HVAC, and heavy duty trucks). Several major research institutions estimate that there is a large (20%–30%) technically feasible and economically practicable potential to reduce the energy consumption of most households, including electricity, natural gas, gasoline, and diesel (Gold et al., 2009; McKinsey & Company, 2009; National Research Council, 2009; Wang & Brown, 2014). The reduction in operating costs more than offsets the initial costs of the technology, resulting in substantial potential net economic benefits. Yet consumers do not choose to purchase the more efficient goods that result in net economic savings.

At an aggregate scale, statistics document the value-action gap by showing a discontinuity between increasingly strong environmental values and a growing concern over climate change in combination with the persistence of unsustainable behaviors such as the dominance of automobile travel, wasteful water consumption, and the purchase of energy-inefficient appliances. While vehicle use has declined among younger populations in the United States, it has not decreased in most other cohorts despite higher levels of general public understanding and concern about climate change (Waitt & Harada, 2012). In farming communities, Gilg (2009) has documented a disconnect between people's perceptions of the land use damage that they are causing and their willingness to change agricultural practices.

A lack of knowledge has been shown to be a strong barrier to pro-environmental behaviors, including energy-efficient products and practices. In general, consumers have limited understanding of the cost and consequences of their energy use. Many citizens are unaware that electricity generation is a principal cause of air pollution. When asked about ways to expand the supply of electricity, consumers have been known to suggest adding more plugs to their home! Consumers are also unaware of the energy imbedded in the products they buy—their "indirect energy use."

It is therefore not surprising that options for reducing energy consumption are also poorly understood (Brown & Wang, 2015), which can cause energy-efficiency and carbon-reduction strategies to fail. For example, Whitmarsh, Seyfang, and

O'Neill (2011) found that the concept of a "personal carbon budget" was difficult to communicate to consumers. Pesonen, Josko, and Hämäläinen (2013) examined the pro-environmental actions taken by staff and customers of a swimming facility. They found that the lack of knowledge about the facility's environmental impacts and possible mitigation options was the greatest obstacle to pro-environmental behavior. In businesses and industry, workers lack specialized knowledge about how to install, operate, maintain, and evaluate energy-efficient technology, and facility managers often distrust hired experts (Prindle, 2010). In addition to being incomplete, information is also often asymmetric, which is why "lemons" can be sold by used car dealers, and leaky apartments can be leased by landlords. Such asymmetries undermine trust in marketplace signals.

This review suggests that research (and policies) should focus on "information deficits." Indeed, policy assessments have shown that "standard" information tools such as appliance labeling and benchmarking can motivate consumers to buy more energy-efficient products (Coller & Williams, 1999; NMR, 2012). Real-time feedback about energy consumption, enabled by new information and communication-enabled gadgets, has shown particular promise. When coupled with information about air pollution and health consequences, information feedback can be even more effective at promoting energy efficiency (Asensio & Delmas, 2015).

However, addressing information deficits has not delivered large-scale impacts in terms of reductions in energy demand or changes in energy related practices. In a world that needs deep decarbonization, broader and mass-scalable behavioral solutions are needed. Policies must be multifaceted, by integrating information tools with pricing instruments and financing programs, grounded by the results of sound social science theories, conceptual frameworks, and empirical research (Brown & Wang, 2015). Blake (1999)'s analysis of sustainable communities in the United Kingdom highlighted tensions between policies focused on the "information deficit" and those that reflected the complex relationships between individuals and institutions. Information alone is insufficient to catalyze transformational behavioral change. As a case in point, while information and concern about climate change and clean energy options are expanding, behavioral engagement is still relatively limited. A broader conceptual framework is needed to explain and address the value-action gap.

THEORIES AND CONCEPTUAL FRAMEWORKS

A plethora of theories of practice have been used to analyze the greening of consumption (Spaargaren, 2011). Several of these conceptual frameworks and theories have also been applied to the energy-efficiency value-action gap, including Fishbein and Ajzen's theory of reasoned action (Fishbein & Ajzen, 1975; Ajzen & Fishbein, 1980); attitude-behavior connection models (ABC) (Stern, 2000); consumer-motivation theories (Hargreaves, Nye, & Burgess, 2008; Shove, 2010); and the U.K. Global Action

Plan (GAP)'s group-based approach (Hargreaves, Nye, & Burgess, 2008). Indeed, one meta-assessment of the theoretical literature looking at behavior and energy technology choices identified no less than 95 potentially applicable theories, cutting across disciplines ranging from behavioral science to marketing and political science (Sovacool, 2016; Sovacool & Hess, 2017). The most relevant are 50 "agency-centered" conceptual frameworks and theoretical approaches. We divide these in two tables (Tables 11.1 and 11.2), depending on their emphasis.

The 27 approaches shown in Table 11.1 emphasize the beliefs, attitudes, and values of the individual decision-maker. Concepts include rational deliberation; expected gains, losses and utility; habit, lifestyle, and self-concept; and communication, persuasion, and messaging.

The 23 approaches shown in Table 11.2 emphasize contextual factors and social norms, in addition to beliefs, attitudes, and values. Concepts include social norms and expectations; institutions and social systems; networks and stakeholder influence; copying and conformity; and constraints beyond one's personal control.

Of these 50 total approaches across both tables, the theory of reasoned action (TRA) has a particularly strong publication record focused on household energy-efficient behavior (Barr, 2004, 2006; Barr & Gilg, 2005; Brown, 1984; Brown & Macey, 1983, 1985; Gadenne et al., 2011; Macey & Brown, 1983). TRA links behavior with several psychological antecedents that include both attitudes and social norms (Ajzen & Fishbein, 1980). By moving backward from behavior to intention, from intention to the corresponding attitude and subjective norm, and from these to underlying beliefs, values, and expectations, increasing understanding of the factors influencing behavior can be gained (Figure 11.1).

The theory of reasoned action links behavior with several psychological antecedents (Ajzen & Fishein, 1980). It does not explicitly link broad energy and environmental attitudes to energy-efficient behaviors, but rather focuses on the attitudes of individuals toward their adoption of specific energy-efficient purchases and practices. Such specificity is employed, for instance, by Brown and Macey (1983, 1985) in their analysis of repetitive household behaviors such as changing furnace filters, nighttime thermostat setback, and caulking. Using panel data, repetitive behavior was found to be strongly influenced by past behavior (e.g., "habits") and also by concerns about comfort, reducing energy bills, and home values. This research also underscored the fact that people vary in the extent that intrinsic states (such as attitudes) and extrinsic influences (in particular, the views of spouses) influence behavior.

Using TRA, Barr (2004) concluded that the factors influencing stated intention and behavior are significantly different so as to suggest that public rhetoric toward environmental action may be influenced by different antecedents from those of actual behavior (Barr, 2004). Employing a similar conceptual framework of consumer environmental behavior and its antecedents, a survey of green consumers showed that both intrinsic and extrinsic environmental drivers, together with social norms and community influence, are associated with environmental attitudes and behavior (Gadenne et al., 2011; Lukman et al., 2013).

Table 11.1 Twenty-seven Theoretical Approaches to Energy Technology Choices
and Behavior That Emphasize Beliefs, Attitudes, and Values

Name and Discipline	Key Author(s)	Application
Cognitive Dissonance Theory– Behavioral science	Leon Festinger	Argues that people in general are motivated to avoid internally inconsistent (dissonant) beliefs, attitudes, and values, including when they adopt new technologies or practices
Consumer Preference Theory– Behavioral science	George Homans, Jon Elster	The underlying basis of most economic theories of consumer preference and several other social-psychological theories of behavior. Suggests that behavior is the outcome of rational deliberations in which individuals seek to maximize their own expected "utility." Suggests that people will adopt new technology when they can afford its price, it aligns with tastes and preferences, and it maximizes the purchaser's utility.
Deficit Model– Behavioral science	J. Burgess, C. Harrison, P. Filius	Understanding about technology is based on the linear progression of knowledge leading to awareness and concern (attitudes), which in turn is assumed to link to behavior
Expectancy-Value Theory–Behavioral science	Martin C. Fishbein, Icek Azjen	A broad class of theories based on the idea that behavior about purchasing new technologies or changing behavior is motivated by the expectations we have about the consequences of our behavior and the values we attach to those outcomes
Four Dimensions of Behavior (4DB) Framework– Behavioral science	Tim Chatterton, Charlie Wilson	Attempts to characterize multifaceted behaviors related to technologies (in this instance, in the domains of energy, electricity, and transport) along the four dimensions of an actor, a domain, durability, and scope
Integrated Framework for Encouraging Pro-environmental Behavior (IFEP)– Behavioral science	Jan Willem Bolderdijk, Kees Keizer, Goda Perlaviciute	Pro-environmental or sustainable behavior often involves a conflict between different goals. People may be motivated to adopt new technologies for hedonic reasons (e.g., because it is enjoyable), for gain reasons (e.g., because it saves money), or for normative reasons (e.g., because they think protecting the environment is the right thing to do).
Lifestyle Theory– Behavioral science	Anthony Giddens, Jonn Axsen	Social acceptance of new technology is mediated by lifestyle, a package of related behaviors, objects, and skills that both expresses and shapes consumer identity
Motivation-Ability-Opportunity Model–Behavioral science	Folke Ölander, John Thøgersen	An integrated behavioral model that combines both internal motivational variables—usually based on the theory of reasoned action (TRA)—with external contextual variables of ability including habit and task knowledge and opportunity
Means End Chain Theory–Behavioral science	Jonathan Gutman, Thomas J. Reynolds, Jerry C. Olson	A qualitative form of expectancy-value theory which posits that preferences for behavior—including new technology adoption—are based on a "laddered" relationship between attributes, consequences, and values

Table 11.1 Continued

Name and Discipline	Key Author(s)	Application
Persuasion Theory—Behavioral science	Carl Hovland, Richard E. Petty	A set of theoretical approaches to the "art of persuasion" that identifies (1) the credibility of the source, (2) the message, and (3) the thoughts/feelings of the receiver as critical. When these three elements align, users and consumers can be convinced to change their behavior or adopt new technical systems.
Protection Motivation Theory—Behavioral science	R. W. Rogers, M. Bockarjova, Linda Steg	Attempts to explain pro-environmental or sustainability choices by employing a wide set of predictors, such as the costs and benefits of current (maladaptive) behavior as well as prospective adaptive behavior
Self-Discrepancy Theory—Behavioral science	E. Tory Higgins	Suggests that people are motivated to act—to change behavior, or adopt new technology—according to feelings aroused by the perceived gap between their actual and "ideal" selves.
Self-Perception Theory—Behavioral science	Daryl Bem	Proposes that people infer their attitudes and willingness to engage in pro-environmental or sustainable behaver by observing themselves
Subjective Expected Utility (SEU)—Behavioral science	Martin C. Fishbein, Icek Azjen. A. H. Eagly, S. Chaiken	A form of expectancy value theory closely related to the rational choice model, it suggests that change in behavior is a function of the expected outcomes of the behavior and the value assigned to those outcomes.
Symbolic Self-Completion Theory—Behavioral science	Robert A. Wicklund, Peter M. Gollwitzer	A symbolic interactionist theory which suggests that people create their sense of identity through the appropriation of symbolic resources to complete the "self- image"
Transtheoretical Model—Behavioral science	James Q. Prochaska, Carlo C. DiClemente	People's attempt to change is viewed as a process of increasing readiness. People move through five stages when attempting to change a behavior: pre-contemplation, contemplation, preparation, action, and maintenance
Domestication Theory—Consumption studies	Roger Silverstone	The integration of technological objects into daily life involves a taming of the wild and a cultivation of the tame in which such novel technologies must be transformed from unfamiliar and exciting to familiar
Bounded Rationality—Economics	Herbert Simon	In decision-making situations, actors face both uncertainties about the future and costs in acquiring information about the present. People therefore make satisfactory rather than truly optimal choices about new technologies.
Prospect Theory—Economics	D. Kahneman, A. Tversky	According to this theory, adopters base their decisions on subjective values that can be modeled by a function that is concave for gains, convex for losses, and steeper for losses than for gains; low probabilities are often over-weighted and moderate to high probabilities under-weighted. Potential adopters will often mis-estimate the costs and benefits of new technologies.

(continued)

Table 11.1 Continued

Name and Discipline	Key Author(s)	Application
Rational Choice Theory—Economics	Gary Becker, James S. Coleman, Thomas Fararo	People are rational economic actors, assessing costs and benefits, and will seek to maximize their own welfare when making informed decisions about new technologies.
Initial Trust Model—Information science and management studies	D. H. McKnight, N. L. Chervany	The willingness of persons to adopt a new technology is explained by their ability to take risks in order to fulfill a need without prior experience, or credible, meaningful information. New technologies will be accepted based on their convenience, flexibility, or perceived benefits.
Motivational Model—Information science and management studies	F. D. Davis, Viswanath Venkatesh, Cheri Speier, R. J. Vallerand	The adoption of new technology is mediated by extrinsic motivations (instrumental value) and intrinsic motivations (desire to perform an activity).
Task Technology Fit Model—Information science and management studies	Dale L. Goodhue, Ronald L. Thompson	Users will adopt a new technology based on four constructs: task characteristics, technology characteristics, task technology fit, and use.
Technology Acceptance Model (TAM)—Information science and management studies	F. D. Davis, Viswanath Venkatesh	Technology acceptance and usage will be based on perceived usefulness, perceived ease of use, and subjective norms.
Theory of Buyer Behavior—Marketing	John A. Howard, Jagdish N. Sheth	Effective marketing programs that convince consumers to adopt a new product (or technology) rely on a mix of perceptual constructs such as information and bias, learning constructions such as attitudes and confidence, previous behaviors such as past purchases, and current intentions and attitude.
Action Theory—Sociology	Max Weber	Social action to achieve a new goal (or accept a new technology) can be based on value-rational actions or value relational (instrumental) ones.
Reflexive Layers of Influence—Transport studies	Jonn Axsen, Kenneth S. Kurani	Identifies and integrates three processes of influence pertaining to new products: diffusion, translation, and reflexivity. Respectively, these processes describe increasingly complex forms of social interaction, ranging from communicating awareness of the product to integrating the product's perceived benefits into lifestyle and self-concept.

Table 11.2 Twenty-three Theoretical Approaches to Energy Technology Choices and Behavior That Include Contextual Factors and Social Norms

Name and Discipline	Key Author(s)	Application
Attitude-Behavior-Context (ABC) Theory—Behavioral science	Paul C. Stern, Stuart Oskamp	A kind of field theory for behavior intended to be environmentally sustainable, inclusive of accepting environmentally friendly technologies. Behavior (B) is an interactive product of "internal" attitudinal variables (A) and "external" contextual factors (C).
Attribution Theory—Behavioral science	Kelvin Lancaster, F. Heider	Attempts to explain why ordinary people explain events as they do, including the adoption of new technology, and it suggests that the two most influential factors are internal attribution to characteristics of the individual or external attribution to a situation or event beyond personal control.
Comprehensive Technology Acceptance Framework—Behavioral science	N. M. A. Huijts, Linda Steg	Proposes a complex model of technological diffusion predicated on experience and knowledge, which are then mediated by trust, issues of procedural and distributive fairness, social norms, attitudes, and perceived behavioral control
Field Theory—Behavioral science	Kurt Lewin	Influential early social-psychological theory positing behavior and agency as a function of a dynamic "field" of internal and external influences. Behavioral change relies on unfreezing (existing behaviors), shifting to a new level, and then refreezing.
Interpersonal Behavior (TIB)—Behavioral science	Harry C. Triandis	Attempts to explain why people behave the way they do. It includes both expectancy-value and normative belief constructs as well as the influence of habitual, social, and affective factors on behavior.
Norm Activation Theory/Model—Behavioral science	S. H. Schwartz	One of the better known attempts to model pro-social or altruistic behaviors: a personal norm to behave in a pro-social way is activated by awareness of the consequences of one's actions and the ascription of personal responsibility for them.
Focus Theory of Normative Conduct—Behavioral science	Robert B. Cialdini	Proposes that behavior is guided by social norms that are either descriptive (what is done) or injunctive (what should be done) in nature. The strength or "salience" of these different kinds of norms in a given context depends on a variety of dispositional and situational factors.
Social Learning Theory—Behavioral science	Albert Bandura	Rewards or punishments influence the likelihood that a person will perform a particular behavior in a given situation. People will learn to adopt a new technology by observing others, in addition to learning by participating. Moreover, individuals are most likely to copy and mimic behavior observed by others they identify strongly with.
Theory of Reasoned Action (TRA)—Behavioral science	Martin C. Fishbein, Icek Azjen	Perhaps the best-known social-psychological attitude-behavior model, TRA adjusts expectancy value theory to incorporate normative social influences on behavioral intention.

(continued)

Table 11.2 Continued

Name and Discipline	Key Author(s)	Application
Theory of Planned Behavior (TPA)—Behavioral science	Icek Azjen	Adjusts the TRA to incorporate the actor's perceived control over the outcomes of his or her behavior
Values-Beliefs-Norms Theory—Behavioral science	Paul C. Stern, Thomas Dietz	An attempt to adjust Schwartz's Norm Activation theory to incorporate a more sophisticated relationship between values, beliefs, attitudes and norms
Critical Stakeholder Assessment—Conflict resolution and project management	R. K. Mitchell, B. R. Agle, D. J. Wood	Identifies relevant stakeholders for a specified project or policy, maps out their relative power, influence, and interests, and assesses the broader context in which they interact. New technologies are likely to succeed when they can garner the support of broad constellations of stakeholders
Energy Cultures Framework—Energy studies	Janet Stephenson	Behaviors related to adopting new, more sustainable energy systems or choices are defined by the interactions among the materials, energy practices, and norms over which an individual or collective has agency.
Social Cognitive Theory—Information science and management studies	Deborah Compeau, Christopher Higgins, Sid Huff, Robert Wood, Alberto Bandura	Proposal that knowledge acquisition of new innovations could be connected to observing others within the context of social interactions, experiences, and outside media influences
Theory of Human Behavior—Information science and management studies	Ronald L. Thompson, Christopher A. Higgins, Jane M. Howell	Individual acceptance of new technologies or practices at the workplace will be based on a mix of job-fit, complexity, long-term consequences, affect towards use, and social factors.
Unified Theory of Acceptance and Use of Technology (UTAUT)—Information science and management studies	Viswanath Venkatesh	In the adoption of new technology, perceived usefulness (performance expectancy), perceived ease of use (effort expectancy), and social influence (norms) affect use via behavioral intention, whereas facilitating conditions directly antecede behavior. Hedonic motivation, price value, and habit are later added as factors.
Diffusion of Innovations Theory—Innovation studies	Everett M. Rogers	Four essential factors influence the diffusion of new technologies: the innovation itself, communication channels, time, and a social system. Moreover, adopters can be categorized into different typologies: innovators, early adopters, early majority, late majority, and laggards.
Initiative-Based Learning—Innovation studies	C. Argyris, Rob Raven, P. Reason, H. Bradbury	Sustainable transitions require that relevant actors are involved in defining and legitimizing new technologies and practices. Understanding the motives and strategies of actors on the ground is critical to making transitions socially robust and sustainable.

Table 11.2 Continued

Name and Discipline	Key Author(s)	Application
Theory of Institutional Entrepreneurship— Organization studies	Paul DiMaggio, Raghu Garud, Cynthia Hardy, Steve Maguire, Julie Battilana	Activities of actors who have an interest in particular institutional arrangements and who leverage resources are able to create new institutions or to transform existing ones.
Advocacy Coalition Framework— Political science and public policy	P. A. Sabatier	Major policy change in technically complex issue areas occurs when strong groups of advocates or stakeholders align to create coalitions.
Social Action Theory—Sociology	Talcott Parsons	Individual decisions to act are based on the structure of social order as well as micro factors related to agency.
Social Capital Theory—Sociology	Pierre Bourdieu, James S. Coleman, Robert Putnam	Social capital has been defined as the connections and relationships among and between individuals. These consist of the networks, norms, relationships, values, and informal sanctions that shape society's social interactions.
Perspectives of Interpersonal Influence— Transport studies	Jonn Axsen, Kenneth S. Kurani	A synthetic framework that proposes the adoption of new technologies is based on diffusion and contagion, conformity, dissemination, translation, and reflexivity.

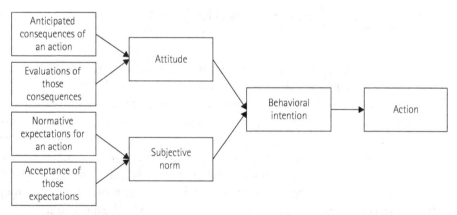

FIGURE 11.1 Fundamental concepts of the theory of reasoned action.

The salience of behavioral economics in contemporary analysis must be highlighted. Increasingly, non-financial factors are being considered and are found to be important in influencing energy use in buildings (Claudy & O'Driscoll, 2008; Wilson & Dowlatabadi, 2007), as was found to be the case with pro-environmental values in the adoption of energy-efficient measures (Asensio & Delmas, 2015). In this approach, many of the structural, endemic, and transaction costs are identified as filtering through the behavioral determinants of action to produce the outcome observed in the market. Consumers and firms highly value their time. As a result, the effort required for them to research available options, bargain with vendors, and process incentive payments can easily convert enthusiasm for finding the best option into exhaustion and acceptance of a standard (and often sub-optimal) fix (Brown and Wang, 2017).

The findings of behavioral economics can be usefully divided into four categories—motivation, influence, perception, and calculation—and described at two levels, foundational and advanced (Cooper, 2017; Wilkinson, 2008).

Motivation: Foundations: values, attitudes, preferences, and choice;
    Advanced: fairness, social preferences
Influence: Foundations: reference points, nature and measurement of utility;
    Advanced: signaling, learning
Perception: Foundations: decision-making under risk and uncertainty, utility theory, prospect theory, loss aversion, decision weighting;
    Advanced: behavioral game theory, bargaining
Calculation: Foundations: mental accounting, framing and editing, budgeting and fungibility, choice bracketing
    Advanced: discounted utility model, alternative intertemporal choice.

OTHER PERSONAL DRIVERS
AND TRADE-OFFS

In addition to attitudes, TRA and other theories of technology choice and behavior highlight the role of subjective norms in determining an individual's behavioral intentions and subsequent behavior. Subjective norms are influenced by the awareness of a norm to act (e.g., noticing that most people purchase high-efficiency light bulbs) and the acceptance of that norm (e.g., internalizing the norm to purchase high-efficiency light bulbs). According to TRA, the immediate determinants of subjective norms are the individual's beliefs that relevant referents approve or disapprove of his or her performing the behaviors and his or her motivation to comply with these referents. However, these components appear to be the most controversial elements in the theory and are thus not elaborated upon here. More recent literature has emphasized the role of social groups and community systems.

The salience of environmental and climate change issues varies across social groups; for some, there are other more significant priorities. For example, a study of UK citizens who have adopted lower-carbon lifestyles found that concerns about social justice, community, frugality, and personal integrity were more influential motivations for low-carbon actions compared with concerns about the environment per se. Reinforcing this finding, participants' narratives about their climate actions revealed strong links to human rights groups as well as environmental organizations (Howell, 2013).

Energy-efficient products often force trade-offs on their users, such as higher prices, risks associated with novelty, and inconveniences of nascent distribution systems (Olson, 2013). All of these trade-offs can expand the value-action gap. Waitt and Harada (2012) highlight the trade-off between traveling less to cut fuel consumption, which compromises the pleasure and passion of driving. Similarly, car attributes, such as cost, reliability, brand, and design, often outweigh environmental performance (Mairesse et al., 2012). Only "dark green" consumers are willing to buy green products that have negative trade-offs and few compensatory qualities. In contrast, a broader array of consumers will purchase green products if they have strong compensatory advantages over conventional attributes such as attractiveness and convenience (Olson, 2013).

SITUATIONAL VARIABLES, INSTITUTIONAL CONTEXT, AND INFRASTRUCTURE

Socio-psychological and personal drivers operate within a system of constraints and conditions that are largely beyond the participants' immediate control. These include policies, programs, and other institutional arrangements, as well as markets, product distribution systems, broadband assets, fuel cost and availability, and other physical infrastructure. Underscoring such factors, residents have been found to drive less and walk or bike more in areas with high residential density, land use mix, connectivity, and transit access (Brown, Southworth, & Sarzynski, 2009; Frank et al., 2010; Saelens, Sallis, & Frank, 2003). The influence of these structural conditions and infrastructures is moderated by personal circumstances. Thus, it is helpful to contextualize consumption practices (Farrelly & Tucker, 2014; Spaargaren, 2011), recognizing that socio-psychological frameworks are most valuable in explaining the value-action gap within the limits of structural constraints. This argues against taking an excessively narrow focus on the individual, as Fudge and Peters (2011) argue has occurred over the last decade in UK government debates. This can oversimplify the discussion and obscure some of the wider institutional and infrastructure issues.

The discovery of "inadvertent environmentalists" by Hitchings, Collins, and Day (2015) underscores the importance of context. Sometimes the situation of everyday life can cause people to cut back on their energy consumption. They may just happen to live close to work, to occupy an energy-smart apartment, to have an abundance of day light, and so on, without consciously choosing a resource-efficient lifestyle. In this case, there could be a fortuitous gap between their attitudes and their behavior.

A fuller explanation of the value-action gap requires an understanding of situational and external factors that influence behavior. Recognizing this need, a wide-spanning approach that adds depth to the behavioral analysis framework is offered in a detailed analysis of efficiency in the building sector prepared by McKinsey & Company (2010). The McKinsey conceptualization of barriers and obstacles to energy efficiency uses three broad categories—behavioral, structural, and availability. Put another way, it cuts across or synthesizes multiple dimensions from Table 11.1. About two dozen specific barriers are described. Moreover, McKinsey identifies nine different clusters of activity in the building sector. The manifestation of the barriers is different in the clusters, so McKinsey ends up with 50 discrete barriers.

Situational variables describe the circumstances of the individual within his or her behavioral setting, which in general are a function of the characteristics of the individual (socio-demographics). It has long been known that households engaging in more energy-efficient behaviors tend to be better educated and wealthier, and they participate in more energy-efficiency programs (Brown & Macey, 1983). Their greater education and wealth result in a higher "carbon capacity," or individual ability to reduce GHG emissions (Whitmarsh, Seyfang, & O'Neill, 2011). The strong positive association between wealth and consumption complicates this relationship.

In the area of energy consumption, there is a need to take into account the social, cultural, and institutional contexts that shape and constrain people's choices (Owens & Driffill, 2008). Evidence suggests the existence of forms of excitement generated by shared practices of sustainable consumption (Spaargaren, 2011). Such experiences may provide consumers with the drive to act more consistently on their moral attitudes. Consistent with this notion, it has been suggested that while individual-level theories offer the best explanation of the value-action gap, community-level theories may offer the best solution (Antimova, Nawijn, & Peeters, 2012). Several studies have found social interaction to be strongly linked to energy-saving behaviors. Community-based activities, in particular, can be influential (Hori et al., 2013).

Numerous studies highlight ease of action and convenience as facilitating factors (Pruneau et al., 2006). These are strongly influenced by such infrastructure characteristics as the density of retail and service providers. The level of effort required to undertake an energy-efficient action can have a dominant influence. This is illustrated by the strong association between recycling and the availability of recycling facilities as a contributor to sustainable living (Chaplin, Gareth, & Wyton, 2014).

Without lapsing into technological determinism, it is clear that such situational, institutional, and infrastructure variables can make crucial contributions to climate governance (Spaargaren, 2011). As Orr (1994) astutely noted, infrastructure such as buildings serve as an important cognitive constraint that acts as a hidden curriculum or "crystallized pedagogy," influencing how occupants think and behave. Hassler (2009) adds that since infrastructure can last hundreds of years, it can lock in patterns of development and growth, foreclosing some choices while opening up others.

OVERCOMING THE VALUE-ACTION GAP

The value-action gap has become a major area of both angst and soul-searching for policymakers. The discrepancy between verbal and actual commitment to sustainable environmental behavior appears to have undermined the effectiveness of many environmental policies and measures. The mobilization of pro-environmental attitudes to address this "value-action gap" has so far had limited success.

Stern et al. (2016) suggest seven design principles for energy-efficiency policies and programs at the household level. Three of them are particularly pertinent to the value-action gap:

1. Provide credible and targeted information at points of decision;
2. Identify and address the key factors, many of them non-financial, inhibiting and promoting the target behaviors in particular populations;
3. Rigorously evaluate programs to provide credible estimates of their impact and to decide where improvements can be made.

Provide Credible and Targeted Information at Points of Decision

Many local, state, and national policies are based on an "information deficit" model of participation, which is undoubtedly effective in some situations where knowledge is limited. Providing credible and readily usable information on the "carbon footprints" of consumer products (Cohen & Vandenbergh, 2012), the energy efficiency of homes and buildings (Cox, Brown, & Sun, 2013), and levels of indirect consumption are promising examples. But to help break out of established ways of thinking and to instigate changes in behavior that are sustained over time, new ways of achieving transformative learning may be required (Sharpe, 2016).

Identify and Address the Key Factors, Many of Them Non-Financial, Inhibiting and Promoting the Target Behaviors in Particular Populations

Understanding the socio-psychological concerns and drivers can lead to the creation of cost-effective and mass-scalable behavioral solutions to encourage household energy efficiency and sustainable energy use (Flynn, Bellaby, & Ricci, 2009). The research and experience reviewed here suggests the need to develop differentiated public policy interventions that effectively reach different subgroups with messages and assistance that motivate change (Blake, 1999). The timing of such interventions can also be key, by exploiting "transformative moments" in the lives of individuals (Hards, 2012). For example, in response to blackouts in the summer of 2001, California utilities were able to quickly transform markets for high-efficiency appliances by exploiting high levels of public concern. By the following summer, peak electricity demand had been significantly shaved, the grid was stabilized, and high-efficiency appliances were mainstreamed.

Rigorously Evaluate Programs to Provide Credible Estimates of Their Impact and to Determine Where Improvements Can Be Made

Without effective program evaluation, it is difficult to identify and remedy weaknesses in program designs. For example, it has been suggested that financial incentives may impair energy-efficiency efforts by changing the frame from a social to a monetary one, undermining the pro-social satisfaction of participants and crowding out other energy-efficiency investments (Rode, Gómez-Baggethun, & Krause, 2015). Incentives may also create a "moral license" effect, where consumers who adopt energy-efficient devices feel that this gives them moral license to increase their electricity consumption in other areas, leading to a rebound effect (McCoy & Lyons, 2016). Progam evaluation can identify such unanticipated consequences and help to identify solutions.

SUGGESTIONS FOR A NEW RESEARCH PARADIGM

Despite the rich empirical record produced by social science research, several issues remain. Why is much relevant social theory so marginalized? Limited data availability and access to resources for survey research are undoubtedly one barrier to the advancement of social theory. How can we make better use of existing intellectual resources pertinent to the value-action gap? (Shove, 2010). Perhaps the existence of so many alternative modeling approaches does not convey consensus on key concepts that need to be understood for the value-action gap to be shrunk.

With these issues in mind, we close by suggesting five fruitful themes that future researchers may want to explore.

First, reconciling the numerous concepts, frameworks, and theoretical platforms that have been applied to this field of research would be useful. Different theories are associated with disparate epistemological assumptions, explanatory power, and applicable scope, but some may yield greater insights when utilized together. Exploring which theories match well—and which do not—would be a clear contribution to the literature.

Second, and critically, focusing on behaviors, actions, and practices together as key methodological units for research and governance provides a way to avoid the pitfalls of the individualistic paradigms that have dominated the field of sustainable consumption studies. These paradigms have often measured purchasing intentions or stated preferences, but not actual actions. In colloquial terms, they measure what people say, but not what they do.

Third, exploring the concept of carbon capability to capture the contextual abilities and motivations of individuals to reduce emissions would help to productively focus information outreach, incentives, and other types of "nudges." Mapping the distribution of carbon capabilities would help show how individual preferences and lifestyles relate to carbon footprints and consequences for climate-change mitigation, and environmental sustainability in general.

Fourth, expanding the examination of the energy-efficiency value-action gap beyond individuals to include households, boards of directors, commercial buying units, government procurement groups, and other decision-making entities would yield different yet important insights. The energy-efficiency gap undoubtedly exists in the business, industrial, and public sectors, but little has been done on the organizational dimension of these decisions.

Fifth and finally, focusing on how and why the value-action gap varies in magnitude across populations, time and space, and policy contexts is essential. This type of research would better capture the heterogeneity and contextual specificity of interventions, data that are needed as programs are tailored up (or down) to accommodate smaller scales.

REFERENCES

Ajzen, I., & Fishbein, M. (1980). *Understanding attitudes and predicting social behaviour.* Eaglewood Cliffs, NJ: Prentice Hall.

Antimova, R., Nawijn, J., & Peeters, P. (2012). The awareness/attitude-gap in sustainable tourism: A theoretical perspective. *Tourism Review, 67*(3), 7–16.

Asensio, O. I., & Delmas, M. A. (2015). Nonprice incentives and energy conservation. *Proceeding of the National Academy of Scie*nces, 112, 510–515.

Barr, S. (2004). Are we all environmentalists now? Rhetoric and reality in environmental action. *Geoforum, 35*(2), 231–249.

Barr, S. (2006). Environmental action in the home: Investigating the "value-action" gap. *Geography, 91*(1), 43–54.

Barr, S., & Gilg, A. W. (2005). Conceptualizing and analyzing household attitudes and actions to a growing environmental problem: Development and application of a framework to guide local waste policy. *Applied Geography, 25*(3), 226–247.

Bertoldi, P., Hirl, B., & Labanca, N. (2012). *Energy efficiency status report Luxembourg.* European Union.

Blake, J. (1999). Overcoming the "value-action gap" in environmental policy: Tensions between national policy and local experience. *Local Environment, 4*(3), 257–278.

Brechin, S. R., & Bhandari, M. (2011). Perceptions of climate change worldwide. *WIREs Climate Change, 2,* 871–885.

Brown, M. A. (1984). Change mechanisms in the diffusion of residential energy conservation practices. *Technological Forecasting and Social Change, 25,* 123–138.

Brown, M. A., & Macey, S. M. (1983). Understanding residential energy conservation through attitudes and beliefs. *Environment and Planning, A, 15,* 405–416.

Brown, M. A., & Macey, S. M. (1985). Evaluating the impact of two energy conservation programs in a Midwestern city. *Applied Geography, 5,* 39–53.

Brown, M. A., Southworth, F., & Sarzynski, A. (2009). The geography of metropolitan carbon footprints. *Policy and Society, 27*(4), 285–304.

Brown, M. A., & Wang, Y. (2015). *Green savings: How policies and markets drive energy efficiency.* Praeger.

Brown, Marilyn A. and Yu Wang. 2017. "Energy-Efficiency Skeptics and Advocates: The Debate Heats Up as the Stakes Rise," *Energy Efficiency* 10(5): 1155-1173 http://link.springer.com/article/10.1007/s12053-017-9511-x

Capstick, S. B., Whitmarsh, L., Poortinga, W., Pidgeon, N., & Upham, P. (2014). International trends in public perceptions of climate change over the past quarter century. *WIREs Climate Change.* Retrieved from http://dx.doi.org/10.1002/wcc.321

Chaplin, G., & Wyton, P. (2014). Student engagement with sustainability: Understanding the value-action gap. *International Journal of Sustainability in Higher Education, 15*(4), 404.

Chung, S.-S., & Leung, M. (2007). The value-action gap in waste recycling: The case of undergraduates in Hong Kong. *Environmental Management, 40*(4), 603–612.

Claudy, M., & O'Driscoll, A. (2008). Beyond economics: A behavioral approach to energy efficiency in domestic buildings. Dublin Institute of Technology.

Cohen, M. A., & Vandenbergh, M. P. (2012). The potential role of carbon labeling in a green economy. *Energy Economics, 34,* S53–S63.

Coller, M. & M. Williams (2009) Eliciting Individual Discount Rates, Experimental Economics, 2 (2): 107-127.

Cooper, M. (2017). *The political economy of electricity: Progressive capitalism and the struggle to build a sustainable power sector.* Greenport, CO: Praegar/ABC Clio.

Cox, M., Brown, M. A., & Sun, X. (2013). Energy benchmarking of commercial buildings: A low-cost pathway for urban sustainability. *Environmental Research Letters, 8*(3), 1–12. Retrieved from http://iopscience.iop.org/1748-9326/8/3/035018/pdf/1748-9326_8_3_035018.pdf

Dietz, T., Gardner, G. T., Gilligan, J., Stern, P. C., & Vandenbergh, M. P. (2009). Household actions can provide a behavioral wedge to rapidly reduce US carbon emissions. *Proceedings of the National Academy of Sciences USA, 106,* 18452–18456.

Farrelly, T., & Tucker, C. (2014). Action research and residential waste minimisation in Palmerston North, New Zealand. *Resources, Conservation & Recycling, 91,* 11–26.

Fishbein, M., & Ajzen, I. (1975). *Belief, attitude, intention and behavior: An introduction to theory and research.* Reading, MA: Addison-Wesley.

Flynn, R., Bellaby, P., & Ricci, M. (2009). The "value-action gap" in public attitudes towards sustainable energy: The case of hydrogen energy. *Sociological Review, 57,* 159–180.

Frank, L. D., Greenwald, M., Winkelman, S., Chapman, J., & Kavage, S. (2010). Carbonless footprints: Promoting health and climate stabilization through active transportation. *Preventive Medicine, 50,* S99–S105.

Frederiks, E., Stenner, K., & Hobman, E. (2015). Household energy use: Applying behavioral economics to understand consumer decision-making and behavior. *Renewable and Sustainable Energy Reviews, 41,* 1385–1394.

Fudge, S., & Peters, M. (2011). Behaviour change in the UK climate debate: An assessment of responsibility, agency and political dimensions. *Sustainability, 3*(6), 789–808.

Gadenne, D., Sharma, B., Kerr, D., & Smith, T. (2011). The influence of consumers' environmental beliefs and attitudes on energy saving behaviors. *Energy Policy, 39*(12), 7684–7694.

Gilg, A. (2009). Perceptions about land use. *Land Use Policy, 26,* S76–S82.

Gold, R., Furrey, L., Nadel, S., Laitner, J., & Elliott, R. N. (2009). *Energy efficiency in the American Clean Energy and Security Act of 2009: Impact of current provisions and opportunities to enhance the legislation.* Washington, DC: American Council for an Energy Efficient Economy, September.

Golove, W. H., & Eto, J. H. (1996). *Market barriers to energy efficiency: A critical reappraisal of the rationale for public policies to promote energy efficiency,* Lawrence Berkeley Laboratory.

Hards, S. (2012). Tales of transformation: The potential of a narrative approach to pro-environmental practices. *Geoforum, 43*(4), 760–771.

Hargreaves, T., Nye, M., & Burgess, J. (2008). Social experiments in sustainable consumption: An evidence-based approach with potential for engaging low-income communities. *Local Environment, 13*(8), 743–758.

Hassler, U. (2009). Long-term building stock survival and intergenerational management: The role of institutional regimes. *Building Research & Information, 37*(5), 552–568.

Hirst, E., & Brown, M. A. (1990). Closing the efficiency gap: Barriers to improving energy efficiency. *Resources, Conservation and Recycling, 3,* 267–281.

Hitchings, R., Collins, R., & Day, R. (2015). Inadvertent environmentalism and the action–value opportunity: Reflections from studies at both ends of the generational spectrum. *Local Environment, 20*(3), 369–385.

Hori, S., Kondob, K., Nogatac, D., & Benb, H. (2013). The determinants of household energy-saving behavior: Survey and comparison in five major Asian cities. *Energy Policy, 52,* 354–362.

Howell, R. A. (2013). It's not (just) "the environment, stupid!" Values, motivations, and routes to engagement of people adopting lower-carbon lifestyles. *Global Environmental Change, 23*(1), 281–290.

Jaffe, A. B. & Stavins, R. N. (1994). The energy paradox and the diffusion of conservation technology. *Resource and Energy Economics, 16,* 2.

Kok, R., Benders, R. M. J., & Moll, H, C. (2006). Measuring the environmental load of household consumption using some methods based on input–output energy analysis: A comparison of methods and a discussion of results. *Energy Policy, 34,* 2744–2761.

Lukman, R., Lozanob, R., Vambergerc, T., & Krajncd, M. (2013). Addressing the attitudinal gap towards improving the environment: A case study from a primary school in Slovenia. *Journal of Cleaner Production, 48,* 93–100.

Macey, S. M., & Brown, M. A. (1983). Residential energy conservation through repetitive household behaviors. *Environment and Behavior, 15,* 123–141.

Mairesse, O., Macharis, C., Lebeau, K., & Turcksin, L. (2012). Understanding the attitude-action gap: functional integration of environmental aspects in car purchase intentions. *Psicologica: International Journal of Methodology and Experimental Psychology, 33*(3), 547–574.

McCoy, D., & Lyons, S. (2016). Unintended outcomes of electricity smart-metering: Trading-off consumption and investment behaviour. *Energy Efficiency,* 1–20.

McCright, A. M., Marquart-Pyatt, S. T., Shwom, R. L., Brechin, S. R., & Allen, S. (2016). Ideology, capitalism, and climate: Explaining public views about climate change in the United States. *Energy Research & Social Science*, 21, 180–189.

McKinsey and Company, Global Energy and Material. (2009). *Unlocking energy efficiency in the U.S. economy*. London, UK: McKinsey and Company, Global Energy and Material.

McKinsey and Company. (2010). *Energy efficiency: A compelling global resource*. London, UK: McKinsey and Company.

National Research Council of the National Academies. (2009). *America's energy future: Technology and transformation, summary edition*. Washington, DC: National Research Council.

NMR Group, with Optimal Energy. (2012). Statewide benchmarking process evaluation. Volume 1: Report. Retrieved from ⟨http://www.calmac.org/publications/Statewide _Benchmarking_Process_Evaluation_Report_CPU0055.pdf⟩

Olson, E. (2013). It's not easy being green: The effects of attribute tradeoffs on green product preference and choice. *Journal of the Academy of Marketing Science*, 41(2), 171–184.

Orr, D. W. (1994). *Earth in mind: On education, environment, and the human prospect* (pp. 112–113). Washington, DC: Island Press.

Owens, S., & Driffill, L. (2008). How to change attitudes and behaviors in the context of energy. *Energy Policy*, 36(12), 4412–4418.

Prindle, W. R. (2010). *From shop floor to top floor: Best business practices in energy efficiency*. Washington, DC: Pew Center.

Pesonen, H.-L., Josko, E., & Hämäläinen, S. (2013). Improving eco-efficiency of a swimming hall through customer involvement. *Journal of Cleaner Production*, 39, 294–302.

Pruneau, D., Doyon, A., Langis, J., Vasseur, L., Ouellet, E., McLaughlin, E., Boudreau, G., & Martin, G. (2006). When teachers adopt environmental behaviors in the aim of protecting the climate. *The Journal of Environmental Education*, 37(3), 3–12.

JRode, J., Gómez-Baggethun, E., & Krause, T. (2015). Motivation crowding by economic incentives in conservation policy: A review of the empirical evidence. *Ecological Economics*, 117, 270–282.

Saelens, B.E., J.F. Sallis & L.D. Frank (2003). Environmental Correlates of Walking and Cycling, Annals of Behavioral Medicine, 25 (2): 80-91.

Sharpe, J. (2016). Understanding and unlocking transformative learning as a method for enabling behaviour change for adaptation and resilience to disaster threats. *International Journal of Disaster Risk Reduction*, 17, 213–219.

Shove, E. (2010). Beyond the ABC: Climate change policy and theories of social change. *Environment and Planning A*, 42(6), 1273–1285.

Sovacool, B. K. (2016). Navigating agency, structure, discourse, and justice: Building theoretical toolkits for the diffusion of new technologies, social studies of science.

Sovacool, B.K. & Hess, D.J. (2017). Ordering Theories: Typologies and conceptual frameworks for sociotechnical change. *Social Studies of Science*, 47(5): 703–750.

Sovacool, B. K., Brown, M. A., & Valentine, S. (2016). *Fact and fiction in global energy policy*. Baltimore, MD: Johns Hopkins University Press.

Spaargaren, G. (2011). Theories of practices: Agency, technology, and culture: Exploring the relevance of practice theories for the governance of sustainable consumption practices in the new world-order. *Global Environmental Change*, 21(3), 813–822.

Stern, P. C. (2000). Towards a coherent theory of environmentally significant behavior, *Journal of Social Issues*, 56.

Stern, P. C., Janda, K. B., Brown, M. A., Steg, L., Vine, E. L., & Lutzenhiser, L. (2016). Opportunities and insights for reducing fossil fuel consumption by households and organizations. *Nature Energy, 1*(16043). doi:10.1038/NENERGY.2016.43

Stoknes, P. E. (2014). Rethinking climate communications and the "psychological climate paradox." *Energy Research & Social Science, 1,* 161–170.

United Nations Environment Programme (UNEP). (2008). *Kick the habit: A UN guide to climate neutrality.* Paris: UNEP.

Vandenbergh, M. P., Stern, P. C., Gardner, G. T., Dietz, T., & Gilligan, J. M. (2010). Implementing the behavioral wedge: designing and adopting effective carbon emissions reduction programs. *Environmental Law Reporter, 40*(6), 10547–10554.

Waitt, G., & Harada, T. (2012). Driving, cities and changing climates. *Urban Studies, 49*(15), 3307–3325.

Wang, Y., & Brown, M. A. (2014). Policy drivers for improving electricity end-use efficiency in the U.S.: An economic-engineering analysis. *Energy Efficiency, 7*(3), 517–546.

Whitmarsh, L., Seyfangc, G., & O'Neill, S. (2011). Public engagement with carbon and climate change: To what extent is the public "carbon capable"? *Global Environmental Change, 21*(1), 56–65.

Wilkinson, N. (2008). *An introduction to behavioral economics.* New York: Palgrave.

Wilson, C., & Hadi, D. (2007). Models of decision making and residential energy use. *Annual Review of Environmental Resources, 32,* 183.

CHAPTER 12

....

ENERGY CULTURES AS SOCIOMATERIAL ORDERS OF ENERGY

....

THOMAS PFISTER AND MARTIN SCHWEIGHOFER

INTRODUCTION

....

WHEN exploring the manifold relationships between energy and society, one of the first insights must be that energy systems are much more than technological hardware. Therefore, most students of energy and society, including the contributors to this volume, commonly depart from the assumption that energy systems are complex sociotechnical arrangements. This chapter has the particular task of discussing the value of investigating energy systems from a perspective of culture. At first sight, there is a plethora of potentially useful cultural theories from which we can draw. What is more, many of the approaches discussed in this chapter do not explicitly self-identify as studies of cultures of energy, but rather focus on practices or sociotechnical imaginaries. Therefore, this chapter must be harshly selective.

We neglect colloquial uses describing energy transitions vaguely as "requiring a change of culture," and we do not view culture in reference to a specific segment of society as in "high" or "popular" culture. In contrast, this chapter suggests that we view culture as a general analytical perspective on social order that can be applied to all segments of society. From this perspective, energy systems transformation is indeed a matter of cultural change, and there is growing agreement among students of energy and society that far-reaching reorderings of energy systems need to be matched by sophisticated cultural analyses (Horta et al., 2014; Rüdiger, 2008; Sarrica et al., 2016; Stephenson et al., 2015; Strauss et al., 2013).

The next section develops a cultural lens on energy and outlines three essential elements of energy cultures: everyday practices as a ground layer, collective representations of the order of energy as a second layer, and knowledge as a dynamic link between them. Following this conceptual outline, the subsequent sections present two examples that illustrate how such a perspective can provide deeper understanding of the characteristics and workings of the order of energy and current attempts to change it.

Energy Systems as Sociomaterial Orders

This section begins by exploring possible uses of the concept of culture for investigating energy. For this purpose, it must find a middle way between trying to cover the entire continuum of different meanings and boiling them down to a single definition. To begin with, culture is a mid-range concept of order. It affects individual agents but does not determine their actions. At the same time, it is constituted by agents, but neither intentionally nor as a mere aggregation of autonomous individuals and their actions. Cultural perspectives focus on the dynamic aspects of order, particularly its emergence and internal diversity. This dynamic and fluent characteristic implies that there is room for variation and that cultures are often based on a plurality of similar elements. There is even room for contestation and resistance, which do not need to refute order at large, but can provide sources of cultural change. Furthermore, contemporary perspectives on culture are increasingly paying attention to the importance of material elements. Cultural studies have shown the many and various ways that energy and its respective material infrastructures are embedded deeply in particular societies. We approach this diversity of accounts by highlighting three aspects of energy cultures that we hold most important with regard to understanding both energy systems as sociomaterial orders and ongoing searches for more sustainable energy. First, we distinguish two main layers of energy cultures: *practices* as the focal unit of analysis on the ground, and *collective representations* that capture particular cultures as a whole. The latter are not so much complete and holistic accessories of an energy culture, but rather the dimension where collective imaginations of the energy system, its use by and value for a society, can be detected. In addition, as a third important aspect, we address the dynamic link mediating between these two layers that is constituted by specific *knowledge practices*.

The Groundwork of Energy Cultures: Practice

The first aspect concerns a widely shared theoretical and empirical predisposition toward (social) practice and practice theory. In fact, practices can be seen as the basic components and therefore the ground layer of each culture. A good starting point is provided by social theorist Andreas Reckwitz:

A "practice" ... is a routinized type of behaviour which consists of several elements, interconnected to one other: forms of bodily activities, forms of mental activities, "things" and their use, a background knowledge in the form of understanding, know-how, states of emotion and motivational knowledge. (Reckwitz, 2002, p. 249)

Such patterns can be understood by other agents, even if they might perform them slightly differently. In particular, regular bodily behavior and use of materials are also connected to "certain routinized ways of understanding, knowing how and desiring" (Reckwitz, 2002, p. 250).

We also follow Reckwitz's insight that practice theories constitute one important strand of cultural theories. Their relevance with regard to understanding the order of energy is demonstrated by the considerable spectrum of accounts investigating energy, society, and sustainability from a perspective on practice—even though they often do not self-identify as cultural theories. At the same time, many of the (relatively few) contributions explicitly employing the theoretical concept of energy culture draw on practice theory.

Several authors in this context have used their practice perspective to criticize dominant views about energy consumption as deliberate choice (Hargreaves, 2011; Shove, 2010). Perhaps the central insight from this perspective is that energy consumption is hardly ever an activity in its own right, but rather is deeply buried within the (often mundane) practices constituting everyday life. Moreover, these patterns of consumption are inscribed into the material artifacts and environments that contemporary societies inhabit. The hidden role of energy and the stability of these arrangements can frustrate, or at least complicate, attempts to make these mundane specific aspects of living more sustainable (for example, Gram-Hansen, 2011; Shove & Walker, 2014; Shove et al., 2015). Hence, practice-theoretical accounts of energy consumption provide important insights into how new technologies are integrated in user practices (Bickerstaff et al., 2016; Ozaki & Shaw, 2014; Ozaki et al., 2013).

From a more general view, this work touches on important questions about stability and change. Practice theories often emphasize the rigidity of cultures. With regard to energy cultures, stability is particularly based on the practice arrangements surrounding energy infrastructures. These infrastructures are not only technological systems, but also markets and regulatory contexts. Often, they are controlled by powerful agents, such as large energy providers with close links to state power, or the state itself. The materialities and the power asymmetries between different social worlds engaging in energy-related practices are mostly overlooked by practice theoretical accounts of energy consumption.

Yet practice and cultural theories not only are about stability, but also allow for analyzing how patterns can change. On the one hand, energy practices and cultures can be disrupted by events such as the oil crises in the 1970s, the 2003 power blackout in the Northeast of the United States, or the 2011 earthquake followed by the nuclear disaster at Fukushima Daiichi in Japan. On the other hand, various actors engage in interventions in the practices of larger groups of people. Examples of such transformation-oriented agents include governments and international organizations (Müller, 2017), civil society and activist groups (Hargreaves et al., 2013; Seyfang & Haxeltine, 2012; Seyfang & Smith, 2007), intermediary organizations (Kivimaa, 2014), and expert communities advocating particular technologies (Gjefsen, 2017) or much larger projects of system innovation (Smith et al., 2010) or transition management (Loorbach, 2007; on its role in governance, see Voss, 2014). Especially large-scale transformation projects of the latter kind will not function without some involvement of the state (for example, Midttun, 2012; Renn & Marshall, 2016; Sovacool, 2010; Verbong & Geels, 2007). In the process, various practice repertoires aiming not only at behavior change, but also at transforming whole energy systems, have emerged, in addition to practices related to energy production and consumption (Scoones et al., 2015; Verbong & Loorbach, 2012). What can be said about most of these practices is that they are mostly knowledge intensive and that new, different expert communities have emerged as their carriers.

We do not need to delve deeper into discussing theoretical variations among practice theories. We only point to one question that arises from reviewing practice theoretical accounts of energy—whether practice should be conceived as the dominant concept, or one among several. For example, in their often quoted definition, Shove, Pantzar, and Watson (2012) describe practice as a combination of three main elements—materials, skills, and meanings. In contrast, Stephenson et.al. (2015) see practices as only one building block of energy cultures alongside norms, which they understand as expectations and aspirations guiding individual action, and material culture, that is, "the physical evidence of culture including objects, buildings, and infrastructure" (Stephenson et al., 2015, p. 119). From an analytical point of view, the composite nature of practices does not require additional elements external to practice. Practices can be thought of as exactly the nexus of all these bodily, material, cognitive, and behavioral elements, which would be sufficient for grounding cultural orders of energy. In principle, this is theoretically consistent. At the same time, since we are interested in the broader picture of energy cultures as sociotechnical orders, it can be confusing to describe them in terms of a myriad of interconnected practices. Therefore, it makes sense to introduce a second layer of energy cultures that comprises a larger whole, rather than the mere sum of its parts (i.e., the underlying practices).

Imagining Sociomaterial Orders: Representations of Energy Cultures

So far, this discussion has addressed practices as the basic units underlying any energy culture on the ground. Since too many accounts employing practice theory or culture focus too narrowly on households and practices of individual consumers, we want to zoom out and take the larger manifestations of culture into account. This top layer is essentially representing larger sociomaterial orders, imaginations of cultural orders of energy, and related collective identities that would not reveal themselves from a perspective of single practices on the ground. These representations draw on collective narratives or symbols; they can be inscribed in technologies and institutions, which does not mean that they do not allow for different collective interpretations.

Without doubt, given their fluent (practice) basis, comprehensive analysis of cultures is elusive. Nevertheless, it is not impossible to investigate cultures from a more comprehensive perspective of the larger whole. For example, historians of electrification have shown how the extension of electricity networks and applications was both manifestation of and trigger for massive social changes from 1880 to the first half of the twentieth century. For example, David Nye traced how massive changes in everyday practices and values in the American family, as well as in the workplace, co-evolved with the widespread extension of electricity in this realm (Nye, 1990). Electricity systems have become central infrastructures providing opportunities for the specific communities operating them (Hughes, 1983). Moreover, such experts are often able to inscribe their values into an energy system affecting much larger parts of a society (Richter et al., 2017). Hence, investigating the attributes of one society's energy systems can reveal much about its social order from a more general perspective.

Looking at the important example of nuclear power, Hecht (2009) studied how it became closely intertwined with politics, the economy, and national identity in France in the decades after World War II. Technological decisions in this context were both driven by and affected much larger political struggles about the meaning and image of modern France as a technological state. Moreover, Jasanoff and Kim (2009) coined the notion of "sociotechnical imaginaries" to describe the ordering role of nuclear technology in two states. Their account is particularly interesting in the context of struggles for energy transformations and more sustainable energy cultures for two reasons. First, they show that technoscientific projects can transport grand narratives about the future of a nation. Second, this relationship is only partially due to the attributes of such projects, but crucially depends on how they are perceived by broader publics. Importantly, the choice of a particular sociotechnical project, as well as influence over its broader reception and its role in a narrated future, is crucially a question of power. Regarding energy, such power is often concentrated in technical and industrial elites. In contrast, Felt (2015) describes how the *absence* of nuclear technology is an important element of Austrian national identity and national energy culture.

Taken together, these accounts emphasize that order is constituted not only by certain sets of practices and technologies, but also by their collective reception and interpretation within a society. With regard to energy, order can only be constituted if particular technoscientific projects (for example, aiming at a more sustainable energy system) are also interpreted in this way by a much broader public than those experts in charge of these programs.

Once such a representation of order is established, it informs practices, but without causally determining them. In other words, these collectively held representations offer accounts about the particular use and value(s) of energy systems within a society. Moreover, energy systems are important anchors for the collective imaginations of states and communities.

Regarding the relationship between the manifold practices on the ground and the encompassing representations of order, they are not strictly separate. Instead, they are linked by a mediating instance: knowledge practices.

Intermediating Between Practices and Collective Representations: Knowledge Practices

A third essential aspect of energy cultures, which we want to discuss in this chapter, is constituted by knowledge and the practices centered on it. It is not a third layer, but rather the dynamic link that mediates between the countless practices on the ground and the order built upon them. We particularly highlight this mediating role of knowledge, as it is crucial for both the stabilization and change of energy cultures.

Knowledge, in this context, can have two forms. On the one hand, knowledge can be implicit and tacit. People constantly have to interpret and to react to the signals they receive from other people and their environment. From a perspective on practice and culture, this is often not a conscious choice. Rather, this can be compared to activating different scripts on the basis of embodied (i.e., learned and internalized rather than consciously rationalized) competences and skills (Berker, 2006; Bickerstaff et al., 2016). Such skills are required for relatively mundane everyday practices such as cooking, laundry, or driving (Shove et al., 2012), as well as for the enormous theoretical and technical activities of scientists in a laboratory (Knorr Cetina, 1999; Latour & Woolgar, 1986).

On the other hand, knowledge can be explicit—something that is produced, debated, claimed, communicated, and contested in terms of concepts, theories, models, and methodologies. From this point of view, knowledge can be seen as a very specific set of practices: practices of knowledge production, communication, and evaluation. While this chapter stresses the importance of practices explicitly involved in making, debating, evaluating, and communicating knowledge, embodied and internalized skills are essential elements of all practices.

All energy infrastructures require highly skilled experts, for example, involved in operating plants, grids, markets, and policies. Also, societal conflicts—for example, about energy technologies, energy consumption, or energy transmission—are mainly fought with knowledge-centered practices. In order to grasp the essential knowledge element of energy systems, Miller, Iles, and Jones (2013) identify "energy epistemics" as a crucial element of the mutually embedded relationship of energy and society: "Who knows about energy systems, what and how do they know, and whose knowledge counts in governing and reshaping energy futures?" (Miller et al., 2013, p. 137).

The concept of energy epistemics comprises the "knowledge practices governing energy systems" (Miller et al., 2013, p. 137), most of which are highly sophisticated expert practices; for example, for estimating energy demand or for metering and billing electricity for consumers. The search for more sustainable energy technologies and energy institutions has amplified the range of these practices in order to design and to assess possible energy systems of the future. The themes and objects in the center of these expert practices are not just objectively given, but rather are representations of phenomena, or epistemic objects. The latter are crucially characterized by the impossibility to know them completely (Knorr Cetina, 2001; Rheinberger, 1997). Their lack of completeness makes them difficult to control and always calls for further attention and elaboration. Formulating a very similar idea for the political realm, Voss and Freeman (2016) claim that policy is crucially tied to knowledge (i.e., epistemic) objects. In contrast to science, where the essential openness of such objects mainly invites further research, there is a broader range of practices and institutions dealing with policy in the public realm, including, for example, judicial review, legislative and regulatory processes, as well as political and social struggles.

Energy cultures and current attempts to transform them are essentially characterized by various epistemic objects, all of them uncertain and often heavily contested. They include elements as diverse as the smart grid (Lösch & Schneider, 2016), communal energy (Islar & Busch, 2016), or electric mobility (Wentland, 2016)—neither of them is just an objective thing. Instead, they are representations of elements that are seen as important and that need to be investigated, governed, financed, or fought over. All those "solutions" need to be translated into practices to design, assess, and realize them with regard to their feasibility, environmental, social, and economic consequences. In addition, they need to be put in relation to competing imagined sociomaterial orders to become meaningful and legitimate projects. In general, most controversies over current energy issues, such as the risks of nuclear power or fracking, are knowledge controversies about the features, potential benefits, and potential harms of envisaged energy systems—the actual future of which is unknown.

The practices targeting transformation and the actors carrying them out—many of which were already mentioned in the first subsection—are particularly enrolled in envisioning and conceptualizing sustainable energy cultures of the future. In order to intervene in existing energy cultures, it is essential that they develop and enact knowledge practices of various kinds. From a theoretical point of view, such knowledge practices aiming at transformation and driven by the uncertainties of the knowledge objects involved are important examples of the dynamic, creative, and productive nature of orders based on practice and culture (Knorr Cetina, 2001). Certainly, these issues are contentious and interwoven with various values, interpretations, and ideas, inevitably leading to different visions for future energy systems and often accompanied by knowledge controversies. These knowledge-intensive political struggles are not only about technological choices or different fuels, but also about the social organization of these systems and their relation to other parts of society (see Miller et al., 2015; Stirling, 2014).

To conclude this first section, energy cultures are sociomaterial orders of energy that are practiced and imagined and in which the two layers of practice and representations of order emerge, become stable, and develop, mostly through practices of knowing. Moreover, as sociotechnical "infrastructures," energy cultures can be nearly invisible stabilizing factors underlying the relationships between energy and society. But they can also be heavily contested with regard to their composition or consequences. Therefore, encounters with energy cultures are essentially political. The following two sections contain two examples that present how energy cultures operate and how they often only become visible when they are contested and become subject to different interventions.

ILLUSTRATION 1: ENERGY CULTURES
OF GREEN ELECTRICITY

The first example centers on current struggles for more sustainable electricity. Its main focus is on EU legislation to foster a transparent market for renewable energy as prerequisite for a demand-led transformation from fossil-nuclear to renewable energy systems, as well as its uptake, and interaction with national renewable resource policy in Germany. In particular, in the process, it demonstrates how the search for more sustainable energy translates into different "projects" that may draw on rather similar knowledge practices but utilizes them to promote rather different envisioned orders of energy.

EU Legislation: Stimulating Practice and Ways of Knowing

It has been a general characteristic of politics in (Western) industrialized societies for several decades that solutions to environmental problems are expected to be compatible with and based on the mechanisms of free markets, addressing environmental problems in a cost-effective way, and ideally generating economic benefits.[1] Before that occurs, however, markets designed to tackle ecological problems need to be created. In particular, this requires the creation of very specific commodities. Important examples include the emissions-trading instruments of the Acid Rain Project established by the US Environmental Protection Agency in 1990 (focusing on sulphur dioxide and nitrogen oxide emissions as tradable commodities), or the EU Emissions Trading System (mainly for the commodity of carbon dioxide), both of which define caps for different pollutants, but also permit pollutant producers to sell or buy emission allowances to balance their output.

Similarly, in a liberalized EU electricity market, the intention is to give consumers greater opportunities to consume electricity from renewables, potentially fostering a demand-led transformation from fossil-nuclear to more sustainable energy systems. However, once electricity is fed into the grid, it is impossible to identify the resources used to produce it. Hence, this example begins with a piece of EU legislation, Directive 2009/28/EC (replacing Directive 2001/77/EC),[2] which constitutes an entire policy framework, including, among other elements: common definitions of key concepts, mandatory national goals for renewable energy production, an EU-wide monitoring regime, and advisory expert committees, as well as the mandatory issuing of guarantees of origin (GOs) as electronic certificates for each megawatt hour (MWh) from renewable resources.

The introduction of GOs as a market-making element is of particular interest for the present illustration. Guarantees of origin (GOs) can be bought and sold independently of the physical electricity they represent. The political intention was to provide transparency and allow consumer choice. Yet doing so also involves several technical and governance challenges. The electronic certificates need to be issued, traded, and devaluated after use. Moreover, there need to be safeguards against double counting or fraud. This involves an information technology (IT) infrastructure, particularly a standardized script, as well as a regulatory oversight. Therefore, Directive 2009/28/EC also obliges the member states to install regulatory bodies and registries at the national level. They formed the Association of Issuing Bodies in 2001 as a transnational network, which operates a hub to transfer these certificates internationally.

Practices in this context are closely intertwined with expert knowledge relevant for measuring, certifying, and trading electricity as well as GOs. People with special training operate a large and highly sophisticated machinery involving energy producers, traders, and GO-issuing bodies. Their knowledge-intensive expert practices are mostly out of eyeshot of the wider public. At the same time, scrutinizing and contesting them also requires analytical skills, substantive evidence, and resources, as controversies are mostly addressed with data, empirical evidence, extensive analyses, and sophisticated theoretical concepts.

Interaction between EU and National Energy Transformations: Struggling for the Right Energy Culture

Due to huge differences with regard to markets for green electricity across EU member states, EU legislation unfolds within very different policy and market contexts. This illustration focuses particularly on Germany, which has a relatively strong market for green electricity, as well as a quite successful national support scheme for renewable energy. Looking at the intersections of these elements reveals important barriers to the objective of sustainable energy consumption and makes competing imaginaries of sustainable energy visible.

In 2013, 22% of all German households had signed up for a "green" electricity tariff.[3] These practices of consumption, which are thought to be driven by knowledge about environmental problems and imaginaries of a greener society, are further nurtured through marketing efforts from utilities that target these sustainable consumers with imageries full of blue skies and green grass (Herbes & Ramme, 2014).

While consumption is only an implicit objective within Directive 2009/28/EC, the focus on production is even stronger in Germany's main policy with regard to climate protection and sustainable energy: the Renewable Energy Sources Act (RES Act), adopted in 2000 and amended repeatedly since then. Its most important component has been a national feed-in tariff for renewable electricity, driving a massive expansion of renewable energy, for example, through photovoltaic (PV) panels on private homes or local energy cooperatives. Directive 2009/28/EC requires that EU policy does not interfere in the very diverse national support schemes for renewable energy. Therefore, electricity receiving the feed-in tariff in Germany is not eligible for GOs. This has the consequence that Germany is meanwhile producing 31.6% of its gross electricity consumption from renewable resources (BMWi, 2016), but most of this energy cannot be sold as (GO-based) green electricity.

This difficult relationship between the approaches of the RES Act and green electricity tariffs is not a coincidence, but rather is the result of conflicting views about a sustainable society and its energy system. Some had hoped that the German energy transformation based on the RES Act could lead to a more fundamental transformation of society at large. Such a sustainable society should be 100% fueled by renewable energy, but also more democratic and equitable. Change, in this context, should be far-reaching and quick. For example, the late Hermann Scheer, a member of the German parliament and main initiator of the German RES Act, campaigned not only for renewable energy, but also for a decentralized energy system that would give citizens control and autonomy—in particular, from the global fossil-nuclear energy industries (Scheer, 2007). From this perspective, an energy transformation is not a question of technological feasibility, but one of political and economic power.[4] Moreover, designing green products for sustainable consumption was certainly not seen as the most important transformation strategy. Others, in particular established electricity producers and their associations, do not share the view that change should be quick, radical, and led by the state or its citizens. Established industrial players warn that competitive markets and grid stability could be undermined by an uncoordinated increase of renewable energy fostered by the RES Act. EU law and policy, and the EU's emphasis on markets and market-based approaches, constitute crucial political and legal resources in this context. From such a perspective, electricity products targeting sustainable consumers would be considered much more appropriate than state subsidies handed out to a very diverse range of producers.

These perspectives are not independent of each other, nor are they represented by clearly distinct sets of actors; rather, they are overlapping and interacting. On the technical side, both approaches share very similar practices focusing on the creation of energy knowledge based on expert skills. They require electricity to be measured, and its sources and producers to be accounted for. The main difference is that in one case, the producer gets a GO that can be traded, and in the other case a direct remuneration, but prevention of double accounting, for example, is central for both systems. Yet both systems are linked to differing visions of sustainable energy systems in combination with different practices and knowledge about appropriate pathways and strategies. Therefore, agents operating within these emerging energy cultures often must navigate ambivalence, face controversies, and settle for compromises.

In this manner, environmentalist nongovernmental organizations (NGOs) and research institutes (a key element of German environmentalism) got involved in green electricity. Most important, they are involved in two specific labels (*Ok-power, Grüner Strom*) designed to certify electricity with real ecological value.[5] Others act as producers (Greenpeace Energy), and the Oeko-Institute even became involved as a German registry in the first voluntary system to issue, exchange, and cancel GOs established by the European electricity industry in 2001—to massive criticism from other German supporters of renewable energy. Interestingly, these actors again draw on and extend similarly sophisticated knowledge practices of certification and accounting that aim at navigating ambivalence and settling controversies. After its latest amendments, the RES Act looks much more suited for European energy markets and industrial actors than as an instrument to build a decentralized energy system along with a society of democratic and autonomous energy citizens. The act still values and protects the newly won diversity of actors within the emerging renewable energy culture in Germany, but promoters of citizens' energy will need to find new strategies and new niches to put their visions into practice.

ILLUSTRATION 2: ENERGY CULTURES OF SUSTAINABLE INDOOR CLIMATE

The second example illustrates changing energy cultures related to indoor climate, with a particular focus on space heating. Heat consumption is embedded in complex constellations of user practices rather than simply a matter of heating technologies, features of buildings, or outside temperatures (e.g., Gram-Hanssen, 2014). These practices form the groundwork of an energy culture that contains a diverse set of possibilities to reduce embedded energy consumption for space heating. This case study discusses selected changes in practices targeting energy savings, with a particular view on the role of knowledge practices. We map different "projects" of sustainable indoor climate along two bigger representations: ecological modernization as basic idea for a future energy order, and bottom-up efforts of local communities to develop new energy cultures of sufficiency.

Searching for a Sustainable Indoor Climate: Innovative Technologies and Novel Practices

In a quest for more sustainable ways to provide comfortable indoor climates, different actors have elaborated very different pathways. Many of them relate to heating technologies that are more efficient or that utilize renewable energy sources. Examples include advanced biomass utilization, for example automatic wood pellet heating systems or solar thermal heating systems and heat pumps. While these technical efforts offered relative improvements in ecological performance, the operation of modern, highly automatized heating systems has led to changed practices of heating buildings (e.g., Gram-Hanssen, 2010). For instance, shared conventions regarding indoor climate and comfort often develop in a way that leads to higher resource use (see Shove, 2003).

As a result, such newly adopted user practices may cancel out energy savings from more efficient technology, a phenomenon known as the rebound effect (for an overview, see Hertwich, 2005).

Beyond innovating heating systems, another strategy with huge potential to increase sustainability is reducing heat losses from buildings (e.g., McKinsey & Company, 2010). Policies to support building insulation and energy-efficient renovation often also seek economic benefits from environmental protection. For instance, the Green Deal of the UK government is presented as "an exciting new initiative, which has a key role to play in significantly increasing the uptake of insulation, creating new jobs, whilst also reducing energy bills and tackling climate change."[6] On the European level, a mandatory energy performance certificate was implemented to boost improved energy efficiency in buildings across Europe (see Buildings Performance Institute Europe, 2010). To that end, the European Commission also rates highly the importance of the construction sector in both economic and environmental terms, as it "[. . .] creates new jobs, drives economic growth, and provides solutions for social, climate and energy challenges."[7]

Among the most radical approaches to increase the energy efficiency of buildings is the so-called Passive House, characterized by high levels of thermal insulation, high-quality windows, airtight buildings without thermal bridges, and mechanical ventilation systems with heat recovery (see Feist et al., 2005). The first Passive House was built in 1991 in Darmstadt, Germany, as a scientific demonstration project.[8] Later, explicit Passive House standards were formulated,[9] which helped to disseminate the concept. Its diffusion was further supported by a calculation tool, the Passive House Planning Package (PHPP), which incorporated the knowledge base necessary to plan and verify Passive Houses (Müller & Berker, 2013). Institutional actors, such as the Passive House Institute and the International Passive House Association, promote passive houses by claiming that energy use for space heating and cooling can be reduced by up to 90%, while increasing living comfort.[10]

The Passive House design also influenced an entire spectrum of interconnected practices. On the one hand, inhabitants have to modify their everyday practices in this high-tech environment, for example, when cooking practices are adapted to advanced ventilations systems (see Ozaki & Shaw, 2014). On the other hand, one should mention the many expert practices of planning, calculation, construction, installation, and maintenance that have emerged along with its spread. They integrate new materials (for example, triple-glazed windows, heat-recovery ventilation systems), skills, and competences (for example, using specific calculation tools, installing and maintaining ventilation systems), as well as shared images. At the same time, expert communities grew around the specific knowledge base, for example certified Passive House designers and consultants,[11] performing a whole set of distinct expert practices, often behind the scenes.

Modern heating systems and Passive Houses both encompass well-established, marketable products and are not reliant on single proponents. However, they are not uncontested, and the range of possible solutions to make housing more sustainable is greater than the options mentioned. Putting these developments in a broader context, the next section points to an important underlying epistemic struggle among competing visions of future energy cultures.

Techno-Optimism Versus Downsizing: Struggles about Representations of Sustainable Heating

The developments discussed in the preceding can be understood as linked to the more general idea that heat consumption could and should be decoupled from its ecological impacts. Such representations of eco-efficient energy cultures often expect investments in alternative heating technologies and energy-saving buildings to create new jobs and stimulate economic growth. Approaches that aim at decoupling heating demand from ecological impacts and combining ecological and economic interests are often linked to a bigger imagination of sociomaterial order described as *ecological modernization* (e.g., Mol et al., 2009). However, such strategies alone frequently fail to achieve an absolute reduction of energy use and related CO_2 emissions, which can be partially attributed to rebound effects (for example, Jackson, 2009).

In contrast, critical voices such as the Simplicity Institute are highlighting "the urgent need to move beyond growth-orientated, consumerist forms of life [...] at a time when the old myths of progress, techno-optimism, and affluence are failing us."[12] They advance the idea of *sufficiency* as an additional but critical and frequently neglected sustainability strategy (for example, Boulanger, 2010; Princen, 2005). Sufficiency refers to simpler and downsized ways of life that allow for lower ecological impacts—in this particular case, a reduction of heating demand. To that end, shared understandings of the size of living space, common conventions of comfortable indoor climate, or time periods in which heating is appropriate would need to be re-evaluated. In contrast to the technology-centered practices tied to ecological modernization, the idea of sufficiency is tied more closely to practices of social innovation. Moreover, informal groups of grassroots activists and organized civil society actors are among the main protagonists who often deliver potentially important but often neglected innovations for new sustainability pathways (Seyfang & Smith, 2007).

Putting New Ideas into Practice: Local Initiatives of Energy Sufficiency

The larger representation of an energy culture of sufficiency found its expression in several practical experiments regarding more sustainable housing. Many of them aim to reduce the space needed per person, but they differ in many ways, for instance with regard to their ecological commitment or their promotion of novel practices of community living. For example, the so-called tiny-house movement has a stronger focus on affordable housing, while putting less emphasis on communal living. Moving along the spectrum, co-housing projects are portrayed as part of a new sharing economy at the forefront of "environmental and socially sustainable neighborhoods" (The Cohousing Association of the United States, 2016, n.p.). The co-housing movement not only has produced various green building designs (for examples, see McCamant & Durrett, 2011), but also has developed specific practices and concepts to build neighborhoods, communities, and new forms of social relationships. Thereby, co-housing is built around shared communal spaces, which is why premises and private apartments can be smaller, thus reducing ecological impacts.

Ecovillages are another, even more pronounced example of sufficiency-oriented innovations. They are designed to combine new ways of community living with sustainable practices of everyday life, including aspects of housing. The Global Ecovillage Network defines ecovillages as a "human-scale settlement consciously designed through participatory processes to secure long-term sustainability."[13] The commitment to principles of sharing and cooperation involves new collaborative practices of building use, which are meant to have a transformative impact. In fact, ecovillages present themselves "as demonstration sites of sustainability in practice and as places of inspiration for the wider society."[14]

A reduction of individual living space as an important element of the more fundamental idea of a sufficient energy culture implies profound social transformations. New materialities and building concepts, images, and norms (with regard to privacy or to shared spaces) and competences (for instance, communication skills to renegotiate commonly used goods) are integrated to form entirely new practices of community living. Regarding an example of those far-reaching experiments, the community of Schloss Tempelhof has created an experimental communal living space around the first Earthship built in Germany[15] (for an introduction to the Earthship concept, see Seyfang, 2011). The Earthship is an innovative building concept that seeks to minimize environmental impact (for an assessment, see Freney, 2014). It is mainly built from natural, recycled, or up-cycled material, seeks to be independent from external resource flows as it produces its own energy (passive solar heating, PV for electricity), utilizes rainwater, and is simple in its construction.[16] At Schloss Tempelhof the Earthship is at the center of a social experiment in community living. As a shared building, it provides a common kitchen, bathroom, and living room for about 25 people.[17] At the same time, private living space is limited to small individual units in the size of a trailer or a yurt, without kitchens, water supply, or bathrooms. While it is obvious that the mundane everyday practices in such experimental environments differ significantly from usual private homes, their inhabitants also develop expert practices of planning (e.g., participatory processes), funding (e.g., crowd funding) or construction (allowing volunteer work and self-organization; applying natural or recycled resources).

Alternative housing projects rooted in local initiatives often have a long history in developing more radical alternatives to dominant energy cultures on both layers: practical groundwork as well as collective imaginations of sociomaterial orders. In these community projects, visions of low-energy futures are linked to knowledge about collaboration, sharing, resilience, or autonomy, which finally gets translated into local practice. Thereby they also challenge established practices of high consumption and representations of ecological modernization. More generally, this can trigger innovations and visions that would not be doable and knowable for actors with a main focus on markets and technology. However, because these projects are so deeply embedded in local contexts, they often remain particular solutions that are difficult to standardize, transfer, or scale up in market environments.

Similar to the previous example of electricity, competing approaches to sustainable housing are not independent of each other and share many (knowledge) practices, for example, of planning and permission seeking, as well as practices to monitor the ecological impacts and gains of sustainable housing. For instance, the Tempelhof Earthship is subject to scientific analysis and detailed monitoring,[18] similar to the first Passive House demonstration projects. Yet, efficiency and sufficiency projects are tied to broader, competing sustainability analyses and concepts drawing on different as well as shared knowledge-centered practices that establish the link to different imagined sociomaterial orders of energy.

CONCLUSION

This chapter introduced the concept of culture as an analytical perspective on sociomaterial orders of energy, in order to grasp the complex and dynamic sociotechnical shifts of current energy systems. From such a perspective, transformations toward greater sustainability are multilayered, highly dynamic, and complex. This perspective allows an analysis of these transformations as broad and contested societal search processes. To a large extent, they are knowledge struggles in which different actors seek to promote their envisioned energy cultures utilizing specific knowledge-centered practices. In the process, knowledge is used to intervene in everyday practices of energy production, use, and distribution, as well as in collective representations of the roles, values, and meanings of energy within a society.

Such struggles are observable along different axes, such as centralized versus decentralized energy systems, top-down regulation versus bottom-up initiatives, fossil fuels versus renewable energy sources, large-scale versus specific local solutions, market-driven approaches versus statist interventions, evolutionary versus radical views of change, fuel switching versus energy saving, modernization versus sufficiency, and so on. While this chapter has provided only brief illustrations, these issues are particularly relevant for industrialized societies in the Global North. In contrast, searches for practices and visions of sustainable energy cultures would be essentially different in the Global South, which was not addressed in this chapter. Moreover, many energy cultures remain quite stable and are hardly visible. For instance, the reliance on large-scale infrastructures like power grids, or the energy dependence of modern lifestyles in general, remain uncontested in many social contexts, while fossil fuels or nuclear power have been under scrutiny for decades.

Both cases highlight the importance of knowledge-centered practices linking the two layers of practices and collectively imagined orders of energy. This particularly applies in times when everyday practices on the ground and broader representations of energy orders are increasingly scrutinized and contested in the context of searches for more sustainable energy cultures. Different actors engage in epistemic work, struggling for particular practices and representations of sociomaterial order. Therefore, questions for further research can be formulated along the different struggles mentioned earlier, but must always answer the questions raised by Miller, Iles, and Jones (2013): who knows what, how do they know it, and whose knowledge counts in the transformation toward more sustainable energy cultures?

Notes

1. This approach also corresponds to the more general orientation toward ecological modernisation that is explained in more detail in the next subsection.
2. In contrast to EU regulations, which create one set of rules applying to the whole Union, directives set common objectives and guidelines but leave implementation to the member states.
3. See https://www.foederal-erneuerbar.de/uebersicht/bundeslaender/BW|BY|B|BB|HB|H H|HE|MV|NI|NRW|RLP|SL|SN|ST|SH|TH|D/kategorie/akzeptanz/auswahl/227-anteil _der_haushalte/sicht/diagramm/#goto_227
4. The feasibility of a completely renewable energy system in Germany is supported by several scientific studies (Henning & Palzer, 2012; Klaus et al., 2010; Quaschning, 2010; Rogall, 2014; SRU, 2011).
5. Reichmuth (2016) provides a comprehensive overview of certification schemes, as well as criteria to assess the ecological quality of green electricity products.
6. See https://www.gov.uk/government/news/green-deal-to-create-green-jobs
7. See https://ec.europa.eu/growth/sectors/construction_en
8. For a historical review, see https://passipedia.org/basics/the_passive_house_-_historical _review
9. See https://passivehouse-international.org/index.php?page_id=150
10. See http://passivehouse.com/02_informations/01_whatisapassivehouse/01_whatisapassive house .htm
11. See http://www.passivhausplaner.eu/index.php?page_id=321&level1_id=277
12. See http://simplicityinstitute.org/about
13. See http://gen-europe.org/home/index.htm
14. See http://gen-europe.org/about-us/ecovillages/index.htm
15. See http://www.schloss-tempelhof.de/experimentelles-wohnen/
16. See https://en.wikipedia.org/wiki/Earthship or http://earthship.org/
17. See http://www.earthship-tempelhof.de/
18. For a detailed monitoring of the Earthship in Tempelhof, see http://monitor.earthship -tempelhof.de

REFERENCES

Berker, T., Hartmann, M., Punie, Y., & Ward, K. J. (Eds.). (2006). *Domestication of media and technology*. Maidenhead: Open University Press.

Bickerstaff, K., Hinton, E., & Bulkeley, H. (2016). Decarbonisation at home: The contingent politics of experimental domestic energy technologies. *Environment and Planning A, 48*(10), 2006–2025.

BMWi. (2016). Erneuerbare Energien in Zahlen. Nationale und internationale Entwicklung im Jahr 2015. Retrieved from www.erneuerbare-energien.de/EE/Redaktion/DE/Downloads /erneuerbare-energien-in-zahlen-2015.pdf?__blob=publicationFile&v=6

Boulanger, P.-M. (2010). Three strategies for sustainable consumption. *S.A.P.I.EN.S. -Surveys and Perspectives Integrating Environment and Society, 3*(2), [Online]. Retrieved from http://sapiens.revues.org/1022

Buildings Performance Institute Europe. (2010). *Energy performance certificates across Europe: From design to implementation*. Retrieved from http://www.buildup.eu/sites /default/files/content/BPIE_EPC%20report%202010.pdf

Feist, W., Schnieders, J., Dorer, V., & Haas, A. (2005). Re-inventing air heating: Convenient and comfortable within the frame of the Passive House concept. *Energy and Buildings, 37*(11), 1186–1203.

Felt, U. (2015). Keeping technologies out: Sociotechnical imaginaries and the formation of a national technopolitical identity. In S. Jasanoff & S.-H. Kim (Eds.), *Dreamscapes of modernity: Sociotechnical imaginaries and the fabrication of power* (pp. 103–125). Chicago: University of Chicago Press.

Freney, M. H. P. (2014). *Earthship architecture: Post occupancy evaluation, thermal performance and life cycle assessment*. PhD Thesis, School of Architecture and Built Environment, University of Adelaide, Australia.

Gjefsen, M. D. (2017). Crafting the expert-advocate: Training and recruitment efforts in the carbon dioxide capture and storage community. *Innovation: The European Journal of Social Science Research, 30*(3), 259–282. Retrieved from http://dx.doi.org/10.1080 /13511610.2017.1279538

Gram-Hanssen, K. (2010). Residential heat comfort practices: Understanding users. *Building Research & Information, 38*(2), 175–186.

Gram-Hanssen, K. (2011). Understanding change and continuity in residential energy consumption. *Journal of Consumer Culture, 11*(1), 61–78.

Gram-Hanssen, K. (2014). New needs for better understanding of household's energy consumption—behaviour, lifestyle or practices? *Architectural Engineering and Design Management, 10*(1–2), 91–107.

Hargreaves, T. (2011). Practice-ing behaviour change: Applying social practice theory to pro-environmental behaviour change. *Journal of Consumer Culture, 11*(1), 79–99.

Hargreaves, T., Hielscher, S., Seyfang, G., & Smith, A. (2013). Grassroots innovations in community energy: The role of intermediaries in niche development. *Global Environmental Change, 23*(5), 868–880.

Hecht, G. (2009). *The radiance of France: Nuclear power and national identity after World War II*. Cambridge, MA: MIT Press.

Henning, H.-M., & Palzer, A. (2012). *100% erneuerbare Energien für Strom und Wärme in Deutschland*. Freiburg: Fraunhofer-Institut für Solare Energiesysteme ISE.

Herbes, C., & Ramme, I. (2014). Online marketing of green electricity in Germany: A content analysis of providers' websites. *Energy Policy, 66*(3), 257–266.

Hertwich, E. G. (2005). Consumption and the rebound effect: An industrial ecology perspective. *Journal of Industrial Ecology, 9*(1–2), 85–98.

Horta, A., Wilhite, H., Schmidt, L., & Bartiaux, F. (2014). Socio-technical and cultural approaches to energy consumption: An introduction. *Nature and Culture, 9*(2), 115–121.

Hughes, T. P. (1983). *Networks of power: Electrification in Western society, 1880–1930.* Baltimore, MD: Johns Hopkins University Press.

Islar, M., & Busch, H. (2016). "We are not in this to save the polar bears!" The link between community renewable energy development and ecological citizenship. *Innovation: The European Journal of Social Science Research, 29*(3), 303–319.

Jackson, T. (2009). *Prosperity without growth: Economics for a finite planet.* London; Stirling, VA: Earthscan.

Jasanoff, S., & Kim, S.-H. (2009). Containing the atom: Sociotechnical imaginaries and nuclear power in the United States and South Korea. *Minerva, 47*(2), 119–146.

Kivimaa, P. (2014). Government-affiliated intermediary organisations as actors in system-level transitions. *Research Policy, 43*(8), 1370–1380.

Klaus, T., Vollmer, C., Werner, K., Lehmann, H., & Müschen, K. (2010). *Energieziel 2050: 100% Strom aus erneuerbaren Quellen.* Dessau-Roßlau: Umweltbundesamt. Retrieved from http://www.umweltbundesamt.de/sites/default/files/medien/378/publikationen/energieziel_2050.pdf

Knorr Cetina, K. (1999). *Epistemic cultures: How the sciences make knowledge.* Cambridge, MA: Harvard University Press.

Knorr Cetina, K. (2001). Objectual practice. In R. S. Theodore, K. Knorr-Cetina, & E. Von Savigny (Eds.), *The practice turn* (pp. 175–188). London: Routledge.

Latour, B., & Woolgar, S. (1986). *Laboratory life: The social construction of scientific facts.* Princeton, NJ: Princeton University Press.

Loorbach, D. (2007). *Transition management: New mode of governance for sustainable development.* Utrecht: International Books.

Lösch, A., & Schneider, C. (2016). Transforming power/knowledge apparatuses: The smart grid in the German energy transition. *Innovation: The European Journal of Social Science Research, 29*(3), 262–284.

McCamant, K., & Durrett, C. (2011). *Creating cohousing: Building sustainable communities.* Gabriola Island, BC: New Society Publishers.

McKinsey & Company. (2010). *Impact of the financial crisis on carbon economics: Version 2.1 of the global greenhouse gas abatement cost curve.* Retrieved from http://www.mckinsey.com/business-functions/sustainability-and-resource-productivity/our-insights/impact-of-the-financial-crisis-on-carbon-economics-version-21

Midttun, A. (2012). The greening of European electricity industry: A battle of modernities. *Energy Policy, 48,* 22–35.

Miller, C. A., Iles, A., & Jones, C. F. (2013). The social dimensions of energy transitions. *Science as Culture, 22*(2), 135–148.

Miller, C. A., Richter, J., & O'Leary, J. (2015). Socio-energy systems design: A policy framework for energy transitions. *Energy Research & Social Science, 6,* 29–40.

Mol, A. P. J., Sonnenfeld, D. A., & Spaargaren, G. (Eds.). (2009). *The ecological modernisation reader: Environmental reform in theory and practice.* London; New York: Routledge.

Müller, F. (2017). IRENA as a glocal actor: Pathways towards energy governmentality. *Innovation: The European Journal of Social Science Research, 30*(3), 306–322. Retrieved from http://dx.doi.org/10.1080/13511610.2017.1279538

Müller, L., & Berker, T. (2013). Passive House at the crossroads: The past and the present of a voluntary standard that managed to bridge the energy efficiency gap. *Energy Policy, 60,* 586–593.

Nye, D. E. (1990). *Electrifying America: Social meanings of a new technology, 1880–1940.* Cambridge, MA: MIT Press.

Ozaki, R., & Shaw, I. (2014). Entangled practices: Governance, sustainable technologies, and energy consumption. *Sociology, 48*(3), 590–605.

Ozaki, R., Shaw, I., & Dodgson, M. (2013). The coproduction of 'sustainability': Negotiated practices and the Prius. *Science, Technology & Human Values, 38*(4), 518–541.

Princen, T. (2005). *The logic of sufficiency.* Cambridge, MA; London: MIT Press.

Quaschning, V. (2010). *Renewable energy and climate change.* Chichester, West Sussex, UK; Hoboken, NJ: John Wiley & Sons.

Reckwitz, A. (2002). Toward a theory of social practices: A development in culturalist theorizing. *European Journal of Social Theory, 5*(2), 243–263.

Reichmuth, M. (2016). Marktanalyse Ökostrom. Final Report of the Umweltbundesamt, Dessau, Germany. Retrieved from https://www.umweltbundesamt.de/publikationen /marktanalyse-oekostrom

Renn, O., & Marshall, J. P. (2016). Coal, nuclear and renewable energy policies in Germany: From the 1950s to the "Energiewende." *Energy Policy, 99,* 224–232.

Rheinberger, H.-J. (1997). *Toward a history of epistemic things: Synthesizing proteins in the test tube.* Stanford, CA: Stanford University Press.

Richter, J. A. , Tidwell, A. S. D., Fisher, E., & Miller, T. R. (2017). STIRring the grid: Engaging energy systems design and planning in the context of urban sociotechnical imaginaries. *Innovation: The European Journal of Social Science Research,* 30(3), 365–384.

Rogall, H. (2014). *100%-Versorgung mit erneuerbaren Energien—Bedingungen für eine globale, nationale und kommunale Umsetzung.* Marburg: Metropolis.

Rüdiger, M. (Ed.). (2008). *The culture of energy.* Newcastle: Cambridge Scholars.

Sarrica, M., Brondi, S., Cottone, P., & Mazzara, B. M. (2016). One, no one, one hundred thousand energy transitions in Europe: The quest for a cultural approach. *Energy Research & Social Science, 13*(3), 1–14.

Scheer, H. (2007). *Energy autonomy: The economic, social and technological case for renewable energy.* London: Earthscan.

Scoones, I., Leach, M., & Newell, P. (Eds.). (2015). *The politics of green transformations.* London; New York: Routledge.

Seyfang, G. (Ed.). (2011). *The new economics of sustainable consumption: Seeds of change.* Basingstoke, UK: Palgrave Macmillan.

Seyfang, G., & Haxeltine, A. (2012). Growing grassroots innovations: Exploring the role of community-based initiatives in governing sustainable energy transitions. *Environment and Planning C: Government and Policy, 30*(3), 381–400.

Seyfang, G., & Smith, A. (2007). Grassroots innovations for sustainable development: Towards a new research and policy agenda. *Environmental Politics, 16*(4), 584–603.

Shove, E. (2010). Beyond the ABC: Climate change policy and theories of social change. *Environment and Planning A, 42*(6), 1273–1285.

Shove, E. (2003). *Comfort, cleanliness and convenience: The social organization of normality.* Oxford; New York: Berg.

Shove, E., Pantzar, M., & Watson, M. (2012). *The dynamics of social practice everyday life and how it changes.* Los Angeles: SAGE.

Shove, E., & Walker, G. (2014). What is energy for? Social practice and energy demand. *Theory, Culture & Society, 31*(5), 41–58.

Shove, E., Watson, M., & Spurling, N. (2015). Conceptualizing connections: Energy demand, infrastructures and social practices. *European Journal of Social Theory, 18*(3), 274–287.

Smith, A., Voss, J.,-P., & Grin, J. (2010). Innovation studies and sustainability transitions: The allure of the multi-level perspective and its challenges. *Research Policy, 39*(4), 435–448.

Sovacool, B. K. (2010). The importance of open and closed styles of energy research. *Social Studies of Science, 40*(6), 903–930.

SRU. (2011). *Sondergutachten: Wege zur 100% erneuerbaren Stromversorgung.* Berlin: Erich Schmidt Verlag.

Stephenson, J., Barton, B., Carrington, G., Doering, A., Ford, R. Hopkins, D., . . . Wooliscroft, B. (2015). The energy cultures framework: Exploring the role of norms, practices and material culture in shaping energy behaviour in New Zealand. *Energy Research & Social Science, 7*(0), 117–123.

Stirling, A. (2014). Transforming power: Social science and the politics of energy choices. *Energy Research & Social Science, 1,* 83–95.

Strauss, S., Rupp, S., & Love, T. (Eds.). (2013). *Cultures of energy: Power, practices, technologies.* Walnut Creek, CA: Left Coast Press.

The Cohousing Association of the United States. (2016). *Cohousing in the United States: An innovative model of sustainable neighborhoods.* Retrieved from http://www.cohousing.org/sites/default/files/attachments/StateofCohousingintheU.S.%204-22-16.pdf

Verbong, G., & Geels, F. (2007). The ongoing energy transition: Lessons from a socio-technical, multi-level analysis of the Dutch electricity system (1960–2004). *Energy Policy, 35*(2), 1025–1037.

Verbong, G., & Loorbach, D. (2012). *Governing the energy transition: Reality, illusion or necessity?* New York: Routledge.

Voss, J.-P. (2014). Performative policy studies: Realizing "transition management." *Innovation: The European Journal of Social Science Research, 27*(4), 317–343.

Voss, J.-P., & Freeman, R. (2016). Introduction: Knowing governance. In J.-P. Voss & R. Freeman (Eds.). *Knowing governance: The epistemic construction of political order* (pp. 63–86). Basingstoke UK: Palgrave Macmillan.

Wentland, A. (2016). Imagining and enacting the future of the German energy transition: electric vehicles as grid infrastructure. *Innovation: The European Journal of Social Science Research, 29*(3), 285–302.

···

CHAPTER 13

THE LIMITS
OF HOUSEHOLD CHANGE
Structural Influences over Individual Consumption

···

JANET A. LORENZEN

INTRODUCTION

ENERGY conservation is a large part of the "every little bit helps" motto of social change, or what academics call the aggregation hypothesis. The narrative suggests that we are all equally responsible for using energy (causing greenhouse gas emissions) and should do our part to reduce this burden on the environment. This perspective has gained serious attention by policymakers because it targets so-called low-hanging fruit (changes that should be easy for consumers to make). Voluntary changes made by households are less controversial than the government regulation of industry. In response, this chapter highlights problems with a consumer-centered policy approach and describes several different ways that consumers are locked into fossil-fuel intensive consumption patterns.

To begin, the "every little bit helps" narrative of easy fixes has several flaws. First, households are not the most significant consumers of energy. According to the US Energy Information Administration, the residential sector accounts for 24% of total energy end use (commercial 19%, industrial 30%, transportation 27%, January–March 2016).[1] Second, doing a little bit helps a little bit. Household changes like adjusting thermostat settings, lowering water-heater temperature, replacing light bulbs, automobile maintenance, and carpooling could reduce greenhouse gas emissions by 7% (Vandenbergh, Barkenbus, & Gilligan, 2008). Other projections are similar and show that changing household practices and increasing efficiency can reduce overall US carbon emissions by 7.4% over 10 years (Dietz et al., 2009) and reduce US energy use by 20% (Gardner & Stern, 2008). While these numbers give us a reason not to ignore the household sector, they do not rationalize a focus on households to the exclusion of other reduction targets—a problematic trend in environmental policymaking (Jackson, 2005).

Third, and most important for this chapter, the idea that we can educate consumers to make better choices fails to recognize that consumers are locked into a context of technological (design), organizational (expert knowledge, supply networks), industrial (industry standards), institutional (government policy), and societal (habits, expectations) systems (Unruh, 2000, 2002). Targeting highly constrained consumers at the end of this supply chain makes little sense if the goal is to significantly alter energy use.

When I say that consumers are constrained or "locked in," I mean that consumers have limited opportunities to influence their own consumption patterns considering the "provision systems" (Briceno & Stagl, 2006, p. 1550), "institutional arrangements (regulatory and normative)" (Mont, 2004, p. 135), "structural forces" (Sanne, 2002, p. 276), or "the frame for consumption choices" (Halme, Jasch, & Scharp, 2004, p. 125) present in the consumer economy. The perfectly informed consumer is a myth (Connolly & Prothero, 2008), who does not exist within the constraints of the system. Even sustainability experts in this study have a difficult time deciding what products are greener because information from producers and distributors is missing or misleading.

In what follows I draw on 45 interviews from three groups who are attempting to reduce their consumption of energy, water, and consumer goods: voluntary simplifiers, religious environmentalists, and green homeowners. I begin by briefly discussing the literature on carbon lock-in in terms of what defines it, reinforces it, and challenges it. I then examine in detail the systematic constraints experienced by these groups. Substantively, I document and organize the chapter around several forms of lock-in: economic, organizational, and societal lock-in. I document different experiences of (1) the prohibitive cost of energy-efficient technology, (2) a focus on energy conservation by changing practices, and (3) challenges from institutions, expertise, and infrastructure. While carbon lock-in presents several constraints for households, I find that informants remain committed to supporting energy-saving designs and broader policy changes that would alter the energy-provision system. I argue that changes to the system must take into account the interconnections and goals within a system, rather than simply reforming elements of the system. I also suggest that the "every little bit helps" motto should be refocused on voting for environmentally friendly candidates and supporting ballot initiatives.

Literature Review

Energy use in the United States is predicted to rise steadily in the next 25 years. Yet, prioritizing and transitioning to energy conservation and alternative energy production has been "extremely slow" (Garrett & Koontz, 2008, p. 1551). One prevailing explanation for this is *carbon lock-in* (Unruh, 2000, 2002), also called *techno-institutional lock-in* or *socio-technical lock-in* (Shove, 2003). In the following I briefly discuss the definition of carbon lock-in, offer several examples, and explore how carbon-intensive systems may be reformed.

Carbon lock-in emphasizes how technological and infrastructural systems interact with and shape paths for household consumption (Shwom, 2011; Shwom & Lorenzen, 2012). Not only are high levels of investments (and profits) made in scaling up technologies, but an entire web of suppliers, expert knowledge, and ways of life grow up around them. The literature on carbon lock-in focuses on how technological systems like personal transportation, housing, and energy use interact with social systems to create a context that blocks the widespread use of alternatives to carbon-based energy (Unruh, 2002). Studies often debate the extent to which consumers are locked into everyday consumption patterns (Briceno & Stagl, 2006; Jackson & Papathanasopoulou, 2008; Mont, 2004; Ropke, 1999; Sanne, 2002; Unruh, 2002).

Single-owner automobile transportation is often cited as the primary example of the co-evolution of technological design, industry standards, and government policies. Policy decisions made at multiple levels of government led to the presence of highways instead of affordable public transportation options (Spangenberg, 2002). There are a few degrees of freedom in this scenario—individuals may move closer to their jobs, carpool, or park 'n' ride, but these have real cost implications (Wilson & Dowlatabadi, 2007). Similarly, energy-efficient housing decisions are a good example of over-determined consumer "choices" (Gram-Hanssen, 2010, 2011). Few consumers have the time and financial resources to build a home to energy-efficient specifications and instead rely on what real estate developers have built. Once systems are in place, incremental changes are more likely than systemic changes due to path dependency (new policies are shaped by existing policies). For example, HOV (high-occupancy vehicle) lanes on highways are a more likely policy choice than investing in public transportation. And retrofitting buildings is less disruptive to the system than altering building codes or passing mixed-use zoning laws. A combination of carbon lock-in, path dependency, upfront costs, and powerful business lobbying focuses policies on incremental changes like energy-efficiency in government buildings and households. One way to avoid confronting these challenges is to focus policymaking on household behavior change, which is less costly and controversial than systemic change.

There is a significant literature on behaviour change in relation to energy conservation and the adoption of alternative energy sources (Anue, 2007; Nye, Whitmarsh, & Foxon, 2010; Stephenson et al., 2010). Motivations to retrofit a home include saving money, technological novelty, ethics, status, and belonging (Zundel & Stieß, 2011). Incentive programs for household changes have wildly different participation rates (10%–90%) depending on how they are designed, programs work best when people make a one-time purchase like insulation, a hybrid or electric vehicle, an Energy Star appliance, or a new heating, ventilation, and air conditioning (HVAC) system (Dietz, Stern, & Weber, 2013). One-time purchases can ensure savings and efficiency without relying on changes in household practices. Unfortunately, when considering how to save energy, people are more likely to think about what they can *do* differently (curtailment such as turning off lights), rather than what material changes they can make to ensure efficiency (Attari et al., 2010). Also, people seem to know the least about things that would conserve the most energy, like buying new appliances (Attari et al., 2010; Buchanan, Russo,

& Anderson, 2014). There is a general disconnect in the United States between how electricity is made and how it is socially perceived (automatic, unlimited), which often leads to public inaction and a lack of understanding about why solar and wind are needed (Sovacool, 2009). These findings make the information-deficit model attractive (if they knew, they would make changes!), but information rarely changes behavior.

We know that information alone fails to change behavior (Chess & Johnson, 2007; Jackson, 2005). Even consumers well informed about environmental harms do not necessarily change their consumption patterns (Connolly & Prothero, 2008; Goldblatt, 2005, p. 40; Kilbourne & Carlson, 2008). And there is no predictable cause-and-effect relationship between information received and enabling rational action (Hargreaves, Nye, & Burgess, 2010). Thus energy monitors or smart meters have mixed results at best (0%–30% reductions in the short term), with little long-term impact (Wilson, 2014). A recent qualitative study by Buchanan, Russo, and Anderson (2014) shows that feedback on energy use only works for motivated users and even for them it has a declining impact over time. Local in-person appeals have better results for energy conservation (Boudet et al., 2016; Hirst, 1987), but these programs are expensive and thus unlikely to be adopted by cities (Dietz, Stern, & Weber, 2013). Given these well-documented limitations, it makes sense to look upstream for changes that alter design and the life cycle of products (Mont & Bleischwitz, 2007), infrastructure, and energy sources.

According to the literature, escaping carbon lock-in requires a combination of the following: "focusing events" (natural disasters, economic or technology-related crisis); technological and scientific innovations (energy storage); niche markets that nurture early adoption (incentives); and creative policies willing to go beyond business as usual (Rudel, 2013; Seyfang & Haxeltine, 2012; Unruh 2002). Confined by carbon lock-in, policies tend to focus on treating emissions and modifying a specific part of the system (solar fed into the existing energy grid)—without changing the system itself (Unruh, 2002). Moving beyond carbon lock-in involves, for example, decentralizing energy production, building a smart grid, or building mixed-use communities to minimize personal transportation needs.

Several scholars look toward the deregulation of energy systems as a way to address carbon lock-in (Carley, 2011; Gangale, Mengolini, & Onyeji, 2013). The deregulation of the energy system that followed the 1973–1974 oil embargo was intended to address inefficiencies and monopolies while lowering prices, allow consumers to choose their supplier, and support technological innovation. About a third of state energy markets in the United States have been deregulated or restructured, allowing for more competition from local, independent companies. One way these new companies distinguish themselves is by offering alternative energy on a regional scale. This looks promising as one way to circumvent carbon lock-in. However, partnerships and mergers by big energy companies have managed to concentrate market power—giving a few providers disproportional influence over the expansion of alternative energy (Carley, 2011). Large energy companies are working to control alternative energy development by supporting legislation that cuts solar credits, creates additional fixed fees like a one-time connection charge or monthly demand charge—fees customers pay before they even start using energy (Garskof, 2016). These policies could disincentivize solar adoption and energy conservation by households. In order for deregulation to enable the diffusion of alternative energy production, state policies like renewable portfolio standards are needed to challenge powerful carbon-based lobbying groups and support broad involvement. This would not be a single policy solution, but rather a process of multiple policy solutions.

Additionally, an exogenous shock to the system may temporarily weaken a system, allowing for change to occur more easily. Triggering events may spur positive policy action such as a reassessment of the power grid (Rudel, 2013). Disasters offer opportunities to circumvent path dependency, to reconsider policy paths, and to set new ones. For example, Hurricane Sandy was followed by fast-tracking smart grid and micro grid (small, independent sources of energy) investments to increase resiliency (LaMonica, 2013). Urban-growth boundaries and mixed-use redevelopment are other examples of working upstream to alter consumption patterns.

My study, described in the following section, examines the different ways that environmentalists, highly committed to energy conservation, are locked into carbon-intensive routines. Previous studies focus on factors that enable household change and the duration of those changes (Boudet et al., 2016). In contrast, I focus on the different ways that consumers experience, challenge, and negotiate carbon lock-in. I draw on a set of 45 interviews and participant observation with members of three groups (15 interviews from each group): voluntary simplifiers, religious environmentalists, and green homeowners.[2]

Voluntary simplifiers in this study are part of a loosely affiliated movement of individuals determined to limit their consumption to an extreme degree in order to address environmental harms (for a review of the literature, see Lorenzen, 2014; Sandlin & Walther, 2009). In some cases, individuals attempt to buy nothing new with the exception of food, medicine, and some items of children's clothing or intimate apparel (Alexander & Ussher, 2012; Ballantine & Creery, 2009). Voluntary simplifiers embrace changes in practices over purchasing efficient technologies (Lorenzen, 2012).

Religious environmentalists believe that caring for the environment is part of a religious duty (Haluza-Delay, 2014; Veldman, Szasz, & Haluza-Delay, 2014). Green religion is diverse because environmental ideas have penetrated every world religion and many smaller religious movements in a kind of ecological zeitgeist (Gardner, 2006; Smith & Pulver, 2009; Taylor, 2007). Religious environmentalists have an approach that brings together progressive interpretations of religious texts and technological solutions to environmental harms, including clean energy.

Green homeowners build or remodel homes in such a way as to use resources more efficiently and decrease unfavorable impacts to human health and the environment. Green homes, nearly 5% of the housing market (Schmidt, 2008, 2008a), typically focus on the efficiency of energy, water, building materials, and indoor air quality (Abair, 2008; Allon, 2011; Fischer, 2010; Groom, 2008). Some green homes in this study are LEED (Leadership in Energy and Environmental Design) certified. Green homeowners are more likely to purchase energy-efficient technologies than change their practices.

EMPIRICAL EXAMPLES OF CARBON LOCK-IN

In this section I explore several different experiences of carbon (or fossil fuel) lock-in: (1) the prohibitive cost of energy-efficient technology, (2) a focus on energy conservation by changing practices, and (3) challenges from institutions, expertise, and infrastructure. While carbon lock-in presents several constraints for households, I find that informants remain committed to supporting energy-saving designs and broader policy changes that would alter the energy provision system.

Economic Lock-in

Informants with a tight budget and a desire to save energy went down two paths. First, energy-efficient changes (e.g., weatherizing homes, new appliances, etc.) were spread out over many years. Second, many informants focused on changing practices rather than purchasing new efficient technologies. The high cost of energy-saving products pushes people to change practices and routines rather than home energy infrastructure (Lorenzen, 2012). And designs that deviate from industry standards (e.g., hybrid hot-water heaters, radiant in-floor heating) have a price premium, pricing many people out of the market (Lorenzen & Harvey, 2016). Research also shows that people default to changing practices and routines when asked how to reduce their energy use (Attari et al., 2010). I find that this preoccupation with changing practices results in a diminishing return as informants address smaller and smaller instances of energy use. Overall, energy savings from household changes are on a much longer time scale than models predict (Dietz, Stern, & Weber 2013), as tight budgets push households toward incremental purchases or changing habits.

For example, Geoff is an architect who has worked on green building projects and recently purchased his first home. Geoff's motto is "reduce, reuse, refuse," and he explains that his technology choices are influenced by financial constraint more than ideological differences:

> Green living is a weird line, where like green is really affordable, living green, because you're reducing and reusing. But then there's that other line where, to get greener things, like low-VOC paints, is much more expensive, because the technology for a lot of things hasn't caught up. So while they're trying to catch up and make things, performance-wise, as good, you know [it costs more]. . . . So, we're definitely towards, I would say, more the reduce-reuse [side]. Because financially, we can't get to that next level. Where the things that we do buy are inherently good.

Geoff and his wife, Kim, also an architect, point out that they purchased a new Energy Star refrigerator recently, but cannot afford a new furnace, on-demand hot-water heater, hybrid vehicle, or solar panels. Upon reflection, Kim identifies two kinds of green living: "commercial green" and "grass roots, hippy green" (i.e., those who can afford new efficient products versus people who focus on changing practices).

Catherine, another voluntary simplifier, keeps a keen eye on her energy bill—comparing this year's bill to last year's bill—and attempts to reduce her household energy use through staged purchases. She replaced her furnace and hot-water heater with Energy Star appliances a couple of years ago. Catherine explains that she considers conservation part of the normal upkeep of her home:

> When I've replaced things—like, I got these new sliding doors; they're very energy efficient. And my front window is double [paned], you know, very energy efficient, when I got them replaced. And I have storm windows. So, I'm trying. But actually, I'm actually kind of planning to put some more insulation in my attic at the moment, but I haven't done it yet. But I'm very aware of those kinds of things.

Several people I spoke with had energy audits on their homes performed and were slowly working through the list of projects recommended in the report—for some, this was taking 10 years or more due to the expense. Instead of making all of the changes at once (like when building a home), most informants wait until they have money saved and something needs to be replaced and then factor energy efficiency into their purchase.

In contrast, many informants focus on changing practices because it is something they can do immediately and it often saves money. Cynthia, a voluntary simplifier, talks about energy saving in terms of her daily routine.

> Everything that we've tried to do with the [home] renovations, we've tried to be [resource conscious]. . . . We do all the compact fluorescent bulbs, even in the lights we have outside and stuff. . . . We try to unplug things or turn them off when they're not in use. We keep lights off if you're not in a room. Anything that has like, a little green light or an LED screen or whatever continues to suck up a lot of energy. So if it's off and it still has that, we usually try to unplug it.

Cynthia also discusses keeping the heat low in the winter (50–60°F) and wearing wool sweaters, while avoiding the use of air conditioning in the summer. She considers her direct energy use as well as "other forms of energy," like the embedded energy in building materials and the indirect energy used to heat water. She also shares a car with her husband, who typically bikes to work. Central to Cynthia's story are the rules that govern her habits, for example, turn off the lights when you leave the room or unplug anything with a stand-by light.

Overall, there is an unusual awareness of energy among the environmentalists I interviewed. In some cases, this leads to upfront investments in alternative energy (solar panels, geothermal systems, or signing up with mass alternative energy providers), which I will return to later in this section. But just as often, informants are preoccupied with the minutia of energy savings. For example, they did not preheat their oven, avoided using their garbage disposal, did not rinse their dishes (or used cold water to rinse their dishes), only ran the dishwasher when it was full, allowed dishes in the dishwasher to air dry (rather than running through the heated drying cycle), used power strips to reduce phantom load for electronics, used their washing machines (only full loads) at night when there was less demand on the energy grid, and some used a clothesline instead of a dryer. Once learned, these habits require little upkeep; however, they also have little impact.

Some of the practices mentioned in this section, such as regulating indoor temperature, make the most of household conservation efforts. The highest energy-intensive aspects of household consumption are driving a private vehicle and heating or cooling homes (Gardner & Stern, 2008). The rest of the changes mentioned, arising as people become more deeply invested in energy efficiency, have a diminishing return. For example, "little energy is used for cooking and running computers and dishwashers" (Gardner & Stern, 2008). In line with previous research, informants are unsure of which changes would save the most energy and, thus, adopted a broad approach.

The programmable thermostat was the most commonly mentioned energy intervention in this study. Mike, a voluntary simplifier, installed a programmable thermostat, although he has never learned how to program it, using it instead as a sophisticated on/off switch (Shove, 2003). Although he complains a little, he doesn't seek out a solution. Mike says:

> The [programmable] thermostat, we [my wife and I] just can't figure out how to use the damn thing, so we use it, we use it, when we wake up in the morning or go to sleep at night or when we leave the house—we will lower it or raise it accordingly. . . . I'm freezing in the morning! But probably because I put it on in the morning when I wake up and it takes it awhile to warm up. But I can live with it.

The new thermostat is used in the same way as the old thermostat. Mike and his wife rationalize that they are saving even more energy because they do not turn up the heat until they wake up, instead of programming the thermostat to increase the temperature a couple of hours before they wake up—which was their original plan when they bought it. Energy Star stopped rating programmable thermostats in 2009 because energy savings depends heavily on user habits. Overall, programmable thermostats contribute little to energy efficiency; data from nearly 200 telephone surveys show that two-thirds of respondents already use non-programmable thermostats in an efficient manner (Malinick et al., 2012). Overall, placing expectations on consumers and end use, while popular, makes only a small impact and does nothing to alter the system or challenge carbon lock-in.

Organizational Lock-in

When policies focus on educating consumers, we forget that consumers exist in context and are not making decisions independently. Industrial and organizational lock-in, in the form of local building codes, installation failures, and confusion over what's greener, results in a great deal of uncertainty for my informants.

For example, Martin, a green homeowner, explains that "educating the town [about green building] takes time and money." Martin says:

> You know, one of the reasons our plumber didn't install the tankless hot-water heaters properly is because they come from Japan [and the installation instructions were in Japanese]. So a barrier would be just the lack of knowledge on the part of most people in the construction industry in the U.S. . . . . It's just a strange thing because you say, yeah, you hear the federal government that can do these tax incentives. And then at the state level, sometimes, there are incentives as well. So you figure: OK. You know, certainly the government's behind this. And then, forget about local [building codes]. Forget about the town, the municipal level. And all of a sudden, you're like: "Oh, my gosh. How're we going to get these people on board?" And you know, sometimes those people can be very tough individuals.

Here incentives run up against knowledge limits and local building codes. In building his LEED-certified home, Martin encountered difficulties at every turn, from improper installation of green products to local ordinances that prohibited the use of rainwater in the home. He describes it as an "early adopter tax" and hopes that months spent getting the local government to approve building permits will pave the way for others to adopt green building practices. Martin identifies two types of lock-in here. First, local building codes conform to industrial standards that constrain the design process because precedent favors existing technologies. Second, once building plans are authorized, Martin encounters organizational lock-in in the form of expertise. Experts support the reproduction of existing systems. Workers who are experts at installing hot-water heaters may not know how to install on-demand hot-water heaters. Installation took longer, and sometimes products had to be installed twice due to errors. Newer models try to address this.

Similarly, Jacob, who is renovating and LEED certifying his home, found a lack of expertise to be an ongoing issue. Jacob says:

> We [he and his wife] wanted to do it [all LED lighting in their house], but we weren't sure what was available and how good the light quality would be. . . . So I went to . . . [a] lighting conference, and looked at a lot of different things. And yeah, so we—I mean, we did do a lot of teaching of, you know—it was definitely a collaborative project with the HVAC guys and certainly with the general contractor, you know, the plumber and the electrician. And the first reaction was, "Why are you doing that?"

Jacob spends a good deal of time conducting research and sharing his knowledge with workers in the building trades, local schools, and the city government. Jacob himself has become an expert on green building—learning more about green building and sustainability than the vast majority of consumers. Yet, even with these extreme efforts I find that educating consumers does not circumvent carbon lock-in. Consumers, like Jacob, who are highly educated remain uncertain about which products are greener, and producers and distributors are little help in figuring it out.

Housing is a prime example of consumer lock-in. A recent study of passive solar explains low adoption rates in the United States (Garrett & Koontz, 2008). From a consumer perspective, there are few passive solar homes available on the housing market. From the producer perspective, there is not enough consumer demand to convince builders to adopt passive solar design. Garrett and Koontz (2008, p. 1563) argue that supply-side incentives are required to alter home design because a "fragmented innovation system prevents widespread adoption" of new ideas by builders. And altering housing stock is critical because homes that are built today lock in energy usage for the next 50–100 years. A representative of the US Green Building Council (USGBC, creators of LEED) interviewed for this study explains that the goal of the USGBC is to change national building codes so people no longer need to opt in to green building. An important part of carbon lock-in exists in the policies that shape institutional inertia (van der Vleuten & Raven, 2006). And once certain policies are in place, they constrain the path for future policies (i.e., path dependency). There is a wide gap between current US building codes and the requirements for LEED certification (silver, gold, or platinum). Building codes change constantly but also incrementally, with little precedent for a major shift to support energy efficiency.

Societal Lock-in

In this section I return to the cost of alternative energy and other aspects involved with its adoption (or non-adoption). I also highlight the business-as-usual context of building large green homes and the habits that make alternative energy use less efficient. Societal lock-in includes the habits, expectations, and financial priorities that ensure comfort, cleanliness, and convenience in everyday life (Shove, 2003). A frequently cited example of societal lock-in is setting air conditioning at 68° in most office buildings. It also affects the adoption of mass-produced alternative energy. People may change energy providers when they move to a new city (Lorenzen, 2012a), but otherwise it is difficult to get people to change energy providers. Brennan (2007) finds that people actually prefer not to choose an energy provider, but would rather have one assigned to them based on where they live.

The expense of alternative energy installations and neighborhood context are also barriers to the adoption of solar and geothermal. For example, Lydia, a religious environmentalist, built a new garage and then purchased a solar system for her garage roof for $23,500, but with the state rebate, she paid about $9,500. The system was paid off in eight years, in part by S-RECS (Solar Renewable Energy Certificates—part of a market for selling solar energy back to local utility companies). Even with incentives like rebates, few people have the capital for upfront expenses. The incentives observed in this study primarily benefited the upper middle class (households with two earners making more than $100,000/year). Subsidies for geothermal lag behind those for solar; a more recent geothermal subsidy was 30% of the total cost of the system (bringing the cost down to about $20,000). Newer financing schemes in rooftop solar allow for leasing panels—"72% of the people who installed residential solar systems in 2014 did so through leasing or another type of third-party arrangement" (Garskof, 2016, p. 13). Unfortunately, leasing offers only modest financial savings, three times less than purchasing solar panels, and contract fine print (an escalator clause) can make a lease more expensive each year (Garskof, 2016).

Companies that reduce upfront costs for alternative energy installations to zero are still facing the difficulties of neighborhood context. For example, Janelle, a voluntary simplifier, was restricted from putting solar panels on the south-facing front roof of her Victorian home by township rules for historic homes. And others in my study, like Mike, lived in older middle-class neighborhoods where lots are smaller and mature trees shade southern exposures. Alternately, new construction means that trees are often cut down and homes (or garages) can be oriented to face south. The majority of people in my study with solar panels had recently built a new home (Lorenzen, 2012).

In addition, alternative energy is often incorporated into business-as-usual systems, like building large, expensive green homes in suburban neighborhoods. Anthony points out that the "green" in green building should include both the operation, and not just the construction, of a building. Anthony explains:

> When you're talking about the concept of green, green, to me, as I say, has no real meaning. But you have to look at it in terms of the issue of sustainability. And when you look at sustainability, you want to utilize resources in as efficient a way as you can in the construction process, with as little waste as possible, *and* you want to have your end result be as efficient as possible so that it is as sustainable as possible, meaning, using as little resources as necessary in order to operate or run that thing you've created.

Here Anthony is speaking out against simply adding alternative energy to homes without changing the way the whole home is designed and used. Jacob, speaking a little more plainly, points out that there are people with "very big houses, who, you know, try to call them 'green,'" which he sees as problematic.

Finally, changing to alternative energy sources may not alter habits; for example, when solar is adopted, it may not be used in an efficient way. Ralph, a green homeowner and art teacher, refers to solar energy as "free." He describes green building as a "win-win-win-win-win situation" referring to (1) the aesthetics of the house, (2) the way the house fits with the environment, (3) clean solar energy that does not pollute like nuclear energy, (4) earning money by selling energy to the grid, and (5) his wife finally got a hot tub out of the deal because it is heated with solar so "it's free to heat it." Ralph said, "I did a lot of extra work [cutting down trees] to make it [the solar ground installation] fit the property. You know, we're blessed with a big enough property that we can have the solar panels." He gets a monthly statement saying "how many pounds of CO_2 we've saved by doing it." This example suggests that solar energy may be used a little less responsibly than energy that is associated with pollution.

The use of efficient technologies is central to the project of sustainability. Green technology, to a large extent, works upstream to address issues of design and efficiency before users become involved. However, green technology does not allow systems or consumer practices to remain unchanged (Lorenzen, 2012). As technologies become more efficient at using resources, we typically consume more of those resources through two types of rebound effects. First, the Jevons paradox (also known as indirect rebound effects) was a term coined in 1865 by Stanley Jevons who hypothesized that the gains in the technological efficiency of machines burning coal in British factories would be offset by falling coal prices that would, in turn, free up capital for investments in many different industries that would use more coal. In other words, studies show that increased energy efficiency and increased energy use in the "medium to long term" are correlated (Dimitropoulos, 2007). Second, at the level of individuals or households, these effects can be measured and are called *direct rebound effects*. Sorrell, Dimitropoulos, and Sommerville (2009) find that 5%–30% of energy efficiency is lost to direct rebound effects. Research tends to focus on driving more due to lower gas prices or heating one's home for longer after installing insulation. Or, for example, between 1990 and 2007 the energy efficiency of refrigerators increased by 10%, but the overall number of refrigerators increased by 20% (Schor, 2010). Suburban homeowners tend to retire old refrigerators to the basement or garage and keep them in use. On the household level, this effect is somewhat constrained by the kind of technology involved and the context in which it is used; for example, the purchase of a high-efficiency washing machine does not lead to doing more laundry (Schor, 2010).

Finally, for those in my study who could not afford their own household alternative energy system, several turned to mass alternative energy providers. Unfortunately, I find that it is difficult for households to decide between alternative energy programs due to a lack of transparency. Some alternative energy programs are not 100% alternative energy, they may not disclose what types of alternative energy the program is based on, and often have a price premium—with little explanation about where the money is going (Lorenzen, 2012). My findings reflect lessons from recent research which shows that consumers do not trust mainstream energy providers to implement alternative energy projects in a way that benefits local communities (Gangale, Mengolini, & Onyeji, 2013; Mumford & Gray, 2010).

Societal lock-in consists of financial constraints, durable habits, and expectations for comfort or convenience. Societal lock-in is also tied to industry standards (which create/reinforce expectations) and organizational lock-in (which guides habits down certain paths). And changes in one part of the system (solar installation) might not affect other parts of the system (household energy efficiency)—leaving households working at cross purposes. Ultimately, the sources or forces of lock-in are intertwined and reinforce each other. For example, building standards influence societal expectations for the size of a house. Altering such a complex system requires multiple, simultaneous policy reforms.

Discussion: Changing Systems

To summarize, I find that environmentalists who are motivated to reduce or alter their use of energy are constrained in several ways: informants are financially and geographically limited in their ability to adopt alternative energy systems, default to changing practices rather than investing in new material goods, are hindered by local building codes and a lack of expert knowledge, and may overuse "free" solar energy to support a comfortable lifestyle. These are examples of economic, organizational, and societal lock-in. Incentives fail to address these constraints and often only succeed in integrating alternative energy technologies into business-as-usual practices like building large suburban homes. On the bright side, informants are supportive of broader policy changes to make energy systems less carbon intensive and more resilient, in part, because they have experienced these drawbacks.

I argue that making more perfect (rational, informed, motivated) consumers is not the answer to reducing energy use or challenging carbon lock-in. Systems that support carbon lock-in are made up of elements (people, physical infrastructure), interconnections (rules/laws, strategies, communication, flows of resources), and purposes (making money) (Meadows, 2008). Meadows (2008) argues that the most effective way of changing a system is to alter interconnections or purposes—rather than elements. She states, "a system generally goes on being itself, changing only slowly if at all, even with complete substitutions of its elements—as long as its interconnections and purposes remain the same" (Meadows, 2008, p. 16). Incentivizing households or communities to adopt solar does change an element in the system, but does little to alter the system as a whole. The most politically feasible projects are typically those that are guided by path dependency and change only elements in the system—which may lead to less than optimal outcomes (Unruh & Carrillo-Hermosilla, 2006). In contrast, feed-in tariffs (potentially nationwide feed-in tariffs) have the power to change relationships and support green niches for energy innovation (Seyfang & Haxeltine, 2012). Additionally, renewable portfolio standards and other benchmarks have the power to alter the purpose of an energy system. Combining goals is also feasible; the US Department of Energy has begun a new grid modernization initiative (http://energy .gov/under-secretary-science-and-energy/grid-modernization-initiative).   Although the future of this initiative is in question, piggybacking efficiency and alternative-energy aims onto existing initiatives is a practical way to take advantage of projects already deemed necessary. Overall, changing an interconnected and competitive system requires comprehensive policies and laws (Sovacool, 2009a).

In order to take advantage of the way consumers have been socialized into the "every little bit helps" motto, I argue that the motto should be repurposed to encompass the support of proenvironmental candidates and policies (Thøgersen & Noblet, 2012). Voting for candidates who support renewable portfolio standards or policies to fund alternative energy would be a small action with potentially broader consequences. In addition, the adoption of solar technology by communities and households (supported by rebates), along with state support of the market for solar energy, puts pressure on larger energy providers to capture those profits by building larger solar farms. While the household adoption of alternative energy sources may not circumvent carbon lock-in due to its exclusivity, it does establish competition within the system and has the potential to drive further changes. Thus, we need not necessarily choose between prioritizing macro versus micro policies because systemic change is an ongoing and interconnected process of transformations at multiple levels: elements, interconnections, and purposes.

Conclusion

The locked-in perspective is a particularly relevant one when we think about how people might move away from fossil fuels embedded in our energy systems. More generally, the notion of carbon lock-in recognizes that institutionalized ideas and formations present in socio-technical systems constrain consumers by guiding them down certain paths. The informants interviewed for this study are constrained by economic, organizational, and societal lock-in. This awareness of structural influences translates into a prescription for multilevel solutions that expose the status quo as an active choice rather than a neutral default.

In order to alter carbon lock-in, we need to remember the limits of individual responsibility and, instead, work to change the relationships and goals within the energy-provision system. Changes "upstream"—long before consumers begin making decisions—have a broader scope, affect more people, and could change how (and where) energy is produced. Rather than voting with our dollars by making decisions in the marketplace, I recommend just voting.

Notes

1. Source: US Energy Information Administration, Monthly Energy Review—Table 2.1, http://www.eia.gov/consumption/
2. I draw from three disparate groups in order to capture a combination of changes in practices and technologies (on case studies, see Small, 2009; for more details on why I studied these groups, see Lorenzen, 2012a). Interviewees are from the Northeastern United States and informants were recommended for inclusion in this study by the founder of a voluntary simplicity community group, the executive director of a nondenominational green religion nonprofit, and the senior technical consultant for residential building at a green building business. Semi-structured interviews lasted 60 minutes. and most interviews were conducted at homes. The interviews were professionally transcribed and coded in Atlas.ti.

REFERENCES

Abair, J. W. (2008). Green buildings: What it means to be 'green' and the evolution of green building laws. *Urban Lawyer*, 40, 623–632.

Alexander, S., & Ussher, S. (2012). The voluntary simplicity movement: A multi-national survey analysis in theoretical context. *Journal of Consumer Culture*, 12(1), 66–86.

Allon, F. (2011). Ethical consumption begins at home: Green renovations, eco-homes and sustainable home improvement. In T. Lewis & E. Potter (Eds.), *Ethical consumption: A critical introduction* (pp. 202–215). London: Routledge.

Anue, M. (2007). Energy comes home. *Energy Policy*, 35, 5457–5465.

Attaria, S. Z., DeKayb, M. L., Davidsonc, C. I., & de Bruin, W. (2010). Public perceptions of energy consumption and savings. *PNAS*, 107, 16054–16059.

Ballantine, P. W., & Creery, S. (2009). The consumption and disposition behaviour of voluntary simplifiers. *Journal of Consumer Behaviour*, 8, 1–12.

Boudet H., Ardoin, N. M., Flora, J., Armel, K. C., Desai, M., & Robinson, T. M. (2016). Effects of a behaviour change intervention for Girl Scouts on child and parent energy-saving behaviours. *Nature Energy*, 1, 1–10. doi:10.1038/nenergy.2016.91

Brennan, T. J. (2007). Consumer preference not to choose: Methodological and policy implications. *Energy Policy*, 35, 1616–1627.

Briceno, T., & Stagl, S. (2006). The role of social processes for sustainable consumption. *Journal of Cleaner Production*, 14. 1541–1551.

Buchanan, K., Russo, R., & Anderson, B. (2014). Feeding back about eco-feedback: How do consumers use and respond to energy monitors?" *Energy Policy*, 73, 138–146.

Carley, S. (2011). Historical analysis of U.S. electricity markets: Reassessing carbon lock-in. *Energy Policy*, 39, 720–732.

Chess, C., & Johnson, B. B. (2007). Information is not enough. In S. C. Moser & L. Dilling (Eds.), *Creating a climate for change: Communication climate change and facilitating social change* (pp. 223–233). Cambridge: Cambridge University Press.

Connolly, J., & Prothero, A. (2008). Green consumption: Life-politics, risk, and contradictions. *Journal of Consumer Culture*, 8, 117–145.

Dietz, T., Gardner, G. T., Gilligan, J., Stern, P. C., & Vandenbergh, M. P. (2009). Household actions can provide a behavioral wedge to rapidly reduce U.S. carbon emissions. *Proceedings of the National Academy of Sciences*, 106, 18452–18456.

Dietz, T., Stern, P. C., & Weber, E. U. (2013). Reducing carbon-based energy consumption through changes in household behavior. *Dædalus*, 142, 78–89.

Dimitropoulos, J. (2007). Energy productivity improvements and the rebound effect: An overview of the state of knowledge. *Energy Policy*, 35, 6354–6363.

Fischer, E. A. (2010). Issues in green building and the federal response: An introduction. *Congressional Research Service*. Retrieved from http://www.policyarchive.org/handle/10207/bitstreams/18960.pdf

Gangale, F., Mengolini, A., & Onyeji, I. (2013). Consumer engagement: An insight from smart grid projects in Europe. *Energy Policy*, 60, 621–628.

Gardner, G. T. (2006). *Inspiring progress: Religions' contributions to sustainable development.* New York: W. W. Norton.

Gardner, G. T., & Stern, P. C. (2008). The short list: The most effective actions U.S. households can take to curb climate change. *Environment*, 50, 12–23.

Garrett, V., & Koontz, T. M. (2008). Breaking the cycle: Producer and consumer perspectives on the non-adoption of passive solar housing in the US. *Energy Policy, 36*, 1551–1566.

Garskof, J. (2016, August). Shedding light on solar power. *Consumer Reports*, 10–15.

Goldblatt, D. L. (2005). *Sustainable energy consumption and society: Personal, technological, or social change?* Norwell, MA: Springer.

Gram-Hanssen, K. (2010). Standby consumption in households analyzed with a practice theory approach. *Journal of Industrial Ecology, 14*, 150–165.

Gram-Hanssen, K. (2011). Understanding change and continuity in residential energy consumption. *Journal of Consumer Culture, 11*, 61–78.

Groom, S. (2008). Making the green-building dean's list: LEED for homes. *Fine Homebuilding, 195*, 94–101.

Halme, M., Jasch, C., & Scharp, M. (2004). Sustainable homeservices? Toward household services that enhance ecological, social, and economic sustainability. *Ecological Economics, 51*, 125–138.

Haluza-Delay, R. (2014). Religion and climate change: Varieties in viewpoints and practices. *Wiley Interdisciplinary Reviews: Climate Change, 5*, 261–279. doi:10.1002/wcc.268

Hargreaves, T., Nye, M., & Burgess, J. (2010). Making energy visible: A qualitative field study of how householders interact with feedback from smart energy monitors. *Energy Policy, 38*, 6111–6119.

Hirst, E. (1987). *Cooperation and community conservation: the hood river conservation project.* Final Report, Hood River Conservation Project, DOE/BP-11287-18

Jackson, T. (2005). Motivating sustainable consumption: A review of evidence on consumer behaviour and behavioural change. Sustainable Development Research Network. Retrieved from http://www.sd-research.org.uk/post.php?p=126

Jackson, T., & Papathanasopoulou, E. (2008). Luxury or "Lock-in"? An exploration of unsustainable consumption in the UK: 1968 to 2000. *Ecological Economics, 68*, 80–95.

Kilbourne, W. E., & Carlson, L. (2008). The dominant social paradigm, consumption, and environmental attitudes: Can macromarketing education help? *Journal of Macromarketing, 28*, 106–121.

LaMonica, M. (2013). One year later, Hurricane Sandy fuels grid innovation. *GreenBiz*. Retrieved from https://www.greenbiz.com/blog/2013/10/24/one-year-later-hurricane-sandy-fuels-grid-innovation

Lorenzen, J. A. (2012). Green and smart: The co-construction of users and technology. *Human Ecology Review, 19*, 25–36.

Lorenzen, J. A. (2012a). Going green: The process of lifestyle change. *Sociological Forum, 27*, 94–116.

Lorenzen, J. A. (2014). Green consumption and social change: Debates over responsibility, private action, and access. *Sociology Compass, 8*, 1063–1081.

Lorenzen, J. A., & Harvey, D. C. (2016). Forced in or left out: Experiencing green from community redevelopment to voluntary simplicity and the potential in-between. In P. Godfrey & D. Torres (Eds.), *Emergent possibilities for global sustainability: Intersections of race, class and gender* (pp. 263–274). New York: Routledge.

Malinick, T., Wilairat, N., Holmes, J., Perry, L., & Ware, W. (2012). Destined to disappoint: Programmable thermostat savings are only as good as the assumptions about their operating characteristics. *ACEEE Summer Study on Energy Efficiency in Buildings* (pp. 162–173). Retrieved from http://aceee.org/files/proceedings/2012/data/papers/0193-000237.pdf

Meadows, D. H. (2008). *Thinking in systems: A primer*. White River Junction, VT: Chelsea Green.

Mont, O. (2004). Institutionalisation of sustainable consumption patterns based on shared use. *Ecological Economics, 50*, 135–153.

Mont, O., & Bleischwitz, R. (2007). Sustainable consumption and resource management in the light of lifecycle thinking. *European Environment, 17*, 59–76.

Mumford, J., & Gray, D. (2010). Consumer engagement in alternative energy: Can the regulators and suppliers be trusted? *Energy Policy, 38*, 2664–2671.

Nye, M., Whitmarsh, L., & Foxon, T. (2010). Sociopsychological perspectives on the active roles of domestic actors in transition to a lower carbon electricity economy. *Environment and Planning A, 42*, 697–714.

Ropke, I. (1999). The dynamics of willingness to consume. *Ecological Economics, 28*, 399–420.

Rudel, T. K. (2013). *Defensive environmentalism and the dynamics of global reform*. Cambridge: Cambridge University Press.

Sandlin, J. A., & Walther, C. S. (2009). Complicated simplicity: Moral identity formation and social movement learning in the voluntary simplicity movement. *Adult Education Quarterly, 59*, 298–317.

Sanne, C. (2002). Willing consumers—or locked-in? Policies for sustainable consumption. *Ecological Economics, 42*, 273–287.

Schmidt, C. W. (2008). Bringing green homes within reach: Healthier housing for more people. *Environmental Health Perspectives, 116*, A24–A31.

Schmidt, C. W. (2008a). Room to grow: Incentives boost energy-efficient homebuilding. *Environmental Health Perspectives, 116*, A32–A35.

Schor, J. B. (2010). *Plenitude: The new economics of true wealth*. New York: Penguin Press.

Seyfang, G., & Haxeltine, A. (2012). Growing grassroots innovations: Exploring the role of community-based initiatives in governing sustainable energy transitions. *Environment and Planning C, 30*, 381–400.

Shove, E. (2003). *Comfort, cleanliness and convenience: The social organization of normality*. Oxford: Berg.

Shwom, R. (2011). A middle range theorization of energy politics: The struggle for energy efficient appliances. *Environmental Politics, 20*, 705–726.

Shwom, R., & Lorenzen, J. A. (2012). Changing household consumption to address climate change: Social scientific insights and challenges. *Wiley Interdisciplinary Reviews: Climate Change, 3*(5), 379–395. doi:10.1002/WCC.182

Small, M. L. (2009). "How many cases do I need?" On science and the logic of case selection in field-based research. *Ethnography, 10*, 5–38.

Smith, A. M., & Pulver, S. (2009). Ethics-based environmentalism in practice: Religious environmental organizations in the United States. *Worldviews: Environment, Culture, Religion, 13*, 145–179.

Sorrell, S., Dimitropoulos, J., & Sommerville, M. (2009). Empirical estimates of the direct rebound effect: A review. *Energy Policy, 37*, 1356–1371.

Sovacool, B. (2009). The cultural barriers to renewable energy and energy efficiency in the U.S. *Technology in Society, 31*, 365–373.

Sovacool, B. (2009a). The importance of comprehensiveness in renewable electricity and energy-efficiency policy. *Energy Policy, 37*, 1529–1541.

Spangenberg, J. H. (2002). Environmental space and the prism of sustainability: Frameworks for indicators measuring sustainable development. *Ecological Indicators, 2*, 295–309.

Stephenson, J., Barton, B., Carrington, G., Gnoth, D., Lawson, R., & Thorsnes, P. (2010). Energy cultures: A framework for understanding energy behaviours. *Energy Policy*, *38*, 6120–6129.

Taylor, S. M. (2007). *Green sisters: A spiritual ecology*. Cambridge, MA: Harvard University Press.

Thøgersen, J., & Noblet, C. (2012). Does green consumerism increase the acceptance of wind power? *Energy Policy*, *51*, 854–862.

Unruh, G. C. (2000). Understanding carbon lock-in. *Energy Policy*, *28*, 817–830.

Unruh, G. C. (2002). Escaping carbon lock-in. *Energy Policy*, *30*, 317–325.

Unruh, G., & Carrillo-Hermosilla, J. (2006). Globalizing carbon lock-in. *Energy Policy* 34: 1185–1197.

van der Vleuten, E., & Raven, R. (2006). Lock-in and change: Distributed generation in Denmark in a long-term perspective. *Energy Policy*, *34*, 3739–3748.

Vandenbergh, M. P., Barkenbus, J., & Gilligan, J. (2008). Individual carbon emissions: The low-hanging fruit. *UCLA Law Review*, *55*, 1701–1758.

Veldman, R. G., Szasz, A., & Haluza-Delay, R. (2014). Social science, religions, and climate change. In R. G. Veldman, A. Szasz, & R. Haluza-Delay (Eds.), *How the world's religions are responding to climate change* (pp. 3–19). New York: Routledge.

Wilson, C. (2014). Evaluating communication to optimise consumer-directed energy efficiency interventions. *Energy Policy*, *74*, 300–310.

Wilson, C., & Dowlatabadi, H. (2007). Models of decision making and residential energy use. *Annual Review Environment and Resources*, *32*, 169–203.

Zundel, S., & Stieβ, I. (2011). Beyond profitability of energy-saving measures: Attitudes towards energy saving. *Journal of Consumer Policy*, *34*, 91–105.

PART IV

....

PERSPECTIVES ON ENERGY EQUITY AND ENERGY POVERTY

....

ENERGY equity, energy poverty, and conceptualization of energy access as a human right describe another emerging area of sociological inquiry with exciting contributions to theory and practice. There remain marked differences in the availability of electricity around the world that cannot be ignored. Previous chapters have noted that sources of the earth's energy resources are not equitably distributed. Scholars working in this vein describe the social implications of these dis-economies of space, to use Ciccantell and Gellert's term. Inequities in energy access are by no means a purely "natural" outcome, however. The developmental trajectories of nations and the distribution of decision-making power within them have at least as much relevance.

It would be folly to discuss the distribution of benefits without also considering the distribution of risks, and this is where we begin our exploration into energy equity. The risks of energy development, as with the benefits that such processes produce, are likewise inequitably distributed. The negative social and environmental impacts of development are borne by communities at the sites of production, while the resources themselves and the wealth they generate are most often exported for consumption elsewhere. Risk is a core field of inquiry in sociology, and many forms of energy development have been subject to extensive risk analysis. All forms of energy entail risks that differ both in kind and in acuity. Debates in the past 10 years regarding nuclear power reflect this dynamic: coal remains the cheapest and most readily available form of electricity, but it also comes with a host of environmental and health impacts, and is greenhouse gas intensive. Nuclear power offers a low-carbon energy alternative, yet the risks associated with accidents and radioactive waste management have been a lightning rod since the Cold War.

While many of the environmental consequences of fossil-fuel development in the West declined over the late twentieth century with the introduction of national environmental regulations, that trend may be reversed in the coming decades, and observations of the hazards of energy development are once again in the limelight. As reserves of conventional fuels decline, investors resort to increasingly risky technologies to extract what is left.

These two co-occurring situations—energy poverty combined with escalating risks—raise uncomfortable questions about how, and the extent to which, the "right" to energy access can be accommodated.

We begin Part IV with a critical analysis of a prominent case of energy production disaster. In Chapter 14, Christine Shearer makes use of extensive documentation of what has been referred to as the most catastrophic of disasters associated with fossil-fuel development to date: the blowout of the Macondo drilling rig, operating in deep waters off the coast of Louisiana by British Petroleum. Communities along the southern US coast continue to suffer the consequences of this disaster, as fisheries have been destroyed, water supplies tainted, and a way of life eradicated, possibly for the foreseeable future. Considering the elevation of risk associated with accessing unconventional fuels—the unconventional nature of this particular operation due to its extreme depth—this blowout can be seen as a "normal accident," to adopt Perrow's depiction of the inevitability of calamity in complex technological systems. Human agency nonetheless played a key role: production pressure and lax regulation clearly increased the probability of this particular accident considerably. These two processes may well be interrelated, as governments are compelled to offer increased incentives and reduced constraints to support the corporate development of resources that have a rather unattractive expected profit margin.

Paulo Manduca, Mauro Berni, Iure Paiva, and José Alexandre Hage then offer a rare, intimate look at energy development dynamics in Latin America in Chapter 15. While many in the developed world complain about increases in the prices of energy, heat, and gasoline when they occur, the authors describe the especially crippling effect of energy price increases in low- and middle-income countries, not only for families and businesses, but for governments that rely on energy-development revenues. The authors, however, go beyond a consideration of energy poverty, which is certainly prevalent in at least some regions of Latin America, to provide an analysis of the interconnections between state-led energy-development projects and poverty. These authors describe the rise, and fall, of a renewable fuel in Argentina and Brazil, the development of which in Brazil at least was specifically designed to support the livelihoods of rural farmers. This story coincided with the fall and subsequent resurrection to prominence of fossil fuels—a story deeply entangled with regional politics, particularly recent emergence of the "pink tide" of populist, center-left governments, which have embraced fossil fuels as the means to economic prosperity, combined with intense international market competition among biofuels producing countries to supply EU markets. To these case studies is added a look at Venezuela, where Hugo Chávez embarked upon a grand experiment with petro-socialism. These are individual stories, and yet this comparative study shows how these stories are interconnected by similar economic conditions, and shared cultural and political imaginaries.

In Chapter 16, Karl-Michael Brunner, Sylvia Mandl, and Harriet Thomson provide a comprehensive overview of the concept of energy poverty and its multiple facets. Energy poverty, the authors note, is a persistent and pressing concern in the developing and the developed world alike, with particular implications for women and girls, who are often responsible for household tasks that require energy. Those lacking adequate and/or affordable access to energy in the developed world are also more likely to be living in housing with lower efficiency, translating into high levels of expense even for basic needs like heat. The authors emphasize that there are multifaceted causes, requiring integrated and gender-sensitive responses, but express hope in the growing acknowledgment of energy poverty as a serious concern: The eradication of energy poverty has been identified as one of the United Nations Sustainable Development Goals. The authors also suggest that there may be tremendous potential in off-grid electrification systems, as they may be more democratic and culturally sensitive, and just plain more pragmatic in some instances.

Part IV closes with Chapter 17 by Marcio Giannini Pereira, Neilton Fidelis da Silva, and Marcos A. V. Freitas that draws crucial links between energy poverty and climate change justice, and importantly, to climate change mitigation as well. As the authors note, there is a need to address energy poverty in climate negotiations. To begin, although we can observe slow but substantial growth in electricity access in some places, such as rural China and Brazil, in other regions such as India and countries in Africa, the obstacles to electrification remain substantial. Importantly, the authors make the case that obstacles to increasing energy access are linked not simply to limits in investment capital, but rather to extreme inequalities in wealth. As they state, "income inequality leads to unequal access to electric power and other modern energy sources worldwide." The authors then provide a powerful definition and elaboration of the concept of climate justice, and its implications for climate negotiations. First, the authors note the need to differentiate emissions associated with meeting basic needs from the comparative "luxury" emissions of the middle and upper classes. Second, considering the limited ecological space available—including the "space" consumed or destroyed due to emissions of greenhouse gases—the distribution of that space becomes a justice issue. The authors provide evidence of enormous discrepancies among countries in levels of historic emissions, which can be interpreted as disproportionate access to ecological space. In other words, historic emitters like the United States owe a large ecological debt to the world, while many other countries have effectively offered an ecological surplus to global society. From this perspective, calls for equal emission reductions targets in climate negotiations lose their credibility.

CHAPTER 14

DECREASING SUPPLIES, INCREASING RISKS IN OIL DEVELOPMENT

CHRISTINE SHEARER

INTRODUCTION

> The Macondo blowout happened in 2010, but to understand how we came to be in a situation where the Deepwater Horizon was drilling 2½ miles into a rock formation, which was itself submerged by a mile of water, for hydrocarbons that were at over 6,000 pounds per square inch of pressure and all of this was considered routine, requires some explanation.
>
> —Gramling and Freudenburg (2012, p. 50)

ON April 20, 2010, a British Petroleum (BP)–controlled oil drilling rig known as Deepwater Horizon exploded off the Gulf of Mexico, releasing an estimated 4.9 million barrels of oil into the ocean. The central cause of the explosion was later identified as a failure of the cement at the base of the 18,000-foot well, which was designed to contain oil and gas within the well bore. That led to a cascade of events that allowed natural gas under tremendous pressure to shoot onto the drilling platform, causing an explosion and fire that sunk the rig.

The event killed 11 of the 126 crewmembers on the rig, and unleashed an oil spill that flowed uncontrollably for 87 straight days. Yet, as stated by environmental sociologists Robert Gramling and William Freudenburg, perhaps the most amazing thing about the event is how the entire risky activity—drilling 2½ miles into a rock formation, which was itself under a mile of water, for hydrocarbons that were at over 6,000 pounds per square inch of pressure—had come to be seen as routine (2012).

The ongoing, large demand for oil in the United States has helped push oil drilling from onshore to offshore, increasing the complexity of the operations and the opportunity for risks and disaster. This has been encouraged by US policy, which has historically encouraged an increase in both national oil demand and domestic oil production. The result has been oil drilling taking place further and further offshore, and deeper and deeper underground.

The increased complexity of these drilling operations increases the potential for what environmental sociologist Charles Perrow has termed "normal accidents" (2011). Using the partial nuclear meltdown at Three Mile Island as a central case study, Perrow argues that increasing technological complexity makes accidents an expected byproduct. This is because safety measures can lessen the potential for failure, but cannot anticipate and prevent all failures, which are bound to occur in unexpected ways. While two or more failures may lead to a "normal accident"—normal since they are almost an unavoidable and inevitable part of increasingly complex systems—Perrow does note that lax regulation, greed, and cutting safety corners makes system failures and thus accidents more likely. Cost-cutting measures are further encouraged when benefits are concentrated among a powerful few, and the majority of risks socialized to the less powerful and vulnerable. When human error or greed plays a large role, many environmental sociologists argue that the "accident" is more accurately characterized as a disaster, highlighting the role of human agency in creating the conditions under which the event occurs (Freudenburg & Gramling, 2011).

This chapter considers offshore oil drilling in the United States in light of normal accident theory, with a particular focus on the 2010 Deepwater Horizon oil spill. The push for more oil has increased the complexity of offshore drilling and thus makes "normal accidents" more likely, according to Perrow's theory. However, it will be argued that the spill was not just a normal accident, due to the social factors surrounding it. Instead, it was a disaster: an arguably preventable result of lax regulation and the prioritization by the US government and oil companies of production over safety.

While the potential for such a disaster can be limited by tightening safety regulations, risk cannot be eliminated completely in complex systems. Further, the incentives for cost-cutting measures will remain if the benefits continue to be concentrated among the powerful and wealthy, and the risks externalized to the less powerful. Increased safety also does not address arguably the biggest risk of all: catastrophic climate change.

THE EARLY DAYS OF US OIL DRILLING

Oil comes from decomposed organic matter that was primarily sea life—zooplankton, algae, and bacteria—that were buried very quickly under sand and silt and deprived of oxygen. Increasing temperature, pressure, and anaerobic material act upon the organic matter and, over millions of years, transform it into hydrocarbons. Since sea life contains fat, oil is fluid, and is often found in layers of water, oil, and gas. The resulting liquid pools into porous rock or collects under layers of hard rock or dried sea salt, and naturally gravitates upward, causing it to sometimes seep out naturally or gush out when drilled.

According to Ida Tarbell's *Standard Oil*, up to the beginning of the nineteenth century oil was found on the surfaces of springs, and was used as kerosene for light (Tarbell, 2009). Then in Kentucky, West Virginia, Ohio, and Pennsylvania, people drilling for salt hit instead upon a dark green substance, which was recognized as the "rock oil" sometimes found in streams. In 1859, after the many uses of oil were gradually realized, Colonel Edwin Drake was sent by the Pennsylvania Rock Oil Company to Titusville, Pennsylvania, to drill for oil. After many fruitless tries, Drake struck oil. Soon the race was on to buy up land, find oil, and refine it for market use.

Drawing on the money he made selling supplies to the US government during the Civil War, John D. Rockefeller started buying up refineries, using competitive pricing and negotiating exclusive shipping deals with railroads to control 90% of US oil refining by 1879 (Yergin, 2011). Rockefeller's Standard Oil was consolidated as a trust in 1882 and quickly moved into production to control supply and thus price. States challenged Rockefeller's power in court, and in 1911 the Supreme Court ruled that Standard Oil was an unlawful trust and had six months to dissolve. However, as the company was put in charge of its own dissolution, it formed separate companies but with the same executives and owners, including Exxon, Mobil, and Chevron (Juhasz, 2009).

After World War II ended in 1945, the United States became increasingly dependent on oil. Cars multiplied and grew in size throughout the 1950s and 1960s. By mid-century, 13 of the 16 largest US corporations were in oil or automobiles (Phillips, 2006). The increased freedom in transportation encouraged flight from the central cities to the suburbs. New single-family dwellings heated by fuel oil also increased national energy consumption for oil and gas. Domestically there was rapid, post–World War II industrial growth in industries such as manufacturing, petrochemicals, and agriculture, all dependent on oil use (Klare, 2007). Oil demand was up and growing, and US oil companies and the US government wanted to increase supply.

OFFSHORE OIL DRILLING

Although the origins of offshore oil can be traced to as early as the late 1800s, Gramling and Freudenburg argue that the real birth of the offshore industry came with the movement into the marshes and estuaries of coastal Louisiana in the late 1920s and 1930s (Gramling & Freudenburg, 2006, 2012). In 1933, the Texas Company (later known as Texaco) introduced the "submersible" drilling barge—a drilling rig mounted on a barge that could be towed to a drilling site and flooded until it fell to the seafloor. Sitting on the shallow bottom, the barge provided a stable base for drilling, and could be re-floated and towed to a new location once the job was completed (Gramling & Freudenburg, 2006). Multiple technological innovations quickly developed to improve offshore drilling and make it larger and more powerful. As Gramling and Freudenburg (2012) state, the development curve for offshore drilling was perhaps only exceeded by the race to the moon, as the three decades following 1933 saw the emergence of sophisticated oil drilling technology capable of working over 60 miles offshore.

To facilitate offshore oil development, two pieces of US federal legislation were quickly passed. The first was the Submerged Lands Act of 1953, assigning to states the title to offshore lands within three miles of the shoreline. Beyond that was considered federal land by the second legislation, the Outer Continental Shelf Lands Act of 1953. That Act authorized the Secretary of the Interior to offer and manage leases for oil and gas on the "Outer Continental Shelf" (OCS), defined as the area beyond state boundaries and up to 200 nautical miles. According to the legislation, there were two primary ways that the federal oil and gas leases would generate income for the US treasury: (a) leases were to be offered for sale in a competitive bidding process, and (b) the holder of the lease paid a royalty to the federal government of one-sixth (16.66%) of the value of the resource (Gramling & Freudenburg, 2012; Shearer, Davidson, & Gramling, 2013).

By the 1960s, oil producers were pushing for OCS drilling off the coast of California, a move resisted by many state residents. Gramling and Freudenburg (2006) argue that Louisiana residents adapted to the oil industry over time—even "overadapted" due to the region's growing economic dependence on the oil industry. Oil exploration started in Louisiana's coastal marshes in the 1920s, working alongside fishermen and employing local residents, and taking place in areas where few people lived. In contrast, offshore drilling in California involved trying to set up oil rigs in often highly populated or tourist coastal areas with few local benefits, making it easy for California residents to see the drilling as an external threat that should be prevented, particularly by the 1960s when environmental consciousness was growing. Despite the opposition, the first of 10 federal offshore lease sales in California was held in 1963 (Gramling & Freudenburg, 2006).

The resistance to offshore oil drilling seemed to be legitimated in 1969, when a large oil spill took place six miles off the coast of Santa Barbara. The event occurred at an offshore drilling rig operated by Union Oil (now Unocal) called platform Alpha, where pipe was being extracted from a 3,500-foot-deep well. The extraction of the pipe was not sufficiently compensated for with the amount of drilling mud poured back down the well, causing pressure to build up. An emergency attempt was made to cap the casing on the well, but it was unsuccessful. The failure further increased the pressure buildup, and natural gas blew out the drilling mud. The explosion was so powerful it split the well casing and cracked the sea floor in five places. Crude oil spewed out of the rupture at a rate of 1,000 gallons an hour for a month before it could be slowed (Molotch, 1970).

Investigators later determined that more steel pipe sheathing inside the drilling hole would have prevented the rupture. Union Oil had been granted a waiver by the US Geological Survey that allowed it to build around the drilling hole a protective casing—a reinforcing element of the well that is supposed to prevent blowouts—that was 61 feet short of the federal minimum requirements at the time. Even though the well head itself was capped, a blowout occurred due to fragmentation of the casing. Also, because the oil rig was beyond California's three-mile coastal zone, the rig did not have to comply with state standards, which at the time were far more rigid than federal government rules (Molotch, 1970).

At around 100,000 barrels, the spill was the largest in US waters at the time, and still the largest to have taken place in the state. The spill became a national media event for months, as televised scenes of helpless birds soaked in oil and unable to fly were coupled with the inability of either the oil companies or the federal government to stop the flow. Environmental sociologist Harvey Molotch noted the striking disjuncture between the sophisticated and expensive technology available for offshore oil drilling versus the decidedly low-tech options available for cleaning up the spill, which included straw, rakes, shovels, and garbage cans (Molotch, 1970). The event was quickly seen as an example of the hubris of the oil industry and a show of its priorities, and also called into question the federal government's dual role of both overseeing and making money from drilling (Molotch, 1970).

The spill was followed by increased opposition to offshore drilling in California, part of a growing national environmental movement that led to the creation of the Environmental Protection Agency (EPA) in 1970 and government policies for protecting air and water. Public support was growing for not just tighter federal and state regulations around oil drilling, but for alternatives to oil altogether (Shearer, 2011). The momentum, however, was short-lived. In 1970, US domestic oil production began to decline. That year, Muammar Gaddafi nationalized Libya's oil, and within a few years more nationalizations took place. Membership in the Organization of Petroleum Exporting Countries (OPEC) grew, and in 1973 the organization raised prices while Arab members declared an embargo in response to the Arab-Israeli War, with another contraction in supply following the Iranian revolution of 1979 (Odell, 1975). Oil shortages followed in the United States, and oil prices soared.

PROJECT INDEPENDENCE

President Richard Nixon seized on the oil embargoes to offer Project Independence, which he claimed would relieve US dependence on foreign oil. The plan tripled offshore acreage for lease in "frontier" areas, which had never seen leasing or were closed following the 1969 Santa Barbara oil spill. After Nixon resigned, President Gerald Ford continued the policy. The first sale also went forth in 1976 on Alaska's OCS. In the Gulf, the acreage leased in 1975 exceeded that of any previous year (Gould, Karpas, & Slitor, 1991).

Offshore leasing accelerated under President Ronald Reagan and his first Secretary of Interior, James Watt. Before Watt took over the Interior Department, only a limited number of blocks was offered in each offshore lease sale, with the resource assessment conducted by the US Geological Survey, and the blocks sold under a competitive bidding process with a fixed 16.66% royalty rate (Gramling & Freudenburg, 2012). To expand OCS leasing, Watts moved toward broader "area-wide" leasing, where all of the blocks in a given area were offered, rather than the more limited selection of tracts that had been in effect. Watts also combined all the leasing, regulation, and royalty collection functions of the OCS program into one government bureau, creating the Minerals Management Service (MMS) (Shearer, Davidson, & Gramling, 2013).

Area-wide leasing not only increased the amount of offshore tracts leased out to oil companies for drilling, but also significantly decreased the public revenues collected per acre for the activity. As noted by Gramling and Freudenburg, federal lease sales fell from an average of $2,225 per acre before 1982 to an average of $263 an acre since 1983, when area-wide leasing went into effect. Area-wide leasing also lowered the royalties collected for a number of leases, from 16.66% to 12.5%. The lower rates were generally for leases with greater water depths, in an attempt to actively encourage leasing and exploration in risky, deepwater frontier areas that would otherwise be deemed uneconomic to drill. Congress also passed the Outer Continental Shelf Deep Water Royalty Relief Act in 1995, which allowed leaseholders to produce royalty-free up to 87.5 million barrels of oil in water depths greater than 800 meters (Gramling & Freudenburg, 2012).

Additionally, area-wide leasing helped privatize offshore oil drilling in the United States. With entire areas being put up for sale every year, only multinational oil companies had the economic resources to contract seismic surveys on most of the areas. Smaller companies were effectively shut out, as the federal government stopped conducting independent offshore surveys. In practice, Watt's area-wide leasing program set up a situation where only the primary buyers (major oil companies) knew the potential value of a given tract (Gramling & Freudenburg, 2012). On the effect of area-wide leasing, Gramling and Freudenburg concluded in 2011 that "contrary to the superficial impression that expanded offshore oil drilling would be 'good for the economy', the reality is that U.S. energy policies over the past quarter-century have conferred most of their benefits to a handful of the world's largest oil companies, with ever lower returns into the federal treasury" (Freudenburg & Gramling, 2011, p. 172).

In short, US policy since the 1950s has encouraged both increased oil demand and increased domestic oil production. The US federal government expanded the acreage of offshore oil leases available, and encouraged oil companies to venture out into riskier drilling endeavors through royalty relief. The relief decreased the revenues collected for the public coffers, even as the potential damages to the public grew. The increased technological complexity increased the risk of a normal accident, and a renewed focus on secure domestic oil supply helped tamp down calls for improved safety precautions and cleanup measures following the 1969 Santa Barbara oil drilling blowout. All of this created ripe conditions for another, even bigger blowout: the Deepwater Horizon explosion of 2010.

DEEPWATER HORIZON

On April 20, 2010, the team aboard the Deepwater Horizon oil rig was preparing to temporarily abandon a well known as Macondo that it had drilled some 70 kilometers from the US coast. The day before, the crew had pumped cement to the bottom of the borehole, a standard procedure intended to prevent oil from leaking out. The following day, the team was conducting checks to determine whether the well had been properly sealed. During the check, high-pressure methane gas from the well expanded and rose into the drilling rig, where it ignited and exploded, engulfing the platform. Eleven workers on the rig were never found, and 94 were rescued by lifeboat or helicopter. Deepwater Horizon eventually sank into the ocean, and the Macondo well hole lay open, gushing out oil for nearly three months straight.

In its own investigation into the event, BP said the accident was caused by the failure of eight different safety systems (Mullins, 2010). First, the cement at the bottom of the borehole did not create a seal, and therefore oil and gas began to leak through it into the pipe leading to the surface. Second, the pipe had two mechanical valves designed to stop the flow of oil and gas, both of which failed. Third, the crew carried out various pressure tests to determine whether the well was sealed or not, the results of which were misinterpreted. Fourth, as a mixture of mud and gas began pouring onto the floor of the rig, the crew immediately attempted to close a valve in a device called the blowout preventer, which sits on the ocean floor over the top of the well bore hole. It did not work properly. Fifth, the crew had the option of diverting the mud and gas away from the rig, venting it safely through pipes over the side. Instead, the flow was diverted to a device on board the rig designed to separate small amounts of gas from a flow of mud. The so-called mud-gas separator was quickly overwhelmed and flammable gas began to engulf the rig. Sixth, the rig had an on-board gas detection system that should have sounded the alarm and triggered the closure of ventilation fans to prevent the gas from reaching potential causes of ignition, such as the rig's engines. This system failed. Seventh, the explosion destroyed the control lines the crew was using to try to close the safety valves in the blowout preventer. Eighth, the blowout preventer has its own safety mechanism in which two separate systems should have shut the valves automatically when it lost contact with the surface. One system seems to have had a flat battery and the other a defective switch. Consequently, the blowout preventer did not close.

While BP's assessment emphasizes the multiple failures of its safety equipment, subsequent federal investigations noted that the failures took place within an environment of cutting corners in safety precautions, which directly or indirectly contributed to many of the failures. The company was running weeks behind schedule and tens of millions of dollars over budget in trying to complete its well. Further, the Deepwater Horizon was scheduled to begin exploratory drilling on another lease held by BP, and the delay was holding up the investigation, thus costing BP more money in potential lost revenue (Freudenburg & Gramling, 2011).

In a 2010 letter to BP, the US House Committee on Energy noted three shortcuts taken by the company that weakened safety measures and thus contributed to the explosion: (1) a change in casing system design that saved time but removed a critical barrier to gas pressure; (2) two changes in the cementing procedure that also saved time but reduced safeguards that help keep the cement casing intact; and (3) failure to acoustically test the final cement bond between the casing and the rock formation (Freudenburg & Gramling, 2011).

In January 2011, the National Commission on the BP Deepwater Horizon Oil Spill and Offshore Drilling concluded that BP, and its partners Halliburton and Transocean, had attempted to work more cheaply and thus helped trigger the explosion. According to the commission's final report on the event, "whether purposeful or not, many of the decisions that BP, Halliburton, and Transocean made that increased the risk of the Macondo blowout clearly saved those companies significant time (and money)" (Spill and Offshore Drilling, 2011). The finding was reinforced by a September 2011 federal investigation by the Coast Guard and the Bureau of Ocean Energy Management, Regulation and Enforcement, which also concluded that BP took many shortcuts that contributed to the disastrous blowout, including seven violations of federal regulations (Griggs, 2011).

Cuts in safety were enabled by cuts in government oversight and regulation. In September 2008, reports by the Interior Department implicated over a dozen MMS officials in unethical and criminal conduct in the performance of their duties. The conduct included using cocaine and marijuana, accepting gifts and free holidays, and literally getting into bed with energy company representatives, leading to "a culture of ethical failure," according to the investigation (Shefrin, 2016). A May 2010 inspector general investigation revealed that MMS regulators in the Gulf region had allowed industry officials to fill in their own inspection reports in pencil and then turned them over to the regulators, who traced over them in pen before submitting the reports to the agency (Urbina, 2010).

The Minerals Management Service also granted BP's drilling plan for the Deepwater Horizon rig a "categorical exclusion" in the months before the 2010 explosion—reserved for actions that are determined not to have a significant effect on the environment and therefore do not require an environmental impact assessment. According to the US Council on Environmental Quality, the categorical exclusions used by the MMS in approving BPs Exploration and Drilling Plan were established in the 1980s, before deepwater drilling became widespread (Woolfson, 2013).

The Service also approved BP's Oil Spill Response Plan, a 582-page report designed to cover all BP operations in the Gulf of Mexico. Once the spill occurred, the plan was revealed as riddled with errors and miscalculations. Under a heading of "sensitive biological resources," the document listed walruses, sea otters, seals, and sea lions as potential victims of an oil spill, none of which actually live in the Gulf region. The document also listed a deceased man as an expert to be located in case of an emergency. Finally, the plan stated that for a leak 10 times worse than what occurred, oil would not reach the shore because drilling operations were too far out to sea. Yet oil contaminated marshland all along the Louisiana coast, with tar balls appearing on beaches as far away as Florida (Freudenburg & Gramling, 2011).

In short, BP's oil response plan may best be characterized as what environmental sociologist Lee Clarke calls a "fantasy document," which are documents used by organizations and experts to normalize danger by claiming that problems are controllable, even when they are not. According to Clarke, fantasy documents help legitimate the insertion of increasingly complex and potentially dangerous technological systems into society by making the systems appear to be safe and subject to expert control—a notion that is, in fact, a fantasy (Clarke, 1999). Fantasy documents are therefore not reliable blueprints for what to do when disaster occurs, but instead are tools to assuage public concern. Indeed, after the BP spill a number of experimental cleanup measures were taken, including the widespread use of chemical oil dispersants totaling an estimated 1.84 million US gallons. Critics argued that the dispersants did not so much address the oil spill as hide it, since its use breaks up floating oil slicks into small droplets that sink underwater, where it can be toxic to marine life (Bond, 2013).

In October 2011, MMS was dissolved after it was determined it had exercised poor oversight over the drilling industry. Three new agencies replaced it, separating the regulation, leasing, and revenue-collection responsibilities, respectively, among the Bureau of Safety and Environmental Enforcement, the Bureau of Ocean Energy Management, and the Office of Natural Resources Revenue (Carpenter, 2015).

In July 2010 it was reported that the spill was already having a "devastating" effect on marine life in the Gulf (Campagna et al., 2011). By June 2010, 143 spill-exposure cases had been reported to the Louisiana Department of Health, believed to be caused by exposure to both the oil and the oil dispersants (Health, 2010). The longer-term health, environmental, and social effects of the spill are still being assessed.

"NORMAL ACCIDENTS" AND DISASTERS

According to Charles Perrow (2011), accidents are an inherent part of increasing system complexity. This is because accidents require only that two or more processes go wrong in unforeseen ways to occur. While precautions and safety measures may decrease the potential for certain failures, they also add to the complexity of the system, and therefore paradoxically increase the potential for new categories of accidents. Further, the more tightly coupled the system, the more quickly failures can cascade before any safety device or personnel can prevent them. In this way, failures are an expected part of system complexity and can lead to "normal accidents"—what happens when two or more failures take place in unexpected ways and defeat safety devices. If the accident brings down a significant part of the system and the system has catastrophic potential, it can lead to a catastrophe: 100 or more immediate deaths, 1,000 longer-term deaths, or irretrievable environmental damage (Perrow, 2011).

In his outlining of the concept, Perrow does not attribute normal accidents to capitalism or greed, because they occur in even government-sponsored programs with low pay-out for the main actors. But Perrow does note that most of the external costs of "normal accidents" are borne by others, both in the short term (e.g., injured workers) and the long term (e.g., people whose environment is negatively affected by the event), making the accidents more acceptable to decision makers (Perrow, 2011).

Later revisiting his theory, Perrow argued that events such as the 1984 Bhopal gas leak in India are not normal accidents under his conception of the term. Bhopal was not the result of two or more failures coming together in unexpected ways, as it was neither unexpected nor inevitable. In contrast to normal accidents, Perrow cited greed and lax oversight as contributory and significant factors to the Bhopal event. This included laying off key people, reducing shift size in operations, cutting maintenance and safety precautions, and allowing safety devices to remain unrepaired. There was also no warning and no evacuation plan (Perrow, 2011). The event was a catastrophe, as it killed thousands if people. But it was not a catastrophe borne of a normal accident, as many of the contributory factors were highly and sadly preventable.

Thus increasing system complexity makes accidents more likely, even "normal." Yet the possibility of accidents is heightened when safety precautions are not being followed; when shortcuts are being made; and when regulation and oversight become lax and loosely enforced. In short, human error and lax oversight transform accidents into what many environmental sociologists refer to as "disasters," highlighting the role of human agency in the event.

With this framework between normal accident and disaster, it is clear that BP was not simply a "normal accident." It was not the unexpected coming together of two failures; BP itself acknowledges eight separate failures. The potential for these failures increased when BP, Halliburton, and Transocean cut corners to save expenses. These shortcuts took place within a lax regulatory environment that prioritized oil production over safety. These cuts in safety and enforcement made failure more likely, and therefore less unexpected. It was a disaster, and given that many of the environmental effects from the BP blowout may be irreversible, it was also a catastrophe.

Conclusion

Drawing upon Charles Perrow's concept of "normal accidents," the 2010 Deepwater Horizon blowout and oil spill would more accurately be characterized not as an accident, but as a disaster. This is because, as argued in this chapter, the event was not due to unexpected failures, but instead highly preventable factors.

Since Colonel Drake first struck oil in the United States in 1904, the United States has become highly dependent on this incredibly energy-dense resource, shaping much of our social, political, and economic lives. Policies of the US government have encouraged both increased national oil demand and increased domestic production, helping create a regulatory and industry environment that prioritized production over safety. This made the social conditions ripe for the 2010 Deepwater Horizon disaster.

In the wake of the disaster, changes have been made to the regulatory agencies in charge of offshore oil development to help tighten and improve oversight and safety. Yet offshore drilling is just one of the numerous ways that oil production has become more unconventional and complex. Other growing innovations include hydraulic fracturing ("fracking"), or the use of chemicals, sand, and water under high pressure to break up existing fissures and access more oil and gas deposits. In 2000, fracking made up just over 2% of US oil production—by 2016, it made up more than half (Kilian, 2016). The practice has helped make the United States the world's top producer of natural gas since 2011 and the world's top producer of petroleum hydrocarbons since 2013 (Kilian, 2016). Yet most of the long-term health and environmental effects from the practice remain unknown, including earthquakes, methane leakage, and water contamination from unidentified chemicals (Ward, Eykelbosh, & Nicol, 2016).

In Canada, oil production is increasingly becoming directed toward development of oil sands, mainly located in the Alberta region. Oil sands (or tar sands) are mixtures of organic matter, quartz sand, bitumen, and water that can either be mined or extracted in situ using thermal recovery techniques. The process for extracting oil from the tar sands is a highly energy- and water-intensive process, with the effects including land degradation, air pollution, and water contamination (Davidson & Gismondi, 2011). In the mid-1990s, government and oil industry representatives projected that Alberta might produce up to 1.2 million barrels per day by 2020; this goal was reached over a decade ahead of schedule, with 2011 production at 1.7 million barrels per day. It is now anticipated that production will exceed 3.7 million barrels per day by 2021—more than three times the high end of earlier projections (Shearer, Davidson, & Gramling, 2013).

In short, the complexity of oil production is growing, as are the risks. As noted by Perrow, one reason accidents are often tolerated as a normal part of technological development is that the external costs are primarily borne by external parties, and not industry owners and decision-makers. This allows people in power to downplay or ignore growing industrial risks, as they predominantly see their own personal risks in terms of losing power and control, not in terms of public health and environmental degradation (Shearer et al., 2013). For example, conservative white men have much lower perceptions of the risks of anthropogenic climate change than any other group in the United States, because they are more concerned with government regulation over industry than the threat of environmental collapse (McCright & Dunlap, 2011).

The complexity, risks, and uncertainty around increasingly unconventional oil drilling are growing. Increased safety and regulation can decrease the potential for accidents and disasters, but not completely, as normal accidents are unavoidable, and many of the risks (e.g., the long-term effects of fracking chemicals in the human body) are unknown. Yet since oil production is taking place within an environment where the risks and rewards are distributed unequally, these risks are portrayed as a normal and seemingly unavoidable part of industrial and technological development. Thus increasingly unconventional oil development continues even as we face the biggest risk ever to human survival, directly linked to the continued pursuit of fossil fuels: the potential for irreversible damage to the climate that sustains us all.

REFERENCES

Bond, D. (2013). Governing disaster: The political life of the environment during the BP oil spill. *Cultural Anthropology*, 28(4), 694–715.

Campagna, C., Short, F. T., Polidoro, B. A., McManus, R., Collette, B. B., Pilcher, N. J., ... Carpenter, K. E. (2011). Gulf of Mexico oil blowout increases risks to globally threatened species. *BioScience*, 61(5), 393–397.

Carpenter, H. (2015). Deepwater Horizon: Agency reorganization and appropriations in offshore oil regulation. *Ecology LQ*, 42, 181.

Clarke, L. (1999). *Mission improbable: Using fantasy documents to tame disaster*: Chicago: University of Chicago Press.

Davidson, D. J., & Gismondi, M. (2011). *Challenging legitimacy at the precipice of energy calamity*. New York: Springer Science & Business Media.

Freudenburg, W. R., & Gramling, R. (2011). *Blowout in the Gulf: The BP oil spill disaster and the future of energy in America*. Cambridge, MA: MIT Press.

Gould, G. J., Karpas, R. M., & Slitor, D. L. (1991). *OCS national compendium*. Herndon, VA: Minerals Management Service. OCS Information Program.

Gramling, R., & Freudenburg, W. R. (2006). Attitudes toward offshore oil development: A summary of current evidence. *Ocean & Coastal Management*, 49(7), 442–461.

Gramling, R., & Freudenburg, W. R. (2012). A century of Macondo United States energy policy and the BP blowout catastrophe. *American Behavioral Scientist*, 56(1), 48–75.

Griggs, J. W. (2011). BP Gulf of Mexico oil spill. *Energy LJ*, 32, 57.

Health, Louisiana Department of. (2010). Louisiana LDH releases oil spill-related exposure information. Retrieved from http://dhh.louisiana.gov/index.cfm/newsroom/detail/108

Juhasz, A. (2009). *The tyranny of oil*. New York: Harper Collins.

Kilian, L. (2016). The impact of the shale oil revolution on US oil and gasoline prices. *CESifo Working Paper Series* 5723.

Klare, M. (2007). *Blood and oil: The dangers and consequences of America's growing dependency on imported petroleum*. New York: Macmillan.

McCright, A. M., & Dunlap, R. E. (2011). Cool dudes: The denial of climate change among conservative white males in the United States. *Global Environmental Change*, 21(4), 1163–1172.

Molotch, H. (1970). Oil in Santa Barbara and power in America. *Sociological Inquiry*, 40(1), 131–144.

Mullins, J. (2010). The eight failures that caused the Gulf oil spill. *New Scientist*, September 8. Retrieved from https://www.newscientist.com/article/dn19425-the-eight-failures-that-caused-the-gulf-oil-spill

Odell, P. R. (1975). *Oil and world power: background to the oil crisis*. London: Penguin Books.

Perrow, C. (2011). *Normal accidents: Living with high risk technologies*. Princeton, NJ: Princeton University Press.

Phillips, K. (2006). *American theocracy: The peril and politics of radical religion, oil, and borrowed money in the 21st Century*. New York: Penguin.

Shearer, C. (2011). *Kivalina: a climate change story*: Haymarket Books.

Shearer, C., Davidson, D., & Gramling, R. (2013). The double diversion of national energy in a globalized era: offshore oil, coal, and oil sand leases. In S. Maret (Ed.), *William R. Freudenburg, a life in social research* (pp. 57–72). Bingley, UK: Emerald Group.

Shearer, C., Rogers-Brown, J. B., Bryant, K., Cranfill, R., & Harthorn, B. H. (2013). Power and vulnerability: Contextualizing "low risk" views of environmental and health hazards.

In S. Maret (Ed.), *William R. Freudenburg, a life in social research* (pp. 235–257). Bingley, UK: Emerald Group.

Shefrin, H. (2016). Risk management profiles: Con Ed, BP, and MMS. In *Behavioral risk management* (pp. 299–317). New York; Springer. Retrieved from https://link.springer.com/chapter/10.1057/9781137445629_18

Spill, National Commission on BP Deepwater Horizon Oil, and Offshore Drilling. (2011). "Deep Water–The Gulf Oil Disaster and the Future of Offshore Drilling." Report to the president. National Commission on the BP Deepwater Horizon Oil Spill and Offshore Drilling. January 2011. Retrieved from https://www.gpo.gov/fdsys/pkg/GPO-OILCOMMISSION/pdf/GPO-OILCOMMISSION.pdf

Tarbell, I. M. (2009). *The history of the Standard Oil company*. New York, NY: Cosimo.

Urbina, I. (2010, May 24). Inspector general's inquiry faults regulators. *New York Times*. Retrieved from http://www.nytimes.com/2010/05/25/us/25mms.html?_r=0

Ward, H., Eykelbosh, A., & Nicol, A. M. (2016). Addressing uncertainty in public health risks due to hydraulic fracturing. *Environmental Health Review*, 59(2), 57–61.

Woolfson, C. (2013). Preventable disasters in the offshore oil industry: From Piper Alpha to Deepwater Horizon. *New Solutions: A Journal of Environmental and Occupational Health Policy*, 22(4), 497–524.

Yergin, D. (2011). *The prize: The epic quest for oil, money and power*. New York: Simon & Schuster.

CHAPTER 15

INDUSTRIALIZING COUNTRIES AS THE NEW ENERGY CONSUMERS

PAULO MANDUCA, MAURO BERNI, IURE PAIVA,
AND JOSÉ ALEXANDRE HAGE

INTRODUCTION

IN the early years of the twenty-first century, petroleum—including oil and gas—was the core theme of political agendas in Venezuela, Bolivia, and Ecuador. Argentina had been reducing production and increasing its foreign dependence, and Brazil had not yet accomplished its goal of self-sufficiency. On the other hand, Brazil and Argentina had been developing massive biofuel production programs and, by the end of the decade, both countries entered the world of big business petroleum.

The long path to ethanol in Brazil that began in the mid-1970s and the comparatively fast start of the biodiesel industry in Argentina in 2000 opened new economic and political integration possibilities for the both countries. Brazil put forward investments in so-called ethanol diplomacy—a term coined to define specific actions the Brazilian government undertook to promote ethanol internationally (Dalgaard, 2012)—and sought to broaden its participation in global policy, fostering an image of an emerging power whose economy was supported by a clean energy matrix, taking a global leadership role in biofuel development.

In 2007, Petrobras discovered oil and gas in the pre-salt geological formations in Brazil's southern Atlantic coast. Then, in 2011, a few months after Petrobras extracted the first gallon of petroleum, the global energy companies YPF (Yacimientos Petrolíferos Fiscales) and Repsol (Repsol S.A.) discovered exploitable reserves of shale gas and oil in the mineral district of Vaca Muerta, in southern Argentina.

Since that time we have observed a great shift in political focus in both countries. Shifts in economic and energy policies, the declarations of national leaders, and the political reactions of civil society suggest that the discovery of petroleum has generated a full-scale rerouting of governments' priorities and investments, and of political agendas as a whole, toward the prioritization of projects associated with fossil fuels (petroleum/shale). Meanwhile, the biofuel sector nearly disappeared from political agendas.

The actions of the two countries are not coincidental. In the period under consideration, the phenomena linked to biofuels and the impacts that have emerged since the discovery of petroleum are more advanced in Brazil than in Argentina. As we will show, the realities are different in each country, but we may also observe historical similarities: the adoption of political models of economic development coincide in the entire region, as have the scourges of dictatorship and cycles of low economic growth. More recently, the region has experimented with the ascension of co-aligned center-leftist governments (the "pink tide"), which have proposed to reissue economical models based on nationalist and statist paradigms. In this context, populist standards of various hues arise. It is the perfect environment for a revitalization of other myths typical of the 1970s (in this case, the myth of the oil industry panacea), and it is through this new Latin American populist frame that we seek to understand the change of priorities related to energy sources.

Populism has been a core subject of interest in recent political sociology since contemporary populist experiments have been observed all over the world. In the tradition of Latin American sociology, populism is associated with low levels of political institutionalization, in which the role of the leader surpasses that of the institution. Analysis over Peron's (1946–1955, 1973–1974) and Vargas's governments (1930–1945) concentrate on this salvationist bias of the leader, who controls and takes advantage of the masses in order to retain his power, while also rewarding his subjects' loyalty by distributing social welfare from which they would otherwise be deprived. Many social scientists do not accept the classification of the pink tide as a populist phenomenon, arguing that this concept does not reflect the linkage that the leftist parties should have with their social bases. Furthermore, the pink tide arises in the process of the democratic consolidation in the region after tovercoming exceptionalist regimes without any breakup of democratic institutions, except perhaps in the Venezuelan case.

Dornbusch and Edwards (1990) present an analysis focused on how governments pursuing this institutional shift cope with economic policies. By studying the governments of Allende (Chile, 1970–1973) and of Garcia (Peru, 1985–1990), Dornbusch and Edwards (1990, p. 247) conceptualized macroeconomic populism as "an approach to economics that emphasizes growth and income distribution and deemphasizes the risks of inflation and deficit finance, external constraints and the reaction of economic agents to aggressive non-market policies." Macroeconomic populism is a very appropriate concept for this study because it describes how governments deal with the main issues common to governments following a pink tide path. While pursuing different approaches, all of these governments prioritize economic growth and wealth distribution, generally against market players' odds. Therefore, such center-leftist governments justify the oil companies' assets expropriation, regulatory framework changes, and so on.

Laclau (2006), on the other hand, challenges what he considers to be pejorative labeling that disqualifies populism as a constructive political path. He considers populism as a regular political characteristic that can be observed in any country, describing broadly based social groups interacting directly with those in political power. Institutional channels are likely to make political relations bureaucratic and distant from social demands. More direct relationships with leaders are seen as a means to shorten the path to demands satisfaction, rather than becoming lost in the state bureaucratic machine. For this reason, populism could be a more evident political process when it succeeds in transforming economic and political structures. De Gaulle and Hugo Chavez would be examples of such populist leadership in their respective times and countries.

In this text we start from the "state of the art" on biofuels in Brazil and Argentina in order to highlight the expertise acquired, as well as the potential that biofuels are supposed to offer for Brazil and Argentina to overcome the challenges of sustainable development. Next we describe the process in which they changed course, almost abandoning their biofuels programs to concentrate efforts in the development of the traditional oil industry. To conclude, we analyze the emergence of leftist governments in Latin America as populist phenomena. In this way Venezuela was a benchmark; leftist-populist governments in both countries were able to manipulate nationalist sentiment around the ideology that oil ownership is the path to development and to the attainment of power. By restoring such typical ideology of the 1970s, which today seems to be outdated in advanced economies, this petroleum populism not only shows how embedded that ideology is in the national identity, but also indicates that biofuels are not yet a phenomenon that changes the economy globally.

THE BIOFUELS ADVENTURE

Argentina and Brazil have become global references for biofuels production. International prices of petroleum in the second half of the first decade of the 2000s provided a great incentive for the two agricultural powers whose biodiversity, lands, and hydro resources made them strong prospective players in the renewable energy market. Brazil has two biofuel programs. The most recent one is the biodiesel program. Brazil's National Program of Production and Use of Biodiesel (PNPB) has been articulated with policies for labor and income generation and for family farming support (Dal Bello Leite, 2014). PNPB established a goal of adding 2% of biodiesel to the diesel traded by January 2008, increasing to 5% by January 2013. In 2015, biodiesel demand in Brazil reached approximately 4 billion liters. Biodiesel producers benefited from tax incentives and credit from BNDES (the National Bank for Economic and Social Development), obtaining the "Social Fuel Seal." Among the criteria for obtaining the Social Fuel Seal are the rural producers' qualification requirement and minimal percentages for the acquisition of feedstock originating from family farms (Finco et al., 2010).

In the beginning, PNPB suffered from high costs of agricultural comodities in the international market, especially soybeans. The program's technicians idealized the introduction of jatropha as feedstock, but they did not succeed at adapting it to Brazil (Bergman et al., 2013). Besides castor bean and palm, the major Brazilian crop is soybean, produced not by small farm owners but by large agricultural corporations in the center-west of the country.

A far more successful biofuel market experience was the ethanol program, in which Brazil has 40 years of experience in the complete cycle: feedstock production, mills, logistics, and flex fuel engines (Goldemberg et al., 2004). The ethanol program started under the name of Proalcool in 1975, as a Brazilian response to the petroleum crisis. The project began in the universities, and when it was taken over by the government it became a substantial national effort, including the development of engines, technology, processes, and logistics. It was a program of massive substitution of petroleum by products by sugarcane ethanol, which has been produced in Brazil since the colonial era. The sugar industry, therefore, offered initial support for the introduction of ethanol, and the flexibility to produce both products at a scale that is convenient for the market, which is a peculiarity of the Brazilian production model—an attribute that has guaranteed the survival of the industry in times of crisis (Leal & Walter, 2010). With Proalcool, sugarcane began to be planted on a massive scale in the southwest of the country, where productivity was better, with a huge impact on the traditional polyculture landscape in the state of São Paulo.

The government of General Geisel—fourth of the military cycle from 1964 to 1985—promoted the production of alcohol-powered vehicles (hydrated alcohol), offered tax incentives and subsidies, and supported the increase of anhydrous alcohol to gasoline—from 1.1% to 25%—which created a fixed demand. In the first years of the 1980s, after the second petroleum crisis, Proalcool achieved its highest production peak. Between 1978 and 1991, the national passenger vehicle fleet running exclusively on ethanol continued to increase, reaching 60% of all road vehicles.

In the second half of the decade, however, the ethanol initiative met two major crises: a substantial decline in incentives due to high government debt levels, followed by the fall in petroleum prices. In response, producers turned to export sugar rather than produce ethanol. The subsequent lack of capacity to fulfill the demand undermined reliability on fuel alcohol, and the owners of vehicles that ran exclusively on ethanol tried to sell their vehicles, or adapt them to run on gasoline. The social and environmental impacts had also begun to take their tolls. Rural workers began to migrate by the thousands from other regions for seasonal work in degrading conditions, resulting in many conflicts. There was a true environmental "hecatomb" in towns neighboring refineries, due to the heavy pollution of rivers, and the burning during harvest. At that time Proalcool began to look like a big mistake.

The 10 years that followed (1986–1995) were a period of stagnation. The crisis in confidence in alcohol-fueled vehicles—the so-called green fleet—is reflected in subsequent car production, which fell from 60% to 1% of produced vehicles. Meanwhile, the subsidies and the international market for sugar guaranteed the survival of the sugarcane producers. With the reform of the state in Collor de Mello's government (1990–1992), the government presence declined, prices were no longer fixed by the government, and the subsidies dwindled away. Proalcool was nearly abandoned by the government.

These extreme difficulties forced the sector to reinvent itself. In 1997, stakeholders created the Sugar Cane Industry Union (UNICA), which gave the sector a professional lobby. The producers, researchers, and defenders of clean energy saw in ethanol a potential substitute for petroleum derivatives. But the deficit of the industry was huge and included cases of slave-like labor, environmental damages, and subsidy dependence, and the risk that the expansion of the sugar-energy sector would involve the destruction of the center-west (Pantanal) and north (Amazon) ecosystems.

Defining a new era, the sugar-energy sector made a series of commitments, such as combating degrading conditions for labor, and improvement of harvest and production processes to internationally acceptable standards. These commitments encouraged the use of tractors for harvest mechanization, the end of burning, and, finally, the adoption of agricultural zoning, which removed the pressure over new lands.

In 1998, when oil prices were quoted around US$100 per barrel, the government aimed to further encourage the sugar-energy industry, by increasing the proportion of anhydrous ethanol in gasoline from 22% to 24%. At the same time, it ended subsidies and forced ethanol to compete directly with gasoline at the gas stations.

The minister of agriculture of the new government that began in January 2003 was a biofuel enthusiast who assumed the post with the goal of making ethanol a government priority. He launched a strategy to promote biofuel, linking the economic advantages of ethanol to positive environmental impacts, including the reduction of emissions of greenhouse gases (GHGs), just at the time when Brazil officially began to engage with international goals of emissions reduction.

Domestically, the government rebuilt the ethanol industry, offering tax incentives, credit for modernization, funding for innovation and ethanol's foreign marketing. Credit feasibility allowed the increase and modernization of industrial facilities between 2002 and 2007, when 120 new mills were installed in the center-southern states in Brazil. The country doubled sugarcane production in only five years. The ethanol program became a rare consensus in Brazilian society.

The first decade of the 2000s was profitable for Brazil's ethanol industry internationally as well. The European Union's (EU) initiatives to enroll biofuels in the energy matrix placed Brazil in a prominent position due to 40 years of accumulated experience in the ethanol market. With the EU initiative, the basis for ethanol's international market were launched. In 2010, the US Environmental Protection Agency (EPA) certified Brazilian ethanol as an advanced biofuel, creating a positive expectation for exporters.

The government then promoted a coordinated action for the international promotion of Brazilian ethanol, dubbed "ethanol diplomacy" (Dalgaard, 2012), with the aim to attract investments, increase foreign production, and open new markets. Ethanol allowed Brazil to occupy a prominent position in environmental international debates, with an energy matrix that consisted of 45% renewable sources. In the following years, Brazil joined the United States and the EU in initiatives to standardize and certify biofuels, thereby creating conditions for a global market.

Ethanol diplomacy has met with difficulties in relations with allied leftist Latin American governments, however, which led to a confrontation in 2007 in the first meeting of the South American energy summit. On that occasion, President Hugo Chávez of Venezuela strongly condemned biofuels and identified them as a risk to food security. This forced Brazilian officials to take immediate action to prevent the final declaration from condemning biofuels.

Back in 2007, President Bush joined President Lula in a visit to an ethanol plant in the state of São Paulo. On that same day, Chávez and Morales (of Bolivia) participated in an anti-American march in Buenos Aires. Brazil agreed to sacrifice ideological solidarity ties with the new leftist Latin American leaders in order to defend ethanol and Brazil's new relations with the United States. At that time, Lula and Bush signed the "ethanol pact," a milestone in Brazilian diplomacy, as the first time that Brazil had signed a bilateral pact with a world power in an equal position.

Despite every effort dedicated to biofuels, as we will see later, since the discovery of petroleum in the South Atlantic, the government's engagement with biofuels has been completely replaced by an interest in offshore petroleum deposits. Although the Ministry of International Affairs has kept biofuels on the agenda, the government only has concentrated on developing new institutional conditions for the drilling of pre-salt.

In the government of da Silva's successor, biofuels disappeared completely from the agenda even of foreign policy. But it was the energy policy of the new president that has caused a deep damage in the ethanol industry. In 2011, petroleum's average price in the international market was over US$110 and remained high until 2014. In the same period, southwest Brazil suffered the most severe drought of the last 80 years, which resulted in a reduction of water supplies in the reservoirs of hydroelectric power plants in the most populous and industrialized area of the country. The reduction of hydroelectric capacity forced the national operator of the electric power system to start up thermoelectric gas plants that generate electricity at a much higher cost. The government avoided passing the high costs of electricity and petroleum to the consumers and kept the prices artificially low. In the case of fossil fuels, the government forced Petrobras to absorb the costs of fuel production and the artificially low sale price (Johnson, 2016). The government reduced to zero the tax rate for gasoline and diesel—in other words, establishing an undeclared subsidy for fossil fuels. Besides the future impacts on the company's financial health and relationships with the shareholders, by keeping the prices low, the government caused significant damage to the ethanol industry, which could not compete with the low gasoline prices.

As a result, companies that had invested heavily in the production growth and modernization of industrial facilities struggled to survive. For more than four years the sugar-energy sector had, unsuccessfully, pressured the government to change its energy policy. In 2015, the producers' lobby convinced the president to increase the proportion of ethanol to gasoline—from 25% to 27%—offering some relief, but not enough to eliminate a crisis situation for the sector. Within 10 years, ethanol producers in Brazil faced two extremes: from the promise of becoming green fuel suppliers for the world, to the greatest economic crisis experienced by the sugar-energy sector.

Biofuels in Argentina are suffering a similar fate. The first Argentinian experience with biofuel started in 1980s, under the milestone Program Alconafta, in which 12 Argentinian provinces were producing 250 million liters of sugarcane ethanol yearly. However, with the increase of international sugarcane prices, followed by frustrating harvests and the lack of a long-term guarantee of consumption, the program lost dynamism little by little until its complete eradication (Dolabella, 2011).

Recently, following global tendencies, Argentina restarted its biofuels policy. In this way it established in 2006 a beneficial taxation regime, credit incentives, and positive regulatory system for the production and consumption of biodiesel and ethanol. The present legislation determines that diesel must consist of 10% biodiesel, and gasoline must consist of 5% ethanol, to guarantee the producers a captive domestic market (Dolabella, 2011). Argentina finally became a great world biofuel producer in 2009 based on a technology-intensive and competitive agriculture and a robust industrial sector producing vegetable oils.

Biodiesel is the most important biofuel in Argentina. Argentina has one of the most modern biodiesel industries in the world, and 85% of plants are located in the provinces of Santa Fé, particularly in Puerto General San Martin, San Lorenzo, and Rosario. These regions have facilities designed specifically for export via the Parana-Uruguay waterway, reducing the average distance from production areas to the loading ports (Dolabella, 2011).

Beyond economic goals, biofuel worked as a national peacemaker during the most difficult conflict in Argentina in the early twenty-first century. In 2008 the clash of interests between the government and farmers was related to the foreign market of agricultural commodities. At that time, Argentinian farmers hoped to increase exportations, taking advantage of the high prices of commodities, while the government wanted to save food prices from rising. As a result, the government instituted the *retenciones* (retentions), a tax penalty intended to reduce the export of grains, in an effort to delink international prices from domestic ones and to neutralize the impact of severe price fluctuations abroad. In the same year, producers responded to the *retenciones* with a national movement called *El paro agropecuario*—a farming lockout led by farmers' unions. When the government established a tax incentive for the exportation of biodiesel, it allowed farmers to export more without breaking the law. So the biofuels incentive policy assumed a role of conciliation between the government and the rural producers since it offered an opportunity to reach the international market by exporting soybean-based biodiesel.

In 2012, 40% of Argentina's soybean oil was processed and exported as biodiesel. The producers expanded the industrial facilities, built biodiesel plants, and increased production capacity from 0.5 million tons in 2007 to 4.1 million tons in 2012. In 2011, Argentina exported 1.7 million tons for US$ 2.1 billion, an increase of 30.7% in volume and 75% in revenue from the previous year. The biofuels sector in Argentina developed rapidly to become the most dynamic activity in the national economy (Chidiak & Rozemberg, 2016). But, by the end of 2012, exports fell by 60% and kept falling in 2013 as a consequence of retaliation imposed by Spain related to the expropriation of the YPF Oil Company, as will be discussed later in the chapter. Spain suspended purchases of Argentinian biodiesel and required the European Commission to adopt measurements against Argentina. Europe, and particularly Spain, was previously the destination of all Argentinian biodiesel. In 2012, the EU raised the tariff from 6.8% to 10.5%, and in 2013 imposed 25% anti-dumping duties on Argentinian biodiesel. The impact was devastating to the producers, who were being squeezed by both domestic and EU taxes. In March 2016, the new Argentinian government (elected in 2015) decided to increase taxes on biodiesel exports from 3.9% to 6.4% and to subsidize petroleum exports as long as international prices were below US$47.5 per barrel, making matters even more difficult for the producers.

Although the future outlook for biofuels in Brazil and in Argentina appears uncertain, the historical development of biofuels represented a great leap for both economies, which had previously been largely dependent on innovation from abroad. The potential of bioproducts and other kinds of bioenergy depends on changes in political and market conditions. Recent data point to industry recovery, but the fact that biofuels are no longer among the national priorities indicates that these countries have chosen a conventional and outdated model of economic development in spite of the journeys traveled, the challenges achieved, and the current potential for expanding the green economy. Biofuels production is likely to proceed, but neither of these governments has yet acknowledged the importance of the green economy, or the looming collapse of the petroleum economy.

PETROLEUM AND NATIONAL IDENTITY

Venezuela was a benchmark for every leftist party in Latin America during first decade of the twenty-first. Although the country has exploited petroleum since 1917, before the Chávez revolution the petroleum income never had been used for a genuinely national development project with the social inclusion of the poor, as the petroleum industry had long been controlled by the elite. The Bolivarian revolution promoted by Hugo Chávez had promised to turn petroleum income into social benefits. It worked while the price of oil was high.

At the time of the highest petroleum prices, Chávez used to use petroleum income for the establishment of what he called the "socialism of the twenty-first century," an ideological mix composed of nationalist authoritarianism, derived from his military bias, and other traditional leftist ideology in Latin America, such as anti-capitalism and anti-Americanism. In this way, Chávez implemented a power centralization policy, re-equipping the armed forces, took steps to militarize several government areas, and nationalized private companies that didn't cooperate with the regime. On the other hand, the government invested strongly in assistance for the poor, and offered petroleum at subsided prices to some countries of the region. In this way, the state-owned oil company—Petróleos de Venezuela S.A. (PDVSA)—became the main instrument for the regime to support every kind of public policy, from social assistance to external policy.

Venezuela's experience inspired other countries, firstl Bolivia and Ecuador, to joined the Bolivarian movement founded by Chávez, which later also included Brazil and Argentina. After oil prices fell, Venezuela entered a deep crisis, but even its crisis was taken as a learning experience by the other leftist governments in region, especially Brazil and Argentina, where the recent discovery of oil was receiving worldwide attention.

Argentina and Brazil spent 200 years as rivals, but in recent years the destinies of both countries have made them more connected. Argentina and Brazil have withstood similar challenges and a desire to join the club of the developed nations in the world. Both countries fell and abandoned military dictatorship at the same time, and in the 1980s faced the challenge of rebuilding democracy and national economies that had been ruined by those regimes. Both crossed the 1990s trying to become connected to the international system through the reform of their politics, and both experimented with leftist populist governments at the end of that process.

In Brazil, the government opted to not privatize the state-owned oil company Petrobras; however, in Fernando Henrique's government (1995–2002) the company was reformed, acquiring governance conditions to be listed in the New York Stock Exchange. But after the ascent of the Workers Party (PT) to the government in 2002, Lula da Silva's government reverted the previous policy of autonomy and semi-privatization, starting a political process of the instrumentalization of Petrobras as a political tool. In this way, Lula da Silva reformed the administrative board in order to increase his own influence and to give power to unions, to the detriment of technicians and minority shareholders.

In 2007, the company found huge oil reserves in the Atlantic off the Brazilian coast below the salt layer, called pre-salt. A dispute soon erupted over the royalties. In 2010, lawmakers changed the petroleum regulatory regime exclusively for the new pre-salt exploitation contracts. They also created a new state company—Pre-Salt Petroleum S.A.—to manage the resources resulting from pre-salt exploitation and imposed a requirement that Petrobras would have to participate in all exploitation projects with a minimum of 30% of capital.

For the leftist wing in power, it was like a revival of "the oil is ours" campaign of the 1950s, when Petrobras was created along with state monopoly. But now the slogan was "the pre-salt is ours." The myth of the existence of an *El Dorado* (the ancient myth of *El Dorado* in which the Spanish conquerors believed they would find an entire city of gold) of petroleum, which once was a feature of the national imaginary, seemed to come true. President Lula da Silva enthusiastically celebrated pre-salt as if it were a "winning ticket" and "our passport for the future" (quoted in the newspaper O Globo, August, #1, 2008). In 2007, he predicted that Brazil would become a very influential member of the Oil Producing and Exporting Countries (OPEC), able to lower prices that had reached over US$130. Petrobras rose like a locomotive, pulling in all sectors of the national economy, including everything from sports, culture, research and development, to the naval industry and petrochemistry.

Pre-salt exploitation never enjoyed universal support in the country. Concerns about costs, technology, and environmental security of pre-salt gave rise to an intense debate among technicians in the sector. According to Petrobras, the average extraction cost was US$8.30 per barrel (2015). Petrobras had announced that the break-even point (the minimum price from which the production would be economically feasible) for pre-salt production projects at the time of discovery was US$45 per barrel, but it has not disclosed the present break-even point. Furthermore, its financial deficit was close to US$126 billion in 2015 (according to Petrobras Balance, first semester, 2016).

Regarding technology, Petrobras has expertise in exploitation in deep waters, but in the case of pre-salt, the depth can be as much as 7,000 meters, and the salt layer can be up to 2,000 meters thick, with temperatures reaching 150°C and the presence of high levels of high sulfur dioxide corroding the pipes and probes. Regarding regulation, the risk-sharing scheme and the compulsory requirement of Petrobras's participation in all projects with at least 30% of capital have received criticism for imposing on the state-run company all development costs and risks incurred. Finally, regarding environmental safety, after BP's accident in the Gulf of Mexico, safety certification for activities under critical conditions of deep sea has aroused fear that safety conditions in the pre-salt project are inadequate.

Following the path set by the government, Petrobras established a US$224 billion investment plan for the acquisition of ships, platforms, refineries, ports, logistic systems, probes, and prospecting equipment. Finally, under the assertion of promoting economic development, the government imposed the "law of national content" that obliged companies to hire national suppliers of equipment and services. In 2010, Petrobras did a third IPO (initial public offering) to raise capital for all the responsibilities it was assigned. The minister of economy, despite his role in a leftist government, celebrated the operation as the "biggest IPO in the history of the capitalism." On that occasion, US$70 billion was collected, which only represented a third of the investment goal of US$224 billion, forcing the company to take out bank loans. That IPO was also strategic to increase the government control over the company and stifle minor shareholders.

In the following years, agents of the capital market strongly criticized the company's financial management because of the lack of transparency and governance, and its high debt level. Even so, the leftist government decided to test the limits of financial capitalism with yet another round of IPO for Petrobras—in this case, to fund the pre-salt project. The success of Petrobras in the stock market at that time was huge, probably because the high prices of oil minimized risk perceptions among investors. Soon the government, the unions, and social movement organizations formed an alliance to create a contagious nationalist atmosphere anchored in and driven by the developmental leap that petroleum had promised, or that they thought it had promised.

Once again, Argentina proceeded in a similar fashion. In Argentina, the government decided to retake control of the YPF Company that had been sold to the Repsol

Company in 1999. In this way, the government expropriated most of its stocks and cut Repsol´s influence in the company.

The relationship between Repsol and the Argentinian government had not been friendly since Kirchner took office in 2003. The production of gas and petroleum had been falling steeply since 2000, which coincided with the YPF's privatization. In 2013, during the inauguration of a fuel supply terminal in an isolated town of a territory up north, President Cristina declared on the relation of YPF to the Argentinians: "The main idea is YPF bringing solutions for the Argentinians['] problems because YPF belongs to the Argentinians."[1]

In 2002 Petrobras had bought Pérez Companc, an Argentinian petroleum company that at the time was the major independent petroleum company in Latin America. This completed the denationalization of the Argentinian petroleum industry.

Repsol/YPF had always complained that the prices of energy goods were kept artificially low by the government, generating losses for the company and discouraging new investments. But in May 2011, it seemed that relationship of Repsol/YPF and the government would greatly improve when the company informed President Cristina Kirchner of the first discovery of profitable shale reserves in Vaca Muerta (dead cow in English)—but it didn't. The Argentinian government expropriated YPF from Repsol just one year later.

Argentina has huge reserves of shale and the Vaca Muerta formation alone retains around 16 billion barrels of oil and 308 trillion cubic feet of natural gas according to US estimatives. This means that Argentina could produce gas and oil for more than 100 years. Just like the Brazilian reserves of pre-salt, the Vaca Muerta reserves have the potential to turn Argentina into a great oil and gas exporter.

YPF's nationalization has generated excitement in the country. Vaca Muerta was soon embraced as "the Saudi utopia" of Argentina (Bercovich & Rebossio, 2014). Politicians engaged with the government predicted a significant impact on the economy on the order of a 3%–4% increase in the country's gross domestic product (GDP). President Cristina Fernandez Kirchner has claimed that Argentina would become "the new Saudi Arabia," but with the advantage that Vaca Muerta is not located in an area of conflict. She went further, insisting on the renaming of Vaca Muerta (dead cow), to "Vaca Viva" (living cow), because from it goods such as as milk and petroleum would be extracted.

That would be a relief to a country that had experienced difficulties since it announced debt default in 2002, unplugging itself from the global credit system. The country was confronting investor fury and a long battle in NY courts because of lawsuits related to the default crisis. Besides, YPF did not have hydraulic fracturing technology, and still needed capital to invest in Vaca Muerta. The government was betting that Vaca Muerta would pose an irresistible attraction for energy companies and investors. And the government was right: Dow Chemical, Chevron, and Exxon Mobil became YPF's partners.

On April 2012, the Spanish government reacted, requesting EU actions against Argentina in response to YPF's nationalization. Spain also announced intentions to retaliate commercially. Vaca Muerta is still the largest major discovery ever made by the Spanish company; biodiesel producers were the largest unintended victims, as we will see.

Although Argentina experienced serious energy safety problems for at least 10 years, the implications of Vaca Muerta are bigger than the eventual energy self-sufficiency that it may offer. Vaca Muerta gave political justification for the government to restore the national acquisition of YPF, and to present that as an asset in reconstructing national pride. Even though the society was being polarized and the economic crisis reduced the government's social support, Repsol's confrontation—in this case representing a kind of European neocolonialism—has risen at a moment of near social consensus,[2] similar to the effect of the Falklands War in 1982[3] (Malamud, 2012). The reaction of the Spanish government and the EU reprisals have only reinforced that perspective.

YPF is part of the Argentinian collective imaginary that nostalgically envisions a time of glory for YPF and the country itself, as can be seen in a speech by Jorge La Peña, the former secretary of energy: "In its moment, regarding energy, it was the flag of the ship. Its badge pictured the Argentinian flag. It was an emblem of independence or of search for energy independence. It was created by the Nation in the beginning of last century, 1922, under the name YPF, but in a way, it had already existed since 1908, only one year after petroleum had been discovered here" (El Pais, February 29, 2012).

As mentioned earlier, YPF lacked the funds and technology to develop the Vaca Muerta, forcing the government to reach out to North American, European, Chinese, and Russian multinational companies. Environmentalists, meanwhile, argued that the state's investments in Vaca Muerta meant reduced investments in renewable energy sources, amounting to an abandonment of goals previously set in the renewable energy area. Finally, there is the problem of local environmental impact. Both the government and YPF dismiss such concerns, arguing that extraction occurs 300 meters deep in a scarcely populated area. The minimization of environmental concerns was an important draw for North American companies that had been confronting obstacles to drill in American soil. The Vaca Muerta region has low population density, but there are indigenous communities that have not yet relinquished legal rights over their traditional land. These communities were the main opposition during the signature of the YPF-Chevron agreement in August 2013 in Neuquén Town. On that day there were street conflicts and police repression; on the following day the protests drew about 10,000 people; and on the three subsequent days the native community of Mapuche blocked the routes to access the YPF fields.

THE PINK TIDE AND PETROLEUM POPULISM

We began this study by trying to associate populist policies in the field of energy with the creation of a populist conceptualization of energy development in several Latin American countries. State manipulation of the prices of energy goods constituted instruments of dependence within countries, empowering leaders of populist government. In fact, Brazil, Argentina, Venezuela, and Bolivia have all attempted to assert control over and intervene in the entire energy supply chain. This included a wide nationalization of energy fields in all countries and the instrumentalization of state oil companies as political tools. In this way, prices of power and fuels must be kept low through subsides or other artificial measures. As a consequence, sometimes, even the government stood tied to these policies. At the end of 2010, the Bolivian government tried to remove subsidies on gasoline, but gave up due to a revolt in the country. In the end, the government decided to increase subsidies instead of take them down. In February 2016, the Venezuelan government decided to increase gasoline prices for the first time in 20 years, from US$0.01 to US$0.95 per liter. Those prices still do not cover production costs, and the government currently faces the highest rate of inflation in the world (720% a year, according to IMF). In Argentina, prices of power have increased by more than 300% since Macri´s government—the first after populist cycle—began, in a commitment to deficit control that endangers social stability. Actually, the regular policies of the leftist governments in the energy field caused big problems in production and in state accounts, but any initiative to restore the proportionality between prices and costs could bring high risks of instability.

So, there is a close association between energy populism and the general populist prescription in which certain social goods should be paid out with no concern over the identity of their supplier—it doesn't matter whether the supplier is the nation or the leader.

This analysis also highlights the importance of state-owned petroleum companies and their role in the political culture and in the collective imaginary. Leftist governments succeeded in creating the ideology that those companies were not only businesses, but also civilizing agents that offer goods supposedly denied by the concentric forces of the international system. Petrobras and YPF should work as an omnipresent branch of the state, the economy's locomotive that is able to restore national sovereignty. Thus they embody national pride.

Regarding the pink tide, our analysis suggests that "petroleum populism" may be a more apt description of contemporary politics in the Latin American countries featured here, highlighting, for example, the centrality of PDVA, of Petrobras, and of YPF as symbols of national resistance within an ideological project that runs counter to prevailing trends.[4]

The theory with which we began was that discoveries of large reserves of fossil fuels have rekindled nationalism, along with the idea that petroleum is the passport to autonomy. The discovery of fossil fuel reserves has encouraged a return to ideologies typical of the 1970s, when petroleum was considered the energy resource that would define national destiny. In this way, it impacted negatively the public policies that prioritize biofuels as a way to achieve a better position in the world economy. Right now, when the importance of petroleum is in decline in many developed countries, where the emphasis is being placed on the development of the green economy, many underdeveloped countries take the opposite direction.

In the time of high prices, Venezuela has become a benchmark for what to do and what not to do. The 1980s crisis and the so-called lost decade forced countries of the region to adopt the requirements of the International Monetary Fund (IMF) and the World Bank in the 1990s. In subsequent years the majority of countries in the region adopted policies to control the public accounts deficit: privatization, tax burden adjustment, cutting of subsidies and tax benefits, and finally, reduction of state intervention in the social arena. As is normal in societies in which inequality is high, the poorest segment of the population paid the highest cost of fixing up the state accounts. In the first decade of the 2000s, the social cost of those adjustments had been great in the form of unemployment and inequality. In this context, support for the leftist parties grew in several Latin American countries.

The pink tide is defined as the emergence of political forces, heirs of Latin American leftist movements of the 1960s, that had lost the revolutionary bias in favor of a traditional social democrat program, marked by the rise of Nestor Kirchner in Argentina in 2003, and of Lula da Silva in Brazil in 2002, together with the rise of Evo Morales in Bolivia (2006), Hugo Chávez in Venezuela (1999), and Rafael Correa in Ecuador (2007). According to Laclau (2006), the two key features of the pink tide were the military dictatorships that these countries had endured from the 1960s to 1980, and the neoliberal structural adjustment policies of the 1990s. Other researchers attribute the pink tide to institutional crises in the region (Roberts, 2007). Those conditions created opportunities for new leadership to rise to power.

Concerning the new populism, we do not associate it with any institutional crisis as all governments ascended to power through a democratic process. The context is related to the deconstruction of the nationalist, paternalist, intervener state, and has strong authoritative reminiscences of the 1990s. In this process, privatizations, increasing the price of social goods, extinction of subsidies, and tax increases—the so-called adjustments—become dominant in the political agenda. Certainly, that was a bankrupt model of the state, but it was the only project of social and economic development known in the region, and its reformers (neoliberals) did not propose anything other than disassembling the old state. From the utopic developmental emptiness that followed the state arose the new leaderships, which offered the hope of rescue through a nationalist project that included a developmental perspective and the recovery of national self-esteem. The historical irony from this is that the center-left had proposed the recovery of a state model that had been created by a rightist authoritative government.

Laclau focuses on the populist bias of Latin American center-leftists. Populism arises when social agents split themselves into two opposing wings that subsequently become crystallized with certain common symbols, and the rise of a leader who assumes those popular demands (Laclau, 2006). As a consequence, when a new leadership is established, all institutional channels become reduced in their legitimacy to absorb social demands because they are surpassed by the leader. In this process, a generic idea about a collective agent— that could be "the people", "the poor people", "the workers"— takes control over the regime. The main component of the identity that shape this collective agent is the individual dissatisfactions that acquire a collective sense and generate ties of solidarity between large strata of society, in opposition to a political system that is not capable or is not aimed at responding positively to those demands.

Laclau has pointed out distinct kinds of Latin American center-leftist populism that we associate here with the pink tide. Venezuela is where the process of rupture was most pronounced, and the political crisis could only be remedied via a populist uprising (Laclau, 2006). It is here, therefore, where one can notice most clearly the components of Latin American populism, as well as its limitations. It happened chronologically with Fidel Castro's decline as a benchmark to Latin American leftism and his substitution by Hugo Chávez, an army colonel who led an attempted military coup in 1992 in a continent where the military was the strongest anti-communist force among all rightist forces.

The rise of populism in Brazil and Argentina was less radical than in Venezuela, though similar. The challenge in these countries was to bring back an old-fashioned national development project without losing certain advances resulting from reform of the state, especially the ties with the financial system. In other words, the center-leftists in Brazil and in Argentina did not propose a rupture with institutions, as in Venezuela, but rather they fought to increase the influence of social movements in politics.

Thus, the close relationship between the leader and his or her supporters deepens as social movements become empowered. The leaders of these countries have become the embodiment of change, as the influence of social movements depends exclusively on the leader and should end with the end of his or her time in office.

LAST WORDS

Access to energy sources has always been a challenge, especially for countries under development, whose means to supply energy needs are more limited than those of rich countries. This was shown in the difficulties faced by poor countries that were dependent on petroleum in the crisis periods in 1973 and 1979. At that time, economic-development projects and programs were strongly impacted by an abrupt increase in petroleum prices and by the secondary effects of the crisis. The default of development programs in the 1960s and 1970s was then attributed to petroleum dependency. Therefore, it seems natural that the governments of the pink tide regard petroleum as an icon to achieve. Perhaps it is the political goal that mostly excites such nationalism, for it is historically placed as a sovereignty issue.

In Latin America, the 1980s are considered the lost decade due to the countries' debt explosion and the failure of the economic model. In the 1990s, the region's reintegration into foreign markets required a reform of the state and the reconstruction of development policies. In this way, the utopias of take advantage of the accessing of the status of power were gone and replaced by a cruel realism tha shows how wider become the breach dividing Latin America from the center of the international economic system.

In this context arose the issue of biofuels. The production of biofuels can be seen as a way to add value to agricultural products and to capitalize the biomass producer. Due to the potential for quick capitalization of biofuels, there is a clear opportunity for investment in new products and in the field of green economy. The potential that Latin American countries, especially Brazil and Argentina, possess in terms of biodiversity, agriculture, and natural resources is huge. These are countries that can step into the future with a new model of economic production, and in a more favorable position.

Though they are countries with the potential to lead this process—a position Brazil enjoyed, although for a very short time—the discovery of fossil reserves triggered opposite feelings and outdated concepts that supposedly had been surpassed. The oil reserves of pre-salt and of Vaca Muerta bring the promise that Petrobras can be what it has never been, and that YPF can go back to be what it was in the distant past. Such petroleum populism succeeded in convincing the society to make robust investments in a fossil-fuel-based energy model, placing biofuels on hold. Symbolic factors such as national pride, sovereignty, and latent national cultures define the new populism, and new leftist leaders in Latin America been able to take advantage of those feelings in order to offer a shortcut to development.

Enthusiasm for the potential represented by biofuels and participation in a new green economy has been subsumed by the discoveries of pre-salt and Vaca Muerta reserves. The tepid phase of international markets for biofuels did not help. In the United States, the consumption of ethanol has stagnated, while protectionism limits entry into European markets. Worldwide, the construction of a green economy exists only as a well-intentioned idea. Thus it would be unrealistic to expect that Brazil and Argentina would decline to develop their own oil industry.

Acknowledgments

The authors thank FAPESP for their support.

Notes

1. http://www.iprofesional.com/notas/162911-Cristina-inaugur-obras-de-YPF-y-propuso-cambiar-nombre-de-Vaca-Muerta-por-Vaca-Viva
2. The survey of *Página 12* journal noted 74% in support of the expropriation of YPF and only 20% against the initiative, while 70% considered that the company should be controlled by the nation.
3. The nationalism of the population was evident once more in April 2, 1982, with the great popular move in support of the military occupation of the Falkland Islands by the military dictatorship. Thirty years after the armed conflict, the government's initiative to recover the control of YPF has great social support, due to its strong emotional ties with the idea of "national sovereignty" (Malamud, 2012).
4. Expression first used by Jose Manuel Roy in El País, May 3, 2006.

REFERENCES

Bercovich, A., & Rebossio, A. (2014). *Vaca muerta*. Buenos Aires: Planeta.

Bergmann, J. C., Tupinambá, D. D., Costa, O. Y. A., Almeida, J. R. M., Barreto, C. C., & Quirino, B. F. (2013). Biodiesel production in Brazil and alternative biomass feedstocks. *Renewable and Sustainable Energy Reviews, 21*, 411–420.

Chidiak, M., & Rozemberg, R. (2015). *Biofuels in Argentina: Lessons learned, challenges pending.* Retrieved from http://www19.iadb.org/intal/icom/en/notas/39-28/

Dal Belo Leite, J., & Silva, J. V., & van Ittersum, M. (2014). Integrated assessment of biodiesel policies aimed at family farms in Brazil. *Agricultural Systems, 131*, 64–76.

Dalgaard, K. (2012). *The energy statecraft of Brazil: Promoting biofuels as an instrument of Brazilian foreign policy, 2003–2010.* PhD dissertation, The London School of Economics and Political Science. Retrieved from http://etheses.lse.ac.uk/585/1/Dalgaard_Energy _Statecraft_Brazil_2012.pdf

Dolabella, R. (2011). Biocombustíveis na Argentina: Políticas públicas e evolução recente, área de agricultura, pecuária, abastecimento e desenvolvimento rural. *Consultoria Legislativa Brasil, 25*. Retrieved from bd.camara.gov.br

Dornbusch, R., & Edwards, S. (1990). Macroeconomic populism. *Journal of Development Economics, 32*, 247–277.

Goldemberg, J., Coelho, S. T., Nastari, P. M., & Lucon, O. (2004). Ethanol learning curve: The Brazilian experience. *Biomass and Bioenergy, 26*(3), 301–304.

Finco, M. V., & Doppler, W. (2010). The Brazilian biodiesel program and family farmers: What is the social inclusion reality in the Brazilian savannah? *Pesquisa Agropecuaria Tropical, 40*, 430-438.

Johnson, K. (2014, February 19). Dilma's power problem: Politics are hobbling Brazil's once-brilliant energy future. *Foreign Policy—Report*. Retrieved from http://foreignpolicy.com /2014/02/19/dilmas-power-problem/

Laclau, E. (2006). La deriva populista y la centro izquierda latino Americana. *Revista de la Cepal, 89*. Retrieved from http://nuso.org/media/articles/downloads/3381_1.pdf

Leal, M. R., & Walter, A. (2010). Sustainability of the production of ethanol from sugarcane: The Brazilian experience. *International Society of Sugar Cane Technology, 27*, 390–396.

Malamud, C. (2012, April 26). *YPF y la política argentina*. Retrieved from http://www .analisislatino.com/notas.asp?id=5027

Roberts, K. M. (2007). Latin America's populist revival. *SAIS Review of International Affairs, 27*(1), 3–15.

CHAPTER 16

ENERGY POVERTY: ENERGY EQUITY IN A WORLD OF HIGH DEMAND AND LOW SUPPLY

KARL-MICHAEL BRUNNER, SYLVIA MANDL,
AND HARRIET THOMSON

INTRODUCTION

THIS chapter deals with energy poverty in its multiple facets. Energy poverty is a multidimensional concept that varies regionally, with no universal definition in place. The term *energy poverty* is most commonly used by the (sustainable) development community in relation to less economically developed regions of the world. It refers to poverty that is exacerbated by a lack of access to modern energy services and end-use technologies. The two main issues are access to electricity and access to clean cooking facilities. For many people in the world, wood is the only lighting and cooking source. The following example can illustrate this kind of dependence: "Rosa lives in Kakuma, a border town located in north-western Kenya. [. . .] She sells foodstuffs at the market but loses one full day per week trekking to the surrounding hills to collect firewood. 'For me getting energy for cooking and lighting is a daily worry. I cook for my family only once a day in the evening. The fire provides the light for cooking and eating a meal with my children. After eating is bedtime.' The lack of lighting means that the children cannot do homework after dark" (Practical Action, 2014, p. 4).

Energy poverty in more economically developed countries is also known as "fuel poverty" or "energy vulnerability," and occurs when a household experiences inadequate levels of essential energy services in the home. Energy poverty in developed countries implies, among other things, an inability to heat or light the home sufficiently; expenses above average for energy provision; energy-inefficient properties, heating systems, and household appliances; and power cuts (Brunner & Mandl, 2014).

To illustrate energy poverty in developed countries, we present an example from the EVALUATE project (www.urban-energy.org): One married couple from Budapest struggles to pay their energy bills and maintain adequate thermal comfort. Despite being relatively highly educated, they have faced periods of unemployment and insecure work. Their apartment not only lacks sufficient insulation and windows, but also has a poor-quality district heating system, which they are unable to control independently. These drivers have been exacerbated by a long-standing billing error, which resulted in them paying twice as much for gas between 2010 and 2013 (Thomson et al., 2016).

Although the situation of the energy poor in the Global North and Global South varies considerably, some similarities can be detected. For instance, due to the economic crisis and the increasing cost of energy, more and more people in Europe are forced to replace modern energy carriers with less technologically advanced and polluting fuels, in what has been termed "energy degradation" (Bouzarovski et al., 2015). In several Scottish islands, peat is being increasingly used for heating purposes (Thomson & Bouzarovski, 2017), as is firewood in many Central and Eastern European countries (Bouzarovski et al., 2015).

In this chapter, we will use the term *energy poverty* for all forms of domestic energy deprivation all over the world. This is in line with authors like Bouzarovski and Petrova (2015), who argue for a global perspective on domestic energy deprivation whereby all forms of energy poverty are underpinned by a common condition, namely the inability to achieve socially and materially necessary levels of domestic energy services.

Until recently, awareness of the problem of energy poverty was limited in many countries. But the situation is changing. On a global level, the world has come to recognize the central role of energy in human and economic development (Halff, Sovacool, & Rozhon, 2014). The United Nations declared 2012 the "International Year of Sustainable Energy for All," and Goal 7 of the 2015 UN Sustainable Development Goals for 2030 calls for "access to affordable, reliable, sustainable and modern energy for all."[1]

Framed within the sustainability debate, energy poverty is tightly connected to normative assumptions of intergenerational and intragenerational equity (Klinsky & Golub, 2016). The latter concerns the distribution of income, poverty, environmental burdens, and other socioeconomic and social-ecological disparities within societies. From a justice perspective, energy poverty in its diverse manifestations is unsustainable and unjust, as it reduces the quality of life of many people worldwide. Recent discussions about energy justice reflect a growing awareness of (in)justices in the energy system, not only from a distributional point of view, but also regarding procedural and recognition-based elements (Jenkins et al., 2016).

Dealing with energy poverty in its various dimensions, we adopt a sociological perspective on energy poverty, based on the assumption that energy practices and societal structures are deeply intertwined. Energy is a basic requirement for everyday life, well-being, and social integration. Energy practices are socially stratified and shaped by inequity and power relations. Energy poverty is not only about technologies, fuels, and infrastructures, but also about social relations of various kinds, cultural practices, social and economic inequalities, political and institutional factors, and specific human-nature-relationships.

The chapter is organized as follows. The following section discusses energy poverty in developed countries, mainly in the European Union (EU). The subsequent section then concentrates on energy poverty in developing countries. Besides general aspects, we pay special attention to rural electrification processes and to gender relations. The chapter concludes with a short discussion of the future of energy poverty.

ENERGY POVERTY IN DEVELOPED COUNTRIES: THE CASE OF THE EU

Causes, Definitions, Measurement

As noted in the introduction to this chapter, energy poverty is a phenomenon that also exists within economically developed countries, with a rapidly growing literature base that suggests the issue is widespread across the EU. A European Commission study found that 11% of the EU population is in a situation where they are not able to heat their homes adequately at an affordable cost, and this situation is estimated to affect around 54 million people in Europe (based on data from 2012) (Pye et al., 2015). The scale of the problem is particularly prevalent in Central, Eastern, and Southern Europe. In terms of key causes, there is broad consensus that energy poverty in Europe is predicated upon poor housing quality, cuts to household income, growing income disparities, and the price of energy. Issues such as austerity agendas and energy-sector reforms compound these drivers to exacerbate energy affordability issues.

However, at the EU level there is no official definition of energy poverty, nor is there a specific legislative program to address the issue (Thomson, Snell, & Liddell, 2016). The limited formal policy interest in energy poverty is also reflected at the member-state level, since at the time of writing only five countries have some form of definition for energy poverty, as summarized in Table 16.1.

It has been suggested by Bouzarovski, Petrova, and Sarlamanov (2012) that the limited number of formal policy definitions of energy poverty may be due to the lack of a strong institutional center within which political initiatives to address the problem can be raised; a limited scientific evidence base; and the unwillingness of some member states to recognize a new form of deprivation. Added to this is the multidimensional nature of the phenomenon, requiring joint multi-agency policy solutions (Thomson, Snell, & Liddell, 2016). And finally, energy poverty is difficult to measure. The difficulty in measurement lies in the fact it is a private condition observed in the home, it varies over time and by place, and it is culturally sensitive (Simcock, Walker, & Day, 2016).

Table 16.1 Summary of Official Definitions of Energy Poverty

England (2013–)
"A household is considered to be fuel poor where:
- *they have required fuel costs that are above average (the national median level)*
- *were they to spend that amount, they would be left with a residual income below the official poverty line" [60% median income]*
(Department of Energy and Climate Change, 2013, p. 3).

France (2009–)
Officially a person is considered fuel poor *"if he/she encounters particular difficulties in his/her accommodation in terms of energy supply related to the satisfaction of elementary needs, this being due to the inadequacy of financial resources or housing conditions"*
(Translation of De Quero & Lapostolet, 2009, p. 16).
In practice, this is complemented by an unofficial definition of spending more than 10% of income on energy costs (Dubois, 2012).

Ireland (2016–)
". . . a household that spends more than 10% of their income on energy is considered to be in energy poverty."
(Department of Communications, Energy & Natural Resources, 2016, p. 8).

Slovakia (2015–)
"Energy poverty under the law No. 250/2012 Coll. Of Laws is a status when average monthly expenditures of household on consumption of electricity, gas, heating and hot water production represent a substantial share of average monthly income of the household"
(Strakova, 2014, p. 3).

UK–wide (2001–2013) and Northern Ireland, Scotland, Wales (2013–)
"A household is said to be in fuel poverty if it needs to spend more than 10% of its income on fuel to maintain an adequate level of warmth"
(Department of Energy and Climate Change, 2010, p. 1).

Source: Adapted from Thomson, Snell, and Liddell (2016).

In terms of measuring energy poverty, a multiplicity of approaches exists within research and policy. Overall, three main measurement approaches are used:

Expenditure approach: where examinations of the energy costs faced by households against absolute or relative thresholds provide a proxy for estimating the extent of domestic energy deprivation;

Consensual approach: based on self-reported assessments of indoor housing conditions, and the ability to attain certain basic necessities;

Direct measurement: where the level of energy services (such as heating) achieved in the home is measured and compared to a set standard.

For specific policy delivery at the local level, these approaches are also supplemented by the following.

Indicators for household identification, such as welfare benefit recipient status.

Despite the complexities associated with measuring energy poverty, statistical indicators of energy poverty form an important and necessary part of the policy landscape; they carry great political weight, and are often used to guide the targeting of energy poverty measures—due to their perceived objectivity. However, as remarked by Boardman (2010, p. 21) "who is fuel poor depends on the definition; but the definition depends on who you want to focus on and this involves political judgment." Who gets assistance depends on prevailing notions of "deserving" and "undeserving" household groups. But these notions do not change the lived experience for households vulnerable to energy poverty. As the subsequent subsection explores, people often employ a diverse range of strategies to help maintain the affordability of energy.

Coping Strategies of Energy-Poor Households in Developed Countries

To date, only a few studies exist that place those concerned in the center of interest, shedding light on living and housing conditions, energy burdens, and coping strategies of energy-poor households (Boardman, 2010).[2] Research findings from Austria reveal that a large number of energy-poor households live in deprived conditions, carrying multiple burdens (lack of financial resources, energy-inefficient dwellings, old appliances, high energy costs, and long-term illnesses, to name just a few) that sometimes aggravate each other (Brunner, Spitzer, & Christanell, 2012). Very often the energy poor have to live in properties with drafty windows and main doors. Among other problems, these circumstances favor the growth of mold.

Many energy-poor households report difficulties in paying their energy bills. Financial shortcomings, debts, arrears in payments to energy providers, and power cuts may lead to stress, anxiety, or depression (Green & Gilbertson, 2008). Feelings of shame and social exclusion aroused by the inability to afford a life in dignity with access to basic energy services should be kept in mind here, too (Brunner, Spitzer, & Christanell, 2012). Sometimes expenditures on other essential items, particularly food, have to be reduced due to financial problems. Findings from the United States show that (energy) poor families tend to spend more on energy in periods of cold weather, but at the same time cut back on their expenses for food in equal amounts, which entails certain health risks. This phenomenon has been termed the "Heat-or-Eat-Dilemma" (Bhattacharya et al., 2003) and was also observed in other countries (O'Neill, Jinks, & Squire, 2006).

Against the backdrop of these housing and living conditions, heating instead of eating is just one coping strategy among others. In general, people adopt a range of behaviors and strategies when confronted with cold inside the home (Gibbons & Singler, 2008; Radcliffe, 2010). In a qualitative study of energy-poor households in Vienna, Austria, a number of different coping strategies regarding heating and lighting practices were identified and divided into strategies for efficiency and strategies for sufficiency. What were termed *efficiency strategies* mainly comprise low-cost investments, which allow for increasing the efficiency of appliances (e.g., water-saving taps) or lighting equipment (e.g., energy-saving light bulbs). They also include sealing drafty windows and/or covering them with thick protective curtains, or installing window blinds, all with the aim of preserving heat. All actions geared toward reducing energy consumption through cutbacks and sacrifices can be considered sufficiency strategies, which were found to be very common. In many households the heating is turned on only in one room of the home. Being energy poor very often means putting on various layers of clothing inside the house during the cold part of the year. Another related strategy for coping with the cold inside the home is "slipping under the covers," even during the daytime.

Generally, energy-poor households often consume less energy than would be necessary for health reasons (Boardman, 2010; Brunner & Mandl, 2014). Under-consuming energy may lead to physical and mental health risks. This particularly affects elderly people, children, and disabled persons. Living in a cold dwelling also curtails other aspects of the quality of life, for example, making it impossible to invite friends (Anderson, White, & Finney, 2010) and thus reducing social interactions (Hills, 2011).

These selected findings clearly show that energy-poor households are characterized by a number of energy burdens and related coping strategies. So the question arises of how energy poverty is dealt with politically.

Recent Discussions and Policy Perspectives

As already mentioned in the introductory section, we have seen strong policy recognition for addressing energy poverty in recent years within the Global South. However, within developed countries, energy poverty has not always been given the same level of attention. Historical analysis of EU policy discourses reveals that concerns about energy poverty were first raised at the EU scale in 2001. Overall, between 2001 and 2014, Thomson, Snell, and Liddell (2016) identify three key phases in EU-level policy discussions and events:

Preliminary discussion on fuel and energy poverty, from 2001 to 2006;
A period of basic legal recognition for energy poverty, from 2007;
An enhanced focus on energy poverty and vulnerable customers, from 2011 onward.

The preliminary discussions between 2001 and 2006 were relatively basic, and just five policy documents were published that briefly mentioned fuel poverty. Beginning in 2007, fuel poverty and energy poverty were discussed more often and in a more meaningful way in EU policy documents. This second phase is characterized by new, basic legal recognition for energy poverty in Europe in Directives 2009/72/EC and 2009/73/EC on the internal markets in natural gas and electricity. During this second phase, the European Parliament, Committee of the Regions (CoR), and the European Economic and Social Committee (EESC) all stressed the importance of vulnerable consumer protection, and the need for a common definition of energy poverty. However, the European Commission positioned itself in opposition to a common pan-EU definition of energy poverty, stating that using energy policy as the sole tool to address energy poverty would distort energy markets (European Commission, 2008). It should come as no surprise, therefore, that a definition of energy poverty was absent from the final wording of the Directives, which failed to offer even a basic description of energy poverty.

The period from 2011 to 2014 marked a new phase in EU discourse, with an enhanced focus on energy poverty and vulnerable consumers. During this time, consultative institutions played a larger role in drawing attention to the issue. Arguably, the biggest development in this phase was the establishment of the Vulnerable Consumer Working Group in 2012, which examined the complex drivers of consumer vulnerability in energy markets.

A key issue across all three policy phases has been the power dynamics inherent within the EU, namely the fact that the European Parliament cannot initiate legislation, and that it shares the powers of amendment and decision with the Council of Ministers. This has led to situations where the European Council has rejected pertinent European Parliament amendments. Since 2014, however, there has been a remarkable shift in the European Commission's attitude toward energy poverty and a thickening of institutional support for direct measures to alleviate the issue. For instance, in the second half of 2015, the European Commission launched the European Energy Union Strategy, and within this document provided a description of energy poverty, and focused on affordability, efficiency, and vulnerable consumers. The European Commission has also provided funding for a new EU Observatory on Energy Poverty, which will be launched in 2017.[3]

A wide range of policy mechanisms has also been developed at the member-state level to combat energy poverty. In a pan-EU review of measures, Pye et al. (2015) categorize these according to four groups:

Financial interventions: primarily short-term relief, aimed at supporting bill payment, mainly under the umbrella of social policy;

Additional consumer protection: measures that use retail markets and other forms of pricing to safeguard specific groups;

Energy efficiency: programs that target the energy performance of the building stock, heating systems, or appliances;

Information provision and raising awareness: measures aimed at improving the ability of consumers to understand their energy rights, as well as energy efficiency investment.

Schemes based on energy efficiency improvements are considered the most beneficial in the long term (Boardman, 2010), particularly deep renovations that can "future proof" the housing stock against future energy price rises. But efficiency measures granted to low-income households often do not yield the desired effect, as the necessary share to be paid by the households themselves is very often impossible for them to finance without assistance (Hills, 2011). Therefore, funds related to energy efficiency often turn into middle- and upper-class subsidies, widening social inequalities rather than narrowing them. Energy-efficiency measures must take the financial constraints of energy-poor households into account, because retrofitting energy-inefficient houses often means higher rent for tenants. It should be kept in mind, too, that energy efficiency schemes alone cannot save those trying to cope with cold weather through extreme sufficiency strategies (Radcliffe, 2010). Financial support mechanisms intended to help certain categories of consumers exist in less than half of the EU member states (Grevisse & Brynart, 2011). But financial interventions are only effective in the short term, and as with additional protection for specific groups, they risk marginalizing certain groups that are not eligible for assistance, raising issues of justice, particularly recognition and procedural justice.

Overall, single measures to fight energy poverty can be sensible and effective, but are likely to have only limited effects in the face of the multifaceted causes of energy poverty and the range of household coping strategies. Therefore, a set of integrated measures aimed at all causes and manifestations of energy poverty, with different time horizons and depths of effects, is needed (Bouzarovski, Petrova, & Sarlamanov, 2012).

ENERGY POVERTY
IN DEVELOPING COUNTRIES

Discussions about energy poverty in developing countries are mainly concentrated on matters of access, the two main issues being access to modern energy services and access to clean cooking facilities. But similar to energy poverty in developed countries, energy deprivation in the Global South also touches upon questions of poverty, affordability, reliability, infrastructure, health, sustainability, and justice, to name just a few.

Huge Challenges, Patchy Progress

The need to improve access to modern energy services has moved into the mainstream of international policymaking, the latest expression of this intention being the adoption of the UN Sustainable Development Goals in 2015. As regards access to electricity, the latest data demonstrate efforts to improve access, "but progress is patchy rather than broad-based" (OECD and IEA, 2015, p. 101). Although the proportion of the global population with access to electricity increased from 79% in 2000 to 85% in 2012, an estimated 1.2 billion people (17% of the global population) did not have access to electricity in 2013, around 80% of them living in rural areas, mainly in sub-Saharan Africa and developing Asia (OECD and IEA, 2015).

The consequences of living without electricity are wide-ranging, from limited access to modern telecommunications, constraints on studying and income generation, through to broader community impacts on health and education facilities, clean drinking water provision, and local businesses. Lighting in energy-poor households that lack electricity access is generally provided by candles or diesel/kerosene lanterns, both of which pose health and safety risks to occupants, including poisoning from ingesting fuel smoke and burns.

But even among populations with physical access to electricity, a lack of affordability and reliable supplies limits consumption. Connection to the grid does not mean that everybody is able to afford electricity and has uninterrupted power supply. The consequence is widespread illegitimate use of electricity by doctoring the meters (Gupta, 2015). Many poor households that are connected face challenges in staying connected, and increasing consumption beyond minimum levels is difficult due to inadequate supply, poor quality, and unaffordable connection costs and tariffs. What is more, even with access to electricity, other options that are detrimental to health (e.g., use of firewood for cooking) are frequently not fully replaced, especially in middle- and low-income households. The speed with which electricity is actually incorporated into the energy basket of households depends inter alia on the number of people living together, the location, the climate, the cost of alternatives, and cultural factors (Davis, 1998).

Access to electricity is one important part of the problem of lacking modern energy services. The use of traditional biomass for cooking is another. In 2014, some 3 billion people (over 40% of the world's population) relied on traditional biomass (wood, dung, agricultural residues) for cooking. Due to population growth, the actual number of people has increased, and limited progress was almost exclusively confined to urban areas, with rural areas "registering no visible change" (International Bank for Reconstruction and Development, The World Bank, and IEA, 2015, p. 282). Households that do not have clean cooking facilities instead use inefficient stoves or open fires and polluting solid fuels, such as biomass or coal. In many instances, households lack adequate ventilation via chimneys or extraction hoods, which exacerbates the situation. As a consequence, indoor air pollution levels can be dangerously high, creating significant health problems. Furthermore, the use of inefficient stoves and wood fuel has serious implications for the environment, resulting in air pollution, deforestation, soil degradation, accelerated loss of biodiversity, and climate change (Goldemberg & Coelho, 2004). Although awareness of problems related to the use of biomass for cooking is increasing, the provision of financial investment is lagging behind. Worldwide in 2013, an estimated $13.1 billion in capital investment was directed to improving access to electricity, but only 3% was directed at increased access to clean cooking facilities (OECD and IEA, 2015).

Ensuring access to modern energy services could benefit the energy poor in diverse ways, by contributing a basis for supporting job creation, economic growth, agriculture, education, commerce, health, and so on (Karekezi et al., 2012). But advocating the benefits of access to modern energy services very often takes a deterministic stance that assumes automatic, equally experienced and wholly beneficial development effects. But simple deterministic relations between access and development outcomes do not reflect reality, as expected impacts of access may not materialize because of high costs, inadequate communication of benefits, differences between priorities of decision-makers and users, behavioral challenges posed by intended beneficiaries, gender relations, cultural traditions, political conditions, and socioeconomic inequalities (Matinga et al., 2016; Ulsrud et al., 2015).

For a long time, a techno-centric view toward the adoption of modern energy services has dominated energy policies. This view assumes that the provision of modern energy is a universally desired and an inherently and wholly positive process. But "[e]nergy use is a practice of culture, not just a matter of technological mastery" (Matinga et al., 2016, p. 153). Very often there is a lack of focus on the socio-cultural contexts in which electricity and clean cooking facilities are introduced. Knowledge about these contexts is crucial for providing solutions that are culturally appropriate, affordable, and accessible to all. Technology and society develop in mutual interaction at the micro level (practical use) as well as at structural levels (e.g., policies, regulations) (Ulsrud et al., 2015). With these perspectives in mind, we will now take a closer look at rural electrification programs to overcome energy poverty.

Rural Electrification to Overcome Energy Poverty

Rural electrification can lead to a significant improvement in energy equity (Pereira et al., 2011). Yet, expanding access to electricity in rural areas cannot be seen as a mere logistic and technological problem (van Els, de Souza Vianna, & Brasil, 2012). Usually rural areas are characterized by low population densities, scattered clusters of premises, as well as dispersed (low-income) consumers with low consumption and load factors (Haanyka, 2006). There are two main possibilities for rural electricity supply: connection to centralized grids or off-grid decentralized systems (e.g., diesel generators or solar power). In some countries (e.g., China), hybrid systems of local and centralized grids are also in place.

Brazil is a country with high ambitions regarding access to modern energy services. An electrification program called "Luz Para Todos (LPT—Light for All)" was launched by the federal government in 2003 in order to bring electricity to rural households (GNESD, n.d.). Within the LPT program, users were not required to pay connection costs. Instead, government funding was used for this purpose (Pereira, Freitas, & da Silva, 2010). Vulnerable electricity customers were offered discounts on their electricity bills up to 100% (GNESD, n.d.). By 2011, 2.3 million households in rural areas of Brazil had benefited from the program. Nevertheless, one fundamental problem of the LPT program is broad electrification of very isolated areas, as in the Northern region (Brazilian Amazonia), where high dispersion requires higher initial investments. There are often not enough incentives for distribution companies to improve energy supply in those areas (Goldemberg, La Rovere, & Coelho, 2004). However, the development of decentralized energy supply in rural areas presents a good opportunity to introduce and expand renewable energy options. For rural areas of Brazil, photovoltaic systems were the preferred option under the LPT program. But the existing energy supply systems with diesel engines and photovoltaics allow only very limited energy consumption. Furthermore, the diesel consumption is especially high in those areas because of the dependency on local boat transport (Goldemberg, La Rovere, & Coelho, 2004). And there are still households without any form of electric light at all. In 2009 this was still the case for 163,000 households in the Amazon, 95% of which were situated in rural areas (IBGE, 2009, quoted in van Els, de Souza Vianna, & Brasil, 2012).

Rural electrification is not just a process of technical supply, but also a social process, inducing various changes at different levels of society. The electrification program in the village of Uroa in Zanzibar may serve as an example (Winther, 2008, 2013; Winther & Wilhite, 2015). From 1986 to 2006 the Norwegian government financed a rural electrification project in Zanzibar through the Norwegian Agency for Development Cooperation, allowing a connection of more than half of the households until 2006 (Winther, 2008). In contrast to the LPT program of Brazil, residents of Zanzibar had to pay for electricity installation, providing electricity only to those who could afford it. Electricity's arrival in Uroa, Zanzibar (as in other places), initiated a complex interaction between local ways of doing things and the multiple potential changes that electricity brings. This interaction infiltrated, for instance, discourses of modernity, senses of place, community and household practices, local economy and politics, social relations of various kinds, perceptions of risk, and rituals and ceremonies. When Uroa's streets were electrically illuminated, its residents started to speak of their village as a town, which shows that electricity tends to be associated with development and modernity and can change the meaning of place (Winther & Wilhite, 2015). With the advent of electric light, the distinction between day and night blurs, making daily activities no longer dependent on natural cycles of sun and moon. Electricity plays an important role in the restructuring of social space and temporality, for instance, when it comes to watching television. As this is an increasingly popular leisure activity of Zanzibaris, households owning a TV often host guests in the evening. Therefore, common times to go to bed have been delayed, shortening the total number of sleeping hours (Winther, 2013). Ironically, with this lengthening of the day enabled by electricity, residents of the village feel their lives have sped up and that they now have too little time (Winther & Wilhite, 2015).

Electricity can also strengthen the social power of existing institutions. In Uroa, Islamic rituals like early prayers were encouraged by the use of amplifiers and speakers. Messages of grand religious leaders were conveyed by television and tape recorders. Furthermore, access to clean water and the bright light from the mosques at night testified to the purity and presence of Islam in the village (Winther, 2013).

Experiences with rural electrification from other countries are quite similar to those in Zanzibar. For example, as regards social inclusion and exclusion, electricity in rural South African villages on the one hand brought a sense of inclusion into the modern world and a sense of improved status of the community and villagers' sense of self. On the other hand, electricity also intensified feelings of exclusion and inequality by highlighting the differences between the poorest and the better off. Televisions have become a new status symbol, and lacking one can become a new marker of poverty (Matinga & Annegarn, 2013). Regarding the impacts of electrification, it is very important to look at the different ways in which different social groups experience electrification and whether social inequalities are reduced or fostered.

What can be learned from the rural electrification of Brazil, Zanzibar, and other countries is that solutions have to be developed together with local residents in order to optimally take into account their specific needs, and cultural as well as geographical circumstances (Andrade, Rosa, & da Silva, 2011; van Els, de Souza Vianna, & Brasil, 2012). To spread energy supply to very remote areas and allow increases in installed power, more electricity access systems based on local energy sources (like hydro) need to be developed. Decentralized renewable energy sources can be provided with local resources and allow energy independence while having much lower environmental impacts (Goldemberg, La Rovere, & Coelho, 2004). However, utilities tend to focus on grid extensions in regions where decentralized systems would be more suitable. A lack of appropriate institutional models is a key barrier to off-grid rural electrification; thus special agents are needed to implement decentralized electricity generation on a municipal level.

The relatively lower level of electricity demand and the high initial costs constitute barriers for potential investors. To make the expansion of renewables in remote areas financially more attractive, tax incentives have to be considered. In order to enable local populations to afford electricity, economic conditions also must be improved (Goldemberg, La Rovere, & Coelho, 2004).

Energy Poverty and Gender

Promoting gender equality and empowering women is a globally agreed-upon goal. But despite advancements in recent decades, gender equality remains a persistent challenge for countries worldwide. Energy poverty has clear gender dimensions. In most developing countries, women experience energy poverty differently and more severely than men. Without access to modern energy services, women and girls spend a lot of their time performing basic subsistence tasks such as collecting fuel and water for their families. Taking India as an example, firewood, cattle dung, and crop waste fulfill 92% of rural domestic household energy needs, all traditionally collected by women. Time allocation for fuel collection can range from one hour to as high as six hours per household per day (Clancy et al., 2012). Very often, time poverty is the result of spending an inordinate amount of time gathering biomass for basic energy needs, preventing women and girls from participating in other beneficial ventures.

Women are also disproportionately affected by serious health problems due to the use of biomass for cooking and the related risk factor of solid fuel smoke. The use of open fires and rudimentary cook stoves is known to be inefficient, unsafe, unclean, and inconvenient (Wickramasinghe, 2016). While cooking, women tend to inhale acrid smoke and fine particulates, and this exposure to harmful gases can last for several hours a day. Indoor air pollution causes an estimated 4.3 million deaths annually due to chronic respiratory diseases, pneumonia, and lung cancer caused by household cooking over coal, wood, and biomass stoves (WHO, 2014). Most of the deaths occur in poor households, affecting mainly women and young children.

Although the disadvantages of an absence of modern energy services to women are well understood, the gender-sensitive transition to modern energy services is slow in some regions. This could be explained, in part, by a failure to address the gender dimensions of energy poverty (Pachauri & Rao, 2013). Gender is a concept that refers to a system of socially defined roles, privileges, attributes, and relationships between men and women, which are not biologically determined, but rather are learned during socialization. Gender describes the relational position of women and men, and very often involves power relations. In many societies, tasks and responsibilities that constitute women's roles are assigned to the private sphere, whereas men's tasks and responsibilities are assigned to the public sphere. But this division does not necessarily result in women's power in decision-making in the home. Very often, men have more power than women to make decisions, and more control over the bodies, lives, and resources of other family members (Clancy et al., 2012). When making decisions about energy access or appliance purchases, men often prioritize their own interests over the needs of women. A study of cook stove adoption in Bangladesh found that husbands frequently exercise authority in cook stove purchasing and do not include the costs and benefits of the new technology that accrue to their wives. Often, the only changes in technology that tend to be adopted are those that benefit male household members. But it is not always men's decision-making power that serves as a barrier to the adoption of modern stoves. In many societies, the cooking fire is seen as the social hub of the family, allowing women to socialize with their families. In South Africa, solar cookers were rejected, as they required a shift to cooking outdoors, which would lead to a breakdown of the social web, weakening women's influence within the family. The widespread resistance to fully adopt clean cooking technologies might also lie in the fact that cooking and the use of fire are deeply embedded in traditional cultures and identities, with preferences for food cooked on traditional fireplaces. Besides, awareness of the dangers of indoor air pollution often is low, even among clinic staff (Clancy et al., 2012).

Modern energy services can offer women benefits that improve their quality of life, and increase their safety, comfort, and convenience, as well as their status as wives and, under specific societal conditions, as daughters-in-law. On the other hand, depending on the specific context, they can also reinforce patriarchal social structures and entrench traditional hierarchies of power that deny women their agency and choice (Standal & Winther, 2016).

Very often, energy interventions and policies are gender blind. Energy and technology are generally considered to be male domains, resulting in men talking to men about energy issues and leaving behind women's needs, views, and participation in energy development. According to Clancy et al. (2016), two major transformations for more gender-aware energy policies will have to take place: first, women have to be empowered to make choices about energy; second, addressing gender issues of energy poverty will require changes on the energy supply side. Results from a case study in Afghanistan suggest that even in a very patriarchal setting, the training and work of women as solar engineers can challenge traditional gender norms of women, changing also men's perspectives on women's abilities and roles in society.

Future Prospects

Some lessons to be learned from electrification processes have already been outlined in different parts of the chapter. Sovacool, in his assessment of factors responsible for success and failures of renewable energy-access programs in 10 different countries of the Asia Pacific, identified a number of factors that correlate with successful national programs (Sovacool, 2013). These include, to name a few: selecting appropriate technologies, by asking local users about their preferences; coupling renewable energy with income-generating activities; providing access to financing and microcredit to overcome start-up cost hurdles with purchasing systems; building capacities and encouraging active participation from communities; avoiding giving away systems for free and instead requiring community contributions and cost-sharing.

When deciding on certain energy systems, aspects of social and ecological sustainability must be weighed against each other. While the use of renewable energies helps to ensure long-term sustainability, in the near term cleaner fossil fuels (e.g., liquefied petroleum gas) combined with more efficient appliances can help to counter energy poverty, due to higher combustion efficiency (Karekezi et al., 2012).

Conventional grid extension has continued to be the predominant mode of electrification in almost all countries of the world, preferred by decision-makers who saw decentralized, off-grid electricity systems at the village level as inferior. But off-grid systems could be a promising path to providing sustainable supply in a more democratic way (Ulsrud et al., 2015), one that is contextually and culturally sensitive and takes into account specific social, economic, and political conditions (Halff et al., 2014).

Concluding Remarks

In this chapter, we have outlined different dimensions, causes, and consequences of energy poverty in the Global South as well as in the Global North. It has been made clear that energy poverty is part and parcel of specific energy-society relations, embedded in wider social, economic, political, and cultural structures, and reflecting inequalities both within and across nations.

Energy poverty is a multidimensional concept, and researchers are responding with theoretical developments to improve our conceptual understanding of the multidimensional nature of the problem. For instance, the application of the energy vulnerability framework set out by Bouzarovski and Petrova (2015) enables a more nuanced examination of the complex issues contributing to and reinforcing energy poverty. Studying energy vulnerability means examining risk factors that contribute to the precariousness of particular spaces and groups of people. One novelty of the vulnerability framework is its emphasis on the spatial and temporal dynamics of energy poverty, which recognizes that households described as energy poor may exit the condition in the future by a change in some of their circumstances, and vice versa. Day, Walker, and Simcock (2016) propose a capability framework for conceptualizing energy use and energy poverty by approaching them from the basis of the energy services accessed or achieved. This approach recognizes that energy is needed for achieving a range of outcomes related in different ways to well-being, and—being a contextually sensitive concept—can be applied to the different manifestations of energy poverty in developing as well as developed countries. What is in demand is not energy per se, but rather the services that energy use can provide, such as cooking, heating, and mobility. Being energy poor therefore means the inability to realize essential capabilities as a direct or indirect result of insufficient access to affordable, reliable, and safe energy services.

As regards policy responses, it is crucial to highlight the necessity of tackling energy poverty as a cross-sectoral phenomenon (Bouzarovski, Petrova, & Sarlamanov, 2012). Energy poverty can be located at the contested crossroads of different areas of politics (energy, health, social policy, environment and climate change, housing, economic affairs, etc.); thus collaboration across ministries will be urgently needed. In many countries, such collaboration rarely takes place, often leading to one-dimensional policy interventions, leaving out potential synergies between policies. Policymaking is always about tensions between policy objectives, balancing between different goals and trade-offs. From an energy justice viewpoint, the question arises whether an energy system fairly disseminates both the benefits and costs of energy services, allows for impartial energy decision-making, and the recognition of different groups of people and their unique energy needs. So far, the various forms of efforts to address global energy poverty show that this is not the case. In many parts of the world, under-consumption of energy in low-income segments of the population coincides with excessive consumption in high-income segments, accompanied by huge differences in carbon footprints. Facing the Sustainable Development Goals, policymakers should acknowledge that those with high environmental impacts should bear the main responsibility of reducing consumption and should be actively targeted in policy. Koch and Fritz (2014) refer to the growing body of literature addressing the distributive consequences and implications of environmental policies for social justice and social policy, showing that responsibilities and impacts sometimes work in opposite ways, since segments of the population likely to be most harmed by environmental issues are the least responsible for causing them and have the least resources to cope with the consequences. The energy poor are among these populations.

In the end, measures and interventions to tackle energy poverty must take into account wider societal structures and power relations. Therefore, policies to fight energy poverty must also be social policies. Some evidence suggests that people in more equitable and socially inclusive societies are better off and report greater amounts of well-being than those in unequal ones (Wilkinson & Pickett, 2010). Equitable policies reducing social, economic, and environmental inequalities could lead to more "successful societies," enhancing solidarity, equity, and environmental performance and thereby allowing a transition toward a low-carbon society that is sensitive to socio-ecological inequalities.

But despite the formulation of Sustainable Development Goals and efforts to tackle poverty and energy deprivation, the world seems to be far away from realizing inter- and intragenerationally just development. Global poverty reduction is lagging behind, and in many countries social and economic inequality has intensified over the last decade. Energy poverty is far from eradicated. Energy systems more or less reflect societal differences. A just energy system requires a just and sustainable society.

Notes

1. https://sustainabledevelopment.un.org/sdg7
2. In this section the term *energy-poor households* is used, although not all households mentioned are energy poor according to the (different) definitions of energy poverty. Some can be located at the intersection between income poverty and energy poverty.
3. http://www.mui.manchester.ac.uk/cure/research/projects/euro-energy-poverty -observatory/

References

Anderson, W., White, V., & Finney, A. (2010). *"You just have to get by": Coping with low incomes and cold homes.* Bristol: Centre for Sustainable Energy.

Andrade, C. S., Pinguelli Rosa, L., & Fidelis da Silva, N. (2011). Generation of electric energy in isolated rural communities in the Amazon Region a proposal for the autonomy and sustainability of the local populations. *Renewable and Sustainable Energy Reviews, 15,* 493–503.

Bhattacharya, J., DeLeire, T., Haider, S., & Currie, J. (2003). Heat or eat? Cold-weather shocks and nutrition in poor American families. *American Journal of Public Health, 93,* 1149–1154.

Boardman, B. (2010). *Fixing fuel poverty: Challenges and solutions.* London: Earthscan.

Bouzarovski, S., & Petrova, S. (2015). A global perspective on domestic energy deprivation: Overcoming the energy poverty–fuel poverty binary. *Energy Research & Social Science, 10,* 31–40.

Bouzarovski, S., Petrova, S., & Sarlamanov, R. (2012). Energy poverty policies in the EU: A critical perspective. *Energy Policy, 49,* 76–82.

Bouzarovski, S., Tirado Herrero, S., Petrova, S., & Ürge-Vorsatz, D. (2015). Unpacking the spaces and politics of energy poverty: path-dependencies, deprivation and fuel switching in post-communist Hungary. *Local Environment, 21,* 1151–1170.

Brunner, K.-M., & Mandl, S. (2014). Energy consumption and social inequality: fuel poverty in Europe. In S. Reiter (Ed.), *Energy consumption: Impacts of human activity, current and future challenges, environmental and socio-economic effects* (pp. 167–184). New York: Nova Science.

Brunner, K.-M., Spitzer, M., & Christanell, A. (2012). Experiencing fuel poverty: Coping strategies of low-income households in Vienna/Austria. *Energy Policy, 49,* 53–59.

Clancy, J., Dutta, S., Mohlakoana, N., Rojas, A. V., & Matinga, M. N. (2016). The predicament of women. In L. Guruswamy (Ed.), *International energy and poverty* (pp. 24–38). London; New York: Routledge.

Clancy, J., Winther, T., Matinga, M., & Oparachoa, S. (2012). *Gender equity in access to and benefits from modern energy and improved energy technologies.* Twente: ETC.

Davis, M. (1998). Rural household energy consumption: the effects of access to electricity—evidence from South Africa. *Energy Policy, 26,* 207–217.

Day, R., Walker, G., & Simcock, N. (2016). Conceptualising energy use and energy poverty using a capabilities framework. *Energy Policy, 93,* 255–264.

Department of Communications, Energy & Natural Resources. (2016). A Strategy to Combat Energy Poverty. Retrieved from http://www.dccae.gov.ie/energy/SiteCollectionDocuments/Energy-Efficiency/A%20Strategy%20to%20Combat%20Energy%20Poverty.pdf

Department of Energy and Climate Change. (2010). *Fuel poverty methodology handbook.* London: HMSO.

Department of Energy and Climate Change. (2013). *Fuel poverty report—Updated.* London: HMSO.

De Quero, A., & Lapostolet, B. (2009). *Plan Bâtiment Grenelle Groupe de travail précarité énergétique rapport.* Paris.

Dubois, U. (2012). Fuel poverty in France. Retrieved from http://fuelpoverty.eu/2012/08/24/fuel-poverty-in-france/

European Commission. (2008). *Communication from the Commission to the European Parliament pursuant to the second subparagraph of Article 251(2) of the EC Treaty concerning the common position of the Council on the adoption of a Directive of the European Parliament and of the Council concerning common rules for the internal market in electricity and repealing Directive 2003/54/EC* (COM(2008)906 final). Brussels: European Commission.

Gibbons, D., & Singler, R. (2008). *Cold comfort: A review of coping strategies employed by households in fuel poverty.* London: Centre for Economic and Social Inclusion.

GNESD. (n.d.). Energy access program in Brazil: "Light for all." Retrieved from http://energy-access.gnesd.org/cases/32-energy-access-program-in-brazil-lighting-for-all.html

Goldemberg, J., Lèbre La Rovere, E., & Teixeira Coelho, S. (2004). Expanding access to electricity in Brazil. *Energy for Sustainable Development, 8,* 86–94.

Goldemberg, J., & Teixeira Coelho, S. (2004). Renewable energy: Traditional biomass vs. modern biomass. *Energy Policy, 32,* 711–714.

Green, G., & Gilbertson, J. (2008). *Warm front, better health: Health impact evaluation of the warm front scheme.* Sheffield: Sheffield Hallam University.

Grevisse, F., & Brynart, M. (2011). *Energy poverty in Europe: Towards a more global understanding.* Stockholm: ECEEE.

Gupta, A. (2015). An anthropology of electricity from the Global South. *Cultural Anthropology, 30*(4), 555–568.

Haanyika, C. M. (2006). Rural electrification policy and institutional linkages. *Energy Policy, 34,* 2977–2993.

Halff, A., Sovacool, B. K., & Rozhon, J. (2014). Introduction: The end of energy poverty. Pathways to development. In A. Halff, B. K. Sovacool, & J. Rozhon (Eds.), *Energy poverty: Global challenges and local solutions* (pp. 1–7). Oxford: Oxford University Press.

Hills, J. (2011). *Fuel poverty: The problem and its measurement. Interim Report of the Fuel Poverty Review.* London: The London School of Economics and Political Science.

IBGE. (2009). PNAD. Retrieved from https://sidra.ibge.gov.br/pesquisa/pnad

International Bank for Reconstruction and Development, The World Bank, and IEA. (2015). *Progress toward sustainable energy 2015.* Washington, DC: The World Bank.

Jenkins, K., McCauley, D., Heffron, R., Stephan, H., & Rehner, R. (2016). Energy justice: A conceptual review. *Energy Research & Social Science, 11,* 174–182.

Karekezi, S., McDade, S., Boardman, B., & Kimani, J. (2012). Energy, poverty, and development. In T. B. Johansson, A. P. Patwardhan, N. Nakicenovic, & L. Gomez-Echeverri (Eds.), *Global energy assessment: Toward a sustainable future* (pp. 151–190). Cambridge: Cambridge University Press.

Klinsky, S., & Golub, A. (2016). Justice and sustainability. In H. Heinrichs, P. Martens, G. Michelsen, & A. Wiek (Eds.), *Sustainability science* (pp. 161–173). Dortrecht: Springer.

Koch, M., & Fritz, M. (2014). Building the eco-social state: Do welfare regimes matter? *Journal of Social Policy, 43*, 679–703.

Matinga, M. N., & Annegarn, H. J. (2013). Paradoxical impacts of electricity on life in a rural South African village. *Energy Policy, 58*, 295–302.

Matinga, M. N., Clancy, J. S., Doyle, V., & Annegarn, H. J. (2016). Behavioral challenges and the adoption of appropriate sustainable energy technologies. In L. Guruswamy (Ed.), *International energy and poverty* (pp. 146–159). London; New York: Routledge.

OECD & IEA. (2015). *World energy outlook.* Paris: OECD, and IEA.

O'Neill, T., Jinks, C., & Squire, A. (2006). "Heating is more important than food": Older women's perceptions of fuel poverty. *Journal of Housing for the Elderly, 20*, 95–198.

Pachauri, S., & Rao, N. D. (2013). Gender impacts and determinants of energy poverty: Are we asking the right questions? *Current Opinion in Environmental Sustainability, 5*, 205–215.

Pereira, M. G., Sena, J. A., Vasconcelos Freitas, M. A., & Fidelis da Silva, N. (2011). Evaluation of the impact of access to electricity: A comparative analysis of South Africa, China, India and Brazil. *Renewable and Sustainable Energy Reviews, 15*, 1427–1441.

Pereira, M. G., Vasconcelos Freitas, M. A., & Fidelis da Silva, N. (2010). Rural electrification and energy poverty: Empirical evidences from Brazil. *Renewable and Sustainable Energy Reviews, 14*, 1229–1240.

Practical Action. (2014). *Poor People's energy outlook 2014: Key messages on energy for poverty alleviation.* Rugby: Practical Action.

Pye, S. T., Dobbins, A., Baffert, C., Brajković, J., Grgurev, I., De Miglio, R., & Deane, J. (2015). *Energy poverty and vulnerable consumers in the energy sector across the EU: Analysis of policies and measures.* London: INSIGHT_E.

Radcliffe, J. (2010). *Coping with cold: Responses to fuel poverty in Wales.* Ebbw Vale: The Bevan Foundation.

Simcock, N., Walker, G., & Day, R. (2016). Fuel poverty in the UK: Beyond heating? *People, Place and Policy, 10*, 25–41.

Sovacool, B. K. (2013). A qualitative factor analysis of renewable energy and Sustainable Energy for All (SE4All) in the Asia-Pacific. *Energy Policy, 59*, 393–403.

Standal, K., & Winther, T. (2016). Empowerment through energy? Impact of electricity on care work practices and gender relations. *Forum for Development Studies, 43*, 27–45.

Strakova, D. (2014). *Energy poverty in Slovakia.* Regulatory Review. Retrieved from https://papers.ssrn.com/sol3/papers.cfm?abstract_id=2546758

Thomson, H., & Bouzarovski, S. (2017). Europe's energy geographies. In B. Solomon & K. Calvert (Eds.), *Handbook on the geographies of energy.* Cheltenham, UK: Edward Elgar Publishing.

Thomson, H., Simcock, N., Bouzarovski, S., & Petrova, S. (2016). Multiple and new vulnerabilities to energy poverty: Findings from Central and Eastern Europe. Paper presented to the Royal Geographical Society Annual Conference, London, August 30–September 2.

Thomson, H., Snell, C., & Liddell, C. (2016). Fuel poverty in the European Union: A concept in need of definition? *People, Place and Policy*, cursive 10, 5–24.

Ulsrud, K., Winther, T., Palit, D., & Rohracher, H. (2015). Village-level solar power in Africa: Accelerating access to electricity services through a socio-technical design in Kenya. *Energy Research & Social Science*, 5, 34–44.

van Els, R. H., de Souza Vianna, J. N., & Pinho Brasil, A. C. (2012). The Brazilian experience of rural electrification in the Amazon with decentralized generation: The need to change the paradigm from electrification to development. *Renewable and Sustainable Energy Reviews*, 16, 1450–1461.

Wickramasinghe, A. (2016). Energy for rural women: Beyond energy access. In L. Guruswamy (Ed.), *International energy and poverty* (pp. 231–244). London; New York: Routledge.

Wilkinson, R., & Pickett, K. (2010). *The spirit level: Why equality is better for everyone.* London: Penguin.

World Health Organization. (2014). *Burden of disease from household air pollution for 2012.* Geneva: WHO.

Winther, T. (2008). *The impact of electricity: Development, desires and dilemmas.* New York; Oxford: Berghahn Books.

Winther, T. (2013). Space, time, and sociomaterial relationships: Moral aspects of the arrival of electricity in rural Zanzibar. In S. Strauss, S. Rupp, & T. Love (Eds.), *Cultures of energy: Power, practices, technologies* (pp. 164–176). London: Routledge.

Winther, T., & Wilhite, H. (2015). Tentacles of modernity: Why electricity needs anthropology. *Cultural Anthropology*, 30, 569–577.

CHAPTER 17

ENERGY POVERTY AND CLIMATE CHANGE

Elements to Debate

MARCIO GIANNINI PEREIRA, NEILTON FIDELIS
DA SILVA, AND MARCOS A. V. FREITAS

INTRODUCTION

THE production and use of energy correspond to about 70% of the emissions of greenhouse gases on the planet. As such, planning the expansion of access to electricity and its use is intrinsically linked to poverty and equity, and also to global climate change. Research shows that the effects of climate change are becoming more intense and accelerated, thus global warming could be significantly greater than projected, with more severe and irreversible consequences. Solomon and associates (2009) state that the outcomes of global warming will still be felt a thousand years after the hypothetical stabilization of emissions. They also affirm that the risks of slow processes such as climate change should not be assumed to be limited, based on a "Promethean" concept that a technological choice will rapidly stabilize emissions and revert all the damage within years or decades. This statement is not valid in the context of carbon dioxide emissions due to the inertia of atmospheric perturbations and ocean warming.

The use of fossil fuels allowed for a great leap of productivity in industry and agriculture in the contemporary world, through the mechanization and substitution of the workforce. This led to a reduction of the rural population, the migration of workers to the service sector, and the growth of commercial and cultural exchanges in an increasingly globalized society. Indubitably, all these advances allowed for great personal and collective gains, such as the reduction and replacement of tiring work, an increase in longevity and life expectancy, improvements in education, higher income, and the expansion of individual freedoms (democracy). However, these advances did not come about in an equitable way.

Globally today, 1.3 billion people do not have access to electric power (WEO, 2011). According to data from the World Energy Outlook (WEO, 2002), if the major trend of electrification rates stays the same, by 2030 a total of 1.4 billion people will still have no access to electric power. To universalize access in South Asia and in Sub-Saharan Africa, the WEO report estimates that more than 40 years and 80 years are needed, respectively.

The lack of access to energy in a society intensifies social asymmetries such as the permanence/expansion of poverty, lack of opportunities for growth, migratory flow toward large cities, and a disbelief in society's future. With electric power, rural communities are expected to reach a higher level of economic and energy sustainability. Energy is essential to human survival; supplying energy to all citizens is also a requirement for social well-being and for a country's economic development. The traditional view of the productive use of energy is that it is associated primarily with the provision of motive power for agricultural and industrial or commercial uses. But access and quality of energy can also help to reduce poverty in terms of income, and can help to improve health, universal primary education, women's empowerment, and gender equality.

If current trends describing access to electric power are maintained, the large social inequality observed between urban areas and rural areas will escalate. Regular and safe access to electricity brings about many social and environmental benefits to the population, especially for communities in rural areas, particularly by improving the quality of life for residents.

Casillas and Kammen (2010) highlight that the expansion of energy services per se will not eradicate poverty, but it will immediately affect the daily life of a population. Energy poverty results in unmet basic needs and depressed economic and educational opportunities that are particularly pervasive among women, children, and minorities. Regular and safe electricity access strengthens economic activities in rural areas, improves the quality of services available to meet internal demands and the demands of small businesses through lighting, domestic appliances, more efficient electronic appliances, and access to information through TV, radio, and cell phones.

Sovacool et al. (2016) state that energy poverty should be interpreted as a violation of distributive justice; for instance, the state of New York (US), with an estimated population of 19.5 million, has the same level of electric power consumption as Sub-Saharan Africa, with a population of 791 million people. The theory of distributive justice affirms that physical safety is a basic right; thus the conditions that guarantee it should be created through jobs, access to food, dignified living conditions, and sustainable access to the environment and its resources. In this context, therefore, people would have the right to a minimum set of energy services, which would provide them with a minimum standard of well-being, and one of these services is electric power.

Researchers have explored the notion of thresholds for basic energy needs (Casillas & Kammen, 2010; Goldemberg et al., 1985; Pereira, Freitas, & Silva, 2011). Energy poverty results in unmet basic needs and depressed economic and educational opportunities that are particularly pervasive among women, children, and minorities. However, there are no international norms for these indicators. Countries often define their own life-line energy entitlements. These typically fall in the range of 20–50 kilowatt hours (kWh) for electricity to households and 6–15 kilograms of liquefied petroleum gas (LPG) for cooking per month, and 10–30 kWh of useful energy per square meter of living space for heating per year. Others institutions such as the United Nations Development Programme and the World Health Organization (UNDP and WHO, 2009) consider energy poverty as a metric of physical availability or access to energy carriers (household or population access).

The traditional use of biomass is estimated to account for 10% of global energy consumption. Its impacts are not insignificant in terms of emissions of pollutants from combustion (CCCD, 2009). The International Energy Agency (2016) estimates that 2.7 billion people use firewood and other solid fuels for cooking and kerosene for lighting, creating an environment contaminated by indoor emissions, which are linked to about 3.5 million deaths per year. This reality is observed particularly in the developing countries of Asia and Sub-Saharan Africa. Burning generally takes place in enclosed spaces with little ventilation, intensifying its harmful effects for human health. According to the International Energy Agency (2016), indoor emissions may contain up to 100 times more particulates than the acceptable level, due to poor ventilation and the use of inappropriate technologies.

Since the 1980s, academic discussions have raised concerns related to the maintenance of an energy-consumption profile based on fossil fuels and the consequences it entails for society, one of these concerns is the climate change. The growing attention it has received is related to the social, economic, and energy consequences of climate change; thus it is necessary to analyze how it affects ecosystems that are more susceptible to extreme weather events and its links to state-of-the-art access to energy on the planet. Solutions should consider the particular context of each country.

At the meetings of the Conferences of the Parties (COP), participants have expressed recognition of the need for a significant drop in the global emissions of greenhouse gases in order to limit the increase of the global temperature to 2°C, and the need for measures to reach this goal in accordance with science and based on equity. The COP-15, held in 2009, affirmed that signatories should cooperate to reduce global and national emissions as soon as possible, while acknowledging that the reduction will take longer for developing countries, and that social and economic development and the eradication of poverty remain the fundamental and supreme priorities of developing countries.

SUSTAINABLE DEVELOPMENT: EQUITY

The most important social outcomes of scientific and technological advances include the increase in life expectancy and the consequent increase of the world population, urbanization, and the production of goods and services, with a reduction of work hours, especially over the last two centuries. Thus, it is possible to state that scientific and technological development has been successful in terms of increasing average life expectancy and work productivity (Longo, 2007).

The majority of global energy resources available in nature is owned by the public domain, and therefore must be managed according to constitutional principles. Hence, public managers have a mandate to work toward making its appropriation socially fair, improving the distribution of the benefits originating from energy resources, as a public good. Some scholars consider energy access to be a basic human right, such as Campos (1984, p. 8): "Isn't there an essential right to energy for the citizen? If energy is such a powerful and necessary factor with the ability to bring an individual out of poverty and to provide access to the benefits brought by technology and culture, shouldn't a right to energy be created, similar to the right to life, to water, to air?"

The world's poorest social stratum is found in developing countries, where public services, such as treated water, health services, education, and electric supply, are limited. As for energy acquisition and use, a significant part of the world population has little or no income, thus energy acquisition through purchase is impossible for them. For this marginalized group, informal access to the network of power supply is the only alternative.

The development of technologies that transform primary energy resources into secondary energy makes electricity a highly valuable tool for the socioeconomic development of a region. Electric power is the basis for many productive activities and services, in addition to bringing about many improvements in the quality of life, and is linked directly to the promotion of health, education, and safety. According to Pope Paul VI (*apud* Campos, 1984 pg. 65) electric power was included on the list of common goods, defined as "the sum of those conditions of the social life whereby men, families and associations more adequately and readily may attain their own perfection."

The electricity used in the productive process and that consumed by the worker in his or her household, although physically identical, assume different social roles. In the production process, it is an auxiliary tool in the making of merchandise, representing a basic input for any operation that transforms raw material into a finished product. In residential consumption, it has a different meaning entirely.

Communities and families living in poverty are particularly vulnerable to energy poverty. They tend to have a more limited capacity to adapt, and they rely to a greater degree on resources that are climate sensitive, such as local supplies of water and food. In regions in which extreme climate events become more intense and/or more frequent, the economic and social costs of these events will rise, becoming substantial in the most directly affected areas.

The impacts of climate change could create social, economic, and technological barriers for most developing countries, adding to the current pressures on natural resources and the environment. Moreover, they are associated with rapid and unplanned urbanization, industrialization, and economic development. For example, the difficulty of populations in areas most vulnerable to the effects of climate change will result in waves of migration to urban centers, which in turn are not prepared for the phenomenon.

In the 1980s and 1990s, the discussion on development entered a new phase with Amartya Sen's contributions from two of his most famous books, *On Ethics and Economics* (1987) and *Development as Freedom* (1999). The author breaks with a prevailing one-dimensional view of the economy by singling out the ethical and political dimension of the pressing economic issues of our time, and by questioning the perspective that the economy should be assessed only with respect to efficiency, for it also encompasses justice and morality issues. By doing so, he also questions the conventional concept of development. According to Sen (1999), development should be interpreted as a process of expanding the real freedoms that the citizens of a country enjoy, thus requiring first of all the removal of constraints to freedom, such as tyranny and poverty, the lack of economic opportunities, systematic social deprivation, neglect of public facilities, and social, political, and economic insecurity.

Hence, the aim of social equity is not limited to the promotion of economic growth. This concept of economic growth, encompassing social factors including ethics, reveals the flaws of a productive system that leads to the concentration of wealth and is characterized by low economic dynamics; in other words, it does not generate wealth and income redistribution. A system that knows how to produce but not to distribute is not sufficient.[1] The social dimension of development is no longer a complement, a humanitarian dimension that has been treated as external to central economic processes. Rather, it becomes an essential component of social reproduction.

The world recognizes the importance of energy services to reach the UN Millennium Goals. Energy was singled out in session nine of the Commission for Sustainable Development (CSD-9) (UNDP, 2003): "To implement the millennium goals, the international community must reduce to half the number of people living with less than US$1/day by 2015, with the access to energy services being a pre-requisite. Increasing access to safe and reliable energy induces the reduction of poverty. . . ."

The Millennium Goals were launched in September 2000, with eight goals measured by indicators. The main objectives are to reduce poverty, to improve health, and to promote peace, human rights, and environmental sustainability (UNDP, 2003). Olav Kjorven, director of the United Nations Development Programme (UNDP, 2011), proposed an expansion of the Millennium Goals, including eight new goals that will last until 2030. Among them, a 50% drop in the emissions of greenhouse gases stands out. The wish to reassess the current modes of consumption and production lies behind the proposal, and countries with economies strongly based in "gray" industries will have to seek other paths of development to reach the established goals, including the eradication of poverty. Simultaneously, other presented proposals were associated with goals to reduce consumption and increase production efficiency, aiming at reducing losses and waste.

In pursuit of the Millennium Goals, many advances have been observed, such as a reduction in the number of people who live in extreme poverty, which went from 1.9 billion in 1990 to 836 million in 2015. Nonetheless, there is still a lot to be done to meet humanity's basic needs. In this sense, the new goals of the millennium were launched in 2014, with the aim of reinforcing the global effort toward social inclusion, associated with development and aligned with universal peace and freedom. According to the

United Nations (2015), Goal 1 states: "By 2030, eradicate extreme poverty for all people everywhere, currently measured as people living on less than US$ 1.25 a day."

A total of 1.3 billion people worldwide still do not have access to electric power, which is vital for the achievement of the Millennium Development Goals (MDG) and thus for reduction of global poverty. According to data from the International Energy Agency (2010), 85% of these people are located in rural areas. Casillas and Kammen (2010) indicate that the environmental impacts caused by climate change will affect the poorest populations first and more severely, particularly those who live in rural areas. Poor people are the most vulnerable and the least resilient to the effects of climate change. Consider, too, that the majority of the poorest among the poor live in the urban periphery and rural areas. Expanding access to electricity at affordable prices and improving the quality of the supply of energy services are essential for human and economic development to adapt in the face of climate change.

The progress observed in increasing access to electric power has been slow, especially in rural areas, due mostly to the high costs associated with the expansion of the electricity grid and the development of systems of decentralized power supply. Two intrinsic features of the rural electricity market are important here: in general, consumers are scattered geographically, and they have a relatively low demand for electric power. These factors limit the interest of electric utilities in supplying this market, especially when investment decisions are strictly limited to financial opportunities.

Over the last 20 years, however, access to electricity in rural areas has expanded, contributing to the social and economic development of populations that previously had no access to electric power in China and Brazil. Table 17.1 shows the access to electric power in Brazil, China, India, and South Africa, illustrating the successful efforts that countries such as China and Brazil have been making to achieve universal access to electric power. India and South Africa still have significant gaps, with the need to expand access to about 268 million people.

Even though coming closer to universalization has its merits, issues related to the quality of energy are generally underestimated, limiting the potential for growth and the social inclusion of projects aimed at reducing energy poverty. While 1.3 billion people

Table 17.1 Access to Electric Power (Selected Countries)

Country	Population with Access, % of total	Urban Population with Access, % of total	Rural Population with Access, % of total	Rural Population Without Access
Brazil	99.5	100	97	1,050,000
China	100	100	100	
India	78.7	98.2	69.7	261,762,791
South Africa	85.4	96.6	66.9	6,363,163

Source: Elaborated by the author based on United Nations Energy for All (2016).

worldwide live in un-electrified communities, as noted earlier, there are perhaps one billion more who have poor-quality electricity services, with limited hours of availability, regular blackouts, under-voltage, and poor frequency stability.

In spite of notable advances over the last decades in electricity access in Brazil, China, India, and South Africa, development in these countries is still far from levels enjoyed in developed countries. Table 17.2 shows additional information, such as the Human Development Index (HDI), life expectancy, population, income concentration (Gini coefficient), and others. These indicators do not directly capture the gains from access to electricity. For countries in which the per capita consumption of electric energy is limited, every increase in energy consumption allows for significant gains in quality of life for the beneficiary communities (bottom of logistic curve). On the other hand, in countries with more organized electricity distribution infrastructure in rural areas, which allows a higher consumption per capita in which consumers already have access to sufficient energy to meet daily needs, the gain in quality of life is less pronounced (top of logistic curve). One alternative is to consolidate and improve indicators that can capture the quality of life gains in these communities, such as the Indicator of Rural Development developed by Pereira and colleagues (2009), and Centro de Pesquisas de Energia Elétrica (CEPEL, 2003, 2006, 2007).

Income concentration still exists and is more intense in countries such as South Africa (0.6338) and Brazil (0.5790). In this case, Stiglitz (2012, p. 60) states that "[i]nequality has high costs. The price of inequality is the deterioration of economy, which becomes less stable and efficient, with less growth, and the subversion of democracy. The significant and increasing gap between the 1 per cent richest and 'the other 99 per cent' is not only one of many concerns, but the defining characteristic of a completely ill society."

Income inequality leads to unequal access to electric power and other modern energy sources worldwide. According to Oxfam (2015), in 2015 the wealth of 80 individuals is now equal to that owned by the bottom 50% of the global population: 3.5 billion people share between them the same amount of wealth as that of the richest 80 people. It is indubitably necessary to think about the historical process of wealth formation, which is associated with the use of fossil fuels. The relevance of this history is not limited to the issue of equity, as it includes the principle of justice as well.

CLIMATE CHANGE AND ENERGY

The processes of development are intrinsically related to climate change. Historically, developed countries are the greatest contributors to the emission of greenhouse gases. According to Hansen and colleagues (2013), from 1751 to 2012, the United States, the United Kingdom, Germany, and Japan were responsible for 26%, 5.4%, 6%, and 4%, respectively, of the historical accumulated emissions of carbon dioxide (CO_2), while Central/South America and Africa accounted for 3.9% and 2.6%.

Table 17.2 Snapshot of Selected Countries

Country	Rank in the HDI (2014)	Population (millions)	Urban Population (% of total)	Population Living below Income Poverty Line, PPP $1.25 a day, %	Inequality-Adjusted HDI	Gross National Income per Capita PPP2011$	Life Expectancy at Birth	Expected Years of Schooling	Gini Coefficient
Brazil	75	202	85.4	3.80	0.557	15,175	74.5	15.2	57.9 (2013)
China	90	1393.8	54.4	6.30	n.a	12,547	75.8	13.1	42.06 (2010)
India	130	1267.4	32.4	23.60	0.435	5,498	68	11.7	33.9 (2009)
South Africa	116	53.1	63.3	9.40	0.428	12,122	57.4	13.6	63.38 (2011)

Note: The closer the Gini coefficient is to 1, the higher is income concentration.

Source: Elaborated by the author based on UNDP (2016) and IndexMundi (2016).

A large segment of the population has no access to the most basic services. Climate negotiations, as well as their agreements, can only be effective if they take into account the priorities of developing countries, as well as the responsibility for historical emissions. In this sense, access to modern sources of energy is central to the discussion of developing countries, whether in the expansion of electric service or in the substitution of wood for LPG, particularly for use in cooking, among other issues associated with the energy context.

As the basis of the world power supply is fossil fuels, access to electric power plays a central role in disputes related to the mitigation of climate change. The supposed conflict between the expansion of energy services and the mitigation of emissions exists partially because the main reference point is the model of energy access adopted by developed countries, with electrification associated with a centralized planning and supply based on fossil fuels and characterized by low efficiency. If developing countries do indeed make the same choices made previously by developed countries with respect to development, based on the exploitation of fossil fuels, the emissions of greenhouse gases will grow rapidly (Yadoo & Cruickshank, 2012). However, the options available today are quite different. According to the International Energy Agency (2016), in 2012 renewable energy accounted for almost 22% of global electricity generation. The generalized adoption of the fossil-fuel model by developing countries becomes a clear barrier to climate stabilization (Alstone, Gerhenson & Kammen, 2015). However, not all developing countries follow this strategy. The electric power supply in Brazil, for instance, is mostly composed of renewable energy, which accounted for 74.2% of its total in 2014.

Yadoo and Cruickshank (2012) state that the use of renewable energy sources to expand access to electric power is an example of a potential strategy of synergy between reducing energy poverty and reducing greenhouse gas emissions, in addition to providing more resilience, considering that access to electric power may improve the ability to adapt to the impacts of climate change. There are many ways to reach this goal, in which renewable energy sources can be integrated into the electrical grid in a centralized way, and the grid can also be expanded to rural areas. Alternatively, off-grid solutions may be encouraged with local small-scale installations, such as photovoltaic panels, small wind turbines, gasifiers, and pico/micro/mini hydropower plants, among other strategies.[2]

Recognizing the differences between developed and developing countries in the context of energy and climate change is important in establishing goals and responsibilities (the principle of common but differentiated responsibilities). The countries with more technological and financial capabilities should also have a stronger commitment with respect to their efforts in climate agreements. Additionally, as for the right to emit (principle of contraction and convergence[3]), it is possible to establish different goals converging to the same deadline (Figure 17.1). These goals categorize countries according to level of development as industrialized countries (IC), advanced developing countries (ADC), and least developed countries (LDC).

A variant of the principle of contraction and convergence refers to common responsibilities but with a differentiated convergence over time (common but differentiated convergence). The central idea of the principle is to support equal per capita emissions in the long term (Figure 17.2).[4]

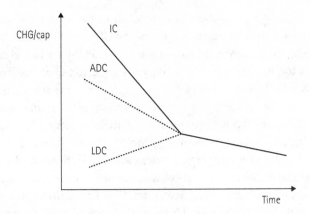

FIGURE 17.1 Contraction and convergence.

Source: Adapted from Höhne, Phylipsen, & Moltmann (2007).

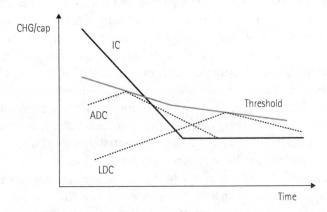

FIGURE 17.2 Common responsibilities with differentiated convergence.

Source: Adapted from Höhne, Phylipsen & Moltmann (2007).

For the proposal of contraction and convergence, historical emissions are more important. Annex I countries (the group of nations referred to under the Kyoto Protocol) could reduce their emissions following the proposal of contraction and convergence, but many of them would have more time for development before they started reducing their emissions. The participation of Non-Annex I countries is conditioned on a gradual reduction of the average emissions of Annex I countries to the average threshold, and there are still no licenses for excessive emissions for less developed countries.

A relevant step in this direction was the Paris Agreement (COP-21) approved by 195 countries part of the United Nations Framework Convention on Climate Change (UNFCCC) to reduce greenhouse gas emissions in the context of sustainable development. The commitment is aimed at maintaining the increase of the average global temperature below 2°C in comparison with pre-industrial levels and aspirations to limit the increase of the temperature to 1.5°C above pre industrial-levels. At COP-21, governments proposed to define their commitments based on intended nationally determined contributions (INDC), in which each government presented its goals according to its social and economic contexts. The role of rapidly developing countries is particularly critical. China and India have committed to reducing their "carbon intensity" per GDP, which still represents an emission increase in absolute terms. Brazil, on the other hand, proposed the absolute goal to reduce its emissions with respect to a historical year, not to a path of reference or a decrease of emission intensity. When compared with other large developing countries, the Brazilian goal restricts emissions to a fixed level. Figure 17.3 shows the (absolute) historical emissions and projections according to the INDCs of China, South Africa, Brazil, and India. Despite Brazil's intended hard limits, the cumulative global projections indicate a continuous increase of absolute emissions.

When considering (absolute) historical emissions and projections according to the INDCs for Japan, the United States, and the European Union (Figure 17.4), climate scenarios show a continuous reduction over time. However, some considerations about scale and metrics can be made:

1. Differences in scale among the analyzed countries are considerable and result from the industrialization process and intensive use of fossil fuels for a long period. For instance, while in 1990 the United States and the European Union had a historical basis of accumulated emissions of about 6,000 Metric tons of carbon dioxide (Mt CO_2) equivalent, the value for Brazil and South Africa was 500 Mt CO_2 equivalent. Additionally, the countries have different populations, as well as different levels of technological development and basic services.

2. It is necessary to evaluate metrics beyond absolute measures, considering the other proposed metrics that are based on intensity (such as per GDP) or that are relative (such as per capita). It is important to acknowledge the social demands of each developing country, in a context of limited resources and the need to expand electric power supply and energy safety, all while ensuring climate justice.

Climate justice is understood as the set of principles that ensure that no group of people (whether an ethnic, racial, or class group) will be allocated a disproportional share of our global climate commons for their emissions, and no group will suffer disproportionally the consequences of those emissions—consequences that may include severe declines in quality of life, compromises to reproduction, and forced migration. Climate injustices associated with our climate crisis are caused by situations of inequality that emerge in many in regions and countries, a result of the pursuit of a development model premised on continuous production and consumption growth and maximization of profits (FBOMS, 2007).

The size of the economy, population, and level of development are also important factors for climate justice. It is argued that per capita consumption is the most appropriate metric for this analysis, although admittedly it does not capture the emissions credited to a country as a result of exports.

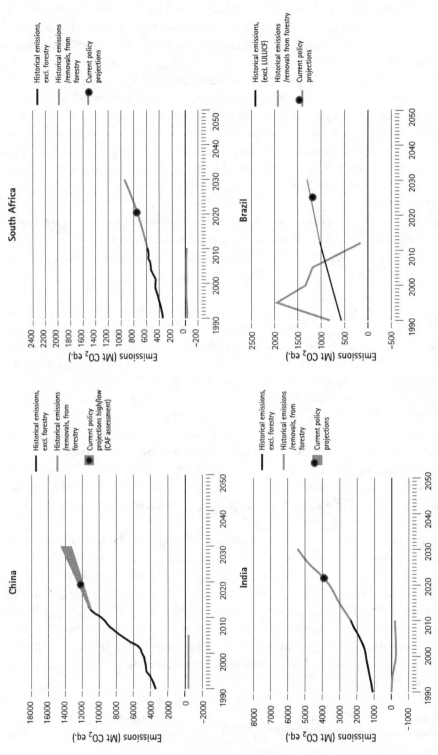

FIGURE 17.3 Contribution goals for the reduction of greenhouse gas emissions (South Africa, Brazil, China and India) (INDC).

Source: Adaptation based on ClimaTracker, 2016; © 2016 by Climate Analytics, Ecofys and New Climate Institute.

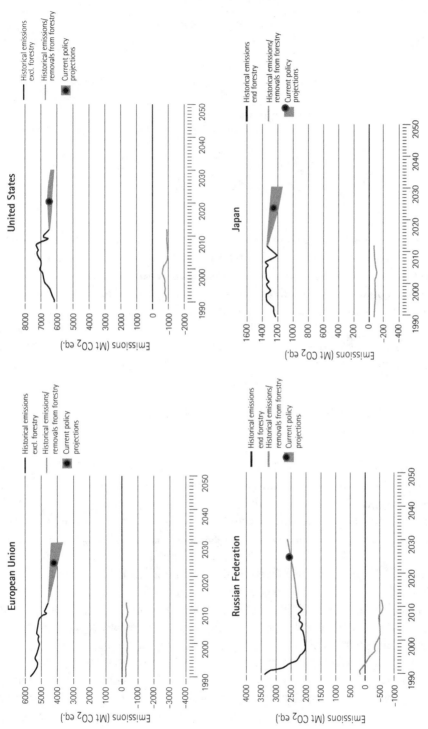

FIGURE 17.4 Contribution goals for the reduction of greenhouse gas emissions (European Union, United States, Russian Federation and Japan) (INDC).

Source: Adaptation based on ClimaTracker, 2016; © 2016 by Climate Analytics, Ecofys and New Climate Institute.

Table 17.3 Benefits and Costs Between Generations and Countries

	Past Generations	Present Generations	Future Generations
Developing Countries	Benefit from emission-generating activities that cause climate change (on a low level)	Benefit from emission-generating activities that cause climate change	Suffer from climate change (on a high level)
Industrialised Countries	Benefit from emission-generating activities that cause climate change (on a high level)	Benefit from emission-generating activities that cause climate change	Suffer from climate change (on a low level)

Source: Elaborated by the author based on Meyer & Roser (2006).

Researchers project an increase of emissions in developing countries in the coming years, confirmed by the INDCs highlighted in Figures 17.3 and 17.4. Meyer and Roser (2006) illustrate in an intuitive way the benefits and costs between generations, considering the level of industrialization of the countries as well. The emission scenarios describe a narrative that imposes precautionary actions based on their anticipated effects on the average temperature increase of the planet. In this way, it is recognized that due to differences between countries, given their stage of development, poorer countries will suffer more from the consequences of climate change (Table 17.3).

REDUCTION OF INEQUALITIES

A reduction of greenhouse gas emissions may have no bearing on levels of inequality. Despite reductions in some developed countries in recent years, the productive structure remained almost unaltered, and technological advances were mostly restricted to developed countries through investments in energy efficiency and renewable energy sources, as exporting industries that pollute and require natural resources from peripheral countries. According to Rawls (1993), the structurally fundamental idea of justice as fairness is that of society as a fair system of cooperation. Sen (1999) states that development should be interpreted as a process of expanding the real freedoms that the citizens of a country enjoy, thus requiring first of all the removal of major impediments to freedom, such as tyranny and poverty, the lack of economic opportunities, systematic social deprivation, neglect of public facilities, and social, political, and economic insecurity.

By contrast, the concept of economic efficiency has been a central theme of economic theory, constituting a basic criterion used by economists to choose between alternative allocations of resources within an economic system. In general terms, economic efficiency means that the economic system is maximizing the use of scarce resources or minimizing the costs of its activities. The multiple forms of utilitarianism based on market mechanisms easily led to the idea that the actions of the dominant public and economic powers have given an effective answer to the promotion of equity based on economic efficiency (Queirós, 2000). The option to prioritize equity or efficiency is the central issue of many public discussions, which are divided into two aspects. The first focuses on how much efficiency should be given up to support equity. The second involves evaluation of how society perceives, commits itself, and is prepared to reduce differences. The decision then is: Should we move toward a greater equality, giving up a certain level of efficiency, or should efficiency come first?

Plato stated that no one should be four times richer than the poorest member of society. In this egalitarian view, inequality matters in terms of the gap between the rich and the poor, which can motivate action, even when the poor obtain no gain. A similar view can be applied to equity and climate change, without aiming at encouraging an increase of historically low-emitting countries, but instead at questioning those who have contributed to global warming historically, especially with the goal of distinguishing luxury emissions from subsistence emissions.

DISCUSSION AND METRICS

Table 17.4 shows the concentration of historical emissions, with 5% of countries accounting for 67.74% of total emissions, and 50% of the lowest-emitting countries representing 0.74% of historic emissions. Even if the uncertainties associated with calculating historical emissions are taken into consideration, this discrepancy among countries reveals in an objective manner the enormous discrepancies in responsibility; the inevitable impacts of climate change due to historic emissions are attributable a small number of countries.

According to Atkinson (2015): "The proportion of differences has a profound effect on the nature of our societies. The fact that some people can buy tickets to travel through space while others make lines at food banks matters greatly." The necessity to reduce greenhouse gas emissions now represents a dominant position in climate policy discourse. This mitigation discourse, however, implies that responsibility for the reduction of emissions should be distributed equally regardless of historic emissions: a proposition

Table 17.4 Accumulated Emissions: CO_2 (Excluding Land Use and Forestry)

Total Accumulated Emissions	%	Number of Countries
5% of countries (top polluters)	67.74	9
50% of countries (lowest polluters)	0.74	92

Source: Author, based on CAIT Climate Data Explorer (2016); © 2016 by Climate Analytics, Ecofys and New Climate Institute.

contrary to the pursuit of equity. Calculating mitigation responsibility according to the amount of potentially fair historical emissions (PFHE) per country, on the other hand, accommodates the needs of every country to meet the basic service needs of its society. The definition of a potentially fair historical emission level is a complex and polemic issue, and its analysis in literature is still in its initial stages.

Seventy-five percent of countries are below the historical average level of emissions. It would be revealing to assess what would be a PFHE level for these countries, considering their societal and energy demands, and the fact that the top-emitting countries benefited from a lower cost of fuels during their development phase. One primary factor allowing for such low fuel prices was the externalization of environmental impacts of fossil-fuel production and consumption. Hence, "productivity" and the generation of wealth both increased. The PFHE concept affirms that opportunities among countries have been unequal historically, which in turn affects the equity of opportunities today. One means by which inequity results is from an advantage or sacrifice credited to the current generation as a result of the benefits or damages generated by previous generations. If there is a global concern about the future equality of opportunities, it is necessary to worry about the inequality of results today.

Hayward (2007) states that there is a strong and positive correlation between ecological space and economic wealth that is more reliable than the correlation between emissions and wealth, highlighting the extent to which all forms of natural resource exploitation involve ecological disruption. Wealth is also determined by access to resources, particularly natural resources. The assumption that there is a determined limit to the ecological space—here referring to nature's absorptive capacity[5]—that can be used by a given country lies behind the definition of the amount of potentially fair historical emissions, and it presumes that countries that surpass that limit will acquire an "ecological debt" with respect to other nations. The consideration is not directed at those countries that have not yet met their emission "quota," but at those which have already surpassed the quota, thereby imposing an ecological debt and its social and environmental costs onto others. The idea is similar to that of a debt to be paid by present and future generations of developing countries. Moreover, this debt should have a discount rate, in which the urgency of short-term and medium-term measures are given preferential status. According to the Intergovernmental Panel on Climate Change (IPCC) (2014), the social discount rate is appropriate for mitigation projects financed by the current reduction of consumption.

It is useful to estimate the amount of PFHE in light of the social and energy needs of countries. In this context, the average emission level of the top 10% historic CO_2 polluters globally (excluding land-use and land-use change) is 60,099 $MtCO_2$ (Table 17.5). The principle of common but differentiated responsibilities recognized in the UNFCCC acknowledges differences in historical emissions and consequent mitigation responsibilities. The theme of intergenerational justice associated with climate change is discussed by Meyer (2013), who concludes that developing countries should have more per capita emission rights than developed countries. In addition, he argues that developed countries should pay for the adaptation costs of the most vulnerable countries as historical compensation, based on the idea of distributive justice.

Table 17.5 Accumulated Emissions from Top
            Polluters: CO_2 (Excluding Land Use)

Country	$MtCO_2$
United States	366,421
China	150,109
Russian Federation	102,709
Germany	84,864
United Kingdom	70,473
Japan	51,005
India	37,976
France	34,457
Canada	28,317
World(total)	1,367,338
Average of top 5% CO_2 polluters	102,926
Average of top 10% CO_2 polluters	60,099

Source: Elaborated by the author based on CAIT Climate Data
Explorer (2016); © 2016 by Climate Analytics, Ecofys and New
Climate Institute.

Table 17.6 Cumulative Debt of Historical
            CO_2 Emissions per Country
            until 2012 (Excluding
            Land Use)

Country	Debt ($MtCO_2$)
United States	(306,322)
China	(90,010)
Russian Federation	(42,610)
Germany	(24,765)
United Kingdom	(10,374)

Source: Elaborated by the author based on CAIT
Climate Data Explorer (2016); © 2016 by Climate
Analytics, Ecofys and New Climate Institute.

Five countries can be seen to have an ecological debt: United States, China, the
Russian Federation, Germany, and the United Kingdom, while remaining countries
have a credit (Table 17.6). Hypothetically, the debt could be converted into financial resources, considering not only carbon's market value, but also its value for the survival
of peoples and ecosystems, with a remuneration for an annual premium rate over the

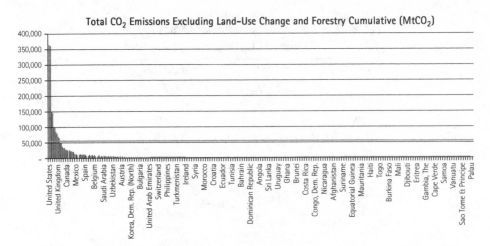

FIGURE 17.5 Accumulated emissions and potentially fair historical emissions (PFHE) limit.

Source: Elaborated by the author based on CAIT Climate Data Explorer (2016); © 2016 by Climate Analytics, Ecofys and New Climate Institute.

stock of debt. The level of 60,099 $MtCO_2$ was determined as the amount of PFHE based on statistical analyses of the distribution of cumulative historical emissions per country. Countries above this value have a debt to other countries (Figure 17.5).

Ecological space refers to the combined available resources, considering that the availability of these resources is limited. Ecological space is relevant to ethics not in virtue of being an evaluative term or referring directly to any determinate object of evaluation. It is primarily a descriptive term. Use of the concept allows capturing, particularly well, something morally important about the way humans' moral relations with one another are mediated through multifarious natural relations (Hayward, 2007).

Even within the top polluting countries, internal differences such as population size, physical space (territory), access to natural resources, and level of technological and social development also translate into inequalities in access to ecological space. The acknowledgment of the debt to the ecological space is a great advance toward reducing historical inequalities in opportunities among countries, but it does not solve the issue of the limited stock of physical space (i.e., there is a physical limit for the amount of greenhouse gases that can be emitted into the atmosphere). Historical emissions and the future emissions projected for countries are two sides of the same coin. And if the discussions are based on only one of these sides, outcomes will be inequitable.

FINAL CONSIDERATIONS

This chapter has two goals. The first is to reaffirm that the production, distribution, and use of energy, in terms of economic and social benefits, is highly unequal. While many in the Western world enjoy high rates of energy consumtion, currently 1.3 billion people have no access to electric power. This number per se reveals the flaw of the hegemonic economic model, and thus how expansion of the supply of electric power services alone does not eradicate energy poverty. The second goal is to provide metrics for climate change discussions from the perspective of climate justice, in regard to developing countries. Regardless of technological advances, if a considerable part of the world population does not have access to the most basic rights, proclaiming victory rings false. A recurring strategy is to deny the problem or apply a reductionist approach to it, characterized in the words of politics as "poverty relief." It is a reduction to the absurd (*reductio ad absurdum*). In the words of Marx (1984 [1852]): "Men make their own history, but they do not make it as they please; under self-selected circumstances, but under circumstances existing already, given and transmitted from the past."

Countries such as Brazil and China achieved significant results over the last few decades, getting closer to the universalization of access to electric power, while 268 million people still go without in just two countries—India and South Africa— combined. Even though achieving universalization has its merits, issues related to the quality of energy in general are underestimated, which limits the potential for growth and social inclusion of projects aimed at reducing energy poverty.

The concentration of historical emissions is noticeable, with 5% of countries accounting for 67.74% of the global total. It is also notable that 50% of countries with the lowest emissions represent 0.74% of global historic emissions. Even if the uncertainties of the calculations of historical emissions are taken into consideration, this discrepancy among countries highlights the issue of responsibility, showing that while the effects of climate change may be global, those responsible represent a small minority of countries.

The amount of PFHE accounts for the social and energy needs of countries. Even though it is in preliminary stages of conceptual development, the premise is entirely valid, acknowledging that the top 10% of emitters are responsible for 60,099 $MtCO_2$ of historical emissions.

The acknowledgment of the debt in the form of ecological space is a great advance toward reducing the historical inequalities of opportunities among countries, but it does not solve the issue of the limited stock of physical space (i.e., the physical limit to the amount of greenhouse gases that can be emitted into the atmosphere). Historical emissions and the future emissions projected for countries are two sides of the same coin. And if the discussions are based on only one of these sides, a global and effective solution will not be attained.

According to Pereira and colleagues (2010), public policies designed to reduce poverty and inequality necessarily permeate education and health matters. Both are directly related to the availability of electricity, mainly insofar as the rural environment is concerned. Electricity is one of the pillars on which education and health lean. As such, the universalization of access to electric energy globally is of fundamental importance for the eradication of poverty and the reduction of social inequality.

The concept of access to energy as a public good to which everyone has a right needs to be adopted urgently and without restrictions. The suppliers' aim of maximizing profit should not be put before collective values based on the maximization of well-being.

Without energy, there is no development and no democracy. Hence, energy should be interpreted as a right and as a fundamental element in the edification of a new humanism that guarantees a dignified life for all human beings.

NOTES

1. According to the Human Development Report (UNDP, 2006), about four hundred people have a personal wealth equal to half of the poorest population of mankind. This income concentration is undignified and brings humanity closer to the time when slavery was economically justified.
2. It is necessary promote studies on future scenarios that reveal which are the impacts of climate change on the potential of renewable energy sources. These potentials may have a regional behavior of intense modifications over time, making it possible or impossible to use a specific source and/or technology.
3. Under contraction and convergence, all countries participate in a global emission reduction with quantified emission targets. As a first step, all countries agree on a path of future global emissions that leads to an agreed long-term stabilization level for greenhouse gas concentrations ("contraction"). As a second step, the targets for individual countries are set in such a way that per capita emissions converge from the countries' current levels to a level equal for all countries within a given period ("convergence").
4. Conceptually, the Brazilian Proposal was built on the "common but differentiated responsibilities" and "polluter pays" principles. These are important principles enshrined in the 1992 UNFCCC. Although these principles are widely accepted, the Brazilian Proposal is not without controversy. The Brazilian Proposal addressed two key issues that pre-Kyoto negotiations were attempting to address (UNFCCC, 1997). First, it addressed the issue of "the future level of emissions to be tolerated from the Annex I Parties" (i.e., the "cap"). Second, the Proposal suggested a "criterion for the sharing of the burden" among industrialized countries (i.e., by historical responsibility for temperature increase).
5. This value is not absolute, which creates space for new discussions and metrics to improve this debate.

REFERENCES

Alstone, P., Gershenson, D., & Kammen, D.M. (2015). Decentralized energy systems for clean electricity access. *Nature Climate Change*, 5: 305–314.

Atkinson, A. B. (2015). *Desigualdade: O que pode ser feito?* São Paulo: Editora Leya.

Campos, J. H. (1984). *Eletrificação rural: Economia e tecnologia*. Texto apresentado no curso de eletrificação rural ministrado pela Energética—Energia, ecologia e informática (mimeo) (p. 36). Rio de Janeiro.

Casillas, C. E., & Kammen, D. M. (2010). The energy-poverty-climate nexus. *Science*, 330: 1181–1182.

Centro de Pesquisas de Energia Elétrica (CEPEL). (2003). *Desenvolvimento e Análise do Indicador de Desenvolvimento Rural (IDR—Qualitativo) para apoio aos estudos de impactos sócio-econômicos do programa de eletrificação rural "Luz no Campo": Fase Ex-Ante—Brasil.* Relatório Técnico CEPEL no. 37.845, Projeto 1437.

Centro de Pesquisas de Energia Elétrica (CEPEL). (2006). *Indicador de Desenvolvimento Rural (IDR): Metodologia e resultados.* Relatório Técnico CEPEL no. 14.601, Projeto 1437.

Centro de Pesquisas de Energia Elétrica (CEPEL). (2007). *Sistema de Impactos Rurais (IMPAR).* Versão 2.3, Rio de Janeiro, No. 1, CD-ROM.

ClimaTracker. (2016). *Climate Action Tracker.* Retrieved from http://climateactiontracker.org /countries/brazil.html

Commission on Climate Change and Development (CCCD). (2009, May). *Energy access, climate and development.* Stockholm: Stockholm Environment Institute (SEI).

Fórum Brasileiro de Organizações Não Governamentais e Movimentos Sociais para o Meio Ambiente e o Desenvolvimento (FBOMS). (2007). *Mudanças Climáticas e o Brasil: Contribuições e diretrizes para incorporar questões de mudanças de clima em políticas públicas.* Brasília: FBOMS.

IndexMundi. (2016). *Data: Income distribution.* Retrieved from http://www.indexmundi.com /facts/south-africa#Poverty-Income distribution

Intergovernmental Panel on Climate Change. (2014). *Technical summary—Climate Change 2014: Mitigation of climate change. Contribution of Working Group III to the Fifth Assessment Report of the Intergovernmental Panel on Climate Change* [Edenhofer, O., R. Pichs-Madruga, Y. Sokona, E. Farahani, S. Kadner, K. Seyboth, A. Adler, I. Baum, S. Brunner, P. Eickemeier, B. Kriemann, J. Savolainen, S. Schlömer, C. von Stechow, T. Zwickel & J. C. Minx (Eds.)]. Cambridge: Cambridge University Press.

International Energy Agency (IEA). (2010). *Energy poverty: How to make modern energy access universal?* Special Early Excerpt of the World Energy Outlook 2010 for the UN General Assembly on the Millennium Development Goals. Paris: International Energy Agency.

International Energy Agency (IEA). (2016). *World energy outlook special report 2016: Energy and air pollution.* Paris: International Energy Agency.

Goldemberg, J., Johansson, T. B., Reddy, A. K. N., & Williams, R. H. (1985). Basic needs and much more with one kilowatt per capita. *Ambio, 14*(4–5), 190–200.

Hansen, J., Kharecha, P., Sato, M., Masson-Delmotte, V., Ackerman, F., Beerling, D. J., . . . Zachos, J. C. (2013). Assessing "dangerous climate change": Required reduction of carbon emissions to protect young people, future generations and nature. *PLoS ONE, 8*(12): e81648.

Hayward, T. (2007). *Human rights versus emissions rights: Climate justice and the equitable distribution of ecological space.* Center for Global Ethics, George Mason University, Virginia. Retrieved from http://s3.amazonaws.com/academia.edu.documents/31542026/eia_117 .pdf?AWSAccessKeyId=AKIAJ56TQJRTWSMTNPEA&Expires=1474396858&Signature =tzl10mNsf%2FstlSvJDaaBDldx6Bc%3D&response-content-disposition=inline%3B%20 filename%3DHuman_Rights_Versus_Emissions_Rights_Cli.pdf

Höhne, N., Phylipsen, D., & Moltmann, S. (2007, May). *Factors underpinning future action 2007 update.* Department for Environment Food and Rural Affairs, United Kingdom.

Longo, W. P. (2007). Alguns impactos sociais do desenvolvimento científico e tecnológico. *Revista de Ciência da Informação, 8*(1): 1–31.

Marx, K. (1984 [1852]). *O 18 de Brumário de Louis Bonaparte* (2nd ed.). Avante. Retrieved from http://www.marxists.org/portugues/marx/1852/brumario/cap01.htm# per cent28N8 per cent29

Meyer, L. H. (2013). Why historical emissions should count (draft). *Chicago Journal of International Law, 13*(2), Article 15. Retrieved from http://chicagounbound.uchicago.edu /cgi/viewcontent.cgi?article=1382&context=cjil

Meyer, L. H., & Roser, D. (2006, December). Distributive justice and climate change: The allocation of emission rights. *Analyse und Kritik, 28*, 223–249.

Oxfam. (2015, January). *Wealth: Having it all and wanting more*. Oxfam Issue Briefing. Retrieved from https://www.scribd.com/doc/252395424/Wealth-Having-it-all-and -wanting more?secret_password=Yb8jp7fmNtWbPScAlyVc#fullscreen&from_embed

Pereira, M. G., Camacho, C. F., Paz, L. R. L., & Rodrigues, A. F. (2009). Indicator of Rural Development (IRD): An instrument for monitoring and evaluation of socio-energy results on public policies for rural electrification in Brazil. *Proceedings of SEEP 2009*, August 12–15, Dublin, Ireland.

Pereira, M. G., Freitas, M. A. V., & Silva, N. F. (2010). Rural electrification and energy poverty: Empirical evidences from Brazil. *Renewable and Sustainable Energy Reviews, 14*(4), 1229–1240.

Pereira, M. G., Freitas, M. A. V., & Silva, N. F. (2011). *The challenge of energy poverty: Brazilian case study*. Energy Policy, 39, 167–175.

Queirós, M. (2000). Utilitarismo ou Equidade? Dilemas para o ambiente e ordenamento. *Finisterra, XXXV*, 103–114.

Rawls, J. (1993). *Uma teoria da justiça*. Lisboa: Editorial Presença.

Sen, A. K. (1987). *On ethics and economics*. Oxford: Basil Blackwell.

Sen, A. K. (1999). *Development as freedom*. New York: Anchor Books.

Solomon, S., Plattner, G.-K., Knutti, R., & Friedlingstein, P. (2009). Irreversible climate change due to carbon dioxide emissions. *Proceedings of the National Academy of Sciences of the United States of America, 106*(6), 1704–1709.

Sovacool, B., Heffron, R., McCauley, D., & Goldthau, A. (2016). Energy decisions reframed as justice and ethical concerns. *Nature Energy, 1*: 16024. Retrieved from https://pdfs .semanticscholar.org/cb91/edc8420fd56a0d058bece081af3344ac62af.pdf

Stiglitz, J. E. (2012). *O preço da desigualdade*. Lisboa, Portugal: Bertand Editora.

United Nations. (2015). *Resolution Adopted by the General Assembly on 25 September 2015 – transforming our world : the 2030 Agenda for Sustainable Development pg. 15*. Retrieved from http://www.un.org/en/ga/search/view_doc.asp?symbol=A/RES/70/1&Lang=E

United Nations. (2016). *United Nations Sustainable Energy for All (SE4All)*. SE4All database. Retrieved from http://databank.worldbank.org/data/home.aspx

United Nations Development Programme (UNDP). (2003). *Millennium Development Goals: A compact among nations to end human poverty*. Human Development Report, UNDP. New York: EUA.

United Nations Development Programme (UNDP). (2006). *Beyond scarcity: Power, poverty and global water crisis*. Human Development Report. New York: Palgrave Macmillan.

United Nations Development Programme (UNDP). (2011). *Millennium Development Goal 8, The global partnership for development: Time to deliver*. MDG Gap Task Force Report 2011. New York: United Nations.

United Nations Development Programme (UNDP). (2016). *Trends in the Human Development Index, 1990–2014*. United Nations Development Programme (UNDP). Retrieved from http://hdr.undp.org/en/composite/trends

United Nations Development Programme and World Health Organization (UNDP & WHO). (2009). *The energy access situation in developing countries: A review focusing on the least developed countries and Sub-Saharan Africa*. New York: United Nations.

United Nations Framework Convention on Climate Change (UNFCCC). (2007). *United Framework Convention on Climate Change—Additional proposals from Parties—UNFCCC, elements of a protocol to the United Nations Framework Convention on Climate Change, presented by Brazil in response to the Berlin Mandate.* Retrieved from http://unfccc.int/cop5 /resource/docs/1997/agbm/misco1a3.htm

World Energy Outlook (WEO). (2002). *World energy outlook.* Retrieved from http://www .worldenergyoutlook.org/media/weowebsite/2011/weo2011_energy_for_all.pdf

World Energy Outlook (WEO). (2011, October). *Energy for all: Financing access for the poor.* Oslo: World Energy Outlook.

World Resources Institute. (2016). *CAIT climate data explorer,.* Retrieved from http://cait.wri .org/

Yadoo, A., & Cruickshank, H. (2012). The role for low carbon electrification technologies in poverty reduction and climate change strategies: A focus on renewable energy mini-grids with case studies in Nepal, Peru and Kenya. *Energy Policy, 42,* 591–602.

PART V

ENERGY
AND PUBLICS

PUBLIC perceptions, their expression in politics and the market, and their emergent effects have more relevance to energy-society relations than they are generally given credit for. Their impact results not only from their consumption decisions; they are, after all, citizens as well as consumers. Public views have had a notable influence on energy policymaking in many circumstances, sometimes pushing for greener, more sustainable energy consumption options; at other times they do not necessarily favor improvements in sustainability, energy conservation, and efficiency.

As Ana Delicado makes clear in Chapter 18, all energy generation infrastructure, whether in the form of a coal mine or a wind farm, must necessarily be located somewhere, leading to impacts on real places and peoples across the globe. Local peoples and politics will play a substantial role in present and future energy-society relations, including the potential for a renewable energy transition. Delicado confirms that local opposition cannot be reduced to the NIMBY ("not in my backyard") syndrome. Those opposed may well have strong climate and environmental predispositions, and yet have very reasonable concerns about specific renewable energy facilities. By the same token, supporters can have a variety of reasons for their support, not all of them "green." Finding resolutions to local conflicts will require closer attention to the contextual factors that affect support.

In Chapter 19, Sampsa Hyysalo and Jouni K. Juntunen uncover another important and yet unrecognized role of consumers/citizens. Renewable energy is often touted for its decentralized character, yet Hyysalo and Juntunen show that this decentralization goes much further than originally recognized. While technological innovations are often attributed to "expertise," we have users—tinkerers and backyard scientists—to thank for creating the very innovations that have allowed for the upscaling of many renewable energy technologies. The real strengths and weaknesses of any tool, after all, are revealed not in the laboratory, but in its use in everyday life.

Chapter 20 closes off this section on a cautionary note. Aleksandra Wagner turns our attention to the role of media, a prevailing source for discourse in every household. According to Wagner, while the political influence of publics may indeed be substantial, the positions and actions they take are reflections of the discursive frames and narratives to which they are subjected. Discourses in public spheres matter to policy and practice, and media has a fundamental influence over those discourses. Wagner notes that the tendency among mainstream mass media institutions to privilege "expertise" discourse can exclude many citizens from engaging in dialogues about energy. Those narratives that dominate the airwaves thus serve to narrow debates and future options to the status quo. Proponents of alternative narratives feel compelled to frame their positions to fit within a dominant economic narrative; as a result, their potential to support a transition in our energy systems currently remains limited.

CHAPTER 18

LOCAL RESPONSES TO RENEWABLE ENERGY DEVELOPMENT

ANA DELICADO

INTRODUCTION

THERE is a wide variation on how local communities respond to reneable energy developments. The following two cases are illustrative.

Case 1

In the late fall of 2015, a small town in North Carolina (United States) made the news all around the world in both conventional and social media. At a town meeting to discuss the construction of a solar farm, residents showed a fierce opposition, sustained on arguments such as that solar panels caused cancer, sucked away the sun from the town, or disrupted photosynthesis. Commentators across the globe made fun of these arguments, denouncing them as irrational and anti-scientific.[1]

However, David Roberts published an insightful piece[2] on the online platform *Vox* showing how this opposition was far from unreasonable and reflected severe economic and social changes, such as the decline of traditional activities (farming), high unemployment, and depopulation, that were eroding the community. Solar farms (three of which were already surrounding the town) were seen as a symbol of these changes. They brought little to no benefit to residents and were seen as impositions from outsiders intent only on extracting profit.

Case 2

At the beginning of 2016, an unfavorable Environmental Impact Assessment Decision rejected the application for the construction of a wind farm in the Torre de Moncorvo municipality in Portugal. After strong complaints from environmental nongovernmental organizations (ENGOs), national authorities upheld their decision on the negative impacts on protected areas, namely the UNESCO classified wine region of Douro and Natura 2000 areas. The promoter vowed to fight this decision in the courts, and local authorities expressed their indignation. The wind farm would bring a direct revenue of €6 million to local authorities and would pay rent to 400 smallholders. According to a television news report, the mayor stated, "we cannot pour down the river 92 million euros just because there might be something [Bonelli eagles] there." A local resident complained, "this [decision] only harms the village. We would have development, we would have jobs, we would have roads. It's the population that will lose. Because of a joke. In my opinion, we don't see here any bats or birds here. It's the population that will lose."[3]

These two cases highlight some of the issues that have made opposition and support for renewable energy development one of the most studied themes in the field of energy and society. The transition to a sustainable energy system, vital for mitigating climate change, demands the replacement of fossil fuel energy with renewable sources, on par with substantial improvements in energy efficiency. However, renewable energy generation requires facilities that, with current technology, take up space, consume resources, transform the landscape, and have some environmental impacts. Their siting is bound to affect communities and thus often gives rise to controversies and disputes.

This chapter discusses the drivers for both opposition and support to local renewable energy developments. Based on the extensive scientific literature published on this issue, as well as the author's own research, it examines the arguments put forward to justify discourses and actions, the local actors that are involved in the controversies, and the results achieved in terms of hindering or promoting renewable energy.

It focuses mainly on wind and solar power, which combined make up 85% of the renewable power capacity in the world in 2015, excluding hydropower (REN21, 2016). It leaves out of the discussion bio-power and geothermal power, since these renewable sources are somewhat less controversial and generate different kinds of impacts. It also excludes hydropower, which has a much longer history, as well as a fairly contested status within energy debates; although it is indisputably a renewable source of energy, its extensive environmental impacts often prevent its classification as sustainable, and it is left out of renewable energy targets in some countries (Frey & Linke, 2002).

The following section of this chapter is devoted to introducing the subject, in particular the apparent mismatch between global support and local opposition to renewables. Next, the most common reasons for opposing wind and solar farms are discussed. The subsequent section explores the reasons that some communities support and even embrace renewable energy developments. A brief conclusion wraps up the discussion.

THE RENEWABLES PARADOX?

Several studies (Afonso & Mendes, 2010; Barry et al., 2008; Bell et al., 2005; Breukers & Wolsink, 2007; Devine-Wright, 2005a; Haggett & Futák-Campbel, 2011; Walker, 1995; Wustenhangen et al., 2007) point to an apparent paradox, in which overwhelming public support for renewable energy at the national level is matched by strong opposition to the siting of energy infrastructures at the local level. International surveys, as well as other published research (Aitken, 2009; Ek, 2005; Wolsink, 2007b), confirm high levels of support for renewable energy. For instance, the latest Eurobarometer survey to address energy and climate issues (European Commission, 2015) shows that 91% of Europeans are in favor of government-set targets to increase the use of renewable energy by 2030. However, some authors have pointed out that public opinion on renewable energy is not homogeneous: there are many "publics," and attitudes vary across social groups, as well as according to the type of renewable energy (with solar being somewhat less contentious than wind) (Ek, 2005; Walker, 1995). Additionally, there is no empirical evidence suggesting a connection between attitudes toward (local) wind farms and attitudes toward renewable energy in general (Ek, 2005; Eltham, Harrison & Allen, 2008; Warren et al., 2005).

This ambivalence is also noticeable in the attitudes and practices of ENGOs, in what Warren et al. (2005) have labeled a "green on green" controversy: "in the case of wind power there are strong 'green' arguments on both sides of the debate. Some environmentalists advocate wind farms because of their 'clean energy' credentials, while others oppose them because of their landscape impacts. Still others are caught awkwardly in the middle, supporting renewable energy in principle but opposing specific wind farm proposals" (Warren et al., 2005, p. 854). This tension within the environmental movement has been confirmed in several other studies (Bell et al., 2005; Breukers & Wolsink, 2007; Cowell, 2010; Delicado et al., 2014; Loring, 2007; Toke, 2005; Toke et al., 2008; Walker, 1995; Wolsink, 2000, 2007a).

Nevertheless, it has yet to be assessed in what measure local opposition plays a role in preventing the development of renewable energy. Given the swift development of renewable energy in some European countries, such as Austria (responsible for 70% of gross electricity consumption), Sweden (63%), Portugal (52%), and Denmark (48%) (EUROSTAT, 2016), but not in others, such as The Netherlands (10%) and the United Kingdom (18%), some authors (Bell et al., 2005; Breukers & Wolsink, 2007; Cowell, 2010; Walker, 1995; Wolsink, 2000, 2007a) attribute varying degrees of success in part to the presence or absence of local support for wind or solar farms. For instance, Van der Horst and Toke (2010) demonstrate that most planning applications for wind farms in the United Kingdom are rejected due to local objections. However, the Portuguese case (Delicado et al., 2014) shows that despite strong opposition to wind farms in the planning stage (through participation in public consultations during Environmental Impact Assessments), this has not prevented a high rate of approval and considerable development of the sector in the country in the past few decades.

Therefore, the connection between local opposition to renewable energy infrastructures and a less successful transition to a sustainable energy system is far from linear. Many other factors are at play, and public policies, as well as economic aspects, may be far more relevant for explaining the development of renewable energy (Bell et al., 2005; Breukers & Wolsink, 2007; Delicado et al., 2014; Jobert et al., 2007; Ringel, 2006; Toke, 2005; Toke et al., 2008; Wolsink, 2000).

Furthermore, few studies address the extent of local opposition or support for energy facilities in each country. The vast majority of literature in this field consists of case studies of localized wind or solar farms, exploring the processes, actors, and justifications that drive social action in these matters. In fact, it can be said that these case studies focus much more frequently on controversies and dissent than on consensus and support for renewable energy infrastructures. This in turn may lead to a somewhat skewed perception that resistance to wind and solar farms is far more widespread than it actually is. There may be a social research bias toward what can be construed as a "social problem," in need of "fixing" due to the urgency of the climate change threat, thus paying much less attention to success stories. Aitken (2009, p. 53) even points out that "the underlying 'pro-wind power' position in this literature could prevent a meaningful engagement with public responses towards wind power developments."

This chapter attempts to redress this imbalance, by looking into both the arguments that justify opposition to and support for wind and solar farms. Though it is crucial to understand the barriers that may impede the much-needed growth of renewable energy, it is also important to look into what drives communities to welcome wind and solar farms and even to protest when planning applications are rejected.

MANY REASONS TO SAY NO TO RENEWABLES

Early studies about wind and solar farms were quick to draw from a tried and tested hypothesis to explain opposition to their construction: the NIMBY "syndrome" (Dear, 1992). The acronym has been used by both policymakers and planners, as well as social researchers, "to describe opponents of new developments who recognise that a facility is needed but are opposed to its siting within their locality" (Burningham, 2000, p. 56). It began to be used to describe protests against the location of waste deposits and other hazardous facilities and has a clear pejorative connotation of "limited and self-interested responses to local environmental change" (Burningham, 2000, p. 60). It is used to withdraw legitimacy from opponents, by labeling them as selfish, irrational, and ignorant.

Although some studies on renewable energy still use this concept (see, for instance, Botetzagias et al., 2013; Fridolfsson & Tangerås, 2013; Groothuis et al., 2008; Ribeiro et al., 2014), many more have a critical stance toward its use. Several authors (Devine-Wright, 2009; Ek, 2005; Van der Horst, 2007; Wolsink 2000, 2007b) looked into evidence from survey data and found little indication that proximity to wind farms had a bearing on attitudes toward them. Warren et al. (2005, p. 866) even found evidence for an "inverse NIMBY" syndrome, whereby those with wind farms in their "backyard" strongly support the technology.

Devine-Wright (2005b) highlights the multidimensionality of public perceptions on renewable energy facilities and draws attention to the role of social identities, social representations, and social networks in generating attitudes. Van der Horst (2007) shows how opponents' arguments can be reasonable and founded in genuine concerns and impacts. Wolsink (2007a) provides evidence that supporters can also have selfish motives. Ellis et al. (2007) realized that critics of renewable development often share the same environmental and climate mitigation values as supporters. Other authors point out that NIMBY approaches focus exclusively on the public and ignore the role played by institutional actors: "No attention is given in such an account to what developers and technology promoters are doing and saying, and how decision processes are structured and enacted" (Walker et al., 2011, p. 4).

Place Attachment

Devine-Wright (2009) was the first to propose an alternative framework to the NIMBY "syndrome" for understanding opposition to renewable energy that has since gained some traction among scholars in this field. The concept of "place attachment," created by human geographers but increasingly used in environmental psychology and related sciences (Lewicka, 2011), refers to "a positive emotional connection with familiar locations such as the home or neighbourhood" (Devine-Wright, 2009, p. 427) and can be used to explain local opposition "as a form of place-protective action, which arises when new developments disrupt pre-existing emotional attachments and threaten place-related identity processes" (Devine-Wright, 2009, p. 426). It is usually connected to the place of residence, but areas that have symbolic value may also generate feelings of attachment from those who live far away (Carlisle et al., 2014). Devine-Wright (2005b) proposes that it is not physical proximity to the facilities, but rather community perceptions of the turbines and social influence that have a bearing on local attitudes. A case study of a proposed offshore wind farm shows that it threatens the identity of residents: "opposition arises from nature/industry symbolic contradictions: between a place represented in terms of scenic beauty that provides a restorative environment for residents and visitors, and a wind farm that will industrialise the area and 'fence' in the bay" (Devine-Wright & Howes, 2010, p. 271). Other authors have also used the concept of place attachment to explore opposition to wind farms (Delicado et al., 2016; Lombard & Ferreira, 2013; Swofford & Slattery 2010) and solar power plants (Brewer at al. 2015; Carlisle et al., 2014) in different countries.

Landscape Concerns

Closely connected to place attachment is the value attributed to landscape and the notion that renewable energy developments somehow deplete that value. Countless case studies have demonstrated how landscape concerns (or seascape, in the case of offshore wind farms) and scenic impact are at the forefront of arguments of anti-renewables campaigners (Carlisle et al., 2014; De la Hoz et al., 2013; Delicado et al., 2016; Devine-Wright & Howes, 2010; Jolivet & Heiskanen 2010; Lombard & Ferreira, 2013; Mason & Milbourne 2014; Pasqualetti, 2000, 2001; Warren et al., 2005; Wolsink, 2010; Woods, 2003). As Warren et al. (2005) synthesise, "The landscape impacts of windfarms are exacerbated by the fact that the locations with the highest wind resource are often precisely those exposed upland areas which are valued for their scenic qualities and which are often ecologically sensitive. Opponents not only highlight the scenic impact of the turbines themselves, but also emphasize the visual impacts of the associated construction and upgrades to the electricity transmission grid. Further, they assert that the landscape impacts of windfarms will damage tourism" (Warren et al., 2005, p. 857).

Countries where landscape quality and preservation values are dominant and where landscape protection organizations are particularly active have higher rates of rejection of planned renewable developments (Breukers & Wolsink, 2007; Loring, 2007; Toke, 2005; Toke, Breukers, & Wolsink, 2008; Wolsink, 2007a, 2010). And yet, as shall be seen in the following, landscape can also be an argument in favor of wind and solar farms.

Opponents of wind and solar farms often claim that they spoil pristine natural environments, causing visual intrusion, not just because they are "machines in the garden," "out of place" technological artifacts, but also because they occupy large spaces, either vertically (wind farms) or horizontally (solar power plants), they require building other infrastructures (power lines, power stations), and they cast shadows (wind turbines) or cause glare (solar panels) (Jolivet & Heiskanen, 2010; Mulvaney, 2013; Rodriguez & Luque, 2010; Rodriguez et al., 2010; Warren et al., 2005). This is particularly acute when landscapes are considered to have an iconic value, such as local landmarks or places of cultural heritage (Afonso & Mendes, 2012; Delicado et al., 2016; Mulvaney, 2013; Rodriguez et al., 2010; Van der Horst, 2007; Wolsink, 2010). Renewable energy developments can also be seen as highly visible symbols of the decline of traditional rural activities, such as agriculture, and the "industrialization" or "mechanization" of rural landscapes (Afonso & Mendes, 2010; Devine-Wright & Howes, 2010; Rodriguez & Luque, 2010; Rodriguez et al., 2010; Woods, 2003). Curiously, several studies point out that it is the "newcomers" (such as second homeowners or retirees who have moved to the countryside), rather than the "natives" of these areas, who invoke these arguments (Anderson, 2013; Van der Horst & Vermeylen 2010). They are often "networked" or "vocal" minorities (Anderson, 2013; Bell et al., 2005; Bell et al., 2013; Carlisle et al., 2014; Ellis et al., 2007; Warren et al., 2005), whose social and economic capital awards them greater power in influencing planning decisions. Van der Horst and Toke (2010, p. 219) show how in more affluent areas in the United Kingdom the approval rate of wind farms is much lower, since "coalitions or special interest groups that are relatively privileged in terms of capital, be it social, human and/or financial, are better equipped to influence and shape the outcomes of the planning process than less organised local publics."

However, several studies demonstrate that resistance to wind and solar farms is higher during the planning stages and declines after their construction, when the actual visual impact is felt (Carlisle et al., 2014; Devine-Wright, 2005a; Pasqualetti, 2001; Van der Horst, 2007; Warren et al., 2005). And in order to overcome landscape concerns, several authors point out how the characteristics of turbines (number, height, color, location) can impact on visual perception (Devine-Wright, 2005a; Jolivet & Heiskanen, 2010; Pasquelatti, 2000; Walker & Cass, 2007; Wustenhangen et al., 2007). Torres Sibile et al. (2009) developed and tested an indicator to assess the magnitude of the objective aesthetic impact on the landscape caused by the installation of wind farms, in order to decrease the likelihood of rejection by populations. Nadai and Labussiére (2013) show how planning procedures based on visualization techniques ("iconographic practices") can succeed in abating local resistance. Ottinger (2013, p. 225) calls for the co-design between "socially conscious engineers" and local populations of "configuration of turbines compatible with the landscape and locals' sense of place."

Procedural and Distributive Justice

Non-acceptance of renewable energy developments is also closely connected to perceptions of injustice in terms of participation in the decision-making and of distribution of benefits. Whereas the literature clearly shows that procedural and distributive justice are crucial for successful planning and development of wind and solar farms (Carlisle et al., 2014; Devine-Wright, 2009; Hall et al., 2013; Wustehangen et al., 2007; Zoellner et al., 2008), several case studies reveal that this is still not a generalized practice.

Based on fieldwork in Australia, Gross (2007, p. 2727) ascertains that there is more resistance to wind farms when it is perceived that only part of the community benefits (for instance, in terms of renting out the land) and when the consultation process is seen as nonexistent or biased: "perceptions of fairness do influence how people perceive the legitimacy of the outcome, and that a fairer process will increase acceptance of the outcome." The author compiles a list of suggestions for increasing legitimacy, which include starting the consultation process early, providing enough impartial information, holding meetings open only to residents and where everyone has a chance to speak, and explaining clearly the impacts on the community. Also in Australia, Anderson (2013) analyzes a case where deficiencies in the public participation process, which was not adequately publicized and did not address community concerns, raised a social network of resistance, with high social capital, that was able to prevent the construction of a wind farm.

Aitken (2009) examines the controversy around a wind farm in Scotland, describing how planning policy devaluates public participation, placing all trust on expert knowledge, even though the technical evidence provided was mostly generalized and did not address local concerns. Opposition campaigners expressed several complaints about the consultation process (access to information, time limitations, absence of a public hearing). A set of case studies in Portugal (Delicado et al., 2014, 2016) also identified severe limitations to public participation in decision-making regarding energy facilities, but a centralized, bureaucratized tradition of administration prevailed over local opposition and planning approval rates were high.

Bringing together this section and the previous one, Mason and Milbourne (2014, p. 106) develop the concept of "landscape justice," a form of justice that is "attentive to space, time, materiality, affect, scale, participation and value." Based on a case study of opposition to a wind farm in Wales (UK), the authors show how "a lack of meaningful participation appears to be the root of all injustices felt by anti-windfarm campaigners" (Mason and Milbourne, 2014, p. 110).

However, Jolivet and Heiskanen's study (2010) of a controversy regarding a proposal for a wind farm in France shows that participation is not a universal panacea for generating acceptance. Although ample opportunities for public consultation were given and the local community embraced the project (more on this case later), surrounding municipalities were not included in the process and their interests (heritage tourism) collided with the setting up of the wind farm, so they opposed the project and submitted a claim to the courts. Breukers and Wolsink (2007) and Bidwell (2013) also draw attention to participation as a means to explore mitigation options and not necessarily for persuading opponents.

Regarding distributive justice, opposition to renewable energy is based not only on an unfair distribution of benefits (see later discussion), but also on uneven distribution of losses. A common concern of residents near wind and solar farms is the devaluation of their property (Bell et al., 2013; Delicado et al., 2014; Devine-Wright & Howes, 2010; Firestone et al., 2015; Gross, 2007; Gulden, 2012; Krogh, 2011; Warren et al., 2005). Equally, local authorities and business owners often fear the impact of renewable energy developments on tourism, dreading that wind turbines or solar panels will deter tourists and jeopardize the local economy (Aitken, 2009; Delicado et al., 2014; Delicado et al., 2016; Devine-Wright & Howes, 2010; Frantál & Kunc 2011; Fridolfsson & Tangerås, 2013; Hall et al., 2013; Lombad & Ferreira, 2013; Nadai & Labussiere, 2010; Warren et al., 2005; Woods, 2003). Yenneti and Day (2016) examine the case of a solar power plant in India and how it reinforced preexisting inequalities by benefiting the more affluent upper castes and hindering the more vulnerable small farmers and shepherds.

Environmental and Health Impacts

Finally, opposition to wind and solar farms is also motivated by very tangible concerns about their impact on the environment and even on human health. Although renewable energies present far fewer risks than other sources, such as fossil fuels and nuclear energy, their effects over wildlife and human life are not negligible. Noise and vibration cause discomfort and can even lead to health problems in local residents (Firestone et al., 2015; Hall et al., 2013; Horner et al., 2012; Knopper & Olson, 2011; Krogh, 2011; McMurtry 2011; Philips, 2011). High-voltage power lines that are needed to connect renewable energy facilities to the grid carry their own risks, which are far from settled in the scientific community (Cotton & Devine-Wright, 2011; Linder, 1995). Water contamination can also be an issue (Aitken, 2009; Delicado et al., 2014).

Wind turbines are known to cause excess bird and bat mortality, which is particularly problematic in protected areas and habitats of at-risk species (Delicado et al., 2014;; Ellis et al., 2007; Lombard & Ferreira, 2013; Nadai & Labussiere, 2010; Sovacool, 2009; Sprague, 2011; Warren et al., 2005; Wolsink, 2010). The same can be said for solar farms, in the case of birds and reptiles (Mulvaney, 2013; Turney & Fthenakis 2011). Also, environmentalists argue that these facilities also disturb wildlife by opening routes into previously safeguarded natural spaces and cutting migration paths of wolves and other mammals (Delicado et al., 2014). Residents and ENGOs also express concerns with waste disposal of technological equipment once it reaches its end of life (Delicado et al., 2016; Mulvaney, 2013).

AND QUITE A FEW REASONS TO SAY
YES TO RENEWABLES

Though the literature is almost unanimous in devaluing NIMBY explanations for the opposition to renewable energy developments, the same cannot be said for its mirror syndrome, PIMBY ("please in my backyard"). Though references to it are far scarcer, some authors point out that some communities do welcome with open arms the opportunity to have wind and solar farms in their vicinity (Jobert et al., 2007; Stigka et al., 2014). Though the literature is far less extensive regarding support to renewable energy developments, two main drivers can be identified: economic rewards and landscape and environmental values.

Economic Rewards

By far the most common motivation for accepting renewables in the literature has to do with the income that wind and solar farms can bring to communities, which is particularly important in a context of crisis in rural areas. First, owners of the land where they are sited benefit from renting or selling their properties (Bell et al., 2013; Brunt & Spooner, 1998; Jobert et al., 2007; Warren et al., 2005). Wind turbines are compatible with agricultural practices such as animal husbandry, so farmers can keep their traditional activities and add an additional source of income (Anderson, 2013; Hall et al., 2013; Lombard & Ferreira, 2013). In the Portuguese case (Afonso & Mendes 2012; Delicado et al., 2016), traditional land-ownership practices are marked by the predominance of smallholdings, which means that usually several families benefit from having wind turbines. In some cases, renewable energy developments are sited in vacant land that is collectively owned (*baldios*) or is the property of the parish, which means that the income is managed by local authorities, in favor (hopefully) of the community. In several countries, renewable energy promotors are required by law to pay a percentage of the revenue to local authorities, which leads to mayors becoming strong supporters of wind and solar farms (Delicado et al., 2016; Fridolfsson & Tangerå, 2013; Pasqualetti, 2001; Walker et al., 2014).

However, going back to opposition to renewable energy development, this added income for some can also be a source of tension, when it is perceived as being not equitably distributed within the community (Delicado et al, 2016; Gross, 2007; Walker et al., 2014). Financial incentives can also be seen as a "bribe" to the community to accept something that is undesirable (Bell et al., 2005; Mason & Millbourne, 2014; Walker et al., 2014). Several studies found that communities often have an expectation of a reduction in electricity bills for putting up with a wind or solar farm in their vicinity and that expectation is usually not met, causing grievances (Delicado et al., 2016; Walker et al., 2014; Warren et al., 2005).

Community ownership of wind and solar farms is also considered as having a positive impact on acceptance (Bell et al., 2005; Breukers & Wolsink, 2007; Ek & Persson, 2014; Loring, 2007; Toke et al., 2008; Walker, 1995; Warren et al., 2005; Wolsink, 2007a, 2010; Wustenhagen et al., 2007). Local communities benefit directly, either from the electricity that is generated or from its income by selling power to the national grid. They can also be involved in the management, as well as having a say in the location and characteristics of the facility (highlighting again the importance of participation).

Second, renewable energy developments can have a positive impact on local employment (Carlisle et al., 2014; Delicado et al., 2016; del Rio and Burgillo 2009; Devine-Wright & Howes, 2010; Hall et al., 2013; Hillebrand et al., 2006; Moreno & Lopez, 2008; Sastresa et al., 2010; Walker et al., 2014). Although solar and wind farms require few permanent personnel for running and maintenance, in communities heavily affected by unemployment even that can make a difference. Also, during the construction stage more manpower (often less qualified) is needed and temporary jobs are created, which also generate revenue for local businesses (accommodation, meals). Furthermore, renewable energies can create additional jobs in connected industries (building or assemblage of solar panels and wind turbines, maintenance, electronics, and components). In parallel, some authors argue that renewable energy developments can have a positive impact on tourism, attracting more visitors, also benefiting the local economy (Delicado et al., 2016; Frantál & Kunc 2011; Frantál & Urbanková, 2017; Lilley et al., 2010).

Local support for renewable energy developments can even spur active protest against planning decisions that reject wind and solar farms. Afonso and Mendes (2010, 2012) examined the case of a proposed wind farm in a natural park in the northeastern tip of Portugal, in one of the poorest areas of the countryside that has been losing population at an accelerated rate. In 2007 the park's development plan required a public debate in which the issues of wind energy were discussed. Whereas park authorities straightforwardly rejected the possibility of including wind farms within the admissible uses of the natural park, the local authorities and population strongly supported this option. They envisioned the future wind farm as a solution for retaining population, generating economic benefits, and bringing innovation and development. The community objected to the official decision and showed their displeasure through small acts of resistance (such as preventing park officials from accessing some areas of the park). They argued that there were already dozens of wind turbines in the Spanish side, just a few feet away from the park border, so the visual and environmental impact was already there. This conflict echoed the distinct visions of the natural park between local residents and park administration already identified by Figueiredo (2008).

Landscape and Environmental Values

Despite the dominance of landscape preservation as an argument against renewable energy, wind and solar farms can also be perceived as an improvement in existing landscapes. This is particularly the case of landscapes perceived as already industrialized (often suffering the effects of deindustrialisation), such as mining areas, or those transformed by human intervention, such as planted forests. Communities see the arrival of renewables as symbols of progress and development or as an opportunity for mitigating industrial stigma by acquiring "green credentials" (Cowell, 2010; Delicado et al., 2016; Firestone et al., 2015; Jobert et al., 2007; Jolivet & Heiskanen 2010; Selman, 2010; Van der Horst, 2007; Warren et al., 2005; Wustenhagen et al., 2007; Zoellner et al., 2008).

Some case studies illustrate this more specifically. Krauss (2010) focused his study on two coastal regions of northern Germany, where landscapes had already been transformed by technology over the centuries (such as the construction of dikes). Familiarity with these technological transformations of nature led communities to actively embrace the wind turbines, as shown in the creation of community-owned wind farms. Furthermore, the land parallel to the dike lines was designated by the land-use plan as a building area for wind turbines. Rodriguez et al. (2010) show how solar farms in the south of Spain can contribute to landscape recovery in spoiled areas, already marked by extensive greenhouses, mining or industrial infrastructures, urban peripheries, or marshlands, or that are close to roads and railways. Jolivet and Heiskanen (2010) address the case of a wind farm in France supported by the local community because it fit the local industrial genealogy and was to be included in a touristic route of a scientific nature, which included deactivated mines.

Renewable energy can even contribute to the generation of a new local identity. Such is the case of a solar farm in the south of Portugal (Delicado et al., 2016): the village where it is situated adopted the brand "Land of the Sun," which appeared in commercial and official logos, a walking tourist route (that included the solar power plant), and even local folk songs.[4] There are cases where wind farms have become local tourist attractions, with walking paths and picnic areas, where families go to see the snow in the mountains in winter or to take wedding pictures (Delicado et al., 2016).

Residents that support renewable energy developments also base their stance in environmental values, such as contributing to fight climate change, to expand clean energy, and to safeguard the planet for future generations (Bidwell, 2013; Delicado et al., 2016; ; Ellis et al., 2007; Firestone et al., 2015; Van der Horst, 2007; Van der Horst & Vermillyen, 2010; Wolsink, 2010; Woods, 2003).

CONCLUSION

Support or opposition of local communities to renewable energy development is strongly contextual. Among the many drivers that influence how communities react to solar and wind farms, we can highlight the following:

- *The economic fabric of localities*: thriving rural communities may be less inclined to accept renewable energy than those that suffer from unemployment and decline of traditional activities and see renewable energy as a new source of revenue that might halt population hemorrhaging.
- *Social capital*: areas that attract affluent second homeowners or retirees are more prone to the generation of opposition movements, which usually have more resources and influence over planning decisions.
- *The characteristics of the renewable energy facilities*: type of energy generated, number and size of turbines or panels, impacts on the landscape and wildlife. The more conspicuous facilities usually generate more opposition.
- *Ownership of the facilities*: Wind and solar farms that are owned by the community or by local promoters tend to attract less resistance. As Wolsink (2000) suggests, opposition to wind farms usually focus on the people (outsiders) who want to build them, rather than on the turbines themselves.
- *Planning traditions and procedures*: transparency, access to information, and involvement of communities in decision-making are crucial for reducing resistance to renewable energy, but not all local or regional authorities enforce these measures.
- *Cultural conceptions of nature*: idyllic representations of rural environments as unspoiled nature usually come into collision with plans for introducing "artificial" artifacts such as turbines or solar panels, whereas acknowledgment that most landscapes have already been transformed by humans (through afforestation, agriculture, or construction) or visions of the rural landscape as a productive space facilitate acceptance (Devine-Wright & Howes, 2010; Woods, 2003). These conceptions, of course, vary according to the kind of landscape where the facilities are sited (more industrial or more rural), but they are also socially constructed and dependent on cultural values and collective emotional attachments.

Thus, simple explanations, like the NIMBY syndrome, or one-size-fits all solutions do little to foster energy transitions. Understanding what is at stake in particular locations is crucial, and that can only be done through participatory engagements between promotors, authorities, and stakeholders.

Both positions often coexist in the same communities. Communities are made up of different kinds of people, from long-time residents to newcomers, from landowners to local authorities, from members of environmental conservation groups to business owners. Different kinds of people have different interests, concerns, and values. Power relations within the community often have a bearing on the planning decisions. Social and economic capital, on one hand, and political authority, on the other, can tip the scales in favor or against renewable energy infrastructures.

The chapter has aimed to demonstrate that we need to pay more attention to success stories, not just to controversies. Even though in some countries the least contentious locations for renewable energies are already taken and disputes are set to rise, the swift development of renewables in the past decade offers some hope for finding solutions to nurture acceptance. Improved technology, a more equitable distribution of benefits, and increased dialogue with citizens can be the key to a more sustainable future.

ACKNOWLEDGMENTS

This chapter is based on research funded by the Portuguese Foundation for Science and Technology (Ref. PTDC/CS-ECS/118877/2010) and the work developed within COST Action TU1401 RELY Renewable Energy and Landscape Quality.

NOTES

1. See, for instance, Todd Miller's piece, "Woodland, N.C. saves earth from dreaded sun sucking solar cells," *Huffington Post*, December 29, 2015, http://www.huffingtonpost.com /todd-r-miller/woodland-nc-saves-earth-f_b_8869968.html
2. David Roberts, "The North Carolina town that's scared of solar panels, revisited," *Vox*, December 18, 2015, http://www.vox.com/2015/12/18/10519644/north-carolina-solar-town
3. Sílvia Brandão, "Autarquias contra chumbo de parque eólico de Moncorvo," *RTP*, February 2, 2016, http://www.rtp.pt/noticias/economia/autarquias-contra-chumbo-de-parque -eolico-de-moncorvo_v893101
4. "So many hours, so many days/So much sun, a vastness/To renew the energies/So many hours, so many days/It's the best solution/Amareleja you are talked about/In heat you have no equal/Beautiful blessed land/Amareleja you are talked about/For the power plant is born." Lyrics to a local folk song about the solar power plant.

REFERENCES

Afonso, A. I., & Mendes, C. (2010). Energía eólica y paisajes protegidos: Controversias en el parque natural de montesinhos. *Nimbus, 25–26*, 5–19.

Afonso, A. I., & Mendes, C. (2012). Wind power in the Portuguese landscape: global concerns and local costs. In G. Welz, F. Sperling, and E. M. Blum (Eds.), *Negotiating environmental conflicts: Local communities, global policies* (pp. 127–142). Frankfurt: Goethe-University.

Aitken, M. (2009). Wind Power planning controversies and the construction of "expert" and "lay" knowledges. *Science as Culture, 18*(1), 47–64.

Anderson, C. (2013). The networked minority: How a small group prevailed in a local windfarm conflict. *Energy Policy, 58,* 1–12.

Barry, J., Ellis, G., & Robinson, C. (2008). Cool rationalities and hot air : A rhetorical approach to understanding debates on renewable energy. *Global Environmental Politics, 8*(2), 67–98.

Bell, D., Gray, T., & Haggett, C. (2005). The 'social gap' in wind farm siting decisions: Explanations and policy responses. *Environmental Politics, 14*(4), 460–477.

Bell, D., Gray, T., Haggett, C., & Swaffield, J. (2013). Re-visiting the "social gap": Public opinion and relations of power in the local politics of wind energy. *Environmental Politics, 22*(1), 115–135.

Bidwell, D. (2013). The role of values in public beliefs and attitudes towards commercial wind energy. *Energy Policy, 58,* 189–199.

Botetzagias, I., Malesios, C., Kolokotroni, A., & Moysiadis, Y. (2013). The role of NIMBY in opposing the siting of wind farms: Evidence from Greece. *Journal of Environmental Planning and Management, 58*(2), 229–251.

Breukers, S., & Wolsink, M. (2007). Wind power implementation in changing institutional landscapes: An international comparison. *Energy Policy, 35*(5), 2737–2750.

Brewer, J., Ames, D. P., Solan, D., Lee, R., & Carlisle, J. (2015). Using GIS analytics and social preference data to evaluate utility-scale solar power site suitability. *Renewable Energy, 81,* 825–836.

Brunt, A., & Spooner, D., 1998. The development of wind power in Denmark and the UK. *Energy and Environment, 9*(3), 279–296.

Burningham, K. (2000). Using the Language of NIMBY : A topic for research, not an activity for researchers. *Local Environment: The International Journal of Justice and Sustainability, 5*(1), 55–67.

Carlisle, J. E., Kane, S. L., Solan, D., & Joe, J. C. (2014). Support for solar energy: Examining sense of place and utility-scale development in California. *Energy Research and Social Science, 3,* 124–130.

Cotton, M., & Devine-Wright, P. (2011). NIMBYism and community consultation in electricity transmission network planning. In P. Devine-Wright (Ed.), *Renewable energy and the public: From NIMBY to participation* (pp. 115–128). London: Earthscan.

Cowell, R. (2010). Wind power, landscape and strategic, spatial planning: The construction of "acceptable locations" in Wales. *Land Use Policy, 27*(2), 222–232.

De la Hoz, J., Martín, H., Martins, B., Matas, J., & Miret, J. (2013). Evaluating the impact of the administrative procedure and the landscape policy on grid connected PV systems (GCPVS) on-floor in Spain in the period 2004–2008: To which extent a limiting factor? *Energy Policy, 63,* 147–167.

Dear, M. (1992). Understanding and overcoming the NIMBY syndrome. *Journal of the American Planning Association, 58*(3), 288–300.

del Río, P., & Burguillo, M. (2009). An empirical analysis of the impact of renewable energy deployment on local sustainability. *Renewable and Sustainable Energy Reviews, 13*(6–7), 1314–1325.

Delicado, A., Figueiredo, E., & Silva, L. (2016). Community perceptions of renewable energies in Portugal: Impacts on environment, landscape and local development. *Energy Research and Social Science, 13,* 84–93.

Delicado, A., Junqueira, L., Fonseca, S., Truninger, M., Horta, A., & Figueiredo, E. (2014). Not in anyone's backyard? Civil society attitudes towards wind power at the national and local levels in Portugal. *Science and Technology Studies*, 27(2), 49–71.

Devine-Wright, P. (2005a). Beyond NIMBYism: Towards an integrated framework for understanding public perceptions of wind wnergy. *Wind Energy*, 8(2), 125–139.

Devine-Wright, P. (2005b). Local aspects of UK renewable energy development: exploring public beliefs and policy implications. *Local Environment*, 10(1), 57–69.

Devine-Wright, P. (2009). Rethinking NIMBYism: The role of place attachment and place identity in explaining place-protective action. *Journal of Community and Applied Social Psychology*, 441, 426–441.

Devine-Wright, P., & Howes, Y. (2010). Disruption to place attachment and the protection of restorative environments: A wind energy case study. *Journal of Environmental Psychology*, 30(3), 271–280.

Ek, K. (2005). Public and private attitudes towards 'green' electricity: The case of Swedish wind power. *Energy Policy*, 33(13), 1677–1689.

Ek, K., & Persson, L. (2014). Wind farms—Where and how to place them? A choice experiment approach to measure consumer preferences for characteristics of wind farm establishments in Sweden. *Ecological Economics*, 105, 193–203.

Ellis, G., Barry, J., & Robinson, C. (2007). Many ways to say "no," different ways to say "yes": Applying Q-methodology to understand public acceptance of wind farm proposals. *Journal of Environmental Planning and Management*, 50(4), 517–551.

Eltham, D. C., Harrison, G. P., & Allen, S. J. (2008). Change in public attitudes towards a Cornish wind farm: Implications for planning. *Energy Policy*, 36(1), 23–33.

European Commission. (2015). *Special Eurobarometer 435 climate change*. Brussels: European Commission.

EUROSTAT. (2016). Electricity generated from renewable sources, Table tsdcc330. Retrieved from http://ec.europa.eu/eurostat/tgm/table.do?tab=tableandinit=1andlanguage=enandpc ode=tsdcc330andplugin=1

Figueiredo, E. (2008). Quiet struggles: Conflicts between residents, visitors and protected and recreational areas' administrations. A. Raschi & S. Trampetti (Eds.), *Proceedings of the MMV4 The Fourth International Conference on Monitoring and Management of Visitor Flows in Recreational and Protected Areas* (pp. 26–32). Montecatini Terme, Italy.

Firestone, J., Bates, A., & Knapp, L. (2015). See me, feel me, touch me, heal me: Wind turbines, culture, landscapes, and sound impressions. *Land Use Policy*, 46, 241–249.

Frantál, B., & Kunc, J. (2011). Wind turbines in tourism landscapes. *Annals of Tourism Research*, 38(2), 499–519.

Frantál, B., & Urbánková, R. (2017). Energy tourism: An emerging field of study. *Current Issues in Tourism*, 20(13), 1395–1412.

Frey, G. W., & Linke, D. M. (2002). Hydropower as a renewable and sustainable energy resource meeting global energy challenges in a reasonable way. *Energy Policy*, 30(14), 1261–1265.

Fridolfsson, S.-O., & Tangerås, T. P. (2013). A reexamination of renewable electricity policy in Sweden. *Energy Policy*, 58, 57–63.

Groothuis, P. A., Groothuis, J. D., & Whitehead, J. C. (2008). Green vs. green: Measuring the compensation required to site electrical generation windmills in a viewshed. *Energy Policy*, 36(4), 1545–1550.

Gross, C. (2007). Community perspectives of wind energy in Australia: The application of a justice and community fairness framework to increase social acceptance. *Energy Policy*, 35(5), 2727–2736.

Gulden, W. E. (2012). A review of the current evidence regarding industrial wind turbines and property values from a homeowner's perspective. *Bulletin of Science, Technology and Society*, 31(5), 363–368.

Haggett, C., & Futák-Campbell, B. (2011). Tilting at windmills? Using discourse analysis to understand the attitude-behaviour gap in renewable energy conflicts. *Mechanism of Economic Regulation*, 51, 207–220.

Hall, N., Ashworth, P., & Devine-Wright, P. (2013). Societal acceptance of wind farms: Analysis of four common themes across Australian case studies. *Energy Policy*, 58, 200–208.

Hillebrand, B., Buttermann, H. G., Behringer, J. M., & Bleuel, M. (2006). The expansion of renewable energies and employment effects in Germany. *Energy Policy*, 34(18), 3484–3494.

Horner, B., Jeffery, R. D., & Krogh, C. M. E. (2012). Literature reviews on wind turbines and health: Are they enough?" *Bulletin of Science, Technology and Society*, 31(5), 399–413.

Jobert, A., Laborgne, P., & Mimler, S. (2007). Local acceptance of wind energy: Factors of success identified in French and German case studies. *Energy Policy*, 35(5), 2751–2760.

Jolivet, E., & Heiskanen, E. (2010). Blowing against the wind: An exploratory application of actor network theory to the analysis of local controversies and participation processes in wind energy. *Energy Policy*, 38(11), 6746–6754.

Knopper, L. D., & Ollson, C. A. (2011). Health effects and wind turbines: A review of the literature. *Environmental Health : A Global Access Science Source*, 10(1), 78.

Krauss, W. (2010). The "Dingpolitik" of wind energy in northern German landscapes: An ethnographic case study. *Landscape Research*, 35(2), 195–208.

Krogh, C. M. E. (2011). Industrial wind turbine development and loss of social justice? *Bulletin of Science, Technology and Society*, 31(4), 321–333.

Lewicka, M. (2011). Place attachment: How far have we come in the last 40 years? *Journal of Environmental Psychology*, 31(3), 207–230.

Lilley, M., Firestone, J., & Kempton, W. (2010). The effect of wind power installations on coastal tourism. *Energies*, 3(1), 1–22.

Linder, S. H. (1995). Contending discourses in the electric and magnetic fields controversy: The social construction of EMF risk as a public problem. *Policy Sciences*, 28(2), 209–230.

Lombard, A., & Ferreira, S. (2013). Residents' attitudes to proposed wind farms in the West Coast region of South Africa: A social perspective from the South. *Energy Policy*, 66, 390–399.

Loring, J. M. (2007). Wind energy planning in England, Wales and Denmark: Factors influencing project success. *Energy Policy*, 35(4), 2648–2660.

Mason, K., & Milbourne, P. (2014). Constructing a "landscape justice" for windfarm development: The case of Nant Y Moch, Wales. *Geoforum*, 53, 104–115.

McMurtry, R. Y. (2011). Toward a case definition of adverse health effects in the environs of industrial wind turbines: Facilitating a clinical diagnosis. *Bulletin of Science, Technology and Society*, 31(4), 316–320.

Moreno, B., & López, A. J. (2008). The effect of renewable energy on employment: The case of Asturias (Spain). *Renewable and Sustainable Energy Reviews*, 12(3), 732–751.

Mulvaney, D. (2013). Opening the black box of solar energy technologies: Exploring tensions between innovation and environmental justice. *Science as Culture*, 22(2), 230–237.

Mulvaney, K. K., Woodson, P., & Prokopy, L. S. (2013). Different shades of green: a case study of support for wind farms in the rural Midwest. *Environmental Management*, 51(5), 1012–1024.

Nadai, A., & Labussiere, O. (2010). Birds, wind and the making of wind power landscapes in Aude, southern France. *Landscape Research*, 35(2), 209–233.

Nadaï, A., & Labussière, O. (2013). Playing with the line, channelling multiplicity: Wind power planning in the Narbonnaise (Aude, France). *Environment and Planning D: Society and Space*, 31(1), 116–139.

Ottinger, G. (2013). The winds of change: environmental justice in energy transitions. *Science as Culture*, 22(2), 222–229.

Pasqualetti, M. J. (2000). Morality, space, and the power of wind-energy landscapes. *Geographical Review*, 90(3), 381.

Pasqualetti, M. J. (2001). Wind energy landscapes: Society and technology in the California Desert. *Society and Natural Resources*, 14(8), 689–699.

Phillips, C. V. (2011). Properly interpreting the epidemiologic evidence about the health effects of industrial wind turbines on nearby residents. *Bulletin of Science, Technology and Society*, 31(4), 303–315.

REN21. (2016). *Renewables 2016: Global status report*. Paris: REN21.

Ribeiro, F., Ferreira, P., Araújo, M., & Braga, A. C. (2014). Public opinion on renewable energy technologies in Portugal. *Energy*, 69, 39–50.

Ringel, M. (2006). Fostering the use of renewable energies in the European Union: The race between feed-in tariffs and green certificates. *Renewable Energy*, 31(1), 1–17.

Rodriguez, E. B., & Luque, D. H. (2010). Energías renovables y paisaje en Castilla y Leon: Estudio de caso. *Nimbus*, 25–26, 21–42.

Rodríguez, M. M., Martín, R. L., & Roselló, M. J. P. (2010). Las plantas fotovoltaicas en el paisaje. tipificación de impactos y directrices de integración paisagística. *Nimbus*, 25–26, 129–154.

Sastresa, E. L., Usón, A. A., Bribián, I. Z., & Scarpellini, S. (2010). Local impact of renewables on employment: Assessment methodology and case study. *Renewable and Sustainable Energy Reviews*, 14(2), 679–690.

Selman, P. (2010). Learning to love the landscapes of carbon-neutrality. *Landscape Research*, 35(2), 157–171.

Sovacool, B. K. (2009). Contextualizing avian mortality: A preliminary appraisal of bird and bat fatalities from wind, fossil-fuel, and nuclear electricity. *Energy Policy*, 37(6), 2241–2248.

Sprague, T., Harrington, M. E., & Krogh, C. M. E. (2011). Birds and bird habitat: What are the risks from industrial wind turbine exposure?" *Bulletin of Science, Technology and Society*, 31(5), 377–388.

Stigka, E., Paravantis, J., & Mihalakakou, G. (2014). An analysis of public attitudes towards renewable energy in Western Greece. *Renewable and Sustainable Energy Reviews*, 32, 100–106.

Swofford, J., & Slattery, M. (2010). Public attitudes of wind energy in Texas: Local communities in close proximity to wind farms and their effect on decision-making." *Energy Policy*, 38, 2508–2519.

Toke, D. (2005). Explaining wind power planning outcomes: Some findings from a study in England and Wales." *Energy Policy*, 33, 1527–1539.

Toke, D., Breukers, S., & Wolsink, M. (2008). Wind power deployment outcomes: How can we account for the differences? *Renewable and Sustainable Energy Reviews*, 12(4), 1129–1147.

Torres Sibille, A. del C., Cloquell-Ballester, V.-A., & Darton, R. (2009). Development and validation of a multicriteria indicator for the assessment of objective aesthetic impact of wind farms. *Renewable and Sustainable Energy Reviews*, 13(1), 40–66.

Turney, D., & Fthenakis, V. (2011). Environmental impacts from the installation and operation of large-scale solar power plants. *Renewable and Sustainable Energy Reviews, 15*(6), 3261–3270.

Van der Horst, D. (2007). NIMBY or not? Exploring the relevance of location and the politics of voiced opinions in renewable energy siting controversies. *Energy Policy, 35*(5), 2705–2714.

Van der Horst, D., & Toke, D. (2010). Exploring the landscape of wind farm developments: Local area characteristics and planning process outcomes in rural England. *Land Use Policy, 27*(2), 214–221.

Van der Horst, D., & Vermeylen, S. (2011). Rights to landscape and the global moral economy of carbon. *Landscape Research, 36*(4), 455–470.

Walker, B. J. A., Wiersma, B., & Bailey, E. (2014). Community benefits, framing and the social acceptance of offshore wind farms: An experimental study in England. *Energy Research and Social Science, 3*, 46–54.

Walker, G. (1995). Renewable energy and the public. *Land Use Policy, 12*(1), 49–59.

Walker, G., et al. (2011). Symmetries, expectations, dynamics and contexts: a framework for understanding public engagement with RE projects. In P. Devine-Wright (Ed.), *Renewable energy and the public: From NIMBY to participation* (pp. 1–14). London: Earthscan.

Walker, G., & Cass, N. (2007). Carbon reduction, "the public" and renewable energy: engaging with socio-technical configurations. *Area, 39*(4), 458–469.

Warren, C., Lumsden, C., O'Dowd, S., & Birnie, R. (2005). Green on green": Public perceptions of wind power in Scotland and Ireland. *Journal of Environmental Planning and Management, 48*(6), 853–875.

Wolsink, M. (2000). Wind power and the NIMBY-myth: Institutional capacity and the limited significance of public support. *Renewable Energy, 21*(1), 49–64.

Wolsink, M. (2007a). Planning of renewables schemes: Deliberative and fair decision-making on landscape issues instead of reproachful accusations of non-cooperation. *Energy Policy, 35*(5), 2692–2704.

Wolsink, M. (2007b). Wind power implementation: The nature of public attitudes: Equity and fairness instead of "backyard motives." *Renewable and Sustainable Energy Reviews, 11*(6), 1188–1207.

Wolsink, M. (2010). Near-shore wind power: Protected seascapes, environmentalists' attitudes, and the technocratic planning perspective. *Land Use Policy, 27*(2), 195–203.

Woods, M. (2003). Conflicting environmental visions of the rural: Windfarm development in Mid Wales." *Sociologia Ruralis, 43*(3), 271–288.

Wustenhagen, R., Wolsink, M., & Burer, M. (2007). Social acceptance of renewable energy innovation: An introduction to the concept. *Energy Policy, 35*(5), 2683–2691.

Yenneti, K., & Day, R. (2016). Distributional justice in solar energy implementation in India: The case of Charanka solar park. *Journal of Rural Studies, 46*, 35–46.

Zoellner, J., Schweizer-Ries, P., & Wemheuer, C. (2008). Public acceptance of renewable energies: Results from case studies in Germany. *Energy Policy, 36*(11), 4136–4141.

....

CHAPTER 19

USER INNOVATION AND PEER ASSISTANCE IN SMALL-SCALE RENEWABLE ENERGY TECHNOLOGIES

....

SAMPSA HYYSALO AND JOUNI K. JUNTUNEN

INTRODUCTION AND OVERVIEW

....

DECENTRALIZED energy production based on renewable sources is a commonly presented vision and solution for future energy needs (Akorede, Hizam, & Pouresmaeil, 2010). Recent years have seen many attempts to include citizens as more active players in the proliferation of renewable energy technologies. Most of these efforts in climate and energy policy have focused on campaigns, means, and measures for how industry-developed products could be diffused and utilized to their full potential by users (Mignon & Bergek, 2016; Nye, Whitmarsh, & Foxon, 2010). There is, however, a growing line of research that shows how users' roles in the diffusion of small-scale renewable energy technologies (S-RET) are not limited to adoption and users' diligence in using them. User activities related to technological domestication, innovation, and market creation are not just "barriers," but also key "enablers" for initial proliferation, further development, and mass-market uptake of S-RET (Caird & Roy, 2008; Nielsen, Reisch, & Thøgersen, 2016; Nyborg & Røpke, 2015; Ornetzeder & Rohracher, 2006; Schot, Kanger, & Verbong, 2016).

Even as many of the renewable and decentralized energy technologies are available off the shelf, their applicability in local situations varies with regard to building location, housing type, and user activities and lifestyles. Users typically need to adapt their routines to suit new technologies in their particular household or occupational settings (Judson et al., 2015; Juntunen, 2014a; Nyborg, 2015). Standardized technologies need to be fitted to different region-specific variations in housing, climate, and regulation, as well as to the often considerable variation that results from the particularities of residential buildings and homeowners' everyday practices (Heiskanen et al., 2014; Judson et al., 2015; Nyborg, 2015; de Vries, Boon, & Peine 2016).

These variable user requirements also lead to users modifying the technologies they use (Heiskanen, Johnson, & Vadovics, 2010; Ornetzeder & Rohracher, 2006; Seyfang & Smith, 2007). This includes making small adaptations and more complex modifications to the S-RET technology to make it suitable for local conditions (Caird & Roy, 2008; Hargreaves et al., 2013; Shove et al., 2007). This phenomenon is well known in other domains, where mass-produced goods do not meet the localized needs of users, and have resulted in what von Hippel calls "user innovation niches": settings that spur a significant amount of innovation by users (Baldwin & von Hippel, 2011; von Hippel, 2005). Indeed, users of S-RET have been important innovative agents in the early period of technology development and have continued to be so in the later expansion phases of the S-RET technologies into new markets and contexts.

In this chapter, we first recount the role of user innovation and local communities in the early phases of S-RET technology development in wind turbine development and the emergence and maturation of solar collector development in new housing forms. We then move to examine a more recent set of findings about the innovation by users in S-RET technology development after the formative years of generic technology. These latter findings are timely, as many S-RETs are proliferating rapidly across the globe to new contexts (even S-RETs that are still in their formative stages, such as wave, tidal, deep geothermal heat, and thin film solar). To examine this, we focus on the only systematic line of research on the matter conducted thus far, on user innovations that have emerged in S-RET in air-source heat pumps, ground-source heat pumps, pellet burning systems, and solar collector technologies in the Finnish market. We review the user motivations, proliferation pathways, and more general effects of user innovations in these S-RETs.

The role of assistance by peers in user communities has been found central for user innovation both in the formative and expansion stages of S-RET, but the forms of community appear to be different. We therefore review the forms of innovative energy communities from locality-based community energy initiatives to distributed and Internet-mediated energy communities. These latter types of communities allow users to provide wide peer support for scaling, choosing, comparing, maintaining, modifying, and funding S-RET systems, and in so doing act as user-side intermediaries that aid other users in a market in which institutions and services are still under formation.

We conclude by outlining the contributions by user innovators to the development and proliferation of S-RET technologies. While climate and energy policymakers voice concerns about citizens' lack of engagement in improving their houses and heating systems, some citizens far exceed expectations. In all, these emerging findings regarding energy users as innovators underscore the importance of citizens' capacities and the role that information platforms can play in the proliferation of micro-generation technology.

User Innovation in the S-RET
Formation Phase

Citizen innovation activities have been documented in the early formative stages of many of today's most important renewable energy technologies. In Austria, Ornetzeder and Rochracher (2006) studied solar collector self-building groups. These groups were highly successful and resulted in improved and widely disseminated technologies. Although Denmark's wind-power industry is currently dominated by large-scale units, citizens' roles were crucial in the formative stages of its technology development. The alternative energy movement gave birth to many entrepreneurial ideas and created a fertile setting for the development of a modern wind-turbine industry in Denmark (Nielsen, 2016; Ornetzeder & Rohracher, 2006). The importance of user innovators and user communities has been equally observed in the early phases of new forms of housing such as passive houses, straw-bale housing, and earthships, which feature an early period of trials and gradual improvements to understand the technical systems and their interplay with houses and everyday life in the household (Ornetzeder & Rohracher, 2006; Seyfang, 2010).

In the renewable energy developments mentioned in the preceding, grassroots movements have played an important role. Grassroots innovation has remained a persistent alternative form with which to seek solutions for both perceived social injustices and environmental problems (Hargreaves et al., 2013; Smith et al., 2014). Grassroots movements pursue socially inclusive innovation processes that benefit local communities not only in terms of outcome, but also through knowledge creation (Walker & Devine-Wright, 2008). Grassroots innovation movements in energy have been predominantly formed by local communities, and thus commonly are called "community energy" projects. Community energy activities consist of a diverse set of activities and include the adoption and adaptation of renewable energy systems, improving energy efficiency, and behavior change (Hielscher, Seyfang, & Smith 2013). Even though many community energy projects do not necessarily feature new innovations from a global perspective, they are novel locally and feature new types of configurations and adjustments from existing technologies (de Vries, Boon, & Peine 2016). Community energy projects can also involve external people and organizations providing expertise that may be lacking in those communities. Engineers, designers, and other experts can provide help and can support local knowledge creation and experiments with alternative energy solutions (Smith, Fressoli, & Thomas 2014).

Scholars have suggested three distinct routes of impact of grassroots innovation on the broader society. The first is the mainstreaming of solutions and practices developed and nurtured within grassroots niches. The second mechanism is shielding and empowering of alternative technologies and consumption practices to be upscaled to the dominant sociotechnical regime, which can exert challenges to the prevailing energy system (Smith et al., 2016). The history of Danish wind power is a well-known case of both these mechanisms of influence at play (Nielsen, 2016; Ornetzeder & Rohracher, 2006). Smith et al. (2016), however, point to a third impact mechanism: "critical niches," which may not directly engage with mainstream energy system change at all, but instead foster alternative discourses, technologies, and ways of life, and in so doing continue to provide exemplars of how things can work significantly otherwise.

User Innovation in S-RET Expansion Phase

Active user engagement with S-RETs has not been limited to the early stages of their development. Users have continued to innovate in the expansion phase of technology development in ground- and air-source heat pumps, pellet burning, solar heat, solar photovoltaic systems, and smart-grid technologies (Heiskanen et al., 2014; Hyysalo, Juntunen, & Freeman, 2013a; Hyysalo, Juntunen, & Freeman, 2013b; Nyborg, 2015). To examine the user innovation in the technology expansion phase, we focus on the Finnish market from 2000 to the present, during which all of these technologies could be considered relatively technically mature and had several commercial designs available. In the Finnish market, over 200 user innovations could be identified in S-RET, such that three independent domain experts as well as Internet searches conducted by authors verified their originality and usefulness (Hyysalo, Juntunen, & Freeman, 2013b; Hyysalo, Johnson, & Juntunen, 2017).

The activities of citizen end-users in energy-related adaptations is predominantly thought of as being limited to add-ons and do-it-yourself (DIY) renovation, which would boil down to simple technical additions such as placing a sledge under an outdoor air-source heat pump unit to remove ice in the winter, or building a housing for it to make it aesthetically more appealing. Such simple add-ons or DIY renovations do ease the use and uptake of new technology (Shove et al., 2007). However, the user inventions found in the Finnish studies also included commercialized products and technically very sophisticated rebuilding of machinery. Let us examine two such innovations, one that spanned the whole of technical configuration and another that was limited to a subsystem.

Example of User Design: Air-Source Heat Pump with Ground Source Outdoor Circuit

The typical ground-source heat pump is connected to a central heating system, which many older houses do not have. Installing new central heating as part of a ground-source heat pump assembly makes the investment difficult to ever recoup, limiting the feasibility of ground-source heat pump proliferation. A user in Northern Finland designed a solution in which an air-source heat pump indoor convector unit was combined with a ground-source outdoor circuit. This suited his own needs, enabling a cost-competitive ground-source heat pump. The new design required that the outdoor heat pump unit, as well as the control logic and connections between inside and outside units, were modified or built anew. The resulting design was successful and provided a new alternative for the non-central-heated northern housing stock. The design was then commercialized by the user with a company, Jääsähkö Oy, in Finland (Hyysalo et al., 2013b; Mattinen et al., 2015).

Example of User Modification and Repurposing: Adding a Resistor to Air Source Heat Pumps to Maintain Temperature at 8°C

In cold winter countries, garages and summer cabins and other non-living spaces are heated to remain just above freezing temperatures, typically with direct electricity heating. A heat pump would cut this maintenance energy use significantly. The latest commercially available models support this type of low indoor-temperature functionality, but their price is typically prohibitively high for such low-level and small-space heating needs. Cheaper heat-pump models, in turn, tend to have a minimum specification temperature, usually 16°C, as they are mass manufactured for cooling, not heating, as their prime purpose. Several users have learned how to fool the indoor temperature sensors of their cheap heat pumps (in various technical ways) so that they can maintain lower indoor temperatures. This way a cheap heat pump costing a few hundred euro, assisted with an extra sensor or relay for a couple of euro, provides a substantial and cost-efficient improvement in heating (Hyysalo et al., 2013; Mattinen et al., 2016).

Both of these innovations were introduced by users themselves. Their carbon reduction potential, moreover, was found to be highly positive when life-cycle carbon assessment was conducted for their use in four Finnish climate zones. Ground-air heat pumps' emissions were over 70% lower than in the case of direct electric heating and were significantly lower than with traditional air-source heat pump heating (Mattinen et al., 2015. Modified air-to-air heat pumps result in a 57% decrease in emissions in heating application in comparison to heat pumps without these modifications (Mattinen et al., 2016).

Examining the user innovations in the technical system in which they were located reveals that, for instance in the case of air-source heat pumps, altogether 79 user innovations were identified, out of which 30 were "system-level designs" that spanned several subsystems of the technology; 25 were "user modifications," technical redesigns that were limited to one subsystem; and were 24 cases of add-ons, repurposing, hacks, relocating, or otherwise working around manufacturer designs to improve the system.

When these innovations are plotted within the technological configuration of typical air-source heat pump systems (Figure 19.1), it becomes evident that users have been able

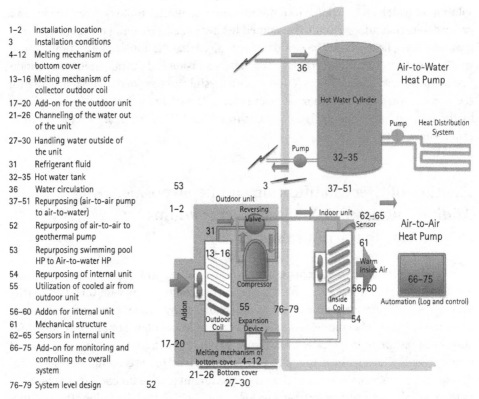

1–2	Installation location
3	Installation conditions
4–12	Melting mechanism of bottom cover
13–16	Melting mechanism of collector outdoor coil
17–20	Add-on for the outdoor unit
21–26	Channeling of the water out of the unit
27–30	Handling water outside of the unit
31	Refrigerant fluid
32–35	Hot water tank
36	Water circulation
37–51	Repurposing (air-to-air pump to air-to-water)
52	Repurposing of air-to-air to geothermal pump
53	Repurposing swimming pool HP to Air-to-water HP
54	Repurposing of internal unit
55	Utilization of cooled air from outdoor unit
56–60	Addon for internal unit
61	Mechanical structure
62–65	Sensors in internal unit
66–75	Add-on for monitoring and controlling the overall system
76–79	System level design

FIGURE 19.1 Range and distribution of user inventions in air-to-air and air-to-water heat pumps.

to innovate in virtually all parts of the technical system, including the coolant gas mixes, control logics, and system-level design. Only three parts of the configuration have been left untouched by innovative users: the inside of the compressor unit, the reversing valve, and the expansion device.

Taken together, user capacity to improve energy technologies is thus considerable. Heat pumps are not the easiest or most likely site for user innovation because of their technical complexity, mass production, low configurability, manufacturer disinterest in niche development, integration of several technology areas (coolant systems, electronics, mechanics, software, and in air- to water-source heat pumps, also plumbing), and the loss of warranty and insurance coverage upon making modifications.

Four major issues stand out as having spurred user innovation: (1) inadequacies of some commercial models in dealing with cold climates and the ensuing room for improvement in their energy efficiency and usability; (2) the emergence of user-run Internet forums where heat-pump owners exchange experience, ideas, and help (see later discussion) (3); the relatively cheap price of particularly lower-end air-source heat pump models, which encourages experimentation with them; and (4) user enchantment with technological projects as either a hobby or an extension of their professional skills and goals (Freeman, 2015; Hyysalo, Juntunen, & Freeman, 2013a, 2013b).

The Diffusion and Impact of User Innovation in S-RET

The impact and diffusion of user innovation in S-RET has thus far remained a relatively nascent research topic, but research to date does provide some initial insights. Most studies merely document that diffusion has happened (Galvin & Sunikka-Blank, 2014; Nygrén et al., 2015; Ornetzeder & Rohracher, 2006, 2013). Historical studies regarding the formative period of technology development in solar collectors and wind energy show that both the commercialization of user innovations and their diffusion within peer-to-peer communities have been important drivers for the early development of these technologies (Nielsen, 2016; Ornetzeder & Rohracher, 2006). The only study to systematically chart the diffusion of user innovation in S-RET concerns the expansion phase, and shows that there are several diffusion routes for user innovations in S-RET (Hyysalo, Johnson, & Juntunen, 2017) (Figure 19.2). Studies show that within these channels, less than 3% of user innovations were diffused through commercialization, either by incumbent companies or by start-ups, 8% were copied as is by peers, and 34% were adapted by peers through further projects, where they were partially replicated and also modified further (Hyysalo, Johnson, & Juntunen, 2017).

These findings of uneven and relatively complex diffusion patterns are in line with research from other fields that identifies structural hindrances to the spread of user innovations. Unlike producers, users do not have to invest in selling the innovation to others to benefit from it—they are innovating for themselves (von Hippel, 1976). From this, it follows that efforts to diffuse the innovation may come as something extra and may require that users appropriate a new role—either helping others (Habicht, Oliveira, & Shcherbatiuk, 2013), raising their professional profile (von Hippel & DeMonaco, 2013) or turning into entrepreneurs (Shah & Tripsas, 2007). The last option aside, the gains that users may enjoy from their efforts to render their innovation diffusible may not be appealing, even if their innovation was socially valuable (Freeman, 2015).

The diffusion and impact of user innovation in the expansion phase, however, also have indirect routes that substantially aid the overall dissemination of S-RET technologies in particular contexts. In Finland, user innovations have been tied to the growth and spread of Internet discussion forums dedicated to S-RET. The forums have considerably aided the market formation of the S-RET; for instance, heat pump installations increased from 50,000 to 700,000 during the decade since Internet discussion forums emerged (Heiskanen et al., 2014), and the forums (in Finnish) had next to 200 million reads during this period, with only very modest levels of state subsidy and suspicions from experts and large retailers. Innovative users were found to provide

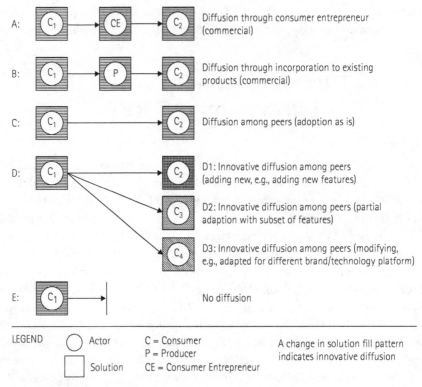

A: C_1 → CE → C_2 Diffusion through consumer entrepreneur (commercial)

B: C_1 → P → C_2 Diffusion through incorporation to existing products (commercial)

C: C_1 → C_2 Diffusion among peers (adoption as is)

D: C_1 → C_2 D1: Innovative diffusion among peers (adding new, e.g., adding new features)

      → C_3 D2: Innovative diffusion among peers (partial adaption with subset of features)

      → C_4 D3: Innovative diffusion among peers (modifying, e.g., adapted for different brand/technology platform)

E: C_1 →   No diffusion

LEGEND   ◯ Actor   C = Consumer   A change in solution fill pattern indicates innovative diffusion
          ▢ Solution   P = Producer
                        CE = Consumer Entrepreneur

FIGURE 19.2 Diffusion channels of user innovation in S-RET.

in-depth peer support for other, less advanced users, in regard to scaling, choosing, comparing, maintaining, and modifying these systems (Hyysalo, Juntunen, & Freeman, 2013a).

INTERNET COMMUNITIES AS CATALYSTS FOR USER INNOVATION

Inventive users tend to get help from their peers, and this help is often vital for realizing their designs (Franke & Shah, 2003; Jeppesen & Molin, 2003). As in more conventional research and development (R&D), inventive users are only proficient in particular aspects related to technology, and hence the scope of design they can master alone remains more limited than when pooling contributions with others (Benkler, 2006; Franke & von Hippel, 2003; Hyysalo, Juntunen, & Freeman, 2013a, 2013b). In many domains, innovating users are deeply embedded in communities of practice (Baldwin, Hienerth, & von Hippel, 2006; Bethwaite, 2008; Flichy, 2007; Franke & Shah, 2003; Hienerth, 2006). It appears to be no accident that in the formative period of renewable energy technologies, user innovation success stories feature self-building groups and cooperatives (Jørgensen & Karnøe, 1995; Ornetzeder & Rohracher, 2006).

Users capable of and motivated to engage in innovation, however, are often geographically dispersed. Internet-enabled services can boost visibility and connectivity among potentially innovative agents. This has been observed in many online game environments (Jeppesen & Molin, 2003; Prügl & Schreier, 2006) and also in designing physical products, even if only some aspects of these products can be shared across the web (Hyysalo & Usenyuk, 2015; Jeppesen & Frederiksen, 2006; Sawhney, Verona, & Prandelli, 2005; Usenyuk, Hyysalo, & Whalen, 2016). The pattern of moving from local to distributed peer assistance networks is visible in S-RET user innovation studies when user innovation is compared in the formative and expansion stages. In the Finnish cases, users' capacity to carry out projects owed much to their exchanges at user-run online forums, which have helped otherwise dispersed and heterogeneous users to create a repository of knowledge and an effective peer-learning environment (Hyysalo, Juntunen, & Freeman, 2013a). Hyysalo and colleagues (2013b, 2016) found that all innovating users had some presence in these online environments. Most innovating users received various kinds of help from other users, most commonly from two to five people, interacted in broader Internet forums, and received inputs from a range of users (Heiskanen et al., 2014; Hyysalo, Johnson, & Juntunen, 2017; Hyysalo, Juntunen, & Freeman, 2013a, 2013b). The forums provided asynchronous discussion boards, private messaging, sharing of images and blueprints, running how-to videos, and soliciting help or collaboration, even as they were not set up for innovation in mind.

The S-RET internet forums in Finland all exist for other reasons than innovation among the members. Their espoused rationale is well captured by a subheading of the largest forum, the heat pump forum, which states it provides "unbiased peer knowledge" among people who run similar technologies and thus face similar questions in acquainting themselves to technological options, scaling the system(s), choosing among available brands, combining different S-RET forms, implementing, adapting, and improving their systems. The range of orientations and questions addressed in these forums is wide, as different people are interested in different aspects of the heating systems. Also the depth of participation varies, with some site visitors merely finding information on a single issue that is pressing for them, such as scaling of a heat pump installation they are planning, whereas others have made hundreds, even thousands of posts. The participation, furthermore, seems to form "paths" as users move from simpler issues in heat pump acquisition to more complex ones in monitoring their performance and improving it. When users were interviewed, many related histories of learning, which can be captured well by the concept of "legitimate peripheral participation" (Lave & Wenger, 1991), in which users initially joined with some specific question in mind, and then gradually grew more competent as their engagement with the technology deepened. Within this ecology of knowledge sharing, the innovating users were found to provide the deepest level of peer support for other, less advanced users in regard to scaling, selecting, comparing, maintaining, and modifying these systems. This was often a result of their background training in one or other speciality related to the

S-RET technology in question (electronics, programming, mechanics, etc.) and having grown inventive in the course of gradually deepening engagement with the technology (Hyysalo, Juntunen, & Freeman, 2013a).

At the same time, the Internet discussion forums that currently exist allow only partial pooling of user contributions and competencies. Users can share ideas, and verbally and visually share solutions, but the forums do not allow them to effectively work on the same project, verify the adequacy of each other's solutions, or easily gain detailed instructions for how to implement each others' solutions. This feeds into a dispersed "innofusion," whereby many user solutions develop independently but do not develop into widely applicable solutions. It thus forms a user-complemented market, in which user solutions and knowledge support commercial offerings, rather than forming a user-competed market in which user solutions could compete head-on with commercial possibilities (Hyysalo, Johnson, & Juntunen, 2017; Hyysalo & Usenyuk, 2015; Raasch & von Hippel, 2012). This may well change in the future as the digital discussion and sharing platforms evolve.

Community Energy Versus Distributed and Dispersed Energy Communities

Traditional community energy has been locality bound and premised on the sharing of finance and production (Hargreaves et al., 2013; Smith et al., 2016), but the new citizen energy communities are geographically dispersed, and share an interest in the same class of technology and in digitally mediated infrastructure without committing to shared finance or production (Juntunen, 2014b).

Community energy activities have been commonly defined through their local participation: energy produced "by" and "for" local stakeholders. In this they have an open, participatory, and collective character, even as particular projects vary in regard to just how open and participatory or local they ultimately are (Walker & Devine-Wright, 2008). In the community energy context, community is often defined as a local unit, which operates inside a limited geographical area. The community typically features a shared ownership and financing structure as well as shared decision-making rules. Often, the maintenance and further development of the S-RET remains with the community, contributing to the upkeep and deepening of energy competences among the community members. The communities can further foster alternative critical discourse on technological options, which can present an important alternative to mainstream views and occasionally lead to convergence of elements of community energy becoming adopted in mainstream energy policy (Smith et al., 2016).

However, locality-bound community energy no longer appears to be the only important community form related to energy users. Distributed energy communities exist through shared energy production outputs over a wide area network, beyond the limits of a specific locale. Currently, these communities have emerged for medium- and large-scale renewable production units. Lumituuli, a wind energy company in Finland, and Solar Energy Cooperative Green Point Batensteinbad Woerden in the Netherlands are examples of cooperatively owned green electricity plants by household investors who share outputs of generation. Wind and solar collectives in these examples are characterized by distributed ownership, and they require minimal direct involvement of local people, and of participants more generally, beyond a small executive group engaged in the endeavor. Here, the outcome is not locally focused and the unit generates energy for wide distribution, rather than for use in the locality (Walker & Devine-Wright, 2008). The recent development into smart grids is opening the grid in new ways for peer-to-peer networking concepts and virtual power plants that can be used with small-scale production units and with renewable micro-generation technologies. The exact forms of these distributed ownership communities are multiplying, as peer-to-peer networking concepts have brought new models of sharing to community energy systems (Juntunen & Hyysalo, 2015; Steinheimer, Trick, & Ruhrig, 2012).

As described earlier, this second newly emerging form of energy community centers around knowledge sharing through user-run Internet forums among renewable micro-generation prosumers. These energy communities are not a Finnish peculiarity but are found widely, for instance in all Nordic countries and Germany. As noted, in these settings the household users own their S-RET equipment and utilize self-generated electicity for their own consumption, but are actively linked to peers who run similar technologies and thus face similar questions in acquainting themselves to technological options; scaling the system(s); choosing among the available brands; combining different S-RET forms; and implementing, adapting, and improving their systems. They can further feature a subset of users who are interested and active in innovating new features to the technologies they have.

Table 19.1 demonstrates the key differences between the three energy communities: local community energy, distributed output sharing, and dispersed knowledge-sharing communities. Whereas in traditional community energy all aspects are dealt with locally, in distributed wind energy the project is owned, governed together, and outputs shared within the group or sold to other users over the grid. In dispersed knowledge-sharing communities, ownership and control over production are in the hands of each household. However, in terms of knowledge sharing and learning processes, the household can enjoy the benefits of and contribute to a wide energy community, where members share common interests on a much wider scale than in local and distributed forms.

These insights can be illustrated by adapting the well-known community energy mapping by Walker and Devine-Wright (2008). Figure 19.3 illustrates how the traditional forms of community energy contrast with a centralized wind-power utility. Some see community energy fundamentally as an issue of producing energy by open participation (Type A in the upper right corner of the figure); others see community energy primarily as involving generating energy for community benefit (Type B); whereas yet others argue that there is greater variety between and within community energy projects

Table 19.1 Case Examples of Community Energy: Local Community Energy Project and Dispersed Structure Community

	Locality–Centered Community Energy Project (e.g., Wind, Solar)	Distributed Energy Community Through Output Sharing	Dispersed Energy Community Through Knowledge Sharing
Scale of the production unit	Small or medium scale	Medium or large scale	Decentralized small scale
Ownership of the production unit	Community owned	Community owned	Owned by households
Daily operation	By active group inside community (or outsourced)	By active group inside community (or outsourced)	By user, user responsibility
Knowledge sharing and community learning	Social learning when working together locally for common goal	Social learning among those in community who engage beyond mere output sharing	Individual operational work supported by online community. Characterized by common interest.
Scale of community knowledge pool	The participants in the locally owned and run community energy project and their personal networks	The engaged participants in the energy project and their personal networks	Thousands of users with similar equipment and broad range of competences
Governance characteristics	Organized; requires governance structure, community control	Organized; requires governance structure, community control	Household control and autonomy
Distribution of energy production	Microgrid or grid-connected, primarily for a group	Microgrid or grid-connected, primarily for a group	Primarily for own use, mostly grid-connected

(Type C). All these conceptions, however, assume that energy communities that involve important citizen participation and cooperative output distribution must be local and open. This is not the case with the distributed energy community that features distributed output, such as a wind cooperative (Type D), which would clearly map away from the local end and in most empirical cases also from less intensive forms of participation, typically having only a limited number of active members running the cooperative, whereas others are involved mainly through financing and output sharing. The dispersed energy communities such as the Internet discussion forums (Type E in figure) map onto the graph toward the distant and private in terms of outputs, but toward open and collaborative in terms of participation, action, learning, and cooperation.

The form of digitally dispersed knowledge-sharing forums appears to matter as well. Unlike the S-RET communities hitherto studied, the globally dominant form of digital

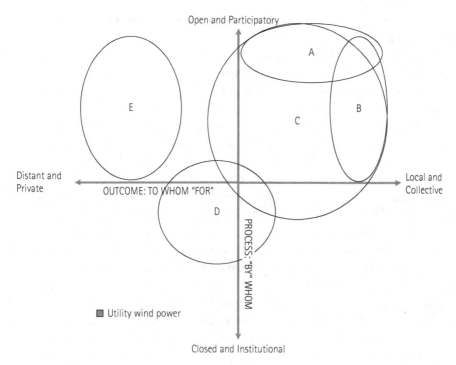

FIGURE 19.3 Mapping energy communities regarding outcome and participation.

user community has been a company-brand focus in which the company has sole control of the forums. Study of user-run online forums indicates that company-run online forums for a single brand—for example, the Ducati motorcycle community (ducati. kontain.com), or the Apple support community (discussions.apple.com)—are an artificial and limiting approach from a user perspective. Before acquisition, help is needed in order to compare different competing solutions from various vendors. During the use period, products are embedded in practices of everyday life, and use is typically linked to other products; in active design engagements, it is by default that users tinker with more than one manufacturer's offering.

DESIGN AND POLICY IMPLICATIONS

Users complement commercial products in the market, in both the early stages of development and the later stages, when the off-the-shelf solutions enter new market contexts. Manufacturers are often well aware of the limitations of products meeting the requirements of all customers. From the manufacturer's point of view, it would be too costly to design, produce, and advertise products that fulfill all market segments and use cases, and typically it is more profitable to identify and serve a few market segments and develop products that meet average within-segment requirements (Franke & von Hippel, 2003).

If manufacturers would take the active user engagement with S-RET seriously, they could enhance it by altering their design strategies. Manufacturers have addressed diverse requirements coming from different users, for example, by design modularity. In preparation for easy extendibility and hybridization of the system, design implications for manufacturers emphasize modularity and multipurposing of products. Recently, especially in the information and communication technology (ICT) industry, the application of ecosystem thinking has changed how innovations emerge in a fast-paced and versatile form. For example, mobile device vendors do not try to fulfill all the customer requirements, but rather develop an open platform that can be utilized by other companies in the business ecosystem through additional (application) products to fulfill specific customer needs. This has made possible a "long tail" approach, in which the available variety of unique items is extended with the sale of small batches of each (Anderson, 2008). Active user engagement with S-RET energy technologies suggests that there may be similar opportunities that do not lock households into specific energy sources and ways of using the technology. For the manufacturer, this type of design approach can be understood as "open pre-configuration," where in the design phase the purpose is not to try to imagine and understand all possible future use cases and needs, but rather to design a product in an enabling manner to open up options for innovative use cases and use practices that can evolve over time (Hyysalo, 2010; Juntunen, 2014a). Open pre-configuration is a forward-looking concept that extends use options from the initial product offering, and gives freedom for easier modification and additions in later stages of use, be they software-based applications or hardware add-ons.

Should manufacturers pursue such modular and open pre-configuration-based design strategies in S-RET, they would likely be assisted by the widespread voluntary sharing among peers that already exists in Internet-mediated discussion forums. Users are willing and able to help their peers to extend their S-RET solutions, and if configuration and improvement of S-RET solutions became easier by design, it is likely that peer help activities involving selecting, improving, and maintaining the systems would likely increase as well—providing manufacturers added benefits.

In terms of policy implications, regulation and supporting schemes can support renewable energy more effectively when they recognize the gradual nature of the adaptation of domestic energy technologies, citizen competency, and willingness to improve their systems. The active user roles and especially modifications typically hinge on ownership of the equipment (Juntunen, 2014b). Devices that are rented or third-party owned through power purchase agreements do not allow for similar adaptations, even if beneficial for the final user. Retaining ownership at the local level is thus important, and credit-based financial products could support this development. Financing agreements offered by financial institutions (credit) should be developed to remove the up-front payment. Local governments can also develop other types of mechanisms. Often the provision of guarantees has been an issue in credit-based financing by banks, and governmental backup might play a role to support the diffusion of household-owned micro-generation.

Another policy implication is the need to retain flexibility in residential energy technologies to enable future extensions and changes of energy sources by users. Practical means to avoid high technology-switching costs can be achieved by a regulatory push toward standardization of system interfaces. Instead of waiting for de facto standards to emerge, a governance approach can be used, whereby a regulator collaborates with industry to define standards. Standardized system interfaces can enable easy modifications, the combining of different small-scale S-RET solutions (an emerging trend in Northern Europe currently), and creation of add-ons, which appear to give greater autonomy and modifiability at the household level.

Third, the newly emerging forms of energy communities such as Internet forums offer formidable support for the diffusion of S-RET technology through user-provided knowledge and solutions in the market. Even as it may be illusory to seek to create such discussion forums through policy measures, allowing (often anonymous) discussions to prevail holds benefits, and some energy and climate policy actors, such as energy advisories, might offer their advice through these discussion forums, as has already happened in work with youth, following the realization that the Internet is where people can be more easily reached today.

Finally, active technological engagement by lead users and user communities offers a potential resource for policymaking. These citizens are highly aware of the limitations of the technology and try to solve them by their own work and inventions. Hence, policymakers might also examine the inventions and engage with the inventors, from the perspective of what needs to be done and where further actions are needed in the S-RET technologies in a given market at a given time.

CONCLUSIONS

Research on innovative energy citizens underscores the importance of the capacities of citizens as innovative energy "prosumers," and the role that capacitating information infrastructures can play in the proliferation of micro-generation technology. The particularities of consumption settings and variation in the competencies of users should not be treated as mere "barriers" or "obstacles" to diffusion of S-RET, but also making space for important improvements and forms of knowledge creation that can significantly augment the development and proliferation of S-RET systems, both in the formative and expansion stage of these technologies.

The research on active user roles with energy technologies has been steadily intensifying, but still remains relatively little studied when it comes to examining users and consumers as innovators—both as individuals and in the energy communities in which they orchestrate their activities. This research area grows in importance through the expanding role of S-RET in energy systems and in the increasing arrays of engagement and community forms taking place in its transformation. We can see that active users can far exceed traditional expectations, but in-depth redesigning of technology will never become something in which all citizens suddenly will engage.

REFERENCES

Akorede, M. F., Hizam, H., & Pouresmaeil, E. (2010). Distributed energy resources and benefits to the environment. *Renewable and Sustainable Energy Reviews, 14*(2), 724–734.

Anderson, C. (2008). *The long tail: Why the future of business is selling less of more.* New York: Hyperion.

Baldwin, C., & von Hippel, E. (2011). Modeling a paradigm shift: From producer innovation to user and open collaborative innovation." *Organization Science, 22*(6): 1399–1417.

Baldwin, C., Hienerth, C., & von Hippel, E. (2006). How user innovations become commercial products: A theoretical investigation and case study. *Research Policy 35*(9), 1291–1313.

Benkler, Y. (2006). *The wealth of networks: How social production transforms markets and freedom.* New Haven, CT: Yale University Press.

Bethwaite, F. (2008). *Higher performance sailing.* London: Adlard Coles Nautical.

Caird, S., & Roy, R. (2008). User-centered improvements to energy efficiency products and renewable energy systems: Research on household adoption and use. *International Journal of Innovation Management, 12*(3), 327–355.

de Vries, G. W., Boon, W. P. C., & Peine, A. (2016). User-led innovation in civic energy communities. *Environmental Innovation and Societal Transitions, 19*(June): 51–65.

Flichy, P. (2007). *The Internet imaginaire.* Cambridge, MA: MIT Press. Retrieved from http://books.google.com/books?id=icwUrZavhHQC

Franke, N., & Shah, S. (2003). How communities support innovative activities: An exploration of assistance and sharing among end-users. *Research Policy, 32*(1): 157–178.

Franke, N., & von Hippel, E. (2003). Satisfying heterogeneous user needs via innovation toolkits: The case of Apache Security software. *Research Policy, 32*(7), 1199–1215.

Freeman, S. (2015). Immersed in pellet technology: Motivation paths of innovative DIYers. *Outlines: Critical Practice Studies, 16*(1), 54–80.

Galvin, R., & Sunikka-Blank, M. (2014). The UK homeowner-retrofitter as an innovator in a socio-technical system." *Energy Policy, 74*(November), 655–662.

Habicht, H., Oliveira, P., & Shcherbatiuk, V. (2013). User innovators: When patients set out to help themselves and end up helping many. *Die Unternehmung, 66*(3), 277–294.

Hargreaves, T., Hielscher, S., Seyfang, G., & Smith, A. (2013). Grassroots innovations in community energy: The role of intermediaries in niche development. *Global Environmental Change, 23*(5), 868–880. Retrieved from http://linkinghub.elsevier.com/retrieve/pii/S0959378013000381

Heiskanen, E., Hyysalo, S., Jalas, M., Juntunen, J. K., & Lovio, R. (2014). The role of users in heating systems transitions: The case of heat pumps in Finland. In S. Junginger & P. R. Christensen (Eds.), *The highways and byways to radical innovation: Design perspectives* (pp. 171–196). Kolding: Design School Kolding, University of Southern Denmark.

Heiskanen, E., Johnson, M., & Vadovics, E. (2010). Learning about users and developing co-design capabilities for energy saving on the local level. Paper presented at the 14th European Roundtable on Sustainable Consumption and Production (ERSCP) and the 6th Environmental Management for Sustainable Universities (EMSU) Conference,

Delft, The Netherlands. Retrieved from https://repository.tudelft.nl/islandora/object/uuid%3A2888ee23-520c-48c4-8d69-239dcc1046a9

Hielscher, S., Seyfang, G., & Smith, A. (2013). Grassroots innovations for sustainable energy: Exploring niche-development processes among community-energy initiatives. In M. J. Cohen, P. P. Vergragt, & H. S. Brown (Eds.), *Innovations in sustainable consumption: New economics, socio-technical transitions and social practices* (pp. 133–158). Cheltenham, UK: Elgar.

Hienerth, C. (2006). The commercialization of user innovations: The development of the rodeo kayak industry. *R&D Management, 36*(3), 273–294.

Hyysalo, S. (2010). *Health technology development and use: From practice-bound imagination to evolving impacts.* London: Routledge.

Hyysalo, S., Johnson, M., & Juntunen, J. K. (2017). The diffusion of consumer innovation in sustainable energy technologies. *Journal of Cleaner Production, 162*, S70–S82.

Hyysalo, S., Juntunen, J. K., & Freeman, S. (2013a). Internet forums and the rise of the inventive energy user. *Science and Technology Studies, 26*(1), 25–51.

Hyysalo, S., Juntunen, J. K., & Freeman, S. (2013b). User innovation in sustainable home energy technologies. *Energy Policy, 55*, 490–500.

Hyysalo, S., & Usenyuk, S. (2015). The user dominated technology era: Dynamics of dispersed peer-innovation. *Research Policy, 44*(3), 560–576.

Jeppesen, L. B., & Frederiksen, L. (2006). Why do users contribute to firm-hosted user communities? The case of computer-controlled music instruments. *Organization Science, 17*(1), 45.

Jeppesen, L. B., & Molin, M. (2003). Consumers as co-developers: learning and innovation outside the firm. *Technology Analysis & Strategic Management, 15*(3), 363–383.

Jørgensen, U., & Karnøe, P. (1995). The Danish wind turbine story: Technical solutions to political visions?" In A. Rip, T. J. Misa, & J. Schot (Eds.), *Managing technology in society: The approach of constructive technology assessment* (pp. 57–82). London; New York: Pinter; St. Martin's Press.

Judson, E. P., Bell, S., Bulkeley, H., Powells, G., & Lyon, S. (2015). The co-construction of energy provision and everyday practice: Integrating heat pumps in social housing in England. *Science and Technology Studies, 28*(3), 26–53.

Juntunen, J. K. (2014a). Domestication pathways of small-scale renewable energy technologies. *Sustainability: Science, Practice, & Policy, 10*(2), 28–42.

Juntunen, J. K. (2014b). Prosuming energy: User innovation and new energy communities in renewable micro-generation. PhD dissertation, Aalto University School of Business, Helsinki. Retrieved from https://aaltodoc.aalto.fi/handle/123456789/14143

Juntunen, J. K., & Hyysalo, S. (2015). Renewable micro-generation of heat and electricity: Review on common and missing socio-technical configurations. *Renewable and Sustainable Energy Reviews, 49*(September), 857–870.

Lave, J., & Wenger, E. (1991). *Situated learning: Legitimate peripheral participation.* Cambridge: Cambridge University Press.

Mattinen, M., Nissinen, A., Hyysalo, S., & Juntunen, J. K. (2015). Energy use and greenhouse gas emissions of air-source heat pump and innovative ground-source air heat pump in cold climate. *Journal of Industrial Ecology, 19*(1), 61–70.

Mattinen, M. K., Tainio, P., Salo, M., Jalas, M., Nissinen, A., & Heiskanen, E. (2016). How building users can contribute to greenhouse-gas emission reductions in Finland: Comparative study of standard technical measures, user modifications and behavioural measures. *Energy Efficiency, 9*(2), 301–320.

Mignon, I., & Bergek, A. (2016). System- and actor-level challenges for diffusion of renewable electricity technologies: An international comparison. *Journal of Cleaner Production*, *128*(August), 105–115.

Nielsen, K. H. (2016). How user assemblage matters: Constructing learning by using in the case of wind turbine technology in Denmark. In S. Hyysalo, T. E. Jensen, & N. Oudshoorn (Eds.), *New production of users: Changing innovation collectives and involvement* (pp. 101–122). New York: Routledge.

Nielsen, K. R., Reisch, L. A., & Thøgersen, J. (2016). Sustainable user innovation from a policy perspective: A systematic literature review. *Journal of Cleaner Production*, *133*(October), 65–77.

Nyborg, S. (2015). Pilot users and their families: Inventing flexible practices in the smart grid. *Science and Technology Studies*, *28*(3), 54–80.

Nyborg, S., & Røpke, I. (2015). Heat pumps in Denmark: From ugly duckling to white swan. *Energy Research & Social Science*, *9*(September), 166–177.

Nye, M., Whitmarsh, L., & Foxon, T. (2010). Socio-psychological perspectives on the active roles of domestic actors in transition to a lower carbon electricity economy." *Environment and Planning A*, *42*(3), 697–714.

Nygrén, N. A., Kontio, P., Lyytimäki, J., Varho, V., & Tapio, P. (2015). Early adopters boosting the diffusion of sustainable small-scale energy solutions. *Renewable and Sustainable Energy Reviews*, *46*(June), 79–87.

Ornetzeder, M., & Rohracher, H. (2013). Of solar collectors, wind power, and car sharing: Comparing and understanding successful cases of grassroots innovations. *Global Environmental Change*, *23*(5), 856–867.

Ornetzeder, M., & Rohracher, H. (2006). User-led innovations and participation processes: Lessons from sustainable energy technologies. *Energy Policy*, *34*(2), 138–150.

Prügl, R., & Schreier, M. (2006). Learning from leading-edge customers at the Sims: Opening up the innovation process using toolkits. *R&D Management*, *36*(3), 237–250.

Raasch, C., & von Hippel, E. (2012). Modeling interactions between user and producer innovation: User-contested and user-complemented markets. Retrieved from http://conference.druid.dk/acc_papers/gqgfi1okh3rq83cv1fo1dm608f48.pdf

Sawhney, M., Verona, G., & Prandelli, E. (2005). Collaborating to create: The Internet as a platform for customer engagement in product innovation. *Journal of Interactive Marketing*, *19*(4), 4–17.

Schot, J., Kanger, L., & Verbong, G. (2016). The roles of users in shaping transitions to new energy systems. *Nature Energy*, *1*(5), 16054.

Seyfang, G. (2010). Community action for sustainable housing: Building a low-carbon future. *Energy Policy*, *38*(12), 7624–7633.

Seyfang, G., & Smith, A. (2007). Grassroots innovations for sustainable development: Towards a new research and policy agenda. *Environmental Politics*, *16*(4), 584–603.

Shah, S. K., & Tripsas, M. (2007). The accidental entrepreneur: The emergent and collective process of user entrepreneurship. *Strategic Entrepreneurship Journal*, *1*(1–2), 123–140.

Shove, E., Watson, M., Hand, M., & Ingram, J. (2007). *The design of everyday life*. Oxford: Berg.

Smith, A., Fressoli, M., & Thomas, H. (2014). Grassroots innovation movements: Challenges and contributions. *Journal of Cleaner Production*, *63*(January). 114–124.

Smith, A., Kern, F., Raven, R., & Verhees, B. (2014). Spaces for sustainable innovation: Solar photovoltaic electricity in the UK. *Technological Forecasting and Social Change*, *81*, 115–130.

Smith, A., Hargreaves, T., Hielscher, S., Martiskainen, M., & Seyfang, G. (2016). Making the most of community energies: Three perspectives on grassroots innovation. *Environment and Planning A, 48*(2), 407–432.

Steinheimer, M., Trick, U., & Ruhrig, P. (2012). Energy communities in smart markets for optimisation of peer-to-peer interconnected smart homes. In *2012 8th International Symposium on Communication Systems, Networks & Digital Signal Processing (CSNDSP)*, 1–6. Poznan University of Technology, Poznan, Poland. Retrieved from http://ieeexplore .ieee .org/xpls/abs_all.jsp?arnumber=6292732

Usenyuk, S., Hyysalo, S., & Whalen, J. (2016). Proximal design: Users as designers of mobility in the Russian north. *Technology and Culture, 57*(4), 866–908.

von Hippel, E. (1976). The dominant role of users in the scientific instrument innovation process. *Research Policy, 5*(3), 212–239.

von Hippel, E. (2005). *Democratizing innovation*. Cambridge, MA: MIT Press.

von Hippel, E., & DeMonaco, H. (2013). Market failure in the diffusion of user innovations: The case of "off-label" innovations by medical clinicians. Retrieved from http://papers.ssrn.com /sol3/papers.cfm?abstract_id=2275562

Walker, G., & Devine-Wright, P. (2008). Community renewable energy: What should it mean? *Energy Policy, 36*(2), 497–500.

....

CHAPTER 20

THE ROLE OF MEDIA INFLUENCE IN SHAPING PUBLIC ENERGY DIALOGUES

....

ALEKSANDRA WAGNER

INTRODUCTION

....

THE ways in which energy is discussed, what is said and what is not said, as well as who speaks and who is absent in media discourse, are crucial sources of influence on the pathways of transformation of the world's relationship to energy. Despite this, media discourses on energy are relatively seldom the subject of systematic scientific analyses. The objective of this chapter is to provide an overview of the main mechanisms and processes observed in media discourses with the potential to shape political and economic responses to energy issues. We shall adopt a critical perspective to attempt to answer the following questions:

- Which groups of actors dominate in the media discourses on various energy issues?
- Which perspectives on energy issues are most visible in the public sphere?
- Which processes form the basis of the argumentative strategies that are adopted?
- And what are the consequences for public dialogues on energy—concerning inclusiveness, openness, and symmetry?

Political debate in various countries over the last two decades has been characterized by energy issues connected to climate change, intersecting with economic and geopolitical (matters Happer, Philo, & Froggatt, 2012). Mass media are a significant element of the process of creation and implementation of public policies, especially at the initial stage of "agenda setting," whereby the problems requiring state intervention are highlighted, and then at the next stage, when legitimation is sought for proposed actions and solutions (Jann & Wegrich, 2007). In the discursive approach to public policy analysis, developed mostly since 1990 (Fischer & Gotweiss, 2012), media debates can also be seen as an important dimension of the following stages: creation of solutions (if we treat the media as a deliberative space), implementation (informational support), and evaluation (articulation of appraisal). This makes the discourses conducted in the public—including media—space especially important. The argumentative model of public-policy analysis (Majone, 1989) assumes research on argumentative structures in the narratives of members of a society. When discussing these, researchers often employ the notion of "epistemic communities," which serve as "informal linkages of knowledge that collectively influence policy actors, but in a micro-political manner" (O'Riordan & Jordan, 1996, p. 87). These communities have the capacity to mobilize around specific discourses (Cotton, Rattle, & Alstine, 2014), which provide them with a framework and define who is entitled to speak in the name of a given community and according to which principles (Fischer & Forester, 1993). Within these discourses, sets of rules are produced that specify the permissible topics and identify and negotiate the symbolic resources that may be used: knowledge and ignorance, values and anti-values. The most widespread and accessible (but not the only) narratives are those transmitted through the mass media, as these are capable of reaching a wider audience. Their visibility in the public sphere becomes the object of competition between the various epistemic communities.

From the perspective of sociological constructivism, analysis of media discourse is crucial for understanding the mechanisms by which public opinion and people's attitudes toward energy issues are formed, since media representations are part of the collective construction of meanings (Heras-Saizarbitoria, Cilleruelo, & Zamanillo, 2011; Świątkiewicz-Mośny & Wagner, 2012). Two key processes are identified in media studies literature: first, *agenda setting* (McCombs & Shaw, 1972) and *priming* (Iyengar & Kinder, 1987), which involve controlling social attention by devoting time, space, and significance to specific issues, depicting them as particularly significant, and presenting selected points of view while ignoring others; and second, *framing* (Scheufele, 1999, 2000), which is the creation of interpretation frameworks and constructing narratives connecting specific events, values, and actors (for more on models of media effects, see McQuail, 2005; Scheufele & Tewksbury, 2007).

Media communication on energy-related topics encompasses many levels: international communication (between states, when the media message creates the context of mutual relations), inter-system communication (between various social systems, e.g., economies and polities, when it is not the taking of a decision, but rather making it public, that produces real systemic effects), and finally, communication between the media and individuals.

Several problems emerge from this final dimension, which is crucial for public dialogue. The first of these problems concerns the complexities of the subject, and the numerous geopolitical, macroeconomic, and technological contexts, making it a challenge to construct a text that does not require specialist knowledge from the reader. As a result, publishers and journalists often use ready-made information packages, allowing well-organized groups equipped with economic and social capital to influence media content, albeit not necessarily aiding in comprehension. The language adopted in the discussion of energy issues becomes a barrier to participation by citizens lacking in the resources of expert knowledge—information remains abstract and incomprehensible for them. The second problem is the knowledge of consumers, which they themselves tend to overstate; research shows disproportions between the scant understanding of basic facts or ability to interpret bills and people's relatively high assessment of their own knowledge (cf. Bittle, Rochkind, & Ott, 2009; Southwell et al., 2012).[1] Third, a general lack of interest in energy issues and perception of their importance among many consumers poses a problem. The residents of European countries do not see energy as a vital issue. Only 4% of EU citizens regard questions of climate, energy supplies, and the environment as issues of particular concern (by way of comparison, the equivalent figures for such topics as immigration, unemployment, and the economy are around 35%–40%) (Eurobarometer, 2015). In addition, previous research on energy technologies indicated that Europeans hold a generally low opinion of those who are to a large extent responsible for creating the media discourse on this topic: journalists and politicians. Yet they view the credibility of scientists and nongovernmental organizations (NGO) as greater (Eurobarometer, 2007).

For most people, however, the media continue to be the main source of information on energy issues (Schmoyer, Truett, & Cooper, 2006 Stankiewicz & Stasik, 2014). The Internet is also growing in importance as a means of searching for specific information (Westerman, Spence, & Van Der Heide, 2014). The aforementioned complexity of the issues further increases public dependence on media information (Littlefield, 2013; Nisbet, 2009; Weagel, 2015). Nevertheless, political debates on energy issues remain mediatized to a great extent, although not all narratives are represented in the media to an equal degree. However, they are of potential significance for public engagement. The basis of civic participation is access to information. The mass media are able to offer wide distribution of information in a short period of time.

MEDIA AND THE PUBLIC SPHERE

One of the main meanings of the public sphere is its understanding as a communicative space (Ferree et al., 2002) in which actors—passive and active participants in the public debate—observe one another, compare their opinions and positions, and strive for a consensus or seek to gain the initiative in defining social situations. In the political public sphere, issues are identified and problematized, to which the political system can then respond (Habermas, 1992). Public opinion is also created, meaning that views are articulated in the public sphere with the power to exert influence on the decisions of the governing administration. In this sense, public opinion provides something of a background for the political system to generate decisions on administering the community.

The normative demands of media theories concerning the role of the mass media are reflected in a series of metaphors whose impacts exceed the framework of academic discourse. Among the most fundamental, referring to the oldest democratic traditions, is the notion of the media as "agora," or forum—a common space where views can be aired. The agora is assumed to be open to citizens, fortified with the conditions of freedom of speech and communicative equality of its participants, and a symbolic area of persuasive actions subjected to the authority of the better argument. The debating actors strive to reach an agreement or to persuade others of their point of view, making use of the criterion of the common good and seeking to legitimize their actions through the process of social dialogue. The metaphor of the agora and more specifically the return to the key meaning of content-based, substantial debate and the resulting reflexive public opinion are at the heart of the concept of deliberative democracy (Dryzek, 2000; Fishkin, 2009). This is also close to the vision of the agora as a space of civic competition, as in Arendt's agonistic model of the public sphere (Benhabib, 1992).

The relationship between power and the media is also revealed, albeit in a different way, by several metaphors ("watchdog," "a mirror for society," or "window on events") that help to define the media as institutions of public trust. They are based on a kind of deontology to a great extent produced and sustained by the media themselves, which defines the demands of publishers and journalists, as well as other participants in media debates. These include responsibility and freedom of speech, reliability, and pursuit of the truth. The normative requirements reproduced in media self-descriptions fulfill additional functions: they guarantee the independence of media institutions from other systems (mostly political) and legitimize their status as a foundation of democracy.

These normative premises lead to critical analyses of contemporary media institutions and their actual role in democratic systems. The main charges leveled at modern media include the following: appropriation of public opinion (Fishkin, 2009); confining the debate to elites by concocting a strange marriage of government, the media, and the experts that legitimize them (Bohman, 2000); and commercialization of the media, triggering profound changes in the functioning of democracy (Habermas, 1992). Critics point to the monopolization of production and distribution of media communication, which, despite the growth of the Internet (which lowers entry barriers, but does not break them down entirely) and civil journalism, remains in the hands of a tiny group of private actors (Cammaerts, 2015).

Critical analyses produce a metaphor that differs somewhat from those presented in the preceding, portraying the media rather as an arena in which actors with conflicting interests do battle. This metaphor assumes inequality in the power and status of the participants in communication, and encompasses processes of manipulation and exclusion. It is not just the visible skirmishes between actors that are of key importance, but also, and perhaps above all, those invisible to the audience: hidden processes of restricting access, concealing, suppressing topics and arguments, arbitrarily assigning communicative positions and equipping actors with particular attributes to strengthen or marginalize them.

The critical approach to media analysis is multifaceted, encompassing analysis of the functioning of media institutions, demonstration of the financial connections between key interest groups, the media, and politicians, and also reconstruction of the symbolic power of the discourse to shape the patterns in audiences' thinking. We can observe a dialectic between the visible and invisible (Cammaerts, 2015). These concepts, however, refer not only to the semiotic availability of actors in the public sphere (Adut, 2012), their positions and reported events, and capacity to attract attention (Fuchs, 2014), but also to the immanent ideological mechanisms that permeate the discourses, imperceptibly to most readers or viewers (Cammaerts, 2015). The critical discourse analysis (CDA) approach is hugely important, its fundamental objective being to reconstruct discursive power relations and domination of interests in the media. CDA perceives the media as a key field of the public sphere, and treats media discourse as an instrument of power (Wodak & Busch, 2004, pp. 109–111). The language used in the media is analyzed within the broad context of sociocultural practices, both referring to communicative actions in specific situations and, in its post-structuralist current, treating discourse as a form of knowledge, a social construction of reality (Fairclough, 2011).

Mainstream and Social Media

Most studies on media discourses on energy issues are based on the content of printed newspapers and magazines. This is because the press is perceived as something of a prototype, with an opinion-forming influence and linear organization of ideas, as well as offering relatively accessible material. Analyses of Internet discourse are also growing in importance, with institutional sources (editorial and news sites) being more accessible than social media (dispersed, fragmentary, with closed channels). The latter, according to techno-optimists, offer opportunities for a renaissance of the democratic public sphere and civic participation. Fuchs (2014) calls this approach "technological determinism," attributing it to such researchers as Shirky (2008), Castells (2009), Jenkins (2008), Howe (2008), and Benkler (2006). Critical researchers contradict this idea, pointing to the inequalities that exist outside of the WorldWideWeb (Graaf, Otjes, & Rasmussen, 2016; Rasmussen & Carroll, 2014). Fuchs takes issue with Castells, highlighting the need for careful assessment of the counter-power released online: "Political counter-power on the Internet faces a massive asymmetry that is due to the fact that the ruling powers control more resources such as money, decision-making power, capacities for attention generation, etc." (Fuchs, 2014 p. 77). He also stresses that the capacity to mobilize communicative counter-power through new media has potential, but is not automatic, showing that the Internet in its present form is a stratified and non-participatory space (Fuchs, 2014). A further element of the discussion on the significance of Internet communication for dialogue and civic participation is its support for "slacktivism," which entails replacing civic activity with a form of undemanding communicative activity in social media, such as expressing support, sharing material on one's profile, or signing an online petition (Morozov, 2009). Current research indicates that it is impossible to verify unequivocally the influence of Internet activism on actual participation, yet slacktivism itself can help to make a problem visible and build civic engagement (Christensen, 2016).

The fundamental role of the new media in dialogues on energy issues could be its ability to introduce into the public sphere topics that are excluded from or marginalized in the mainstream media, and its empowerment of social actors, for example by removing the institutional barriers to their participation in communication. The presence of informal organizations and groups in the social media space appears to confirm their mobilizing nature, also in a manner that goes beyond state borders (e.g., the transnational cooperation of groups in organizing anti-nuclear protests). Yet what remains problematic is the issue of media visibility and hetero-reference, understood as the ability to enter into dialogue with people outside one's own group. The colonization of the Internet by corporate interests (Fuchs, 2014) can effectively counteract this. Even today, constructing a mass range or noticeable presence on Internet search engines, for example, requires significant economic capital. Lockwood (2008) also shows that the web-based skeptical discourses regarding climate change in effect support, and boost the visibility of, the dominant discourses of the mainstream media. Replication of the characteristics of mainstream discourses in the Internet space is also described by Graff et al. (2015), while those to note the online domination of political actors have included McNutt and Marchildon (2009) and Hubert (2017).

Internet discourse on energy problems is also formed by marketing and political communications. Modern marketing and public relations (PR), based on a relational approach to the consumer, make extensive use of social media channels, seeking to involve consumers in dialogical communication, building their engagement and loyalty. This communication goes beyond the sphere of economic relations, and has an impact on the processes of path creation and path dependency, discussed later in the chapter.

New media play an important role as communication channels and tools for organizing social movements, including protest movements. The ability to transmit information instantly and increase the visibility of a problem by sharing specific contents leads to a change in communication dynamic. It remains an open question how much of an effect this type of activity actually has on the political agenda and pluralism of the public sphere. Other effects of Internet-based communication are the danger of fragmentation of the public sphere (social networks often develop around one idea or a specific issue) and the capacity to support homogeneous networks (we usually contact people similar to us in terms of lifestyle or views) (Fishkin, 2009; Juza, 2016). As a result, first, there might be a lack of space in which contrasting views and different lines of argument can become visible to each other. Second, remaining in the niche of a specific social network can give an illusory impression of the homogeneity of society, or that the views represented by the participants of one's own network are dominant. However, "one needs unity in diversity in order to struggle for participatory democracy and maintaining this condition once it is reached. It is preferable and more effective to have a few widely accessible and widely consumed broad critical media than many small-scale special interest media that support the fragmentation of struggles" (Fuchs, 2014, p. 182). At present, these roles continue to be played by traditional media—especially television and the press (Scheufele & Nisbet, 2002). Although they are closely related to new media (reinforcing each other's dynamic of generation and circulation of information), to the greatest extent they provide actors and issues with social visibility on a mass scale. This is aptly summed up by the authors of a book on geothermal energy: "Whether geothermal energy will become a critical issue in the social media will depend on whether the local initiatives to get national attention and/or incidents such as earthquakes receive national or even international press coverage" (Hirschberg, Wiemer, & Burgherr, 2015, p. 405). The balancing act between the global and the local seems to characterize media discourses on energy as a whole.

TOPICS AND FRAMES

There are huge differences in the subjects covered in discourses on energy issues, which encompass technology, energy resources, politics, social practices, transition, economic indicators, markets, and many others. One of the more popular approaches to analyzing these is the reconstruction of the "frames" represented in so-called media packages (Gamson & Modigliani, 1989): sets of concepts and values in which actors and events are placed. These present events and processes from a particular perspective. Individual frames often compete with or are oppositional to one another. They include metaphors, used to reinforce individual frames to create media representations (Luokkanen, Huttunen, & Hildén, 2014; Świątkiewicz-Mośny & Wagner, 2012). The classic study that reconstructs frames in media discourse, using the example of nuclear energy, is that of Gamson and Modigliani (1989). Contemporary researchers frequently employ this methodology, inquiring as to the functions that frames fulfill in communications on energy: "Framing is vital to shaping public opinion, changing policies, and fostering collective action" (Fishendler, Boymel, & Boykoff, 2014, p. 2). The convergence of frames constructed in the mainstream media with those to which people discussing energy issues refer has been confirmed empirically in both focus group studies and research on Internet discourse (Gamson & Modigliani, 1989; Hirschberg, Wiemer, & Burgherr, 2015; Wagner, 2017), although not all narratives are represented equally in media discourses.

One of the most visible frames, the occurrence of which has been recorded in many countries, is that of civilizational development (cf. Chan 2012; Cherry et al., 2015; Gamson & Modigliani, 1989; Lis & Stankiewicz, 2017; Wagner, 2017). The key concepts of economic development, identified with progress and civilizational development, are the foundations of capitalism and neoliberal ideology. This frame is used by the most visible actors in global discourses—politicians and businesses. Governments, which always aim to gain influence over the way in which problems are presented in the media, frequently legitimize their point of view by referring to expert studies. They also make use of the technological frame, employing the construction of the "big chance" (cf. Cotton, Rattle, & Alstine, 2014; Lis & Stankiewicz, 2017; Wagner 2014), or referring to security threats to the same end (cf. Boersma & Johnson, 2013; Fishendler, Boymel, Boykoff, et al., 2014). The technological frame of presenting energy problems is also often used for deligitimizing opponents and asserting their lack of competence, accusing them of obstinacy and wielding unrealistic visions of development, in order to drive them out of mainstream channels of communication (Lis & Stankiewicz, 2017). Contrary to the belief that the media concentrate on negative contents and conflict (Luhmann, 2000a), many studies have shown the prevalence of generally positive overtones of media discourses on energy technologies (Feldpausch-Parker et al., 2011: Heras-Saizarbitoria, Cilleruelo, & Zamanillo, 2011; Horsbøl, 2013; Pilibaityte, Balockaite, & Juraite 2011; Waegel, 2015; Wagner, 2014).

The economic development and technology frames are often contrasted with the environmental frame (Gamson & Modigliani, 1989; Lis & Stankiewicz, 2017). Here we can observe a discursive opposition between economic security and environmental concerns ("jobs" or "environment") (Evans & Phelan, 2016). Environmental non-governmental organizations (ENGOs) employ a media frame of environmental protection, and call for minimized interference in the natural state of the earth. This frame is often presented in either a utopian form (as a chance for a better, cleaner future) or a dystopian one (a catastrophic narrative), while a technology frame tends to be more oriented to problem-solving (Müller, 2015). In recent years a frame constructed to link the economic viewpoint with the objectives of climate policy has also been evident. In ideological terms, this serves the line of development adopted by the European Union (EU) (Fishendler, Boymel, & Boykoff, 2014; Uusi-Rauva & Tienari, 2010), which presents itself as a pioneer in addressing climate change, and to which are addressed expectations of becoming an actor that can engage the global community in collective action (cf. Zoller & Fairhurst, 2007).

This linking of discourses of climate policy and energy issues leads to demands for energy transition. This perspective is often juxtaposed with the problem of energy security, to which it confers the status of *raison d'état*. Securitization helps to gain the attention of policymakers as well as support for the implementation of new solutions and technologies (Fishendler, Boymel, & Boykoff, 2014). The subject of energy security began to play an important role in public discourses following the terrorist attacks of September 11, 2001 (Brown & Huntington, 2008). Usually this refers to assuring the continuity of energy supplies, yet the concept also has much broader connotations (Baumann, 2008). Energy is generally treated here as an instrument of foreign policy. The securitization and politicization of the discourse is often connected with the weaponization of energy and the use of natural resources for political purposes (Belyi, 2015; Newnham, 2011).

While the gravity of problems of stability of supplies and prices of energy is widely accepted, there are sharp differences in the way the media of various countries present the same issues, reflecting different geopolitical interests. An example is the presentation of energy cooperation between the EU and Russia (Kratochvil & Tichy, 2013), or the portrayal of shale gas in Russia (Ocelik & Osicka, 2014), the United Kingdom (Cottone, Rattle, & Alstine 2014; Upham et al., 2015 and Poland (Jaspal, Nerlich, & Lemańczyk, 2014; Lis & Stankiewicz, 2017; Wagner, 2017).

A question that is indirectly connected to this is *framing risk* in energy discourses. This is presented in various ways: from economic and political risk (e.g., resulting from a state withdrawing its support for a given technology or from international political conflicts), to risks to the environment, health, and/or a community (e.g., a region's changing character as a result of industrialization). Strategies in this respect involve targeted selection of information in order to create a desired picture and making strategic use of it. Yet it is important to remember that the potential risks of a new technology can be presented through its advantages and disadvantages as well (cf. Heras-Saizarbitoria, Cilleruelo, & Zamanillo, 2011). Both can be "subject to amplification as a consequence of how they are reported in the media—a process known as "risk amplification" (Kang & Jang, 2014). In dominant political-economic discourses, even where questions of environmental risk are acknowledged, they are often treated in a simplified way, and the preventive mechanisms are reduced to standard procedures (Kratochvil & Tichy, 2013; Wagner, 2017). It is also often the case that risk is discursively exported beyond a distant time frame, thus blurring the problem of threat and responsibility (e.g., in the case of nuclear waste disposal).

Those marginalized perspectives in discourses on energy issues that are adopted most frequently are those of the residents of areas earmarked for investments, or citizens in general. When these perspectives do appear, they are most likely to be invoked in reference to social protests, and tend to be caricatured within hegemonic media discourses as the "NIMBY phenomenon" (Devine-Wright, 2005), characterizing citizens' concerns as irrational fears resulting from lack of knowledge of technology (Stankiewicz, 2009). Various interest groups often co-opt the voices of concerned residents, assigning them to particular positions in a discourse. Rarely in media do we encounter instances in which the representatives of local communities speak for themselves.

The media are geared toward drama, and prefer surprising events or those that arouse emotions, yet the discourse of emotions does not fulfill the criteria of rational argument favored in deliberation (Zabdyr-Jamróz, 2016). Local communities are often depicted in the context of protests or dramatic events, such as the terrorist attack on a rally for energy justice taking place in Kabul on July 23, 2016. Owing to the 80 deaths and hundreds of injuries, participants in the demonstration attracted international media attention.

ACTORS

The actors speaking out on energy-related issues with the greatest exposure in the media are politicians, a tendency recorded by research on discourse in numerous countries, including Germany, Portugal, the United States, China, Poland, Lithuania, the United Kingdom, and Israel. Researchers have also consistently observed the domination of political and economic perspectives, followed by technological and environmental ones (Feldpausch-Parker, 2011; Horsbøl, 2010; Sojak, Afeltowicz, & Stankiewicz, 2013; Stephens, Rand, & Melnick 2009). In some cases, however, such as discussion of specific technological options, scientists are increasingly visible in the media (cf. Schmidt et al., 2013).

Alongside politicians, influential representatives of business and economic experts occupy a privileged position in energy discourses. This is demonstrated not only by their greater media exposure (more frequent presence in the media, more attractive places and times of programs or publications, opportunity to speak independently—interview, participation in discussion panels), but also by symbolic representations of attention and their status—for example, the roles of specific guests, with their quoted statements portrayed as influential and opinion-forming. These statements are placed in the context of socioeconomic events and subjects that are labeled as important, and are accompanied by figures and graphs. They are often observed in the context of formal events, and newspaper interviews feature photographs of the people, whose formal clothing accentuates their high social status.

Also visible in the media are well-organized governmental, nongovernmental, and industry groups, which often use professional means to solicit media attention. The privileged treatment of large governmental organizations and corporate interest groups is supported by the aforementioned mechanism whereby these entities, which the media treat as reliable sources, provide ready-made information packages. The resultant effect is known in the literature as "sourcing"—influencing media content by delivering extensive, free packages of current information (Herman & Chomsky, 1988). The presence of recognizable social actors increases the status and adds to the credibility of the news item, making it attractive for the media (Luhmann, 2000a).

Research reveals an ambivalent role for scientists in discourses on energy issues—in some cases their presence is minimal (Waegel, 2015), and they even deliberately withdraw from media discourse (Wagner, 2014), while in others their roles as experts legitimizing various positions are accentuated (Schmidt et al., 2013). It is a similar case with NGOs, and especially ENGOs. Although usually present in the media discourse, they often receive unequal treatment compared to dominant actors. Their arguments are frequently overlooked (Feldpausch-Parker et al., 2011; Kittle & Kelly, 2012; Uusi-Rauva & Tienneri, 2010) or deprecated as unscientific, irrational, utopian, controversial, and so on. The visibility of NGOs' positions in the media grows, however, when they represent a symbolic coalition with other actors, for example politicians or labor movements (Norman, 2016). The growing visibility of civil society actors in the public sphere makes it easier for those actors to introduce alternative points of view into the discourse, and thus to wield influence on the shaping of energy policy, yet we should note that this does not happen automatically. For example, the wide representation of discursive topics in the case of shale gas in the United Kingdom has not caused the hegemonic discourse of economic-political elites to be broken: "The dominant story line within Government concerns global competitiveness, energy security and profitability—over-riding not only activist concerns with environmental impacts, climate ethics, procedural justice and renewable energy development but also framing shale gas more and more as destination, rather than transition fuel" (Cotton, Rattle, & Alstine, 2014, p. 436).

The marginalization of environmental organizations and civil society actors contradicts the paradigm of ecological modernisation (Breukers & Wolsink, 2007), which considers them to be key actors in shaping environmental policies. Ecological modernization theory (EMT) proposes that environmental policy can stimulate modernization of the economy and technological innovation (Hajer, 1995), underlining the necessity of, and yet not problematizing, wider representations of stakeholders in public debate. Weak representation of environmental actors also fails to satisfy the requirements of democratic deliberation—a condition of which is inclusion in the debate of everyone who has an interest in providing input. Exclusion can lead to the exacerbation of protest actions, as these "myriad stakeholder actors attempt to reassert the dominance of their competing story lines in shaping policy outcomes" (Cotton, Rattle, & Alstine, 2014, p. 436).

The relations between the various categories of social actors are very diverse: from evident opposition, to attempts to engage in dialogue, and the construction of epistemic coalitions. The representation of different types of actors also differs in various societies, with some actors receiving more prominence in some contexts and less in others, because different countries exhibit differences in the communicative public sphere (Ferree et al., 2002), media cultures (cf. Esser, 1999), and level of development of the critical public sphere (Teräväinen, Lehtonen, & Martiskainen, 2011). Research suggests that the energy discourses in countries with mature democracies—Germany, France, the United Kingdom, and the Netherlands—are more inclusive, whereas younger democracies tend to restrict the media representation of actors engaged in the discourse, marginalizing NGO representatives, social activists, and representatives of local communities (cf. Lis & Stankiewicz, 2017; Pilibaityte, Balockaite, & Juraite 2011; Wagner, Grobelsky, & Harembski, 2016).

MEDIA AND ENERGY TRANSITION

Media discourses on energy are particularly consequential, because those discourses can support path dependence or transition. The power of the media institution lies in its ability to make discourses visible and, as a consequence, it has the symbolic power to shape citizens' consciousness. Therefore, the media space is an important arena, where different interest groups fight for public attention and legitimation of their positions. Putting particular problems on the public agenda gives actors a chance to evoke a political response in the form of public policy. Not only actual benefits, but also future possibilities, are here at stake.

Path dependence refers to the reliance of energy systems on decisions made in the past. The opposite concept is energy transition, described as path creation, "involving distributed and active agency, where new opportunities are created by a collective through mindful deviation" (SYKE, 2016). There is no doubt that the media have the potential to create a new path by educating and distributing information on innovations.

On the other hand, they serve to maintain the status quo. Diverse interests clash here—some actors will be very eager to implement changes, while others are likely to block them. Rinkinen (2011) distinguishes four sources of innovations in energy systems: new market entrants, old incumbent companies, civic activity, and policy interventions. He also points to their potential interactions. Actors representing all these areas are capable of generating the narratives present in the mainstream media, which can affect social thought patterns. The conditions of effective communicative action are access to the public sphere, and the capacity to attract the attention of the general public and ultimately support for one's position. Media support, shaping the consciousness of citizens, is a necessary condition, although it is certainly insufficient for effective transition to more sustainable technologies. This also requires changes in the field of direct and indirect economic and social mechanisms of supporting them in order "to form a landscape where sustainable new energy technologies may develop in more favorable conditions" (SYKE, 2016).

In global energy systems on the whole, fossil-fuel interests continue to dominate. Despite scientists' calls for profound transformations to energy policies and the advanced discourse on anthropogenic climate change, energy systems exhibit strong resistance to radical changes (Scrase & Ockwell, 2010), tending instead to concentrate on improving individual indicators, and this is reflected in mainstream media. The mainstream media prefer to adopt the lines of argument of government administrations rather than draw from those of scientific discourse (Weagel, 2014). If the main tasks of governments in liberal democracies include maintaining domestic order, surviving internationally as an independent state and raising revenue, economic growth, and civil legitimacy (Dryzek et al., 2003), this results in institutional limitations, as well as physical limitations on discourse—in other words, social practices, which "governed by energy policy have direct physical consequences for human beings, animals and nature which can result in their health suffering and, sometimes, their death" (Scrase & Ockwell, 2010).

Scrase and Ockwell (2010) argue that only actors capable of discursive construction of a frame to respond to core imperatives will be able to join the discourse that influences energy policy. Illustrating this point, the discourse on renewable energy sources is increasingly anchored in the field of economics (new jobs, cheap energy). "A policy discourse framed solely around the environmental and social benefits of renewables would be unlikely to meet with any fundamental success in influencing policy" (Scrase & Ockwell, 2010, p. 2228).

Path creation/path dependency is linked to public acceptance and social resistance. Whereas indicators of public acceptance usually appear in the media in the form of cited statistics, such methods do not capture the extent of social resistance to technology, which is generated by small but well-organized groups capable of using the media instrumentally (Devine-Wright, 2005). They might be invisible in aggregated statistics of opinion polls, yet remain visible in the media. In the latter, issues of social resistance are either presented in a NIMBY context, or placed within archetypal narratives such as that of David and Goliath: poor and disorganized residents/citizens, defending their world from callous, gigantic corporations whose economic interests are guarded by an army of lawyers. A question that arises is whether resistance groups making effective use of the media, capable of achieving short-term benefits including concessions from investors and politicians, are also able to convert the media visibility they have success-fully mobilized into influence on long-term energy policy. Are they able to introduce an alternative narrative to the discourse and become empowered in the public sphere? Previous events suggest that this influence is very limited. To a great extent, the media discourse is subordinated to the ideological hegemony of neoliberalism.

Growing uncertainty and disruption in politics in many parts of the world today favor the production of future governance visions in strictly ideological terms (Ekenburg, 2012). Discursive control over areas of uncertainty can become a source of political power (Luhmann, 2000b). Such dominance structures are reproduced through media communication: they define the parameters of that communication, within which other actors must operate. This communication is a space in which the past and the future can meet in the present (Luhmann, 1976), in the form of experiences and expectation. Therefore the visions of the future that are presented in current media discourse, the ways in which the future is anticipated and negotiated between different actors, can be another significant dimension of public dialogues on energy.

The mechanisms of futurization and de-futurization discussed by Luhmann (1976) describe how the future is "opened," by allowing the possibility of different scenarios (futurization), or "closed," by reducing them to one of the most likely or desired scenarios (de-futurization). Defining the future can serve the interests of legitimacy or revolution, protecting the status quo or changing the reality. It is associated with diag-nosis capabilities (including resources such as knowledge and technological develop-ment) and based on value systems. Visions of the future in relation to energy are crucial because of the need for setting goals and providing a framework for the activities of various actors in the sector and the long-term and multidimensional effects of their decisions, gaining acceptance for them and building a sense of responsibility for their actions.

The visions of the future in current media discourse can be interpreted in different ways: the design of development can be subject to reflection in the context of coloniza-tion of the future (Adam, 2004), and the narration of a crisis can serve to mobilize im-mediate action and will support the focus on alternative visions of the future (Luhmann, 2000b).

The dominance of the technological, economic, and political perspectives (including securitization) described earlier favors mechanisms of de-futurization. The narrowing of potential future scenarios to one, the most desirable and impending, this dominant perspective has as its main goal the protection of the current system of power and hege-monic interests. Alternative scenarios are often labeled as utopian, relegated to the role of critiquing the status quo rather than identifying alternative future pathways.

Although some voices advocate formulating energy policy on an international level (Szulecki & Westphal, 2014), media discourses on energy issues do not contribute signif-icantly to such discussions. This is partly related to the dominant structure of economic interests. Ideas serving the expansion of fossil fuel markets are strongly embedded in today's predominantly technocratic and nationalistic energy policy discourses (Dryzek et al., 2003). Media discourses seem to be influenced by short-term events, while the energy and climate crises we face refer to the long-term horizon of human existence. Energy discourse in the media is influenced by accidents and current economic and political events, and rarely embraces the challenge of constructing a long-term vision of the future, instead focusing on the near future.

Energy Public Discourse as a Post-Hegemonic Discourse

Hard as it is to argue with the pragmatic belief that only the narratives of actors who remain within the fundamentals of a liberal state can exert a real influence on energy policy, radical and alternative narratives are crucial for deliberation and social dialogue, as they have the potential to question hegemonic discourses and introduce new narratives of knowledge (Ojha, Cameron, & Kumar, 2012). As a result, alternative narratives support the process of change to public policies and increase flexibility in responses to our currently turbulent reality. Yet, Cammaerts (2015) describes contemporary media discourse as a post-hegemonic discourse, in which the ideological premises of neoliberalism are treated as obvious and ideologically neutral, constructing the framework of rationality and responsible governance. As a result, they become invisible.

The discourse on energy issues is no different—the logic of power and money continues to apply. Individuals are therefore treated mainly as consumers, not as citizens (Brondi et al., 2014). The epistemic groups connected with the governing administration, and the world of politics and large corporate interests, are clearly dominant over other actors when it comes to opportunities for articulating visions, demands, and values. This discourse absorbs narratives that are potential counter-powers, yet, by marginalizing their importance and depreciating them, at the same time it removes their revolutionary power (Cammaerts, 2015). A fundamental fault in the development of civic dialogue on energy issues is its elite nature (using technical language, expert knowledge—economic, political, technological—as a prerequisite for participation), as well as elimination of alternative narratives. The influence of economic and political elites on the media is excessive in contemporary societies (Cammaerts, 2015; Domhoff, 2013), especially considering their perceived lack of effectiveness in solving the problems the world is facing (Dryzek et al., 2003; Klein, 2014).

The blank spaces on the map of problems and topics present in media discourses on energy include issues raised by representatives of social studies: energy poverty and justice—unequal distributions of costs and benefits linked to energy—around the world. In some countries, climate issues are presented separately from energy issues, or climate policy goals are discussed as formal political obligations without building a deeper awareness of the problem. Media also does not provide space for expression of political ideas that might create an alternative to the neoliberal vision of future development. While the link between energy and environmental problems is undoubted, some argue that the current structure of the economy poses a hurdle to effective actions. Economic efficiency is today one of the main foundations of the system, and cannot be endangered by, for example, radical restrictions on production (Baker, 2000).

Meanwhile, according to some researchers, counter-power narratives are currently weak and poorly visible because of the need to situate such narratives within the field of economic rationality (Teräväinen, Lehtonen, & Martiskainen, 2011). As Fischer and Gottweiss (2012) argue, however, it was agreement on values and ideas that drove social movements to make the key steps in the development of democracy of Western societies. Klein makes a similar argument, stressing the agency of political ideas and the language of morality. She calls for a departure from pragmatic arguments, pointing to costs and benefits in favor of speaking about what is good and bad (Klein, 2014). Today, attempts to create new, alternative narratives tend to find their place outside of the mainstream of media communication—for example in nonfiction prose, presenting both the global perspective (Klein, 2014) and the local one, giving a voice to residents, as in the reportages of Nobel Prize–winner Svetlana Alexievich (2016), and in alternative media, including social media. For now, their visibility in the public sphere, and thus also their true impact on the hegemonic discourse and politics, remains limited.

NOTE

1. This has important consequences. In Australia, for example, it has been observed that perception of issues related to the coal industry that deviates from the facts supports the hegemony of this energy sector (Richardson & Denniss, 2011).

REFERENCES

Adam, B. (2004). *Minding futures: An exploration of responsibility for long term futures. (Working Paper 67)* Retrieved from www.cardiff.ac.uk/socsi/futures/

Adut, A. (2012). A theory of the public sphere. *Sociological Theory, 30*(4), 238–262.

Alexievich, S. (2016). *Chernobyl prayer: A chronicle of the future.* New York: Penguin Modern Classics.

Baker, S. (2000). The EU: Integration, competition and growth—and sustainability. In W. M. Lafferty & J. Meadowcraft (Eds.), *Implementing sustainable development* (pp. 303–336). Oxford: Oxford University Press.

Baumann, F. (2008, March). Energy security as multidimensional concept. *Policy Analysis.* Retrieved from http://www.cap.lmu.de/download/2008/CAP-Policy-Analysis-2008-01.pdf

Belyi, A. (2015). *Transnational gas markets and Euro-Russian energy relations.* London: Palgrave Macmillan.

Benhabib, S. (1992). Models of public space: Hannah Arendt, the liberal tradition, and Jürgen Habermas." In C. Calhoun (Ed.), *Habermas and the public sphere* (pp. 73–98). Cambridge, MA: MIT Press.

Benkler, Y. (2006). *The wealth of networks* New Haven, CT: Yale Universty Press.

Bittle, S., Rochkind, J., & Ott, A. (2009). *The Energy Learning Curve™: Coming from different starting points, the public sees similar solutions. A report from Public Agenda.* Retrieved from www.publicagenda.org/reports/energy

Boersma, T., & Johnson, C. (2013). Energy (in)security in Poland the case of shale gas. *Energy Policy, 53*, 389–399.

Bohman, J. (2000). The division of labour in democratic discourse: Media, experts, and deliberative democracy. In S. Chambers & A. Costain (Eds.), *Deliberation, democracy and media* (pp. 47–64). Lanham, MD: Rowman and Littlefield.

Breukers, S., & Wolsink, M. (2007). Wind energy policies in the Netherlands in stitutional capacity-building for ecological modernisation. *Environmental Politics, 16*(1), 92–112.

Brondi, S., Armenti, A., Cottone, P., Mazzara, B. M., & Sarrica, M. (2014). Parliamentary and press discourses on sustainable energy in Italy: No more hard paths, not yet soft paths. *Energy Research & Social Science, 2*, 38–48.

Brown, S. P. A., & Huntington, H. G. (2008). Energy security and climate change protection: Complementary or trade off? *Energy Policy, 36*, 3510–3513.

Cammaerts, B. (2015). Neoliberalism and the post-hegemonic war of position: The dialectic between invisibility and visibilities. *European Journal of Communication, 30*(5), 522–538.

Castells, M. (2009). *Communication power.* Oxford: Oxford University Press.

Chan, C.-W. (2012). *A study on media discourse on nuclear energy in China.* PhD dissertation. Retrieved from http://hdl.handle.net/10722/180102.

Cherry, C., Hopfe, C., MacGillivray, B., & Pidgeon, N. (2015). Media discourses of low carbon housing: The marginalisation of social and behavioural dimensions within the British broadsheet press. *Public Understanding of Science, 24*(3), 302–310.

Cotton, M., Rattle, I., & Alstine, J. (2014). Shale gas policy in the United Kingdom: An argumentative discourse analysis. *Energy Policy, 73*, 427–438.

Christensen, H. S. (2016). *Political activism on the Internet: Slactivism or political participation by other means?* Retrieved from http://firstmonday.org/ojs/index.php/fm/article/view/3336/2767

Devine-Wright, P. (2005). Beyond NIMBYism: towards an integrated framework for understanding public perceptions of wind energy. *Wind Energy, 8*, 125–139.

Domhoff, W. G. (2013). *The myth of liberal ascendancy: Corporate dominance from the Great Depression to the Great Recession.* Boulder, CO: Paradigm.

Dryzek, J. S. (2000). *Deliberative democracy and beyond: Liberals, critics, contestations.* Oxford: Oxford Univeristy Press.

Dryzek, J. S., Downs, D., Hunold, C., Schlosberg, D., & Hernes, H.-K. (2003). *Green states and social movements: Environmentalism in the United States, United Kingdom, Germany and Norway.* Oxford: Oxford University Press.

Ekengren, M. (2002). *The time of European governance.* Manchester, UK: Manchester University Press.

Evans, G., & Phelan, L. (2016). Transition to a post-carbon society: Linking environmental justice and just transition discourses. *Energy Policy, 99*, 329–339.

Esser, F. (1999). Tabsloidisation of News: A Comparative Analysis of Anglo-American and German Press Journalism. *European Journal of Communication, 14*(3), 291–324.

Eurobarometer. (2007). *Energy technologies: Knowledge, perception, measures.* Retrieved from http://ec.europa.eu/commfrontoffice/publicopinion/archives/ebs/ebs_262_en.pdf

Eurobarometer. (2015). *Public Opinion in the EU*, no. 83. Retrieved from http://ec.europa.eu/commfrontoffice/publicopinion/index.cfm

Fairclough, N. (2011). *Media discourse.* London; New York: Bloomsbury Academic.

Feldpausch-Parker, A. M., Ragland, C. J., Melnick, L. L., Chaudhry, R., Hall, D. M., Peterson, T. R., Stephens, J. C., & Wilson, E. J. (2011). A comparative state-level analysis of Carbon Capture and Storage (CCS) discourse among U.S. energy stakeholders and the public. *Energy Procedia, 4,* 6368–6375.

Ferree, M. M., Gamson, W., Gerhards, J., & Rucht, D. (2002). Four models of the public sphere in modern democracies. *Theory & Society, 31*(3), 289–324.

Fischer, F., & Forester, J. (1993). *The argumentative turn in policy analysis and planning.* Durham, NC; London: Duke University Press.

Fischer, F., & Gottweiss, H. (2012). *The argumentative turn revisited: Public policy as communicative practice.* Durham, NC: Duke University Press.

Fishendler, I., Boymel, D., & Boykoff, M. T. (2014). How competing securitized discourses over land appropriation are constructed: The promotion of solar energy in the Israeli Desert. *Environmental Communication.* Retrieved from http://sciencepolicy.colorado.edu/admin/publication_files/2014.48.pdf

Fishkin, J. S. (2009). *When the people speak: Deliberative democracy and public consultation.* Oxford: Oxford University Press.

Fuchs, C. (2014). *Social media: A critical introduction.* London: Sage, 2014.

Gamson, W., & Modigliani, A. (1989) Media discourse and public opinion on nuclear power: A constructionist approach. *American Journal of Sociology, 95*(1), 1–37.

van der Graaf, A., Otjes, S., & Rasmussen, A. (2016). Weapon of the weak? The social media landscape of interest groups. *European Journal of Communication, 31*(2), 120–135.

Habermas, J. (1992). Further reflections on the public sphere and concluding remarks. In C. Calhoun (Ed.), *Habermas and the public sphere* (pp. 421–479). Cambridge, MA: MIT Press.

Hajer, M. A. (1995). *The politics of environmental discourse: Ecological modernization and the policy process.* New York: Oxford University Press.

Happer, C., Philo, G., & Froggatt, A. (2012). *Climate change and energy security: Assessing the impact of information and its delivery on attitudes and behaviour.* London: UK Energy Research Centre.

Heras-Saizarbitoria, I., Cilleruelo, E., & Zamanillo, I. (2011). Public acceptance of renewables and the media: an analysis of the Spanish PV solar experience. *Renewable and Sustainable Energy Reviews, 15,* 4685–4696.

Herman, E., & Chomsky, N. (1988). *Manufacturing consent.* New York: Pantheon Books.

Hirschberg, S., Wiemer, S., & Burgherr, P. (2015). *Energy from the Earth: Deep geothermal as a resource for the future?* Retrieved from http://e-collection.library.ethz.ch/eserv/eth:46999/eth-46999-01.pdf

Horsbøl, A. (2013). Energy transition in and by the local media: The Public emergence of an "energy town." *Nordicom Review, 34*(2), 19–34.

Howe, J. (2008). *Crowdsourcing: Why the power of crowd is driving the future of business.* New York: Three Rivers Press.

Hubert, W. (2017). Representation of selected energy topics on the Polish Internet. In A. Wagner (Ed.), *Visible and unvisible: Nuclear energy, shale gas, wind power in the Polish media discourse* (pp. 159–176). Krakow: Jagiellonian University Press (WUJ).

Iyengar, S., & Kinder, D. (1987). *News that matters*. Chicago: University of Chicago Press.

Jann, W., & Wegrich, K. (2007). Theories of the policy cycle. In F. Fischer, G. J. Miller, & M. S. Sidney (Eds)., *Handbook of public policy analysis* (pp. 43–62). London: CRC Press.

Jenkins, H. (2008). *Convergence culture*. New York: New York University Press.

Juza, M. (2016). Internet w życiu społecznym: Nadzieje, obawy, krytyka [Interent in social life: hopes,concerns, critics]. *Studia Socjologiczne, 1*(220), 199–221.

Jaspal, R., Nerlich, B., & Lemańczyk, S. (2014). Fracking in the Polish press: Geopolitics and national identity. *Energy Policy, 74*, 253–261.

Kang, M., & Jiho, J. (2014). NIMBY or NIABY? Who defines a policy problem and why: Analysis of framing in radioactive waste disposal facility placement in South Korea. *Asia Pacific Viewpoint, 54*(1), 49–60.

Kittle, M. A., & Kelly, A. R. (2012). Merging Duke Energy and Progress Energy: Online public discourse, post-Fukushima reactions, and the absence of environmental communication. *Environmental Communication, 6*(2), 278–284.

Klein, N. (2014). *This changes everything: Capitalism vs. climate*. New York: Penguin.

Kratochvıl, P., & Tichy, L. (2013). EU and Russian discourse on energy relations. *Energy Policy, 56*, 391–406.

Lis, A., & Stankiewicz, P. (2017). Framing shale gas for policy-making in Poland. *Journal of Environmental Policy & Planning, 19*, 53–71.

Littlefield, S. R. (2013). Security, independence, and sustainability: Imprecise language and the manipulation of energy policy in the United States. *Energy Policy, 52*, 779–788.

Lockwood, A. (2008, September 12). Seeding doubt: How sceptics use new media to delay action on climate change. Paper delivered to the Association for Journalism Education (AJE) annual conference on New Media, New Democracy. Sheffield University.

Luhmann, N. (1976). The future cannot begin: Temporal structures in modern society. *Social Science Social Research: An International Quarterly Interaction Between European and American, 43*(1), 130–152.

Luhmann, N. (2000a). *The reality of the mass media*. Stanford, CA: Stanford University Press.

Luhmann, N. (2000b). *Die Politik der Gesellschaft*. Frankfurt am Main: Suhrkamp.

Luokkanen, M., Suvi, H., & Hildén, M. (2014). Geoengineering, news media and metaphors: Framing the controversial. *Public Understanding of Science, 23*(8), 966–981.

Majone, G. (1989). *Evidence, argument, and persuasion in the policy process*. New Haven, CT: Yale University Press.

McCombs, M. E., & Shaw, D. L. (1972). The agenda-setting function of mass media. *Public Opinion Quarterly, 36*(2), 176–187.

McNutt, K., & Marchildon, G. (2009). Think tanks and the web: Measuring visibility and influence. *Canadian Public Policy, 35*, 219–235.

McQuail, D. (2005). *Mass communication theory*. London: Sage.

Morozov, E. (2009). *Foreign policy: Brave new world of slacktivism*. Retrieved from http://www.npr.org/templates/story/story.php?storyId=104302141

Müller, M. (2015). Changing climates: Findings on the German print media discourse. Presentation held at the Workshop *Changing Climates and the Media,*" September 21, 2015, University of Lancaster.

Newnham, R. (2011). Oil, carrots, and sticks: Russia's energy resources as a foreign policy tool. *Journal of Eurasian Studies, 2,*(2), 134–143.

Nisbet, M. (2009). Communicating climate change: Why frames matter for public engagement. *Environment: Science and Policy for Sustainable Development, 51*(2), 12–23.

Norman, H. (2016). Mining Gomeroi country: Sacred lands, economic futures and shifting alliances. *Energy Policy*, *99*, 242–251.

Ocelik, P., & Osicka, J. (2014). The framing of unconventional natural gas resources in the foreign energy policy discourse of the Russian Federation. *Energy Policy*, *72*, 97–109.

Ojha, H., Cameron, J., & Kumar, C. (2012). Deliberation or symbolic violence? The governance of community forestry in Nepal. *Forest Policy and Economics*, *11*(5), 365–374.

O'Riordan, T., & Jordan, A. (1996). Social institution and climate change. In T. O'Riordan & J. Jager (Eds.), *Politics of climate change: an European perspective* (pp. 65–106). London: Routledge.

Pilibaityte, V., Balockaite, R., & Juraite, K. (2012). Energy security discourse in Lithuanian media: Comparative assessment of energy security in Lithuania and Belarus: A cross-disciplinary study, 2011–2012. Research report: NORDISCO 2012, Nordic and Baltic Interdisciplinary Conference on Discourse and Interaction, Linkoping, Sweden, November 21–23, 2012.

Rasmussen, A., & Carroll, B. (2014). Determinants of upper-class dominance in the heavenly chorus: Lessons from European Commission online consultations. *British Journal of Political Science*, *44*(2), 445–459.

Richardson, D., & Denniss, R. (2011). *Mining the truth: The rhetoric and reality of the commodities boom*. Institute Paper No. 7. Canberra: The Australia Institute.

Rinkinen, J. (2011). The role of media discourse in path creation: The case of energy use of Finnish personal transport system. Paper presented at the Second International Conference on Sustainability Transitions Diversity. University of Lund, Sweden.

Scrase, I., & Ockwell, D. G. (2010). The role of discourse and linguistic framing effects in sustaining high carbon energy policy- an accessible introduction. *Energy Policy*, *38*, 2225–2233.

Scheufele, D. A. (1999). Framing as a theory of media effects. *Journal of Communication*, *49*(1), 103–122.

Scheufele, D. A. (2000). Agenda-setting, priming, and framing revisited: Another look at cognitive effects of political communication. *Mass Communication and Society*, *3*, 297–316.

Scheufele, D. A., & Nisbet, M. (2002). Being a citizen online: New opportunities and dead ends. *The International Journal of Press/Politics*, *7*(3), 55–75.

Scheufele, D. A., & Tewksbury, D. (2007). Framing, agenda setting, and priming: The evolution of three media effects models. *Journal of Communication*, *57*(1), 9–20.

Schmidt, L., Horta, A., Pereira, S., & Oliveira, C. (2013). *Comparative analysis of the public discourse about fusion and nuclear energy before and after Fukushima*. WP12-SER-ACIF-1 Final Report. Retrieved from http://hdl.handle.net/10451/8678

Schmoyer, R. L., Truett, T., & Cooper, C. (2006). *Results of the 2004 knowledge and opinions surveys for the baseline knowledge assessment of the U.S. Department of Energy Hydrogen Program*. Research Report. Retrieved from https://info.ornl.gov/sites/publications/Files/Pub1840.pdf

Shirky, C. (2008). *Here comes everybody*. London: Penguin.

Sojak, R., Afeltowicz, L., & Stankiewicz, P. (2013). *Transnational media discourse on nuclear energy before and after the Fukushima accident*. Unpublished report prepared for EFDA: WP12-SER-ACIF-1 by Nicolaus Copernicus University (NCU).

Southwell, B., Murphy, J. J., DeWaters, J. E., & Le Baron, P. A. (2012). *Americans' perceived and actual understanding of energy*. RTI Press publication No. RR-0018-1208. Research Triangle Park, NC: RTI Press. Retrieved from http://www.rti.org/rtipress

Stankiewicz, P. (2009). The role of risks and uncertainties in technological conflicts: Three strategies of constructing ignorance Innovation. *The European Journal of Social Science Research*, 22(1), 105–124.

Stankiewicz, P., & Stasik, A. (2014). *Raport: Poszukiwanie i wydobycie gazu łupkowego w Polsce—wiedza, opinie, oceny*. Retrieved from http://infolupki.pgi.gov.pl/sites/default/files /czytelnia_pliki/1/sondaz_pig_raport_gaz_lupkowy.pdf

Stephens, J. C., Rand, G. M., & Melnick, L. L. (2009). Wind energy in US media: A comparative state-level analysis of a critical climate change mitigation technology. *Environmental Communication*, 3(2), 168–190.

Świątkiewicz-Mośny, M., & Wagner, A. (2012). How much energy in energy policy? The media on energy problems in developing countries (with the example of Poland). *Energy Policy*, 50, 383–390.

Syke. (2016). The project description. Retrieved from http://www.syke.fi/en-us/Research __Development/Research_and_development_projects/Projects/Path_Dependence_and _Path_Creation_in_Energy_Systems__A_MultiLevel_Perspective_on_Technological _Business_and_Policy_Innovations_EnPath

Szulecki, K., & Westphal, K. (2014). The cardinal sins of European energy policy: Nongovernance in an uncertain global landscape. *Global Policy*, 5(1).

Teräväinen, T., Lehtonen, M., & Martiskainen, M. (2011). Climate change, energy security, and risk: Debating nuclear new build in Finland, France and the UK. *Energy Policy*, 39, 3434–3442.

Upham, P., Lis, A., Riesch, H., & Stankiewicz, P. (2014). Addressing social representations in socio-technical transitions with the case of shale gas. *Environmental Innovation and Societal Transitions*, 16, 120–141.

Uusi-Rauva, C., & Tienari, J. (2010). The EU energy and climate package: A showcase for european environmental leadership? *Environmental Policy and Governance*, 20, 73–88.

Wagner, A. (2014). Shale gas: Energy innovation in a (non-)knowledge society: A press discourse analysis. *Science and Public Policy*, 42(2), 273–286.

Wagner, A. (2017). *Visible and unvisible: Nuclear, shale gas and wind mills in media discourses in Poland*. Krakow: WUJ.

Wagner, A., Grobelski, T., & Harembski, N, (2016). Is energy policy a public issue? Nuclear power in Poland and implications for energy transitions in Central and East Europe. *Energy Research and Social Science*, 13, 158–169.

Weagel, A. (2015). *The use of language and its impact on energy policy discourse: A case study of the hydrogen economy and the news media during the G. W. Bush administration*. PhD Thesis, University of Delaware. Retrieved from http://udspace.udel.edu/handle/19716/17198

Westerman, D., Spence, P. R., & Van Der Heide, B. (2014). Social media as information source: Recency of updates and credibility of information. *Journal of Computer-Mediated Communication*, 19(2), 171–183.

Wodak, R., & Busch, B. (2004). Approaches to media texts. In J. Dowling, D. McQuail, P. Schlesinger, & E. Wartella (Eds.), *Handbook of media studies* (pp. 105–123). Thousand Oaks, CA; London; New Delhi: Sage.

Zabdyr-Jamróz, M. (2016). *Combining emotions, self-interests and expertise: Three discourses in deliberation assembled*. Retrieved from https://www.researchgate.net/publication /304451397_Combining_Emotions_Self-Interests_and_Expertise_Three_Discourses_in _Deliberation_Assembled

Zoller, H. M., & Fairhurst, G. T. (2007). Resistance leadership: The overlooked potential in critical organization and leadership studies. *Human Relations*, 60(9).

PART VI

....

ENERGY (RE)TAKES CENTER STAGE IN POLITICS

....

EMPHASIS in this section will be on the growing rise to prominence of energy issues in social movements activity, which has emerged in several guises. Once outside of the limelight of civil society, energy has increasingly become the subject of attention by a diverse spread of social movement organizations. As Delicado has described in Chapter 18, local peoples have special interest in energy development that takes place near their homes. In some cases, these interests coalesce into mobilized opposition. Local opposition to risky development is not new, but the growth in number, and successes, of those efforts directed specifically toward energy development is noteworthy.

Ion Bogdan Vasi offers an overview of the growth and coalescence of this movement activity in Chapter 21. He notes in particular that movements originally confined to local opposition to existing and proposed new energy infrastructure and facilities have a tendency to expand in scope. Initially dominated by attention to nuclear energy, fossil fuels have today received the lion's share of social movement attention, with campaigns critiquing the entire production chain, from extraction (mines) to transport (pipelines) to combustion (electricity plants). Particularly in developing countries, hydro power is subject to increasing criticism and organized opposition. Other forms of renewable energy are not immune to critique either; however, wind and solar have also received extensive social movement support. All this has culminated an increasingly global phenomenon, especially regarding the integration of climate change with energy issues. According to Vasi, this energy-based social movement activity has had an effect on current energy-society relations on par with technological innovations and market forces, perhaps best illustrated by the 2015 Paris Agreement, a political feat unimaginable just a year prior.

The next two chapters look more closely at specific social movement campaigns that have shaken up energy politics, and serve as confirmation of Vasi's statements on the potential influence of social movement activity. In Chapter 22, Jennifer Dodge traces the development of conflicts over hydraulic fracturing in New York, which culminated in the banning of those practices, despite the touted scale of shale deposits in the region. This conflict, as is the case with so many others, hinged on discourse, particularly divergent depictions of the potential, and risks, associated with the techniques deployed to access unconventional oil and gas reserves. Dodge finds three mutually exclusive "sociotechnical imaginaries" present in the media analysis of this conflict. One imaginary depicts dreams of riches and plenty; another offers nightmares of environmental and health tragedies; and yet a third is situated somewhere in between. The nightmare imaginary ultimately prevailed, and New York's governor eventually banned fracking from the state. Dodge attributes this outcome to the association of this nightmare imaginary with strong narratives of place attachment that served as a notable departure from the scientific and technical frames that often constitute energy imaginaries. Perhaps unexpectedly, this nightmare imaginary has taken hold in many regions of the world, even within the United States, where progressive dream imaginaries still prevail at the national level.

In Chapter 23, Mark C.J. Stoddart, Jillian Rene Smith, and Paula Graham direct our gaze north of New York, to observe oil politics in Canada, a nation-state that is perhaps even more enmeshed in a "carbon complex" than is the United States, in which oil and gas industries have become a financial mainstay. And yet even here, fossil fuel dependence is becoming problematized, and once again, the expansion of non-conventional oil and gas development activities seems to be a key instigator. One particular set of players has emerged at the forefront, representing a unique position in oil politics. Indigenous peoples in Canada have become formidable opponents of oil and gas development, portraying such development as merely the latest chapter in a long colonial history of expropriation, constituting a fundamental breach of their rights. Alliances among Indigenous and environmental groups have allowed for powerful arguments that integrate treaty rights with environmental justice, and social protest tactics including "Healing Walks." This alliance is not without friction, however, as each contingent tends to represent different depictions of justice. As with Dodge, Stoddart and his colleagues highlight the means by which divergent visions of place transpire in divergent local positions toward fracking.

We then move from defensive to proactive social movements, in support of renewable energy. In Chapter 24, Cyria Emelianoff compares Germany and Sweden, both of which are well along the path toward a substantial transition to renewable energy. Yet the pathways to transition taken in these two countries are starkly different, highlighting the fact that there is no single transition pathway. While the differences in these cases, however, are often attributed to national actors and laws as well as international events, Emelianoff tells a different story through in-depth interviews with actors in other realms. As with other chapters in this section, her work highlights the relevance of the local level, which "can be the origin of 'path creation.' " In both countries, organized activism in a small handful of cities became instrumental in leading national transitions.

CHAPTER 21

SOCIAL MOVEMENTS AND ENERGY

ION BOGDAN VASI

INTRODUCTION

ENERGY is sometimes described as the "lifeblood of society" because of the essential role it plays in economic development and technological progress. Yet, energy is also an increasingly contentious topic in countries around the world. The growing number of mobilizations against energy projects is the result of skyrocketing global consumption of energy and rising awareness about the environmental problems associated with energy production. To understand this, it is useful to first ponder a few facts: in 1971 the world total primary energy supply was 6,101 Mtoe; by 2014 that number had increased to 13,699 Mtoe (million tons of oil equivalent, where a ton of oil equivalent is the amount of energy released by burning one ton of crude oil); the vast majority of the energy nowadays is produced by burning fossil fuels such as oil (36%), natural gas (26%), and coal (18%), which contributes to global climate change; global consumption of energy is estimated to increase by about 50% by 2040; in recent years, approximately 7 million premature deaths annually have been linked to air pollution; if climate change proceeds as expected, one in six species could face extinction.[1]

Traditionally, activism related to energy has been directed against local energy-production facilities. During the 1970s, for example, many environmental protests have targeted nuclear power plants and polluting coal power plants. This has gradually changed, as activists have started to organize not only reactive campaigns against existing power plants, but also proactive protests against proposed ones. In developing countries, activists have also opposed plans to build large-scale energy projects, such as electricity-producing dams. At the same time, environmental activists around the world have been increasingly organizing to not only anti-"dirty" energy protests, but also campaigns that support decentralized governance structures and forms of energy operation. This has led to the emergence of pro-"clean" energy campaigns that contribute to growing demand for renewable energy. Governments and electric utilities have responded to the mounting pressure from energy-focused campaigns organized by environmental activists in different ways; while some have continued to support investment in fossil fuels, others have begun transitioning to a renewable energy future. This chapter identifies the main energy-focused campaigns organized by activists in developed and developing countries, discusses the ways in which governments and energy companies have responded to these campaigns, and explores current and future trends in energy production around the world.

Reactive Opposition to Energy Projects

While the rise of the environmental movement is often associated with the issue of pesticides and the publication of Rachel Carson's *Silent Spring* in 1962, the first large and sustained environmental protests were directed against energy production, particularly from nuclear power. The anti-nuclear protests can be described as reactive mobilizations, since they emerged in response to existing or proposed power plants. While some of the (early) protests were directed against the construction of nuclear power plants in specific locations, many of the (later) protests were opposing the construction of nuclear power "in anybody's backyard"—in other words, they supported a nationwide moratorium on nuclear power.

In the United States, local opposition to nuclear power plants goes back to the late 1950s, when activists from the San Francisco area organized protests against the building of the Bodega Bay power plant. Strong opposition from local activists contributed to the abandonment of plans to build this power plant and launched the anti-nuclear movement in the United States (Wellock, 1998). The efficiency of nuclear power created the perception that nuclear power could be used to produce electricity that is "too cheap to meter," and led to ambitious plans to build hundreds of nuclear power plants.[2] For example, in 1973 President Nixon launched Project Independence, which called for a massive expansion of nuclear power that would help the United States reach energy independence by 1980. In 1975 President Ford announced a plan to build 200 nuclear power plants by 1985 and an additional 600 by 2000 (Joppke, 1993).

One of the first US environmental groups to mobilize against nuclear power was the National Resources Defense Council (NRDC). In 1974 the NRDC published a report that demanded drastic tightening of plutonium regulation; in 1975 the NRDC took the lead in organizing opposition against the fast breeder program, which was supposed to become the core of the coming plutonium economy. The Union of Concerned Scientists (UCS) is another group that has been at the forefront of anti-nuclear opposition. In 1975 the UCS launched a signature drive that resulted in the collection of over 2,000 signatures from scientists who demanded a drastic reduction in the construction of

new reactors. As more and more environmental groups joined the coalition against nuclear power, the anti-nuclear opposition had grown from a loose network of concerned
individuals to a popular movement (Joppke, 1993). The anti-nuclear campaign peaked
in late 1970s, when the UCS, the Clamshell Alliance, and other environmental groups
organized large protests following the Three Mile Island nuclear accident.

Opposition to nuclear power was also at the forefront of the environmental movement
in many European countries. In Germany, activists organized a vigorous campaign in
Wyhl in 1975, which evolved into a permanent siege of a nuclear power plant construction
site and resulted in the arrest of thousands of people and the eventual decision to cancel
construction by local authorities. Other protests at Brokdorf and Grohnde resulted in
violent clashes with police and temporary damage of the image of the anti-nuclear campaign in public opinion and mass media (Wagner, 1994). By the late 1980s, however,
the anti-nuclear campaign in Germany has become widely recognized and politically
influential—it is estimated that almost 50% of the environmental protests in Germany in
the late 1980s and early 1990s were directed against nuclear power (Rucht & Roose, 2003).

Another country with influential anti-nuclear protests is Denmark. While
Denmark has no nuclear power plants today, during the early 1970s the Danish government launched a plan to build nuclear power plants in approximately 10 locations.
Immediately following the government's announcement to build nuclear power plants,
a new environmental group was formed: the Organization for Information about
Nuclear Power (OOA). OOA's goal was simple—to stop nuclear power in Denmark.
The organization's strategy was two-pronged: first, it demanded that the decision to
build nuclear power be taken away from the central administration and handed over
to the parliament; second, it asked for more public debate and information. Since the
government feared that a national referendum would be unfavorable to nuclear power,
it repeatedly postponed its plans for nuclear power (Jamison et al., 1990). By 1980 the
Danish anti-nuclear movement has grown to approximately 130 local groups and had
mobilized vigorously. For example, over the course of two years, anti-nuclear activists
distributed information about nuclear power to almost all households in the country,
a campaign that is considered to have "led to a Danish renunciation of nuclear power"
(Jamison et al., 1990, p. 98).

Other countries have also experienced strong anti-nuclear protests, albeit with various degrees of success. In Spain anti-nuclear protests were unable to prevent the construction of nuclear power plants, but turned public opinion against nuclear power
more rapidly than in countries such as United Kingdom, France, Italy, or Sweden (Kolb,
2007). In Sweden, the anti-nuclear demonstrations resulted in a minor reduction of
planned nuclear power plants in 1979, from 13 to 12; yet, once the policy course was set
for these power plans, "no deviations from this course could be observed on the implementation side" (Flam & Jamison, 1994). In France, the weak anti-nuclear mobilizations
were not capable of preventing the government from realizing its plan to power the
vast majority of the country with nuclear power. In contrast, the Austrian anti-nuclear
movement was able to influence the government's energy policy and to prevent the construction of nuclear power plants (Preglau, 1994).

Similarly to the anti-nuclear campaigns, protests against fossil-fuel power plants were predominantly reactive in nature. Early protests against fossil-fuel power plants were organized by environmental justice activists concerned about pollution in specific locations, for example, in Los Angeles and San Jose (Cole and Foster 2000; Pellow, 2005; Mascarenhas 2015). Local protests against coal-burning power plants have been organized in communities around the United States, and some of them have succeeded in reducing pollution or even closing power plants (Grant & Vasi, 2017). More recently, however, protests against the combustion of fossil fuels have shifted to regional and global problems. During the 1980s many environmental demonstrations were organized against coal-burning power plants because they caused regional acid rain. In Germany, for example, activists from Greenpeace and Robin Wood staged demonstrations that included climbing buildings and unfurling banners that read "Stop Acid Rain" and "The Forest Is Dead, Long Live Politics." These and other protests have contributed to the adoption of "more stringent environmental regulation of coal power plants, the closing of many domestic coal mines, decreasing public support for tax subsidies for the coal industry, and a gradual decline in overall coal production" (Vasi, 2011, p. 60).

Environmental activists have mobilized not only against coal-burning power plants but also against fossil-fuel extraction. Mountaintop removal (MTR) coal mining has been an area of intense mobilization in recent years, particularly in the Appalachian region in the United States. One of the organizations at the forefront of the campaign to stop MTR coal mining in the United States is Mountain Justice, a local group that worked tirelessly to "escalate resistance to mountain top removal from a regional to a national level" and "debunk the myth of 'clean coal' and of 'jobs versus the environment.'"[3] While Mountain Justice specialized in direct action against MTR sites in West Virginia, Tennessee, Virginia, and Kentucky, other organizations (Earthjustice, Appalachian Mountain Advocates, West Virginia Highlands Conservancy, Ohio Valley Environmental Coalition, Coal River Mountain Watch, and Natural Resources Defense Council) have used litigation and lobbying to influence national policymaking. These organizations have failed to pass national legislation to ban MTR because "the loopholes in the Surface Mining Control and Reclamation Act, the vague definitions of 'approximate original contour,' and the permitting process for mountaintop removal are all classic examples of how the coal companies are permitted to pollute" (Fox, 2005, p. 27). However, anti-MTR activists have succeeded in delaying some local projects such as the Spruce Mine, which is considered the largest MTR proposal in West Virginia and would have resulted in dynamiting 2,200 acres of mountains and forest lands.

Another method of fossil-fuel extraction that has been the target of environmental activists is that of tar sands extraction. Because this method has been used primarily in remote regions in Alberta, Canada, environmental activists have organized few direct campaigns against tar sand operations. However, activists have targeted the oil industry indirectly, by organizing campaigns against pipelines that are supposed to transport Alberta's oil to various regions in the United States and Canada. For example, environmental activists in Canada have organized blockades to stop the construction of the Trans Mountain pipeline, which is proposed to carry tar sands from Edmonton,

Alberta, to Burnaby, British Columbia. Similarly, environmental activists in the United States have organized large protests against the proposed Keystone XL pipeline, which is supposed to carry oil from Alberta to Oklahoma and Texas. Numerous groups such as National Resources Defense Council, Sierra Club, National Wildlife Federation, Friends of the Earth, and the League of Conservation Voters have joined forces to protest the Keystone XL pipeline in locations across the United States. A 2011 protest in front of the White House resulted in the arrest of over 1,000 people and challenged President Barack Obama to stand by his 2008 call to "be the generation that finally frees America from the tyranny of oil" (Mayer, 2011, p. 19).

Hydraulic fracturing is another method of fossil-fuel extraction that has been opposed in communities around the world. In the United States, local activists have organized anti-fracking campaigns in hundreds of communities; in the Marcellus Shale region in the northeastern United States, for example, over 240 cities have adopted bans against hydraulic fracturing between 2010 and 2014. Many of these cities have organized events that included gatherings, demonstrations, debates, or screenings of documentaries such as *Gasland* (Vasi, Walker, Johnson, & Tan, 2015). According to Vasi et al. (2015), local screenings of *Gasland* contributed to anti-fracking mobilizations, which, in turn, influenced the adoption of local bans against fracking in the Marcellus Shale area. Due to the growing number of communities that have opposed hydraulic fracturing, the oil and gas industry has lobbied state legislators to adopt legislation that prevents the adoption of municipal bans; thus, it is now illegal to adopt local bans against fracking in states such as Texas, Oklahoma, Colorado, and Ohio (Vasi, 2016). In contrast, France has banned hydraulic fracturing based on the precautionary principle in 2011, while Romania proposed a moratorium on fracking after a petition was signed by more than 50,000 people.[4]

Activists in developed countries have also organized a growing number of protests against the distribution of oil and gas. Some of the most sustained protests in recent times have been organized against the Dakota Access Pipeline, which was built to carry shale oil from North Dakota to Illinois. The pipeline is opposed by members of the Standing Rock Sioux Tribe and environmental activists because it crosses sacred sites and burial places for the tribe and because of concerns about oil spills that could pollute drinking water. During the summer of 2016, lawyers for the tribe pressed charges against Dakota Access, and months of litigation and protests followed. Activists set up camp near the Standing Rock Sioux Tribe's reservation and clashed with authorities repeatedly. In October, for example, 141 people were arrested as police attempted to remove the camp, and a number of protesters were injured by pepper spray, water hoses in subfreezing weather, and dog bites. Activists, however, have declared their resolve to continue the protests; as one organizer with the Indigenous Environmental Network put it, "We are staying here committed to our prayer. Forced removal and state oppression? This is nothing new to us as native people."[5]

Activists have targeted not only nuclear and fossil fuel projects, but also renewable energy projects. In many cases, however, opposition against renewable energy projects came from groups with ties to the fossil-fuel industry. Cape Wind, the first offshore wind project proposed for the United States, has been opposed by the Alliance to Protect Nantucket Sound (also known as Save Our Sound), an association of homeowners from Cape Cod and the islands of Martha's Vineyard and Nantucket. While the association claims to protect the Nantucket Sound through conservation and environmental action, it has been documented that it received support from fossil-fuel groups. Bill Koch, the younger brother of Charles Koch and David Koch, is a co-chair of the Alliance and the principal funder of opposition to Cape Wind (Sheppard, 2010). Indeed, as Koch himself has said, opposition to Cape Wind was driven by NIMBY ("not in my backyard") attitudes, rather than by concern about the environmental effects of the offshore wind industry: "I was telling one of my guys when this [wind farm] first came up, 'I wish I'd thought of this!' But as a businessman, I said I wouldn't have put it in my backyard—I would have put it in someone else's backyard!" (Blanchard 2005).

In contrast to the United States and Europe, where activists targeted predominantly nuclear power plants and fossil-fuel extraction, distribution, and combustion sites, in many developing countries activists protested primarily against hydro power projects. Most developing countries lack the necessary resources to develop a nuclear industry; moreover, because electricity is often in short supply in these countries, local residents are more likely to tolerate pollution from fossil-fuel power plants. Hydro-electric dams, however, are often very disruptive for local residents, who have to relocate when their villages are inundated. Consequently, although dams were so important for the conception of development that politicians named them "temples of progress" (McCormick, 2006, p. 329), many developing countries have experienced anti-dam protests during the last decades.

While some of the anti-dam protests in developing countries have been unable to delay or prevent the construction of large dams, others have been somewhat successful. In India, for example, the Silent Valley protests from the 1980s were organized by local people who feared being displaced from their ancestral land and by environmentalists concerned about the possible destruction of large rainforests. With support from international organizations such as the World Wildlife Fund, local activists were able to persuade the government to stop construction of the Silent Valley dam in 1983 and, later, construction of three other projects proposed over the Godavari and Indravati rivers (Hemadri, 1999, p. xxvi). During the second half of the 1980s, activists started the Save the Narmada River campaign, which used the Gandhian strategy of resistance: non-cooperation and civil disobedience, refusal to cooperate with project authorities, blocking all project-related works, and refusal to leave their villages. This campaign inspired resistance actions in other parts of India, which led to the withdrawal of other projects in the late 1990s and "succeeded in compelling governments, both at the central and state levels, and powerful funding agencies like the World Bank to rethink their policies on displacement and rehabilitation" (Nayak, 2010, p. 71). Recently, anti-dam protests have flared in the Eastern Himalayas part of India, and hundreds of Buddhist lamas and locals have protested plans to build large dams in an area that is considered "ecologically, culturally, and strategically" sensitive.[6]

In Brazil opposition against dams was initially organized by local activists who took advantage of the democratic transition and drew on national and international church networks. After years of protests, activists succeeded in obtaining better compensation in cash or land for those affected by dam construction, halting the construction of many dams, developing a national organization (The National Movement of People Affected by Dams), and forming the World Commission on Dams in 1999 (Rothman and Oliver 1999). The Brazilian anti-dam movement also succeeded in altering the discourse around dam planning at national and international levels and in creating new governmental and intergovernmental bodies to answer movement concerns (McCormick, 2006). In contrast, the anti-dam opposition in China has been initially weak and did not change the government's decision to build mega-dams such as the Three Gorges Dam. More recently, however, anti-dam activists were successful in convincing the government to suspend the decision to build dams on the Nujiang River. Because these dams would have been constructed in an area that was recognized by UNESCO as one of the most biologically diverse temperate ecosystems in the world and was designated as a World Heritage Site, a group of environmental nongovernmental organizations (NGOs) worked assiduously to persuade the government to suspend the project. Consequently, the Chinese premier's announcement that the project was suspended was "the first time a national leader had acted on the side of caution, and it was also a good demonstration of the growing strength of the coalition of ENGOs in China" (Teh-Chang, 2007, p. 171)

PROACTIVE CAMPAIGNS FOR RENEWABLE ENERGY

The environmental movement underwent a major transformation in the early 1990s, when it started to shift from a more confrontational to a more collaborative and consultative approach. While many environmental groups continue to organize direct actions against polluting power plants and fossil-fuel extraction sites, a number of environmental organizations have developed collaborations with companies and governments in order to stimulate the adoption of clean technologies. Consider the example of Greenpeace, an organization that is known primarily for its use of sensational, nonviolent tactics to bring attention to environmental destruction. Starting in the 1990s, Greenpeace has moved from protesting against environmentally damaging practices such as nuclear power or fossil-fuel combustion to offering solutions to those practices. As one Greenpeace organizer from Germany states,

> In the 1990s you could still be against something, but it was also required that you have a solution. Greenpeace developed solutions very early. We developed a CFC-free refrigerator, and then we developed a very fuel-efficient car. We have very high standards: we work with scientific institutions that have a very good reputation.

We've been working with renewable industries for over ten years because we need them to confirm our results. From my point of view, it makes sense to have energy demands that are not only ambitious but also achievable (as cited in Vasi, 2011, p. 63).

The environmental movement used a YIMBY ("yes in my backyard") discourse to promote renewable energies, emphasizing that climate change cannot be addressed without massive investments in wind and solar projects. To attract investments in renewables, German environmental groups such as Greenpeace-Germany have worked with energy institutes and other organizations such as the Eco-Institute and Eurosolar to promote feed-in tariffs (FIT), which are pricing laws stipulating that renewable energy producers are paid a set rate for their electricity depending on the technology used and the size of the installations. The first FIT policy adopted in 1990 in Germany is credited with launching both the solar and the wind energy industry in this country. The second FIT policy was adopted in 2000 and amended in 2004; without it, the solar and wind industries would have been unable to compete; in the words of the German Wind Industry Association, "without this state-controlled minimum price, the wind energy sector would have had no chance against the billion Euro heavy-weights of the coal and atomic energy industries on the cartel-organized energy market" (Vasi, 2011, p. 65).

In other countries, environmental groups have supported renewable energy projects by promoting the adoption of production tax credits (PTC), renewable portfolio standards (RPS), and other types of policies. In the United States, for example, virtually every major environmental group joined with the American Wind Energy Association to lobby for the introduction of production-based tax credit to support wind energy in the early 1990s. Environmental groups lobbied to extend the PTC, with mixed results: while their efforts were successful in 1999, when they succeeded in extending the credit until 2001, they were unsuccessful in 2003 and 2004, when the PTC was left to expire. Similarly, environmental groups lobbied for the adoption of RPS policies at the state level; in fact, the Union of Concerned Scientists was involved in designing the RPS policy in California in the late 1990s. In Texas, environmental groups such as Environmental Defense helped regulators design the initial RPS in 1999, and also negotiated with utilities and lobbied for subsequent revisions (Vasi, 2011).

Environmentalists have also shaped the renewable energy sector by increasing local demand for green power. Since the 1990s, Greenpeace and other German NGOs organized campaigns that targeted electricity consumers and encouraged them to demand green power. In the United States, environmental groups have contributed to hundreds of decisions by colleges and universities to "declare independence from dirty energy" (Vasi, 2011, p. 117). Additionally, environmental organizations have nudged many local businesses and large corporations into purchasing green power. The World Resources Institute, for example, has launched the Safe Climate, Sound Business initiative in 1998 to show that addressing climate change and promoting economic growth are not incompatible. In 2000 this program was developed into the Green Power Market Development Group, a commercial and industrial partnership dedicated to building voluntary markets for green power. Consequently, a significant portion of the renewable energy projects in the United States were developed because energy consumers have been willing to pay more for green power (Bird, Dagher, & Swezey, 2007).

Another way in which the environmental movement has contributed to the expansion of the renewable energy sector has been by stimulating entrepreneurship in the renewable energy industries. In the wind energy industry, many entrepreneurs who literally built wind turbines in their backyards were either members or sympathizers of the environmental movement. Many of the pioneers of the Danish wind energy industry, such as Erik Grove-Nielsen and Henrik Stiesdal, had been involved in the Organization for Renewable Energy (OVE) during the 1970s. OVE influenced many entrepreneurs' decision to enter the wind energy industry by publishing a *Solar and Wind Handbook* that allowed innovators to find each other, and by organizing meetings in which engineers and technicians could disseminate knowledge and solve technological issues. Consider how one organizer describes OVE's role:

> Some of the inventors in Denmark never talked to each other. That's where OVE made a big difference; probably, the biggest difference. In the beginning of 1976 we organized a wind energy meeting where we got together and exchanged ideas and experiences. Small groups were getting together to solve technical problems in the design of the first turbines. After a while, we had groups working on different things. The technical groups had a very big role in the first few years. Everybody who worked with wind energy had to go to those. (Vasi, 2011, p. 154)

The environmental movement has also stimulated entrepreneurial activity in the electric utility industry. One of the companies that has successfully entered the electricity market in the United Kingdom is Ecotricity, a company founded by environmental activist Dale Vince. Unlike traditional utility companies, which have to answer to their shareholders, Ecotricity uses a unique model to turn "bills into mills": because they are a not-for-dividend company, they put all of their profits into their mission—to build more renewable energy projects by "spending more each year per customer on new sources of Green Energy than any other energy company in Britain."[7] The company's commitment to green power resulted in sustained support from environmental groups such as Friends of the Earth, the Royal Society for the Protection of Birds, and Sea Shepherd Conservation Society.

One of the most important ways in which the environmental movement influenced the growth of the wind and solar industries has been to inspire the emergence of renewable energy cooperatives. Indeed, many environmental activists perceived the option to join a wind or solar power cooperative as an opportunity to opt out of dirty electricity. In Germany about one-third of all wind-power capacity has been built by associations or cooperatives of local landowners and nearby residents, while in Denmark about a quarter of the wind-energy capacity has been developed by cooperatives (Gipe, 2009). In fact, one of the first offshore wind farms in the world has been built by a cooperative— the Middelgrunden Wind Turbine Cooperative, which consists of 20 large wind turbines and is considered to be the most photographed wind farm in the world.[8] Wind farm and solar power cooperatives also exist in some US regions, such as Minnesota, Iowa, and Texas, as well as in the Canadian province of Ontario.

Growing concern about global climate change has motivated activists to organize not only campaigns against fossil fuel extraction consumption, but also campaigns to support renewable energy. Environmental activists frustrated with the UK government's inability to rapidly accelerate the growth of renewable energy industries have formed the Westmill Wind Farm Co-operative, a community-owned organization with more than 2,000 members who own an onshore wind farm estimated to produce as much electricity in a year as that used by 2,500 homes. The Westmill Wind Farm Co-operative has inspired local citizens to form the Westmill Solar Co-operative. This solar cooperative produces enough energy to power 1,400 homes, making it the first large-scale solar farm cooperative in the country and, in the words of its members, a visible reminder that solar power represents "a new era of sustainable and 'democratic' energy supply that enables ordinary people to produce clean power, not only on their rooftops, but also at utility scale."[9] Similarly, renewable energy enthusiasts from the United States have founded the Clean Energy Collective, a company that has pioneered "the model of delivering clean power-generation through medium-scale facilities that are collectively owned by participating utility customers."[10]

Raising awareness about global climate change has also shaped the public's energy preferences. Opinion polls show that in many countries the majority of the public prefers solar and wind to fossil fuels. A 2015 survey, for example, shows that 79% of Americans consider that the United States should put more emphasis on solar energy, and 70% would like to see more emphasis on wind energy, but only 41% would like to see more emphasis on oil and 28% would like to see more emphasis on coal.[11] Consequently, a growing number of utilities are beginning to offer their customers the option to choose either an up-front or ongoing payment to support a solar project— what is termed a "utility-sponsored solar project." For example, the Sacramento Municipal Utility District's (SMUD) SolarShares program allows customers to purchase output from a solar project on a monthly basis. Moreover, while regular utilities have few or no incentives to encourage energy conservation, SMUD makes the SolarShares less expensive for their customers who use less electricity. Because the effective rate for solar is locked in when consumers enroll, solar power act as a hedge against future price increases, which diminishes the premium price for solar energy (USDOE, 2011).

Finally, the advent of the sharing economy and the presence of peer-to-peer platforms that empower consumers to buy various products and services directly from producers has the potential to revolutionize the electricity sector. Rather than organizing YIMBY campaigns and investing in local renewable energy cooperatives, individuals concerned about climate change may have the option to buy green power directly from owners of wind turbines, solar panels, and biomass facilities. This is already happening in some countries with deregulated electricity markets. For example, the Dutch company Vandebron offers individuals the option to buy electricity straight from local farmers with excess electricity production from solar panels, wind turbines, or biogas installations and to avoid the utilities, which are "fundamentally unsuited to providing renewable energy because they have legacy investments in fossil fuels, which they need to recover" (Schiller, 2014). Similarly, in the United Kingdom the start-up Open Utility has partnered with the utility Good Energy to match small generators of renewable energy with potential buyers in their local community.[12] Given these recent developments, in the near future a growing number of individuals may become "prosumers"—both producers and consumers of electricity.

AN ENERGY-FOCUSED GLOBAL MOVEMENT AND THE FOSSIL-FUEL COUNTER-MOVEMENT

It has become a ritual for the environmental movement to protest at international negotiations on global climate change. Since the first Conference of the Parties was organized under the United Nations Framework Convention on Climate Change (UNFCCC) in 1995 in Berlin, climate change activists have organized protests every year in cities across the world: Bonn, The Hague, Copenhagen, Buenos Aires, Montreal, and Paris, among others. Frustrated with the inability of national governments to achieve meaningful reductions of greenhouse gases, environmental activists have begun to form a climate- and energy-focused global movement. The main umbrella organization for this movement is 350.org, an organization founded in 2008 that works with hundreds of environmental organizations from around the world in an attempt to build a "global grassroots climate movement that can hold our leaders accountable to the realities of science and the principles of justice."[13] On September 21, 2014, the groups affiliated with 350.org have organized what is considered to be the largest climate change march in history—the People's Climate March—which included approximately 311,000 people in New York City and many others in Melbourne, Berlin, New Delhi, Johannesburg, London, Paris, and other cities around the world (Westbrook, 2014).

The energy-focused global movement, however, does more than organize large protests and demonstrations to attract mass media attention and influence public opinion. Another tactic it frequently uses is to organize direct actions against energy infrastructure projects such as the Dakota Access Pipeline, which is supposed to carry fracked oil from North Dakota to other parts of the country. Another tactic is to target the federal government through petitions to halt offshore drilling, and still another one is to pressure national governments and the Vatican to divest from fossil fuels. In Canada, for example, environmental activists are holding town hall meetings across the country where people can speak up for the "People's Climate Plan," a grassroots initiative demanding that the government develop a national climate strategy that includes a fast transition to renewable energy and a commitment to "keep the majority of fossil fuels in the ground."[14] Arguably the most ambitious tactic used by activists is to pressure the US government to investigate oil and gas companies such as Exxon-Mobil; as the "Exxon knew" petition drive argues,

> Recent reports have shown that Exxon may have known about the threat of climate change decades ago. Yet over the course of nearly forty years, the company has contributed millions of dollars to think-tanks and politicians that have done their best to spread doubt and misinformation—first on the existence of climate change, then the extent of the problem, and now its cause. If Exxon intentionally misled the public about climate change and fossil fuels, then they should be held accountable. We're calling for an immediate investigation.[15]

Given that global climate change has recently become the most important issue for many environmental activists, environmental organizations have organized numerous campaigns that oppose the construction of new coal power plants and advocate for closing old coal plants. One of the best examples of this type of campaign is Beyond Coal, which is organized by Sierra Club. The Beyond Coal campaign started with opposition to a proposed coal power plant in the Chicago area in 2001, but has rapidly grown to be "the most extensive, expensive and effective campaign in Sierra Club's 123-year history, and maybe the history of the environmental movement" (Grunwald, 2015). Before 2008, Sierra Club's strategy has been to focus its efforts on preventing the construction of new coal power plants; by most measures, the strategy has succeeded: only 30 of the 200 coal power plants proposed in 2001 have been constructed. With financial support from philanthropists such as Michael Bloomberg and Tom Steyer, the Beyond Coal campaign also was able to target existing coal power plants and contribute to their retirement. One study estimates that at least 40% of 189 power plants closed since 2001 were retired in part because of the Beyond Coal campaign (Grunwald, 2015).

The growing number of energy-focused campaigns has forced governments to respond to citizens' demands in a number of ways. First, despite initial resistance from a number of states, during the last two decades the vast majorities of the world's governments have signed the Protocol to the United Nations Framework Convention on Climate Change, also known as the Kyoto Protocol. Moreover, by December 2017 a total of 170 of the 197 parties to the convention, accounting for almost 48% of the global greenhouse gas emissions, have signed the Paris Agreement, which attempts "to strengthen the global response to the threat of climate change by keeping a global temperature rise this century well below 2 degrees Celsius above pre-industrial levels and to pursue efforts to limit the temperature increase even further to 1.5 degrees Celsius"[16] Since the Paris Agreement is stipulated to take effect after the threshold for at least 55 Parties to the Convention (accounting in total for at least an estimated 55% of the total global greenhouse gas emissions) has passed, this international treaty entered into force in October 2016.

At the national level, many countries have also adopted policies to stimulate the growth of renewable energy industries. Some governments have adopted FIT policies, which are generally considered to be "the most efficient and effective support schemes for promoting renewable electricity" (European Commission, 2008). By 2010, FITs had been enacted in over 50 countries, including Australia, Austria, Canada, Denmark, France, Germany, Israel, the Netherlands, Turkey, and the United Kingdom. Other countries, such as China, Japan, the United Kingdom, and the United States, have adopted RPS policies, or regulations that require the increased production of energy from renewable energy sources, such as wind, solar, biomass, and geothermal. In the United States, the federal governments has also adopted PTC policies, which is an inflation-adjusted per-kilowatt-hour tax credit for electricity generated by renewable energy resources, and Net Metering, which allows consumers who generate some or all of their own electricity to use that electricity anytime, instead of when it is generated.

But the energy-focused movement has also led to the emergence of a counter-movement led by the fossil-fuel industries. Many fossil-fuel companies have opposed any significant reduction of greenhouse gases, and their lobby has been successful in "defeating Kyoto" in the United States (McCright & Dunlap, 2003). For example, the coal lobby funded a study entitled "Refusing to Repeat Past Mistakes: How the Kyoto Climate Change Protocol Would Disproportionately Threaten the Economic Well-Being of Blacks and Hispanics in the United States" and has supported numerous "AstroTurf" organizations, or "grassroots for hire" (Walker, 2014), that lobbied for the government to reject the Kyoto Protocol (Bullard, 2000). Opposition from the fossil-fuel industries has also led to the periodic expiration of the PTC in the United States in 2000, 2002, 2004, 2010, and 2014, contributing to a 75%–93% drop in the installation of wind turbines and a "boom-bust" cycle in the wind energy industry.[17]

In recent years the fossil fuel and electric utility industries in the United States have also organized direct attacks against Net Metering and RPS policies. The Arizona Public Service, the largest utility in Arizona, and the 60 Plus Association, a group funded by the fossil-fuel companies associated with the Koch Industries, have run anti-solar advertisements and have asked regulators to charge net-metering customers over $50 per month (Elsner & Kasper, 2015). In Colorado, the RPS has been attacked in the legislature and the courts by the Heartland Institute, a conservative think tank with ties to the fossil-fuel industry that promotes climate change denial. In Louisiana the legislature's decision to approve a bill to significantly reduce tax credits available for residents and companies that install solar energy systems was the result of a well-funded campaign of the American Legislative Exchange Council (ALEC) and the Acadian Consulting Group (ACG), two think tanks supported by the fossil-fuel and electric-utility industries. In Ohio, the RPS policy that required that a quarter of the state's electricity come from renewable and alternative sources by 2025 and that utilities increase efficiency by 22% has been frozen due to lobbying from ALEC and Americans for Prosperity, a group funded by the Koch Industries and other conservative groups (Pantsios, 2015). As a study of the attacks on renewable energy policies concludes, "A main component in the strategy to stop the growth of renewable energy is to fund front groups, who then attack clean energy policies across the United States. While corporate interests also lobby politicians and regulators, these front groups serve a fundamental role in these assaults by adding a supposed independent, anti-clean energy voice to energy policy debates" (Elsner & Kasper, 2015, p. 2).

CONCLUSION

Standard accounts of the evolution of the energy sector around the world emphasize the importance of technological innovations and market forces. A common interpretation of the current growth of the wind, solar, and biomass industries is that these industries are capturing a growing market share because the technologies used to build wind turbines, solar photovoltaic panels, concentrated solar, or biomass conversion systems are constantly improving. For clean-technology optimists, renewable energy innovation has taken on an air of inevitability: relentless technological improvements are all but guaranteed to result in lower prices and market dominance of renewables. In the case of solar energy, the so-called Swanson's Law is based on the observation that the price of solar photovoltaic modules tends to drop 20% for every doubling of cumulative shipped volume (Carr, 2012). Following this logic, some energy analysts have estimated that solar power may contribute to as much as 20% of energy consumption by 2027 (Doyne & Lafond, 2016). For those less optimistic about clean technology, however, the rapid diffusion of solar and wind technologies is not guaranteed. In this interpretation, significant problems with intermittence will prevent widespread adoption of solar technology; thus, even under favorable policy conditions, solar photovoltaic technology is estimated to account for only 16% of total electricity by 2050 (International Energy Agency, 2014).

This chapter has argued that the evolution of the energy sector around the world is shaped not only by technological innovations and market forces, but also by social movements. A brief examination of the history of the environmental movement in the developed world shows that environmental protests during the 1970s and 1980s often took the form of reactive campaigns directed against nuclear power plants. While it is difficult to identify the exact causal effects of these protests on the nuclear energy industry, anecdotal evidence shows that in some cases the protests slowed the pace of construction of nuclear power plants, and even contributed to a moratorium on nuclear power. Mountaintop coal mining, tar sand extraction, and hydraulic fracturing have also generated significant local opposition in recent years in many countries, and this opposition has had various degrees of success. In developing countries, opposition against energy projects has targeted primarily large dams in environmentally sensitive areas or in regions that required the relocation of numerous people.

At the same time, environmental activists have been mobilizing to support renewable energy. Campaigns concentrated on building support for renewable energy sources such as wind, solar, and biomass have become increasingly common. As the global climate change issue has become the dominant theme of environmentalism, an energy-focused global movement has emerged in recent years. This movement not only has pressured governments and companies to adopt renewable energy policies, but also has generated a backlash from the fossil fuel industry and the conservative movement, which has argued that "environmentalists want us to return to the Stone Age" (Klein, 2014, p. 91). The complex dynamic between this movement and the counter-movement makes it difficult to predict exactly how much renewable sources of energy will contribute to the energy sector in the coming decades.

The recent election of conservative governments in the United States and some European countries adds significant uncertainly about the prospects of renewable energy in the near future. Indeed, the election of reality TV celebrity and real estate mogul Donald Trump as president of the United States will undoubtedly have a major impact on the energy sector in the coming years. Trump has claimed that "the concept of global warming was created by and for the Chinese in order to make U.S. manufacturing non-competitive," has pledged to "cancel all wasteful climate change spending," and has stated that "wind [turbines] kills all our birds . . . they are rusting and rotting."[18] He has picked the CEO of ExxonMobil, the largest oil company in the world, as secretary of state, and has nominated a climate change denialist as the head of the Environmental Protection Agency. These political changes, however, are also guaranteed to contribute to more contention over energy and to trigger waves of collective action and cycles of protest against fossil fuels in the United States and around the world. When it comes to energy, one thing is for sure: the fight will go on.

NOTES

1. See http://www.iea.org/publications/freepublications/publication/KeyWorld2016.pdf; http://www.eia.gov/forecasts/ieo/world.cfm; http://www.who.int/mediacentre/news/releases/2014/air-pollution/en/; http://science.sciencemag.org/content/348/6234/571.full
2. These plans were based on the observation that, assuming that uranium is readily available, nuclear power plants are very efficient: one ton of natural uranium can produce more than 40 million kilowatt-hours of electricity—this is equivalent to burning 16,000 tons of coal or 80,000 barrels of oil. See http://web.ead.anl.gov/uranium/guide/facts/
3. See Mountain Justice's website, retrieved from https://www.mountainjustice.org/who-we-are/goals/
4. See http://petroglobalnews.com/2013/10/9-countries-or-regions-that-ban-fracking/
5. See http://www.reuters.com/article/us-north-dakota-pipeline-idUSKBN13L00C
6. See http://timesofindia.indiatimes.com/city/guwahati/Tawang-in-Arunachal-Pradesh-erupts-in-anti-dam-protest/articleshow/50695746.cms
7. See Ecotricity's website, retrieved from https://www.ecotricity.co.uk/about-ecotricity
8. See the Middelgrunden Wind Cooperative's website, retrieved from http://www.middelgrunden.dk/middelgrunden/?q=en/node/35
9. See http://inhabitat.com/british-cooperative-launches-worlds-largest-community-owned-solar-park/
10. See Clean Energy Cooperative's website, retrieved from http://www.easycleanenergy.com/index.html#about-cec

11. See Gallup's website, retrieved from http://www.gallup.com/poll/2167/energy.aspx
12. See Open Utility's website, retrieved from https://www.openutility.com/about/
13. See 350.org's website, retrieved from https://350.org/how/
14. See People's Climate Plan, retrieved from http://peoplesclimate.ca/
15. See 350.org, retrieved from https://350.org/campaigns/
16. See the United Nations Framework Convention on Climate Change website, retrieved from http://unfccc.int/paris_agreement/items/9485.php
17. See Union of Concerned Scientists' website, retrieved from http://www.ucsusa.org/clean_energy/smart-energy-solutions/increase-renewables/production-tax-credit-for.html#.V-bgdPArJhE
18. See http://www.nytimes.com/2016/11/19/world/asia/china-trump-climate-change; http://www.motherjones.com/environment/2016/12/trump-wind-power-hotel-soho-manhattan-ivanka-climate; http://www.independent.co.uk/news/world/americas/donald-trump-climate-change-denier-state-department-environmental-spending-questions-a7488281.html

REFERENCES

Bird, L., Dagher, L., & Swezey, B. (2007). Green power marketing in the United States: A status report (10th ed.). Retrieved from http://www.nrel.gov/docs/fy08osti/42502.pdf

Blanchard, J. (2005, September 15). Not just about his view: Put wind farm on dry land, says mogul. *Providence Journal*. Retrieved from https://web.archive.org/web/20120819054424/http://www.providencejournal.com/

Bullard, R. (2000). *Climate justice and people of color*. Environmental Justice Resource Center, Clark Atlanta University. Retrieved from http://www.ejrc.cau.edu

Carr, G. (2012, November 21). Sunny Uplands: Alternative energy will no longer be alternative. *The Economist*. Retrieved from: http://www.economist.com/news/21566414-alternative-energy-will-no-longer-be-alternative-sunny-uplands

Cole, L., & Foster, S. R. (2000). From the ground up: Environmental racism and the rise of the environmental justice movement. New York: New York University Press.

Elsner, G., & Kasper, M. (2015). Attacks on renewable energy policies in 2015. Retrieved from https://d3n8a8pro7vhmx.cloudfront.net/energyandpolicy/pages/472/attachments/original/1438288015/Energy-and-Policy-Institute-Attacks-on-Renewable-Energy-Policies-in-2015-Final.pdf?1438288015

European Commission. (2008, January 23). Commission staff working document, Brussels, 57. Retrieved from http://ec.europa.eu/energy/climate_actions/doc/2008_res_working_document_en.pdf

Farmer, D. & Lafond, F. (2016). How predictable is technological progress? *Research Policy, 45*, 647–665.

Flam, H., & Jamison, A. (1994). The Swedish confrontation over nuclear energy: A case of a timid anti-nuclear opposition. In H. Flam (Ed.), *States and anti-nuclear movements* (pp. 163–201). Edinburgh: Edinburgh University Press.

Fox, J. (2005). Mountaintop removal in West Virginia: An environmental sacrifice zone. In L. King & D. McCarthy (Eds.), *Environmental sociology: From analysis to action* (pp. 16–28). Lanham, MD: Rowman & Littlefield.

Gipe, P. (2009). Community wind: The third way. *Wind-Works*. Retrieved from http://www.wind-works.org/cms/fileadmin/user_upload/Files/presentations/Wind-101/Wind_101-half-4_Community___Urban_Wind.pdf

Grant, D., & Vasi, I. B. (2017). Civil society in an age of environmental accountability: The effects of local NGOs on U.S. power plants' CO_2 emissions. *Sociological Forum, 32*, 94–115

Grunwald, M. (2015). Inside the war on coal: How Mike Bloomberg, red-state businesses, and a lot of Midwestern lawyers are changing American energy faster than you think. Retrieved from http://www.politico.com/agenda/story/2015/05/inside-war-on-coal-000002

Hemadri, R. (1999). Dam, displacement, policy and law in India. Contributing paper, prepared for *Thematic Review*, Social Issue 1.3, Displacement, resettlement, rehabilitation, reparation and development, World Commission on Dams. Retrieved from http://siteresources.worldbank.org/INTINVRES/214578-1112885441548/20480074/DamsDisplacementPolicyandLawinIndiasoc213.pdf

International Energy Agency. (2014). *Technology roadmap: Solar photovoltaic energy*. Technical Report. Paris: OECD/IEA. Retrieved from https://www.iea.org/publications/freepublications/publication/TechnologyRoadmapSolarPhotovoltaicEnergy_2014edition.pdf

Jamison, A., Eyerman, R., Cramer, J. & Læssøe, J. (1990). *The making of the new environmental consciousness: A comparative study of the environmental movements in Sweden, Denmark, and the Netherlands*. Edinburgh: Edinburgh University Press.

Joppke, C. (1993). *Mobilizing against nuclear power: A |comparison of Germany and the United States*. Berkeley: University of California Press.

Klein, N. (2014). *This changes everything: Capitalism vs. the climate*. New York: Simon & Schuster.

Kolb, F. (2007). *Protest and opportunities: The political outcomes of social movements*. Frankfurt: Campus Verlag.

Kumar, N. A. (2010). Big dams and protests in India: A study of Hirakud Dam. *Economic & Political Weekly, XLV*(2), 69–73.

Lin, T.-C. (2007). Environmental NGOs and the anti-dam movements in China: A social movement with Chinese characteristics. *Issues & Studies, 43*(4), 149–184.

Mascarenhas, M. (2015). Environmental inequality and environmental justice. In K. Gould & T. Lewis (Eds.), *Twenty lessons in environmental sociology* (pp. 161–178). Oxford: Oxford University Press.

Mayer, J. (2011). Taking it to the streets. *The New Yorker*. Retrieved from http://www.newyorker.com/magazine/2011/11/28/taking-it-to-the-streets#ixzz1eftWuSRW

McCormick, S. (2006). The Brazilian anti-dam movement: Knowledge contestation as communicative action. *Organization and Environment, 19*(3), 321–346.

McCright, A. & Dunlap, R. (2003). Defeating Kyoto: The conservative movement's impact on U.S. climate change policy. *Social Problems, 50*, 348–373.

Pantsios, A. (2015). 4 States where solar is under attack by Koch-funded front groups. *EcoWatch*. Retrieved from http://www.ecowatch.com/4-states-where-solar-is-under-attack-by-koch-funded-front-groups-1882023460.html

Pellow, D. (2005). The movement for environmental justice in the U.S.: Confronting challenges and charting a new course. Transatlantic Initiative to Promote Environmental Justice. Budapest, Hungary, October 27–30.

Preglau, M. (1994). The state and the anti-nuclear power movement in Austria. In H. Flam (Ed.), *States and anti-nuclear movements* (pp. 37–69). Edinburgh: Edinburgh University Press.

Rothman, F. D., & Oliver, P. E. (1999). From local to global: The anti-dam movement in southern Brazil, 1979–1992. *Mobilization: An International Journal, 4*(1), 41–57.

Rucht, D., & Roose, J. (2003). Germany. In C. Rootes (Ed.), *Environmental protests in Western Europe* (pp. 80–108). Oxford: Oxford University Press.

Schiller, B. (2014). The sharing economy takes on electricity, so you can buy your power from neighbors. Retrieved from https://www.fastcoexist.com/3036271/the-sharing-economy -takes-on-electricity-so-you-can-buy-your-power-from-neighbors

Sheppard, K. (2010). Cape Wind delay a big win for dirty energy interests. *Mother Jones.* Retrieved from http://www.motherjones.com/mojo/2010/01/cape-wind-delay-big-win -dirty-energy-interests

USDOE. (2011). *A guide to community solar: Utility, private and non-profit project development.* Retrieved from http://www.nrel.gov/docs/fy11osti/49930.pdf

Vasi, I. B. (2011). *Winds of change: The environmental movement and the global development of the wind energy industry.* Oxford: Oxford University Press.

Vasi, I. B., Walker, E., Johnson, J., & Tan, S. (2015). No fracking way! Media activism, discursive opportunities and local opposition against hydraulic fracturing in the United States, 2010–2013. *American Sociological Review, 80,* 934–959.

Vasi, I. B. (2016). This (gas) land is your (truth) land? Documentary films and cultural fracturing in Marcellus, Barnett, and Woodford shale communities. In A. Ladd (Ed.), *Fractured communities.* (pp. New Brunswick, NJ: Rutgers University Press.

Walker, E. (2014). *Grassroots for hire: Public affairs consultants in American democracy.* Cambridge: Cambridge University Press.

Wagner, P. (1994). Contesting policies and redefining the state: Energy policy-making and the anti-nuclear movement in West Germany. In H. Flam (Ed.), *States and anti-nuclear movements* (pp. 264–295). Edinburgh: Edinburgh University Press.

Wellock, T. R. (1998). *Critical masses: Opposition to nuclear power in California, 1958–1978.* Madison: The University of Wisconsin Press.

Westbrook, L. (2014). Climate change summit: Global rallies demand action. *BBC News.* Retrieved from http://www.bbc.com/news/science-environment-29301969

CHAPTER 22

NIGHTMARES AND DREAMS

Contested Framing of Unconventional Fossil Fuels

JENNIFER DODGE

> ... one person's dream can be another person's nightmare, and there may
> never be full harmony between those who want to profit from their unex-
> pected good fortune and those who don't want to be disturbed. ...
>
> —Anonymous editorial commenting on the possibility of developing the
> Marcellus Shale in New York (Anonymous, 2008, p. B2)

INTRODUCTION

IN the United States and around the world, there has been a heated controversy over shale gas development since horizontal drilling and high-volume hydraulic fracturing techniques, often referred to as "fracking," made it possible to develop previously in-accessible oil and gas reserves. In public discourse, the vision of a prosperous energy future based on plentiful shale gas has promised abundant energy supplies, economic development, personal enrichment, and independence from foreign gas and oil. Some challengers have questioned this vision by juxtaposing the supposed benefits of shale gas with negative consequences such as increased greenhouse gas emissions and polluted aquifers and private drinking water supplies, among other problems. An alternative energy vision has also arisen to reject reliance on fossil fuels altogether and to direct attention toward the development of sustainable or renewable sources of energy.

We can think of these competing visions as "sociotechnical imaginaries," or "collectively imagined forms of social life and social order reflected in the design and fulfillment of nation-specific scientific and/or technological projects" (Jasonoff & Kim, 2009, p. 120). Energy imaginaries are sociotechnical imaginaries centered on energy projects that order, for example, "the risks and benefits of energy choices . . . and the way public policy has adjudicated the ownership of those risks and benefits" (Jasonoff & Kim, 2013, p. 190). This concept is useful for understanding shale gas development in the United

States. A shale gas imaginary emerged when new hydraulic fracturing and horizontal drilling techniques were created, opening up the possibility of developing vast but previously inaccessible oil and gas reserves. As I explain later, this imaginary perpetuates and revitalizes a long-standing fossil-fuel energy imaginary, which has been realized in large part, as 18 states have some development from fracking (EIA, 2015a).

Despite the power of the shale gas energy imaginary in the United States, decision-makers in New York banned shale gas development in the massive Marcellus Shale. This is surprising given that fracking was on the agenda in New York at a time of deep economic recession, high oil and gas prices, and unpopular engagement in conflicts abroad where the United States draws gas supplies. Moreover, communities where shale gas development would have been possible in New York had experienced decades of economic decline, and many residents were ready for economic development, even at an environmental price. In contrast to New York, states with similar reserves had begun developing shale gas at breakneck speed, including neighboring Pennsylvania. The divergence of the New York case raises important questions about how political actors in New York managed to debunk a powerful energy imaginary to valorize an alternative approach. More generally we might ask: How are old imaginaries—even if refashioned as new opportunities—dismantled or debunked? How do new imaginaries gain acceptance and take hold?

Understanding the dynamics by which competing actors contest alternative visions of the energy future is an important entry point for answering these questions. The controversy over fracking is emblematic of a key struggle in society today over the perpetuation of the fossil-fuel economy through the development of unconventional fossil fuels or the transition to a "greener" social order (Dodge & Metze, 2017). Focusing on the contest over energy imaginaries exposes the heart of this struggle, drawing attention not only to different visions of energy futures, but also to the ways they are realized or thwarted. The results will have significance for both the literature on "sociotechnical imaginaries" in science and technology studies (Eaton et al., 2014; Jasonoff & Kim, 2009; Smith & Tidwell, 2016) and the policy studies literature, which similarly examines how imaginaries in a range of policy fields shape public policy (Jessop, 2009; Levy & Spicer, 2013).

While these literatures recognize that energy imaginaries can be contested (Smith & Tidwell, 2016), they tend to focus on broadly accepted imaginaries operating at the national level and over long periods of time. The fracking controversy, in contrast, alerts us to the specific dynamics by which political and social actors contest competing energy imaginaries in moments of potential energy transitions and how one alternative becomes accepted and another rejected. We learn how entrenched imaginaries are supplanted with alternatives that promise a "better" future.

New York is an important case. It is one of the few places in the United States where considerable shale gas reserves were passed over in favor of developing alternative energy, despite the broad acceptance of the shale gas energy imaginary at the national level. Furthermore, citizens, public officials, civic organizations, industry associations, and a host of other actors from across the spectrum became highly mobilized in a robust contest over the shale gas imaginary and its alternative, founded on renewables. This makes New York a particularly interesting case in which to observe not only how national energy imaginaries are being translated into local contexts (Eaton et al., 2014), but also how dominant energy imaginaries are challenged in an interpretive struggle to the point where they fail to cohere. I explore these dynamics by focusing on the ways actors in one region of New York framed the national imaginary of shale gas, and how an alternative was ultimately embraced over it.

I begin by situating the shale gas imaginary in growing literatures on sociotechnical and policy imaginaries, then describe the framing approach I use to analyze contestation over the shale gas imaginary in New York. I conclude with a discussion about the significance of the New York case for theory and for practical aspects of energy transitions.

FRAMING SOCIOTECHNICAL IMAGINARIES

As collectively imagined forms of social life, sociotechnical imaginaries both "describe attainable futures and prescribe futures that states believe ought to be attained" (Jasonoff & Kim, 2009, 120). As such, they reflect moral, political, and social choices about desirable futures and thus incorporate definitions of the public good. As they articulate what is desirable in the social world, they also inform action; they have "the power to influence technological design, channel public expenditures, and justify the inclusion or exclusion of citizens with respect to the benefits of technological progress" (Jasonoff & Kim, 2009, p. 120).

Imaginaries may drive policies in this way, but it is not inevitable that national imaginaries will prevail in diverse localities, or that actors across the spectrum will interpret them in similar ways (Eaton et al., 2014; Smith & Tidwell, 2016). They must be interpreted for local projects. Even as imaginaries are "associated with active exercises of state power, such as the selection of development priorities, the allocation of funds, the investment in material infrastructures, and the acceptance or suppression of political dissent" (Jasonoff & Kim, 2009, p. 123), they are not inevitable. Local actors may challenge dominant imaginaries and offer alternatives. But this requires the exercise of countervailing political power and the development of alternative material infrastructures that help to support alternative imaginaries. Without this political power, local actors may not successfully challenge dominant national sociotechnical imaginaries (Smith & Tidwell, 2016).

A frame analytical approach is useful for understanding how coalitions contest the interpretation of national energy imaginaries, and their social and political meanings. A *frame* is a schemata of interpretation (Goffman, 1974) that enables people "to locate, perceive, identify, and label occurrences within their life space and their world at large. By rendering events or occurrences meaningful, frames function to organize experience and guide action," (Davidson, 1985 [1973] in Rein & Schon, 1996, p. 89). *Framing* involves processes of alignment that are negotiated in interaction (Dewulf et al., 2009). In political controversies, different coalitions will engage in framing and counter-framing moves (Abolafia, 2004) to create and recreate interpretations of policy issues in inter-action over time. This process involves weaving together normative claims and facts to orient participants to the issues (Fischer, 2003).

Framing can play an important role in shaping how national sociotechnical imaginaries are translated into local contexts, including whether they are transformed or rejected outright. For example, Eaton et al. (2014) uses frame analysis to show how local actors frame national imaginaries and interpret them for local contexts. They show how frames are "keyed" toward either more "flattened" institutional interpretations or "sharpened" into more critical understandings of national imaginaries. In the case of bi-oenergy, they "argue that flattened keys reinforce and reproduce the extant assertions of the national imaginary of bioenergy, whereas sharpened, critical keys problematize and challenge the imaginary" (Eaton et al., 2014, p. 229). This chapter applies Eaton et al.'s approach, and adds the idea that keying involves linking sociotechnical imaginaries to various notions of power.

To explain, when coalitions key a sociotechnical imaginary in a "flattened" way, they may justify existing institutions as fair, capable, or efficient. In contrast, keying a sociotechnical imaginary in a "sharpened" way may involve critiquing existing institutions for failing to be inclusive, democratic, or transparent. Coalitions may thus critically key a sociotechnical imaginary to justify the transfer of power to different levels or scales of government (Cotton et al., 2014; Smith & Fergueson, 2013), or to civil society and/or private institutions. As such, flattened keying of an imaginary might have the effect of supporting the existing power structures, while a critical keying would justify a change in the balance of power. Envisioning the future thus includes framing institutions as supportable or not, and articulating a normative argument for how they should be reorganized to meet energy needs and to support alternative notions of the public good.

Exploring how alternative imaginaries are contested—and how specific policies result—requires an interactive approach to analysis that focuses on the interpreta-tion and reinterpretation of energy imaginaries over time. This approach unpacks the different moral, social, and/or political meanings that are attached to shale gas develop-ment and its alternative.

FRACKING FOR SHALE GAS AS AN ENERGY IMAGINARY IN THE UNITED STATES

The sociotechnical imaginary for shale gas in the United States began to form when in-dustry refined development techniques in the Barnett Shale in Texas in 1992 (US DOE, 2009), introducing high-volume hydraulic fracturing and horizontal drilling techniques to "conventional" gas development. "Conventional" gas development uses *vertical* drilling, and hydraulic fracturing techniques developed in the 1950s to extract discrete pockets of natural gas close to the earth's surface. As "unconventional" gas development, fracking takes place deeper underground; drilling is completed vertically and then expanded horizontally. Then, the shale is fractured by pumping high volumes of hydraulic fracturing fluid—which contains water, sand, and chemical additives such as friction reducers, scale inhibitors, and biocides (Vidic et al., n.d., p. 827)—into less permeable shale formations to break them up and release the gas (Rao, 2012). Paired with rising gas prices and successful recovery operations, the advancements in these techniques made development of formerly inaccessible shale economically viable (US DOE, 2009). A few states, including Texas and Pennsylvania, began developing shale gas in the early 2000s. Development expanded considerably between 2007 and 2012 (EIA, 2015a), with 12 states in the United States developing shale gas by 2010 (Richardson et al., 2013). Currently, 18 of the 50 states have some fracking development (EIA, 2015a).

As the idea spread that shale gas development was becoming possible on a large scale, many supporters began articulating considerable positive benefits. Some argued that it would reduce carbon emissions compared to other sources of energy such as coal, thus serving as a "bridge fuel" in the transition toward more sustainable forms of energy (Cathles et al., 2012). This was paired with the hope that shale gas could meet growing energy demands. Others focused on the considerable economic benefits that shale gas could provide, for individual owners of shale gas reserves or for governments who would see increased tax revenue, not to mention general economic benefits in the form of job growth and economic activity. Others focused on its potential to reduce dependence on foreign energy and create greater energy independence.[1]

Various government agencies, gas companies, and think tanks initiated studies of shale gas reserves to assess the possibilities of shale gas development. According to the Energy Information Administration (EIA), the United States has an estimated 622.5 trillion cubic feet of wet shale gas reserves and 78.2 billion barrels of tight oil that is still recoverable (EIA, 2015b). Between 2001 and 2010, shale gas development increased from 1% to over 20% of the energy production of the United States and is expected to increase to 35% by 2035 (EIA, 2014; Paltsev et al., 2011). Total shale production in the country increased from 1,293 billion cubic feet in 2007 to 13,447 billion cubic feet by 2014 (EIA, 2015c), with shale gas production expected to increase by 50% from 2015 to 2040 (EIA, 2016). While estimates vary widely (Brady & Crannell, 2012), the overarching message is that shale gas is a "game changer" (IHS, 2010).

This imaginary evolved in a policy context that already favored oil and gas development. For example, under the Resource Conservation and Recovery Act and the Solid Waste Disposal Act, solid wastes produced from oil and gas development are exempted from categorization as a hazardous waste unless the Environmental Protection Agency (EPA) "could prove that the wastes posed a hazard to human health and the environment" (Brady & Crannell, 2012, 46–47). The consequences are that protective requirements for storing, transporting, treating, and disposing of wastes produced from hydraulic fracturing are lower than they would be if classified as hazardous wastes. Similar exemptions are found in the Emergency Planning and

Community Right-To-Know Act (where the EPA excludes the oil and gas industry from reporting requirements on its Toxics Release Inventory), the Clear Air Act (where the EPA excludes oil and gas industry from regulating hazardous air pollutants largely by exempting it from an aggregation rule: since single wells do not emit the threshold limit of hazardous air pollutants, they do not need a permit and are essentially unregulated), and the Comprehensive Environmental Response, Compensation, and Liability Act (which excludes petroleum[2] from hazardous substances in the Superfund program).

In addition, the 2005 Energy Policy Act, signed into law by President George W. Bush, created and strengthened expansive exemptions specific to "fracking" in various environmental statutes (Brady & Crannell, 2012). Since 1997, for example, the EPA and state-level Underground Injection Control (UIC) programs were required to regulate hydraulic fracturing under the Safe Drinking Water Act (SDWA). However, the Energy Policy Act created the "Halliburton loophole," which exempts fracking from the SDWA regardless of whether it threatens drinking water (Brady & Crannell, 2012). While some US senators and representatives attempted to pass bills to end this exemption, they failed. The 2005 Act also effectively excludes oil and gas activities from the National Environmental Policy Act's procedural requirements through "categorical exclusions," which presume that these activities will have no significant environmental impact unless the public can prove otherwise. Finally, while the Energy Policy Act amended the Clean Water Act to exclude oil and gas development activities associated with hydraulic fracturing from storm-water permitting requirements, it was overturned by the Ninth Circuit Court of Appeals in a lawsuit filed by the Natural Resources Defense Council. These requirements would have prevented sediment from construction sites from being released into navigable waters (Brady & Crannell, 2012). This version of the national shale gas imaginary promotes "unfettered" energy and economic development (Forbes, 2012), favoring loose regulations and minimal government intervention. It also removes environmental protections that would "hamper" such unfettered development.

More recently, the Obama administration supported natural gas development. But the EPA also has revisited several exemptions in environmental regulations for hydraulic fracturing, including new standards under the Clean Air Act requiring all newly fracked wells to reduce emissions, and new standards for wastewater discharges resulting from shale gas development (Brady & Crannell, 2012). In addition, the Government Accountability Office has issued a report detailing exemptions in key federal and state regulations for hydraulic fracturing, presumably as a means to adjust them (USGAO, 2012). The Trump administration is actively reversing some of these efforts, has appointed pro-development figures to lead the EPA, the Department of Interior, and the Department of Energy, and has claimed he will attempt to shut down the EPA.

Although the United States has taken a lead in the expansion of fracking globally, the technique has grown increasingly controversial. In 2012, Vermont's governor signed a bill banning hydraulic fracturing outright (Brady & Crannell, 2012); New York's governor placed an indefinite moratorium on fracking of the Marcellus Shale in December 2014, citing health concerns (Keep Tap Water Safe, 2014); and Maryland moved to ban fracking in 2015 (Cama, 2015). Even in states without bans, battles over its permissibility and regulation continue at the local level. Local ballot initiatives in three states where fracking was permitted passed in November 2014, including Denton, Texas, which already had 275 fracked wells (Gaworecki, 2014). The pollution of the water table over the Barnett Shale seemed to figure prominently in Denton, though companies immediately filed an injunction to block the ban. While San Benito, California voted to ban fracking, Santa Barbara County voted against a ban (Gaworecki, 2014).

To understand how this imaginary was translated for New York, I analyze data related to one county, Broome County, where shale gas was a real possibility, and situate this in the state context. First, I obtained hearing transcripts produced by the Department of Environmental Conservation (DEC), available through its website and a freedom of information request. Three hearings took place in Broome County and provided citizens an opportunity to offer feedback on proposed new regulations for fracking for shale gas: a scoping hearing in 2008, and public hearings in 2009 and 2011. Second, I collected 3,759 news articles that referenced the terms "fracking," "hydraulic fracturing," or "hydrofracturing" in four newspapers covering the controversy across the state: *New York Times, Albany Times Union, Ithaca Journal*, and *Binghamton Press & Sun*. I selected for analysis 452 articles in "media peaks," months when fracking was covered more frequently (Dodge & Lee, 2017). Third, I interviewed 16 people in Broome County representing local governments, grassroots and mainstream environmental organizations, and landowner coalitions that were active in the controversy.

FRAMING THE SHALE GAS IMAGINARY AND ITS ALTERNATIVE

The EIA estimates that the portion of the Marcellus Shale located in the "Southern Tier" region of New York has 141 trillion cubic feet of recoverable shale gas (2014). Despite the enormous potential of the Marcellus Shale, New York rejected shale gas development in 2014 and opened the potential to transform its energy policy to favor "alternative energy." This decision did not come easily. Citizens, landowner coalitions, mainstream and grassroots environmental organizations, and many others contested the national imaginary for shale gas from mid-2007 through December 2014. I explore these dynamics by focusing on the ways New Yorkers, particularly in one county, framed the national imaginary of shale gas, and how an alternative was ultimately embraced.

Drill, Baby, Drill: A Gas Rush with New Landowner Controls

Once landowners, developers, and an assortment of staff from local Farm Bureaus and the Cooperative Extension learned that large-scale oil and gas development in the Southern Tier of New York was possible, they began organizing themselves to prepare for it. As they did so, they perpetuated the national energy imaginary for shale gas, translating it for New York, and organizing their ideas and actions to make development possible.

These groups positively keyed the national shale gas imaginary by framing it as beneficial for New York. For instance, as various groups estimated the enormous quantities of recoverable shale gas in the Marcellus Shale, industry representatives and pro-development landowners equated these quantities with economic benefits. One landowner testified at a hearing "that the natural gas in the Marcellus that's extractible is 50 billion cubic feet per square mile. And you take the size of the Marcellus in New York State which is 20 to 25,000 square miles, you come up with a huge sum of money" (DEC, 2008, 130). Brad Gill, of the Independent Oil and Gas Association, claimed that a "total annual economic impact of approximately 1.4 billion dollars is within reason" in the Marcellus Shale (DEC, 2008, p. 59). For Gill, the positive economic impact also included considerable tax benefits for local and state governments, and the enrichment of individual landowners. Given that the Southern Tier region had been in economic decline for decades, pro-development landowners were eager to emphasize how these benefits could bring prosperity back to the area.

In framing the national imaginary for New York, landowners and industry representatives also framed its "win-win-win" logic, almost in a mantra-like fashion. First, developing the Marcellus Shale would produce an abundance of affordable natural gas, contributing to an energy supply that would support the American way of life. Second, it would reduce dependence on foreign oil by increasing the development of "indigenous" energy. Finally, it would serve as a "bridge fuel" that would support the transition to cleaner forms of energy. This positive keying supported the idea of shale gas as a "game changer."

Rather than emphasizing that shale gas development was *good for this place*, as many landowners interested in economic development would do, industry representatives instead framed *this place as good for development*. This occurred during the DEC's scoping hearings, where members of the public provided feedback on the scope of analysis the DEC would conduct to assess proposed development. Grant Seabolt from STW Resources, an industry services organization based in Houston, Texas, noted, ". . . in order to have successful gas production, you need to have a good formation, you certainly have that in [the] Marcellus [Shale]. You also need to have a good supply of water. [You] certainly also have a good supply of water. But the third thing you need also is you have to have a way to deal with the waste water produced in the operations" (DEC, 2008, p. 98).

In part, he was selling his wastewater treatment services, but also revealing a common interpretation of the shale gas imaginary for New York. While landowners were focusing on economic benefits, industry representatives were focusing on whether or not the conditions for development were favorable. They especially expressed interest in the high quality of the gas trapped in the Marcellus Shale, the availability of large quantities of water necessary for production, and the proximity of development to pipelines and other infrastructure (DEC, 2008). Several companies had been testing wells that showed promising production levels, which further sparked interest among these groups to develop in the area. In this scoping meeting, pro-development groups showed their confidence that development was inevitable.

These ways of interpreting the shale gas imaginary were deeply resonant at a time of economic crisis and high oil and gas prices, and helped to support considerable activity. In the first decade of the 2000s, prospectors began developing nearby formations to position themselves to develop the Marcellus Shale (Wilber, 2012). "Landmen" began pitching leasing deals to landowners. Landowners—after word got out about a few bad leasing deals—began educating themselves on the legal aspects of oil and gas leasing, and forming landowner coalitions to gain negotiation leverage (Jacquet & Stedman, 2011). With support from the Farm Bureau and Cooperative Extension, these groups moved forward to implement development projects under existing rules and regulations. In April 2008, the DEC asked the state legislature to consider a bill that would streamline permitting processes and update spacing requirements to allow for horizontal drilling (Nearing, 2008), a move that signaled the advent of broad-scale development.

In this context, industry insiders played an important role in perpetuating the national imaginary of shale gas for New York. They did so by framing the challenges of development in practical terms. For example, industry insiders framed the time it would take to organize equipment and labor to scale up production as considerable. They further used this framing to suggest that impacts would be minimal, as they would be spread out over time. This logic extended to regulatory and infrastructure capacity. For instance, when confronted with concerns that water produced from development activities posed a threat—because it contained toxins from fracturing fluid and materials that would surface through development activities—industry leaders expressed faith that the capacity to handle wastewater would develop as production rolled out, and that producers should be allowed to use the existing capacity (DEC, 2008).

Industry also framed the volume of water that would be needed as relatively small. For example, Dave Cornue, a geologist at ALL Consulting, explained,

> As of the year 2000 there were 3.6 trillion gallons of water used in a 79 county area that included the majority of the Marcellus Shale play. The primary use of that water was for electrical generation, industrial uses, public water supply, irrigation and livestock. . . . Hypothetically, if we are to assume that 1,000 Marcellus wells will be drilled in a year, this yields a total water usage of approximately 3.9 billion gallons, just over one-tenth of one percent of the total water consumption for this area. While fresh water volumes are larger than what was considered in [conventional development], they are still relatively small in comparison to all current water uses. (DEC, 2008, p. 112)

By comparing the amount of water needed to develop shale gas to the total amount of water needed for all other uses in the area, Cornue was attempting to make the amount seem insignificant, although it is doubtful that calling 3.9 billion gallons "small" was an effective strategy. Even so, the argument was consistent with the "roll-out" thesis: through proper planning and coordination with local government, operators could spread out the withdrawal of large volumes of water over space and time, making their impact negligible. In addition, other nuisances—such as increased emissions from truck traffic—would be "temporary" or "transient."

Another way industry leaders framed shale gas for New York was to equate fracturing for shale gas with conventional development. By promoting this framing, industry leaders were justifying minimal changes to New York's environmental regulations. First, they framed existing regulations as adequate, including the 1992 Generic Environmental Impact Statement, which set the standards for conventional oil and gas development in all of New York. In addition, they framed development activities as already highly regulated, including a requirement to use fracturing fluid only for designated purposes, and to allow truck traffic only on roads that were designated for industrial use.

As part of this flattened keying of the national shale gas imaginary, pro-development landowners and industry representatives sought to empower two different groups to manage shale gas development. First, both groups framed industry operators and their "best practices" as important controls to minimize impacts. Several industry represent-atives, for example, discussed how they could reuse stimulation fluids, thus minimizing the volumes of water they would extract from rivers and other water bodies, and dis-pose back into those rivers. This, in turn, would minimize the spread of invasive species and reduce the capacity needed to treat wastewater. To justify industry operators as protectors of the environment, these representatives referred to development in other places where industry standards were already working. One noted how fracking was happening safely below schools, churches, and airports in Fort Worth, Texas. Second, in addition to empowering industry leaders, landowners also favored placing control in the hands of newly forming landowner coalitions who could oversee development activities. These coalitions had educated themselves about the best ways to develop landowner-friendly leases that would give them control over development activities on their property. Some of these coalitions supported the "drill, baby, drill" national imag-inary, but as I describe later, many supported a modified version of it. Both approaches, at least in theory, provided a mechanism by which shale gas development could pro-ceed to generate economic benefits and remain flexible and unconstrained, while also protecting the environment.

In parallel to this "flattened" keying of the national imaginary, diverse political actors began developing a modified version called "responsible development" in the hopes they could create greater protections for the environment and human health than the "drill, baby, drill" imaginary.

"Chill, Baby, Chill": Slowing Down for Responsible Development

The proposed development activity alerted public officials, environmental organiza-tions, and even some members of pro-development landowner coalitions, who called for a moderated version of the national imaginary. On the surface, this group appeared to share a consensus that fracking for shale gas should be done, but only under strict regulations. Yet, a closer look at their discourse reveals diverse perspectives. Public officials came close to supporting the national imaginary reflected in the policies of the Bush administration, but also saw value in additional state regulations to protect the environment while realizing the "tremendous" economic benefits. Well-established environmental organizations expressed great ambivalence about the "drill, baby, drill" imaginary. They helped debunk the national imaginary by supporting "responsible development" while also raising deep doubts that even strict regulations could mitigate risks to the environment and human health. Others framed fracking as unsafe, and advocated for strict regulations under the assumption they had no choice but to accept fracking.

These three groups all framed fracking in terms of (1) "safety" and (2) "balance" between the competing demands of environmental protection and economic development. Yet, they attached very different meanings to these frames. For the first group, mostly public officials and pro-development landowners, "safe development" was possible with some new regulations, such as requiring closed-loop drilling, steel tanks for water storage, and secondary containment. But in the balance between environmental protection and economic development, it leaned toward economic development. It framed economic gains of developing the Marcellus Shale as potentially huge, and sought to speed up the regulatory process so economic benefits could be realized. For example, one landowner said, "A foolhardy tradeoff would be to seek and recover a valuable resource such as natural gas and denigrate or destroy another, especially one so vital to all life such as water" (DEC, 2008, 145), but went on to argue that the regulations should be completed quickly to allow development to proceed. Another proposed removing the New York City watershed from development plans, not to protect the watershed but to avoid regulatory delays for the rest of the state. As with their "drill baby drill" counterparts, this group framed impacts of fracking mostly in economic terms, and the region as economically desperate. For instance, Harry Carlson, a landowner and resident of Windsor, New York, said, "The positive and likely continuing economic impact of the anticipated gas recovery projects here . . . appear to be huge. It comes at a time when the region is desperate for it, not only for the monetary gain but also for the gas energy itself" (DEC, 2008, pp. 146–147). Landowners came out in large numbers during the hearings on the environment department's draft regulations, continuing to further this storyline (DEC, 2009/2011).

For the second group—largely made up of environmental organizations—development could never be completely safe, but it could be done responsibly. Responsible development meant creating strict regulations to protect the environment and public health. This position implicitly framed fracking as inevitably risky and as a matter of public health and environmental protection. For example, Chris Burger, from the Binghamton Regional Sustainability Coalition (BRSC), claimed that "nothing can be done to eliminate the dangers posed by gas drilling. BRSC has, however, taken time to develop a list of concerns and suggestions that we feel can reduce these dangers" (DEC, 2008, pp. 46–47). This group proposed more robust regulations, such as the use of alternative, "green" fracturing fluid and full disclosure of fracturing fluid contents to both the

DEC and to the public. They also wanted regulations to account for cumulative impacts not required in the current state regulations or proposed revisions to them. For example, Burger advocated that the DEC create a "fully built out scenario" that would account for cumulative impacts to water quality and air quality, among other considerations. He proposed the creation of pollution thresholds that when reached would "kick in" additional environmental reviews.

For this group, the balance between economic development and environmental protection tipped toward environmental protection. They framed "great rewards" of fracking in relation to its "great risks," posing this question for regulators: "How do you get the rewards without creating destruction?" While the regulations they proposed would be more expensive, they framed the protections for human health and environment as worth the additional costs.

A third group—of environmental organizations and environmentally minded citizens—framed fracking as *not* safe. This group cited incidents and accidents in other states as examples of an industry out of control. While this group promoted similar regulations as those actors advocating for responsible development, they also sought more radical changes, based on the idea that "the Marcellus play" was "a revolutionary change" (DEC, 2008, p. 43). Adam Flint advocated for returning home rule to local governments in oil and gas development, reversing a long-standing environmental statute. Others called on the DEC to scrap its proposed supplement to the existing generic regulations and "go back to the drawing board," or to create an entirely new set of generic regulations to account for the uniqueness of shale gas. One citizen summarized this group's view: "Political pressure by puppet government officials with conflicts of interest need to be quieted with a chill, baby chill. For what is at stake here is the most basic of human rights: clean, unfettered and uncontaminated water" (DEC, 2008, p. 105).

This group also framed economic gains as compatible with environmental protection but reversed the formulation. Rather than seeing fracking as an economic engine that could be controlled enough to protect the environment, this group framed a clean environment as a necessary resource for businesses such as tourism and outdoor recreation. From this perspective, fracking was a threat to a clean environment and thus to business. Consistent with this view, this group framed the costs of weak regulations as considerable, not only in terms of the potential destruction of the purity of the environment, but also in terms of the economics of the region. Several citizens pleaded with the DEC not to allow development on such a broad scale without identifying the capacity to provide adequate oversight, and to handle the scale of development.

In reaction to these criticisms, Governor Patterson signed a bill that would enable fracking of the Marcellus Shale, and also directed the DEC to create supplementary regulations to the existing generic ones for oil and gas development. A draft of the new supplementary regulations was released in 2009, but the final draft was delayed amidst controversy, and a revision was not made public until 2011. Over that period, several municipalities banned fracking through zoning laws, while the state legislature actively proposed and passed legislation relevant to fracking (NCSL, 2014).

While these groups held different perspectives, they all shared a view that one could not rely on past regulations to manage the impacts of shale gas. Their critical keying framed federal regulations as failing to protect human health and the environment. To make their case, they repeatedly referred to the "Halliburton loophole" and research done by Theo Colburn, which documented 300 chemicals found in water bodies near fracking sites, 65 of which were hazardous according to federal laws but were exempted from regulation in the 2005 Energy Bill. This group also framed the current Generic Environmental Impact Statement, which governed all oil and gas development to date in New York, as outmoded. They cited new technologies that the DEC could use, such as geospatial mapping, to assess cumulative impacts. This "chill baby chill" group sought regulations that would draw on the best new science and technology to evaluate potential impacts and mitigate risks.

The criticisms of existing regulations extended to the *new* regulations that the DEC proposed to regulate shale gas. Environmental organizations launched the most fundamental critique. They did so by framing as inappropriate the DEC's reliance on information from New York to assess the impacts of shale gas development. These environmental groups urged the DEC to use information and scientific reports about places where shale gas development was already happening. They framed these places as "labs" that provided important information for New York about the likely effects of shale gas development. They also pointed out myriad problems of the national "drill baby drill" imaginary that these places demonstrated. Roy Lackner said, "We are sitting on an incredibly unique ecosystem that needs to be safeguarded with whatever it might possibly take. This [environment department's approach to regulation] is a clear affront to what needs to be responsibly done in this area, the science is still out" (DEC, 2008, pp. 107–108).

Looking to other places for information about the effects of shale gas was not only about shale gas being "totally different" in volume, scale, and geography from conventional development. These groups were also pointing out the myriad problems of the "drill baby drill" energy imaginary. Using information about development in New York would have provided evidence about development under a different imaginary—one prior to the Bush administration. Only by examining what was happening in other states under the "drill baby drill" imaginary could one get a fair assessment of how this imaginary was playing out in practice, and the effects it would have on valuable environmental resources and human health. For this group, the evidence was overwhelming that the "drill baby drill" approach had major shortcomings. It exposed the population to toxic, cancer-causing chemicals, among other problems. Even the stricter environmental regulations already in New York were not sufficient to handle the limitations of national policy because they were created when more strident regulations existed at the federal level, and when the new techniques for developing shale gas were as yet unknown.

Unlike their "drill baby drill" counterparts, many framed the DEC's capacity to oversee large-scale development as grossly inadequate and its practices as negligent. The DEC had claimed there had never been one instance of groundwater contamination in

New York's history of regulating oil and gas development, and it used this statement as evidence that it would maintain this track record for shale gas development. But environmental organizations framed this information as distorted. For example, Scott Lauffer, of the Atlantic Chapter of the Sierra Club, argued at a scoping hearing that

> [a]lthough the Draft Scope states that gas production has existed in New York for 50 years without any known incident of drinking water contamination, it is not know that contamination hasn't occurred. We note that for the past 50 years the State of New York has not known what chemicals it has been permitting in subsurface injections. It's known that Project Drinking Water Wells have been blown out by drilling activity in North Brookfield and obvious groundwater contamination has occurred in areas of Chenango County which were reported to the DEC. This event was never properly addressed. By the time DEC got to the site four days later, the contamination had dispersed down stream (DEC, 2008, pp. 65–67).

He and other environmentalists called on the DEC to do random sampling of existing wells in New York to accurately assess whether aquifers and private wells had been contaminated in the past.

The overlap of the "safety" and "balance" frames enabled these three groups to discuss the kinds of regulations needed to realize the economic and energy benefits of fracking while protecting the environment and human health. But it also revealed deep cleavages about the desirability of the fracking for shale gas imaginary. The environmentalists' critical keying refocused attention on specific practical and political questions that would eventually create an opening for the emergence of a powerful anti-fracking movement. They were planting the seeds of dissent against the national imaginary.

Environmentalists advocating for "responsible development" argued to shift regulatory authority and rebalance the power of regulatory agencies in New York. For example, Dereth Glance, the executive program director of Citizen's Campaign for the Environment, proposed stronger coordination between the DEC's mineral division—which was responsible for developing new regulations for shale gas—and its water division—which took a stronger stance on protecting water resources. Others sought to elevate the power of diverse water resource councils to give them the same authority as interstate water commissions whose jurisdiction did not reach into the Marcellus Shale region. And others proposed inter-agency coordination, for example, between the DEC and the Public Service Commission, which could help assess and manage the impacts on power lines and transmission stations. The "fracking is unsafe" faction, in contrast, emphasized the importance of citizen action. For example, Adam Flint, a local environmental activist, said "the history . . . in other hazardous industrial processes tells us that only those citizens who are organized and active with community interests can have any real assurance that their health and safety are protected" (DEC, 2008, p. 45).

The ambivalence within this coalition appeared in its reactions to public policies. When Governor Cuomo proposed approving the development of a few wells in the Southern Tier on a pilot scale as a compromise, environmentalists vehemently rejected it, while landowner coalitions strongly supported it. Ultimately the idea of small-scale development was shut down amidst the controversy. To understand this outcome, it is important to understand a final, even more critical approach in New York to framing the national shale gas imaginary.

"It's Not the Right Thing To Do": Rationale for an Alternative Energy Imaginary

As these diverse actors were translating the shale gas imaginary for New York, another group was keying it even more critically. Individual citizens and a small number of environmental organizations raised doubts about the promised economic benefits and shamed DEC regulators and landowners for recklessly rushing in with "dollar blind sight" to support development activities (DEC, 2008, p. 104). While sharing concerns over the economic crisis, they framed existing rules and regulations at both the federal and state level as deeply flawed, as they supported the destruction of the environment and public health for economic gains.[3] For example, one claimed that the federal 2005 Energy Policy Act provides oil and gas companies unreasonable rights, allowing them to conduct dangerous industrial activities with virtually no regulation or oversight. They derided federal policies that treat fracturing fluid as a trade secret, and discredited reports held up as evidence that fracking was "safe." For example, this group referenced a 2004 EPA study, which finds that 88 out of every 220 wells in Wyoming have been contaminated and demonstrates that gas laced with fracking fluid and other toxic subsurface materials can migrate through well casings and fractures in layers of rock to contaminate aquifers. At the state level, this group critiqued the DEC's proposed state regulations for shale gas— which in theory should overcome the limitations of federal policy. One said the DEC "would be laughed out of the long house," referencing a Native American principle of assessing actions based on their impact for the next five generations. Rather than framing delays as "bad for business," they posited them as necessary for protecting landowners and the environment from the nefarious practices of the oil and gas industry.

While many local residents shared the view of the environmental organizations that strict regulations were needed to protect the environment, at least in the initial parts of the controversy, their perspective took on a much more local flavor. Their deepest concerns were over the impact that widespread oil and gas development would have on their quality of life. This was paired with deep doubts about the ability of the DEC, or any other regulatory body, to really protect the local community from the risks of fracking. They also raised doubts about whether or not landowners could really protect themselves and their neighbors from these risks through oil and gas leases. While few specifically mentioned new leasing practices as a problem, they discussed how landowners would be "outgunned" by billion-dollar oil and gas companies if anything would go wrong. One came to the conclusion "that this operation cannot be done right because it's not the right thing to do" (DEC, 2008, p. 154).

These concerns were closely tied to meanings that residents held of the places they lived. Many spoke about the area as a "beautiful place" or a "wonderful area" with a "strong community." For example, Evan Romer explained in a hearing, "One of the biggest assets in this area is the natural scenery, the hills, the rivers, the streams. That's why many of us value living here" (DEC, 2008, p. 137). Others framed the natural resources in the area as "precious gifts" that should be preserved. For example, one resident, Charlotte Schotanus, testified at a hearing that

> "[t]he bottom line is to preserve the water, air and the health of our community for the present and for the future, our generation and for all future generations after us. We are, after all, our brother's keeper. Purity of our water and air and the health of our citizens are of the utmost importance, even more so than the money. We need to preserve these gifts" (DEC, 2008, p. 75).

For these residents, the effort to create regulations to manage fracking was not an intellectual exercise, but was linked concretely to fears of how their communities would change, and how the natural environment where they lived would be destroyed. As Evan Romer explained, "If the Supplement [revised regulation] allows the density of drilling that's being proposed, it will absolutely destroy the quality of life in this area. We'll be living in an industrial zone" (DEC, 2008, p. 136). Others described how the county would be devastated by the infusion of tens of thousands of gallons of fracturing fluid in each of the hundreds of wells that would be developed.

Their specific concerns, while overlapping at times with those who favored "responsible development," were much more focused on the overall impact on their quality of life and community health. These concerns were tied directly to their doubts about the DEC's ability to protect them from harms. At a public hearing, several residents appealed to DEC representatives directly. One asked, ". . . do you honestly believe—and I really wish that you could tell me because you represent the DEC—do you honestly believe that there will be good regulations in place to protect us? Do you honestly believe that?" (DEC, 2008, p. 79).

These residents framed their doubts in relation to the DEC's past record regulating other polluting industries in the area. One woman spoke about the DEC's inability to properly regulate the dairy industry. She explained how her aquifer had been contaminated when a neighboring farmer had "spread liquid effluent over an uncased wellhead" (DEC, 2008, p. 203), while others were dumping effluent into unlined lagoons regulated by the DEC. According to her, it took the DEC a year and a half to respond to her request for information about the contamination, while she was forced to buy water for her livestock for $300 a month. She connected this experience to fracking: "So I'm living it and I'm here to tell you that there is a correlation between an unregulated industry 65 miles north of here and what you're about to see with another unregulated industry, that being the oil and gas" (DEC, 2008, pp. 204–205).

Others framed fracking in relation to previous experiences with toxic pollution. Several made reference to Endicott, New York, where a "toxic plume" of trichloroethylene

(TCE) left behind at an IBM microelectronics plant contaminated homes and businesses in the area (*Press & Sun Bulletin*, 2016). Others connected fracking to Love Canal, where a school and working-class neighborhood were erected on top of a toxic waste site, and where high levels of chemicals had leached into the air and soil in the homes, causing reproductive and other health problems (CHEJ, n.d.). Diane Lisek stated simply, "I don't want to be the Love Canal of the state" (DEC, 2008, p. 190). Both the connection to Love Canal and to Endicott animated fears that the toxic chemicals in fracturing fluid could migrate in unexpected ways to cause devastating harms to the environment and human health. In her testimony at a public hearing, Charlotte Schotanus put these concerns together with the fear that the community would not be protected:

> The number of fluids used for fracing is quite astounding and the number of those on the federal hazardous list is overwhelming. What are you going to do to protect the public from another Love Canal or another Endicott? What about the landowners who want no part of this but end up with contaminated water and air? Are you going to protect the public by preserving their clean water and air and help with the expense caused in their water if their water is tainted? (DEC, 2008, p. 76).

Diane Liske pointed out that when these types of incidents occur, public officials "solve nothing" or "just drag their feet and shift the blame of liability" (DEC, 2008, p. 185). She explained the same thing could happen with fracking: "It's like milk when it spoils it never goes back again. And in life we have to look to what gets spoiled that can't be fixed and we have to ask ourselves is . . . who's going to provide the umbrella [when it rains]? Who takes liability? Who will address things?" One person summed up the experience this way, "Let's not repeat mistakes that have been made for economic reasons in the past" (DEC, 2008, p. 44).

These residents discussed regulations, often in ways similar to leaders in the environmental organizations. But many of their concerns were also more proximate, that is, relating to the effects they expected to experience. One women asked the DEC to "[d]o your studies of what has happened in states such as Colorado, Wyoming, Texas, etcetera. Check how their water and air has been tainted and how their lives have been changed forever due to the resulting health issues" (DEC, 2008, pp. 73–74). Another said, without good regulations, "we're all going to be doomed" (DEC, 2008, pp. 79–80).

For these reasons, this group framed doubts about the economic value of fracking. Some pointed out that property values would go down, or that the companies would be benefiting more than local residents. One questioned whether the economic benefits were worth the risks when she said, "So there will be people in the surrounding area that may have economic gain but they don't know what they pass on to their neighbor" (DEC, 2008, pp. 187–188). One man at a scoping hearing talked about leaving a landowner coalition when he found out he would be protected if the aquifer under his property was contaminated, but his neighbor would not.

Many began framing a new way of thinking that they variously called "creative thinking," "green thinking," and "long-term thinking." For example, one woman testifying at the scoping hearing said, "This 'drill, baby drill' attitude has got to stop. We've got to start thinking in a green fashion" (DEC, 2008, p. 79). Even in the beginning of the controversy, when most of the "alternatives" focused on making shale gas development less disruptive, residents began framing a "truer" alternative to the "drill baby drill" national imaginary. Several, for example, began calling for alternative energy, in the form of solar collectors or windmills. In a 2008 scoping meeting, one resident claimed, "The alternative energy should really be developed" (DEC, 2008, p. 155).

As the controversy evolved, residents and activists founded new anti-fracking organizations such as New Yorkers Against Fracking, Frack Action, Fleased, and New York Residents Against Drilling. Many existing environmental and other citizens' organizations also became mobilized against fracking, such as Food & Water Watch, Citizen Action of New York, and Toxics Targeting, among others. These groups organized a large grassroots campaign across the state, initiated protests, and engaged health professionals and other experts who provided information about the negative impacts of fracking.

This group developed the critical keying of the shale gas imaginary, forming a more stridently anti-fracking discourse. It framed fracking as an inherently dangerous process that could not be controlled through regulation (Allstadt et al., 2012). It framed evidence to support this claim, including visible accidents such as the British Petroleum oil spill in the Gulf of Mexico, and the *Gasland* movie, which highlighted the relationship between fracking and water contamination. This group challenged the pro-fracking and "responsible development" groups, asserting that fracking was not inevitable in New York, contrasting private economic benefits with broader social and environmental harms, and arguing that fracking was not worth the risks. It also discussed fracking as a public not a private decision, debunking the notion, for example, that frack fluid could be considered a trade secret (Dodge & Lee, 2017). It challenged economic arguments by asserting that fracking would harm existing business in tourism and outdoor recreation (Urban, 2008).

This group framed the DEC as "unprepared" and lacking objectivity and inclusiveness, and requested studies to address deficiencies in its review (Environmental Working Group of Physicians, Scientists and Engineers for Healthy Energy, 2012; Lifton et al., 2012; Sierra Club, 2012). It also called the energy industry secretive and accident-prone (Allstadt et al., 2012). For these reasons, its policy solution was not stronger regulations or better planning, but a statewide ban on fracking. In step with this view, several municipalities banned fracking under local zoning laws, which were upheld in New York's highest court (*Wallach v. Town of Dryden et al./Cooperstown Holstein Corporation v. Town of Middlefield*, 2014).

This group importantly linked fracking to two broader issues. It framed fracking as a matter of public health (Advocates for Cheery Valley, Inc., et al., 2012), and introduced the idea of the public's right to health, safety, and welfare in the state's constitution. It also linked fracking to climate change, calling fracking a "false solution" to an energy transition toward renewables (Shackford, 2009).

This group was not without its critics. Some local residents framed alternative energy as unrealistic. For example, Clif Tamsell said, "We've been told for 20 years by the 'environmentalists' that renewable energy is going to be a huge factor in electrical production. At this point it's two to three percent [of energy production in New York] in spite of the billions and billions of dollars that have been spent. It's not realistic to expect that that's going to increase significantly during our lifetime" (DEC, 2008, pp. 131–132). But the residents who opposed fracking successfully linked fracking to ongoing dependence on fossil fuels and the dangers of global climate change.

Governor Cuomo eventually announced that the state would ban fracking. He would later issue his energy strategy, which included a goal that 50% of New York's energy would be produced by renewable sources, and that it would cut greenhouse gas emissions by 80% of 1990 levels, by 2050 (New York State, 2015). While it is beyond the scope of this chapter to explore the form that this alternative energy future would take, it is important to note that the adoption and creation of a renewable energy imaginary does not easily follow from a ban on fracking, and instituting an alternative energy imaginary is not straightforward. Since fracking was banned in 2014, for instance, an important debate has emerged about what form renewable energy would take. The Cuomo administration has spent a good deal of time focusing on reviving an old nuclear energy infrastructure, as this would help hit reduction targets for greenhouse gas emissions (McGeehan, 2015a). Others have pointed out that this is not a desirable energy solution but a cynical interpretation of the renewable energy imaginary, meant more to protect jobs in key districts than to address climate change (McGeehan, 2015b; Wasserman, 2016). Only more recently, after outrage has been expressed over this interpretation of alternative energy, has the attention begun to turn more seriously toward wind farms and other forms of renewable energy such as solar or hydropower (McGeehan, 2016).

Conclusion: Fracking as an Emblematic Struggle over Energy Imaginaries

While most scholars assert that national energy imaginaries have considerable power to shape policy, this case exemplifies a different dynamic, where political actors contest competing imaginaries and shape them over time. The resulting images of the future are intimately connected to efforts to rebalance power. The New York case reveals not only the ways in which a movement against fracking was able to shift the power dynamics of the energy sector in New York, but also how it faces serious constraints to its transformation.

The alternative and critical ways of framing the shale gas imaginary ensured that it would fail to cohere in New York. Mainstream environmental organizations contributed to this, at least initially, by framing shale gas as inherently risky, and the DEC as unprepared and outmoded. Their "responsible development" approach, while allowing a broad conversation about how to develop shale gas and protect the environment, also revealed deep divisions over the risks of fracking and how to balance environmental protection with economic development. Citizens and grassroots environmental organizations framed proponents of the "drill baby drill" imaginary as greedy and out of touch with the realities of climate change. They also framed the imaginary as perpetuating and ushering in to New York a dangerous industrial process, raising doubts about its purported economic benefits and about the ability of landowner coalitions or gas companies to regulate fracking through leasing deals or industry best practices. Individual citizens linked the effects of fracking to proximate concerns, such as protecting the natural beauty of the area, their quality of life, and the health of their communities. They also associated fracking with toxic incidents in the past, including Endicott and Love Canal.

Consistent with their views, these groups sought to shift power away from the environment department to regulate fracking, which was seen as captured by industry. Existing mainstream environmental organizations sought to empower the Public Service Commission, various water resource councils, and the Department of Health, among other formal institutions. They also enjoyed insider access to shape the regulatory response. Citizens emphasized independent citizen action, forming grassroots organizations focused on building their own countervailing power, and working in coalition with national groups.

These findings build on the growing literature that shows how energy imaginaries can be contested (Smith & Tidwell, 2016). They add to the discussion by showing how political and social actors contest competing energy imaginaries during potential energy transitions and how one alternative becomes accepted and another rejected. We learn how entrenched imaginaries are supplanted with alternatives that involve a new way of thinking and acting. It also reveals that sociotechnical imaginaries are not singular; they do not exist in isolation, but compete with other conceptualizations of energy futures.

This controversy over fracking in New York reflects a broader, global struggle over energy production and the organization of society (Dodge & Metze, 2017). The shale gas imaginary perpetuates yet also transforms the fossil-fuel energy imaginary by opening a pathway for the development of unconventional fossil fuels. Yet, as people implement the shale gas imaginary, they perpetuate a fossil-fuel system with greater risks than conventional forms of development. Environmentalists and their allies are highlighting the increased risks associated with the perpetuation of a fossil-fuel economy and the industrial social order (while those who are protecting it seek to deny those risks). The fight over fracking is emblematic of this broader struggle to refashion the energy imaginary for a "greener" future.

ACKNOWLEDGMENTS

Many thanks to Bill Sisk for his excellent research assistance. This research was supported by the Paul A. Volcker Junior Scholar Research Grant Award, Public Administration Section, American Political Science Association, 2016.

NOTES

1. At the global level, the energy independence argument was particularly relevant for countries dependent on authoritarian oil and gas producers (De Jong et al., p. 2014).
2. Petroleum includes crude oil, natural gas, natural gas liquids, liquefied natural gas, and mixtures of natural gas and synthetic gas (Brady & Crannell, 2012, p. 51).
3. Energy benefits were mentioned but were not in the forefront of the discussion.

REFERENCES

Abolafia, M. (2004). Framing moves: Interpretive politics at the Federal Reserve. *Journal of Public Administration Research and Theory, 14*(3), 349–370.

Advocates for Cheery Valley, Inc., et al. (2012). Letter to Governor Cuomo on fracking. [Open Letter]. Retrieved from http://www.psr.org/resources/letter-to-governor-cuomo-on-fracking.html

Allstadt, L., et al. (2012). Open letter to Governor Cuomo: Signed by Ingraffea; Steingraber; Howarth; Barth & many others. [Open Letter]. Retrieved from http://www.ernstversusencana.ca/open-letter-to-governor-cuomo-signed-by-ingraffea-steingraber-howarth-barth-many-others

Anonymous (2008, July 25). Well timed. *Press & Sun-Bulletin*, pp. 2–B2. Retrieved from http://search.proquest.com/docview/440994193?accountid=14168

Brady, W. J., & Crannell, J. P. (2012). Hydraulic fracturing regulation in the United States: The laissez-faire approach of the federal government and varying state regulations. *Vermont Journal of Environmental Law, 14*, 39–70.

Cama, T. (2015). Mayland bans fracking. *The Hill*. Retrieved from http://thehill.com/policy/energy-environment/243625-maryland-bans-fracking

Cathles, L. M., III, Brown, L., Taam, M., & Hunt, H. (2012). A commentary on "The greenhouse-gas footprint of natural gas in shale formations by R.W. Howarth, R. Santoro, and Anthony Ingraffea." *Climate Change, 113*, 525–535.

Center for Health and Environmental Justice (CHEJ). (n.d.). Love Canal. Retrieved from http://chej.org/about-us/story/love-canal/

Cotton, M., Rattle, I., & Van Alstine, J. (2014). Shale gas policy in the United Kingdom: An argumentative discourse analysis. *Energy Policy, 73*, 427–438.

Davidson, D. (1985 [1973]). On the very idea of a conceptual scheme. In J. Rajchaman & C. West (Eds.), *Post-analytic philosophy* (pp. 183–198). New York: Columbia University Press.

De Jong, S., Auping, W., & Govers, J. (2014). *The Geopolitics of Shale Gas: The implications of the US' shale gas revolution on intrastate stability within traditional oil and natural gas exporting countries in the EU neighborhood.* The Hague: The Hague Centre For Strategic Studies (HCSS) and TNO.

Department of Environmental Conservation (DEC). (2008, November 17). Supplemental generic environmental impact statement draft scoping meeting on DEC's oil and gas regulatory program for the Marcellus Shale. [Hearing transcription]. Broome Community College, Binghamton, NY.

Department of Environmental Conservation (DEC). (2009, November 12). Supplemental generic environmental impact statement draft scoping meeting on DEC's oil and gas regulatory program for the Marcellus Shale. [Hearing transcription]. Chenango Valley High School, Chenango Bridge, NY.

Department of Environmental Conservation (DEC). (2011, November 17). In re: Draft supplemental generic environmental impact statement and draft regulations for high-volume hydraulic fracturing. [Hearing transcription]. The Forum, Binghamton, NY.

Dewulf, A., Gray, B., Putnam, L., Lewicki, R., Aarts, N., Bouwen, R., & van Woerkum, C. (2009). Disentangling approaches to framing in conflict and negotiation research: A meta-paradigmatic perspective. *Human Relations*, 62(2), 155–193.

Dodge, J., and Lee, J. (2017). Framing dynamics and political gridlock: The curious case of hydraulic fracturing in New York. *Journal of Environmental Policy & Planning*, 19(1), 14–34. doi:10.1080/1523908X.2015.1116378

Dodge, J., & Metze, T. (2017). Hydraulic fracturing as an interpretive policy problem: lessons on energy controversies in Europe and the U.S.A. *Journal of Environmental Policy and Planning*, 19(1), 1–13.

Eaton, W. M., Gasteyer, S. P., & Busch, L. (2014). Bioenergy futures: Framing sociotechnical imaginaries in local places. *Rural Sociology*, 79(2), 227–256.

Energy Information Administration (EIA). (2014). *Annual energy outlook report: With projections to 2040*. Washington, DC: US Energy Information Administration.

Energy Information Administration (EIA). (2015a). EIA shale gas production. Retrieved from http://www.eia.gov/dnav/ng/ng_prod_shalegas_s1_a.htm

Energy Information Administration (EIA). (2015b). Technically recoverable shale oil and shale gas resources: US. Retrieved from http://www.eia.gov/forecasts/aeo/assumptions/pdf/oilgas.pdf

Energy Information Administration (EIA). (2015c). US shale production (billion cubic feet). Retrieved from http://www.eia.gov/dnav/ng/hist/res_epg0_r5302_nus_bcfa.htm

Energy Information Administration (EIA). (2016). *Annual energy outlook early release: Annotated summary of two cases*. Washington, DC: US Energy Information Administration. Retrieved from http://www.eia.gov/forecasts/aeo/er/pdf/0383er%282016%29.pdf

Environmental Working Group of Physicians, Scientists and Engineers for Healthy Energy. (2012). Ten problems with New York's shale gas drilling plan. Retrieved from http://static.ewg.org/pdf/Top-Ten-NY-Drilling-Problems.pdf

Fischer, F. (2003). *Reframing public policy: Discursive politics and deliberative practices*. Oxford: Oxford University Press.

Forbes. (2012). *2012 U.S. energy sector outlook*. New York: Forbes Insight.

Gaworecki, M. (2014). Voters ban fracking in Texas, California, and Ohio. *DeSmogBlog*. Retrieved from http://www.desmogblog.com/2014/11/05/voters-ban-fracking-texas-california-and-ohio

Goffman, E. (1974). *Frame analysis*. Cambridge, MA: Harvard University Press.

IHS Cambridge Energy Research Associates. (2010). Fueling North America's energy future: The unconventional natural gas revolution and the carbon agenda. Cambridge, MA: IHS CERA.

Jacquet, J., & Stedman, R. C. (2011). Natural gas landowner coalitions in New York State: Emerging benefits of collective natural resource management. *Journal of Rural Social Sciences*, 26(1), 62.

Jasonoff, S., & Kim, S. H. (2009). Containing the atom: Sociological imaginaries and nuclear power in the United States and South Korea. *Minerva*, 47, 119–146.

Jasonoff, S., & Kim, S. H. (2013). Sociotechnical imaginaries and national energy policies. *Science as Culture*, 22(2), 189–196.

Jessop, B. (2009). Cultural political economy and critical policy studies. *Critical Policy Studies*, 3(3–4), 336–356.

Keep Tap Water Safe. (2014). Global Bans on Fracking. Retrieved from https://keeptapwatersafe.org/global-bans-on-fracking/

Levy, D. L., & Spicer, A. (2013). Contested imaginaries and the cultural political economy of climate change. *Organization, 20*(5), 659–678.

Lifton, B., et al. (2012). Seventy six legislators send bipartisan letter to Governor Cuomo. . . [Letter]. Retrieved from http://toxicstargeting.com/MarcellusShale/documents /letters/2012/06/13/legislators-letter

McGeehan, P. (2015a, November 22). Gov. Cuomo to order large increase in renewable energy in New York by 2030. *New York Times*. Retrieved from https://www.nytimes.com/2015/11/23 /nyregion/gov-cuomo-to-order-large-increase-in-renewable-energy-in-new-york-by -2030.html?_r=0

McGeehan, P. (2015b, November 16). Plan to close nuclear plant in upstate New York rattles its neighbors. *New York Times*. Retrieved from https://www.nytimes.com/2015/11/17/nyregion /plan-to-close-nuclear-plant-in-upstate-new-york-rattles-its-neighbors.html?action=click &contentCollection=N.Y.%20%2F%20Region&module=RelatedCoverage&region=EndOf Article&pgtype=article

McGeehan, P. (2016, January 17). Cuomo confirms deal to close Indian Point nuclear plant. *New York Times*. Retrieved from https://www.nytimes.com/2017/01/09/nyregion /cuomo-indian-point-nuclear-plant.html

National Conference of State Legislatures. (2014). Fracking update: What states are doing to ensure safe natural gas extraction. Retrieved from http://www.ncsl.org/research/energy /fracking-update-what-states-are-doing.aspx

Nearing, B. (2008, July 24). Paterson approves law on risky gas drilling. *Albany Times Union*, A1.

New York State. (2015). New York State energy overview: The energy to lead: 2015 New York State Energy Plan. Retrieved from https://energyplan.ny.gov/Plans/2015.aspx

Paltsev, S., Jacoby, H. D., Reilly, J. M., Ejaz, Q. J., Morris, J., O'Sullivan, F., Rausch, S., Winchester, N., & Kragha, O. (2011). The future of U.S. natural gas production, use, and trade. *Energy Policy, 39*, 5309–5321.

Press & Sun Bulletin. (2016, May 20). Timeline: Endicott's TCE dilemma. Retrieved from http://www.pressconnects.com/story/news/local/2016/05/20/timeline-endicotts-tce -dilemma/84566228/

Rao, V. (2012). *Shale gas: The promise and the peril*. Research Triangle Park, NC: RTI Press.

Rein, M. & Schon, D. (1996). Reframing policy discourse. In F. Fischer and J. Forester (Eds), *The argumentative turn in policy analysis and planning* (pp. 145–166). Durham, NC: Duke University Press.

Richardson, N., Gottlieb, M. Krupnick, A., & Wiseman, H. (2013). *The state of state shale gas regulation* [Report]. Washington, DC: Resources for the Future.

Shackford, S. (2009, November 19). Ithaca gas protesters: Payout not worth risk. *Ithaca Journal*. Retrieved from http://search.proquest.com/docview/378069435?accountid=14166

Sierra Club. (2012). Sierra Club reacts to Governor's Plan to limit drilling to economically disadvantaged counties of New York. Retrieved from http://atlantic2.sierraclub.org/content /sierra-club-reacts-governors-plan-limit-drilling-economically-disadvantaged-counties-new

Smith, M. F., & Ferguson, D. P. (2013). "Fracking democracy": Issue management and locus of policy decision-making in the Marcellus Shale gas drilling debate. *Public Relations Review, 39*, 377–386.

Smith, J. M., & Tidwell, A. S. D. (2016). The everyday lives of energy transitions: Contested sociotechnical imaginaries in the American West. *Social Studies of Science, 46*(3), 327–350.

US DOE. (2009). *Modern shale gas development in the United States: A primer* (Report). Washington, DC: US Department of Energy.

US GAO. (2012, September). Unconventional oil and gas development: Key environmental and public health requirements. Retrieved from http://www.oilandgasbmps.org/workshops /COGCCgroundwater/GAO_health.pdf

Urban, R. (2008, August 19). Protecting our resources: A priority. *Albany Times Union*, A1.

Vidic, R., Brantley, S., Vandenbossche, J., Yoxtheimer, D., & Abad, J. (n.d). Impact of shale gas development on regional water quality. *Science, 340,* 6134.

Wallach v. Town of Dryden et al./Cooperstown Holstein Corporation v. Town of Middlefield. (2014, June 30). Retrieved from http://www.nycourts.gov/ctapps/decisions/2014/jun14/130 -1310pn14-decision.pdf

Wasserman, H. (2016, September 2). Nuclear's last stand? New York's Cuomo rushes in to save dying plants. *The Progressive.* Retrieved from http://www.progressive.org/news/2016 /09/188931/nuclear%E2%80%99s-last-stand-new-york%E2%80%99s-cuomo-rushes-save -dying-plants

Wilber, T. (2012). *Under the surface: Fracking, fortunes, and the fate of the Marcellus Shale.* Ithaca, NY: Cornell University Press.

....

CHAPTER 23

OIL OPPOSITION

Creating Friction in Energy Politics

....

MARK C. J. STODDART, JILLIAN RENE SMITH,
AND PAULA GRAHAM

Introduction

....

ANTI-OIL protests in Canada have increased in recent years. This includes protests aimed directly at the Alberta oil sands, as well as those against new oil pipeline infrastructure, such as the proposed Northern Gateway, Kinder Morgan, Keystone XL, and Energy East projects. South of the Canadian border, Indigenous-led protests have emerged at Standing Rock, North Dakota against the Dakota Access pipeline which, if constructed, would transport oil in an underground pipeline across several US states. Hundreds of Indigenous and environmental activists have gathered to protect local land and water sources and preserve Indigenous cultural heritages. However, as McAdam and Boudet (2012) argue in their analysis of the United States, social movement mobilization against new energy development is exceptional, rather than the norm. More often, critical attention to the oil industry does not emerge until the aftermath of a disaster, such as the 1982 sinking of the *Ocean Ranger* offshore oil platform in Newfoundland and Labrador, Canada (Dodd, 2012); the massive oil spill from the *Exxon Valdez* tanker in 1989 in Prince William Sound, Alaska (Ritchie, 2012; Widener & Gunter, 2007); or the 2010 blowout at British Petroleum's (BP) Macondo oil well in the Gulf of Mexico (Freudenburg & Gramling, 2011; Hoffbauer & Ramos, 2014). Opposition to all of these oil developments became most contentious *after* disastrous events occurred.

Beyond these specific highly visible moments of contention, the normal operation of the oil industry is so tightly bound up with capitalist economies that we can define contemporary societies using terms like "fossil capitalism" (Altvater, 2007) or "petro-capitalism" (Carter, 2014; Haluza-DeLay, 2014). Similarly, Urry (2013) notes that contemporary capitalist societies are highly dependent on a "carbon complex" that is made up of the "carbon capital" interests of oil and gas companies, transportation and shipping companies, and car and airplane manufacturers. But the carbon complex has an even broader reach, as carbon capital provides royalties and tax revenues to governments, advertising income to mass media companies, and access to consumer goods and highly mobile lifestyles (Urry, 2013). The global impacts of recent oil price declines and ongoing volatility underscores the point that our energy systems, economic systems, and political systems are deeply connected through the carbon complex.

In this chapter, we focus on examples from Canada, where the normal operation of the carbon complex has been opposed and problematized. In particular, we examine mobilization against new oil development by Indigenous and environmental activists, with examples from Alberta and Atlantic Canada. Our discussion identifies two key themes. First, we find diverse approaches within anti-oil activism in terms of both discursive and tactical links between particular oil development projects and broader socio-environmental issues such as colonialism and climate change. Environmental opposition often reflects a conservationist approach that emphasizes ecological risks, which often compartmentalizes opposition to specific oil projects from broader analyses of the social-ecological harms of the carbon complex. By contrast, Indigenous opposition is more often grounded in a rights-based approach that emphasizes Canada's long history of colonization through resource extraction on Indigenous lands. Second, where there are alignments between Indigenous and environmental opposition against oil projects, we see that appeals to treaty agreements and environmental justice are used by both Indigenous and non-Indigenous anti-oil activists to contest energy projects.

The Alberta Oil Sands

The Athabasca River Basin in northern Alberta contains one of the world's largest fossil energy reserves, making the province of Alberta one of Canada's key oil development regions. The Alberta oil sands are set in a vast boreal forest landscape, which includes the territory of Cree, Dene, and Métis peoples (Weis et al., 2014). The Alberta oil sands are responsible for a significant proportion of Canada's carbon footprint, which is one of the highest in the world, per capita (Davidson & Gismondi, 2011; Murphy & Murphy, 2012). Under the Conservative government of Prime Minister Stephen Harper (2006–2015), the Canadian government offered a supportive political environment for the Alberta oil industry, reinforcing the long-term support of the Alberta provincial government for the oil industry (MacNeil, 2014; Murphy & Murphy, 2012). The notion that the oil sands are economically and socially beneficial for Alberta and for Canada—an idea promoted by governments and by industry associations such as the Canadian Association of Petroleum Producers (CAPP)—obtained near-hegemonic status in Alberta, and a great deal of cultural resonance in the rest of Canada (Haluza-DeLay, 2014).

Indigenous communities in northern Alberta challenge the social and environmental legitimacy of the oil sands on environmental justice grounds, focusing on the disproportionate amount of suffering endured by Indigenous communities in Alberta. The Indigenous organizations and networks who have been involved in this issue include "the Unist'ot'en Camp, the Yinka Dene Alliance, Moccasins on the Ground gatherings, the Healing Walk, and the Idle No More movement" (Weis et al., 2014, p. 16). As well, the Beaver Lake Cree, the Athabasca Chipewyan First Nation, and the Fort McKay First Nation have put forward legal challenges to the oil sands industry (Weis et al., 2014). In particular, the Lubicon Lake Cree Nation has struggled with extensive oil and gas development on their ancestral lands for over three decades (Laboucan-Massimo, 2014; Ominayak & Thomas, 2009).

Activists voice concerns around exposure to water pollution, leading to increased rates of illness in Indigenous communities, as well as disruption and harm to fish and wildlife populations that remain key parts of Indigenous diets and cultural practices. Ecological devastation occurs in the form of large-scale deforestation of boreal forests, alteration of the water cycle to extract bitumen, wetland destruction, and the accumulation of toxins in wastewater "tailings ponds" (Weis et al., 2014). Health problems overrepresented in Alberta Indigenous communities include "asthma and other respiratory problems, cancers of all kinds, skin diseases, and miscarriages" (Ominayak & Thomas, 2009, p. 112). According to Lubicon Cree Chief Bernard Ominayak, many Indigenous communities of the Athabasca region once characterized by self-sufficiency have experienced a "significant decline in our land-based livelihood [which has] reduced us to a state of poverty and dependency" (p. 111). Ongoing land-claim disputes between Indigenous communities and the Canadian government are complicated by the environmental politics of resources allocation in the province (Coats, 2014; Ominayak & Thomas, 2009; Thomas-Muller, 2014). These injustices fuel Indigenous resistance to oil sands development and its accompanying network of roads and pipelines (Laboucan-Massimo, 2014).

The oil sands industry is understood by many Indigenous activists as a colonizing force, "both in the sense that it disproportionately affects Indigenous communities and in the sense that it coercively plunders resources from Indigenous lands" (Awâsis, 2014, p. 254). The sociocultural impacts of the industry on local Indigenous communities are significant, as oil development "intensifies experiences of disconnection from the land and each other" (Awâsis, 2014, p. 254). Resistance to the oil sands, then, often occurs in the form of protesting any further development through decolonizing practices that assert Indigenous rights to self-determination and traditional ways of life (Awâsis, 2014).

Indigenous mobilization has drawn on a variety of tactics for protecting "land, water, and autonomy" (Weis et al., 2014, p. 16), which include the presentation of "critical evidence and arguments to the public hearings and environmental impact assessments surrounding pipeline and shipment plans"; the use of direct action and peaceful blockades in attempts to "physically disrupt production," as well as establishing encampments on culturally significant sites (Weis et al., 2014, p. 18). Banners have also been dropped in protest on oil sands sites and Canadian Parliament buildings in Ottawa (Weis et al., 2014). Some community organizers engage in public education activities through "speaking tours and the creation of a range of Internet resources" such as

Keepers of the Athabasca (www.keepersofthewater.ca/athabasca) and the Indigenous Environmental Network (www.ienearth.org/what-we-do/tar-sands) (Weis et al., 2014, pp. 18–19).

Indigenous-led Healing Walks are also a demonstration of oil sands opposition, coupled with critique of Canada's colonial history and calls for the assertion of Indigenous and treaty rights. The Tar Sands Healing Walk was "born out of the need to heal from the destruction produced by the rapid rate of tar sands extraction in Alberta" and is understood as a "ceremonial walk of prayer" (Cardinal, 2014, p. 130). Through the Healing Walk, participants of Indigenous and settler origins engage in exercises of building community by sharing stories and resources, attending workshops, and experiencing firsthand the impacts of oil sands development on local eco- and social systems (Cardinal, 2014). The Walk also strives to maintain hope: "Healing turns the greatest adversities into the warmest and highest hopes, which our children and grandchildren can carry to light their way. This is the spirit we have brought to the Tar Sands Healing Walk" (Cardinal, 2014, p. 128). For participants in this form of action, building communities of healing is as much a part of the decolonizing process as activist organizing against the oil sands.

Specific concerns with the Alberta oil sands have been linked to broader movements for Indigenous recognition and resurgence through the Idle No More movement (Thomas-Muller, 2014; Wood, 2015). Idle No More was initiated in 2012 by a small group of Indigenous women who connected specific concerns in their communities to a broader critique of the Harper government's omnibus Bill C-45, which weakened a slate of environmental regulations (Coates, 2015; Coburn & Atleo, 2016; Palmater, 2015). Idle No More spread into a series of social movement activities online (particularly through the extremely successful #IdleNoMore Twitter hashtag) and offline, including protests and drum circles (Coates, 2015; Palmater, 2015). The movement simultaneously put forth concerns about Indigenous treaty rights and land claims, environmental justice concerns regarding water quality, social inequalities around housing, health care, education, and missing and murdered Indigenous women. Idle No More became another site to amplify concerns with the Alberta oil sands and link this issue to a broader movement.

Environmental organizations have also mobilized against the Alberta oil sands, though environmental claims have focused on localized ecological harms such as water and air pollution and wildlife impacts (Coats, 2014; Davidson & Gismondi, 2011). However, environmental organizations have also targeted the Alberta oil sands as part of broader campaigns around climate change. The Alberta oil sands and the Canadian government have come under particular scrutiny in international venues of environmental protest, and imagery of the oil sands has been key to framing Canada as a climate villain internationally. For example, in our research on media representations of the climate policy debate, we examined coverage from the *Globe and Mail* and the *National Post* in the lead-up and aftermath of the 2009 Copenhagen Conference of the Parties meetings (Stoddart, Smith, & Tindall, 2016). We found that environmental organizations, such as the David Suzuki Foundation, Pembina Institute, and World Wildlife

Fund, gained access to media coverage and served as critics of Canadian climate policy. Much of the environmental movement critique in media coverage of the Copenhagen Conference linked Canada's poor performance on emission reductions to the economic power and influence of the oil sands industry. The relationship between Stephen Harper's Conservative government and the Alberta oil industry was highlighted and problematized by environmentalists.

Environmental activists have often worked in coalitions or as allies with Indigenous activists opposed to oil sands development (Awâsis, 2014). For example, the Tar Sands Healing Walk has been a site for alliance building between Indigenous and environmental activists. As Cardinal notes (2014, pp. 130–131), "Many organizers who work on environmental protection in other parts of Canada attended the Healing Walk and have hosted workshops, including alliance building between First Nations and the growing non-Indigenous resistance to pipelines across the continent." After repeatedly being denied a voice during decision-making processes around oil and gas development, the Lubicon Cree enlisted international support, informing journalists and environmental groups of their ongoing struggles (Laboucan-Massimo, 2014; Ominayak & Thomas, 2009). Attempts to reach out to a broader network of international supporters appear to have been successful. A 2005 United Nations Human Rights Committee declared that "Canada is violating the Lubicon people's human rights" (Ominayak & Thomas, 2009, p. 121). Similarly, in 2006, the United Nations Committee on Economic, Social, and Cultural Rights concluded that Canada has not adequately consulted with the Lubicon Nation (Laboucan-Massimo, 2014; Ominayak & Thomas, 2009).

There are also key differences between environmental-focused opposition to the oil sands and Indigenous-led campaigns, which tend to position oil development as a continuation of colonization. Coats (2014), for example, describes a tension between a "conservationist approach" that characterizes much environmental movement activism and an "Indigenous Rights approach" to the oil sands. The conservationist perspective "views the tar sands as a polluting industry that needs to be stopped and cleaned up to prevent further destruction of forests, habitats, and freshwater, and to prevent further climate change" (Coats, 2014, p. 270). This perspective generally emphasizes technological solutions, and promotes action by provincial and federal governments and corporations. Environmental groups who adopt this conservationist perspective are often concerned with connecting opposition to the oil sands with critiques of Canadian climate change policy, and frame economic dependence on the oil sands as a key factor in explaining the Alberta and Canadian governments' poor performance on greenhouse gas mitigation (Haluza-DeLay, 2014; Stoddart, Smith, & Tindall, 2016). By contrast, the Indigenous Rights perspective "holds that the colonial system in Canada and abroad fails to protect Indigenous peoples' rights" (Coats, 2014, p. 271). Here, the oil sands are perceived as a particularly pernicious and harmful example of colonial injustices that require more substantial transformations to Canadian politics and society.

Environmentalist and Indigenous campaigns against the oil sands also differ in how much emphasis is given to the distributional and procedural environmental justice impacts of the oil sands for Indigenous communities (Thomas-Muller, 2014; Vasey,

2014). The distributional dimension of environmental justice refers to which groups are more exposed to environmental health risks and environmental degradation. By contrast, the procedural dimension of environmental justice refers to which groups are incorporated into the procedures of governance that decide whether or not the environmental risks of a project are acceptable, and who should be exposed to those risks. In mobilization against the Alberta oil sands, Indigenous activists are more likely to assert claims based on both dimensions of environmental justice, with a broader perspective on the social needs of Indigenous communities. By contrast, environmental claims that invoke environmental justice are more likely to focus on distributional justice issues of the increased environmental health risks for downstream communities near the oil sands.

FRACKING AND OFFSHORE OIL
IN ATLANTIC CANADA

The Alberta oil sands have garnered a great deal of attention and opposition from Indigenous activists and environmental groups, resulting in national and international attention for this specific mobilization against the Canadian carbon complex. Atlantic Canada, which includes the eastern provinces of Newfoundland and Labrador, Nova Scotia, New Brunswick, and Prince Edward Island, offers a valuable contrast to Alberta. Other than a few recent, episodic, and regionally specific moments of mobilization, the oil and gas industries in this region are less commonly targets of social resistance and protest, compared to Alberta. Instead, oil exploration and extraction are often presumed to be economically and socially beneficial, and offer an example of what Freudenburg (2005) terms "the social construction of non-problematicity." We provide an overview of specific instances where the non-problematicity of oil and gas development has been destabilized.

Indigenous groups in New Brunswick were among the first to act in defense against hydraulic fracturing, or fracking, in eastern Canada. Fracking is an unconventional resource extraction technique in which water, chemicals, and sand are shot into impermeable shale rock to harvest oil and natural gas (de Rijke, 2013). Seismic testing in search of natural gas began near Elsipogtog First Nation, one of New Brunswick's largest reserves, in 2011. Industrial activity by Southwestern Energy intensified in May 2013, when Elsipogtog band members, settler allies, and the Mi'kmaq Warrior Society united in defense of clean water by blocking workers from accessing equipment (Howe, 2015). Peaceful anti-shale gas protests were ongoing for many months, culminating in October 2013 when the Royal Canadian Mounted Police, equipped with assault rifles and "less lethal" rounds, stormed onto the scene to enforce a court injunction against a road blockade on Highway 134, resulting in five flaming police cars and 40 arrests (Howe, 2015). New Brunswick's anti-fracking movement can be characterized by a unique dynamic between Indigenous and settler communities. As non-Indigenous communities recognized that their concerns were not being heard by the government, many turned to treaty rights and the province's constitutional duty to consult with Indigenous populations as a way to halt shale gas development (Howe, 2015). In many Canadian cases, Indigenous resistance to oil development is predicated on a (re) assertion of constitutionally protected Indigenous treaty rights (Howe, 2015).

An anti-fracking movement gained momentum as Indigenous-led resistance to the hotly debated form of drilling in New Brunswick earned international attention. In 2012, Toronto-based oil and gas corporations Black Spruce Exploration and Shoal Point Energy proposed onshore to offshore fracking projects in three locations on the west coast of the island portion of Newfoundland and Labrador, Canada's easternmost province. The proposed projects are near—and in the case of Sally's Cove, actually fall within—Gros Morne National Park, one of the province's most important tourist attractions and a UNESCO World Heritage site (Smith, 2016). Against the backdrop of intense critique from local communities, as well as resistance from outside the province, the provincial government declared a moratorium in November 2013, which was renewed with the release of the final report by the Newfoundland and Labrador Hydraulic Fracturing Review Panel in 2015.

A diverse network of individuals and groups coalesced against fracking development along the west coast of Newfoundland. The NL-Fracking Awareness Network, composed of over 20 organizations from various environmental and non-environmental sectors, serves as an umbrella organization and key network for mobilization and awareness-raising. Networks of anti-fracking or "fracking awareness" organizations communicate and organize both online (emails, listservs, online conference calls, social media platforms, and blogs) and offline (hosting public movie screenings, educational events, petitions, and letter-writing campaigns) (Smith, 2016).

However, research by Smith (2016) shows that local residents' perceptions of rural places differ, and correlate with either supportive or oppositional positions on fracking. While proponents conceptualize "place" as a resource extraction landscape, opponents understand "place" as a restorative landscape for leisure/tourism activities. Fracking opponents understand rurality as idyllic and restorative and employ a discourse of protection by calling on the provincial government to enact a buffer zone around Gros Morne National Park. Those against development near Gros Morne share concerns about fracking's potentially negative impacts on tourism, the fishery, and ground and surface water reservoirs. Apprehensions are expressed about fracking diminishing the coastline's unique "sense of the rural" (Smith, 2016). As well, some opponents link local fracking risks to global climate change. There is also worry about how fracking might hinder residents' and tourists' experiences of hunting, fishing, hiking, and star-gazing (Smith, 2016).

Fracking opponents value expert (scientific, technical) and local ecological knowledge forms, but criticize the government-appointed Newfoundland and Labrador Hydraulic Fracturing Review Panel for lacking objectivity, diversity in representation, and for omitting topics they identify as important, such as community consent and climate change considerations (Smith, 2016). The panel's composition received public criticism for being too industry- and engineering-heavy, lacking women and Indigenous panelists, and for lacking representatives from health, environment, tourism, and fisheries sectors (Fusco, 2015; Rollmann, 2015). Opponents emphasized the need for a strong precautionary principle approach with regard to fracking in Newfoundland (Smith, 2016), whereby industry ought to prove "in advance of the risk" that proposed projects are not exceedingly harmful to human or environmental health (Agyeman, 2005, p. 21).

Another oil development controversy in Atlantic Canada emerged around the Old Harry proposal for offshore oil exploration in the Gulf of St. Lawrence (Bourgault et al., 2014). This development, proposed by Corridor Resources, would be located off the west coast of the island of Newfoundland. In Newfoundland and Labrador, offshore oil development is rarely criticized in public discourse because of the economic and social benefits it brings to the province in terms of employment and provincial revenues (Fusco, 2007). In our research on the Newfoundland and Labrador tourism industry, we find that tourism operators often view nature-based tourism and offshore oil as separate forms of development that do not intersect, as tourism uses of the coastal environment do not share the same ecological space with offshore oil (Stoddart & Graham, 2018). The main concern is risk of an oil spill, but this risk is often viewed as relatively minor and appropriately managed by government regulation. If anything, the oil industry is sometimes seen as providing positive spillover effects for nature-based tourism, as the industry draws new people to the region, or contributes resources to local amenities and infrastructure that support tourism. The tourism industry, which relies on images of unspoiled landscapes and wildlife to draw visitors, often demonstrates an acceptance of the oil industry as separate and coexisting modes of development for coastal environments. This makes the controversy over the Old Harry development unusual and a particularly valuable case to examine in more depth.

The Old Harry proposal has drawn together opposition from tourism operators and organizations, environmental groups, and community organizations in Newfoundland and Labrador, as well as across the other four provinces that border the Gulf of St. Lawrence: Nova Scotia, Prince Edward Island, New Brunswick, and Quebec. In our research on the Old Harry case, we identify four related discourses that are used to articulate opposition to the project, and which build and maintain an environmentalism-tourism alignment grounding opposition to this specific oil development (Stoddart & Graham, 2018). These discourses are circulated by environmental organizations (including national groups like the David Suzuki Foundation) and by coalitions of environmentalists, tourism operators, fishers, local communities, and Indigenous groups. Two organizations, the St. Lawrence Coalition / Coalition Saint-Laurent and Save Our Seas and Shores (SOS), serve as contact points for bridging environmental concerns and the concerns of regional Indigenous groups. Furthermore, in 2013 the Innu, Maliseet, and Mi'gmaq Nations of Quebec formed their own National Coalition to speak out against oil extraction in the Gulf, in part because of risks to crab fisheries and their economic importance for Indigenous communities (St. Lawrence

Coalition, 2013). These discourses enable bridges to be built across environmental groups, tourism organizations, and community organizations in ways that problematize the specific Old Harry development, but rarely disturb the normalized acceptance of the Atlantic Canadian offshore oil industry in general or engage in broader critiques of the regional carbon complex.

First, there is a "wilderness and wildlife" discourse that focuses on the potential harms of oil spills and exploratory seismic activity for whales and other marine life in the Gulf of St. Lawrence that serve as an important tourism attraction. This discourse also argues that Old Harry will pose ecological risks to Gros Morne National Park. Besides the ecological risks, local residents also worry that the visual presence of oil-related activity will harm visitors' experience of this protected area and make it less desirable as a destination. This is also a prominent theme in Smith's (2016) study of community interpretations of fracking near Gros Morne.

Second, there is a discourse focused on protecting the existing social-ecological networks of tourism and fisheries communities in the Gulf of St. Lawrence. This discourse creates a distinction between offshore oil development elsewhere in the province, which doesn't pose direct risks to established tourism economies, and potential development in the Gulf of St. Lawrence, where tourism development is already established in the social-ecological space of potential oil development.

Third, there is a discourse that focuses on the ecological impacts of a potential large-scale oil spill. While the wilderness and wildlife discourse relies on imagery of whales and wildlife, unspoiled seascapes, and rugged coastlines, this ecological risk discourse repeatedly invokes the BP Macondo blowout and oil spill in the Gulf of Mexico as an iconic image of oil disaster. This imagery is often coupled with assertions that the Gulf of St. Lawrence is a more rugged and difficult operating environment due to sea ice, high winds, and rough weather, and that it is a more enclosed ecosystem, which would make the dispersion of an oil spill even more difficult.

Finally, there is a discourse that focuses on contesting the political jurisdiction of oil governance in the Gulf of St. Lawrence. The Old Harry project falls within the political jurisdiction of Newfoundland and Labrador, which is the province that will gain the most economically from the development. However, it would create risks for ecosystems and communities in all five provinces that border the Gulf. As such, the development is problematized, particularly in provinces other than Newfoundland and Labrador, for representing an illegitimate distribution of risks and benefits. The issue of intersecting social and ecological scales is also raised to problematize the notion that Old Harry is an object of concern only for the Newfoundland and Labrador governments, rather than the much broader region of the Gulf of St. Lawrence.

The discourses used in mobilizing against the Old Harry project are productive for bridging the tourism industry and environmentalist interests in protecting the Gulf of St. Lawrence. These discourses work in part because they compartmentalize Old Harry, which is positioned as a specific controversial project, from the rest of the Newfoundland oil industry, which is treated as non-problematic. By contrast, there are signs that Indigenous resistance to oil development in the Gulf of St. Lawrence is less characterized by this compartmentalized approach and bears similarities to Indigenous resistance to the Alberta oil sands and fracking in Elsipogtog. For example, the objectives of the Innu, Maliseet, and Mi'gmaq National coalition for the protection of the Gulf of St. Lawrence are to recalibrate relationships between government and decision-makers regarding oil extraction in the Gulf (The Innu, Maliseet, and Mi'gmaq National Coalition for the Protection of the Gulf of St. Lawrence, 2013).

CONCLUSION

In this chapter, we have provided an overview of environmental and Indigenous-led protest over oil extraction in Alberta and Atlantic Canada, offering insight into the different ways in which energy can become controversial. In Atlantic Canada, criticisms of the oil industry tend to be project-specific, making anti-oil mobilization more of a sporadic than an ongoing campaign. In Alberta, opponents to the oil sands make connections to a broader resistance to the oil industry and concerns about global climate change, as well as assertions of Indigenous rights. By contextualizing the oil sands mobilization as a component of climate change activism and a step toward decolonizing Canada, the basis of support for anti-oil activism in Alberta includes international organizations and groups seeking to "green the economy," as well as groups fighting for environmental justice. These types of global linkages are not as prevalent in the examples of Atlantic Canadian oil and gas protest (an exception being the fracking protests at Elsipogtog, which were also linked to Idle No More). These differences do not necessarily mean that oil sands protests have been more successful or meaningful than mobilization in Atlantic Canada. It is possible that the Atlantic Canadian protests, because they are more regional and project-specific, are able to recruit more new activists at the local level and may have more direct influence over local government and industry decision-making. By contrast, in Alberta the level of involvement by organizations and activists from outside the province has led to public debates about foreign money and influence, and the degree to which anti-oil sands activism reflects local interests. Whether a more localized model of resistance or a more internationalized model of resistance is more politically effective remains a key question for further comparative research on Indigenous and environmental movement mobilization against oil development.

Indigenous and environmental movements often use similar strategies to encourage opposition to oil development, as they highlight environmental degradation and potential environmental health impacts on communities near the sites of oil extraction. However, there are also key differences. Environmental groups often put more emphasis on environmental destruction and environmental health impacts of specific projects, without necessarily engaging in critique of the carbon complex as a whole. By contrast, Indigenous-led resistance to oil development appears less likely to adopt this compartmentalized approach that focuses on project-specific environmental harms.

Instead, Indigenous-led resistance more often positions oil extraction within a broader critique of colonial and cultural assimilation projects. Indigenous mobilization to oil development is often based on reasserting cultural values and upholding treaty rights, and protecting land and water from environmentally compromising activities is inherently linked with preserving Indigenous ways of life. This demonstrates a more all-encompassing approach to oil resistance, which goes beyond the "isolate and regulate" approach put forth by many conservationists. As such, our discussion echoes Naomi Klein's (2015) recent assertions that Indigenous groups can play a pivotal role in making the transition toward less carbon-intensive societies as a response to climate change. However, while we agree that Indigenous mobilization offers a productive model of engaging with the social-environmental issues of oil development, we are wary of projecting a romanticized role as heroes and saviors of petro-capitalist societies onto Indigenous groups. Rather, Indigenous movement discourse should encourage environmental organizations to also work toward more holistic engagements with the environmental and social impacts of oil development, both in relation to specific projects and the industry as a whole.

As in many countries, the Canadian political economy is heavily tied to the success of what has been called "fossil capitalism" (Altvater, 2007), "petro-capitalism" (Carter, 2014; Haluza-DeLay, 2014), or the "carbon complex" (Urry, 2013). The cases we have examined are examples of unconventional oil and natural gas, which are often more energy intensive and expensive to extract and are located in more challenging operating environments. Corporations are increasingly turning to unconventional forms of oil development, such as hydraulic fracturing, oil sands, and offshore extraction in deep ocean or northern environments, due to technological advancements as well as the depletion of conventional sources. An increased focus on tough oil and gas around the world means that we are likely to see more episodes of contention over oil development. This is likely to be exacerbated as societies grapple with the need to respond to climate change and decisions about whether to continue the pursuit of unconventional fossil fuels, or to make the transition to more renewable energy systems.

ACKNOWLEDGMENTS

We would like to thank Howard Ramos for his comments on the development of this chapter. This chapter builds on research supported by the Social Sciences and Humanities Research Council of Canada (SSHRC).

REFERENCES

Agyeman, J. (2005). *Sustainable communities and the challenge of environmental justice.* New York: New York University Press.

Altvater, E. (2007). The social and natural environment of fossil capitalism. *Socialist Register,* 43, 37–59.

Awâsis, S. (2014). Pipelines and resistance across Turtle Island. In T. Black, S. D'Arcy, T. Weis, & J. K. Russell (Eds.), *A line in the tar sands: Struggles for environmental justice* (pp. 253–266). Toronto: Between the Lines.

Bourgault, D., Cyr, F., Dumont, D., & Carter, A. (2014). Numerical simulations of the spread of floating passive tracer released at the Old Harry Prospect. *Environmental Research Letters*, 9(5), 1–14.

Cardinal, J. (2014). The Tar Sands Healing Walk. In T. Black, S. D'Arcy, T. Weis, & J. K. Russell (Eds.), *A line in the tar sands: Struggles for environmental justice* (pp. 127–133). Toronto: Between the Lines.

Carter, A. V. (2014). Petro-capitalism and the tar sands. In T. Black, S. D'Arcy, T. Weis, & J. K. Russell (Eds.), *A line in the tar sands: Struggles for environmental justice* (pp. 23–35). Toronto: Between the Lines.

Coates, K. (2015). *#IdleNoMore and the remaking of Canada*. Regina, SK: University of Regina Press.

Coats, E. (2014). A proposal for a coherent, powerful, indigenous-led movement." In T. Black, S. D'Arcy, T. Weis, & J. K. Russell (Eds.), *A line in the tar sands: Struggles for environmental justice* (pp. 267–278). Toronto: Between the Lines.

Coburn, E., and Atleo, C. K. (2016). Not just another social movement: Indigenous resistance and resurgence. In W. K. Carroll & K. Sarker (Eds.), *A world to win: Contemporary social movements and counter-hegemony* (pp. 116–194). Winnipeg, MB: ARP Books.

Davidson, D. J., & Gismondi, M. (2011). *Challenging legitimacy at the precipice of energy calamity*. New York: Springer.

de Rijke, K. (2013). Hydraulically fractured: Unconventional gas and anthropology. *Anthropology Today*, 29(2), 13–17.

Dodd, S. (2012). *The Ocean Ranger: Remaking the promise of oil*. Halifax, NS: Fernwood.

Freudenburg, W. R. (2005). Privileged access, privileged accounts: Toward a socially structured theory of resources and discourses. *Social Forces*, 84(1), 89–114.

Freudenburg, W. R., & Gramling, R. (2011). *Blowout in the Gulf*. Cambridge, MA: MIT Press.

Fusco, L. (2007). *The invisible movement: The response of the Newfoundland environmental movement to the offshore oil industry*. Master's thesis, Memorial University of Newfoundland.

Fusco, L. (2015). Newfoundland fracking panel lacks diversity and key areas of expertise. *Rabble.ca*. Retrieved from http://rabble.ca/news/2015/03/newfoundland-fracking-panel-lacks-diversity-and-key-areas-expertise

Haluza-DeLay, R. (2014). Assembling consent in Alberta: Hegemony and the tar sands. In T. Black, S. D'Arcy, T. Weis, & J. K. Russell (Eds.), *A line in the tar sands: Struggles for environmental justice* (pp. 36–44). Toronto: Between the Lines.

Hoffbauer, A., & Ramos, H. (2014). Social and political convergence on environmental events: The roles of simplicity and visuality in the BP oil spill. *Canadian Review of Sociology*, 51(3), 216–238.

Howe, M. (2015). *Debriefing Elsipogtog: The anatomy of a struggle*. Black Point, NS: Fernwood.

The Innu, Maliseet, and Mi'gmaq National Coalition for the Protection of the Gulf of St. Lawrence. (2013). Memorandum of understanding. Retrieved from http://saveourseasandshores.ca/wp-content/uploads/2013/11/The-Innu-Maliseet-and-Mi%E2%80%99gmaq-National-coalition-for-the-protection-of-the-Gulf-of-St.-Lawrence.pdf

Klein, N. (2015). *This changes everything: Capitalism vs. the climate*. New York: Simon & Schuster.

Laboucan-Massimo, M. (2014). Awaiting justice: The ceaseless struggle of the Lubicon Cree. In T. Black, S. D'Arcy, T. Weis, & J. K. Russell (Eds.), *A line in the tar sands: Struggles for environmental justice* (pp. 113–117). Toronto: Between the Lines.

MacNeil, R. (2014). Canadian environmental policy under Conservative majority rule. *Environmental Politics, 23*(1), 174–178.

McAdam, D., & Boudet, H. S. (2012). *Putting social movements in their place: Explaining opposition to energy projects in the United States, 2000–2005.* Cambridge: Cambridge University Press.

Murphy, R., & Murphy, M. (2012). The tragedy of the atmospheric commons: Discounting future costs and risks in pursuit of immediate fossil-fuel benefits. *Canadian Review of Sociology, 49*(3), 247–270.

Newfoundland and Labrador Hydraulic Fracturing Review Panel. (2015). Retrieved from http://nlhfrp.ca

Ominayak, B., & Thomas, K. (2009). These are Lubicon lands: A First Nation forced to step into the regulatory gap. In J. Agyeman, P. Cole, R. Haluza-DeLay, and P. O'Riley (Eds.), *Speaking for ourselves: Environmental justice in Canada* (pp. 111–122). Vancouver, BC: UBC Press.

Palmater, P. (2015). *Indigenous nationhood: Empowering grassroots citizens.* Halifax, NS: Fernwood.

Ritchie, L. A. (2012). Individual stress, collective trauma, and social capital in the wake of the Exxon Valdez oil spill. *Sociological Inquiry, 82*(2), 187–211.

Rollmann, H. (2015). Fracking review panel: Independent of what, exactly? *The Independent.ca.* Retrieved from http://theindependent.ca/2014/11/19/fracking-review-panel-independent-of-what-exactly/

Smith, J. R. (2016). *When petro-capitalism comes knocking: Community interpretations and responses to the Gros Morne Fracking Controversy.* Master's thesis, Memorial University of Newfoundland.

St. Lawrence Coalition. (2013). Oil and gas exploration in the Gulf: Innu, Maliseet, and Mi'gmaq National Coalition for the protection of the Gulf of St. Lawrence. *Coalitionsaintlaurent.ca.* Retreived from http://www.coalitionsaintlaurent.ca/wp-content/uploads/2014/04/2013-10-29-Appui-Coalition-autochtone-EN.pdf

Stoddart, M. C., & Graham, P. (2018). Offshore oil, environmental movements, and the oil-tourism interface: The old Harry conflict on Canada's East Coast. *Sociological Inquiry.* doi:10.1111/soin.12192

Stoddart, M. C. J., Smith, J., & Tindall, D. B. (2016). Blame Canada: Environmental movements, national media and Canada's reputation as a climate villain. In W. K. Carroll & K. Sarker (Eds.), *A world to win: Contemporary social movements and counter-hegemony* (pp. 250–266). Winnipeg, MB: ARP Books.

Thomas-Muller, C. (2014). The rise of the native rights-based strategic framework: Our last best hope to save our water, air, and earth. In T. Black, S. D'Arcy, T. Weis, & J. K. Russell (Eds.), *A line in the tar sands: Struggles for environmental justice* (pp. 240–252). Toronto: Between the Lines.

Urry, J. (2013). *Societies beyond oil: Oil dregs and social futures.* London: Zed Books.

Vasey, D. (2014). The environmental NGO industry and frontline communities. In T. Black, S. D'Arcy, T. Weis, & J. K. Russell (Eds.), *A line in the tar sands: Struggles for environmental justice* (pp. 64–75). Toronto: Between the Lines.

Weis, T., Black, T., D'arcy, S., & Russell, J. K. (2014). Introduction: Drawing a line in the tar sands. In T. Black, S. D'Arcy, T. Weis, and J. Kahn Russell (Eds.), *A line in the tar sands: Struggles for environmental justice* (pp. 1–20). Toronto: Between the Lines.

Widener, P., & Gunter, V. J. (2007). Oil spill recovery in the media: Missing an Alaska native perspective. *Society and Natural Resources, 20*(9), 767–783.

Wood, L. J. (2015). Idle No More, Facebook and diffusion. *Social Movement Studies, 14*(5), 615–621.

CHAPTER 24

THE LOCAL AT THE FOREFRONT OF ENERGY TRANSITION

The Example of the Development of Renewable Electricity in Germany and Sweden

CYRIA EMELIANOFF

INTRODUCTION

GERMANY and Sweden are among the most advanced countries in the field of renewable energy owing to certain common factors: influential environmental movements whose ideas have passed on to the public and the Parliament; a latitude for action granted to local governments, which have local energy companies and are pioneers for the phasing out of fossil and fissile fuels (Collier & Löfstedt, 1997; Bulkeley & Kern, 2006; Emelianoff, 2014); Social Democratic governments in power in the late 1990s, when implementation of the Kyoto Protocol began; and the most ambitious targets for reducing carbon dioxide (CO_2) emissions in the European Union (EU).

Both countries, however, differ in all respects regarding the nature of their energy resources and their settlement patterns, fairly clearly for the structure of their energy operators and their position on the nuclear issue. Although Germany and Sweden produce an increasing share of their electricity from renewable sources, 30% and 57% respectively, their transition paths differ profoundly. For 20 years, the share of renewable electricity has risen slowly in Sweden (49% of the electricity mix in 1997), while its growth has been meteoric in Germany (4.5% in 1997). The dynamics of transformation of the electricity sector are therefore not comparable. However, if we expand the view to include the heat sector, we see that the two countries are facing a regime shift in their energy system. In Sweden, this shift mainly concerns the heating sector and, in a nascent manner, that of mobility, and tends to exacerbate electrification.

The legacy of coal and lignite mining has made electricity a high CO_2-emitting sector in Germany (more than a third of national emissions, for 42% of the electricity produced), while this sector is largely carbon-free in Sweden, due to the early development of hydro and nuclear power. In addition to the geohistorical determinant, the organization of the electrical sectors is contrasted, for reasons not unrelated to the political structure of these countries. In 2014, 79% of electricity is produced in Sweden by three energy companies, and two-thirds in Germany by the "big four" energy providers. For renewable electricity, the difference is even more pronounced: half of German production between 2000 and 2010 was by private actors, not energy companies (40% by citizens, 11% by farmers, etc.). Besides the 450 power companies, the existence of 586 energy cooperatives and over 800 Stadtwerke means that the four major energy groups produced only 7% of renewable electricity in 2011 (Rudinger, 2012). The re-municipalization of the energy sector is well established in Germany, while Swedish municipalities and cooperatives have lost ground. They produced 20% of Sweden's electricity in 1990, versus less than 14% in 2006, three large companies having structured an oligopoly since the liberalization of the energy market in 1996 (Chen & Johnson, 2008). The new sectors of renewable power, such as wind power, developed mainly by local or regional companies, municipalities, and citizens (Wizelius, 2013), are being taken over by the major energy operators.

A comparative analysis allows the identification of the political differences that shape these two trajectories of energy transition. To understand them, we should leave the stage of state actors and the national electricity sector regulations. It is not at this level that the oppositions are very marked, with governments primarily trying to protect large energy operators, on which their industries rely, as well as the attendant jobs and their electoral bases (the Social Democrats in Germany being a party of miners and workers). We propose, in order to enter into the mysteries of this transition, a territorial and multi-scale history of the transition to renewable energy, electricity being coupled to heat by co-generation. This history will bring to light the political differences between local authorities and between states, but also between local and national or federal policies, which are, to a varying degree, integrated.

This analysis of multilevel climate governance examines the interplay and coordination of climate action at all scales and across scales, in a non-hierarchical way. The empirical work employed in this chapter has been undertaken in the framework of research projects on the European Campaign of Sustainable Cities and Towns, and on urban energy transitions in Europe. Non-directional interviews were conducted in Hanover, Freiburg im Breisgau, Växjö, Malmö, and Stockholm with civil servants heading municipal climate policies and sustainable urban planning, with politicians, and with leaders of environmentalist associations.

The chapter reviews the history of the development of renewable electricity in the two study countries, affected by three geopolitical processes, giving birth to three rationales: the oil shocks, the anti-nuclear movement with its Cold War backdrop, and climate-change negotiations. It shows how certain Swedish and German territories have challenged the dominant energy system by deploying local energy production. The discussion presents some key points of the comparative analysis, identifying the political differences between these transition paths, via a multi-scale analysis.

REVISITING THE POLITICAL HISTORY OF RENEWABLE ENERGY: THE WEIGHT OF LOCAL CHALLENGERS

The growth of renewable electricity in Germany and Sweden is a well-documented history (Chen & Johnson, 2008; Evrard, 2013; Lauber & Mez, 2004; Sahr, 1985), including on the comparative level (Roggenkamp, 2010). However, this story is often told as involving national actors, laws, and financial incentives (feed-in tariffs [FIT] or renewable energy certificates), as well as "exogenous" catalysts such as the oil shocks, nuclear disasters, and climate change, or European policies. The catalysts are more rarely analyzed in a bottom-up or trans-scalar manner, evaluating local consequences triggered by global changes. The role of the local level in the energy transition has long been minimized (Bulkeley et al., 2011) or is seen as being downstream, as if the only issue was how local government or citizen groups deploy new energy potentials via the tools put in place to upper levels.

This vision ignores the specific, complex, and contentious history of this, or rather these, transitions, where conflicts are waged not only in Parliament or in talks with the major energy operators. National accounts of energy transition serve the interpretation that, since the postwar period, only states have legitimate control of energy resources and the right to the political and economic dividends. Other histories are woven, however, behind energy transitions: those of local governments, citizen groups who dispute the prerogative of states and major energy groups, challenging traditional energy players. Today, we can consider that there are as many energy transitions in Germany as there are Länder, i.e. states of the German federal republic (Evrard, 2013), but this vision could ramify locally.

We begin by recalling that the deployment of renewable energy has been driven by local initiatives, often involving scientists, in the United States and Germany since the 1970s (Morris, 1982; Scheer, 2007; Vasi, 2011), and in Sweden in the 1990s, for the development of wind power and biomass by municipal energy companies (Collier & Lofstedt, 1997; Wizelius, 2013). The vision of phasing out fossil fuels emerged in Swedish cities, which carried this ambition to the state level (Emelianoff, 2014). The idea of a "fossil fuel–free municipality" was born in the early 1980s in Övertornea, a small town in recession in the far north, where a project of local and ecological development was developed with the help of two scientists (James & Lahti, 2004). Taken up by the Naturskyddsföreningen (Swedish Society for Nature Conservation), this idea found fertile ground in Växjö, in the second half of the 1990s, then in Stockholm, and was discussed in a national city net-work in the 2000s, before becoming a state policy. In Germany, the idea and the term *Energiewende* were introduced by the Öko-Institut, established in 1977 and funded by the anti-nuclear movement, in a report published in 1980, subtitled "Growth and Prosperity without Oil and Uranium." Some anti-nuclear activists occupy positions of responsibility in municipal administrations and elected bodies due to the growing power of the Green vote. After the Chernobyl disaster, these actors piloted local policies for nuclear power phase-out and for renewable energy production, based on municipal energy companies, the Stadtwerke, the strategies of which they managed to redirect.

These pioneer territories can be considered the missing link between the prototypes from research and market entry of renewable energy. Faced with resistance from na-tional energy operators to develop renewable power after the oil shocks (Evrard, 2013; Scheer, 2007), local communities have been on the forefront of change (Bulkeley & Betsill, 2003; Hinderer & Fuchs, 2016; Morris, 1982). To reread the history of energy transition through the optic of local struggles, victories, and failures, the networking of actors of renewable energy and pioneering communities (i.e., to territorialize the his-tory of energy transitions) is important in order to understand not only the conflicts, complexity, and diversity, but also the political dissonances, which foster a plurality of scenarios for the future (Emelianoff, 2010). Local or regional levels can be the origin of "path creation" by partially freeing themselves from path dependencies (Lafferty & Ruud, 2008; Rohracher & Späth, 2014; Späth & Rohracher, 2012). The geographical contexts are not understood here as imposing downstream adaptations to the dominant models, but rather as opening up new political options whose confluence, divergent paths, and conflicts form the skein of what is commonly called "energy transition," a process that is far from unified.

It would be too simple to oppose schematically local and national or federal policies. Regime shift in electrical systems occurs in a multi-scalar and trans-scalar way, articulating local, national, and transnational networks, parliamentary battles, gov-ernmental allies, and European and national incentive schemes, in a game of alliances that disqualifies "bottom-up" and "top-down" approaches (Bulkeley, 2005). Rather than opposing levels of government, it is inter-scalar coalitions of actors that should be analyzed in their confrontations, notably the coalitions around fossil fuels, nuclear energy, and centralized and decentralized renewables. We will provide an overview of these struggles over the rationales that served as their central themes.

RENEWABLE ELECTRICITY: A GEOPOLITICAL PLAYTHING

Renewable electricity is taking off in a context marked by the oil shocks, the end of the cold war and the entry into an era of global change. In this new geopolitical landscape, renewable electricity has been successively an alternative to nuclear power and an alternative to fossil fuels.

An Alternative to Nuclear

In both contexts under study, rejection of nuclear energy is the predominant reason for the deployment of renewable energy from 1970 (Sahr, 1985; Scheer, 2007). Germany is now the largest producer of solar energy; it was also the principal hotbed of the anti-nuclear movement, grounded in movements against arms and the nuclear bomb in the postwar period (Keller, 1993). The context of the Cold War and nuclear deterrence could only feed hostility and terror concerning the power of the atom, in a country split in two by a wall. Solar thermal energy was one of the first alternatives developed by anti-nuclear activists; scientists, environmentalists, and craftsmen were soon to become solar professionals. Even so, after the oil shocks, the federal government favored coal and nuclear power, which gave rise to violent conflicts in the second half of the 1970s, shaking a number of cities (Kitschelt, 2009). Nevertheless, nuclear power continued its expansion, coal being uncompetitive despite subsidies, providing 40% of electricity production in the 1980s (against 14% today) (Roggenkamp, 2010).

The Chernobyl disaster triggered a threshold effect that interrupted this tendency, first locally and then gradually at the federal level. Some local authorities decided to get rid of nuclear power by developing energy-saving, photovoltaic electricity, micro-combined heat and power (CHP) plants, and wind power. Federal support for renewable energy was reduced at that time to a few research programs, until climate concerns forced a change starting from 1990, with the introduction of the first FITs (Lauber & Mez, 2004). Renewable energy nevertheless continued to develop on the margins of the dominant system until the late 1990s (Evrard, 2013).

In Sweden, the environmental movement is focused on conservation and the right to nature, so important to Swedish culture. It has been opposed to centralized renewables more than nuclear, especially in 1966–1967, when large dam projects resulted in strong mobilization. In the absence of fossil resources apart from uranium, the government, which had been a pioneer for hydropower and energy savings, reoriented its policy and implemented the second-largest nuclear program in the world after France (Sahr, 1985). As in Germany, this trend was reinforced by the oil shocks, but was not without controversy in Parliament, as early as 1973, on the issue of nuclear waste. The municipal energy companies obtained an increase of district heating via CHP plants, limiting the use of nuclear energy (Sahr, 1985). Major research and development programs were devoted to wind energy and biomass, but energy companies lost interest (Chen & Johnson, 2008). In 1976 the growing anti-nuclear sentiments led to the fall of the Social Democrats, in power since 1930 (Sahr, 1985).

From 1977 all municipalities were requested to elaborate energy plans. However, local energy utilities often prioritized energy production and exportation rather than energy savings (Palm, 2006). The Three Mile Island accident (in the United States,

1979) led to a referendum vote in favor of phasing out nuclear energy. Energy savings were reinforced: the country has adopted the most restrictive thermal regulations of all Organisation of Economic Co-operation and Development (OECD) countries (Löfstedt, 1997). But government policy with regard to nuclear power was at least hesitant, especially with the emergence of climate change issues. Nuclear power was again challenged with the coming to power of a coalition between Social Democrats and Greens in 2014. Previously, nuclear energy supplied 41% of the electricity production in a country that has reduced its CO_2 emissions by 61% between 1973 and 2013 (and by a quarter since 1990, like Germany).

An Alternative to Fossil Fuels

In the late 1980s, concerns related to oil shocks and nuclear power in the context of the Cold War gave way to those of climate change, particularly in Germany, the largest European emitter of CO_2. Already in 1987, the issue was seriously discussed in the Bundestag and led to two federal programs that were a great success in a receptive context: the "100 megawatts (MW)" of wind power and "1,000 solar roofs" programs. Besides equipment subsidies, FITs were introduced in 1990 (obligatory buy-back at 65%–90% of the consumer selling price). The major energy operators were oriented toward East German markets and underestimated the importance of the law (Lauber & Mez, 2004).

In 1995, 1,100 MW of wind power had already been installed, allowing the sector to become an economic pressure group (Roggenkamp, 2010). Since 1989, towns and consumers have obtained the right to pay a higher rate for renewable electricity and thereby subsidize the emerging sectors. This was the principal mechanism that ensured the growth of solar, involving dozens of cities and Stadtwerke (Lauber & Metz, 2004). However, the Länder set the price of electricity, and some refused to pass on the surcharge to the consumer, which was borne by the energy companies, leading to legal disputes. The major companies alerted in vain the European Commission, and sought to rescind the FITs, also in vain due to mass protests in 1997, which led to the withdrawal of the project. The FITs were nevertheless capped the following year (Lauber & Metz, 2004).

In Sweden, the fiscal incentives in favor of renewable energy were less controversial, for the simple reason that they did not penalize a national production sector, but rather fossil fuel imports. The introduction of a carbon tax in 1991, today the highest in the world, was a strong incentive, as its price climbed, for energy utilities to convert district heating to biomass. But the use of bioenergy for electricity production was very modest before 2003, due to the low cost of electricity (Jacobsson, 2008).

The national targets for wind-power generation, established following the closure of a nuclear plant near Copenhagen in 1997, did not solicit much response from the local authorities, who at that time decided against wind farm developments, curbing installations in the name of preserving landscapes (Roggenkamp, 2010). They were not stakeholders in the means of production and were therefore not interested. Local authorities asserted themselves in the 1990s as a centerpiece in the transition to renewable energy.

CENTRALIZED OR DECENTRALIZED RENEWABLE ELECTRICITY? GERMAN AND SWEDISH CITIES AT WORK

The emergence of local energy policies is due to the appropriation by some local authorities of the geopolitical issues mentioned earlier, because environment or climate activists were members of their teams. Some focused on energy-saving measures in the wake of the oil shocks, others on emancipation from nuclear power after Chernobyl, the latest target the phasing out of fossil fuels in the context of climate negotiations. The four transnational networks of cities dedicated to issues of sustainability, energy, and climate (ICLEI, Climate Alliance, Energy Cities, and more broadly the European Sustainable Cities and Towns Campaign) provided key assistance to the cities, furnishing tools, methods, recognition, appreciation, and emulation within Europe. Some local authorities became proponents of the interface between housing, urban planning, and energy, operationalizing a turn toward sustainable urbanism (Emelianoff, 2007), as well as for the production of renewable electricity.

"The Solar Offensive" in Freiburg im Breisgau

Freiburg im Breisgau (220,000 habitants) in Baden-Württemberg was one of the main European centers of anti-nuclear protest, which was crucial to its political and economic future. This university town was a cradle of the German Greens, who took the municipality from the Social Democrats in 2002. A constellation of local actors supporting solar energy snowballed, creating a niche economy that structured the solar sector in Germany. The 1970s saw a network of solar thermal artisans develop. After Chernobyl, the first municipal environment department in Germany was created and instituted a local energy production plan. The head of this department incited ICLEI to establish its European headquarters in Freiburg and assumed the post of secretary general of ICLEI (Emelianoff & Stégassy, 2010). The early 1990s were marked by experimental buildings that attracted solar power militants: a heliotrope house, an energy-positive housing estate, and solar air conditioning for the hospital, among others. "The solar offensive" of the municipality relied on a partnership with independent research centers and universities. In 1993, the regional association for renewable energies already federated a host of activists and experts (Rohracher & Späth, 2014). Their projects attracted other solar professionals, such as the International Solar Energy Society (ISES), which transferred from Melbourne to Freiburg in 1995, the photovoltaic panels manufacturer Solar Fabrik, a vocational training center in solar energy, and an information center. Research institutions working with the municipality came to the forefront internationalally, such as the Öko-Institute and the Fraunhofer Institute for Solar Energy Systems (IES). Citizens were not absent from this innovative environment. In 1995, the first citizen-owned photovoltaic plant was installed on the stadium, and the municipality has made available other roofs for citizen investment.

The local authority has been working on the restructuring of local energy companies in order to "recommunalize" energy production. The slogan "Freiburg Solar City" hides a paradox, but responds to a political and economic challenge: deploy the solar sector and its potential beyond the municipal boundaries. Within these boundaries, gas and wood CHP is central to the strategy for phasing out nuclear power: CHP produced 52% of the electricity consumed in the city in 2006 against 3% in 1992, via some central and 90 micro power plants. The share of nuclear power has declined at the same time from 60% to 30%. The objectives of the Climate Plan adopted in 1996 have been partly achieved: the reduction of CO_2 emissions is estimated to be 20% per capita by the end of 2000, each inhabitant emitting 8.53 tons of CO_2 per year. Photovoltaic provides less than 1% of the electricity consumed in the city in 2007. But in choosing to install photovoltaic panels on the most exposed sites (schools, churches, the trade show center, brewery, expressway, etc.), Freiburg raised the visibility of photovoltaic power.

Hanover: A Network Leader

The protagonists of the energy and climate policy in Hanover, capital of Lower Saxony (521,000 inhabitants), are also from the anti-nuclear movement. In the late 1970s, the director of the department of environmental and economic affairs of the city had opened a training center for renewable energy in an alternative community (Emelianoff & Stégassy, 2010). His colleague in charge of the Agenda 21 also worked for various alternative community projects. Both led an ambitious policy within the coalition "red-green," in power since 1989, representing a remarkable continuity.

As in Freiburg, the energy policy was initiated in order to phase out nuclear energy, in 1987. Hanover participated in the founding congress of ICLEI in New York and in the pilot program "Urban CO_2 Reduction Plans," launched in 1991 with 12 other cities around the world. This program was a preparatory step for the Cities for Climate Protection campaign, which brought about a change of scale in the mobilization of local authorities and a rescaling of climate public policies. At this time, the city could not find support from federal or state governments for its climate policy. So the environmental department developed a strong connection with transnational municipal networks, in order to gain recognition and power to act at the local level. The city played a particular role in the European dynamic of sustainable development, being a founding member of ICLEI, of the Climate Alliance, and one of the three coordinating cities of the European campaign of sustainable cities and towns (Emelianoff, 2014).

The urban CO_2 reduction plan adopted in 1995 prioritized energy efficiency in housing, public buildings, and industry, in partnership with the municipal energy company, which was at first reluctant (as in Freiburg) but was obliged to follow the municipal strategy. The German Stadtwerke were indeed organized to generate profits to fund local public policies (Lauber & Mez, 2004). Then the Hanover Stadtwerke worked on local energy production and decentralized co-generation, reducing energy loss: in 2007, 149 CHPs and micro-CHPs were installed, 240 wind generators in the surrounding region, small hydro-electric stations, and solar energy and biomass installations; co-generation produced 29% of the electricity consumed in Hanover, compared to 12% in Germany as a whole. In 2014, half of the electricity sold by the Stadtwerke came from renewable sources (35% supported by FITs), 7% from nuclear, and 35% from coal. The sharp reduction in the share of nuclear and higher electricity consumption, and the difficulty in reducing car traffic in the city of Volkswagen, explain why CO_2 emissions have fallen by only 7.3% per capita between 1990 and 2010 (11.4 t CO_2 per year per inhabitant).

Växjö, a "Fossil Fuel–Free City in 2050"?

The search for greater energy independence after the oil shocks is behind the policy of Växjö (85,000 inhabitants). The municipal energy company (VEAB) was the first in Sweden, starting in the early 1980s, to use biomass for some of its district heating, it being a cheaper energy source than oil, locally abundant, and capable of generating local jobs. The prospect of nuclear power plants being shut down in southern Sweden reinforced this orientation (Jacobsson, 2008). This was fertile ground for the proposal from the Swedish Society for Nature Conservation, which led the city's Agenda 21, to program a phase-out of fossil fuels. The Social Democrats, the Greens, and the Conservatives were unanimously in favor of the program because the leader of the Conservative Party in Växjö was a convinced environmentalist, an non-conformist figure who became mayor in 2006. The city enjoyed the support of the LIP (Lokala investeringsprogrammen) and KLIMP (klimatinvesteringsprogram) national programs to co-finance its actions in favor of sustainability and action on climate change. Synergies between industry and the university gave birth, with the help of national and European funds, to the Centre for Bioenergy. Researchers are working on development of second-generation biofuels, which would assure a second step toward a transition to biomass (Emelianoff, 2014).

The "fossil fuel–free city" strategy adopted in 1996 had the goal of reducing CO_2 emissions by half by 2010. Electricity was already carbon-free, so the main means of action was the conversion to biomass of the district heating network. The Sandvik II CHP plant (110 MW) came online in 1997, 70% financed by the European program Thermie and by a national program, and fueled by wood detritus collected within a radius of 100 kilometers; 20% of this energy is converted into electricity. The transition to biomass heating has led to a decrease by more than 40% of CO_2 emissions. The municipality estimated that emissions per inhabitant were 2.7 tonnes in 2012, with the decarbonation of transport constituting the next challenge.

On the initiative of the Swedish Society for Nature Conservation, a national network of cities was created in 1998 in order to exchange solutions to reduce fossil-fuel dependence, and to enable local politicians to lobby ministers to support policies. In 2006, after the Kyoto Protocol took effect, Swedish Prime Minister Göran Persson created the Swedish Commission on Oil Independence and embraced a cause that had become national: putting an end to the use of fossil fuels.

In Germany, Michael Huber wonders if local authorities may be the real political leaders on climate policy (Huber, 1997). In Sweden, according to Tore Wizelius, local officials assumed more responsibility in the area of transition to renewables than the government, with the state-owned Vattenfall being reluctant to develop renewable energy and emitting more CO_2 in Germany than that emitted by the entire country of Sweden. This explains the civic battles, especially in Berlin, to try to buy the electric grid and the means of energy production from Vattenfall (Blanchet, 2015).

THE EUROPEANIZATION
OF ENERGY POLICIES

Last but not least, the multi-scalar history of energy transition owes much to the battles waged within European institutions. Both the signing of the Kyoto Protocol in 1997 and its entry into force in 2005 significantly impacted local and national energy policies. Moreover, the liberalization of the electricity market, in 1996 in Sweden and 1998 in Germany, gave various producers access to the power grid, while concentrating the means of production, with states seeking to strengthen competitiveness of the major energy operators.

Following the adoption of the Kyoto Protocol, the Social Democrats who came to power in 1998 in Sweden and Germany tried to make renewable energies both inevitable and profitable. We know the parliamentary work in 2000 of the German Social Democrat Herman Scheer, and the efforts of the Greens and the Öko-Institut, in favor of the adoption of the EEG (Erneuerbare-Energien-Gesetz) law to strengthen FITs, against the advice of the minister of economy. It was preceded by fiscal reform, which taxed mineral oils and reduced labor taxes, while financing, on the side, a program of "100,000 solar roofs" (Lauber & Mez, 2004). In 2002, the electoral weight of the Greens carried the decision to phase out nuclear power. FITs were revised upward in 2004, greatly accelerating the transition to renewable energy. In 2015, for the 30% of renewable electricity generation, 5.9% is supplied by solar, 13.3% by wind, and 6.8% from biomass.

In Sweden, under the leadership of Prime Minister Göran Persson and in order to deal with a period of economic recession, the Social Democrats funded a two € billion program of green modernization of the economy, partially relying on local communities. One-third of the budget was allocated to renewable energy and energy efficiency, notably through the LIP and KLIMP programs for local authorities (Eckerberg, 2001), until the center-right government came to power in 2006. However, it was not until the EU directive on renewable energy in 2001, during the Swedish presidency of the EU (fiercely negotiated over five years), which set a target of 22% renewable electricity in EU consumption by 2010, that a decisive instrument was implemented at the national level in 2003. Prior to that, the use of renewables grew only slightly in Sweden (Chen & Johnson, 2008). With tradable green certificates, electricity users have the obligation to acquire green certificates in proportion to their consumption, which helps local energy companies in their transition to biomass (Lundgvist & Biel, 2007). The CHPs are central to the operationalization of the energy transition in the 2000s. According to the size of municipalities, they use wood waste, unconventional waste (agribusiness, cosmetics, etc.), and cereal crops. In 2015 they provided 60% of heating and 10% of the consumed electricity, with 7% coming from biomass.

The renewable energy certificates have supported the most profitable energy sources and have not promoted innovation (Chen & Johnson, 2008). The higher cost of wind generation explains the disinterest of major operators, leading to nearly 60% of wind power in the country, representing 5% of the electricity mix in 2012, being produced by municipal energy companies, various territorial operators, and citizens (Wizelius, 2013). The recent taking in hand of the wind-energy sector by large energy operators has resulted in large or giant wind farms in the north, where opposition to wind power is less. The wind power share in the energy mix has increased to 10% in 2015 and should undergo rapid changes. Sweden hosts the largest wind projects in the EU. The entry into government of the Greens for the first time in their history, in 2014, in coalition with the Social Democrats, resulted in an engagement to phase out nuclear power; taxes on nuclear power were increased, and investment was redirected toward renewable energy. In 2015, nuclear power had fallen to 34% of the electricity mix.

The entry into force of the Kyoto Protocol in 2005 reinforced the objectives of the EU, which has stipulated that by 2020 renewables should represent 20% of final energy consumption in each country. These objectives were translated into German law by the Law on Energiewende in 2010, which fixed very ambitious levels of renewable energy consumption (60% in 2050) and a halving of primary energy consumption. The coalition between Conservatives and Liberals in power since 2005 continues to make life difficult for small projects, focusing on centralized renewable energy and the extension of the lifespan of nuclear power plants (Hinderer & Fuchs, 2016). However, the global financial crisis curbed foreign investors, and the movement toward energy remunicipalisation continued. Between 2007 and 2012, 170 electricity and gas concessions were transferred to local authorities; 60 Stadtwerke and 600 energy cooperatives have been created. More generally, local authorities have discovered the economic potential (for jobs and tax revenue) of local energy management (Hinderer & Fuchs, 2016).

This evolution and the unexpectedly rapid development of renewable electricity led to, in 2014, the denial of access to the network for very small power producers, especially solar energy and biomass, and to opposition to the rebirth of auto production (Hinderer & Fuchs, 2016). This time the European Commission took the side of the major energy operators. The latter had not invested in the transmission grids, nor had the 884 heterogeneous operators invested in the distribution grids. Faced with this opposition, challengers to the electricity system have developed other strategic work fields, such as energy independence in rural areas or the citizen takeover of operating concessions for energy grids (Blanchet, 2015; Hinderer & Fuchs, 2016; Moss et al., 2014).

DISCUSSION

Confronting two models of electricity transition such as Sweden and Germany supposes the review of some geo-historical and cultural fundamentals. These two countries are at the extremes of the spectrum as regards their population distribution, the nature of their energy resources, and their relationship to these resources. The attachment to coal in Germany, a symbol of industrial success, is an element of fossil-fuel path dependence that cannot be underestimated. The abundance of renewable energy in Sweden does not mean that it can all be exploited, as shown by the environmental conflicts over hydro, wind, and biomass use in the name of attachment to nature. These cultural and identity factors weigh in the modalities and rhythms of the energy transition.

Second, the relationship to nuclear power, which is the determinant of the development of renewable electricity in the two case studies (Chen & Johnson, 2008; Roggenkamp, 2010), is not charged with the same meanings. The postwar peace movement permeates the environmental movement in Germany, while the latter is essentially the heir to the nature conservation movement in Sweden. The first challenge to nuclear power in the Swedish Parliament (in 1973) was due to the concerns about nuclear waste management (Sahr, 1985), not to its potential for war or catastrophe. Located on the dividing line between the East and West, Germans were much more vigilant about the major nuclear risks. The Chernobyl and Fukushima disasters have profoundly marked public opinion, leading to local and national decisions to phase out nuclear power. The Chernobyl disaster was responsible for the creation of the Federal Ministry of Environment in 1987 (Huber, 1997) and the first municipal environment service in Germany, in Freiburg im Breisgau.

The nuclear path dependence in Sweden is reinforced by the political centralism of a country where local authorities have a lot of resources and latitude of action, but whose political orientations are determined by the state, with a strong vertical integration of power. Skepticism about the cost of decentralized plants (Chen & Johnson, 2008) is fed by the oligopolistic structure of the energy sector, an abundant resource (green gold), and high energy needs for the paper industry. On the contrary, German political structures and culture instead gave strong legitimacy to decentralized energy management, including scientific production in transition studies. This culture has allowed many challengers—associations, groups, local governments—to develop renewable electricity production in some Länder, and explains the public support for federal schemes. The modalities and rhythms of the energy transition continue to vary according to Länder, by virtue of path dependence on fossil fuels, difficult economic situations for certain sectors of East Germany, and political orientations.

These factors partly explain why Swedish policy has relied on market mechanisms (green certificates), rather than strong state regulation, through FITs, in order not to jeopardize the nuclear sector. In Germany, FITs have served to affirm federal policy over the Länder, which notably determine the price of electricity. They contributed to the initiation of multi-scalar governance of the energy transition, which is already firmly established in Sweden. Sweden is the European country that has most solicited its local authorities in order to attain CO_2 emission reduction objectives (Lundgvist & Biel, 2007). Political actors work together in relative proximity and mutual acquaintance, in a somewhat non-hierarchical partnership, which is facilitated by the size of the country.

On the contrary, in Germany we find a plurality of energy policies in a fragmented, dissonant, and complex landscape. The pioneering cities were not supported by the federal government in the beginning, focusing rather on professional and political actor networks to structure an alternative to the dominant power system. The transnational dimension of these networks should not be neglected in understanding the lobbying efforts of local authorities. The German cities are the leaders of two main European networks that have worked since the beginning of the 1990s to put in place a multilevel climate governance and a new diplomacy of cities for climate: ICLEI Europe, based in Freiburg im Breisgau, and Climate Alliance, in Frankfurt am Main. They have also been invested in the European campaign for sustainable cities. This international detour is probably more effective in a political structure in which each level of government has a relative independence. The involvement of Swedish cities in transnational municipal networks is mainly attributable to a will to assert ecological leadership. The engagement of German cities in the climate battle has been of a more political and conflictive nature. It has contributed to the rise of the Greens, lending more weight to political ecology in the transition process.

In both contexts studied, a handful of cities governed by a red-green coalition have paved the way for changes in energy regime. National accounts of the energy transition often emphasize the role of renewable energy research and development programs. We tend to forget that these programs can be territorially driven and supported by local communities. The research institutes on solar power in Freiburg and bioenergy in Växjö were established as a result of local dynamics. Backed by industry in Växjö and anti-nuclear activists in Freiburg, they themselves reflect the divergent policy approaches in these cities.

The liberal conservatives who succeeded the Social Democrats in Sweden in the early 2000s, at the local and national levels, have bet on technological innovation, green growth, and carbon markets. Greater political stability has allowed Social Democrat cities in Germany to partly resist the neoliberal agenda. Both political camps are convinced of the necessity of a transition toward an ecological economy, but for different reasons: strong public regulation, notably via eco-fiscality, conditions innovation and economic competitiveness, yielding an advantage for Swedish enterprises on the world market, whereas for the German Greens, it is the responsibility of political ecology to work profound transformations on the nature of economic activities in the direction of energy sobriety (Emelianoff, 2014). To undertake the exit from both nuclear energy and fossil fuels requires a heavy reduction of electricity usage. Energy decentralization is a central part of the solution. These divergent political orientations, greening of capitalism versus eco-political economy, explain the divergent positioning of these cities (but not of the national governments) as regards centralized energy and the role of technological innovations. This also explains why the liberalization of the energy market in Sweden has produced a concentration of energy operators, with privatization of municipal power companies, while in Germany ultimately encouraging a re-municipalization and re-politicization of energy.

For Hinderer and Fuchs (2016), local interest in renewable energy is inseparable from the search for decentralized energy control. More broadly, we believe that this local control is the mainspring of action in favor of transition of local authorities in Europe. This more or less explicit struggle turns local authorities into challengers of the dominant electrical system. Energy resources are political resources, whether it is a question of securing energy supply, overcoming the dangers of nuclear power and the "electrocracy" (Moss, 2014), increasing financial income and therefore the empowerment of local governments to develop local jobs, reducing the carbon footprint of the area, or embodying a political alternative. As was the case in the early twentieth century (Schott, 2008), local management energy empowers local communities, and reactivates old battles for greater local self-determination.

Yet in both study contexts, national or federal policies have strengthened centralized forms of power generation. This trend does not appear to benefit the low-carbon energy transition. By delocalizing renewable energy, the logics of mutualization, local distribution networks, and chaining of energy sources no longer work. The coupling with architecture, urban planning, and landscaping, which determine the microclimates and allow the resizing of some energy needs, becomes inoperative. The rebound effects related to gray energy generated by renewable power facilities do not seem to be taken into account. Nor does the distance between the consumer and the producer of electricity promote civic responsibility with regard to energy transition. It also creates externality effects between municipalities that are consumers or producers energy, causing conflicts regarding renewable energy facilities (Quitzow et al., 2016).

Territorial energy management allows, on the contrary, to understand energy resources as multidimensional and "embodied," in opposition to the view of energy as an industrial sector, which extracts resource management from its environment and at the same time limits its potential. The local energy systems that have, for example, coupled water, energy, and waste systems in sustainable neighborhoods in Stockholm and Malmö have made inhabitants—their warmth and their waste—a promising source of renewable energy. Energy innovation can be spatial, not just technical. Furthermore, the fundamentally political nature of energy systems becomes the subject of multifaceted citizen struggles to retake "power" in a world given over to increasing climatic and environmental injustices. So we can say, without much risk, that territories play a central role not only upstream, but also downstream of the energy transition, by redefining its goals, its forms, its potentials, and its latent resources.

Conclusion

Activist and community initiatives taken up by some local governments in Germany and Sweden have driven a movement to phase out fossil and fissile fuels, in turn relayed by other levels of government and other European states. The nonlinear path of the transition to renewable energy calls for conceptualization of this process as multi-scalar and trans-scalar. Transnational networking of local actors and city governments has allowed the distribution and circulation of ideas, innovations, and action models, with the complicity of a part of the European Commission. Parliamentary allies and battles have been successful in partially modifying the regulatory, legal, and tax frameworks governing the electricity market. The tardy intervention of national or federal authorities caused a change of scale in the production of renewable electricity, FITs having shown, in this regard, their effectiveness.

The comparative analysis of German and Swedish electrical transitions allows us to highlight the political dimensions of these two transition paths. The contrasted relationship to nuclear energy, the decentralized culture of Germany, and the weight of political ecology prove crucial to understanding the rhythms and modalities of transition toward renewable energies. The multi-scalar governance of the energy transition, also contrasted, has paradoxical effects. Less developed and more confrontational in Germany, space is opened for a strong territorial heterogeneity and for alternatives and citizen initiatives, creating a potential for the questioning and evolution of this transition. Contrariwise, the strong multi-scalar integration of Swedish policies left less space for dissension and in the end might disserve the low carbon transition, in terms of climate change issues. Vertical integration of policies is thus not a guarantee of successful multilevel climate governance, at least in the short term, since it strengthens the neoliberal alignment of energy transition policies.

References

Blanchet, T. (2015). Struggle over energy transition in Berlin: How do grassroots initiatives affect local energy policy-making? *Energy Policy, 78,* 246–254.

Bulkeley, H. (2005). Reconfiguring environmental governance: Towards a politics of scales and networks. *Political Geography, 24,* 875–902.

Bulkeley, H., & Betsill, M. (2003). *Cities and climate change: Urban sustainability and global environmental governance.* London, New York: Routledge.

Bulkeley, H., Castan Broto, V., Hodson, M., & Marvin S. (2011). *Cities and low carbon transitions.* London; New York: Routledge.

Bulkeley, H., & Kern, K. (2006). Local government and the governing of climate change in Germany and the UK. *Urban Studies, 43*(12), 2237–2259.

Chen Y., Johnson F. (2008). Sweden: Greening the power market in a context of liberalization and nuclear ambivalences. In W. Lafferty & A. Ruud (Eds.), *Promoting sustainable electricity in Europe: Challenging the path dependence of dominant energy systems* (pp. 219–240). Cheltenham, UK: Edward Elgar.

Collier, U., & Löfstedt, R. (1997). Think globally, act locally? Local climate change and energy policies in Sweden and the UK. *Global Environmental Change, 1*(7), 25–40.

Eckerberg, K. (2001). Sweden: Problems and prospects at the leading edge of LA21 implementation. In W. Lafferty (Ed.), *Sustainable communities in Europe* (pp. 15–39). London: Earthscan.

Emelianoff, C. (2007). La ville durable: L'hypothèse d'un tournant urbanistique en Europe. *L'information Géographique, 71*, 48–65.

Emelianoff, C. (2010). Pioneer cities for climate protection (Freiburg im Breisgau, Grenoble): The 1960–70s inheritance. *Informationen zur Modernen Stadtgeschichte, 2*, 34–44.

Emelianoff, C. (2014). Local energy transition and multilevel climate governance: Lessons from two pioneer cities (Hanover, Germany, and Växjö, Sweden). *Urban Studies, 51*(7), 1376–1391.

Emelianoff, C., & Stegassy, R. (2010). *Les pionniers de la ville durable: Récits d'acteurs, portraits de villes en Europe*. Paris: Autrement.

Evrard, A. (2013). *Contre vents et marées: Politiques des énergies renouvelables en Europe*. Paris: Les Presses de Sciences Po.

Hinderer, G., & Fuchs, N. (2016). One or many transitions: Local electricity experiments in Germany. *Innovation: The European Journal of Social Science Research, 29*(3), 320–336.

Huber, M. (1997). Leadership and unification: Climate change policies in Germany. In U. Collier & R. Löfstedt (Eds.), *Cases in climate change policy: Political reality in the European Union* (pp. 65–86). London: Earthscan.

Jacobsson, S. (2008). The emergence and troubled growth of a biopower innovation system in Sweden. *Energy Policy, 36*(4), 1491–1508.

James, S., & Lahti, T. (2004). *The natural step for communities: How cities and towns can change to sustainable practices*. Gabriola Island, Canada: New Society.

Keller, T. (1993). *Les Verts allemands: Un conservatisme alternatif*. Paris: L'Harmattan.

Kitschelt, H. (2009). Political opportunity structures and political protest: Anti-nuclear movements in four democracies. *British Journal of Political Science, 16*, 57–85.

Lafferty, W., & Ruud, A. (Eds.). (2008). *Promoting sustainable electricity in Europe: Challenging the path dependence of dominant energy systems*. Cheltenham, UK: Edward Elgar.

Lauber, V., & Mez, L. (2004). Three decades of renewable electricity policies in Germany. *Energy & Environment, 15*(4), 599–623.

Löfstedt, R. (1997). Sweden: The dilemna of a proposed nuclear phase out. In U. Collier & R. Löfstedt (Eds.), *Cases in climate change policy: Political reality in the European Union* (pp. 165–183). London: Earthscan.

Lundgvist, B. (2007). *From Kyoto to the town hall: Making international and national climate policy work at the local level*. London: Earthscan.

Morris D. (1982). *Self-Reliant Cities. Energy and the Transformation of Urban America*, San Francisco, Sierra Club Books.

Moss, T. (2014). Socio-technical change and the politics of urban infrastructure: Managing energy in Berlin between dictatorship and democracy. *Urban Studies, 51*(7), 1432–1448.

Moss, T., Becker, S., & Naumann, M. (2014). Whose energy transition is it, anyway? Organisation and ownership of the *Energiewende* in villages, cities and regions. *Local Environment, 20,* 1547–1563.

Palm, J. (2006). Development of sustainable energy systems in Swedish municipalities: A matter of path dependency and power relations. *Local Environment, 11*(4), 445–457.

Quitzow, L., Weert, C., Grundmann, P., Leibenath, M., Moss, T., & Rave, T. (2016). The German *Energiewende*: What's happening? Introducing the special issue. *Utilities Policy, 41,* 163-171.

Roggenkamp, K. (2010). *The success of sustainability: A comparaison of policies towards renewable energies in Germany and Sweden.* Saarbrücken: Lambert Academic.

Rohracher, H., & Spath, P. (2014). The interplay of urban energy policy and socio-technical transitions: The eco-cities of Graz and Freiburg in retrospect. *Urban Studies, 51*(7), 1415–1431.

Rudinger, A. (2012). *L'impact de la décision post-Fukushima sur le tournant énergétique allemand.* Working Paper no. 05, IDDRI.

Sahr, R. (1985). *The politics of energy policy change in Sweden.* Ann Arbor: University of Michigan Press.

Scheer, H. (2007). *L'autonomie énergétique: Une nouvelle politique pour les énergies renouvelables.* Arles: Actes Sud.

Schott, D. (2008). Empowering cities: The incorporation of gas and electricity in the European urban environment. In M. Hård & T. J. Misa (Eds.), *Urban machinery: Inside modern European cities* (pp. 165–186). Cambridge: Cambridge University Press.

Späth, P., & Rohracher, H. (2012). Local demonstrations for global transitions: Dynamics across governance levels fostering socio-technical regime change towards sustainability. *European Planning Studies, 20*(3), 461–479.

Vasi, I. (2011). *Winds of change: The environmental movement and the global development of the wind energy industry.* Oxford: Oxford University Press.

Wizelius, T. (2013). *Windpower ownership in Sweden: Business models and motives.* London; New York: Routledge.

PART VII

EMERGING
TRENDS IN THE
ENERGY-SOCIETY
RELATIONSHIP

WE are experiencing rapid shifts in several aspects of contemporary society, with direct or indirect implications for energy-society relationships, many of which have been alluded to throughout this volume. Drivers of these changes include technology, politics, risks associated with unconventional fuel extraction, and the growing political salience of climate change, among others. One trend of note involves the prosumer movement: the rapid expansion of household-level micro-generation of renewable energy, including the purchase of solar arrays, but also citizen-led developments of new technologies, such as the geothermal heat pump developed in Germany. The growth of an energy-focused social movement, and the formation of the International Renewable Energy Agency, described by Sybille Roehrkasten in Chapter 25, are other trends to watch. Other observations have opened up new lines of sociological inquiry, including case studies of local energy transition; complex systems-based analyses of our transportation systems; and critical inquiries into the adoption of new technologies, with a particular focus on science and technology studies. But how do we know how far along we are on the transition pathway? Authors of the chapters in this closing section explore this question, offering both hope and caution.

In Chapter 25 Sybille Roehrkasten expands on the opening provided by Emelianoff in Part VI, to explore macro-trends that can offer us insight into how far we are along a pathway to renewable energy transition. In terms of kilowatts, renewable energy additions to our global energy portfolio are certainly increasing—more than doubling since the turn of the twenty-first century—and expansion appears to be happening across the globe, notably including developing country locations. Yet, discouragingly, they have not made a dent in the volume of fossil fuels extracted and burned each year. This is the case for a number of reasons, including strong political support for fossil fuels that includes heavy subsidies, and technical challenges in energy storage and grid integration for renewables. Nonetheless, there are signs of groundwork being done to support future expansion, including the continued fall in prices for wind and solar (which are important because decisions to adopt renewable energy often hinge on economics), and in particular, the establishment of an International Renewable Energy Agency, of which 150 states currently are members. Symbolically and substantively, this agency, headquartered in the United AraB Emirates, marks a turning point in the political legitimacy of renewable energy.

Jennie C. Stephens and Nils Markusson in Chapter 26 offer cautious reflection on that element of institutional change in which we often place an undue amount of faith: technology. Can advances in, for example, carbon capture and storage (CCS) prevent climate catastrophe while allowing for continued exploitation of fossil fuels? It has certainly received enthusiastic policy attention among the suite of mitigation options on the table. The prevalence of such "solutions" in policy debates reflects a long cultural history of technological optimism in Western society, a predilection that dangerously narrows our mitigation options and overlooks cultural avenues for climate mitigation. Enthusiasm for CCS is on the wane, as expectations have not been realized, but this, as often as not, only motivates attention to other technological fixes. Renewable energy is itself a technological fix of sorts, after all, that diminishes attention on the very real potential that what we need, in addition to technological advances in our energy production and consumption systems, are strategies to *reduce* energy consumption. Ultimately, the authors remind us that technology does indeed need to be recognized as a necessary element to energy-society relations, but our tendency to privilege technology may in fact serve as a barrier to transition.

Martin David, in Chapter 27, also urges caution in our optimism toward transition. Analogous to the previous chapter, it is the very privileging of innovation as the solution—by scholars as often as activists and policymakers—that may ultimately present a barrier to transition. As David makes clear, *innovations* can only really emerge after *exnovation* has taken place: the dismantling of preexisting political structures and infrastructures supporting fossil-fuel use. As a compelling point of note, David begins his historical case study analysis by acknowledging that Germany's electricity grid has indeed undergone an impressive renewable energy transition. But because the structures supporting the coal industry in Germany remained in place, that coal continued to be mined, and was merely exported, rather than consumed domestically. And frankly, *where* the coal gets burned is of no consequence to the climate, so what is really gained in the form of decarbonization? Very little, it would seem, according to David, until Germany's coal-production enterprise is dismantled.

CHAPTER 25

··

ARE WE ON THE CUSP OF A GLOBAL RENEWABLE ENERGY TRANSITION?

··

SYBILLE ROEHRKASTEN

WHILE global capacity additions in renewable electricity already outpace capacity additions in conventional power, the global energy system is still heavily dependent on fossil energy. The international community needs to immediately curtail and then completely phase out the global use of fossil fuels in order to limit global warming to well below 2°C. This primarily applies to coal and oil, which are the most climate-damaging energy sources, but also to natural gas in the longer term. This chapter analyzes global energy trends to assess whether a global renewable energy transition is already underway, and what steps are needed to further accelerate the global deployment of renewables. It furthermore links changing trends in global energy to global governance dynamics. Here, dramatic changes have been observed in recent years. While the United Nations for a very long time remained almost silent on renewables, renewables are today a core pillar of the UN sustainability agenda. Moreover, while many were speaking about the crisis of multilateralism, in 2010 a new intergovernmental organization was formed—the International Renewable Energy Agency (IRENA)—which currently has more than 150 member states (now, there are 154 members).

THE EXPANSION OF RENEWABLE ENERGY IN LIGHT OF GLOBAL ENERGY TRENDS

Since the beginning of the millennium, global renewable energy capacities have experienced impressive growth. Renewable energy derives from naturally regenerative

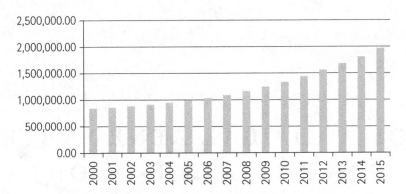

FIGURE 25.1 Installed renewable energy capacities worldwide, 2000–2015 (in MWe).

Source: Author's illustration based on IRENA, Data and Statistics, http://resourceirena.irena.org/gateway/dashboard
/?topic=4&subTopic=16

sources. It comprises hydropower, wind energy, solar energy, bioenergy, geothermal energy, and tidal and wave energy. As visible in Figure 25.1, worldwide renewable energy capacities more than doubled from 842,452 megawatts of electricity (MWe) in 2000 to 1,964,688 MWe in 2015.

Hydropower has been the most prevalent renewable energy source so far. In 2015, 62% (1,207,659 MWe) of installed renewable energy capacities were based on hydropower. However, since 2000 non-hydro renewable energy sources have gained more and more ground. In 2000, these sources only accounted for 7% of installed renewable energy capacities. In 2015, wind, solar, and bioenergy made up substantial shares, with wind energy accounting for 21% (416,639 MWe), solar energy for 11% (223,949 MWe), and bioenergy for 5% (102,853 MWe) of installed capacities. The shares of geothermal energy and wave energy are still negligibly small. It is important to note that hydropower and bioenergy have higher capacity factors than wind and solar energy, so that their shares in renewable electricity *generation* are higher than in installed capacities. In 2014,[1] hydropower provided 74% of electricity generation (compared to 65% of installed capacities), wind energy 13% (19% of capacities), bioenergy 7% (5% of capacities) and solar energy 4% (10% of capacities). Wind and solar energy are the renewable energy technologies that experienced the highest growth rates in installed capacities between 2000 and 2015: wind energy increased more than 24-fold, and solar energy by 183-fold.[2] Nowadays, solar energy leads global investments in non-hydro renewables, making up a share of 56% in 2015 (161.04 billion US$). Wind energy follows with 38% (109.64 billion US$).[3]

The expansion of renewable energy capacities has been a truly global phenomenon: renewable energy capacities have been growing in all regions of the world. Today, almost all countries of the world have adopted renewable energy targets. This is a stark contrast to the situation 10 years ago: while in 2005 only 43 countries had renewable energy targets in place, in 2015 164 countries had adopted such targets. It is striking that most renewable energy targets concentrate on the electricity sector: 150 countries had

Table 25.1 Top Five Countries in Installed Renewable Energy Capacities, 2015

	1	2	3	4	5
Hydropower	China	United States	Brazil	Canada	Russia
Wind	China	United States	Germany	India	Spain
Solar	China	Germany	Japan	United States	Italy
Bioenergy	Brazil	United States	China	Germany	India
Geothermal	United States	Philippines	Indonesia	Mexico	New Zealand
Marine	Korea	France	Canada	China	United Kingdom

Source: Author's illustration based on IRENA, Data and Statistics;http://resourceirena.irena.org/gateway/dashboard/?topic=4&subTopic=18

renewable electricity targets in 2015, while renewable energy targets for the transport sector and for heating/cooling existed only in 59 and 47 countries, respectively.[4]

While in the past, industrialized economies led in global renewable energy investments, this has changed recently. In 2015, emerging and developing economies for the first time invested more in renewable energies than did industrialized economies.[5] This is primarily due to the dominating role of China, which has been leading the world in renewable energy investments since 2012. In 2015, China accounted for more than a third of global investments in renewables (102.9 billion US$).[6] China, furthermore, leads the world in terms of installed hydropower, wind, and solar capacities (see Table 25.1).

A Global Energy Transition: Not Yet a Reality, But Urgently Needed

To assess whether a global energy transition toward renewables is already happening, looking at the expansion trends of renewables alone is not sufficient—they have to be examined in the context of overall energy developments. And here, one message is still very clear: global energy supply is still dominated by fossil fuels. In 2014, the fossil energy sources oil, gas, and coal accounted for 78.3% of global final energy consumption. Modern renewables made up 10.3%, while traditional biomass accounted for 8.9% and nuclear energy for 2.5% (REN21, 2016). Data from the International Energy Agency (IEA, 2016a), furthermore, reveal that the fossil-fuel share in global primary energy demand has not decreased between 1990 and 2014. So, it is far too early to affirm that a global energy transition toward renewables is already happening. Even within the electricity sector, where the expansion of renewables has been most advanced, non-renewable sources still accounted for more than three-quarters of power generation in 2015 (REN21, 2016). Data from IEA (2016a) further show that even in the electricity sector, there has been only a slight increase in the share of renewable power generation, from 20% in 1990 to 22% in 2014. In the heating and cooling sector, final energy was 92% conventional, while 96% of global fuel for road transport was based on fossil energy in 2015 (REN21, 2016). One message is very clear: in order to achieve a global energy transition toward renewables, it is not sufficient to merely expand renewables; they actually have to *replace* other energy sources.

However, in the electricity sector at least, there are some very positive signs that a transition toward renewables is likely to happen. Figures by IRENA reveal that in this sector, the world experienced an important turnaround in 2013: for the first time, renewables outpaced fossil fuels and nuclear energy in capacity additions, making up a share of 58% (IRENA, 2014). IEA's *World Energy Outlook 2015* presents slightly different numbers and speaks of an almost 50% share of renewables in capacity additions in 2013. According to the IEA's *World Energy Outlook 2016*, capacity additions in renewables for the first time exceeded fossil fuels and nuclear in 2014 (IEA, 2016a). In addition, worldwide investments in renewables have outpaced those for fossil and nuclear energy in the electricity sector since 2008. In 2015, renewables accounted for 70% of total global investments in new electricity production capacity. The IEA expects that in the future, one unit of renewable energy investment will generate one-third more electricity on an annual basis, due to technological progress and unit cost reductions (IEA, 2016b). In the transport and heating/cooling sector, we are still far away from such a turnaround.

In more than 50 countries around the world, in fact, renewables already account for over 50% of electricity generation (see Quitzow, Roehrkasten, & Jaenicke, 2016). Almost all of these countries have significant hydropower capacities. In these countries, hydropower emerged to dominate the sector early on against other energy sources. Denmark provides a striking contrast: in 2014 it reached a renewables share of almost 50% in its electricity supply without relying on hydropower. Some countries aim at achieving a 100% renewable electricity supply. Among these are countries with significant hydropower capacities, such as Costa Rica, Dominica, Fiji, Papua New Guinea, Samoa, Scotland, and Vanuatu. But other countries like Cabo Verde, Denmark, and Tuvalu have also set a goal of 100% renewable electricity supply, without having significant hydropower resources at their disposal. Renewable electricity supply in Denmark primarily relies on wind power and bioenergy; in Cabo Verde on wind and solar energy. The main renewable energy source in Tuvalu and Djibouti is solar energy (REN, 2016).[7]

As noted earlier, implementing the climate protection goals of the international community requires that renewable energies do not only expand, but actually *replace* fossil fuels. In the Paris Agreement, member-states of the United Nations committed to the goal of limiting global warming to well below 2°C. After an unprecedentedly rapid ratification process, the Paris Agreement entered into force in November 2016. Since the energy sector accounts for two-thirds of global greenhouse gas emissions (IEA, 2015b), the goal of the Paris Agreement is not achievable without a fundamental transformation of the global energy system—covering all sectors, electricity, transport, and heating/cooling. In order to limit global warming to well below 2°C, the international community needs to immediately curtail and then completely phase out the global use of fossil fuels—primarily coal and oil, which are the most climate-damaging energy sources, but also natural gas in the longer term (IEA, 2014, 2015b). This poses paramount challenges for all countries around the world—for industrialized countries with saturated energy markets, but even more so for emerging and developing economies that confront strongly rising energy demand. Unlike in saturated markets with stable or even declining energy demand, in developing and emerging markets the expansion of renewable energy technologies is not automatically accompanied by a reduction or substitution of conventional energy sources. However, recent figures from the IEA point at a positive development: in 2014, global energy-related emissions stalled, marking the first time in 40 years that such a stall did not occur as a result of an economic downturn. Preliminary estimates by the IEA for the year 2015 suggest that emissions stayed flat in 2015 as well. According to the IEA, this is the first indication of a decoupling of energy-related carbon emissions from economic growth. The IEA attributes this to three major developments: the global expansion of renewables, reduced coal consumption in China, and improvements in energy efficiency (IEA, 2015b, 2016a). Whether this decoupling is a temporary phenomenon or will be a long lasting trend, however, it is still too early to assess.

A significant increase in the global deployment of renewables is also needed to reach the Sustainable Development Goals (SDGs) that the United Nations adopted in September 2015. The SDGs include the following goal on energy: to ensure access to affordable, reliable, sustainable, and modern energy for all by 2030. The energy SDG encompasses three major targets by 2030: (1) to ensure universal access to affordable, reliable, and modern energy services; (2) to increase substantially the share of renewable energy in the global energy mix; and (3) to double the global rate of improvement in energy efficiency. Here, the challenges are formidable. An estimated 1.1 billion people worldwide[8]—more people than living in the Organisation for Economic Co-operation and Development (OECD) world—lack access to electricity. In Sub-Saharan Africa, this is the case for two out of three people (see also Quitzow et al., 2016). Worldwide, 2.9 billion people[9]– almost 40% of the global population—rely on traditional biomass for cooking, which is responsible for indoor air pollution. The prevalence of traditional biomass, in addition to the burning of oil and coal, has significant negative impacts on air quality and human health.

To enhance a sustainable energy supply around the world, the international community needs to satisfy a globally rising energy demand while simultaneously mitigating the environmental damages caused by energy production and use. With a growing world population and worldwide efforts to climb the ladder of socioeconomic development, global energy demand is increasing sharply: the IEA (2016a) estimates that it will increase by more than a third up to 2040, from 13,684 million tons of oil equivalent (Mtoe) in 2014 to 17,866 Mtoe in 2040. In the mitigation of energy-induced environmental risks, renewable energies have a key role to play. In addition to contributing to climate mitigation, they help to reduce local environmental pollution. Air pollution is a major environmental problem in large urban centers, causing an estimated 6.5 million deaths worldwide each year. Energy production and use—particularly traditional biomass, coal, and oil—are by far the largest man-made sources of air pollutants. Next to improving air pollution control technologies, it is necessary to substitute these energy sources with cleaner ones, such as modern renewable energy technologies (IEA, 2016c). While nuclear energy mitigates climate change and local air pollution, it cannot be regarded as a sustainable energy source: next to the well-known safety risks, permanent and environmentally secure storage of radioactive waste remains an unsolved problem around the world. Wind and solar energy, furthermore, can contribute to sustainable water use. Already today, many regions in the world suffer from water scarcity. And competition over scarce water resources will increase in the future: the UN *World Water Report 2015* estimated that by 2030, 40% of global water demand will not be met (UNESCO, 2015). At the same time, the water demand of the energy sector is growing sharply. According to estimates by the IEA (2016a), water consumption in the global energy sector will increase by almost 60% between 2014 and 2040. Wind power and solar photovoltaics are the least water-intensive electricity sources and can thus play a major role in reducing the energy-induced water demand (Roehrkasten, Schaeuble, & Helgenberger, 2016.

However, it must be emphasized that no energy source, including renewables, is free of environmental risks. The possible negative impacts of hydropower and bioenergy on ecosystems are well known. Large hydroelectric dams alter river ecosystems, with significant impacts on downstream water-flow regulation, sediment transport, and fisheries. If not managed wisely, this can lead to massive negative consequences for biodiversity and can undermine the healthy functioning of ecosystems (see, for example, UNESCO, 2014). Large-scale use of bioenergy compromises biodiversity and might lead to deforestation, soil degradation, air pollution, and disrupted local water cycles.[10] The environmental risks that go along with the extraction of rare earths—metals used for the construction of wind turbines and solar panels—are less known and will require much more attention in the future. In a comprehensive analysis of the environmental impacts of rare-earth mining in China—the country that dominates the global market for rare earths—China Water Risk (2016) reveals massive contamination of water sources and soils. Deploying renewable energies in a way that minimizes the associated environmental risks is of utmost importance for enhancing an environmentally sustainable energy transition.

Drivers and Barriers for an Accelerated Expansion of Renewables

While renewable energies do entail many environmental benefits, their expansion in most parts of the world is not driven by environmental concerns, but by economic cost-benefit analyses. Hydropower, bioenergy, and geothermal energy have been cost-competitive with fossil fuels for a while. Solar and wind energy for a long time were considered to be expensive energy technologies. However, this has drastically changed in recent years. With the global scaling up of solar and wind energy and recent technical breakthroughs, prices for solar and wind energy are dropping around the globe. Solar photovoltaic (PV) module prices experienced the most dramatic drop: prices in 2015 were 80% lower than in 2009. Wind turbines experienced a price drop of 30%–40% from 2008/2009 to 2015 (IRENA, 2015, 2016a). Over the last five years, the global weighted average of levelized costs of electricity for hydropower, biomass, onshore wind, and geothermal energy has been within the estimated fossil-fuel costs range, from US$0.04 to 0.14 per kilowatt hour (KWh) (see Table 25.2). Solar PV recently reached cost parity. Offshore wind is still slightly above the fossil-fuel cost range, while solar thermal energy remains comparatively expensive. While these figures present global average numbers, each technology has a substantial cost range, depending on factors such as location, availability of resources and technologies, and financing costs.

Efforts to increase energy security and to foster economic development have been additional key drivers for renewable energy investments around the world (see also Quitzow, Roehrkasten, & Jaenicke, 2016). Meeting rapidly rising domestic energy demand is a challenge that most developing and emerging economies confront. In these countries, investments in renewable energy capacities are seen as an important instrument to meet rising demand while diversifying the energy mix. For countries that are struggling to provide their population with access to electricity, the decentralized deployment of renewable energies provides a great opportunity, as it facilitates a rapid scaling up at relatively low cost, reducing the need for costly electricity grid expansion. For countries without significant domestic fossil-fuel reserves, reducing import dependency has also been an enduring concern. In these countries, investments in renewables offer the opportunity to deploy domestically available energy sources, and thus to reduce import spending, political dependence on exporting countries, and vulnerability to possible interruptions of supply. Interestingly, even fossil-fuel-rich and exporting countries, such as the United Arab Emirates, have begun to invest in renewables in order to secure long-term export strength: investments in renewables are viewed as a means

Table 25.2 Cost Comparison of Different Renewable Energy Technologies and Fossil Fuels, 2015

	Weighted average (USD/KWh)
Hydropower	0.046
Biomass	0.055
Onshore wind	0.060
Geothermal	0.080
Solar PV	0.126
Fossil fuel cost range: 0.04–0.14	
Offshore wind	0.159
Solar thermal	0.245

Source: IRENA, Data and Statistics;http://resourceirena.irena.org/gateway/dashboard/?topic=3&subTopic=33

to not only reduce domestic consumption of fossil fuels and thus free up resources for export, but also to ensure their leadership in the global energy sector by diversifying business models (Qader & Roehrkasten, 2018). For countries such as Germany, the United States, and China, enhancing export strength through industrial leadership in an expanding global renewable energy industry has been an additional important driver behind the domestic expansion of renewables.

To accelerate the global expansion of renewables, several barriers need to be overcome. These comprise technical, economic, and political challenges. Among the technical challenges, the storage and grid integration of large shares of fluctuating renewable energy sources such as wind and solar remain key issues. In addition, more efforts are needed to develop sustainable and practically implementable renewable energy solutions in the transport sector, as well as in the heating/cooling sector (IRENA, 2016b). In several countries, for example in Sub-Saharan Africa, there is still limited data on renewable energy resource availability, such as solar radiation levels and wind speed, and local expertise on the new technologies is still lacking (Quitzow et al., 2016). From an economic point of view, the cost structure of renewable energy investments has various challenges. Renewable energy projects have very low running costs, with large upfront investments accounting for most overall costs. Therefore, a stable long-term financing framework is even more important for renewable energy projects than for fossil-fuel projects. In addition, leveling the playing field between renewable and conventional energy is challenging. In many countries, fossil fuels are still heavily subsidized, and even if prices are not subsidized, they typically do not account for negative externalities on the environment and human health. Third, there are several political challenges. In various countries, renewable energy targets are not backed by dedicated policies and regulatory frameworks. However, such policies are crucial to facilitate a stable investment environment. Overcoming path dependencies and vested interests in fossil and nuclear energy remains challenging in most countries of the world (see, for example, Araujo, 2014; Roehrkasten, Thielges, & Quitzow, 2016; Stirling, 2014). Powerful stakeholders linked to fossil and nuclear industries are often reluctant to change existing business models and infrastructure, and seek to prevent competition from new market players. It remains an important task for energy research to improve the understanding of existing drivers and barriers and to find context-specific and practically implementable solutions.

Renewables Moving from the Sidelines to the Center Stage of Global Energy Governance

The global expansion of renewable energies has compelled a major shift in global energy governance: renewables have moved from the sidelines to the center stage (see also Roehrkasten, 2015). Since the turn of the millennium, many initiatives for transboundary cooperation on renewables have been launched. In addition to growing support for the domestic expansion of renewables in many countries, energy security concerns during periods of high oil prices and global efforts to mitigate climate change were important drivers behind these developments.

The most notable step has been the creation of a new intergovernmental organization on renewable energy, the IRENA. Founded in 2009, since 2011 it has been a full-fledged international organization, more than 150 member states (currently there are 154).[11] IRENA is the first international organization dedicated to promoting renewable energies. What distinguishes IRENA from most other institutions in international energy governance is its truly global scope, as it is open to all UN member-states. Its wide-spread membership provides it with a high degree of legitimacy. In its activities, IRENA concentrates on knowledge services and policy advice: it provides renewable energy data and statistics, advice on best practices and policy development, and insights on financing and technologies, and it engages in capacity development.[12]

IRENA's mere creation and more so its widespread membership were remarkable developments considering the long history of failed attempts to address renewables in global forums prior to the establishment of IRENA (Roehrkasten, 2015; Roehrkasten & Westphal, 2013). Reaching UN-wide consensus has been a particularly difficult (and oftentimes impossible) undertaking. At the 2002 World Summit on Sustainable Development in Johannesburg, South Africa, the promotion of renewables was among the most controversial issues (IISD, 2002; Karlsson-Vinkhuyzen, 2010; Najam & Cleveland, 2005; Rowlands, 2005). At the 2006 and 2007 sessions of the UN Commission on Sustainable Development, several irreconcilable cleavages on renewable energy arose (IISD, 2007).

This began to change in the year of IRENA's official creation, a time when the United Nations began to take an active stance on sustainable energy. The UN Secretary-General set up the Sustainable Energy For All (SE4All) initiative, aiming at three major goals by 2030: doubling the share of renewables in global energy supply, doubling the improvement rate for energy efficiency, and ensuring access to modern forms of energy. SE4All was the first major UN initiative on sustainable energy (Roehrkasten & Westphal, 2013). With the adoption of the SDGs in 2015, sustainable energy finally became an integral part of the UN agenda on sustainable development. The energy SDG builds on the goals set out by SE4All, albeit with one major difference: SE4All aims at *doubling* the share of renewables in global energy supply, while the energy SDG comprises a less specific target of "*significant* increase" for renewables.

IRENA's creation furthermore impacted the IEA's work on renewables. When the member countries of the OECD founded the IEA in 1974 as a response to the oil price shock, they put emergency mechanisms for oil supply shortages at the core of IEA's activities. However, over time IEA has expanded its activities significantly. It is currently the leader in international energy market analysis and related policy advice. Next to its emergency measures to deal with oil supply disruptions, it serves "as the outstanding official organizational forum for information sharing and analysis on international energy matters" (Leverett, 2010, p. 252). Its activities cover not only oil, but all energy sources.

The IEA issues regular publications on energy topics, annually reviews the national energy policies of its member-states, and engages in dialogue with energy-exporting countries and non-IEA energy consumers (Colgan, 2009). The IEA, however, has been criticized repeatedly that its research and policy advice favors conventional energy over renewables (see, for example, Lesage, Van de Graaf, & Westphal, 2010; Metayer, Breyer, & Fell, 2015; Röhrkasten & Westphal, 2013; Van de Graaf, 2012a, 2012b;). Yet, interestingly, in parallel to the founding of IRENA, the IEA also stepped up its attention toward renewables (see also Heubaum & Biermann 2015; Van de Graaf, 2012a). Under pressure to modernize, the IEA today aims to become a hub for clean energy technologies and energy efficiency.[13] However, it still provides more conservative figures on the global expansion of renewable energies than IRENA;[14] recent analysis by Metayer, Breyer, and Fell (2015) suggests that it consistently underestimates the expansion trajectories of solar and wind energy in its yearly flagship publication, the *World Energy Outlook*.[15]

International climate protection efforts have been a key driver behind the worldwide promotion of renewables.[16] According to Dubash and Florini (2011, p. 10), the rise of environmental protection as a major objective in global energy governance was "the single most dramatic shift in the global energy landscape over the last two decades." With the adoption of the UN Framework Convention on Climate Change (UNFCCC) in 1992, the international community committed itself to mitigate global greenhouse gas emissions. As the energy sector still accounts for two-thirds of global greenhouse gas emissions (IEA, 2015b), it has been a central target of global mitigation efforts. Cherp, Jewell, and Goldthau (2011, p. 82) even claim that within global governance, climate protection has been "the arena with the clearest and most ambitious goals of systematic energy transition." While it is indisputable that the UNFCCC process has been very important for the worldwide promotion of renewables, its supportive role has been rather indirect. The main outcomes of the process—the framework convention itself, as well as the Kyoto Protocol and the Paris Agreement—hardly even mention renewable energy (see also Hirschl, 2009).

Politics Behind IRENA's Creation

It seems rather puzzling that IRENA was formed during a time when many were speaking about a crisis of multilateralism (Roehrkasten & Westphal, 2013). Urpelainen and Van de Graaf (2015, p. 162) even refer to its inception as a "miracle" and ask if IRENA's creation can serve as a model of institutional innovation in global governance. In order to understand this puzzle, it is necessary to shed light on the politics behind IRENA's creation.[17]

The German government has been the brain and main engine behind IRENA's creation. The promotion of renewable energies has been a key pillar of the German *Energiewende*, which started in 2000, and Germany's international energy policies (see Quitzow, Roehrkasten, & Jaenicke, 2016; Roehrkasten & Steinbacher, 2016). Prior to IRENA's creation, Germany tried to strengthen UN action on renewables several times, without success. In 2008 it decided to push for renewable energy outside of the UN framework, building on a coalition of the willing, instead of trying to achieve a UN-wide consensus. Four context factors opened an important window of opportunity for creating a new international organization on renewable energy: the worldwide expansion of renewables had already started, fossil fuel prices were rising tremendously, the political attention toward climate protection peaked in the wake of the Copenhagen Climate Summit in 2009, and the global financial crisis that emerged in 2008 had not yet relented. Early supporters of the initiative were Spain and Denmark—two countries that also strongly supported the expansion of renewables within their own countries.

With its initiative to create IRENA, the German government also wanted to establish a counterweight to the IEA in global energy governance (see also Urpelainen & Van de Graaf, 2014, 2015; Van de Graaf, 2012a, 2013a, 2013b). First, Germany joined the criticism of the IEA for favoring conventional over renewable energy in its analysis and policy advice. This criticism had been fueled by the accusation that the IEA keeps its cards very close to its chest when it comes to the modeling assumptions of its energy supply scenarios, which are a powerful tool used by governments to guide decisions about different energy paths. In addition, its major reports must be approved by its member-states, some of which have clear economic interests in the production of conventional and unconventional fossil fuels as well as nuclear energy. So the German government wanted IRENA to challenge IEA analysis and advice, advocating for the global expansion of renewables. Second, Germany wanted to create an international energy organization that was open to universal membership—in contrast to the IEA being limited to members from the OECD world. The IEA's restricted membership increasingly challenged its credibility, as emerging and developing countries outside the OECD are becoming key drivers of developments in global energy markets. Non-OECD countries already accounted for 60% of global energy demand in 2013, and the IEA expects this share to rise to 70% by 2040 (IEA, 2015a).

The initiative to create IRENA met widespread political support. In 2009, IRENA's founding statute was signed by 75 countries. However, a number of influential countries were missing from the list of signatories. At that time, creating IRENA did not receive the support of the emerging countries of Brazil, China, India, Indonesia, Mexico, and South Africa, nor the G8 countries Canada, Japan, Russia, the United Kingdom, and the United States (Van de Graaf, 2012a). Some countries opposed IRENA's creation due to general reservations against renewable energy, or regarding the creation of new international organizations in general. Other countries, such as China and Brazil, raised sovereignty concerns. They feared that IRENA would engage in standardization and impose restrictions on the energy policies of its member-states. Some IEA member-states did not want to create competition with the IEA.

Reasons for joining IRENA varied as well. Next to the countries that were actually supportive of the mandate to promote renewable energy worldwide, there were those that expected to gain access to financial resources by joining IRENA. Yet others joined simply to ensure the ability to influence a new intergovernmental organization. The IEA member states of the United Kingdom, United States, Japan, and Australia, for example, finally decided to join IRENA, but formed an alliance to try to limit IRENA's budget and restrict its activities to developing countries—and thus protect IEA's role as the central energy organization of the OECD states. As of January 2017, Brazil and Canada are the only large countries that have refrained from joining IRENA.

During IRENA's founding, several issues were highly controversial among the member-states. First, the degree to which IRENA activities should be binding was a topic of debate. While some countries wanted IRENA to engage in standard-setting and regulation, it was ultimately agreed that IRENA would work from the principle of voluntariness. The scope of renewable energy that fell under the auspices of IRENA was also discussed. Some governments raised sustainability concerns with regard to biofuels and large hydropower. Here, agreement was reached to promote all kinds of renewable energy—with the restriction that they have to be produced and used in a sustainable way. The scope of membership was also debated: Should IRENA build on a small front-runner coalition or on broad membership? Finally, it was decided to follow a UN-wide approach. Controversies also concerned the geographical scope of IRENA's activities. While some countries argued that IRENA should concentrate its activities on the developing world, it was finally decided that IRENA should aim at the *global* expansion of renewables, covering both developing and industrialized countries.

To the surprise of many, IRENA's headquarters were located in the United Arab Emirates. As a member of the Organization of the Petroleum Exporting Countries (OPEC), the Emirates belongs to the group of countries that used to oppose UN action on renewable energies. However, not only the Emirates but also the OPEC member Nigeria expressed support for IRENA's creation in the early stages. This illustrates an important policy shift that has become prevalent in many fossil-fuel-rich countries around the world: their strategies for enhancing long-term energy security and export strength are no longer restricted to fossil fuels; in their search for alternative business models and for means to satisfy rising domestic energy demand, they also invest in renewable energy (see also Qader & Roehrkasten, 2018). For the United Arab Emirates, gaining IRENA's headquarters was furthermore a question of national prestige: IRENA is the first intergovernmental organization located in the Arab world.

Current Challenges for Global Governance on Renewable Energy

While in the past it was a common criticism that global governance on (renewable) energy is weakly developed (see, for example, Florini, 2008; Florini & Sovacool, 2011; Gupta, 2012; Karlsson-Vinkhuyzen, Jollands, & Staudt, 2012; Lesage, Van de Graaf, & Westphal, 2010), this is no longer the case. Today, there is no lack of institutions in global energy governance; in addition to IRENA, many others have been created since the 2000s (Roehrkasten & Westphal, 2016). These institutions contribute to the promotion of renewables in various ways. Some of them aim to encourage governments and other policy actors to commit to increasing the use of renewable energy within their spheres of influence; others aim to facilitate free trade of renewable energy technologies and services, or the transfer of financial and technological know-how. Still others target knowledge creation and exchange, publishing data and analysis on renewables, and advise governments and other decision-makers on how to expand renewables in an effective way (see also Roehrkasten, 2015).

While for a long time energy has been regarded as an issue that primarily concerns national interests, today it is increasingly considered in its global dimensions. More and more policymakers and researchers recognize that energy is a central precondition for and a key component of a globally sustainable development, and that energy policymaking involves a range of transboundary interdependencies. These interdependencies are also the starting point for an emerging global governance perspective on energy, which began to gain ground in academic debates during the second half of the 2000s (among the first publications were Najam & Cleveland, 2005; Rowlands, 2005; Suding & Lempp, 2007; Florini, 2008; Hirschl, 2009; Lesage, Van de Graaf, & Westphal, 2010). A central argument of global governance research is the assertion that transboundary cooperation can lead to better policy outcomes than unilateral action, and that there are many policy problems that cannot be tackled by single governments alone (Roehrkasten, 2015). However, sovereignty concerns remain important in global energy governance, as energy is commonly seen as a strategic good that is crucial for the economic development of countries and the political power of states (see, for example, Gupta, 2012; Hirschl, 2009; Karlsson-Vinkhuyzen, 2010; Karlsson-Vinkhuyzen, Jollands, & Staudt, 2012; Lesage, Van de Graaf, & Westphal, 2010). Therefore, several energy policymakers fear that multilateral processes could limit their freedom to determine energy priorities at the national level (Karlsson-Vinkhuyzen, 2010). Political processes at the national level remain essential building blocks of global energy governance (Dubash & Florini, 2011; Karlsson-Vinkhuyzen, Jollands, & Staudt, 2012). Strengthening the understanding of the interlinkages between global and national energy policymaking remains an important challenge in research on global energy governance (see also Sovacool, 2014; Van de Graaf & Colgan, 2015).

The governance structure on (renewable) energy remains highly fragmented, with different aspects dealt with by different bureaucratic silos and analyzed by separate groups of experts and policymakers. Several authors emphasize that the fragmented structure of global energy governance leads to an increased need for coordination (see, for example, Dubash & Florini, 2011; Falkner, 2014; Florini & Sovacool, 2009, 2011; Goldthau & Sovacool, 2012; Lesage, Van de Graaf, & Westphal, 2010). Yet, different understandings, languages, and expertise make communication between different actors and governance spheres difficult (Dubash & Florini, 2011). Fragmentation occurs along two major lines: between different energy sources and between different issue areas. International organizations and networks rarely cover the whole range of energy sources, but instead concentrate on selected energy sources. As a consequence, there is no holistic approach to energy-related issues in global governance: "To date, there is no single venue for international discussions on energy issues. There is no World Energy Organization. Instead, global energy governance is fragmented and dispersed into a patchwork of various overlapping and sometimes overtly competing organizations" (Lesage et al., 2010, p. 51). According to Florini and Sovacool (2011) and Dubash and Florini (2011), the major policy actors in global energy governance are therefore failing to address complex and interconnected energy challenges adequately, including the trade-offs between different objectives of energy policymaking. Cherp, Jewell, and Goldthau (2011) add that global efforts to enhance energy security, energy access, and climate protection are not coordinated but instead build on three largely autonomous governance arenas, characterized by different origins, paradigms, and policy actors. Actors in related issue areas, such as climate protection, might not even be aware of the side effects their actions have on energy issues. Therefore, decisions made in other arenas often shape energy policies in an uncoordinated way (Dubash & Florini, 2011; Falkner, 2014). Future research on global energy governance needs to address how to improve coordination and coherence.

A very important, but still under-researched area in global energy governance pertains to the contested nature of knowledge and social understandings in global energy governance (see Roehrkasten, 2015). The creation and diffusion of knowledge and social understandings are important fields of action for the international organizations and initiatives dealing with renewables on a global scale, confirming the assertion of Breitmeier, Young, and Zürn (2006) that transboundary cooperation not only is focused on solving transboundary problems, but also involves encouraging new thinking about transboundary issues. This also entails struggles over the prerogative of interpretation, as the relationship between IEA and IRENA reveals. However, most global governance approaches assume the existence of an unambiguously "given" reality (on this critique, see Avant, Finnemore, & Sell, 2010; Barnett & Duvall, 2005; Overbeek et al., 2010). They thus miss one important aspect of political action at the global level: global governance involves heterogeneous groups of actors with highly diverse backgrounds and views; the varying levels of influence of actors determine whose ideas prevail in the end. Creating and structuring knowledge and social understandings is an important way of exercising power in global governance, as it influences what policymakers and researchers consider "real" or "relevant." Against this background, it would for example be very interesting to investigate if the IEA has deliberately underestimated the potential of renewables and to what extent the outcomes of its analyses are influenced by its member-states.

Last but not least, the rising influence of emerging and developing countries will have important repercussions on global energy governance and related research. The comprehensive analysis of global governance in the realm of renewable energies (Roehrkasten, 2015) reveals that the old North-South paradigm still plays an important role, even though it does not align with new realities. This old paradigm builds on North-South flows of finance and technical cooperation, which also implies North-South flows of ideas and knowledge. Likewise, Sovacool (2014) demonstrates in his analysis of the national affiliation of energy studies journal authors from 1999 to 2013 that 87% of all authors were based in either North America or Europe. This certainly undermines the capacity of energy research to adequately reflect the heterogeneity of backgrounds and views that need to be taken into account when shaping the future direction of a global energy transition. Such a regional bias is particularly problematic for global governance research, as analyses that concentrate on the "common good" easily lose sight of the fact that what is perceived as the "common good" may look very different, depending on the perspective of the perceiver. Therefore, an important task for future research is not only to improve the understanding of new actors in global energy governance, but also to become more diverse itself.

CONCLUSION

Since the beginning of the millennium, global renewable energy capacities have experienced impressive growth. Hydropower has been the most prevalent renewable energy source so far, but wind and solar energy account for the highest growth rates. Renewable energy capacities are increasing in all regions of the world, and emerging economies today are taking the lead in global renewable energy investments. Despite the growth in renewable energy capacities, however, global energy supply is still dominated by fossil fuels—indeed, the fossil-fuel share in global primary energy demand has not decreased since 1990. The expansion of renewables has been most advanced in electricity generation, moreover; the transport and heating/cooling sectors are lagging behind. So, it is far too early to affirm that a global energy transition toward renewables is already happening. However, such a transition is urgently needed in order for the international community to reach the goals of the Paris Agreement and the SDGs. To accelerate the global expansion of renewables, further energy research is needed to improve our understanding of existing drivers and barriers and to find context-specific and practical, implementable solutions.

At the same time, renewables have started to move from the sidelines to the center stage of global energy governance. A number of initiatives for transboundary cooperation on renewables have been launched, the creation of IRENA being the most notable. The brain and main engine behind IRENA's creation has been Germany, a global frontrunner in the promotion of an energy transition. To the surprise of many, IRENA's headquarters are based in the OPEC member-state the United Arab Emirates. This illustrates an important policy shift: while fossil-fuel-rich countries have for a long time blocked global action on renewables, many nowadays also invest in renewables. In addition, around the world, energy is increasingly viewed in its global dimensions. Strengthening the understanding of the linkages between global and national energy policymaking remains an important challenge for future research. Future research should furthermore investigate how to improve coordination and coherence in a fragmented global governance structure and address a very important but still under-researched area: the contested nature of knowledge and social understandings of global energy governance. Gaining a better understanding of new policy actors from the emerging and developing world is a crucial building block of this endeavor. However, this can only be achieved if energy research itself becomes more diverse.

Notes

1. Data for renewable electricity generation are not yet available for the year 2015.
2. Significant capacity additions in solar energy only started in 2008. The expansion of wind energy started earlier.
3. All data cited in this section are based on IRENA, Data and Statistics, http://resourceirena .irena.org/gateway/
4. IRENA, Data and Statistics, http://resourceirena.irena.org/gateway/
5. Please note that the data on renewable energy investments exclude large hydropower. To the author's knowledge, there are no publicly available data on renewable energy investments including large hydropower.
6. Data are based on joint analysis of IRENA, Frankfurt School UNEP Centre, and Bloomberg New Energy Finance. They are available on IRENA, Data and Statistics, http://resourceirena.irena.org/gateway/
7. Information on the prevailing renewable energy technologies in the countries is based on IRENA, Data and Statistics, http://resourceirena.irena.org/gateway/
8. SE4All, Our mission, http://www.se4all.org/our-mission
9. SE4All, Our mission, http://www.se4all.org/our-mission
10. For a comprehensive list of environmental sustainability indicators for bioenergy see Global Bioenergy Partnership (2011).
11. Next to its 150 members, a further 27 governments are in the process of accession. See IRENA, membership, http://www.irena.org/menu/index.aspx?mnu=cat&PriMenuID=46 &CatID=67
12. IRENA, What we do, http://www.irena.org/Menu/index.aspx?PriMenuID=53&mnu=Pri
13. See Roehrkasten (2015): International Energy Policy: Shifting towards renewables, IASS Blog, available at http://blog.iass-potsdam.de/2015/11/international-energy-policy -shifting-towards-renewables/ On the changing role of the IEA, see also Heubaum & Biermann (2015) and Van de Graaf (2012b).
14. As mentioned earlier, IRENA and IEA data differ for example on the renewables share in global capacity additions in 2013. While IRENA (2014) states that the renewables share was 58%, the IEA in its World Energy Outlooks 2015 and 2016 speaks of a share of less than 50% in 2013 and claims that renewable energy capacity additions for the first time exceeded fossil and nuclear energy in 2014.
15. However, consistent underestimations of the expansion of renewables does not necessarily mean that this is done on purpose.
16. For a comprehensive analysis on the interlinkages between global environmental politics and energy, see Falkner (2014).
17. This subsection is based on Roehrkasten (2015) and Roehrkasten/Westphal (2013).

References

Araújo, K. (2014). The emerging field of energy transitions: Progress, challenges, and opportunities. *Energy Research & Social Science, 1,* , 112–121.

Avant, D. D., Finnemore, M., & Sell, S. K. (2010). Conclusion: Authority, legitimacy, and accountability in global politics. In D. D. Avant, M. Finnemore, & S. K. Sell (Eds.), *Who governs the globe?* (pp. 356–370). Cambridge: Cambridge University Press.

Barnett, M., & Duvall, R. (2005). Power in global governance. In M. Barnett & R. Duvall (Eds.), *Power in global governance* (pp. 1–32). Cambridge: Cambridge University Press.

Breitmeier, H., Young, O. R., & Zürn, M. (2006). Analyzing international environmental regimes: From case study to database. Cambridge, MA: MIT Press.

Cherp, A., Jewell, J., & Goldthau, A. (2011). Governing global energy: Systems, transitions, complexity. *Global Policy*, 2(1), 75–88.

China Water Risk. (2016). Rare earths: Shades of grey—Can China continue to fuel our clean and smart future? Retrieved from http://chinawaterrisk.org/wp-content/uploads/2016/07/CWR-Rare-Earths-Shades-Of-Grey-2016-ENG.pdf

Colgan, J. (2009). The International Energy Agency: Challenges for the 21st century. *GPPi Policy Papers Series*, 6. Retrieved from http://www.gppi.net/fileadmin/user_upload/media/pub/2009/Colgan_2009_The_International_Energy.pdf

Dubash, N. K., & Florini, A. (2011). Mapping global energy governance. *Global Policy*, 2, 6–18.

Falkner, R. (2014). Global environmental politics and energy: Mapping the research agenda. *Energy Research & Social Science*, 1, 188–197.

Florini, A. (2008). Global governance and energy. *CAG Working Paper Series*, 1.

Florini, A., & Sovacool, B. K. (2009). Who governs energy? The challenges facing global energy governance. *Energy Policy*, 37(12), 5239–5248.

Florini, A., & Sovacool, B. K. (2011). Bridging the gaps in global energy governance. *Global Governance*, 17, 57–74.

Global Bioenergy Partnership. (2011, December 20). The Global bioenergy partnership sustainability indicators for bioenergy. Retrieved from http://www.globalbioenergy.org/fileadmin/user_upload/gbep/docs/Indicators/Report_HYPERLINK_updated_CM_25-05-2017.pdf

Goldthau, A., & Sovacool, B. K. (2012). The uniqueness of the energy security, justice, and governance problem. *Energy Policy*, 41, 232–240.

Gupta, J. (2012). Global energy governance in the twenty-first century: Challenges and opportunities. In M. P. Amneh & Y. Guang (Eds.), *Secure oil and alternative energy: The geopolitics of energy paths of China and the European Union*(pp. 427–447). Leiden; Boston: Brill.

Heubaum, H., & Biermann, F. (2015). Integrating global energy and climate governance: The changing role of the International Energy Agency. *Energy Policy*, 87, 229–239.

Hirschl, B. (2009). International renewable energy policy: Between marginalization and initial approaches. *Energy Policy*, 37, 4407–4416.

IEA. (2014). *World energy outlook 2014*. Paris: International Energy Agency (IEA).

IEA. (2015a). *World energy outlook 2015*. Paris: International Energy Agency (IEA).

IEA. (2015b). *Special report on climate change*. Paris: International Energy Agency (IEA).

IEA (2016a). *World energy outlook 2016*. Paris: International Energy Agency (IEA).

IEA. (2016b). *World energy investment*. Paris: International Energy Agency (IEA).

IEA. (2016c). Energy and air pollution. *World energy outlook special report*. Paris: International Energy Agency (IEA). Paris

IISD. (2002). Summary of the World Summit on Sustainable Development: 26 August–4 September 2002. *Earth Negotiation Bulletin*, 22(51).

IISD. (2007). Summary of the Fifteenth Session of the Commission on Sustainable Development: 30 April–11 May 2007. *Earth Negotiation Bulletin*, 5(254).

IRENA. (2014). *REThinking energy: Towards a new power system*. Abu Dhabi: International Renewable Energy Agency (IRENA).

IRENA. (2015). *Renewable power generation costs in 2014*. Abu Dhabi: International Renewable Energy Agency (IRENA).

IRENA. (2016a). *The power to change: Solar and wind cost reduction potential to 2025*. Abu Dhabi: International Renewable Energy Agency (IRENA).

IRENA. (2016b). *REmap: Roadmap for a renewable energy future, 2016 edition*. Abu Dhabi: International Renewable Energy Agency (IRENA).

Karlsson-Vinkhuyzen, S. I. (2010). The United Nations and global energy governance: Past challenges, future choices. *Global Change, Peace & Security, 22*(2), 175–195.

Karlsson-Vinkhuyzen, S. I., Jollands, N., & Staudt, L. (2012). Global governance for sustainable energy: The contribution of a global public goods approach. *Ecological Economics, 83*, 11–18.

Lesage, D., Van de Graaf, T., & Westphal, K. (2010). Global energy governance in a multipolar world. Farnham, UK: Ashgate.

Leverett, F. (2010). Consuming energy: Rising powers, the international energy agency, and the global energy architecture. In A. S. Alexandroff & A. F. Cooper (Eds.), *Rising states, rising institutions: Challenges for global governance* (pp. 240–265). Baltimore, MD: Brookings Institution Press.

Metayer, M., Breyer, C., & Fell, H.-J. (2015). The projections for the future and quality in the past of the World Energy Outlook for solar PV and other renewable energy technologies. Energy Watch Group and the Lappeenranta University of Technology. Retrieved from https://www.lut.fi/documents/10633/70751/The-projections-for-the-future-and-quality-in-the-past-of-the-World-Energy-Outlook-for-solar-PV-and-other-renewable-energy-technologies-EWG-WEO-Study-2015.pdf

Najam, A., & Cleveland, C. J. (2005). Energy and sustainable development at global environmental summits: An evolving agenda. In L. Hens & B. Nath (Eds.), *The world summit on sustainable development: The Johannesburg Conference* (pp. 113–134). Dordrecht: Springer.

Overbeek, H., Dingwerth, K., Pattberg, P., & Compagnon, D. (2010). Forum: Global governance: Decline or maturation of an academic concept? *International Studies Review, 12*, 696–719.

Qader, M., & Roehrkasten, S. (2018). Renewable energy: A recent, but dynamic trend in the MENA region. In D. Jalilvand & K. Westphal (Eds.), The political and economic challenges of energy in the Middle East and North Africa. London: Routledge.

Quitzow, R. Roehrkasten, S., Jacobs, D., Bayer, B., Jamea, E. M., Waweru, Y., & Matschoss, P. (2016). *The future of Africa's energy supply*. IASS Study, Institute for Advanced Sustainability Studies (IASS), Potsdam.

Quitzow, R., Roehrkasten, S., & Jaenicke, M. (2016). *The German energy transition in international perspective*. IASS Study, Institute for Advanced Sustainability Studies (IASS), Potsdam.

REN21. (2016). *Renewables global status report*. Paris: Renewable Energy Policy Network for the 21st Century (REN21).

Roehrkasten, S. (2015). *Global governance on renewable energy*. Wiesbaden: Springer VS Research.

Roehrkasten, S., Schaeuble, D., & Helgenberger, S. (2016). *Secure and sustainable energy in a water-constrained world*. IASS Policy Brief 1/2016, Institute for Advanced Sustainability Studies (IASS), Potsdam.

Roehrkasten, S., & Steinbacher, K. (2016). Germany: Promoting an energiewende domestically and globally. In S. Roehrkasten, S. Thielges, & R. Quitzow (Eds.), *Sustainable energy in the G20* (pp. 51–56). IASS Study, Institute for Advanced Sustainability Studies (IASS), Potsdam.

Roehrkasten, S., Thielges, S., & Quitzow, R. (Eds.). (2016). *Sustainable Energy in the G20*. IASS Study, Institute for Advanced Sustainability Studies (IASS), Potsdam.

Roehrkasten, S., & Westphal, K. (2013). *IRENA and Germany's foreign renewable energy policy*. Working Paper, Stiftung Wissenschaft und Politik (SWP), Berlin .

Roehrkasten, S., & Westphal, K. (2016). The G20 and its role in global energy governance. In S. Roehrkasten, S. Thielges, & R. Quitzow (Eds.), *Sustainable energy in the G20* (pp. 12–18). IASS Study, Institute for Advanced Sustainability Studies (IASS), Potsdam.

Rowlands, I. H. (2005). Renewable energy and international politics. In P. Dauvergne (Ed.), *Handbook of global environmental politics* (pp. 78–94). Cheltenham, UK: Edward Elgar.

Sovacool, B. K. (2014). What are we doing here? Analyzing fifteen years of energy scholarship and proposing a social science research agenda. *Energy Research & Social Science, 1*, 1–29.

Stirling, A. (2014). Transforming power: Social science and the politics of energy choices. *Energy Research & Social Science, 1*, 83–95.

Suding, P. H., & Lempp, P. (2007). The multifaceted institutional landscape and processes of international renewable energy policy. *International Association for Energy Economics Newsletter*, Second Quarter, 4–9.

UNESCO. (2014). *Water and energy: The United Nations world water development report 2014*. Paris: United Nations Educational, Scientific and Cultural Organization (UNESCO).

UNESCO. (2015). *Water for a sustainable world: The United Nations world water development report 2015*. Paris: United Nations Educational, Scientific and Cultural Organization (UNESCO).

Urpelainen, J., & Van de Graaf, T. (2014). Your place or mine? Institutional capture and the creation of overlapping international institutions. *British Journal of Political Science, 45*, 799–827.

Urpelainen, J., & Van de Graaf, T. (2015). The International Renewable Energy Agency: A success story in institutional innovation? *International Environmental Agreements, 15*, 159–177.

Van de Graaf, T. (2012a). How IRENA is reshaping the global energy architecture. *European Energy Review, 29*. Retrieved from https://biblio.ugent.be/publication/7125631/file/7125632.pdf

Van de Graaf, T. (2012b). Obsolte or resurgent? The International Energy Agency in a changing global landscape, *Energy Policy, 48*, 233–241.

Van de Graaf, T. (2013a). Fragmentation in global energy governance: Explaining the creation of IRENA. *Global Environmental Politics, 13*(3), 14–33.

Van de Graaf, T. (2013b). *The politics and institutions of global energy governance*. New York: Palgrave Macmillan.

Van de Graaf, T., & Colgan, J. (2015). Global energy governance: A review and research agenda. *Palgrave Communications, 2*. Retrieved from https://www.nature.com/articles/palcomms201547.pdf

CHAPTER 26

....

TECHNOLOGICAL OPTIMISM IN CLIMATE MITIGATION

The Case of Carbon Capture and Storage

....

JENNIE C. STEPHENS AND NILS MARKUSSON

INTRODUCTION

....

SINCE anthropogenic climate change was first identified as a problem in need of mitigation (Marchetti, 1977; PSAC, 1965), technological changes, rather than social changes, have dominated both the scientific and political discourse on the issue. The presumption has been that technological innovation in energy and carbon management will be the primary mechanism for society to address climate change. As the transition to lower-carbon energy systems proceeds, technological innovation continues to be consistently prioritized in climate policy discourse, despite well-established recognition of the critical need for social, cultural, and institutional changes in reducing fossil-fuel reliance and transitioning toward more renewable-based energy systems.

The technological focus in climate mitigation relates to a broader societal phenomenon of technological optimism, which has been described as the assumption that technological developments will consistently perpetuate and sustain human civilization (Basiago, 1994). Technological optimism is a powerful cultural phenomenon with a long history. The current manifestation of technological optimism is rooted in a long-standing Western cultural tradition. The belief in technological progress as the primary measure of societal reform is so embedded in our culture that it shapes our very conception of history (Marx, 1982). Our shared assumptions of progress and commitment to instrumentalism go back at least as far as the Renaissance and the scientific revolution. Faith in the potential of technology to solve societal problems is not just about a generalized use value; technology also has a strong symbolic value. As such, technological optimism can obscure the scope for other, non-technical forms of societal changes and diminish the perceived potential for non-technical solutions to societal problems.

The term "technical fix" is frequently used by academics and activists to describe the application of a technological solution to a social problem, where a reductive problem definition leads to only a partial and superficial solution (Drengson, 1984; Rosner, 2004; Scott, 2011). First coined in the 1960s (Weinberg, 1966) as a pragmatic attempt to save the reputation of technology from the onslaught of anti-establishment critique, the notion of a technical fix was already couched in caveats by its creator, and soon was heavily critiqued by others. The main arguments have been that technical fixes are only ever partial or temporary and so risk just shifting or delaying the problem. They fail to address the need for deeper sociopolitical change and so are used to defend problematic entrenched political regimes. This line of argument is now so well established that the very term "technical fix" is now often used with a negative connotation (Sarewitz & Nelson, 2008). Despite these critiques, society continues to invest in the promises of technical fixes, as evidenced by climate policy and investment in carbon capture and storage (CCS).

Throughout the past 40–50 years of political discourse surrounding how to respond to climate change, the history of CCS technology provides an illustrative example of technological optimism. This chapter reviews this history to highlight how technological optimism and the perception of a "technical fix" inadvertently perpetuates the status quo by crowding out or postponing other climate mitigation responses, including social and cultural changes.

Carbon Capture and Storage: An Introduction to the Technology

CCS refers to a set of technologies designed to reduce CO_2 emissions from large point sources, including coal-fired power plants, by capturing the CO_2 and then storing the carbon in a reservoir other than the atmosphere. CCS incorporates various technologies associated with capturing and transporting CO_2 and storing the compressed gas. Most current conceptualizations of CCS focus on the potential of storing the CO_2 in underground geologic formations, although ocean storage and terrestrial storage have also been considered (de Figueiredo et al., 2002; IPCC, 2005).

A complete CCS system involving geologic carbon storage includes four basic steps with different technologies required for each step: (1) capture the CO_2 from a power plant or other concentrated source; (2) transport the CO_2 gas from the capture location to an appropriate storage location; (3) inject compressed CO_2 gas into a suitable underground formation; and (4) monitor the injected CO_2 to verify its storage. Technologies that are used commercially in other sectors are currently available for each of these components. Carbon dioxide capture technology is widely used in ammonia production and several other industrial manufacturing processes; CO_2 gas has been transported through pipelines and injected underground for decades, most notably in

West Texas, where it is used to enhance oil recovery (EOR) of wells with declining production (rather than to store). Several CO_2 storage demonstration projects (including Sleipner in the North Sea and Weyburn in Saskatchewan, Canada) have been injecting millions of tons of CO_2 underground for several years. Yet, the integration and scaling up of these technologies to demonstrate CO_2 capture and storage with a power plant has been slower and more expensive than many had projected (Reiner, 2016).

An additional important technological consideration for CCS is the possibility of combining bio-energy with CCS (BECCS), which offers unique climate mitigation potential because it could actually draw down and reduce CO_2 already accumulated in the atmosphere (Vergragt et al., 2011). If carbon is captured and stored from a power plant that is burning biomass, there could be net movement of CO_2 from the atmosphere to geologic formations. While CCS coupled with coal or natural gas offers possible reductions in CO_2emissions, CCS coupled with bio-energy has been considered a negative emissions technology because it has potential to reduce atmospheric CO_2 concentrations (Anderson and Peters, 2016; Azar et al., 2010).

History of Carbon Capture
and Storage

The concept of engineering systems to deliberately capture and store CO_2 has evolved in the past 20 years from a relatively obscure idea to an increasingly recognized set of climate change mitigation options. As the need to reduce greenhouse gas emissions is increasingly accepted as a societal objective to mitigate climate change, reducing atmospheric concentrations of CO_2, the greenhouse gas with the largest impact on the climate system, has become an international priority (Anderson & Peters, 2016). Given the societal challenges of rapidly reorganizing society to function without fossil fuels, technological options that enable a continued use of fossil fuels while reducing CO_2 emissions from fossil fuel burning or drawing down atmospheric CO_2 concentrations have broad appeal (Anderson & Peters, 2016).

Government Investment

The appeal of the potential of CCS to reconcile continued fossil-fuel use with CO_2 emissions reductions has led to large government investments to advance CCS technology. Many of the countries that have invested the most in CCS are countries whose energy systems are heavily reliant on coal, including the United States, Australia, Canada, and China (Tjernshaugen, 2008; Meadowcroft & Langhelle, 2009; Torvanger & Meadowcroft, 2011). Norway has also been a major investor in CCS, not because the country is heavily reliant on coal but because of its ambitious climate policy ambitions and national-level involvement in oil and gas extraction in the North Sea (Tjernshaugen & Langhelle, 2009). The Global CCS Institute (GCCSI), which maintains a website with updated descriptions of current CCS projects around the world, reports that there are 15 large-scale CCS project in operation, 7 others under construction, and an additional 18 in various stages of planning and development (GCCSI, 2014). Among the current priorities for advancing CCS are enhancing the capture process to reduce the energy intensity and cost of capture, demonstrating underground CO_2 capture in a geologically diverse set of geologic formations, and demonstrating and deploying integrated and scaled-up CCS power-plant systems that allow for "learning-by-doing" (Watson et al., 2014).

Interest and investment in CCS have resulted in an international CCS community of scientists, engineers, and energy policy experts working on CCS who have become strong advocates for sustaining government investment (Stephens et al., 2011). To perpetuate CCS advancement, the CCS community has developed training and recruitment efforts (Gjefsen, 2017).

Slow Pace of Demonstration

The high price of CCS demonstration has slowed down the pace of CCS advancement, but this has not eliminated the technological optimism (Martínez Arranz, 2016; Reiner, 2016). Despite a period of strong CCS support, investment, and excitement in the first decade of the 2000s, it was not until October 2014 that the world's first commercial-scale demonstration of a coal-fired power plant with CCS began operation—the Boundary Dam Project in Saskatchewan (Black, 2014). This project, a 110 MW retrofit of a coal-fired power plant, has been viewed by many as a milestone for CCS development. In the United States, a US$5 billion coal-fired power plant project with CCS in Kemper County, Mississippi, came online in 2015 (Goldenberg, 2014), yet expensive delays and cancellations of multiple other CCS demonstrations projects, including the Peterhead project in Scotland (Shell, 2014) and the Barendrecht project in the Netherlands (Feenstra et al., 2010), illustrate the multiple challenges of CCS implementation.

So for over a decade, governments around the world have invested billions of dollars in developing CCS technology with the hope of reconciling sustained use of fossil fuels with climate mitigation objectives (Markusson et al., 2012; Torvanger & Meadowcroft, 2011). A peak in interest in the technology during the first decade of the 2000s was followed by very slow progress for CCS demonstration, as well as international climate policy generally (Martínez Arranz, 2016). Carbon prices remained low or absent, and only a few CCS projects materialized (Scott et al., 2013). While future carbon reduction potential from CCS continues to feature prominently in climate policy modeling and is assumed by many to be a technology critical to "solving" climate change (Anderson and Peters, 2016, IEA, 2013, GCCSI, 2013) scepticism about the high costs of CCS and the uncertain societal benefits are widespread (Greenpeace International, 2008, Goldenberg, 2014, Stephens, 2014).

Bio-Energy with Carbon Capture and Storage (BECCS) and Carbon Capture Utilization and Storage (CCUS)

As the controversial future of CCS continues to be debated (Reiner, 2016), two variations on CCS configurations have gained attention and have impacted CCS development: bio-energy with CCS (BECCS) and carbon capture utilization and storage (CCUS). BECCS has been particularly influential in climate policy because this is one of the most technologically feasible options for actually reducing the concentration of CO_2 that is already in the atmosphere (i.e., producing negative emissions). Although decoupling CCS research from fossil fuels and expanding CCS research related to bio-energy may reduce controversy regarding CCS investments because BECCS is more explicitly focused on the long-term climate mitigation potential of CCS, most CCS research and investments remain focused on CCS with fossil fuels rather than CCS with bio-energy. This is despite very optimistic assumptions about the feasibility of BECCS made in scenarios informing international climate policy; the integrated models used to specify details for the 2015 international Paris climate agreement assume a significant amount of future negative emissions, with BECCS technology assumed to be a predominant contributor (Anderson & Peters, 2016).

The concept of carbon capture utilization and storage (CCUS) emerged in the United States as CCS advocates began emphasizing *utilization* as a pathway to CCS development after the 2009 failure of key legislation that could have sparked a carbon trading system. Utilization includes enhanced oil recovery (EOR) using captured CO_2, a practice largely at odds with climate mitigation. Advocates of CCS in the United States promoted the acronym "CCUS" (carbon capture utilization and storage) to emphasize the commercial viability of CCS-related technologies applied primarily to EOR (Atlantic Council, 2012). The CCUS reframing was an attempt to maintain momentum with the hope that technology development would spillover back to CCS (Endres et al., 2016). The US government took several steps to support this reframing, and CCUS became established as the official US policy lingo in CCS-related efforts. In 2012, the Department of Energy renamed its annual meeting on CCS the "Annual Carbon Capture, Utilization and Sequestration Conference," while the US-led, ministerial-level international Carbon Sequestration Leadership Forum instituted a CO_2 utilization taskforce (Gjefsen, 2013), spreading the term to other countries.

The CCUS reframing hinged on the scope for revenue from enhanced oil (or gas) extraction to help finance development of capture technology, rather than emissions markets or other climate policy funding mechanisms. Adding monitoring, measurement, and verification of injected CO_2 for EOR could conceivably enable the incorporation of EOR operations into emissions markets mechanisms, which would have the effect of channeling climate policy support toward fossil extraction. Technology optimism is here really pushed to its limits, making its role in defending ongoing industrial concerns easy to spot.

TECHNOLOGICAL OPTIMISM
AND CCS CONTROVERSY

Given that the main human activity contributing to climate change is the burning of fossil fuels for energy, energy production and use are central to climate mitigation efforts. Technological optimism has led to a stronger focus in climate mitigation on technological innovation than on social innovations that could reduce energy demand (Gallagher et al., 2012; Holdren, 2006).

This focus on energy technology has led to renewed interest in renewables and nuclear energy framed as low-carbon options, but also in CCS and its promise to decarbonize fossil fuel energy.

While nuclear technology and some renewables have already been deployed at scale, CCS requires further development and demonstration efforts. In this sense, a positive outlook on CCS technology in particular requires an additional measure of optimism.

The optimistic view of the potential of CCS to contribute to climate mitigation has provided powerful motivation for large public and private investments in CCS technology. But continued investment in CCS continues to be controversial as the scale and urgency of climate change grow and CCS advancement continues to be slow and expensive (Reiner, 2016). Although CCS is still considered by some to be a critical climate-mitigation technology, especially the BECCS potential, others view CCS investment as an expensive fossil-fuel subsidy that could inadvertently perpetuate, rather than reduce, fossil-fuel reliance (Greenpeace International, 2008; Stephens, 2014).

As energy and climate experts explore future scenarios that result in lower CO_2 concentrations in the atmosphere to attempt to keep global temperatures below an increase of 2°C, CCS remains a critically important technology (IEA, 2008, 2014). With dominant status-quo assumptions regarding a continued trajectory of fossil-fuel use, achieving climate goals without CCS is very difficult (IEA, 2014). However, the dominant assumptions regarding continued fossil-fuel consumption are increasingly being challenged. Analysis by the International Energy Agency (IEA) shows that if CCS is not widely deployed, the only way that emissions can be reduced to prevent even less than a 2°C warming is if more than two-thirds of current proven fossil fuel reserves are kept in the ground (IEA, 2014). While some view sustained fossil-fuel consumption as inevitable and consider the possibility of not using proven fossil reserves as an impossibility, others are working toward and advocating for a future in which fossil-fuel consumption will be drastically reduced and fossil-fuel resources will be kept in the ground (McKibben, 2016). Controversy surrounding CCS technology is due, in large part, not to the technological feasibility of this approach, but to differences in assumptions regarding the potential for change in future fossil-fuel extraction and consumption patterns.

The emergence of the possibility of CCS in the last 20 years has enabled many fossil fuel-dependent actors, particularly individuals and institutions in coal-dependent regions of the world, to stop denying the existence of climate change. Because CCS provides the possibility of continuing coal use while also addressing climate change, CCS technology has influenced climate-change policy providing additional justification for pricing and trading carbon (Stephens, 2013). And with recent increases in natural gas reliance, CCS similarly offers the possibility of reconciling climate mitigation goals with growth in natural gas power plants. Indeed, the promise of CCS to reconcile fossil-fuel use with the climate change imperative has been instrumental in bringing countries including the United States on board with international climate policy agreements (Narita, 2012). As the climate threat grows, and mitigation efforts progress slowly, the belief in such reconciliation is ever harder to sustain. Many current scenarios that keep warming within tolerable levels now rely not only on CCS technology to mitigate emissions, but also on BECCS technology drawing down CO_2 from the atmosphere.

CHALLENGES TO CCS OPTIMISM

Despite the technological optimism surrounding CCS, various specific characteristics of CCS are challenging that optimism. The energy penalty, the amount of additional energy required to capture and store CO_2, is one recurring challenge to the optimism. This energy penalty has been estimated to be about 30%, within a range from 11% to 40% (House et al., 2009). This means roughly that for every three coal-fired power plants utilizing CCS, an additional power plant would be required simply to supply the energy needed to capture and store the CO_2. The magnitude of this energy penalty (including even the lower estimates) is so high that it is difficult to imagine a future scenario in which generating and then consuming this much additional energy to enable CCS would actually make sense.

Another set of CCS characteristics that challenges optimistic future visions relates to political difficulties in managing and preventing leakage of the underground storage of CO_2 for thousands of years after it is injected (Wilson et al., 2007). Optimism about the potential of CCS is based primarily on research on technical feasibility, but less attention has been paid to the sociopolitical requirements of regulating and enforcing long-term monitoring and maintenance of CO_2 stored underground (Wilson et al., 2003). Global institutional structures with the capacity to enforce liability for thousands (or even hundreds) of years do not exist. Even with nuclear waste, we have not developed a long-term international institution. And political instability, corruption, and inevitable tensions among countries create severe and constant risks of any proposed global CO_2 storage management scheme.

The health and safety risks of perpetuating the use of fossil fuels represent another set of challenges to CCS optimism (Muller, 2011). Fossil-fuel power plants result in major health and safety risks to both the communities surrounding the plant (including water and air pollution) and those impacted by fossil-fuel extraction (including coal mining, hydraulic fracturing for natural gas extraction, and fossil-fuel transport) (Markandya & Wilkinson, 2007). Strong public concern about the health and safety risks of storing CO_2 underground has derailed several large-scale CCS demonstration projects in the past four years, including the Vattenfall project in Germany and the Barendrecht project in the Netherlands (GCCSI, 2014). In addition, concern about earthquakes triggered by the injection of large volumes of CO_2 underground is motivating enhanced technical understanding of the risks of leakage (Zoback & Gorelick, 2012).

CCS optimism and the vision of CCS as an essential part of climate mitigation has also enabled complacency about the growing dangers of sustained fossil fuel dependence (Fehrenbacher, 2016; Princen et al., 2015; Stephens, 2014). By reinforcing fossil-fuel infrastructure, these investments could be promoting the notion that our current fossil-based energy systems can be safely continued. CCS skepticism is often coupled with concern that large government investments in CCS are slowing down the transition to renewable energy. If the support devoted to CCS technology development was invested, instead, in facilitating and encouraging the transition toward renewable-based energy, this could contribute to more rapid and dramatic energy-system changes. Investments in CCS also have been recognized as one of many fossil fuel subsidies (Victor, 2009), so CCS investments are also viewed by some as incentivizing continued use of fossil fuels.

The high costs and long time frame of CCS provide additional challenges to the optimistic view. Despite over a decade of investment, widespread CCS deployment remains a distant and expensive possibility (Boretti, 2013). While some view the Canadian Boundary Dam Project, the first full-scale power plant with CCS that came on line in October 2014, as a historic demonstration of the potential of CCS, others see this project as reflecting the improbability of CCS ever becoming commercially viable due to the exorbitant costs that required huge government subsidies, and the prolonged time frame for this first full-scale demonstration plant. The total project cost has been estimated at US$1.24 billion, with some being contributed by the federal and provincial governments and costs being recovered by selling the captured CO_2 for EOR.

For skeptics, the slow pace and high cost of demonstrating CCS result in a problematically long time horizon for scaling up CCS deployment to the point that any significant climate mitigation benefits can be realized (Watson et al., 2012). Though CCS has often been described as a "bridging" technology (Hansson & Bryngelsson, 2009) to provide CO_2 reductions during the transition to renewable-based energy systems, the past decade of slow progress suggests to some that building the CCS bridge may take longer than the transition to renewables (Boretti, 2013).

In the current global economic situation, government expenditure of the magnitude required to advance CCS is becoming more difficult to justify. A single CCS demonstration plant is estimated to cost on the order of US$1 billion, and those advocating more investment in CCS are asking governments to spend US$3–4 billion each year for the next decade (IEA, 2013; McKinsey, 2008).

Promises of rolled-out CCS plants also have come with promises of reduced costs, due to technological learning. One potential contribution of this Boundary Dam project is badly needed evidence about what the actual operating costs of CCS will be. So far there have been reports about cost over-runs and technical problems, but also denials of this by the company (Austen, 2016; Johnstone, 2016), so it is not yet clear whether costs are going down, or whether costs are actually increasing.

Conclusions: Technological Optimism and a Controversial, Uncertain Future for Carbon Capture and Storage

The case of CCS illustrates both the appeal and the challenges of technological optimism. The appeal lies largely in the enabling power of stability; CCS provides a technological vision for mitigating climate while continuing to rely on fossil fuels and sustaining high levels of energy consumption. Despite multiple practical near-term challenges to CCS advancement, the technologically optimistic vision of CCS has persisted. A major societal risk is that this technical optimism overshadows and detracts from societal attention and investment in other non-technical strategies for confronting climate change. Transitioning away from fossil fuels toward lower-carbon renewable-based systems not only demands technical change, but also involves social and cultural change. Given the high costs, slow pace, and long time horizon for realizing actual greenhouse gas reductions from CCS, investments in reducing energy demand and expanding renewable energy technologies are likely to offer more concrete, near-term societal benefits that would be less risky than investing in CCS.

Advocates and Skeptics

Advocating for government support for CCS technology has become a passionate priority for many deeply committed, technologically optimistic energy professionals. With growing international realization of the magnitude of CO_2 reductions that is required, a reliance on optimism surrounding BECCS as a negative emissions technology has grown since the Paris climate accord. This optimism makes sense for those who are unable to envision deeper social change and those who are unwilling to consider the possibility of drastically reducing fossil-fuel combustion. Given all the forces contributing to multiple types of fossil-fuel "lock-in," a mainstream energy policy perspective assumes an inevitability of continued fossil-fuel reliance due to its low cost, abundance, and reliability. Justifications for this perspective include the potential for fossil fuels to expand electricity access in the developing world, provide unparalleled economic development opportunities, and sustain societal stability. One problem with this narrative is that the extremely negative social, economic, environmental, and human health impacts of coal and other fossil fuels (Muller, 2011) are dismissed and are not explicitly acknowledged.

As the risks and impacts of climate change become more apparent, accelerating a transition away from fossil fuels to renewable-based energy systems has become a priority not only to mitigate climate change, but also to enhance resilience as communities prepare for and adapt to climate change. During this transition, all energy investments must be carefully considered with regard to their long-term influence on energy-system change. As the world attempts to prepare for dramatic changes ahead, deep societal change—far beyond technological innovation—is in desperate need of consideration. Long-held assumptions regarding the inevitability of future fossil-fuel extraction, energy consumption, and infinite continued growth need to be re-evaluated. If the political imperative to strive toward perpetual economic growth was altered to align with actual physical constraints (D'Alisa et al., 2014), our dominant material culture could be changed and perhaps the foundational faith on high-technology solutions would be diminished.

Skepticism about the societal value of investing billions of dollars in CCS, an expensive fossil-fuel-focused technology, has grown. The private sector has recognized the many risks of CCS and has only been willing to invest in CCS in conjunction with rare strong government investment. And emissions markets are (perhaps inevitably) too weak to drive deployment (let alone development).

The Future of CCS: Relying on Uncertainty

Despite these developments, the future of CCS remains uncertain and controversial (Reiner, 2016). As urgency in climate mitigation grows, some activists are calling for different assumptions about fossil-fuel extraction, energy-consumption patterns, and how to facilitate and accelerate the transition to renewable-based energy systems (McKibben, 2016). Others have made the case that CCS for industrial facilities and BECCS is what is important to prioritize now, rather than CCS for power generation (Martínez Arranz, 2016). Depending on how these societal discussions develop, priorities related to advancing CCS could change. Even if CCS advancement is justified in terms of the potential of negative emissions with BECCS technology, the large scale of biomass that would be required to substantially draw down atmospheric CO_2 is very problematic (Anderson & Peters, 2016).

From a technological perspective, it has been suggested that the infrastructural requirements and inflexibility of CCS could exacerbate "technological lock-in" to fossil-fuel use (Meadowcroft & Langhelle, 2009; Vergragt et al., 2011). From a political perspective, the sunk costs associated with the amount of money already invested in CCS also creates "political lock-in." As discussed, CCS is also deeply embedded in the use of emissions markets policies and key policy-supporting scenario production exercises. For governments and institutions that have already invested millions or billions of dollars and considerable political and cultural capital to advance CCS, continued support appears likely, despite growing skepticism about the societal risks of advancing CCS (Pollak et al., 2011).

As hype and investment in CCS continue to decline (Martínez Arranz, 2016), the future of this technology is becoming increasingly uncertain (Scott et al., 2013). The optimism, eagerness, and excitement surrounding CCS just 10 years ago (ACCSEPT, 2007; IPCC, 2005; McKinsey, 2008) have diminished, and expectations for large-scale demonstration projects (Coninck et al., 2009; Gibbins & Chalmers, 2008; Markusson et al., 2011) have plummeted. During this period of slow-down and reduced expectations, any continued investment in CCS must be focused on the long-term climate mitigation potential of the technology, and care must be taken to ensure that investments are no longer coupled with incentivizing and legitimizing prolonged fossil-fuel use.

Beyond CCS

It is easy to criticize CCS for being a technical fix, and as being only a partial and temporary solution, at the very best. And most proponents would readily acknowledge this, talking of it as a bridging solution that buys time for the development of other solutions, and as one choice from a portfolio of mitigation options. As discussed earlier, there are serious question marks around CCS as even a temporary and partial solution to global warming. But the technical fix promise is a powerful one, and countries throughout the world appear to be relying more and more on such promises.

With regard to the daunting challenge of climate change, as CCS deployment at scale has proven to be more difficult and more expensive than previously assumed, other technological fixes to climate change are now being considered (Markusson et al., 2017). This includes technologies that aim to cool the planet to counterbalance global warming, so-called solar radiation-management technologies. Some of these are potentially very fast-acting and powerful, but also inherently very difficult to develop safely, and they are intensely controversial.

At the same time, it is important to acknowledge that renewable energy technologies are another form of technological fix, and the renewable energy transition also relies on technological optimism to transform energy generation. A climate-mitigation strategy that would clearly not be considered a technological fix is drastic reduction of energy consumption (Mitchell, 2012); there is huge potential for social change regarding patterns of energy use (Shove, 2010) and expectations regarding how much energy is needed (Dietz, 2015; Holt, 2012).

As humanity grapples with how to appropriately and effectively respond to climate change, the relative reliance on technological versus social innovation is contested. While technological advancements will clearly play a role, the potential and need for non-technical social changes, for example in energy-consumption patterns and energy-demand expectations, will persist. The case of CCS demonstrates the powerful influence of a potential "technical fix" on climate policy.

References

ACCSEPT. (2007). The ACCSEPT Project: Summary of the main findings and key recommendations. Retrieved from https://www.researchgate.net/profile/Paul_Upham/publication/238102581_Summary_of_the_Main_Findings_and_Key_Recommendations/links/00b49529861e43f84a000000/Summary-of-the-Main-Findings-and-Key-Recommendations.pdf?origin=publication_list

Anderson, K., & Peters, G. (2016). The trouble with negative emissions. *Science*, *354*, 182–183.

Atlantic Council. (2012). *Issue brief: US policy shift to carbon capture, utilization, and storage driven by carbon dioxide enhanced oil recovery*. Washington, DC: Atlantic Council.

Austen, I. (2016, March 29). Technology to make clean energy from coal is stumbling in practice. *New York Times*. Retrieved from https://www.nytimes.com/2016/03/30/business/energy-environment/technology-to-make-clean-energy-from-coal-is-stumbling-in-practice.html

Azar, C., Lindgren, K., Obersteiner, M., Riahl, K., Vuuren, D. P. V., Elzen, K. M. G. J., Mollersten, K., & Larson, E. D. 2010. The feasibility of low CO_2 concentration targets and the role of bioenergy with carbon capture and storage (BECCS). *Climatic Change*, *100*, 195–202.

Basiago, A. D. (1994). The limits of technological optimism. *Environmentalist*, *14*, 17–22.

Black, P. (2014). Worlds first coal-fired power plant CCS operation. *Process Industry Informer*. Retrieved from http://www.processindustryinformer.com/latest-news/news-events/industry-news/worlds-first-coal-fired-power-plant-ccs-operation

Boretti, A. (2013). Is there any real chance for carbon capture to be beneficial to the environment? *Energy Policy*, *57*, 107–108.

Coninck, H. D., Stephens, J. C., & Metz, B. (2009). Global learning on carbon capture and storage: A call for strong international cooperation on CCS demonstration. *Energy Policy*, *37*, 2161–2165.

D'Alisa, G., Dmaria, F., & Kallis, G. (2014). *Degrowth: A vocabulary for a new era*. New York: Routledge.

De Figueiredo, M. A., Reiner, D. M., & Herzog, H. J. (2002). Ocean carbon sequestration: A case study in public and institutional perceptions. *Sixth International Conference on Greenhouse Gas Control Technologies*, October 1–4, 2002, Kyoto, Japan.

Dietz, T. (2015). Altruism, self-interest, and energy consumption. *Proceedings of the National Academy of Sciences*, *112*, 1654–1655.

Drengson, A. (1984). The sacred and the limits of the technological fix. *Zygon*, *19*, 259–275.

Endres, D., Cozen, B., O'Byrne, M., Feldpausch-Parker, A. M., & Peterson, T. R. (2016). Putting the U in carbon capture and storage: Rhetorical boundary negotiation within the CCS/CCUS scientific community. *Journal of Applied Communication Research*, *44*, 362–380.

Feenstra, C. F. J., Mikunda, T., & Brunsting, S. (2010). *What happened in Barendrecht? Case study on the planned onshore carbon dioxide storage in Barendrecht, the Netherlands*. ECN and Global CCS Institute. Retrieved from http://admin.cottoncrc.org.au/files/files/pybx.pdf

Fehrenbacher, K. (2016). What Donald Trump didn't mention about clean coal. *Fortune*. Retrieved from http://fortune.com/2016/10/10/donald-trump-clean-coal/

Gallagher, K. S., Grübler, A., Kuhl, L., Nemet, G. & Wilson, C. (2012). The energy technology innovation system. *Annual Review of Environment and Resources, 37,* 137–162.

GCCSI. (2013). *Global status of CCS: Update Jan. 2013.* Canberra, Australia: Global CCS Institute.

GCCSI. (2014). *Projects website.* Retrieved from http://www.globalccsinstitute.com/projects /browse

Gibbins, J., & Chalmers, H. (2008). Preparing for global rollout: A "developed country first" demonstration programme for rapid CCS deployment. *Energy Policy, 36,* 501–507.

Gjefsen, M. D. (2013). Carbon cultures: Technology planning for energy and climate in the US and EU. *Science & Technology Studies, 26,* 63–81.

Gjefsen, M. D. (2017). Carfting the expert-advocate: Training and recruitment efforts in the carbon dioxide capture and storage community. *Innovation: The European Journal of Social Science Research, 30*(3), 259–282.

Goldenberg, S. (2014, March 12). Can Kemper become the first US power plant to use "clean coal"? *The Guardian.* Retrieved from http://www.theguardian.com/environment/2014/mar /12/kemper-us-power-plant-coal-carbon

Greenpeace International. (2008). False hope, why carbon capture and storage won't save the climate. Retrieved from http://www.greenpeace.org/international/Global/international /planet-2/report/2008/5/false-hope-executive-summary.pdf

Hansson, A., & Bryngelsson, M. (2009). Expert opinions on carbon dioxide capture and storage-A framing of uncertainties and possibilities. *Energy Policy, 37,* 2273–2282.

Holdren, J. P. (2006). The energy innovation imperative, addressing oil dependence, climate change, and other 21st century energy challenges. *Innovations, Technology, Governance & Globalization, 1,* 3–23.

Holt, D. B. (2012). Constructing sustainable consumption: From ethical values to the cultural transformation of unsustainable markets. *The ANNALS of the American Academy of Political and Social Science, 644.*

House, K. Z., Harvey, C. F., Aziz, M. J. & Schrag, D. P. (2009). The energy penalty of post-combustion CO_2 capture and storage and its implications for retrofitting the US installed base. *Energy & Environmental Science, 2,* 193–205.

IEA. (2008). *CO_2 capture and storage: A key carbon abatement option.* Paris: International Energy Agency. Retrieved from https://www.iea.org/publications/freepublications /publication/CCS_2008.pdf

IEA. (2013). Technology roadmap: Carbon capture and storage.

IEA. (2014). IEA hails historic launch of carbon capture and storage project. Paris: International Energy Agency. Retrieved from http://www.noodls.com/viewnoodl /25284530/iea---international-energy-agency/iea-hails-historic-launch-of-carbon -capture-and-storage-proj

IPCC. (2005). *IPCC special report on carbon dioxide capture and storage.* Geneva: Intergovernmental Panel on Climate Change, Working Group III.

Johnstone, B. (2016). SaskPower CEO says CCS project back on track, renewables main focus to 2030. *Regina Leader Post.* Retrieved from https://www.globalccsinstitute.com/news /saskpower-ceo-says-ccs-project-back-track-renewables-main-focus-2030

Marchetti, C. (1977). On geoengineering and the CO_2 problem. *Climatic Change, 1,* 59–68.

Markandya, A., & Wilkinson, P. (2007). Electricity generation and health. *The Lancet, 370,* 979–990.

Markusson, N., Gjefsen, M. D., Stephens, J. C., & Tyfield, D. (2017). The political economy of technical fixes: The (mis)alignment of clean fossil and political regimes. *Energy Research & Social Science, 23*, 1–10.

Markusson, N., Ishii, A. & Stephens, J. C. (2011). The social and political complexities of learning in CCS demonstration projects. *Global Environmental Change, 21*, 293–302.

Markusson, N., Shackley, S. & Evar, B. (Eds.). (2012). *The social dynamic of carbon capture and storage: Understanding CCS representations, governance and innovation*. London: Routledge, Taylor and Francis Group, EarthScan.

Martínez Arranz, A. (2016). Hype among low-carbon technologies: Carbon capture and storage in comparison. *Global Environmental Change, 41*, 124–141.

Marx, L. (1982). Are science and society going in the same direction? *Science, Technology, & Human Values, 8*, 6–9.

McKibben, B. (2016). Why we need to keep 80 percent of fossil fuels in the ground. *YES!* Retrieved from http://www.yesmagazine.org/issues/life-after-oil/why-we-need-to-keep-80-percent-of-fossil-fuels-in-the-ground-20160215

McKinsey (Company). (2008). CCS assessing the economics. Retrieved from http://processnet.org/processnet_media/14_15h_Daal-p-1750.pdf

Meadowcroft, J., & Langhelle, O. (Eds.) (2009). *Caching the carbon: The politics and policy of carbon capture and storage*, Cheltenham, UK: Edward Elgar.

Mitchell, R. B. (2012). Technology is not enough: Climate change, population, affluence, and consumption. *Journal of Environment & Development, 21*, 24–27.

Muller, N. Z., Mendelsohn, R., & Nordhaus, W. (2011). Environmental accounting for pollution in the United States economy. *American Economic Review, 101*, 1649–1675.

Narita, D. (2012). Managing uncertainties: The making of the IPCCs: Special report on carbon dioxide capture and storage. *Public Understanding of Science, 21*(1), 84–100.

Pollak, M., Phillips, S. J., & Vajjhala, S. (2011). Carbon capture and storage policy in the United States: A new coalition endeavors to change existing policy. *Global Environmental Change, 21*, 313–323.

Princen, T., Manno, J. P. & Martin, P. L. (Eds.). (2015). *Ending the fossil fuel era*. Cambridge, MA: MIT Press.

PSAC. (1965). *Restoring the quality of our environment*. Report of the Environmental Pollution Panel. Washington, DC: President's Science Advisory Committee, The White House.

Reiner, D. M. (2016). Learning through a portfolio of carbon capture and storage demonstration projects. *Nature Energy, 1*, 15011.

Rosner, L. (2004). *The technological fix: How people use technology to create and solve problems*. New York: Routledge.

Sarewitz, D., & Nelson, R. (2008). Three rules for technological fixes. *Nature, 456*, 871–872.

Scott, D. (2011). The technological fix criticisms and the agricultural biotechnology debate. *Journal of Agricultural and Environmental Ethics, 24*, 207–226.

Scott, V., Gilfillan, S., Markusson, N., Chalmers, H. & Haszeldine, R. S. (2013). Last chance for carbon capture and storage. *Nature Climate Change, 3*, 105–111.

Shell. (2014). *Shell signs agreement to advance major clean energy project at Peterhead*. Retrieved from http://www.shell.co.uk/gbr/aboutshell/media-centre/news-and-media-releases/2014/shell-signs-agreement-clean-energy-project-peterhead.html: http://www.shell.co.uk/gbr/aboutshell/media-centre/news-and-media-releases/2014/shell-signs-agreement-clean-energy-project-peterhead.html

Shove, E. (2010). Beyond the ABC: Climate change policy and theories of social change. *Environment and Planning A, 42*, 1273–1285.

Stephens, J. C. (2013). Carbon capture and storage (CCS) in the USA. In F. Urban (Ed.), *Low carbon development: Key issues* (pp. 297–307). London: Earthscan.

Stephens, J. C. (2014). Time to stop investing in carbon capture and storage and reduce government subsidies of fossil-fuels. *Wiley Interdisciplinary Reviews: Climate Change, 5*, 169–173.

Stephens, J. C., Hansson, A., Liu, Y., Coninck, H. D., & Vajjhala, S. 2011. Characterizing the international carbon capture and storage community. *Global Environmental Change, 21*, 379–390.

Tjernshaugen, A. (2008). Political commitment to CO_2 capture and storage: Evidence from government RD&D budgets. *Mitigation, Adaptation, Strategy Global Change, 13*, 1–21.

Tjernshaugen, A., & Langhelle, O. (2009). Technology as political glue: CCS in Norway. In J. Meadowcroft, & O. Langhelle (Eds.), *Caching the carbon: The politics and policy of carbon capture and storage* (pp. 98–124). Cheltenham, UK: Edward Elgar.

Torvanger, A., & Meadowcroft, J. (2011). The political economy of technology support: Making decisions about CCS and low carbon energy technologies. *Global Environmental Change, 21*, 303–312.

Vergragt, P. J., Markusson, N., & Karlsson, H. (2011). Carbon capture and storage, bio-energy with carbon capture and storage, and the escape from the fossil-fuel lock-in. *Global Environmental Change, 21*, 282–292.

Victor, D. (2009). *The politics of fossil-fuel subsidies.* Winnipeg, Manitoba: International Institute for Sustainable Development. Retrieved from http://www.iisd.org/library /politics-fossil-fuel-subsidies

Watson, J., Kern, F., Haszeldine, S., Gibbins, J., Markusson, N., Chalmers, H., Ghaleigh, N., Ascui, F., Arapostathis, S., Winskel, M., Gross, R., Heptonstall, P. & Pearson, P. (2012). *Carbon capture and storage: Realising the potential?* London: UK Energy Research Centre. Retrieved from http://www.ukerc.ac.uk/publications /carbon-capture-and-storage-realising-the-potential-.html

Watson, J., Kern, F., & Markusson, N. (2014). Resolving or managing uncertainties for carbon capture and storage: Lessons from historical analogues. *Technological Forecasting and Social Change, 81*, 192–204.

Weinberg, A. M. (1966). Can technology replace social engineering? *American Behavioral Scientist, 22*, 7–10.

Wilson, E. J., Friedmann, S. J., & Pollak, M. F. (2007). Research for deployment: Incorporating risk, regulation, and liability for carbon capture and sequestration. *Environmental Science & Technology, 41*, 5945–5952.

Wilson, E. J., Johnson, T. L., & Keith, D. W. (2003). Regulating the ultimate sink: Managing the risks of geologic CO_2 storage. *Environmental Science & Technology, 37*, 3476–3483.

Zoback, M. D., & Gorelick, S. M. (2012). Earthquake triggering and large-scale geologic storage of carbon dioxide. *PNAS, 109*, 10164–10168.

....

CHAPTER 27

EXNOVATION AS
A NECESSARY FACTOR
IN SUCCESSFUL
ENERGY TRANSITIONS

....

MARTIN DAVID

INTRODUCTION: WHY ENERGY TRANSITION IS NOT JUST ABOUT THE NEW

ENERGY production is based on sociotechnical structures and practices that have evolved over long periods of time. The exponential growth of energy-production systems is actually in and of itself a sociotechnical success story: small-sized decentralized methods of energy production, like wind generators or small hydro-energy units, vanished and made way for big sites of coal-fired or nuclear-fueled energy production and huge hydro-dams, favoring the centralization of energy-producing systems for ever increasing energy use. After a century of innovating energy systems based on "the bigger the better" approach, discourses reflecting on the negative environmental and societal effects caused by these former sociotechnical innovations began to gain traction in different countries. The end result is that sociotechnical and social innovations are again about to transform modes of energy consumption and production, for example, renewables like photovoltaics, hydro, or biomass energy-producing solutions (Karakaya, Hidalgo, & Nuur, 2014).

It could be argued that innovation has become a paradigm inscribed in Western modernizing ambitions, as was amply shown in the past (Gripenberg, Sveiby, & Segercrantz, 2012; Nill & Kemp, 2009). While the issue of energy innovations has generally gained considerable scientific ground (Karakaya, Hidalgo, & Nuur, 2014) and has formed the argumentative cornerstone of energy transitions in various countries

(Podobnik, 2006), there is one troubling aspect regarding energy transitions: the persistence of production patterns of former energy-producing technologies and the resulting environmental impacts, as well as the social practices tied to its use. What is simply designated as "former energy-producing technologies" manifests itself in centralized energy-production structures, and in labor and its conditions, as well as in its sociotechnical path dependencies. This means that an energy transition also necessitates processes of divestment from former (social) structures that sociotechnical innovations are meant to replace. This aspect of energy transitions has received limited attention in the academic community thus far.

The German electricity transition provides a key illustration. Germany's transition has effectively been measured in a lopsided manner: it is assessed in terms of its steadily growing gross-electricity production of renewable energies, but not by its equally steady growth in exports of coal-fired produced electricity to neighboring countries. Low energy pricing has been enabled by renewables entering the German electricity market in which old coal-fired (and nuclear-fueled) production systems prevail. This has enhanced the interest of neighboring countries, with the result that in 2015 about 10% of Germany's coal-fired electricity production was exported (Podewils, 2016). However, while renewable electricity innovations place pressure on markets, the old infrastructure of coal-fired energy production keeps on running a climate-unfriendly export machine. The much-trumpeted success of the German energy transition should therefore be reassessed, taking note of the need for abandoning old structures along the transition pathway in order to institute real decarbonization.

Processes of divesting from fossil-fuel energy technologies and production structures have been described in the past as "exnovation" (Paech, 2013), yet the framing of exnovation as a necessary condition for successful energy transitions is relatively new. Interestingly, the German *Energiewende* is fully premised on the desire to exnovate nuclear energy and to substitute it with renewable sources of energy production, even though this ongoing process is not referred to as exnovation. After the Fukushima disaster, the drive to end nuclear energy production dominated the energy transition discourse. Thus, in 2011 the German administration decided to phase out nuclear energy and to gradually remove all nuclear power plants from the German energy grid by 2022 (Geels et al., 2016). Unfortunately, exnovation processes in energy transitions have not yet been explored in depth, even though the concept of exnovation could decisively change the perception of what is termed the "energy transition" since the German de-carbonization of its electricity-producing structures lags behind. The sustainability of the German energy transition is therefore questionable from the perspective of de-carbonization, a process envisaged by the Kyoto Protocol, which was internationally negotiated in 1997. This chapter therefore aims to describe the exnovation of the German coal- and lignite-fired electricity production system and to analyze why the exnovation of coal-fired electricity production lags behind nuclear energy exnovation in the face of the German energy transition.

The remainder of this chapter is organized as follows: drawing mainly from exnovation literature, the following section explores the concept of exnovation and introduces the conceptual gaps that this chapter will address. The subsequent section introduces the case of the German energy transition and its electricity production, especially with lignite and coal but also with nuclear energy, relying on secondary literature. After providing a rough overview of the physical and institutional structures embedding the sociotechnical system of concern (energy production), design, and re-design principles of the German energy transition, those are drawn upon in the discussion of regime destruction as the major mechanism driving exnovations in the system of concern. This comprises an analysis of the interplay of politics, science, and publics, which the literature on energy transitions has regularly framed as central to envisioning the sociotechnical change of the German energy producing system (e.g., Finetti, 2011; Mautz, 2007; Mautz, Byzio, & Rosenbaum, 2008). The next section of the chapter assesses the exnovation of coal- and lignite-fired energy and contrasts this to the exnovation of nuclear electricity production. It shows how German energy politics, science, and publics articulate exnovation narratives, which then become potentially enacted. A discussion of the findings is then provided and a final section concludes the chapter.

APPROACHING EXNOVATION

Exnovation refers to processes in which existing technologies, for instance in reference to energy systems, become societally framed as obsolete and unacceptable, particularly in regard to their undesired externalities (Gross & Mautz, 2015). Exnovation is therefore not the introduction of "another fancy term" for problems that have already been dealt with long before. Rather, exnovation describes a research strand rooted in organizational innovation studies (Clark, 2003), which emerged during the 1970s (Yin et al., 1978). The holistic perspective of exnovation contrasts with concepts comprising solely particular aspects of endings such as policy termination (deLeon, 1978), organizational termination (Daniels 2006), evolutionary industrial and technological discontinuities (Tushman & Anderson, 1986), creative destruction (Tripsas, 1997), or product elimination (Avlonitis, 1983). Thus, in order to understand exnovation processes in energy transitions, it is not enough to look at a particular aspect or level. Rather, exnovation comprises different aspects and levels of the complex sociotechnical energy-producing system.

Making the concept of exnovation work at the systemic level can be regarded as a methodological challenge, because exnovation has been framed as a part of the transition process of energy-producing systems (Gross & Mautz, 2015; Paech, 2013), and because the concept of exnovation stems empirically from macro-organizational studies (Clark, 2003). Exnovation generally refers to the ending of something that was once new, and may include processes (Yin et al., 1978), rules (Brewer, 1978), factories (Clark & Staunton, 1989), or technical equipment (Kimberly, 1981) in organizations, and thus can be regarded as a holistic perspective on organizational change. An often-cited author in exnovation literature, Kimberly sees exnovation occurring "when an organization divests itself of an innovation in which it had previously invested" (Kimberly, 1981, p. 91). Thus, exnovation drives something out that was previously new to the organization. However, exnovation is a fundamental feature of the enhancement of innovation processes (Rye & Kimberly, 2007), enabling their further adoption effectiveness (Kimberly, 1981) in bringing about the desired change.

Analyzing Exnovation of Complex Sociotechnical Systems

This chapter attempts a "scaling up" of the organizational level of investigation to the national level by exploring the exnovation of the sociotechnical coal-fired electricity production system in Germany. Whereas exnovation stems from macro-organizational research strands (Clark & Staunton, 1989; Kimberly, 1981), the understanding of exnovating complex sociotechnical systems is under researched. To make exnovation work on a systemic level, its conceptual gaps should be carefully identified. In this chapter, exnovation refers to a long-lasting process of divesting from coal-fired electricity production, which means taking coal-fired energy plants off the electricity grid. According to Kimberly, the decision to exnovate something that once started as an innovation depends on why it was previously introduced by the organizations that introduced it in the first place. It may be that an organization evaluates a new innovation as better than the one previously adopted, or that an innovation shows unsatisfying effects, or even that a change in rules and events beyond the organization's control occurs, such as shifts in demand, regulation, and availability of raw materials (Kimberly, 1981).

Analyzing exnovation at the complex system level is a challenging task, but can be described with a structure and agency framework. Kimberly (1981, p. 91) exemplifies structure by referring to the replacement of medical equipment: "An organization, in other words, can discontinue using the equipment; but discontinued use does not necessarily imply exnovation." This means that unless a structure that enables a particular practice is eradicated, the practice in question will prevail even under changed institutions, for example in the case of environmental law. Therefore, coal facilities producing electricity need to be actively removed, as well as the associated enabling and conserving structures. In contrast to most other organizations, Germany's coal sectoral structure is polycentric in the sense that it comprises different sets of actors, each of them related to each other in specific ways. Its performance—and this includes exnovation—depends on the coal sector's culture, determined by its organizational history (see, e.g., Poole et al., 2000; Ulijn & Weggeman, 2001). This relates to lignite and coal miners, electricity production plants and administrations, as well as to the communal, domestic, and international arenas, and supranational politics and norms. Consequently, this sociohistorical embedding should be recognized as drawing on the structural characteristics of the German lignite and coal exnovation, because the institutional structure depends on the interplay of different actors' practices and rules.

Additionally, exnovation is normative to the extent that proponents take the position that something needs to be exnovated, highlighting the role of agency. Organizational actors make decisions to deliberatively leave practical or technological pathways into which they have been locked. Exnovation is also likely to become a conflict-ridden stakeholder process in which exnovators and status quo-(coal-)actors have very different interests at stake (Kimberly, 1981). Hence we may think of "exnovators" as actors pushing a certain exnovation agenda and trying to overcome political and economic burdens. Thus, exnovation cannot be thought of as an autonomous process, as suggested for instance by the heurism of "creative destruction," which assumes that "old things" disappear when innovations emerge. However, in contrast to organizational agency, agency in exnovating complex sociotechnical systems like the German electricity-production system can be expected to be distributed in a polycentric manner. This means that the interacting actors of the German electricity-production system base their actions on their own interests and capacities, which can differ from the agency of others.

The Embedding Infrastructure of the Coal- and Lignite-Fired Electricity-Production System in Question

Currently 44 lignite- and 68 coal-fired energy plants are in use in Germany (Bundesnetzagentur, 2017). Coal mines "declined from 146 in 1960 to 39 in 1990 to 12 in 2000, and (intended) full closure in 2018" (Geels et al., 2016, p. 902). Lignite mines in East Germany are still being exploited and continue to meet the lignite demands for electricity production. Coal-fired energy production has geologically benefited from large lignite and coal repositories that have been extensively exploited throughout German history and have formed the bases of German industrialization as well its post–World War II capitalist structure (Lauber & Jacobsson, 2016). Nearly half of Germany's electricity is provided by coal-fired production as of this writing, a fact that makes it an especially promising field for targeting by decarbonization policies. To achieve the international climate goals as internationally outlined in the Paris Agreement in 2015, Germany would need to completely forgo coal-powered electricity by 2050 at the very latest (Schrader, 2016).

German coal- and lignite-fired energy production is shaped by European supranational policy structures that were established in the aftermath of World War II. In May 1950 the European Coal and Steel Community (ECSC) was formed, whose founding members—France, West Germany, Italy, the Netherlands, Belgium, and Luxembourg—shared coal and steel resources. This was done in order to, in the words of its founder, French Foreign Minister Schumann, "make it plain that any war between France and

Germany becomes not merely unthinkable, but materially impossible" (Schuman [1950] 2017). Thus, the idea of this first supranational body, founded in 1951, was to put German and French coal and steel production under supranational jurisdiction in order to secure European peace and economic growth, by using economic structures to make future war between any European country impossible (Orlow, 2002). This development, along with the absorption of all the ECSC by subsequent treaties until the Lisbon Treaty, links the foundation of the exnovation discussed here to not only the foundation of postwar European history and its basic economic principles, but also to current European politics.

The climate regulation instrument of the European Union—the European Union Emissions Trading System (EU ETS)—which was promulgated by the European Climate Change Programme (ECCP) in January 2005, supposedly governs German emissions reduction. The system aims to fulfill the emission goals as defined by the EU according to the Kyoto Protocol, which suggested a CO_2 reduction for Germany of 8% between 2008 and 2012 (Convery, 2009). The EU ETS is based on pricing tons of greenhouse gases (GHGs) emitted by businesses, which in turn buy certificates according to their emissions. This system covers about 45% of the GHGs in the EU, and the number of certificates artificially shrinks by 1.75% per year, and can be regarded as the mechanism and speed of this exnovation strategy. Some argue that this rate is not progressive enough (Helm & Hepburn, 2009). Moreover, in its national emission-reduction plan, Germany granted extra certificates to its coal-fired power stations, which naturally puts the German EU ETS implementation behind its reduction goals (Ziehm, 2008). As it turns out, Germany's policy has favored compulsory decoupling from its international and supranational levels.

Destroying the Lignite and Coal Regime

Whereas transition management has intensely highlighted regime construction as a possible way of changing toward sustainable lifestyles (Geels et al., 2016), little attention has been paid thus far to the processes of niche destruction necessary for a change toward sustainable energy provision. From this perspective, German coal exnovation provides an interesting example in which decarbonization would require the destruction of the coal and lignite niche provided by the German state.

As one key illustration, intentions to reduce emissions are thwarted by the immense subsidies for lignite and stone coal in Germany. Subsidies are mainly intended to secure labor that would otherwise vanish. Securing coal-related jobs has been the endeavor of Social Democrat politics in Germany for decades and hence embodies the political and social mobilization potential of many worker unions tied to the German coal business (Jacobson & Lauber, 2006). A study from 2010 found that between 1958 and 2008 anthracite was cumulatively supported with €295.2 billion, and lignite with €56.9 billion—whereas nuclear energy accounts for €131.8 billion (Meyer, Küchler, & Hölzinger, 2010). These amounts consisted of €187 billion in financial subsidies, €101 billion in tax incentives, as well as €42 billion that should have been paid to the state but were not, at least as far as could be investigated (Meyer, Küchler, & Hölzinger, 2010: 9). Subsidies were granted in research and development (R&D) on mining technology and in domestic and European carbon capture and storage (CCS)—pilot projects, market subsidies, modernization, social service, phase-out subsidies, energy tax incentives, liberation of royalties, liberation of water bills in anthracite mining, and subsidies of miners' associations. Due to open-cast extraction of lignite, cleanup operations and relocations were also part of the many components that helped the German coal industry to survive (Meyer, Küchler, & Hölzinger, 2010, p. 9). This underscores how deeply incorporated coal- and lignite-fired electricity production really is in Germany, leaving aside the externalized environmental and health costs of coal firing. To sustain coal-fired (and also nuclear) electricity production after the closure of most German coal mines by 2000 (Geels et al., 2016), coal was increasingly imported: coal imports to Germany comprised 28.9 million tons in 2004, and 50.6 million tons in 2013 (Destatis, 2014). Here a technological path dependency is revealed: whereas coal mining vanished due to skyrocketing costs caused by exhausted domestic repositories, coal-fired energy plants kept firing. This illustrates a factor in exnovation that is rarely reflected upon: there is not a single exnovation regarding lignite- and coal-fired electricity production, but instead a complex system of interacting subsystems that can be differentiated in both domestic lignite and coal extraction and in both lignite and coal-fired electricity production. Consequently, a complex organizational termination (Daniels, 2006) (e.g., lignite- and coal-fired energy plants and procurement infrastructure) must be pushed to completely divest from lignite and coal in order to not fall back on discontinued use and back-door policies.

From a decarbonization perspective, as strengthened with the 2015 Paris Agreement, the successful establishment of sociotechnical niches represented by renewable electricity-producing systems depends on the niche destruction of coal- and lignite-fired electricity production, as this German case illustrates. From this point of view, niche destruction is a fundamental mechanism for the exnovation of German coal- and lignite-fired electricity generation, as well as for nuclear electricity production.

Assessing the Exnovation of Coal-Fired Energy in the Face of the German *Energiewende*

German coal and lignite policymaking is anything but predictable. After a long traditional practice of lignite and coal funding by the German state, subsidies in 1997 were reduced for the very first time by the coalition of the Christian Democratic Union of Germany (CDU) and Free Democratic Party (FDP) parties (Umweltbundesamt, 2003), and then again by the SPD and Green Party coalition in 2005 (CDU/CSU, 2005). This made German coal less competitive internationally and led to a discussion in February 2007 about when coal subsidies should be completely stopped. After months of negotiation between the coal lobby, representatives of the Bundesländer and the German federal government, a coal- and lignite-fired electricity exnovation by 2018 was announced for the first time (BMWi, 2009).

Then, in July 2015, protests from the German trade union IG Bergbau, Chemie, Energie (a trade union representing mining and chemistry jobs), as well as from the lignite, coal, and energy industries, led to the rejection of the coal and lignite exnovation policy incentive of the German Ministry of Economic Affairs. According to this initiative, emissions would have been forced into accordance with the EU ETS and would have placed inefficient coal-fired energy plants at the end of the energy-production chain, since additional emissions exceeding the cap would have cost extra certificates (Gawel & Strunz, 2015). The proposal aimed to remove 2.7 gigawatts of lignite-firing plants and to introduce a tax on coal- and lignite-firing plants if they exceeded production as defined in the EU ETS emission reduction plan (Spiegel Online, 2015). Instead, a proposal of the German trade union IG Bergbau, Chemie, Energie was discussed in July 2015, which set incentives to put lignite-fired energy plants into a silent reserve to fully take all plants bigger than 6 gigawatts (GW) off the grid from 2020 onward (FÖS, 2015).

This setback was not to be the end of the story, however. At the end of 2015, in the aftermath of the Conference of the Parties 21 in Paris, the German Environmental Ministry proposed the German Climate Plan 2015. The plan made clear suggestions for when to exnovate completely from coal in order to fulfill climate-protection goals. However, the proposal was rejected by the German Ministry of Economic Affairs in July 2016 without stating any reason for the refusal (Handelsblatt, 2016).[1] Consequently, the German Climate Plan 2015 leaves the exnovation date of coal and lignite-fired electricity wide open.

Coal and Lignite Exnovation Modeling: Between Utopia and Windows of Opportunity

In preparation for the 2009 United Nations Climate Change Conference negotiations in Copenhagen, the World Wildlife Fund (WWF) ran a study on renewable energy in Germany. The authors referred to scenarios of technological pathways toward climate-friendly energy production by 2050, and with this study set a hallmark in carbon-relevant technology scenario modeling in Germany. In this study, Kirchner and colleagues (2009) argued for a scenario called "Model Germany," which relies heavily on sociotechnical innovations such as renewable energies and CCS. Further, the study underscored that a moratorium for coal-fired energy plants was necessary, but did not explicate *when*. Instead, the authors defined a life span for coal-fired energy plants of 45 years and by this pushed exnovation up to this 45-year cap (Kirchner et al., 2009). Relying on the EU ETS as a decarbonization measure, the study puts emphasis on innovative technology development to capture and store carbon, but not necessarily on the exnovation process regarding the politics of coal- and lignite-fired technologies.

Five years later, a discursive shift toward the discussion of costs around the cessation of using coal- and lignite-fired electricity occurred due to an emerging discussion about the electricity sector's contribution toward climate protection (Geels et al., 2016; Lauber & Jacobsson, 2016). However, in 2014 a study of the German Institute for Economic Research looked at the exnovation of coal and introduced three different scenarios for taking coal-fired energy production off the electricity grid. Reitz and associates (2014) emphasize that the growth of the German renewable energy portfolio led to an overproduction of electricity, which made the closure of coal- and lignite-firing energy plants likely. Consequently, and contrary to the WWF proposal, the study builds on the success of renewable energy innovations. Further, the authors show that both producer and supplier profit due to an increase of prices caused by shutting down coal-fired energy production. However, the study remains open concerning an exact date of exnovation.

The discourse on coal and lignite exnovation shifted again in 2015 when the non-governmental think tank Agora Energiewende proposed scenarios that focused on an earlier time of exnovation of lignite- and coal-fired electricity production than the scenarios described in the preceding. One scenario proposed phasing out coal- and lignite-fired electricity production from 2020 onward, accompanied by a retrofitting of coal-fired electricity plants, thus reducing emissions. Another climate-protection scenario argued for gradually phasing out coal, starting from 2016 and ending by 2040, without a retrofitting of coal-fired electricity plants (Rosenkranz et al., 2015). This study decisively argued in favor of exnovating independently of the EU ETS frame with the proposal for national policy initiatives (Gawel & Strunz, 2015).

Prompted by the discussion in 2015 around the proposal put forward by the German trade union IG Bergbau, Chemie, Energie, another turning point in the debate on coal and lignite exnovation was reached in 2016, leading to the development of three different scenarios of how to move away from coal and lignite. In May 2016 the Energy Research & Scenarios gGmbH suggested a scenario in which all coal-fired electricity plants would be successively removed from the electricity grid according to their age (Hecking et al., 2016). The study backed up the scenario of Agora Energiewende to progressively exnovate coal until 2040, instead of solely relying on the EU ETS to enhance decarbonization effects. In August 2016, a more progressive scenario to phase out coal-fired electricity production was proposed in a study by the Berlin University of Applied Sciences, underscoring the necessity of ceasing coal-fired electricity production by 2030 in order to achieve German climate-protection goals (Quaschning, 2016). Later, in September 2016, the trade union ver.di and the Hans Böckler Foundation published a scenario that envisaged a complete cessation of coal-fired electricity production by 2040 (Ecke, 2016). Notably, ver.di once opted against an exnovation of coal, but has since suggested that turning away from coal would be bearable with regard to employment. This could mark a decisive turning point in the public perception of climate-unfriendly technologies in Germany; the scenarios suggest that the coal and lignite exnovation discourse has moved toward a more progressive use of domestic policy, independently from the EU ETS.

The Articulation of Anti-Coal and Anti-Lignite Narratives by Publics

The public discourse on the (potential) exnovation of coal-fired energy in Germany has long since been overshadowed by events around nuclear energy (Renn & Marshall, 2016). The German policy discourse on coal- and lignite-fired electricity, focusing on the international climate-protection goals, emerged only recently and put only limited pressure on domestic coal politics. The German anti-nuclear movement, evolving in the 1960s and gaining ground after the Chernobyl nuclear accident in 1986, was characterized as the most intense protest against nuclear energy among all the anti-nuclear movements in Europe (Roose, 2010).

Public discourse on the exnovation of lignite- and coal-fired energy have since the 1980s been framed as a health issue. Anti-coal protests have been much smaller than anti-nuclear protests after Chernobyl and Fukushima, and are mostly of a local and regional nature. Anti-coal protests nonetheless have grown and have become more organized after the emergence of official plans from the government to build more coal-fired energy plants (Heinrich-Böll-Stiftung & BUND, 2015). In April 2007, the nongovernmental organization (NGO) Climate-Alliance Germany was founded, consisting of about 100 organizational members, among them churches, development organizations, environmental organizations, trade unions, consumer protection organizations, youth associations, and other groupings. The organization successfully picked up on the international climate-protection discourse. When plans for new plants became official, the young organization took action and launched an anti-coal campaign in 2008, and 18 planned facilities were subsequently blocked through juridical means (Climate-Alliance Germany, 2016). Since then, various protests have been carried out in coal-field areas such as the region of Lusatia (Eastern Germany) in 2014, where NGOs including Campact and Greenpeace organized a human chain of eight kilometers consisting of 7,500 people. In 2015, 6,000 people blocked extraction activities at the Garzweiler coal mine in the Rhineland (Western Germany) (Heinrich-Böll-Stiftung & BUND, 2015). Nevertheless, compared to the anti-nuclear movement, the anti-coal movement is still in its infancy.

An international movement opposing lignite- and coal-fired energy production is the so-called divestment movement. The fossil fuel divestment movement dates back to the founding of the environmentalist advocacy group 350.org organized by Bill McKibben, who first mobilized on US university campuses in 2011 (Ayling & Gunningham, 2015). In 2012, a global divestment movement arose that aimed to redirect finances from emitting industries (McKibben, 2012). The movement spread to Germany by 2014, but remains a rather loosely organized social movement in Europe. We can observe that the articulation of anti-lignite and anti-coal narratives by publics have changed through the years; once centering on health and climate as a rhetorical vehicle to argue against heavy-emitting technologies, the divestment movement engages in a rather indirect manner as a political bottom-up strategy.

DISCUSSION

Why is the exnovation of lignite- and coal-firing electricity production and its associated technologies lagging behind the exnovation of nuclear energy in Germany? The German political scene is uncertain regarding policy goals on coal- and lignite-fired electricity production. Policy termination literature has long underscored the fact that the dismantling of policies is itself a political act that can be reversed, for instance by changes in administrations (Bardach, 1976; Bauer & Knill, 2014; deLeon, 1978). This also has been the case for the phase-out of nuclear energy. After the 1990s, the environmental political field became dominated by a coalition of the SPD and the Green Party. The coalition revised the nuclear statute in 2002 with a view to divesting from nuclear energy. Nevertheless, in 2010 this revision was redrawn in what could be literally termed the "phase-out from the phase-out," enacted by the first Merkel cabinet under massive civil protest (Uekoetter, 2012), but was revised yet again after the Fukushima disaster. Considering the complex structure of the sociotechnical system in question, however, the assessment of exnovation cannot be reduced to the policy cycle alone and to only one policy field. It is rather the case that understanding of the exnovating of lignite- and coal-fired electricity production requires a focus on different policy stakes of implicated actors and different policy fields. Yet it has been shown that coal exnovation takes place in international, and supranational, as well as domestic policy structures, all of which have emerged over long periods of time with their own symbolic meanings. The idea of exnovating lignite- and coal-firing electricity production is strongly opposed to these structures and their path dependencies (e.g., labor, infrastructure), known under the rubric of carbon lock-in (McLellan, Chapman, & Aoki, 2016; Unruh, 2000). Differing from the mainly domestic issue of nuclear-policy termination (Geels et al., 2016), the lignite and coal exnovation is being pushed by a complex policy structure proposed by the Kyoto Protocol since 1997 and the EU ETS, in power since 2005. It has further been shown that a better interplay between domestic exnovation policy and international and supranational policy levels is needed in order to meet climate goals. German administrations have understood how to manipulate the supranational EU ETS policy frame by allowing extra emission certificates for coal-firing energy-producing facilities. This marks a tendency to move away from supranational policy instruments toward domestic sectoral protectionism, which could partially explain the lag in German lignite and coal exnovation.

Another possible reason why the exnovation of nuclear energy production was more successful in Germany than coal exnovation is perhaps the lower employment level of nuclear energy production compared to that of the lignite- and coal-fired electricity production, an industry that has had a long tradition of employment in Germany (Meyer, Küchler, & Hölzinger, 2010). As a result, trade unions opposed to the lignite and coal exnovation exerted strong political pressure.

Nevertheless, it could be argued that supranational and international environmental policies are more progressive, stable, and effective than domestic policies in their ability to promote and direct the exnovation of lignite- and coal-fired technologies. Seen from this perspective, international and supranational environmental policy could be interpreted as an exnovation-securing structure outside the reach of the German lignite- and coal-fired electricity-producing sector. This means that exnovation-enabling policy structures are mainly formed by knowledge materialized in institutions on the international and European level, challenging the domestic status quo of lignite and coal politics on sustainability grounds.

The German energy transition is based on problem-oriented knowledge production in applied sociotechnical contexts (Finetti, 2011). However, decarbonization practices like the exnovation of coal-fired electricity production have not been studied extensively, and thus insights from doing so have yet to be applied. It has furthermore been shown that the modeling of coal and lignite exnovation pathways has changed over the years, as has energy transition design overall. The German word "Energiewende" (energy transition) first appeared in 1981 in the book *Energy transition: Growth and Wellbeing Without Crude Oil and Uranium* (Krause, Bossel, & Müller-Reißmann, 1981), published by the Institute for Applied Ecology (German: Öko-Institut), which emerged from the German anti-nuclear movement in 1977. It proposed an ecological scenario in which Germany would withdraw from crude oil and nuclear electricity production by 2030, substituting these energy sources with renewable production, especially coal-fired electricity (Simon, 2013). The scenario, which positively reflected on the German anti-nuclear movement (Maubach, 2014), found its way between 1979 and 1980 to a parliamentarian committee of inquiry on future nuclear energy politics. The committee found the scenario economically too risky (Bartosch, Hennicke, & Weiger, 2014, pp. 11–15), since at that time nuclear energy was perceived as key to the German postwar economy (Hüttl & Ossing, 2011). However, during this time period, coal was seen as a fundamental component to replacing nuclear energy production in this particular energy-transition plan, and climate protection did not possess as strong a narrative for a potential energy transition. Presentation of the scenario beyond party politics marks a decisive turning point: knowledge articulation found its way into decision-making circles (Vowe, 1987). This means that the exnovation of coal-fired energy was originally not part of the energy transition rhetoric; to the contrary, coal was even pondered as a means of supporting the abolishment of nuclear energy, as noted by Krause, Bossel, and Müller-Reißmann (1981). From this point of view, it becomes clear that the design principles of the German energy transition, which were largely sustained by the anti-nuclear movement, also influenced scientific accounts on lignite and coal exnovation.

Whereas the 1990s witnessed a heavy emphasis on the nuclear debate, the question of when to resign from lignite and coal remained open (Geels et al., 2016; Renn & Marshall, 2016). Nevertheless, since 2009 and in anticipation of the COP meetings, sustainability-oriented think tanks have ably introduced into debates more detailed and progressive exnovation scenarios. In 2014 exnovation was directly envisaged and was described in more depth concerning the consequences of agency and structure, with the discussions yielding proposals that consecutively produced scientific knowledge in the field. The 2016 proposals agree that exnovation from lignite and coal is economically feasible. This underscores that the vision to exnovate lignite and coal technologies had yet to be developed in accordance with public discourses.

The German energy transition actually builds on an exnovation that already was strongly determined by the public. What seems to have been triggered only by the severe effects of the nuclear disasters and then pushed by governmental administration was actually socio-historically "pre-structured" long before, by decades of anti-nuclear protesting (Manow, 2013). The catastrophic event in Chernobyl on April 26, 1986, only strengthened the German anti-nuclear movement, which already was growing during the Cold War amidst a peace movement that had been in development since the 1960s (Roth, 1994). After this evidence came to light, nuclear energy phase-out became a dominant frame in the pubic energy transition-discourse. Whereas a consensus between the anti-nuclear movement, the CDU/CSU, and energy industries did not occur (Matthes, 2000), the events in Fukushima on March 11, 2011, pushed the German government to issue the official declaration of the German "Energiewende" and to commit to completing the exnovation of nuclear energy by 2022 (Bundesregierung, 2011). This exclusive focus on nuclear-exnovation biased the discourse away from attention to the exnovation of lignite- and coal-fired energy. Consequently, one reason for the late public discourse on lignite and coal exnovation might be the different framing of the risk of both coal- and lignite-fired electricity production compared to that of nuclear energy. Unlike the tragic externalization of risks of nuclear electricity provision in Chernobyl and Fukushima, the risks of coal are "largely internalized within the production system, in the form of damage to miners' lives and health" (Jasanoff & Kim 2013, p. 191). Whereas domestic uranium extraction has not been a recently disputed issue, civil society is beginning to emphasize the climate-change discourse and use it against coal- and lignite-fired energies. If the use of this discourse by the German anti-coal movement prevails, it could play a decisive role in stabilizing domestic anti-coal policy initiatives. as was done by the anti-nuclear movement in the past. Meanwhile, early concerns regarding serious health damages associated with the use of coal- and lignite-firing electricity plants remain salient. A study from 2013 estimated approximately 3,100 early deaths per year in Germany due to emissions resulting from the use of coal- and especially lignite-firing energy production (Greenpeace, 2013).

Lignite- and coal-exnovation does not have the background of a social movement tradition that was triggered by a tragic accident, subsequently leading to a process of shifting away from the energy technology in question, as was the case with nuclear energy technologies. Today the anti-nuclear movement continues to hold the advantage in that it learned that protesting against top-down enacted technologies pays dividends. However, what sounds like a disadvantage for the exnovation of coal in the face of the *Energiewende* in first place can turn out to be a helpful "pilot project" for the exnovation of coal in Germany: it proved that the exnovation of nuclear energy could be put in motion. The consequent next step for the anti-lignite and anti-coal movement is therefore to push for the exnovation of coal technology in order to get the process of decarbonization started. At the same time, the support for the 2016 exnovation scenario by the German trade union ver.di, which is linked to the German Confederation of German Trade Unions, shows that even the organizational field of pro-exnovation actors has changed.

As for innovation, the public plays a decisive role in articulating exnovation narratives in energy transitions. It has been shown that the public influences both policymaking and scientific endeavors on lignite and coal exnovation. To put it in the words of Kimberly (1981, p. 92), the anti-coal movement represents "a result of internal opposition generated by the impact of an innovation on existing interests, power, and control."

CONCLUSION

In this chapter, exnovation has been examined at the systemic level through the case of German lignite and coal exnovation in the face of energy transition. From the perspective of decarbonization goals, the exnovation of coal-fired electricity production, as a fundamental part of the German energy transition, still lags behind the exnovation of nuclear energy, although nuclear waste issues are still a high-ranking unsolved issue on the agenda. It took nearly 40 years to decide to withdraw from lignite and coal subsidies.[2]

Regime destruction during the course of exnovation is a challenge, and yet also a requirement for successful energy transitions. Innovation research has long stressed that the "termination of existing practices, procedures, and institutions needs to be considered in advance of initiating an innovation" (Brewer, 1980, p. 337). The discussion on exnovation, however, is unlikely to effect change if it solely relies on processes of creative destruction that are triggered by sociotechnical renewable energy innovations. Energy transition proponents need to actively envision exnovation and plan it. Exnovation might be harder to push than innovation, as suggested by the relatively unspectacular introduction of the German feed-in scheme in 1990 (Greiner & Hermann, 2016).

The physical, institutional, and practice structures of a complex sociotechnical electricity-producing system cannot be cut loose from agency, nor can agency alone determine structure. Rather, both are interdependently intertwined and a result of the interactions with different actors. This has methodological consequences for exnovation research. It is not enough to look for solutions at the policy level, or to rely on science or social movements. Rather, it is the interplay of all these factors that determines the pace of an exnovation, as this chapter has demonstrated. Publics are not yet a set of agents that is well represented in exnovation literature; here they have been mainly discussed in terms of their role in articulating exnovation narratives that science and policy act upon. For instance, early scientific accounts on German lignite and coal exnovation still framed coal as a bridging technology that could be used during the withdrawal from nuclear energy. The example examined here suggests that an articulation of the exact exnovation steps to be taken is essential. The international climate protection discourse has thus aided in a shift toward such a decarbonization vision. This was also enshrined in the international policy structure of the Kyoto Protocol that came into effect in 2005, after the introduction of the German feed-in tariff, introduced in 1990 and then modified in 2000 to set the basis for sociotechnical energy innovations. The EU ETS, initiated due to the Kyoto Protocol, seems to be a stabilizing supranational structure for the German lignite and coal exnovation process, considering the unpredictable "back and forth" of German lignite and coal politics.

ACKNOWLEDGMENTS

The author would like to thank the German Ministry of Education and Research for funding the research project GORmin—Governance Options for Acceptable Primary and Secondary Scarce-Resource Mining in Germany (support code: 033R148). The author is especially grateful to Nona Schulte-Römer, Debra Davidson, and Matthias Gross.

NOTES

1. The heads of both government departments (Barbara Hendricks, minister of the German Ministry of Environmental Affairs, and Sigmar Gabriel, minister of the German Ministry of Economic Affairs) were members of the same party, the Social Democratic Party of Germany (SPD).
2. The sustained protection of the niche of lignite- and coal-firing energy technologies underscores the unprofitability of the sector since the early post–World War II era.

REFERENCES

Avlonitis, G. J. (1983). Ethics and product elimination. *Management Decision, 21*(2), 37–45.

Ayling, J., & Gunningham, N. (2015). Non-state governance and climate policy: the fossil fuel divestment movement. *Climate Policy, 17*(2). 1–15.

Bardach, E. (1976). Policy termination as a political process. *Policy Sciences, 7*(2), 123–131.

Bartosch, U., Hennicke, P., & Weicker, H. (2014). Kurzer Aufriss einer langen Vorgeschichte. In P. Hennicke, H. Weicker, & U. Bartosch (Eds.), *Gemeinschaftsprojekt Energiewende—Der Fahrplan zum Erfolg* (pp. 11–18). München: Oekom Verlag.

Bauer, M. W., & Knill, C. (2014). A conceptual framework for the comparative analysis of policy change: Measurement, explanation and strategies of policy dismantling. *Journal of Comparative Policy Analysis: Research and Practice, 16*(1), 28–44.

BMWi (Bundesministerium für Wirtschaft). (2009). Kohlepolitik. Retrieved from http://www
.bmwi.de/BMWi/Navigation/Energie/kohlepolitik.html

Brewer, G. D. (1978). Termination: Hard choices—harder questions. *Public Administration Review, 38*(4), 338–344.

Brewer, G. D. (1980). On the theory and practice of innovation. *Technology in Society, 2*(3), 337–363.

Bundesnetzagentur. (2017). Aktuelle Kraftwerkliste. Retrieved from https://www
.bundesnetzagentur.de/DE/Sachgebiete/ElektrizitaetundGas/Unternehmen_Institutionen
/Versorgungssicherheit/Erzeugungskapazitaeten/Kraftwerksliste/kraftwerksliste-node.html

Bundesregierung. (2011). Energiewende mit Augenmaß. Retrieved from www.
bundesregierung.de/ContentArchiv/DE/Archiv17/Artikel/2011/03/2011-03-29
-energiewende-hin-zu-erneuerbaren-energien.html

CDU/CSU (Christian Democratic Union of Germany/Christian Social Union in Bavaria).
(2005). *Deutschlands Chancen nutzen. Wachstum. Arbeit. Sicherheit. Regierungsprogramm 2005–2009.* Berlin: CDU/CSU.

Clark, P. A. (2003). *Organizational innovations.* London: SAGE Publications.

Clark, P. A., & Staunton, N. (1989). *Innovation in technology and organization.* Routledge: London.

Climate-Alliance Germany. (2016). Climate-Alliance Germany. Retrieved from http://www
.climate-alliance-germany.de/

Convery, F. J. (2009). Origins and development of the EU ETS. *Environmental and Resource Economics, 43*(3), 391–412.

Daniels, M. R. (2006). Policy and organizational termination. *International Journal of Public Administration, 24*(3), 249–262.

deLeon, P. (1978). Public policy termination: An end and a beginning. *Policy Analysis, 4*(3), 369–392.

Destatis. (2014). Import von Steinkohle 2013 um 15,2 % gestiegen. Retrieved from https://www
.destatis.de/DE/PresseService/Presse/Pressemitteilungen/2014/04/PD14_141_51.html

Ecke, J. (2016). *Gutachten: Sozialverträgliche Ausgestaltung eines Kohlekonsens.* Berlin: ver.di
—Vereinte Dienstleistungsgesellschaft.

Finetti, M. (2011). Interview: "Ohne Forschung keine Energiewende." *Forschung, 36*(2), 22–23.

FÖS (Forum Ökologisch-Soziale Marktwirtschaft). (2015). *Teurer Klimaschutz mit Kapazitätsreserve.* Berlin: Forum Ökologisch-Soziale Marktwirtschaft.

Gawel, E., & Strunz, S. (2015). Klimaabgabe für Kohlekraftwerke: Ein richtiger Schritt zur Erreichung des Klimaziels? *ifo Schnelldienst, 68*(14), 8–11.

Geels, F. W., Kern, F., Fuchs, G., Hinderer, N., Kungl, G., Mylan, J., Neukirch, M., & Wassermann, S. (2016). The enactment of socio-technical transition pathways: A reformulated typology and a comparative multi-level analysis of the German and UK low-carbon electricity transitions (1990–2014). *Research Policy, 45*(4), 896–913.

Greenpeace. (2013). Tod aus dem Schlot. Wie Kohlekraftwerke unsere Gesundheit ruinieren. Retrieved from https://www.greenpeace.de/presse/publikationen/studie-tod-aus
-dem-schlot

Greiner, B., & Hermann, H. (2016). *Erstellung und Begleitung des Klimaschutzplans 2050.* Berlin: Öko-Institut, Fraunhofer ISI, IREES GmbH.

Gripenberg, P., Sveiby, K.-E., & Segercrantz, B. (2012). Challenging the innovation paradigm: The prevailing pro-innovation bias." In K.-E. Sveiby, P. Gripengerg, & B. Segercrantz (Eds.), *Challenging the Innovation Paradigm* (pp. 1–14). London: Routledge.

Gross, M., & Mautz, R. (2015). *Renewable energies.* London: Routledge.

Handelsblatt. (2016, June 26). Gabriel streicht Hendricks' Klimaschutzplan zusammen. Retrieved from www.handelsblatt.com/politik/deutschland/kein-datum-fuer-kohleausstieg-gabriel-streicht-hendricks-klimaschutzplan-zusammen/13807130.html

Hecking, H., Kruse, J., Paschmann, M., Polisadov, A., & Wildgrube, T. (2016). *Ökonomische Effekte eines deutschen Kohleausstiegs auf den Strommarkt in Deutschland und der EU.* Berlin: ewi Energy Research & Scenarios gGmbH.

Heinrich-Böll-Stiftung & BUND (Bund für Umwelt und Naturschutz Deutschland). (2015). *Kohleatlas, Daten und Fakten über einen globalen Brennstoff.* Berlin: Heinrich-Böll-Stiftung; Bund für Umwelt und Naturschutz Deutschland.

Helm, D., & Hepburn, C. (2009). *The economics and politics of climate change.* Oxford: Oxford University Press.

Hüttl, R. F., & Ossing, F. (2011). Der Ausstieg aus der Atomenergie und die Energiebilanz Deutschlands. *System Erde, 1*(2), 8–15.

Jacobsson, S., & Lauber, V. (2006). The politics and policy of energy system transformation-explaining German diffusion of renewable energy technology. *Energy Policy, 34*(3), 256–276.

Jasanoff, S., & Kim, S.-H. (2013). Sociotechnical imaginaries and national energy policies. *Science as Culture, 22*(2), 189–196.

Karakaya, E., Hidalgo, A., & Nuur, C. (2014). Diffusion of eco-innovations: A review. *Renewable and Sustainable Energy Reviews, 33,* 392–399.

Kimberly, J. R. (1981). Managerial innovation. In P. C. Nystrom & W. H. Starbuck (Eds.), *Handbook of organizational design* (pp. 84–104). Oxford: Oxford University Press.

Kirchner, A., Schlesinger, M., Weinmann, B., Hofer, P., Rits, V., Wünsch, M., . . . Mohr, L. (2009). *Modell Deutschland, Klimaschutz bis 2015: Vom Ziel her denken.* Berlin: WWF.

Krause, F., Bossel, H., & Müller-Reissmann, K.-F. (1981). *Energie-Wende: Wachstum und Wohlstand ohne Erdöl und Uran.* Frankfurt: Fischer.

Lauber, V., & Jacobsson, S. (2016). The politics and economics of constructing, contesting and restricting socio-political space for renewables: The German Renewable Energy Act. *Environmental Innovation and Societal Transitions, 18*(2), 147–163.

Manow, P. (2013). Die Energiewende: Beiträge der Wissenschaft. In J. Radtke & B. Hennig (Eds.), *Die deutsche "Energiewende" nach Fukushima* (pp. 11–12). Weimar: Metropolis-Verlag.

Matthes, F. C. (2000). *Stromwirtschaft und deutsche Einheit: Eine Fallstudie zur Transformation der Elektrizitätswirtschaft in Ost-Deutschland.* Berlin: edition energie + umwelt.

Maubach, K.-D. (2014). *Energiewende, Wege zu einer bezahlbaren Energieversorgung.* Berlin: Springer.

Mautz, R. (2007). The expansion of renewable energies in germany between niche dynamics and system integration: Opportunities and restraints. *Science, Technology & Innovation Studies, 3*(2), 113–130.

Mautz, R., Byzio, A., & Rosenbaum, W. (2008). *Auf dem Weg zur Energiewende: Die Entwicklung der Stromproduktion aus erneuerbaren Energien in Deutschland.* Göttingen: Universitätsverlag.

McKibben, B. (2012). Global warming's terrifying new math. *Rolling Stone,* July 19. Retrieved from https://www.rollingstone.com/politics/news/global-warmings-terrifying-new-math-20120719

McLellan, B. C., Chapman, A. J., & Aoki, K. (2016). Geography, urbanization and lock-in—considerations for sustainable transitions to decentralized energy systems. *Journal of Cleaner Production, 128,* 77–96.

Meyer, B., Küchler, S., & Hölzinger, O. (2010). *Staatliche Förderungen der Stein und Braunkohle im Zeitraum 1950–2008*. Berlin: Greenpeace.

Nill, J., & Kemp, R. (2009). Evolutionary approaches for sustainable innovation policies: From niche to paradigm? *Research Policy, 38*(4), 668–680.

Orlow, D. (2002). *Common destiny: A comparative history of the Dutch, French, and German Social Democratic Parties, 1945–1969*. Oxford: Berghahn Books.

Paech, N. (2013). Economic growth and sustainable development. In A. Michael, B. Andreas, & H. Lehmann (Eds.), *Factor X, re-source: Designing the recycling society* (pp. 31–44). Amsterdam: Springer.

Podewils, C. (2016). 2015 war Rekordjahr für Erneuerbare Energien, Stromerzeugung und Stromexport, Agora Energiewende.Retrieved from https://www.agora-energiewende.de /de/presse/agoranews/news-detail/news/2015-war-rekordjahr-fuer-erneuerbare-energien -stromerzeugung-und-stromexport/News/detail/

Podobnik, B. (2006). *Global energy shifts: Fostering sustainability in a turbulent age*. Philadelphia: Temple University Press.

Poole, M. S., Van de Ven, A. H., Dooley, K., & Holmes, M. E. (2000). *Organizational change and innovation processes, theory and methods for research*. Oxford: Oxford University Press.

Quaschning, V. (2016). *Sektorkopplung durch die Energiewende, Anforderungen an den Ausbau erneuerbarer Energien zum Erreichen der Pariser Klimaschutzziele unter Berücksichtigung der Sektorkopplung*. Berlin: HTW University of Applied Sciences Berlin.

Reitz, F., Gerbaulet, C., von Hirschhausen, C., Kemfert, C., Lorenz, C., & Oei, P.-Y. (2014). *Szenarien einer nachhaltigen Kraftwerksentwicklung in Deutschland*. Berlin: German Institute for Economic Research.

Renn, O., & Marshall, J. P. (2016). Coal, nuclear and renewable energy policies in Germany: From the 1950s to the "Energiewende." *Energy Policy, 99*(1), 224–232.

Roose, J. (2010). Der endlose Streit um die Atomenergie. Konfliktsoziologische Untersuchung einer dauerhaften Auseinandersetzung. In P. H. Feindt & T. Saretzki (Eds.), *Umwelt- und Technikkonflikte* (pp. 79–103). Berlin: Springer.

Rosenkranz, G., Praetorius, B., Litz, P., Ecke, J., Hilmes, U., & Steinert, T. (2015). *Der Klimaschutzbeitrag des Stromsektors bis 2040. Entwicklungspfade für die deutschen Kohlekraftwerke und deren wirtschaftliche Auswirkungen*. Berlin: Agora Energiewende.

Roth, R. (1994). Lokale Bewegungsnetzwerke und die Institutionalisierung von neuen sozialen Bewegungen. In F. Neidhardt (Ed.), *Öffentlichkeit, öffentliche Meinung, soziale Bewegungen* (pp. 413–436). Opladen: VS Verlag für Sozialwissenschaften.

Rye, C. B., & Kimberly, J. R. (2007). The adoption of innovations by provider organizations in health care. *Medical Care Research and Review, 64*(3), 235–278.

Schrader, C. (2016). Can Germany engineer a coal exit? *Science, 351*(6272), 430–431.

Schuman, R. (2017 [1950]). The Schuman Declaration: 9 May 1950. European Union. Retrieved from   https://europa.eu/european-union/about-eu/symbols/europe-day/schuman -declaration_en

Simon, K.-H. (2013). Energiewende—nichts Neues?! Aber was bleibt auf der Strecke? In D. Gawora & K. Bayer (Eds.), *Energie und Demokratie* (pp. 125–140). Kassel: Kassel University Press.

Spiegel Online. (2015, July 2). Energiegipfel: Koalition beerdigt Klimaabgabe. Retrieved from http://www.spiegel.de/wirtschaft/soziales/energie-koalition-streicht-klimaabgabe-fuer -kohlekraftwerke-a-1041662.html

Tripsas, M. (1997). Unraveling the process of creative destruction: Complementary assets and incumbent survival in the typesetter industry. *Strategic Management Journal, 18*(1), 119–142.

Tushman, M. L., & Anderson, P. (1986). Technological discontinuities and organizational environments. *Administrative Science Quarterly, 31*(3), 439–465.

Uekoetter, F. (2012). Fukushima and the lessons of history: Remarks on the past and future of nuclear power." In J. Kersten, M. Vogt, & F. Uekoetter (Eds.), *Europe after Fukushima: German perspectives on the future of nuclear power* (pp. 9–32). München: Rachel Carson Center Perspectives, No. 1.

Ulijn, J., & Weggeman, M. (2001). Towards an innovation culture: What are its national, corporate, marketing and engineering aspects, some experimental evidence. In C. Cooper, S. Cartwright, & C. Early (Eds.), *Handbook of organisational culture and climate* (pp. 487–517). London: John Wiley & Sons.

Umweltbundesamt. (2003). *Hintergrundpapier: Abbau Steinkohlesubventionen—Ergebnisse von Modellrechnungen.* Dessau: Umweltbundesamt.

Unruh, G. C. (2000). Understanding carbon lock-in. *Energy Policy, 28*(12), 817–830.

Vowe, G. (1987). Zum Verhältnis von Wissen, Interesse und Macht bei der Gestaltung technischer Entwicklungen. Das Beispiel der Enquete-Kommissionen. In J. Friedrichs (Ed.), *23. Deutscher Soziologentag 1986* (pp. 405–408). Berlin: Springer.

Yin, R. K., Quick, S. S., Bateman, P. M., & Marks, E. L. (1978). Changing urban bureaucracies, how new practices become routinized. RAND Corporation. Retrieved from http://www.rand.org/pubs/reports/R2277.html

Ziehm, C. (2008). Eine Kritik am Emissionshandel. *Solarzeitalter, 6*(2), 34–39.

CHAPTER 28

··

IN CLOSING

From "energy" to "Energy"

··

MATTHIAS GROSS AND DEBRA J. DAVIDSON

THE future is open—defined by multiple, emergent outcomes of a confluence of processes unfolding today. And thus we as social scientists must also be open—to alternative paradigms that may be unsettling, to theories and knowledge offered by other disciplines, to methodological creativity, to close scrutiny of those "outlier" observations that might otherwise be swept under the rug.

Having said this, there are certainly things we can say with confidence regarding our future at this point in time. First, our relationships with energy are changing, and rapidly, whether the result of intentional social action or the result of a confluence of events and processes. Sager reminds us in Chapter 5 of this volume that economic development has always gone hand in hand with increased energy access, and yet he highlights that we cannot count on the continuation of economic development enjoyed in the West into the future, as the costs of assuring energy access increase. Yet the prospects of continuing to grow our economies while reducing energy are slim, if history is any indication; thereby Sager's is the first of several chapters in this volume that imply caution regarding the prospects for "decoupling" our economies from greenhouse gas emissions, as long as we continue to rely on fossil fuels for our energy.

Thus, we also can say with confidence that society's continued reliance on fossil fuels is highly likely to lead to escalating climate, as well as social and environmental, disruptions. The disruptions already occurring have become ever more difficult to conceal or explain away, and growing awareness of their severity has compelled increasing calls for transition toward low-carbon energy-society systems—calls that have begun to carry weight in various political arenas. Many such calls, however, are met with enthusiastic forecasts of technological revolution, or calls for market-intervening policies such as carbon levies. Still others are met with passionate pleas for voluntary cultural change. As the chapters in this volume show, neither of these approaches is sufficient, particularly on their own, as they are so frequently considered.

In response, just as a business-as-usual approach to energy development will not be adequate to addressing our shifting energy-society relationships in a manner that ensures equity and socio-ecological well-being, a science-as-usual approach to energy-society scholarship in the social sciences is also inadequate. We close this volume with a synthesis of the valuable contributions offered by the authors of the previous chapters, and a nod of commendation to the numerous other scholars who have invested their intellectual energy into understanding energy-society systems despite the fact that, in many social science disciplines, doing so posed a challenge to mainstream theories and areas of inquiry. And yet, we offer a friendly challenge to our many colleagues working in this area, to open up the many black boxes that may prevent further advances in the ability of social scientists to understand complex energy-society systems, and to bring those insights to bear on energy planning.

What Are the Key Contributions Offered by Contributors to This Volume?

As many chapters imply, sociologists and other social scientists have struggled to integrate energy into preexisting disciplinary theories and methods, much as has been the case for many other non-social elements, such as ecosystems, biodiversity, and the environment. Energy, however, given its many forms and states, may be an even tougher conceptual challenge than, say, trees and birds. Energy transitions may not only be the most crucial challenge that twenty-first century societies will have to face, but they may also be the most crucial challenge for, and ultimately the acid test of, the environmental social sciences, and sociology in particular.

As we know from many historical studies, energy transitions of the past have been inherently long-term processes, and there is no reason to believe it should be different this time (Smil, 2010). On the other hand, there is also no reason to believe that such a transition will proceed in a smooth and orderly fashion, as presumed in many bold, prescriptive formulas that call for, say 20% renewable energy by 2030, 50% by 2050, and so on. Since the future trajectories of complex systems are emergent and thus cannot be "controlled" in this manner, the best we can do is identify crisis-inducing elements and trends and ways to constrain them, as well as positive trends and ways to nurture them. The identification of these trends is ultimately our central purpose for this volume. This collection of chapters offers competing perspectives, a diversity of theoretical approaches, and a broad geographical canvas of observation, which we as the editors of this volume celebrate. Yet from this diverse body of scholarship we can derive a number of resonant themes regarding the current trends that will influence future trajectories. The primary change agents that have drawn attention are supply shifts, demand shifts, and political and governance shifts. Then there is a suite of mediating factors, particularly technology and social movements. And as with any complex system, each of these is interrelated.

Supply

On the supply side, our chapter authors articulate three prevailing themes. First, the pressures and opportunities for continued development of fossil-fuel resources are not dissipating. On coal in particular, Ciccantell and Gellert in Chapter 7 warn that we will likely suffer the consequences of coal-fired electricity generation for many years to come, due in large part to China's reliance on this resource. Coal still supplies almost three-quarters of domestic electricity in China, although the amount of new coal power being built has been declining lately (cf. Vaughan, 2017). Indeed, despite the attention put on renewables in many social science research streams, as of 2016 nearly half of global electricity is still produced by coal-fired power plants. Although as a share of the source of electricity generation coal is projected to decline steadily in most countries, even in Germany—often deemed a renewable energy pioneer—one-quarter of electricity produced comes from brown coal, and as noted by David in Chapter 27, additional coal mined here is exported to be burned elsewhere. Given the phase-out of nuclear power and current political constellations, this is unlikely to change significantly in the next decades.

Manduca, Berni, Paiva, and Hage also note in Chapter 15 the quick reversal of direction observed in Latin America with the discovery of new offshore oil reserves, and of course Venezuela continues to sit upon one of the largest reserves of petrochemicals in the world, in the form of bitumen and heavy oil. With prospects of an ice-free Arctic, development of deposits there, estimated to be quite large, is sure to follow. Second, and closely related to this first point, although reserves of fossil fuels are still quite large, they exist in lower quality forms, such as shale, and in less accessible places, such as under deep seabeds. These characteristics translate into the need for application of riskier technologies, which, especially when combined with political economic conditions that favor maximizing production at the expense of risk management, will lead to increasing occurrences of major catastrophes like the blowout of the Macondo well in the Gulf of Mexico. Development of such unconventional fuels also leads to escalating impacts associated with routine operations, leading to escalating public reactions, as Dodge observes in Chapter 22 in response to the hydraulic fracturing of shale reserves in New York.

The third prevailing theme is strong agreement that renewables will not be a panacea. First, as York and David both observe (Chapters 9 and 27), the dramatic increase in development of renewables in recent decades has not deterred fossil-fuel consumption, highlighting David's point that "exnovation" is just as critical as innovation in facilitating system transition. Furthermore, as Mares warns in Chapter 6, renewables are no more equitably distributed than fossil fuels, and thus geopolitics inevitably enters the equation. Manduca, Berni, Paiva, and Hage, in Chapter 15, show that a renewable sector can fall as quickly as it rises, subject to the whims of politics and markets. And renewables are by no means "impact free." Their development comes with environmental impacts and social impacts that can be opposed by local peoples, as described by Delicado in Chapter 18.

Demand

On the demand side, four key themes emerge from this volume, beginning with the vast inequities in consumption identified by York in Chapter 9, which means pockets of energy poverty, described in detail by Brunner, Mandl, and Thomson in Chapter 16. This in turn can place pressure on governments to meet that demand, by using the least costly options available, often coal. Second, as outlined by Pereira, da Silva, and Freitas in Chapter 17, this energy poverty is crucially linked to climate justice, and a failure to incorporate acknowledgment of energy poverty and a justice perspective into international efforts to mitigate climate change will doom those efforts themselves. Third, the overriding tendency to attribute responsibility for changing energy consumption to middle-class families by voluntary means is both undue and of limited utility. In fact, as noted by Lorenzen in Chapter 13, states and industries are responsible for much larger shares of our energy-consumption portfolios. And aside from this, as several authors in this volume have noted, but particularly Brown and Sovacool in Chapter 11, as well as Pfister and Schweighofer in Chapter 12, attempts to influence individual consumption behaviors, particularly when they are voluntary, often fail because consumption practices cannot be separated from culture, and this fact is rarely accommodated in policy measures.

Fourth, and on a positive note, Hyysalo and Juntunen describe in Chapter 19 the important but often unrecognized role that citizens play in enabling the upscaling of alternative energy practices, playing the roles of "prosumers" and citizen innovators. Whereas the traditional world of research has only allowed certified experts to develop novel technologies, today the energy user and non-scientist can potentially play an active part in this. These forms of research are also characterized by high complexity in terms of both the range and number of actors involved and the framework conditions that govern these real-world experiments taking place there. Finally, the rise of cities as main sites of consumption, as discussed by Sadorsky in Chapter 10, is foreboding—as urbanization is far from complete, and per capita energy consumption in cities is higher than elsewhere. On the other hand, there are numerous opportunities for innovative shifts in consumption practices in cities, and both governmental and nongovernmental organizations in cities have become important political actors in energy and climate dialogues.

Markets, Politics, and Governance

These shifts in supply and demand then influence markets, with multiple emergent and unexpected outcomes. Markets are also inevitably shaped by politics, not only in the form of subsidies and taxes, but also as mediators of production and distribution, as highlighted by Sharples in Chapter 8.

Shifts in energy politics and governance are myriad, and many chapters have focused on these. The first key point made by several authors, particularly Mares in Chapter 6, but also Manduca et al. (Chapter 15), as well as Ciccantell and Gellert (Chapter 7), emphasizes a force that has *not* changed substantially. Namely, global and domestic energy politics are still subject to an entrenched elite connected to fossil-fuel development. Moreover, governing and civil society organizations are often weakest in production (petro) states, representing what may turn out to be the linchpin for any prospects of low-carbon transition. Without substantial exnovation in places of production, fossil-fuel consumption will likely continue. Second, although Vogler cautions in Chapter 2 that the international energy governance regime has not developed nearly as quickly as the international climate governance regime, the recent establishment of an international renewable energy agency described by Roehrkasten in Chapter 25 is certainly notable, as is the recognition of energy poverty as a key UN development issue (Brunner, Mandl, and Thompson, Chapter 16).

Third, a factor that is not new but no less important, the spatial location of resources determines whether a given country is an exporter or an importer of those resources. Yet as Mares makes clear in Chapter 6, the trade relations that result are by no means stable, but as often as not, are conflict-ridden, with direct implications for security and well-being across the geographic map of the production chain. Importantly, as sites of production and consumption shift rapidly, so too do trade relations, and the potential for conflict. A fourth key point made by authors in this volume is the growth in citizen awareness and engagement in energy issues, especially at sites of production, the focus of both Delicado and Dodge (Chapters 18 and 22).

Growing instances of local opposition to pipelines, mountaintop removal (coal), coal/open-cast mining in general, and hydraulic fracturing, as well as renewable energy developments, raise the possibility that we are experiencing the emergence of a new energy-focused global-scale social movement, one with direct links to the politics of climate change. At the same time, in the past decade, established environmental organizations have elevated climate change, and by extension energy systems, to the top of their agenda, while new organizations specifically devoted to climate change have emerged, such as 350.org. This growing movement has become a regular player in international governmental meetings, and has facilitated some of the largest civil disobedience protest activities of the twenty-first century. Their tactics have also diversified, in some cases to great effect. Although estimates vary of the aggregate impact of the fossil fuel divestment movement, for example, in just five years movement actors have convinced over 700 institutions around the globe to divest their financial holdings in fossil fuels.

On social movements, one of the highlights that can be taken away from this research record is the growing momentum and internationalization of both resistance to fossil fuels (which may assist exnovation), and support for alternatives—which supports innovation (Vasi, Chapter 21). Recent mobilizations are not always from expected sources, such as established environmental organizations, either. Many have erupted in rural, resource-dependent regions, where citizens are increasingly concerned about the effects of production, and there are a growing number of youth movements in the West as well, playing key roles in divestment campaigns in particular. Resistance grows even in countries with a long history of fossil fuel production, such as Canada, as described by Stoddart, Smith, and Graham in Chapter 23. Stoddart et al.'s chapter also notes the emergence of Indigenous peoples in Canada onto the energy politics stage, something observed in many other regions as well. Importantly, and resonating with other chapters in this volume, Emelianoff in Chapter 24 describes the efficacy of bottom-up, grassroots action: even national-scale shifts can be attributed to the actions of key local agents, in her case in cities across Germany and Sweden. Key to at least some of these mobilizations is a shift in the imaginaries through which energy developments are interpreted (Dodge, Chapter 22), particularly in relation to unconventional fossil fuels. Analysis of media coverage of energy issues has the potential to constrain this momentum, however. In Chapter 20, Wagner describes how narratives that dominate the airwaves serve to narrow debates and future options to the status quo, thus potentially discouraging expansion of social movement support.

Technology

On technology, authors throughout the volume agree that optimism regarding the potential for future technological advances to foster a low-carbon transition in energy-society relations without requisite shifts in cultural, political, and economic systems is unwarranted. First, as history illustrates, increases in consumption efficiency induced by technology tend not to lead to reductions in consumption; in fact, the opposite is often the case. Such rebound effects are an under-researched area in sociology, but it is an enduring characteristic of almost all areas of energy efficiency and technology development. Just as crucial, technological optimism has tended to direct attention away from the many other factors that influence energy-society relations, and away from the need to take reductions in consumption seriously (Stephens & Markusson, Chapter 26).

How Can We Improve upon the Contributions Made by Social Science?

The first black box to be opened begins with our conceptual understanding of the earth. Many environmental social scientists conceive of the earth as a closed system with finite resources. In approaching many areas of inquiry, this conceptual approach is reasonable, and appropriate. But especially when it comes to "energy," strict adherence to such a finite earth perspective technically does not make much sense. Strictly speaking, there is no shortage of energy. Rather, we face a limited supply of economically and/or technologically feasible means of converting this unlimited energy into the power and fuels we use. After all, the sun provides the ultimate source of energy for life on earth, initially in the form of light energy generated through processes of nuclear fusion. The earth itself is also a sphere made out of fire, which continues to produce radiogenic heat underneath the earth's crust. Only the thin surface of the earth (a maximum of 35 km in depth) has been cooled to the annual average temperatures between 0°C and 24°C to which human inhabitants are exposed, depending on the climatic zone. At some 5,000 kilometers in depth we find the threshold between earth's inner and outer core, the temperature of which has recently been estimated at 6,000°C (cf. Howell, 2013), roughly the same temperature as the average surface of the sun, and representing an extraordinary reserve of energy. The gravitational forces of the sun and the moon also generate mechanical energy effects that manifest in the power of the tides and waves, as well as wind.

In short, from a geological point of view there is no energy shortage, or even a finite earth. The "energy crisis" is, rather, a social crisis: a disconnect between the energy demands of contemporary social systems and our ability to access sufficient energy to meet those needs. This depiction may challenge the notions of Mother Nature and ecology implicitly or explicitly expressed in the work of many social scientists, but it is geologically accurate. More crucially, opening up our conceptions of energy-society relations to embrace this view can stimulate substantial advances in research. Our failure to do so, on the other hand, amounts to a failure on the part of the social sciences to respect the knowledge offered by natural scientists and engineers, while at the same time we continue to urge greater respect for ours. In the long run, such disconnections between the social and natural sciences compromise the perceived value of the social sciences in the wider society and in policymaking.

The Only Thing We Can Be Confident about Is Uncertainty

Another black box to be opened has to do with uncertainty, and our level of comfort with it. As noted at the beginning of this chapter, the future is open. In other words, the outcomes of current shifts in energy-society relations are not at all clear. Perhaps energy transitions best exemplify what Anthony Giddens (1990) once described as the juggernaut of modernity; that is, the modern world needs to be understood as a forward-moving process analogous to a powerful locomotive that cannot be steered or directed but only adjusted. The more complex the world gets, the more we need to accept that we cannot know everything, and we also must rely on others' expertise. In such a world, trust in processes and organizations that we may not fully understand is absolutely necessary. We may not have complete knowledge and understanding of the inner workings of a subway train or airplane, but in order to get where we want to go, we must board anyway, and we do so, every day. While embracing this degree of trust may appear anathema to science, founded as it is upon generating knowledge, a dose of this trust is becoming increasingly necessary.

Research in new fields of inquiry such as chaos theory and complex systems provides some key insights, not only for revealing the extent of uncertainty in complex systems, but also as a means of embracing that uncertainty epistemologically. Complex systems are difficult, perhaps impossible, to control or "steer," or even comprehend in their entirety (Cushing et al., 2003; Perrow, 1984), and a failure to account for these complexities can limit the effectiveness of energy policies. Novel risks and uncertainties have become a regular feature of daily life, and significant sources of change are as likely to come from unexpected sources below the surface of our vision as they are from sources in plain view. With each problem solved, awareness of new problems emerges, and thus new horizons regarding the unknown become visible. Horta and Rohracher both discuss in different ways (Chapters 3 and 4) how energy-society relations describe complex systems—complexity that sociologists are only beginning to understand. Both of these chapters, as well as others in this volume, emphasize a distinct mismatch between the long-term, global, and systemic challenges we face, and the short-term, national/regional, and incremental activities initiated to address those challenges so far. This gap may be widening in the future, and inadequate accommodation for uncertainty in scholarship may well contribute to this gap. For one thing, on either side of this gap, knowledge about "what is sustainable" changes and is often highly situational. Sociology in particular has not seriously dealt with this tension.

Comfort with lack of knowledge is increasingly required. In regard to energy-society systems, we face a multitude of knowledge gaps. Non-knowledge will not go away; it can only change. As important as approaches to closing knowledge and data gaps are, we must also be cognizant that gaps cannot always be closed, so decisions need to be made in the face of not knowing. Yet scholars in many disciplines, trained in Western scientific methods, have been indoctrinated in the beliefs that (a) all new knowledge derives from direct observation, and (b) only new (empirical) knowledge can inform our conceptual understanding. Thus, knowledge gaps continue to be seen as a problem to solve. However, even with the emergence of the Internet, new computing and remote-sensing technologies, and other avenues through which new information emerges and becomes increasingly accessible, the goal of eliminating knowledge gaps is just as unrealizable today as ever. Yet, so strictly do many researchers adhere to this doctrine (indeed, they are sanctioned when they do not) that we often ascribe greater levels of certainty in our analyses than is valid. This is often done, for example, in risk assessments that assume the calculability of hazard, and sustainability assessments that presume to characterize the long-term stability of a social system on the basis of a collection of static proxy indicators. The problem here that so often transpires is that official rhetorics—of confidence or safety, of anticipated policy outcomes—that conceal our knowledge gaps may only serve to increase the chances of hazard, or policy failure.

Instead of glossing over knowledge gaps, sociologists and other social scientists should acknowledge them, and mind them. The relation between the known and the unknown can be seen as a continuous circuit, in which the production of knowledge is a prerequisite for perceiving new ignorance, and vice versa. Uncertainties surrounding energy systems might better be interpreted or at least accompanied, first and foremost, not in terms of concepts of safety, risk, or big data, but increasingly in terms of strategic or accidental constructions of ignorance.

A Strong Dose of Conceptual Flexibility Is Required

Not only must we grapple with what we do not know, we must also accommodate dynamic shifts in what we do know. Indeed, we must not only accommodate, but actively seek, new knowledge by casting our knowledge-gathering nets broadly across the academy. Knowledge across the social and natural sciences about the complex relations between science, ecology, technology, and society changes over time, sometimes rapidly, sometimes in fundamental ways. Despite this dynamic context, we in the social sciences often approach energy-society relations with static and even normative assumptions about the natural world. Those normative assumptions often predetermine, for instance, what constitutes "good" and "bad" solutions, and which new innovations are deemed (usually incorrectly) as either unproblematic, or impossible, despite dramatic changes in the knowledge and technologies associated with those innovations over time. By doing so, we not only narrow our sociological gaze considerably, but our prescriptions can also appear biased and politically one-sided. Understanding of the expected environmental benefits and risks of different practices (such as nuclear power, electric vehicles, or recycling), for example, can shift dramatically with the emergence of new knowledge, or new technologies. Likewise, previous assessments have turned out to have omissions, unreliable data, or simply errors. Sustainability needs to be understood as a moving target, and so also does the future of energy demand and production in and of society. One vivid illustration of the need to adjust our lens with the emergence of new knowledge is the growing body of empirical evidence of rebound effects associated with energy-efficiency technologies, just as William Jevons might have predicted back in 1865. Unintended effects are nothing new to sociologists, and there is an urgent need for greater sociological attention to such rebound effects; an opening for doing so has already been provided by York and McGee (2016). In sum, we should openly acknowledge and reflect upon our assumptions, and continuously ask, "What if I am wrong?"

Rebound effects are not the only place to look. Negative social and environmental side effects of many heralded renewable energy technologies such as solar power, wind turbines, electric vehicles, or geothermal energy do indeed exist, but are not critically evaluated. Battery-driven electric vehicles are a particularly pertinent case, as they are associated with multiple side effects that manifest beyond the operation of the car itself, evident in the production (including mining for rare earths) and recycling of batteries, among many other factors. And of course, depending on where a car owner lives, electric vehicles just might be less environmentally friendly than their fossil-fuel-burning counterparts if they are recharged on an electric grid powered by coal.

On the other end of the spectrum, we may be overlooking potentially revolutionary avenues toward energy transition, again based on normative beliefs. Recent improvements in developing synthetic fuels as an alternative to petrochemical-based fuels, for example, has not received any attention from environmental social scientists. Yet there have been some striking new research and technology developments in this field that render synthetic fuels worthy of consideration. Not only have synthetic fuels been shown to have the capacity to withstand mechanical loads up to 10 times more than the capacity of usual lubricants available in the market, there is also potential to develop carbon-neutral synthetic fuels. A few "outlier" researchers (working within major German research institutions) even believe that, due to the development of synthetic fuels, the classical combustion engine will have a "Second Spring" by 2030, due to its ability to outperform the current alternatives in efficiency and environmental performance (cf. Fröhndrich, 2017). While the inclination among environmental social scientists may be to disregard these voices as conservative outliers or as being "in the pockets of industry," sociologists and other social science researchers should critically assess these new developments, despite their potential incompatibility with established views.

In short, we urge our colleagues to be conscious of their tendencies to unquestionably embrace mainstream positions. In Norway or Germany, for instance, it often goes unquestioned that a ban on gas-powered cars is a good thing per se and that traditional combustion engines must be phased out by a certain date. Some EU countries have already set a phase-out date of 2030 for doing so. A ban on a particular type of engine, however, may well be a rather ineffective and possibly even *counter*-effective means of achieving the ultimate goal, which is the elimination of greenhouse gas emissions. Given recent research on synthetic fuels, it may very well be that combustion engines can be emissions neutral (considering all factors involved in a cradle-to-cradle life-cycle evaluation, cf. McDonough and Braungart 2002) even earlier than electric vehicles for reasons mentioned earlier.

As a final example illustrating the need for conceptual flexibility, environmental social scientists have been complicit in a tendency across the environmental sciences to elevate CO_2 to a position of superiority, as an indicator of global warming, and even environmental impact generally. CO_2 emission levels thus have a tendency to serve as the sole indicator determining support for given energy sources or technologies. Even a hypothetical CO_2-free society, however, can be replete with many forms of social and ecological ills, and indeed can continue to experience global warming as, for example, methane sources expand.

Challenging Paradigms by Looking under the Rug

Inclinations toward drawing, on the basis of rather limited indicators, grandiose conclusions regarding the potential revolutionary changes we are experiencing are similarly folly. Many scholars have been all too eager to pronounce epochal, systemic breaks that mark, say, a shift from a risk society to reflexive modernity, as sociologist Ulrich Beck (1992) notably did decades ago, or other proclamations that the limits to growth have been irrevocably breached. Sociologists in particular have expressed a certain eagerness to demarcate epochal shifts. Many of the most important sociolog-ical monographs of the last half-century contain one or more such proclamations. Enthusiastic pronouncements of "peak oil," or renewable energy transitions, are rele-vant contemporary examples.

Each of these pronouncements has as many counter-indicators as there are indicators. Historians and philosophers of science would remind us that those who are themselves immersed in historical processes cannot themselves recognize the potential revolu-tionary character of those processes, as they lack the necessary distance to perceive the many indications that define system-wide change (cf. Schiemann 2011). In other words, while it is indeed crucial for social scientists to continue to inquire into those social processes that appear to hold promise for facilitating an energy transition, such as the increase in adoption of renewable energy, doing so to the exclusion of consideration for counter-indicators, such as the continued development of coal and oil reserves, can lead to egregious miscalculations of future trajectories both near and far.

One way of doing so is to look under the proverbial rug—instead of discarding the outliers from our models, bring them to the center of scrutiny. Sociology, which has also been called the science of the unexpected (Portes, 2000), would seem to already have an aptitude for doing so. But, perhaps with the rise to prominence of statistical analysis methods that are overly preoccupied with avoiding Type I errors, and a much longer sociological tradition of confirming adherence to prevailing paradigms—what Thomas Kuhn (1963) and Ludwik Fleck (1979) once referred to as "normal science"—we are far more likely to exclude from analysis the very observations that demand close attention in complex systems. As described by Fleck, a paradigm, or "thought style" (including certain moods, unquestioned assumptions, political directions) becomes sufficiently accepted after a certain amount of time to become dominant. Then the research field organizes itself into an esoteric "inner circle," within which scholars who express accept-ance of the dominant paradigm enjoy the affirmation and collegiality of membership, and a perimeter populated by those outside of the accepted circle. The cost of member-ship in the inner circle, however, is continued allegiance to dominant paradigms, which translates into unconscious or even conscious exclusion of new information, anomalies, outliers, and counterintuitive empirical results. Continued ascription to dominant paradigms leads inevitably to a loss of legitimacy before an eventual "scientific revolu-tion," though this process can take place over decades, if not, as in the past, centuries. In the context of energy-society relations, however, continued ascription to dominant but folly paradigms also runs the risk of very real consequences in the form of failures to foresee crises and develop effective policies.

Careful deciphering of outliers needs to become part of energy research today. Environmental social scientists as a rule have often been relegated to the outer circle of their home disciplines, but we have also been shown to be perfectly capable of organizing into our own inner and outer circles. We thus call on our colleagues to ex-pand the ranks of that outer circle, perhaps even moving toward a dismantling of inner circles entirely. One important member of that outer circle in sociology was William Freudenburg. His persistent courage to question has resulted in a number of important, even foundation-shaking new findings. An exemplar of his contributions is his work on the "double diversion," one of his last major research projects before his untimely death in 2010. The basis of this work began with an analysis of outliers. In his 2005 paper in *Social Forces*, Freudenburg evaluated the distribution of pollution emissions in the United States, first across industries, then across companies within industrial sectors, and finally across individual facilities within companies. What he discovered was a stark divergence from the largely accepted paradigm that pollution is necessarily (and thus equitably) associated with material production. To the contrary, he found such wide disproportions in pollution emissions—measured creatively with an application of the Gini coefficient—that in his final analysis that coefficient was about as close to 1.0 (absolute inequality) as one can achieve. In other words, a highly disproportionate share of pollution emissions in the United States not only comes from a small handful of industries that do not have a particularly large role to play in the national economy, but also comes from a mere handful of companies, even facilities.

What's Next?

We recognize the extent to which heeding our calls to action can and likely will elicit sanctions from peers, but we view the contributions in this *Handbook* as representative of a growing aptitude and courage to move forward anyway. We hope, however, that these contributions are merely the beginning. Sociologists and their colleagues in other disciplines have played important roles in bringing change processes in energy transitions into sharper critical relief, and identifying those elements that have the potential for outcomes that support climate mitigation, equity, and well-being. But our contributions can also be greatly substantiated when we challenge ourselves—our own normative assumptions, predispositions, and particular knowledges, and reach out to other disciplines, including the natural sciences and engineering, to ground our own analyses in material and biophyscial realities, and stay abreast of these equally dynamic terrains.

History may repeat itself, but the odds are against it, and thus, the knowledge and theories we have accumulated based on historical circumstances need to be revisited, and we need to begin to look beyond our own disciplinary borders, and epistemic communities, for learning opportunities. Will fossil-fuel companies necessarily resist transition? Are carbon capture and storage never to hold potential? Will the strongest leaders in supporting transition emerge from unlikely places, like indigenous communities in the North, and rural, resource-dependent communities, rather than international governmental forums and well-resourced nongovernmental organizations? Can we break from the historical, positive association between social complexity and energy consumption? We don't have definitive answers to any of these questions, but we do believe, strongly, that they are valid questions to ask. True knowledge creation comes from the courage to question, to tinker, to think outside the box, to imagine.

References

Beck, U. (1992 [1986]). *Risk society: Towards a new modernity.* London: Sage.

Cushing, J. M., Costantino, R. F., Dennis, B., Deshanais, R., & Henson, S. M. (2003). *Chaos in ecology: Experimental nonlinear dynamics.* Oxford: Elsevier.

Fleck, L. (1979 [1935]). *Genesis and development of a scientific fact.* Chicago: University of Chicago Press.

Freudenburg, W. R. (2005). Privileged access, privileged accounts: Toward a socially structured theory of resources and discourses. *Social Forces, 84*(1), 89–114.

Fröhndrich, S. (2017, January 5). Zweiter Frühling für den Verbrenner. *Deutschlandfunk.* Retrieved from http://www.deutschlandfunk.de/automobilindustrie-zweiter-fruehling -fuer-den-verbrenner.724.de.html?dram:article_id=375623

Giddens, A. (1990). *The consequences of modernity.* Palo Alto, CA: Stanford University Press.

Howell, E. (2013, April 25). Earth's core 1,000 degrees hotter than expected. *LiveScience.* Retrieved from http://www.livescience.com/29054-earth-core-hotter.html

Kuhn, T. (1963). *The structure of scientific revolutions.* Chicago: University of Chicago Press.

McDonough, W., & Braungart, M. (2002). *Cradle to cradle: Remaking the way we make things.* New York: MacMillan.

Perrow, C. (1984). *Normal accidents: Living with high risk technologies.* New York: Basic Books.

Portes, A. (2000). The hidden abode: Sociology as analysis of the unexpected. *American Sociological Review, 65*(1), 1–18.

Schiemann, G. (2011). We are not witnesses to a new scientific revolution. In A. Nordmann, H. Radder, & G. Schiemann (Eds.), *Science transformed? Debating claims of an epochal break* (pp. 31-42). Pittsburgh, PA: University of Pittsburgh Press.

Smil, V. (2010). *Energy transitions: History, requirements, prospects.* Santa Barbara, CA: Praeger.

Vaughan, A. (2017, March 22). Coal in "freefall" as new power plants dive by two-thirds. *The Guardian.* Retrieved from https://www.theguardian.com/environment/2017/mar/22 /coal-power-plants-green-energy-china-india

York, R., & McGee, J. A. (2016). Understanding the Jevons paradox. *Environmental Sociology, 2*(1), 77–87.

INDEX

....

Tables and figures are indicated by an italic *t* and *f* following the page number.